HTML and CSS Quick Reference

 W9-APR-338

STRUCTURE TAGS

`<!--...-->`	Creates a comment
`<html>...</html>`	Encloses the entire HTML document
`<head>...</head>`	Encloses the head of the HTML document
`<meta />`	Provides general information about the document
`<style>...</style>`	Style information
`<script>...</script>`	Scripting language
`<noscript>...</noscript>`	Alternative content when scripting is not supported
`<title>...</title>`	The title of the document
`<body>...</body>`	Encloses the body (text and tags) of the HTML document

HEADINGS

`<h1>...</h1>`	Heading level 1
`<h2>...</h2>`	Heading level 2
`<h3>...</h3>`	Heading level 3
`<h4>...</h4>`	Heading level 4
`<h5>...</h5>`	Heading level 5
`<h6>...</h6>`	Heading level 6

PARAGRAPHS

`<p>...</p>`	A plain paragraph

LINKS

`<a>...</a>`	Creates a link or anchor; includes common attributes
`href="..."`	The URL of the document to be linked to this one
`name="..."`	The name of the anchor
`target="..."`	Identifies the window or location in which to open the link
`rel="..."`	Defines forward link types
`rev="..."`	Defines reverse link types
`accesskey="..."`	Assigns a hotkey to this element
`shape="..."`	Is for use with object shapes
`coords="..."`	Is for use with object shapes
`tabindex="..."`	Determines the tabbing order
`onClick`	Is a JavaScript event
`onMouseOver`	Is a JavaScript event
`onMouseOut`	Is a JavaScript event

LISTS

`<ol>...</ol>`	An ordered (numbered) list
`<ul>...</ul>`	An unordered (bulleted) list
`<menu>...</menu>`	A menu list of items
`<dir>...</dir>`	A directory listing
`<li>...</li>`	A list item
`<dl>...</dl>`	A definition or glossary list
`<dt>...</dt>`	A definition term
`<dd>...</dd>`	The corresponding definition to a definition term

CHARACTER FORMATTING

`<em>...</em>`	Emphasis (usually italic)
`<strong>...</strong>`	Stronger emphasis (usually bold)
`<code>...</code>`	Code sample
`<kbd>...</kbd>`	Text to be typed
`<var>...</var>`	A variable of placeholder for some other value
`<samp>...</samp>`	Sample text
`<dfn>...</dfn>`	A definition of a term
`<cite>...</cite>`	A citation
`<b>...</b>`	Boldfaced text
`<i>...</i>`	Italic text
`<tt>...</tt>`	Typewriter font
`<u>...</u>`	Underlined text
`<pre>...</pre>`	Preformatted text

OTHER ELEMENTS

`<hr />`	A horizontal rule
` `	A line break
`<blockquote>...</blockquote>`	Used for long quotes or citations
`<address>...</address>`	Signatures or general information about a document's author
`<font>...</font>`	Change the size, color, and typeface of the font
`size="..."`	The size of the font from 1 to 7
`color="..."`	The font color
`face="..."`	The font type
`<basefont />`	Sets the default size of the font for the current page
`size="..."`	The default size of the font from 1 to 7

SAMS Teach Yourself

When you only have time for the answers™

HTML and CSS Quick Reference

IMAGES

`<img />`		Inserts an inline image into the document; includes common attributes
	`usemap="..."`	A client-side imagemap
	`src="..."`	The URL of the image
	`alt="..."`	A text string that will be displayed in browsers that cannot support images
	`align="..."`	Determines the alignment of the given image
	`height="..."`	Is the suggested height in pixels
	`width="..."`	Is the suggested width in pixels
	`vspace="..."`	The space between the image and the text above and below it
	`hspace="..."`	The space between the image and the text to its left and right

CSS TEXT AND FONT STYLE PROPERTIES

`color`	Sets the color of text
`direction`	Sets the direction of text, as in left-to-right or right-to-left
`font`	A shorthand property that allows you to set all the font properties in one declaration
`font-family`	A prioritized list of font family names and/or generic family names for an element
`font-size`	Sets the size of a font
`font-style`	Sets the style of the font
`font-variant`	Displays text in a small-caps font or a normal font
`font-weight`	Sets the weight (boldness) of a font
`letter-spacing`	Increase or decrease the space between characters of text
`text-align`	Aligns the text within an element
`text-decoration`	Applies a decoration to text
`text-indent`	Indents the first line of text in an element
`text-transform`	Controls the capitalization of letters of text
`white-space`	Establishes the handling of white space within an element
`word-spacing`	Increases or decreases the space between words

TABLES

`<table>...</table>`		Creates a table
	`background="..."`	Background image for the table
	`bgcolor="..."`	Background color of the table
	`border="..."`	Width of the border in pixels
	`cols="..."`	Number of columns
	`cellspacing="..."`	Spacing between cells
	`cellpadding="..."`	Spacing in cells
	`width="..."`	Table width
`<caption>...</caption>`		The caption for the table
`<tr>...</tr>`		A table row
	`align="..."`	The horizontal alignment of the contents of the cells within this row; possible values are `left`, `right`, `center`, `justify`, and `char`
	`bgcolor="..."`	Background color for the row
	`valign="..."`	The vertical alignment of the contents of the cells within this row; possible values are `top`, `middle`, `bottom`, and `baseline`
`<th>...</th>`		A table heading cell
	`align="..."`	The horizontal alignment of the contents of the cell
	`valign="..."`	The vertical alignment of the contents of the cell
	`bgcolor="..."`	Background color for the cell
	`rowspan="..."`	The number of rows this cell will span
	`colspan="..."`	The number of columns this cell will span
	`nowrap="..."`	Turns off text wrapping in a cell
`<td>...</td>`		Defines a table data cell
	`align="..."`	The horizontal alignment of the contents of the cell
	`valign="..."`	The vertical alignment of the contents of the cell
	`bgcolor="..."`	Background color for the cell
	`rowspan="..."`	The number of rows this cell will span
	`colspan="..."`	The number of columns this cell will span
	`nowrap="..."`	Turns off text wrapping in a cell

Laura Lemay
Rafe Colburn

Sams **Teach Yourself**

Web Publishing with HTML and CSS

in **One Hour** a Day

 800 East 96th Street, Indianapolis, Indiana 46240

Copyright © 2006 by Sams Publishing

International Standard Book Number: 0-672-32886-0

Library of Congress Catalog Card Number: 2005909528

Printed in the United States of America

Fifth Printing: March 2008

11 10 09 08   5 6 7 8 9 10

Trademarks

All terms mentioned in this book that are known to be trademarks or service marks have been appropriately capitalized. Sams Publishing cannot attest to the accuracy of this information. Use of a term in this book should not be regarded as affecting the validity of any trademark or service mark.

Warning and Disclaimer

Every effort has been made to make this book as complete and as accurate as possible, but no warranty or fitness is implied. The information provided is on an "as is" basis. The author(s) and the publisher shall have neither liability nor responsibility to any person or entity with respect to any loss or damages arising from the information contained in this book or from the use of the CD or programs accompanying it.

Bulk Sales

Sams Publishing offers excellent discounts on this book when ordered in quantity for bulk purchases or special sales. For more information, please contact

U.S. Corporate and Government Sales
1-800-382-3419
corpsales@pearsontechgroup.com

For sales outside of the U.S., please contact

International Sales
international@pearsoned.com

Acquisitions Editor
Betsy Brown

Development Editor
Songlin Qiu

Managing Editor
Charlotte Clapp

Project Editor
Mandie Frank

Indexer
Aaron Black

Proofreader
Jessica McCarty

Technical Editor
Martin Psinas

Publishing Coordinator
Vanessa Evans

Multimedia Developer
Dan Scherf

Book Designer
Gary Adair

Page Layout
Nonie Ratcliff

Contents at a Glance

Table of Contents

About the Authors

Rafe Colburn is a software developer and author living in North Carolina. His other books include *Sams Teach Yourself CGI in 24 Hours* and *Special Edition Using SQL*. If you'd like to read more of his writings, check out his home page at http://rc3.org/.

Laura Lemay is a technical writer, author, web addict, and motorcycle enthusiast. One of the world's most popular authors on web development topics, she is the author of *Sams Teach Yourself Web Publishing with HTML, Sams Teach Yourself Java in 21 Days,* and *Sams Teach Yourself Perl in 21 Days*.

Dedication

For Patricia.

Acknowledgments

I'd like to acknowledge the hard work of all of the people at Sams Publishing who clean up my messes and get these books out on the shelves. Special thanks go to Betsy Brown, Songlin Qiu, Mandie Frank, Andrew Beaster, and technical editor Martin Psinas. I'd also like to thank my wife for suffering through yet another one of these projects.

—Rafe Colburn

We Want to Hear from You!

As the reader of this book, *you* are our most important critic and commentator. We value your opinion and want to know what we're doing right, what we could do better, what areas you'd like to see us publish in, and any other words of wisdom you're willing to pass our way.

You can email or write me directly to let me know what you did or didn't like about this book—as well as what we can do to make our books stronger.

Please note that I cannot help you with technical problems related to the topic of this book, and that due to the high volume of mail I receive, I might not be able to reply to every message.

When you write, please be sure to include this book's title and author as well as your name and phone or email address. I will carefully review your comments and share them with the author and editors who worked on the book.

E-mail: webdev@samspublishing.com

Mail: Mark Taber
            Associate Publisher
            Sams Publishing
            800 East 96th Street
            Indianapolis, IN 46240 USA

Reader Services

Visit our website and register this book at www.samspublishing.com/register for convenient access to any updates, downloads, or errata that might be available for this book.

Introduction

Over the past decade, the Web has become completely integrated into the fabric of society. Most businesses have websites, and it's rare to see a commercial on television that doesn't display a URL. The simple fact that most people now know what a URL *is* speaks volumes. People who didn't know what the Internet was several years ago are now sending me invitations to parties using web-based invitation services.

Perhaps the greatest thing about the Web is that you don't have to be a big company to publish things on it. The only things you need to create your own website are a computer with access to the Internet and the willingness to learn. Obviously, the reason you're reading this is that you have an interest in web publishing. Perhaps you need to learn about it for work, or you're looking for a new means of self-expression, or you want to post baby pictures on the Web so that your relatives all over the country can stay up to date. The question is, how do you get started?

There's more than enough information on the Web about how to publish websites like a seasoned professional. There are tutorials, reference sites, tons of examples, and free tools to make it easier to publish on the Web. However, the advantage of reading this book instead is that all the information you need to build websites is organized in one place and presented in an orderly fashion. It has everything you need to master HTML, publish sites to a server on the Web, create graphics for use on the Web, and keep your sites running smoothly.

But wait, there's more. Other books on how to create web pages just teach you the basic technical details, such as how to produce a boldface word. In this book, you'll also learn why you should be producing a particular effect and when you should use it. In addition, this book provides hints, suggestions, and examples of how to structure your overall website, not just the words on each page. This book won't just teach you how to create a website—it'll teach you how to create a good website.

Also, unlike other books on this subject, this book doesn't focus on any one platform. Regardless of whether you're using a PC running Windows, a Macintosh, some flavor of UNIX, or any other computer system, many of the concepts in this book will be valuable to you. And you'll be able to apply them to your web pages regardless of your platform of choice.

Who Should Read This Book

Is this book for you? That depends:

- If you've seen what's out on the Web and you want to contribute your own content, this book is for you.
- If you work for a company that wants to create a website and you're not sure where to start, this book is for you.
- If you're an information developer, such as a technical writer, and you want to learn how the Web can help you present your information online, this book is for you.
- If you're just curious about how the Web works, some parts of this book are for you, although you might be able to find what you need on the Web itself.
- If you've created web pages before with text, images, and links, and you've played with a table or two and set up a few simple forms, you may be able to skim the first half of the book. The second half should still offer you a lot of helpful information.

If you've never seen the Web before but you've heard that it's really nifty, this book isn't for you. You'll need a more general book about the Web before you can produce websites yourself.

What This Book Contains

This book is intended to be read and absorbed over the course of several one-hour lessons (although it depends on how much you can absorb in a day). On each day you'll read one lesson on one area of website design. The lessons are arranged in a logical order, taking you from the simplest tasks to more advanced techniques.

Part I: Getting Started

In Part I, you'll get a general overview of the World Wide Web and what you can do with it, and then you'll come up with a plan for your web presentation. You'll also write your first (very basic) web page.

Part II: Creating Simple Web Pages

In Part II, you'll learn how to write simple documents in the HTML language and link them together using hypertext links. You'll also learn how to format your web pages and how to use images on your pages.

Part III: Doing More with HTML and XHTML

In Part III, you'll learn how to create tables and forms and place them on your pages. You'll also learn how to use cascading style sheets to describe how your pages are formatted instead of tags that are focused strictly on formatting.

Part IV: JavaScript and Dynamic HTML

In Part IV, we'll look at how you can extend the functionality of your web pages by adding JavaScript to them. First, I'll provide an overview of JavaScript, and then I'll provide some specific JavaScript examples you can use on your own pages. Finally, I'll describe how you can dynamically modify the look and feel of your pages using Dynamic HTML.

Part V: Designing Effective Web Pages

Part V will give you some hints for creating a well-constructed website, and you'll explore some sample websites to get an idea of what sort of work you can do. You'll learn how to design pages that will reach the types of real-world users you want to reach, and you'll learn how to create an accessible site that is usable by people with disabilities.

Part VI: Going Live on the Web

In Part VI, you'll learn how to put your site up on the Web, including how to advertise the work you've done. You'll also learn how to use some of the features of your web server to make your life easier.

Part VII: Appendixes

In the appendixes you'll find reference information about HTML, Cascading Style Sheets, the HTML color palette, and common file types on the Web. You'll also find a list of useful websites that complement the information in the book.

What You Need Before You Start

There are lots of books about how to use the World Wide Web. This book isn't one of them. I'm assuming that if you're reading this book, you already have a working connection to the Internet, you have a web browser such as Microsoft Internet Explorer or Mozilla Firefox, and you've used it at least a couple of times. You should also have at least a passing acquaintance with some other elements of the Internet, such as email and FTP, because I refer to them in general terms in this book.

In other words, you need to have used the Web in order to provide content for the Web. If you meet this one simple qualification, read on!

NOTE

> To really take advantage of all the concepts and examples in this book, you should consider using the most recent version of Microsoft Internet Explorer (version 6.0 or later) or Mozilla Firefox (version 1.0 or later).

Conventions Used in This Book

This book uses special typefaces and other graphical elements to highlight different types of information.

Special Elements

Three types of "boxed" elements present pertinent information that relates to the topic being discussed: Note, Tip, and Caution. Each item has a special icon associated with it, as described here.

NOTE

> Notes highlight special details about the current topic.

TIP

> It's a good idea to read the tips because they present shortcuts or trouble-saving ideas for performing specific tasks.

CAUTION

> Don't skip the cautions. They help you avoid making bad decisions or performing actions that can cause you trouble.

DO	DON'T
DO/DON'T sections provide a list of ways that the techniques described in a lesson should and shouldn't be applied.	

▼ Task:

Tasks demonstrate how you can put the information in a lesson into practice by giving you a real working example.

HTML Input and Output Examples

Throughout the book, I'll present exercises and examples of HTML input and output.

Input ▼

An input icon identifies HTML code that you can type in yourself.

Output ▼

An output icon indicates the results of the HTML input in a web browser such as Microsoft Internet Explorer.

Special Fonts

Several items are presented in a monospace font, which can be plain or italic. Here's what each one means:

> `plain mono`—Applied to commands, filenames, file extensions, directory names, Internet addresses, URLs, and HTML input. For example, HTML tags such as `<TABLE>` and `<P>` appear in this font.

> `mono italic`—Applied to placeholders. A placeholder is a generic item that replaces something specific as part of a command or computer output. For instance, the term represented by `filename` would be the real name of the file, such as `myfile.txt`.

Workshop

In the workshop section, you can reinforce your knowledge of the concepts in the lesson by answering quiz questions or working on exercises. The Q&A provides additional information that didn't fit in neatly elsewhere in the lesson.

PART I:
Getting Started

LESSON 1:
Navigating the World Wide Web

A journey of a thousand miles begins with a single step, and here you are at the beginning of a journey that will show you how to write, design, and publish pages on the World Wide Web.

In this Lesson

Before beginning the actual journey, you should start simple, with the basics. You'll learn the following:

- How the World Wide Web really works

- What web browsers do, and a couple of popular ones from which to choose

- What a web server is, and why you need one

- Some information about uniform resource locators (URLs)

These days the Web is pervasive, and maybe most if not all of today's information will seem like old news. If so, feel free to skim it and skip ahead to Lesson 2, "Preparing to Publish on the Web," where you'll find an overview of points to think about when you design and organize your own Web documents.

How the World Wide Web Works

Chances are that you've used the Web, perhaps even a lot. However, you might not have done a lot of thinking about how it works under the covers. In this first section, I'm going to describe the Web at a more theoretical level so that you can understand how it works as a platform.

I have a friend who likes to describe things using many meaningful words strung together in a chain so that it takes several minutes to sort out what he's just said.

If I were he, I'd describe the World Wide Web as a global, interactive, dynamic, cross-platform, distributed, graphical hypertext information system that runs over the Internet. Whew! Unless you understand all these words and how they fit together, this description isn't going to make much sense. (My friend often doesn't make much sense, either.)

So, let's look at all these words and see what they mean in the context of how you use the Web as a publishing medium.

The Web Is a Hypertext Information System

The idea behind hypertext is that instead of reading text in a rigid, linear structure (such as a book), you can skip easily from one point to another. You can get more information, go back, jump to other topics, and navigate through the text based on what interests you at the time.

Hypertext enables you to read and navigate text and visual information in a nonlinear way, based on what you want to know next.

When you hear the term *hypertext*, think *links*. (In fact, some people still refer to links as hyperlinks.) Whenever you visit a web page, you're almost certain to see links throughout the page. Some of the links might point to locations within that same page, others to pages on the same site, and still others might point to content stored on other servers. Hypertext was an old concept when the Web was invented—it was found in applications such as HyperCard and various help systems. However, the World Wide Web redefined how large a hypertext system could be. Even large websites were hypertext systems of a scale not before seen, and when you take into account that it's no more difficult to link to a document on a server in Australia from a server in the United States than it is to link to a document stored in the same directory, the scope of the Web becomes truly staggering.

NOTE

Nearly all large corporations and medium-sized businesses and organizations are using web technology to manage projects, order materials, and distribute company information in a paperless environment. By locating their documents on a private, secure web server called an *intranet*, they take advantage of the technologies the World Wide Web has to offer while keeping the information contained within the company.

The Web Is Graphical and Easy to Navigate

In the early days, using the Internet involved simple text-only applications. You had to navigate the Internet's various services using command-line programs (think DOS) and arcane tools. Although plenty of information was available on the Net, it wasn't necessarily pretty to look at or easy to find.

Then along came the first graphical web browser: Mosaic. It paved the way for the Web to display both text and graphics in full color on the same page. The ability to create complex, attractive pages rivaling those founds in books, magazines, and newspapers propelled the popularity of the Web. These days, the Web offers such a wide degree of capabilities that people are writing web applications that replace desktop applications.

A *browser* is used to view and navigate web pages and other information on the World Wide Web. Currently, the most widely used browser is Microsoft Internet Explorer, which is built into Microsoft Windows.

Hypertext or Hypermedia?

If the Web incorporates so much more than text, why do I keep calling the Web a hypertext system? Well, if you're going to be absolutely technically correct about it, the Web is not a hypertext system—it's a hyper*media* system. But, on the other hand, you might argue that the Web began as a text-only system, and much of the content is still text-heavy, with extra bits of media added in as emphasis. Many very educated people are arguing these very points at this moment and presenting their arguments in papers and discursive rants as educated people like to do. Whatever. I prefer the term *hypertext*, and it's my book, so I'm going to use it. You know what I mean.

The Web Is Cross-Platform

If you can access the Internet, you can access the World Wide Web, regardless of whether you're working on a low-end PC or a fancy expensive workstation. More recently, people began accessing the Internet through their mobile phones, portable handheld PCs, and personal information managers. If you think Windows menus and buttons look better than Macintosh menus and buttons or vice versa (or if you think both

Macintosh and Windows people are weenies), it doesn't matter. The World Wide Web isn't limited to any one kind of machine or developed by any one company. The Web is entirely cross-platform.

Cross-platform means that you can access web information equally well from any computer hardware running any operating system using any display.

The Cross-Platform Ideal

The whole idea that the Web is—and should be—cross-platform is strongly held to by purists. The reality, however, is somewhat different. With the introduction over the years of numerous special features, technologies, and media types, the Web has lost some of its capability to be truly cross-platform. As web authors choose to use these nonstandard features, they willingly limit the potential audience for the content of their sites. For example, a site centered around a Flash animation is essentially unusable for someone using a browser that doesn't have a Flash player, or for a user who might have turned off Flash for quicker downloads. Similarly, some programs that extend the capabilities of a browser (known as *plug-ins*) are available only for one platform (either Windows, Macintosh, or UNIX). Choosing to use one of those plug-ins makes that portion of your site unavailable to users who are either on the wrong platform or don't want to bother to download and install the plug-in.

The Web Is Distributed

Web content can take up a great deal of space, particularly when you include images, audio, and video. To store all of the information, graphics, and multimedia published on the Web, you would need an untold amount of disk space, and managing it would be almost impossible. (Not that there aren't people who try.) Imagine that you were interested in finding out more information about alpacas (Peruvian mammals known for their wool), but when you selected a link in your online encyclopedia, your computer prompted you to insert CD-ROM #456 ALP through ALR. You could be there for a long time just looking for the right CD-ROM!

The Web succeeds at providing so much information because that information is distributed globally across millions of websites, each of which contributes the space for the information it publishes. These sites reside on one or more computers, referred to as web servers. A *web server* is just a computer that listens for requests from web browsers and responds to that request. You, as a consumer of that information, request a resource from the server to view it. You don't have to install it, change disks, or do anything other than point your browser at that site.

A *website* is a location on the Web that publishes some kind of information. When you view a web page, your browser connects to that website to get that information.

Each website, and each page or bit of information on that site, has a unique address. This address is called a *uniform resource locator* or *URL*. When people tell you to visit a site at http://www.yahoo.com/, they've just given you a URL. Whenever you use a browser to visit a website, you get there using a URL. You'll learn more about URLs later today in "Uniform Resource Locators."

The Web Is Dynamic

If you want a permanent copy of some information that's stored on the Web, you have to save it locally because the content can change any time, even while you're viewing the page.

If you're browsing that information, you don't have to install a new version of the help system, buy another book, or call technical support to get updated information. Just launch your browser and check out what's there.

If you're publishing on the Web, you can make sure that your information is up-to-date all the time. You don't have to spend a lot of time re-releasing updated documents. There's no cost of materials. You don't have to get bids on numbers of copies or quality of output. Color is free. And you won't get calls from hapless customers who have a version of the book that was obsolete four years ago.

Consider a book published and distributed entirely online, such as *Thinking in Java* by Bruce Eckel (which you can find at www.mindview.net/Books/TIJ/). He can correct any mistakes in the book and simply upload the revised text to his website, making it instantly available to his readers. He can document new features of Java and include them in the latest version of the book on his site. The website for the book appears in Figure 1.1.

NOTE

> The pictures throughout this book usually are taken from Firefox running on Mac OS X. The only reason for this use is that I'm writing this book on an Apple Powerbook. If you're using a different operating system, don't feel left out. As I noted earlier, the glory of the Web is that you see the same information regardless of the platform you're using. So, ignore the buttons and window borders and focus on what's inside the window.

FIGURE 1.1
The website for
Thinking in Java.

For some sites, the capability to update the site on the fly, at any moment, is precisely why the site exists. Figure 1.2 shows the home page for Yahoo! News, an online news site that's updated 24 hours a day to reflect up-to-the-minute news as it happens. Because the site is up and available all the time, it has an immediacy that neither hard-copy newspapers nor most television news programs can match. Visit Yahoo! News at http://news.yahoo.com.

The Web Is Interactive

Interactivity is the capability to "talk back" to the web server. More traditional media, such as television, isn't interactive in the slightest; all you do is sit and watch as shows are played at you. Other than changing the channel, you don't have much control over what you see. The Web is inherently interactive; the act of selecting a link and jumping to another web page to go somewhere else on the Web is a form of interactivity. In addition to this simple interactivity, however, the Web also enables you to communicate with the publisher of the pages you're reading and with other readers of those pages.

For example, pages can be designed to contain interactive forms that readers can fill out. Forms can contain text-entry areas, radio buttons, or simple menus of items. When the form is submitted, the information typed by readers is sent back to the server from which the pages originated. Figure 1.3 shows an example of an online form for a rather ridiculous census.

FIGURE 1.2
Yahoo! News.

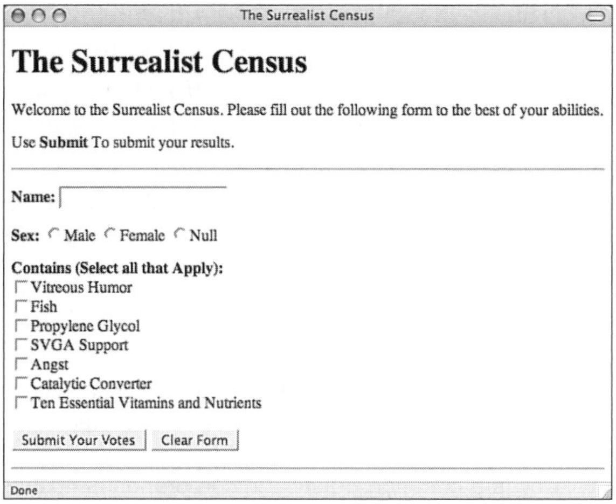

FIGURE 1.3
The Surrealist
Census form.

As a publisher of information on the Web, you can use forms for many different purposes, such as the following:

- To get feedback about your pages.
- To get information from your readers (survey, voting, demographic, or any other kind of data). You then can collect statistics on that data, store it in a database, or do anything you want with it.

- To provide online order forms for products or services available on the Web.
- To create guestbooks and conferencing systems that enable your readers to post their own information on your pages. These kinds of systems enable your readers to communicate not only with you, but also with other readers of your pages.

In addition to forms, which provide some of the most popular forms of interactivity on the Web, advanced features of web technologies provide even more interactivity. Flash, JavaScript, Java, and Shockwave, for example, enable you to include entire programs and games inside web pages. Software can run on the Web to enable real-time chat sessions between your readers. As time goes on, the Web becomes less of a medium for people passively sitting and digesting information (and becoming "Net potatoes") and more of a medium for reaching and communicating with other people all over the world.

Web Browsers

A web browser, as mentioned earlier, is the program you use to view pages and navigate the World Wide Web. A wide array of web browsers is available for just about every platform you can imagine. Most browsers are freeware or shareware (try before you buy) or have a lenient licensing policy. Microsoft Internet Explorer, for example, is included with Windows and Safari is included with Mac OS X. Mozilla Firefox, Netscape Navigator, and Opera are all available for free. Currently, the most widely used is Microsoft Internet Explorer (sometimes called just *Internet Explorer* or *IE*). Despite the fact that Internet Explorer has the lion's share of the market, however, it isn't the only browser on the Web. This point will become important later, when you learn how to design Web pages and learn about the diverse capabilities of different browsers. Assuming that Internet Explorer is the only browser in use on the Web and designing your pages accordingly limits the audience you can reach with the information you want to present.

NOTE

> Choosing to develop for a specific browser, such as Internet Explorer, is suitable when you know a limited audience using the targeted browser software will view your website. Developing this way is a common practice in corporations implementing intranets. In these situations, it's a fair assumption that all users in the organization will use the browser supplied to them and, accordingly, it's possible to design the web pages on an intranet to use the specific capabilities of the browser in question.

What the Browser Does

The core purpose of a web browser is to connect to web servers, request documents, and then properly format and display those documents. Web browsers can also display files on your local computer, download files that are not meant to be displayed, and in some cases even allow you to send and retrieve email. What the browser is best at, however, is dealing with retrieving and displaying web documents. Each web page is a file written in a language called the *Hypertext Markup Language (HTML)* that includes the text of the page, a description of its structure, and links to other documents, images, or other media. The browser takes the information it gets from the web server and formats and displays it for your system. Different browsers might format and display the same file in diverse ways, depending on the capabilities of that system and how the browser is configured.

Retrieving documents from the Web and formatting them for your system are the two tasks that make up the core of a browser's functionality. Depending on the browser you use and the features it includes, however, you also might be able to play Flash animations, multimedia files, run Java applets, read your mail, or use other advanced features that a particular browser offers.

An Overview of Some Popular Browsers

This section describes the most popular browsers currently on the Web. They're in no way the only browsers available, and if the browser you're using isn't listed here, don't feel that you have to use one of these. Whichever browser you have is fine as long as it works for you.

Microsoft Internet Explorer

Microsoft's browser, Microsoft Internet Explorer, is included with Microsoft Windows. It was also included with the Mac OS, but has since been discontinued. You can still install and use other browsers if you want, but if you're not picky, you don't need to do anything more.

NOTE

If you're serious about web design, you should install all the popular browsers on your system and use them to view your pages after you've published them. That way, you can make sure that everything is working properly. Even if you don't use a particular browser on a day-to-day basis, your site will be visited by people who do. If you are interested in checking cross-browser compatibility issues, you should start with Microsoft Internet Explorer and Mozilla Firefox, and perhaps include Opera as well.

Microsoft Internet Explorer has become the most widely used web browser, in large part due to the fact that it has been tightly integrated with the latest versions of Windows. As of January 2006, Internet Explorer makes up more than 80% of the overall browser market. Figure 1.4 shows Internet Explorer running under Windows XP.

FIGURE 1.4
Microsoft Internet
Explorer
(Windows XP).

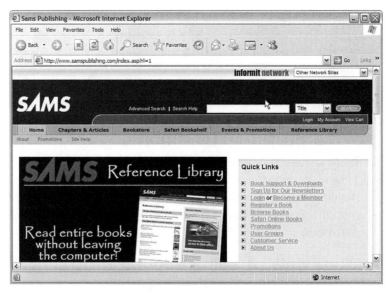

Mozilla Firefox

Mozilla Firefox is the new kid on the web browser block. In 1998, Netscape Communications opened the source code to their web browser and assigned some staff members to work on making it better. Seven years and many releases later, the result of that effort is Mozilla Firefox. Netscape Communications, since acquired by America Online, no longer has any official ties to the Mozilla Foundation, which is now an independent nonprofit organization.

Microsoft released Internet Explorer 6 in October 2001. Firefox and its predecessor Mozilla have seen many revisions over that time, and currently offer more comprehensive support for web standards than does Internet Explorer. Firefox is available for Windows, Mac OS X, and Linux, and is a free download at http://www.mozilla.com.

Internet Explorer still dominates the web browser market, but Firefox is becoming increasingly popular, especially with people who create websites.

Netscape Navigator

Once the dominant web browser, Netscape Navigator is now a version of Mozilla Firefox that has been modified to have the Netscape brand rather than the Mozilla brand. In terms of how they display web pages, Netscape Navigator and Mozilla Firefox are identical. You can download Netscape at http://browser.netscape.com.

The important thing to remember about Netscape is that the browser has a long history, and once dominated the market. Netscape went nearly four years between browser releases, and at one time Netscape 4.7 was extremely popular. Unfortunately, now it exists mainly to cause pain to web designers. The problem with Netscape 4.7 is that it's old, and its support for current web standards is woefully lacking. With Firefox, much effort was put into making it adhere as closely as possible to published standards. When Netscape 4.7 was released, Netscape was taking a more cavalier attitude toward standards. The bottom line is that pages that look great in Internet Explorer, Firefox, and other current browsers can look awful in Netscape 4.7. You'll have to decide whether you take this into consideration as you design your pages.

Other Browsers

When it comes to browsers, Microsoft Internet Explorer and Mozilla Firefox are the big two. And in terms of market share, Internet Explorer dominates, but there are plenty of other browsers floating around as well. You'd think that given the fact that the browser market has been dominated by Microsoft or Netscape almost since its inception, there wouldn't be a lot of other browsers out there, but that's not the case.

For example, Opera (http://www.operasoftware.com/) has a niche market. It's small, fast, free, and available for a number of platforms, including Windows, Mac OS X, and Linux. It's also standards compliant. Apple has developed a browser named Safari that is the default web browser for Mac OS X. For UNIX users who use KDE, there's Konqueror. There are various Mozilla offshoots, such as Camino for Mac OS X, and Flock, a browser derived from Firefox that is integrated with a number of websites that enable you to publish your own content on the Web. Likewise, command-line browsers such as Lynx and Links are available to provide an all-text view of web pages. There are also a number of browsers that provide access to the Web for people with various disabilities; I'll discuss them in detail in Lesson 17, "Designing for the Real World." It makes sense to code to common standards to accommodate all these types of browsers.

Using the Browser to Access Other Services

Internet veterans know that there are dozens of different ways to get information: FTP, Usenet news, and email. Before the Web became as popular as it is now, you had to use a different tool for each of these, all of which used different commands. Although all these choices made for a great market for *How to Use the Internet* books, they weren't very easy to use.

Web browsers changed that. Although the Web itself is its own information system with its own Internet protocol (the *Hypertext Transfer Protocol* or *HTTP*), web browsers can read files from other Internet services also. Even better, you can create links to information on those systems just as you would create links to web pages. This process is seamless and available through a single application.

1

To point your browser to different kinds of information on the Internet, you use different kinds of URLs. Most URLs start with http:, which indicates a file at an actual website. To download a file from a public site using FTP, you'd use a URL like ftp://_name_of_site/directory/filename. You can also view the contents of a directory on a publicly accessible FTP site using an ftp: URL that ends with a directory name. Figure 1.5 shows a listing of files from the iBiblio FTP site at ftp://ftp.ibiblio.org/.

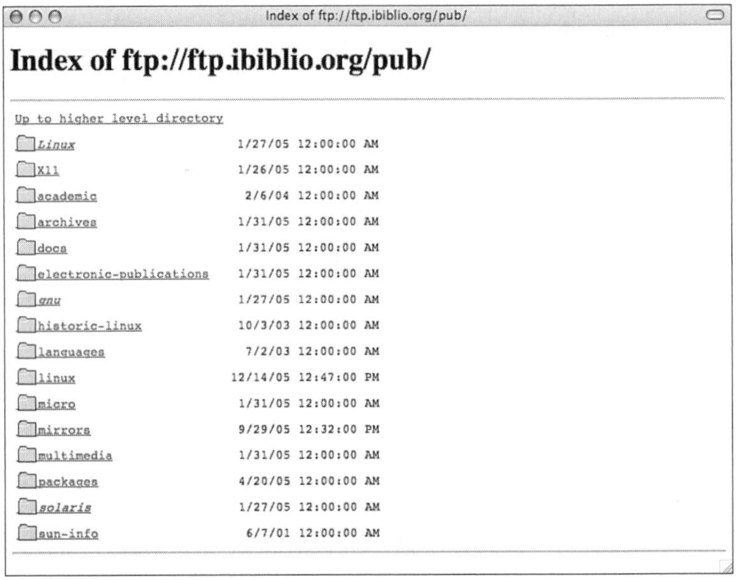

FIGURE 1.5

A listing of files and directories available at the iBiblio FTP site.

Index of ftp://ftp.ibiblio.org/pub/

Index of ftp://ftp.ibiblio.org/pub/

```
Up to higher level directory
  Linux                        1/27/05 12:00:00 AM
  X11                          1/26/05 12:00:00 AM
  academic                      2/6/04 12:00:00 AM
  archives                     1/31/05 12:00:00 AM
  docs                         1/31/05 12:00:00 AM
  electronic-publications      1/31/05 12:00:00 AM
  gnu                          1/27/05 12:00:00 AM
  historic-linux               10/3/03 12:00:00 AM
  languages                     7/2/03 12:00:00 AM
  linux                       12/14/05 12:47:00 PM
  micro                        1/31/05 12:00:00 AM
  mirrors                      9/29/05 12:32:00 PM
  multimedia                   1/31/05 12:00:00 AM
  packages                     4/20/05 12:00:00 AM
  solaris                      1/27/05 12:00:00 AM
  sun-info                      6/7/01 12:00:00 AM
```

To access a Usenet newsgroup through your web browser (thereby launching an external news-reading program), you can simply enter a news: URL, such as **news:alt.usage. english**.

You'll learn more about different kinds of URLs in Lesson 5, "Adding Links to Your Web Pages."

Web Servers

To view and browse pages on the Web, all you need is a web browser. To publish pages on the Web, you need a web server.

A *web server* is the program that runs on a computer and is responsible for replying to web browser requests for files. You need a web server to publish documents on the Web. One point of confusion is that the computer on which a server program runs is also referred to as a server. So, when someone uses the term *web server*, she could be referring to a program used to distribute web pages or the computer on which that program runs.

When you use a browser to request a page on a website, that browser makes a web connection to a server using the HTTP protocol. The server accepts the connection, sends the contents of the requested files, and then closes the connection. The browser then formats the information it got from the server.

On the server side, many different browsers can connect to the same server to get the same information. The web server is responsible for handling all these requests.

Web servers do more than just serve files. They're also responsible for managing form input and for linking forms and browsers with programs such as databases running on the server.

As with browsers, many different servers are available for many different platforms, each with many different features and ranging in cost from free to very expensive. For now, all you need to know is what the server is there for; you'll learn more about web servers in Lesson 18, "Putting Your Site Online."

Uniform Resource Locators

As you learned earlier, a URL is a pointer to some bit of data on the Web, be it a web document, a file available via FTP, a posting on Usenet, or an email address. The URL provides a universal, consistent method for finding and accessing information.

In addition to typing URLs directly into your browser to go to a particular page, you also use URLs when you create a hypertext link within a document to another document. So, any way you look at it, URLs are important to how you and your browser get around on the Web.

URLs contain information about the following:

- How to get to the information (which protocol to use: FTP, HTTP, or file)
- The Internet hostname of the computer where the content is stored (www.ncsa.uiuc.edu, ftp.apple.com, netcom16.netcom.com, and so on)
- The directory or other location on that site where the content is located

You also can use special URLs for tasks such as sending mail to people (called *Mailto URLs*) and running JavaScript code. You'll learn all about URLs and what each part means in Lesson 5.

Summary

To publish on the Web, you have to understand the basic concepts that make up the parts of the Web. Today, you learned three major concepts. First, you learned about a few of the more useful features of the Web for publishing information. Second, you learned about web browsers and servers and how they interact to deliver web pages. Third, you learned about what a URL is and why it's important to web browsing and publishing.

Workshop

Each lesson in this book contains a workshop to help you review the topics you learned. The first section of this workshop lists some common questions about the Web. Next, you'll answer some questions that I'll ask you about the Web. The answers to the quiz appear in the next section. At the end of each lesson, you'll find some exercises that will help you retain the information you learned about the Web.

Q&A

Q Who runs the Web? Who controls all these protocols? Who's in charge of all this?

A No single entity owns or controls the World Wide Web. Given the enormous number of independent sites that supply information to the Web, for any single organization to set rules or guidelines would be impossible. Two groups of organizations, however, have a great influence over the look and feel and direction of the Web itself.

The first is the World Wide Web Consortium (W3C), based at Massachusetts Institute of Technology in the United States and INRIA in Europe. The W3C is made up of individuals and organizations interested in supporting and defining the languages and protocols that make up the Web (HTTP, HTML, XHTML, and so on). It also provides products (browsers, servers, and so on) that are freely available to anyone who wants to use them. The W3 Consortium is the closest anyone gets to setting the standards for and enforcing rules about the World Wide Web. You can visit the Consortium's home page at http://www.w3.org/.

The second group of organizations that influences the Web is the browser developers themselves, most notably Microsoft and the Mozilla Foundation. The competition to be the most popular and technically advanced browser on the Web can be fierce. Although both organizations claim to support and adhere to the guidelines proposed by the W3C, both also include their own new features in new versions of their software—features that sometimes conflict with each other and with the work the W3C is doing.

Things still change pretty rapidly on the Web, although not as rapidly as they did in the height of the so-called browser wars. The popular browsers are finally converging to support many of the standards defined by the W3C, so writing to those standards will work most of the time. I'll talk about the exceptions throughout this book.

1

Q I've heard that the Web changes so fast that it's almost impossible to stay current. Is this book doomed to be out of date the day it's published?

A Although it's true that things do change on the Web, the vast majority of the information in this book will serve you well far into the future. HTML and XHTML are as stable now as they have ever been, and once you learn the core technologies of HTML, CSS, and JavaScript, you can add on other things at your leisure.

Quiz

1. What's a URL?
2. What's required to publish documents on the Web?

Quiz Answers

1. A URL, or uniform resource locator, is an address that points to a specific document or bit of information on the Internet.

2. You need access to a web server. Web servers, which are programs that serve up documents over the Web, reply to web browser requests for files and send the requested pages to many different types of browsers. They also manage form input and handle database integration.

Exercises

1. Try navigating to each of the different types of URLs mentioned today (http:, ftp:, and news:). Some links you might want to try are http://www.tywebpub.com, ftp://ftp.cdrom.com, and news:comp.infosystems.www.

2. Download a different browser than the one you ordinarily use and try it out for a while. If you're using Internet Explorer, try out Mozilla, Netscape, Opera, or even a command-line browser such as Lynx or Links. To really see how things have changed and how some users who don't upgrade their browser experience the Web, download an old browser from http://browsers.evolt.org/ and try it out.

LESSON 2:
Preparing to Publish on the Web

When you write a book, a paper, an article, or even a memo, you usually don't just jump right in with the first sentence and then write it through to the end. The same goes with the visual arts—you don't normally start from the top-left corner of the canvas or page and work your way down to the bottom right.

A better way to write, draw, or design a work is to do some planning beforehand—to know what you're going to do and what you're trying to accomplish, and to have a general idea or rough sketch of the structure of the piece before you jump in and work on it.

Just as with more traditional modes of communication, the process of writing and designing web pages takes some planning and thought before you start flinging text and graphics around and linking them wildly to each other. It's perhaps even more important to plan ahead with web pages because trying to apply the rules of traditional writing or design to online hypertext often results in documents that are either difficult to understand and navigate online or that simply don't take advantage of the features that hypertext provides. Poorly organized web pages also are difficult to revise or to expand.

In this Lesson

Today, I describe some of the things you should think about before you begin developing your web pages. Specifically, you need to do the following:

- Learn the differences between a web server, a website, a web page, and a home page

- Think about the sort of information (content) you want to put on the Web
- Set the goals for the website
- Organize your content into the main topics
- Come up with a general structure for pages and topics
- Use storyboarding to plan your website

After you have an overall idea of how you're going to construct your web pages, you're ready to actually start writing and designing those pages in Lesson 4, "Learning the Basics of HTML." If you're eager to get started, be patient! You'll have more than enough HTML to learn over the next three days.

Anatomy of a Website

First, here's a look at some simple terminology I use throughout this book. You need to know what the following terms mean and how they apply to the body of work you're developing for the Web:

- **Website**—A collection of one or more web pages linked together in a meaningful way that, as a whole, describes a body of information or creates an overall effect (see Figure 2.1).
- **Web server**—A computer on the Internet or an intranet that delivers Web pages and other files in response to browser requests. (An intranet is a network that uses Internet protocols but is not publicly accessible.)
- **Web page**—A single document on a website, usually consisting of an HTML document and any items that are displayed within that document, such as inline images.
- **Home page**—The entry page for a website, which can link to additional pages on the same website or pages on other sites.

Each website is stored on a web server. Throughout the first week or so of this book, you'll learn how to develop well–thought out and well-designed websites. Later, you'll learn how to publish your site on an actual web server.

A *web page* is an individual element of a website in the same way that a page is a single element of a book or a newspaper (although, unlike paper pages, web pages can be of any length). Web pages sometimes are called *web documents*. Both terms refer to the same thing. A web page consists of an HTML document and all the other components that are included on the page, such as images or other media.

FIGURE 2.1
Websites and pages.

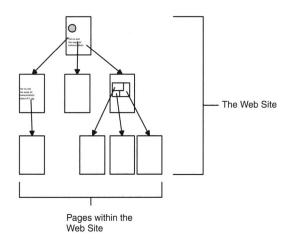

The Web Site

Pages within the
Web Site

One problem with the term *home page* is that it means different things in different contexts. If you're browsing the Web, you usually can think of the home page as the web page that loads when you start your browser or when you click the Home button. Each browser has its own default home page, which generally leads to the website of the browser's creator or one that makes them some money through advertising when you visit.

Within your browser, you can change that default home page to point to any page you want. Many users create a personalized page linking to sites they use often and set that as their browser's home page.

If you're publishing pages on the Web, however, the term *home page* has an entirely different meaning. The home page is the first or topmost page on your website. It's the intended entry point that provides access to the rest of the pages you've created (see Figure 2.2).

CAUTION   Most of your users will access your site through your home page, but some will enter your site through other pages. The nature of the Web is that people can link to any page on your site. If you have interesting information on a page other than your home page, people will link directly to that page. On the other pages of your site, you shouldn't assume that the visitor has seen your home page.

FIGURE 2.2
A home page.

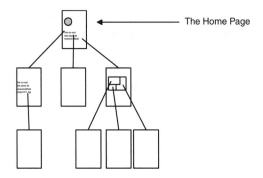

The Home Page

A home page usually contains an overview of the content of the website, available from that starting point—for example, in the form of a table of contents or a set of icons. If your content is small enough, you might include everything on that single home page—making your home page and your website the same thing. A personal home page might include a link to a person's resume and some pictures from a recent vacation. A corporate home page usually describes what the company does, and contains links like "About the Company," "Products and Services," and "Customer Support."

What Do You Want to Do on the Web?

This question might seem silly. You wouldn't have bought this book if you didn't already have some idea of what you want to put online. But maybe you don't really know what you want to put on the Web, or you have a vague idea but nothing concrete. Maybe it has suddenly become your job to put a page for your company on the Web, and someone handed you this book and said, "Here, this will help." Maybe you just want to do something similar to some other web page you've seen and thought was particularly cool.

What you want to put on the Web is what I'll refer to throughout this book as your *content*. *Content* is a general term that can refer to text, graphics, media, interactive forms, and so on. If you tell someone what your web pages are about, you're describing your content.

What sort of content can you put on the Web? Just about anything you want to. Here are some of the types of content that are popular on the Web right now:

- **Stuff for work**—Perhaps you work in the accounting department and you need to publish the procedure for filing expense reports on your company's intranet. Or you're a software developer and you need to publish the test plan for your company's next software release on an internal web server. Chances are that you can publish some information on a web page at work that will save you from having to type it into an email every time someone asks you about it. Try it!

- **Personal information**—You can create pages describing everything anyone could ever want to know about you and how incredibly marvelous you are—your hobbies, your resume, your picture, things you've done.

- **Weblogs and journals**—Many people use the Web to publish their journals or their opinions on a weblog. Many people use content management applications to publish their journals or weblogs, but knowing HTML is still helpful for changing the look and feel of your site and sprucing up your individual entries or articles.

- **Hobbies or special interests**—A web page can contain information about a particular topic, hobby, or something you're interested in; for example, music, *Star Trek*, motorcycles, cult movies, hallucinogenic mushrooms, antique ink bottles, or upcoming jazz concerts in your city.

- **Publications**—Newspapers, magazines, and other publications lend themselves particularly well to the Web, and websites have the advantage of being more immediate and easier to update than their print counterparts. Delivery is a lot simpler as well.

- **Company profiles**—You could offer information about what a company does, where it's located, job openings, data sheets, white papers, marketing collateral, product demonstrations, and whom to contact.

- **Online documentation**—The term *online documentation* can refer to everything from quick-reference cards to full reference documentation to interactive tutorials or training modules. Anything task-oriented (changing the oil in your car, making a soufflé, creating landscape portraits in oil, learning HTML) could be described as online documentation.

- **Shopping catalogs**—If your company offers items for sale, making your products available on the Web is a quick and easy way to let your customers know what you have available as well as your prices. If prices change, you can just update your web documents to reflect that new information.

- **Online stores**—It's turned out that the Web is a great place to sell things. There are any number of sites that let just about anybody sell their stuff online. You can auction your goods off at eBay or sell them for a fixed price at half.com. Amazon.com lets you do both. You can also create your own online store if you want. There's plenty of software out there these days to make the task of selling things online a lot easier than it used to be.

- **Polling and opinion gathering**—Forms on the Web enable you to get feedback from your visitors via opinion polls, suggestion boxes, comments on your web pages or your products, or through interactive discussion groups.

2

- **Online education**—The low cost of information delivery to people anywhere with an Internet connection via the Web makes it an attractive medium for delivery of distance-learning programs. Already, numerous traditional universities, as well as new online schools and universities, have begun offering distance learning on the Web. For example, the Massachusetts Institute of Technology is placing teaching materials online for public use at http://ocw.mit.edu/.
- **Anything else that comes to mind**—Hypertext fiction, online toys, media archives, collaborative art…anything!

The only thing that limits what you can publish on the Web is your own imagination. In fact, if what you want to do with it isn't in this list or seems especially wild or half-baked, that's an excellent reason to try it. The most interesting web pages are the ones that stretch the boundaries of what the Web is supposed to be capable of.

You might also find inspiration in looking at other websites similar to the one you have in mind. If you're building a corporate site, look at the sites belonging to your competitors and see what they have to offer. If you're working on a personal site, visit sites that you admire and see if you can find inspiration for building your own site. Decide what you like about those sites and you wish to emulate, and where you can improve upon those sites when you build your own.

If you really have no idea of what to put up on the Web, don't feel that you have to stop here; put this book away, and come up with something before continuing. Maybe by reading through this book, you'll get some ideas (and this book will be useful even if you don't have ideas). I've personally found that the best way to come up with ideas is to spend an afternoon browsing on the Web and exploring what other people have done.

Setting Your Goals

What do you want people to be able to accomplish on your website? Are your visitors looking for specific information on how to do something? Are they going to read through each page in turn, going on only when they're done with the page they're reading? Are they just going to start at your home page and wander aimlessly around, exploring your world until they get bored and go somewhere else?

Suppose that you're creating a website that describes the company where you work. Some people visiting that website might want to know about job openings. Others might want to know where the company actually is located. Still others might have heard that your company makes technical white papers available over the Net, and they want to download the most recent version of a particular paper. Each of these goals is valid, so you should list each one.

For a shopping catalog website, you might have only a few goals: to enable your visitors to browse the items you have for sale by name or price, and to order specific items after they're done browsing.

For a personal or special-interest website, you might have only a single goal: to enable your visitors to browse and explore the information you've provided.

The goals do not have to be lofty ("this website will bring about world peace") or even make much sense to anyone except you. Still, coming up with goals for your Web documents prepares you to design, organize, and write your web pages specifically to reach these goals. Goals also help you resist the urge to obscure your content with extra information.

2

If you're designing web pages for someone else—for example, if you're creating the website for your company or if you've been hired as a consultant—having a set of goals for the site from your employer definitely is one of the most important pieces of information you should have before you create a single page. The ideas you have for the website might not be the ideas that other people have for it, and you might end up doing a lot of work that has to be thrown away.

Breaking Up Your Content into Main Topics

With your goals in mind, try to organize your content into main topics or sections, chunking related information together under a single topic. Sometimes the goals you came up with in the preceding section and your list of topics will be closely related. For example, if you're putting together a web page for a bookstore, the goal of being able to order books fits nicely under a topic called, appropriately, "Ordering Books."

You don't have to be exact at this point in development. Your goal here is just to try to come up with an idea of what, specifically, you'll be describing in your web pages. You can organize the information better later, as you write the actual pages.

Suppose that you're designing a website about how to tune up your car. This example is simple because tune-ups consist of a concrete set of steps that fit neatly into topic headings. In this example, your topics might include the following:

- Change the oil and oil filter
- Check and adjust engine timing
- Check and adjust valve clearances
- Check and replace the spark plugs
- Check fluid levels, belts, and hoses

Don't worry about the order of the steps or how you're going to get your visitors to go from one section to another. Just list the points you want to describe in your website.

How about a less task-oriented example? Suppose that you want to create a set of web pages about a particular rock band because you're a big fan, and you're sure other fans would benefit from your extensive knowledge. Your topics might be as follows:

- The history of the band
- Biographies of each of the band members
- A *discography*—all the albums and singles the band has released
- Selected lyrics
- Images of album covers
- Information about upcoming shows and future albums

You can come up with as many topics as you want, but try to keep each topic reasonably short. If a single topic seems too large, try to break it up into subtopics. If you have too many small topics, try to group them together into a more general topic heading. For example, if you're creating an online encyclopedia of poisonous plants, having individual topics for each plant would be overkill. You can just as easily group each plant name under a letter of the alphabet (A, B, C, and so on) and use each letter as a topic. That's assuming, of course, that your visitors will be looking up information in your encyclopedia alphabetically. If they want to look up poisonous plants by using some other method, you'd need to come up with another system of organization as well.

Your goal is to have a set of topics that are roughly the same size and that group together related bits of information you have to present.

Ideas for Organization and Navigation

At this point, you should have a good idea of what you want to talk about as well as a list of topics. The next step is to actually start structuring the information you have into a set of web pages. Before you do that, however, consider some standard structures that have been used in other help systems and online tools. This section describes some of these structures, their various features, and some important considerations, including the following:

- The kinds of information that work well for each structure
- How visitors find their way through the content of each structure type to find what they need
- How to make sure that visitors can figure out where they are within your documents (context) and find their way back to a known position

As you read this section, think about how your information might fit into one of these structures or how you could combine these structures to create a new structure for your website.

Hierarchies

Probably the easiest and most logical way to structure your web documents is in a hierarchical or menu fashion, as illustrated in Figure 2.3. Hierarchies and menus lend themselves especially well to online and hypertext documents. Most online help systems, for example, are hierarchical. You start with a list or menu of major topics; selecting one leads you to a list of subtopics, which then leads you to a discussion about a particular topic. Different help systems have different levels, of course, but most follow this simple structure.

FIGURE 2.3
Hierarchical
organization.

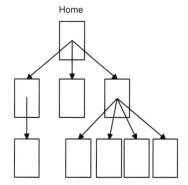

Home

In a hierarchical organization, visitors can easily see their position in the structure. Their choices are to move up for more general information or down for more specific information. If you provide a link back to the top level, your visitors can get back to some known position quickly and easily.

In hierarchies, the home page provides the most general overview to the content below it. The home page also defines the main links for the pages farther down in the hierarchy. For example, a website about gardening might have a home page with the topics shown in Figure 2.4.

If you select Fruits, you then follow a link "down" to a page about fruits (see Figure 2.5). From there, you can go back to the home page, or you can select another link and go farther down into more specific information about particular fruits.

FIGURE 2.4
A Gardening home page with a hierarchical structure.

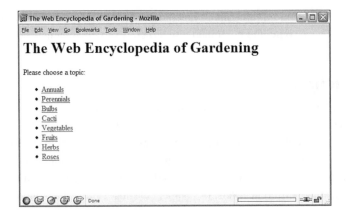

FIGURE 2.5
Your hierarchy takes you to the Fruits page.

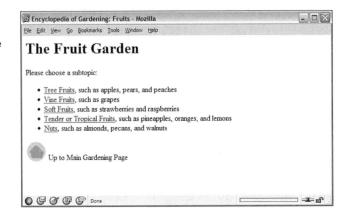

Selecting Soft Fruits takes you to yet another menu-like page, where you have still more categories from which to choose (see Figure 2.6). From there, you can go up to Fruits, back to the home page, or down to one of the choices in this menu.

Note that each level has a consistent interface (up, down, back to index), and that each level has a limited set of choices for basic navigation. Hierarchies are structured enough that the chance of getting lost is minimal. This especially is true if you provide clues about where up is; for example, an Up to Soft Fruits link as opposed to just Up.

Additionally, if you organize each level of the hierarchy and avoid overlap between topics (and the content you have lends itself to a hierarchical organization), using hierarchies can be an easy way to find particular bits of information. If that use is one of your goals for your visitors, using a hierarchy might work particularly well.

FIGURE 2.6
From the Fruits page, you can find the Soft Fruits page.

Avoid including too many levels and too many choices, however, because you can easily annoy your visitors. Having too many menu pages results in "voice-mail syndrome." After having to choose from too many menus, visitors might forget what they originally wanted, and they're too annoyed to care. Try to keep your hierarchy two to three levels deep, combining information on the pages at the lowest levels (or endpoints) of the hierarchy if necessary.

Linear

Another way to organize your documents is to use a linear or sequential organization, similar to how printed documents are organized. In a linear structure, as illustrated in Figure 2.7, the home page is the title or introduction, and each page follows sequentially from that structure. In a strict linear structure, links move from one page to another, typically forward and back. You also might want to include a link to Home that takes the user quickly back to the first page.

FIGURE 2.7
Linear organization.

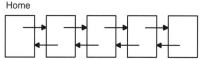

Context generally is easy to figure out in a linear structure simply because there are so few places to go.

A linear organization is very rigid and limits your visitors' freedom to explore and your freedom to present information. Linear structures are good for putting material online when the information also has a very linear structure offline (such as short stories, step-by-step instructions, or computer-based training), or when you explicitly want to prevent your visitors from skipping around.

For example, consider teaching someone how to make cheese by using the Web. Cheese making is a complex process involving several steps that must be followed in a specific order.

Describing this process using web pages lends itself to a linear structure rather well. When navigating a set of web pages on this subject, you'd start with the home page, which might have a summary or an overview of the steps to follow. Then, by using the link for going forward, move on to the first step, Choosing the Right Milk; to the next step, Setting and Curdling the Milk; all the way through to the last step, Curing and Ripening the Cheese. If you need to review at any time, you could use the link for moving backward. Because the process is so linear, you would have little need for links that branch off from the main stem or links that join together different steps in the process.

Linear with Alternatives

You can soften the rigidity of a linear structure by enabling the visitors to deviate from the main path. You could, for example, have a linear structure with alternatives that branch out from a single point (see Figure 2.8). The offshoots can then rejoin the main branch at some point farther down, or they can continue down their separate tracks until they each come to an end.

FIGURE 2.8
Linear with
alternatives.

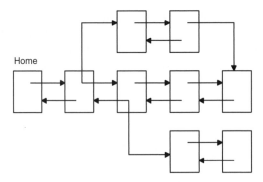

Suppose that you have an installation procedure for a software package that's similar in most ways, regardless of the computer type, except for one step. At that point in the linear installation, you could branch out to cover each system, as shown in Figure 2.9.

After the system-specific part of the installation, you could link back to the original branch and continue with the generic installation.

FIGURE 2.9
Different steps for
different systems.

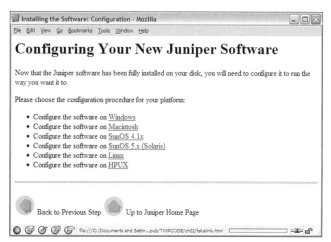

2

In addition to branching from a linear structure, you could also provide links that enable
visitors to skip forward or backward in the chain if they need to review a particular step
or if they already understand some content (see Figure 2.10).

FIGURE 2.10
Skip ahead or
back.

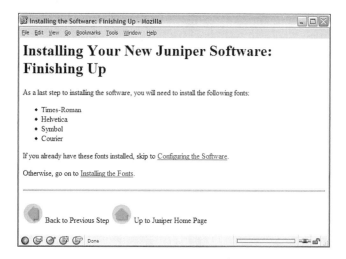

Combination of Linear and Hierarchical

A popular form of document organization on the Web is a combination of a linear structure
and a hierarchical one, as shown in Figure 2.11. This structure occurs most often when
very structured but linear documents are put online; the popular Frequently Asked
Questions (FAQ) files use this structure.

FIGURE 2.11
Combination
of linear and
hierarchical
organization.

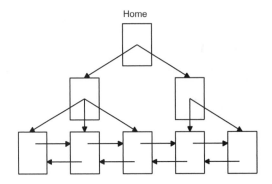

Home

The combination of linear and hierarchical documents works well as long as you have appropriate clues regarding context. Because the visitors can either move up and down or forward and backward, they can easily lose their mental positioning in the hierarchy when crossing hierarchical boundaries by moving forward or backward.

Suppose that you're putting the Shakespeare play *Macbeth* online as a set of web pages. In addition to the simple linear structure that the play provides, you can create a hierarchical table of contents and summary of each act linked to appropriate places within the text, similar to what is shown in Figure 2.12.

FIGURE 2.12
Macbeth's
hierarchy.

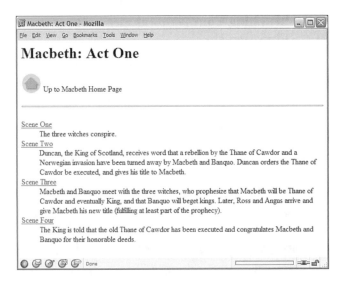

Because this structure is both linear and hierarchical, you provide links to go forward, backward, return to beginning, and up on each page of the script. But what is the context for going up?

If you've just come down into this page from an act summary, the context makes sense: *Up* means go back to the summary from which you just came.

But suppose that you go down from a summary and then go forward, crossing an act boundary (say from Act 1 to Act 2). Now what does *up* mean? The fact that you're moving up to a page you might not have seen before is disorienting given the nature of what you expect from a hierarchy. Up and down are supposed to be consistent.

Consider two possible solutions:

- Do not allow forward and back links across hierarchical boundaries. In this case, to read from Act 1 to Act 2 in *Macbeth*, you have to move up in the hierarchy and then back down into Act 2.

- Provide more context in the link text. Rather than just Up or an icon for the link that moves up in the hierarchy, include a description of where the user is moving to.

Web

A web is a set of documents with little or no actual overall structure; the only thing tying each page together is a link (see Figure 2.13). Visitors drift from document to document, following the links around.

For an example of such a site, visit Wikipedia at http://wikipedia.org. Wikipedia is an encyclopedia written and maintained by the public. Anyone can write a new article or edit an existing article, and the site is very loosely organized. Articles that reference topics discussed in other articles link to them, creating a web organization scheme. Wikipedia has no hierarchical organization; you're expected to find the topics you're interested in by following links or using the site's search functionality.

FIGURE 2.13
A web structure.

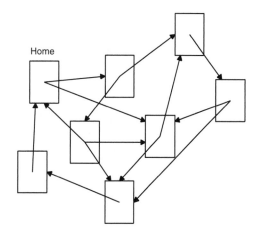

Web structures tend to be free-floating and enable visitors to wander aimlessly through the content. Web structures are excellent for content that's intended to be meandering or unrelated or when you want to encourage browsing. The World Wide Web itself is, of course, a giant web structure.

In the context of a website, the environment is organized so that each page is a specific location (and usually contains a description of that location). From that location, you can move in several different directions, exploring the environment much in the way you would move from room to room in a building in the real world (and getting lost just as easily). The initial home page, for example, might look something like the one shown in Figure 2.14.

From that page, you then can explore one of the links, for example, to go into the building, which takes you to the page shown in Figure 2.15.

FIGURE 2.14
The home page for a web-based virtual environment.

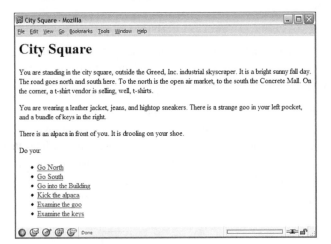

FIGURE 2.15
Another page in the web environment.

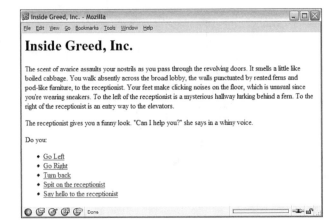

Each room has a set of links to each adjacent room in the environment. By following the links, you can explore the rooms in the environment.

The problem with web organizations is that you can get lost in them too easily—just as you might in the world you're exploring in the example. Without any overall structure to the content, figuring out the relationship between where you are, where you're going and, often, where you've been, is difficult. Context is difficult, and often the only way to find your way back out of a web structure is to retrace your steps. Web structures can be extremely disorienting and immensely frustrating if you have a specific goal in mind.

To solve the problem of disorientation, you can use clues on each page. Here are two ideas:

- Provide a way out. Return to Home Page is an excellent link.
- Include a map of the overall structure on each page, with a "you are here" indication somewhere in the map. It doesn't have to be an actual visual map, but providing some sort of context goes a long way toward preventing your visitors from getting lost.

Storyboarding Your Website

The next step in planning your website is to figure out what content goes on what page and to come up with some simple links for navigation between those pages.

If you're using one of the structures described in the preceding section, much of the organization might arise from that structure—in which case, this section will be easy. However, if you want to combine different kinds of structures or if you have a lot of content that needs to be linked together in sophisticated ways, sitting down and making a specific plan of what goes where will be incredibly useful later as you develop and link each individual page.

What's Storyboarding and Why Do I Need It?

Storyboarding a website is a concept borrowed from filmmaking in which each scene and each individual camera shot is sketched and roughed out in the order in which it occurs in the movie. Storyboarding provides an overall structure and plan to the film that enables the director and staff to have a distinct idea of where each individual shot fits into the overall movie.

The storyboarding concept works quite well for developing web pages. The storyboard provides an overall rough outline of what the website will look like when it's done, including which topics go on which pages, the primary links, and maybe even some conceptual idea of what sort of graphics you'll be using and where they'll go. With that representation in hand, you can develop each page without trying to remember exactly where that page fits into the overall website and its often complex relationships to other pages.

In the case of really large sets of documents, a storyboard enables different people to develop various portions of the same website. With a clear storyboard, you can minimize duplication of work and reduce the amount of contextual information each person needs to remember.

For smaller or simpler websites, or websites with a simple logical structure, storyboarding might be unnecessary. For larger and more complex projects, however, the existence of a storyboard can save enormous amounts of time and frustration. If you can't keep all the parts of your content and their relationships in your head, consider creating a storyboard.

So, what does a storyboard for a website look like? It can be as simple as a couple of sheets of paper. Each sheet can represent a page, with a list of topics each page will describe and some thoughts about the links that page will include. I've seen storyboards for very complex hypertext systems that involved a really large bulletin board, index cards, and string. Each index card had a topic written on it, and the links were represented by string tied on pins from card to card.

The point of a storyboard is that it organizes your web pages in a way that works for you. If you like index cards and string, work with these tools. If a simple outline on paper or on the computer works better, use that instead.

Hints for Storyboarding

Some things to think about when developing your storyboard are as follows:

- **Which topics will go on each page?**

  A simple rule of thumb is to have each topic represented by a single page. If you have several topics, however, maintaining and linking them can be a daunting task. Consider combining smaller, related topics onto a single page instead. Don't go overboard and put everything on one page, however; your visitors still have to download your document over the Net. Having several medium-sized pages (such as the size of two to ten pages in your word processor) is better than having one monolithic page or hundreds of little tiny pages.

- **What are the primary forms of navigation between pages?**

  What links will you need for your visitors to navigate from page to page? They are the main links in your document that enable your visitors to accomplish the goals you defined in the first section. Links for forward, back, up, down, and home all fall under the category of primary navigation.

- **What alternative forms of navigation are you going to provide?**

    In addition to the simple navigation links, some websites contain extra information that's parallel to the main web content, such as a glossary of terms, an alphabetical index of concepts, copyright information, or a credits page. Consider these extra forms of information when designing your plan, and think about how you're going to link them into the main content.

- **What will you put on your home page?**

    Because the home page is the starting point for the rest of the information in your website, consider what sort of information you're going to put on the home page. A general summary of what's to come? A list of links to other topics? Whatever you put on the home page, make sure that it's compelling enough so that members of your intended audience want to stick around.

- **What are your goals?**

    As you design the framework for your website, keep your goals in mind, and make sure that you aren't obscuring your goals with extra information or content.

TIP

> Several utilities and packages can assist you in storyboarding. Foremost among them are site-management packages that can help you manage links in a site, view a graphical representation of the relationship of documents in your site, move documents around, and automatically update all relevant links in and to the documents. Some examples include consumer products such as Microsoft FrontPage and Adobe Dreamweaver.

Summary

Designing a website, like designing a book outline, a building plan, or a painting, can sometimes be a complex and involved process. Having a plan before you begin can help you keep the details straight and help you develop the finished product with fewer false starts. Today, you learned how to put together a simple plan and structure for creating a set of web pages, including the following:

- Deciding what sort of content to present
- Coming up with a set of goals for that content
- Deciding on a set of topics
- Organizing and storyboarding the website

With that plan in place, you now can move on to the next few days and learn the specifics of how to write individual web pages, create links between them, and add graphics and media to enhance the website for your audience.

Workshop

The first section of the workshop lists some of the common questions people ask while planning a website, along with an answer to each. Following that, you have an opportunity to answer some quiz questions yourself. If you have problems answering any of the questions in the quiz, go to the next section where you'll find the answers. Today's exercises help you formulate some ideas for your own website.

Q&A

Q **Getting organized seems like an awful lot of work. All I want to do is make something simple, and you're telling me I have to have goals and topics and storyboards. Are all of the steps listed here really necessary?**

A If you're doing something simple, you won't need to do much, if any, of the stuff I recommended today. However, if you're talking about developing two or three interlinked pages or more, having a plan before you start will really help. If you just dive in, you might discover that keeping everything straight in your head is too difficult. And the result might not be what you expected, making it hard for people to get the information they need out of your website as well as making it difficult for you to reorganize it so that it makes sense. Having a plan before you start can't hurt, and it might save you time in the long run.

Q **You talked a lot today about organizing topics and pages, but you said nothing about the design and layout of individual pages. Why?**

A I discuss design and layout later in this book, after you've learned more about the sorts of layout that HTML (the language used for web pages) can do and the stuff that it just can't do. You'll find a whole day and more about page layout and design in Lesson 16, "Writing Good Web Pages: Do's and Don'ts."

Q **What if I don't like any of the basic structures you talked about today?**

A Then design your own. As long as your visitors can find what they want or do what you want them to do, no rules say you *must* use a hierarchy or a linear structure. I presented these structures only as potential ideas for organizing your web pages.

Quiz

1. How would you briefly define the meaning of the terms *website*, *web server*, and *web pages*?
2. In terms of web publishing, what's the meaning of the term *home page*?
3. After you set a goal or purpose for your website, what's the next step to designing your pages?
4. Regardless of the navigation structure you use in your website, there's one link that should typically appear on each of your web pages. What is it?
5. What's the purpose of a storyboard?

Quiz Answers

1. A *website* is one or more web pages linked together in a meaningful way. A *web server* is the actual computer that stores the website (or, confusingly enough, the piece of software that responds to requests for pages from the browser). *Web pages* are the individual elements of the website, like a page is to a book.
2. A *home page*, in terms of web publishing, is the entry point to the rest of the pages in your website (the first or topmost page).
3. After you set a goal or purpose for your website, you should try to organize your content into topics or sections.
4. You should try to include a link to your home page on each of the pages in your website. That way, users can always find their way back home if they get lost.
5. A storyboard provides an overall outline of what the website will look like when it's done. It helps organize your web pages in a way that works for you. They are most beneficial for larger websites.

Exercises

1. Come up with a list of several goals that your visitors might have for your web pages. The clearer your goals, the better.
2. After you set your goals, visit sites on the Web that cover topics similar to those you want to cover in your own website. As you examine the sites, ask yourself whether they're easy to navigate and have good content. Then make a list of what you like about the sites. How would you make your website better?

LESSON 3:
Introducing HTML and XHTML

After finishing up the discussions about the World Wide Web and getting organized, with a large amount of text to read and concepts to digest, you're probably wondering when you're actually going to get to write a web page. That is, after all, why you bought the book. Wait no longer!

In this Lesson

Today, you get to create your very first (albeit brief) web page, learn about HTML (the language for writing web pages), and learn about the following:

- What HTML is and why you have to use it

- What you can and cannot do when you design HTML pages

- What HTML tags are and how to use them

- How to write pages that conform to the XHTML standard

- How you can use Cascading Style Sheets to control the look and feel of your pages

What HTML Is—And What It Isn't

Take note of just one more thing before you dive into actually writing web pages. You should know what HTML is, what it can do, and most importantly what it can't do.

HTML stands for *Hypertext Markup Language*. HTML is based on the *Standard Generalized Markup Language (SGML)*, a much larger document-processing system. To write HTML pages, you won't need to know a whole lot about SGML. However, knowing that one of the main features of SGML is that it describes the general structure of the content inside documents—rather than its actual appearance on the page or onscreen—does help. This concept might be a bit foreign to you if you're used to working with WYSIWYG (What You See Is What You Get) editors like Adobe's Dreamweaver or Microsoft FrontPage, so let's go over the information carefully.

HTML Describes the Structure of a Page

HTML, by virtue of its SGML heritage, is a language for describing the structure of a document, not its actual presentation. The idea here is that most documents have common elements—for example, titles, paragraphs, and lists. Before you start writing, therefore, you can identify and define the set of elements in that document and give them appropriate names (see Figure 3.1).

FIGURE 3.1
Document elements.

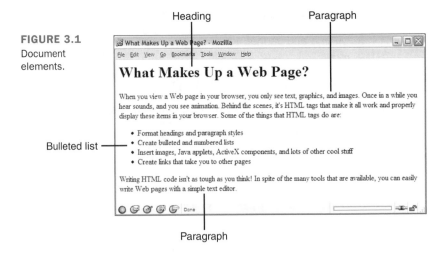

If you've worked with word processing programs that use style sheets (such as Microsoft Word) or paragraph catalogs (such as FrameMaker), you've done something similar; each section of text conforms to one of a set of styles that are predefined before you start working.

HTML defines a set of common styles for web pages: headings, paragraphs, lists, and tables. It also defines character styles such as boldface and code examples. These styles are indicated inside HTML documents using *tags*. Each tag has a specific name and is set off from the content of the document using a notation that I'll get into a bit later.

HTML Does Not Describe Page Layout

When you're working with a word processor or page layout program, styles are not just named elements of a page—they also include formatting information such as the font size and style, indentation, underlining, and so on. So, when you write some text that's supposed to be a heading, you can apply the Heading style to it, and the program automatically formats that paragraph for you in the correct style.

HTML doesn't go this far. For the most part, HTML doesn't say anything about how a page looks when it's viewed. HTML tags just indicate that an element is a heading or a list; they say nothing about how that heading or list is to be formatted. So, as with the magazine example and the layout person who formats your article, the layout person's job is to decide how big the heading should be and what font it should be in. The only thing you have to worry about is marking which section is supposed to be a heading.

3

NOTE

> Although HTML doesn't say much about how a page looks when it's viewed, Cascading Style Sheets (CSS) enable you to apply advanced formatting to HTML tags. Many changes in HTML 4.0 favor the use of CSS tags. And XHTML, which is the current version of HTML, eliminates almost all tags that are associated with formatting in favor of Cascading Style Sheets. I'll talk about both XHTML and CSS later today.

Web browsers, in addition to providing the networking functions to retrieve pages from the Web, double as HTML formatters. When you read an HTML page into a browser such as Netscape or Internet Explorer, the browser interprets, or *parses*, the HTML tags and formats the text and images on the screen. The browser has mappings between the names of page elements and actual styles on the screen; for example, headings might be in a larger font than the text on the rest of the page. The browser also wraps all the text so that it fits into the current width of the window.

Different browsers running on diverse platforms might have various style mappings for each page element. Some browsers might use different font styles than others. For example, a browser on a desktop computer might display italics as italics, whereas a handheld device or mobile phone might use reverse text or underlining on systems that don't have italic fonts. Or it might put a heading in all capital letters instead of a larger font.

What this means to you as a web page designer is that the pages you create with HTML might look radically different from system to system and from browser to browser. The actual information and links inside those pages are still there, but the onscreen appearance changes. You can design a web page so that it looks perfect on your computer system, but when someone else reads it on a different system, it might look entirely different (and it might very well be entirely unreadable).

How the Visual Styles for Tags Evolved

In practice, most HTML tags are rendered in a fairly standard manner, on desktop computers at least. When the earliest browsers were written, somebody decided that links would be underlined and blue, visited links would be purple, and emphasized text would appear in italics. They also made similar decisions about every other tag. Since then, pretty much every browser maker has followed that convention to a greater or lesser degree. These conventions blurred the line separating structure from presentation, but in truth it still exists, even if it's not obvious.

Why It Works This Way

If you're used to writing and designing documents that will wind up printed on paper, this concept might seem almost perverse. No control over the layout of a page? The whole design can vary depending on where the page is viewed? This is awful! Why on earth would a system work like this?

Remember in Lesson 1, "Navigating the World Wide Web," when I mentioned that one of the cool things about the Web is that it's cross-platform and that web pages can be viewed on any computer system, on any size screen, with any graphics display? If the final goal of web publishing is for your pages to be readable by anyone in the world, you can't count on your readers having the same computer systems, the same size screens, the same number of colors, or the same fonts that you have. The Web takes into account all these differences and enables all browsers and all computer systems to be on equal ground.

The Web, as a design medium, is not a new form of paper. The Web is an entirely different medium, with its own constraints and goals that are very different from working with paper. The most important rules of web page design, as I'll keep harping on throughout this book, are the following:

DO	DON'T
DO design your pages so that they work in most browsers.	**DON'T** design your pages based on what they look like on your computer system and on your browser.
DO focus on clear, well-structured content that's easy to read and understand.	

Throughout this book, I'll show you examples of HTML code and what they look like when displayed. In examples in which browsers display code very differently, I'll give you a comparison of how a snippet of code looks in two very different browsers. Through these examples, you'll get an idea for how different the same page can look from browser to browser.

TIP

Although this rule of designing by structure and not by appearance is the way to produce good HTML, when you surf the Web, you might be surprised that the vast majority of websites seem to have been designed with appearance in mind—usually appearance in a particular browser such as Microsoft Internet Explorer. Don't be swayed by these designs. If you stick to the rules I suggest, in the end, your web pages and websites will be even more successful simply because more people can easily read and use them.

3

How Markup Works

HTML is a *markup language*. Writing in a markup language means that you start with the text of your page and add special tags around words and paragraphs. The tags indicate the different parts of the page and produce different effects in the browser. You'll learn more about tags and how they're used in the next section.

HTML has a defined set of tags you can use. You can't make up your own tags to create new styles or features. And just to make sure that things are really confusing, various browsers support different sets of tags. To further explain this, take a brief look at the history of HTML.

A Brief History of HTML Tags

The base set of HTML tags, the lowest common denominator, is referred to as HTML 2.0. HTML 2.0 is the old standard for HTML (a written specification for it is developed and maintained by the W3C) and the set of tags that all browsers must support. In the next few lessons, you'll primarily learn to use tags that were first introduced in HTML 2.0.

The HTML 3.2 specification was developed in early 1996. Several software vendors, including IBM, Microsoft, Netscape Communications Corporation, Novell, SoftQuad, Spyglass, and Sun Microsystems, joined with the W3C to develop this specification. Some of the primary additions to HTML 3.2 included features such as tables, applets, and text flow around images. HTML 3.2 also provided full backward-compatibility with the existing HTML 2.0 standard.

NOTE   The enhancements introduced in HTML 3.2 are covered later in this book. You'll learn more about tables in Lesson 8, "Building Tables." Lesson 11, "Integrating Multimedia: Sound, Video, and More," tells you how to use Java applets.

HTML 4.0, first introduced in 1997, incorporated many new features that gave designers greater control over page layout than HTML 2.0 and 3.2. Like HTML 2.0 and 3.2, the W3C maintains the HTML 4.0 standard.

Framesets (originally introduced in Netscape 2.0) and floating frames (originally introduced in Internet Explorer 3.0) became an official part of the HTML 4.0 specification. Framesets are discussed in more detail in Lesson 14, "Working with Frames and Linked Windows." We also see additional improvements to table formatting and rendering. By far, however, the most important change in HTML 4.0 was its increased integration with style sheets.

NOTE   If you're interested in how HTML development is working and just exactly what's going on at the W3C, check out the pages for HTML at the Consortium's site at http://www.w3.org/pub/WWW/MarkUp/.

At one time, Microsoft and Netscape were releasing new versions of their browsers frequently, competing to see who could add the most compelling new features to HTML without waiting for the standards process to catch up. These days, browser releases are less frequent, and HTML is more "finished" than it was in the late nineties. Now developers must mostly concern themselves with slight differences between how the browsers handle the HTML they support rather than deciding against competing sets of features. Confused yet? You're not alone. The extra work involved in dealing with variations between browsers has been a headache for Web developers for a very long time. Keeping track of all this information can be really confusing. Throughout this book, as I introduce each tag, I'll explain any browser specific issues you'll run into.

The Current Standard: XHTML 1.0

The Internet is no longer limited to computer hardware and software. MSN TV enables you to access the Internet, giving you more reason to become a couch potato. Personal information managers and palmtop computers enable you to access the Internet while you're on the road. More and more people are accessing the Internet with mobile phones and other wireless devices. Special interfaces and hardware enable physically challenged individuals to access the Internet. As it has matured, the Internet has become an effective means of communication and education for the masses. Many of the newer portable technologies, however, pose problems for the old HTML specification. They simply don't have the processing power of a desktop computer, and aren't as forgiving of poorly written HTML as web browsers. The developers of the HTML specification have struggled to accommodate these ongoing changes, and the limitations of HTML have become evident. We're stretching and distorting the HTML specification far beyond its capabilities. The future of the Internet demands a markup language that's more extensible and portable than HTML. The direction is heading toward the use of XML (short for *Extensible Markup Language*), a subset of SGML that allows for custom tags to be processed. And that's where XHTML 1.0 comes into play.

3

XHTML 1.0 is written in XML, and is the current standard that will help web designers prepare for the future. Documents written in XHTML can be viewed on current browsers, but at the same time they're valid XML documents. The purpose of this book is not only to teach you HTML 4.01, but also to teach you how to format your HTML so that it's compliant with the XHTML 1.0 specification.

Technically, XHTML 1.0 and HTML 4.01 are *very* similar. The tags and attributes are virtually the same, but a few simple rules have to be followed in order to make sure that a document is compliant with the XHTML 1.0 specification. Throughout this book, I'll explain how to deal with the different HTML tags to make sure that your pages are readable and still look good in all kinds of browsers.

What HTML Files Look Like

Pages written in HTML are plain text files (ASCII), which means that they contain no platform- or program-specific information. Any editor that supports text (which should be just about any editor—more about this subject in "Programs to Help You Write HTML" later today) can read them. HTML files contain the following:

- The text of the page itself
- HTML tags that indicate page elements, structure, formatting, and hypertext links to other pages or to included media

Most HTML tags look something like the following:

`<thetagname>`*`affected text`*`</thetagname>`

The tag name itself (here, *`thetagname`*) is enclosed in brackets (< >). HTML tags generally have a beginning and an ending tag surrounding the text they affect. The beginning tag "turns on" a feature (such as headings, bold, and so on), and the ending tag turns it off. Closing tags have the tag name preceded by a slash (/). The opening tag (for example, `<p>` for paragraphs) and closing tag (for example, `</p>` for paragraphs) compose what is officially called an *HTML element.*

CAUTION

> Be aware of the difference between the forward slash (/) mentioned with relation to tags, and backslashes (\), which are used by DOS and Windows in directory references on hard drives (as in `C:\window` or other directory paths). If you accidentally use the backslash in place of a forward slash in HTML, the browser won't recognize the ending tags.

Not all HTML tags have both an opening and closing tag. Some tags are only one-sided, and still other tags are containers that hold extra information and text inside the brackets. XHTML 1.0, however, requires that *all* tags be closed. You'll learn the proper way to open and close the tags as the book progresses.

Another difference between HTML 4.0 and XHTML 1.0 relates to usage of lowercase tags and attributes. HTML tags are not case sensitive; that is, you can specify them in uppercase, lowercase, or in any mixture. So, `<HTML>` is the same as `<html>`, which is the same as `<HtMl>`. This isn't the case for XHTML 1.0, where all tag and attribute names must be written in lowercase. To get you thinking in this mindset, the examples in this book display tag and attribute names in bold lowercase text.

▼ Task: Exercise 3.1: Creating Your First HTML Page

Now that you've seen what HTML looks like, it's your turn to create your own web page. Start with a simple example so that you can get a basic feel for HTML.

To get started writing HTML, you don't need a web server, a web provider, or even a connection to the Web itself. All you really need is an application in which you can create your HTML files and at least one browser to view them. You can write, link, and test whole suites of web pages without even touching a network. In fact, that's what you're going to do for the majority of this book. I'll talk later about publishing everything on the Web so that other people can see your work.

▼

To get started, you'll need a text editor. A *text editor* is a program that saves files in ASCII ▼
format. ASCII format is just plain text, with no font formatting or special characters. For
Windows, Notepad and Microsoft WordPad are good basic text editors (and free with
your system). Shareware text editors are also available for various operating systems,
including DOS, Windows, Mac OS, and Linux. If you point your web browser to
www.download.com and enter `Text Editors` as a search term, you'll find many resources
available to download. If you're a Windows user, you might want to check out HTML-Kit
in particular. It's a free text editor specifically built for editing HTML files. You can
download it at http://www.chami.com/html-kit/. By the same token, Mac users might
want to look at TextWrangler, available from http://www.barebones.com. If you prefer to
work in a word processor such as Microsoft Word, don't panic. You can still write pages
in word processors just as you would in text editors, although doing so is more complicated.
When you use the Save or Save As command, you'll see a menu of formats you can use
to save the file. One of them should be Text Only, Text Only with Line Breaks, or DOS
Text. All these options will save your file as plain ASCII text, just as if you were using a
text editor. For HTML files, if you have a choice between DOS Text and just Text, use
DOS Text, and use the Line Breaks option if you have it.

3

CAUTION

> If you do use a word processor for your HTML development, be very
> careful. Many recent word processors are including HTML modes or
> mechanisms for creating HTML or XML code. This feature can produce
> unusual results or files that simply don't behave as you expect. If
> you run into trouble with a word processor, try using a text editor
> and see whether it helps.

What about the plethora of free and commercial HTML editors that claim to help you
write HTML more easily? Some are text editors that simplify common tasks associated
with HTML coding. If you've got one of these editors, go ahead and use it. If you've got
a fancier editor that claims to hide all the HTML for you, put it aside for the next couple
of days and try using a plain text editor just for a little while. Appendix A, "Sources for
Further Information," lists many URLs where you can download free and commercial
HTML editors that are available for different platforms. They appear in the section titled
"HTML Editors and Converters" (in Appendix A).

Open your text editor and type the following code. You don't have to understand what
any of it means at this point. You'll learn more about much of this today and tomorrow.
This simple example is just to get you started.

```
<!DOCTYPE html PUBLIC "-//W3C//DTD XHTML 1.0 Transitional//EN"
 "http://www.w3.org/TR/xhtml1/DTD/transitional.dtd">
```
▼

▼
```
<html>
<head>
<title>My Sample HTML Page</title>
</head>
<body>
<h1>This is an HTML Page</h1>
</body>
</html>
```

NOTE

Note that the `<!DOCTYPE>` tag in the previous example doesn't appear in lowercase like the rest of the tags. This tag is an exception to the XHTML rule and should appear in uppercase. This is explained in detail in Lesson 17, "Designing for the Real World." In fact, you don't have to specify a `DOCTYPE` at all to get your pages to work. The purpose of the `DOCTYPE` is to tell validators and browsers which specification your page was written to. I'll include them in all examples in the book, but you can leave them out if you like.

After you create your HTML file, save it to your hard disk. Remember that if you're using a word processor like Microsoft Word, choose Save As and make sure that you're saving it as "Text Only". When you choose a name for the file, follow these two rules:

- The filename should have an extension of `.html` (`.htm` on DOS or Windows systems that support only three-character extensions)—for example, `myfile.html`, `text.html`, or `index.htm`. Most web software requires your files to have these extensions, so get into the habit of doing it now. (If you are using Windows, make sure that your computer is configured to show file extensions. If it isn't, you'll find yourself creating files named things like `myfile.html.txt`, which your browser will not think are HTML files.)

▲
- Use small, simple names. Don't include spaces or special characters (bullets, accented characters)—just letters and numbers are fine.

▼ Task: Exercise 3.2: Viewing the Result

Now that you have an HTML file, start your web browser. You don't have to be connected to the Internet because you're not going to be opening pages at any other site. Your browser or network connection software might complain about the lack of a network connection, but you should be able to work offline.

After your browser is running, look for a menu item or button labeled Open, Open File, or maybe Open Page. Choosing it enables you to browse your local disk. The Open com-
▼ mand (or its equivalent) opens a document from your local disk, parses it, and displays it.

By using your browser and the Open command, you can write and test your HTML files on your computer in the privacy of your own home. (On most operating systems, you can just drag the icon from your HTML file into an open browser window if you prefer.)

If you don't see something similar to what's shown in Figure 3.2 (for example, if parts are missing or if everything looks like a heading), go back into your text editor and compare your file to the example. Make sure that all your tags have closing tags and that all your < characters are matched by > characters. You don't have to quit your browser to do so; just fix the file and save it again under the same name.

FIGURE 3.2
The sample HTML file.

3

Next, go back to your browser. Locate and choose a menu item or button called Reload (for Netscape users) or Refresh (for Internet Explorer users). The browser will read the new version of your file, and voilà! You can edit and preview and edit and preview until you get the file right.

If you're getting the actual HTML text repeated in your browser rather than what's shown in Figure 3.2, make sure that your HTML file has an .html or .htm extension. This file extension tells your browser that it's an HTML file. The extension is important.

If things are going really wrong—if you're getting a blank screen or you're getting some really strange characters—something is wrong with your original file. If you've been using a word processor to edit your files, try opening your saved HTML file in a plain text editor (again, Notepad will work just fine). If the text editor can't read the file or if the result is garbled, you haven't saved the original file in the right format. Go back into your original editor, and try saving the file as text only again. Then try viewing the file again in your browser until you get it right.

Text Formatting and HTML

When an HTML page is parsed by a browser, any formatting you might have done by hand—that is, any extra spaces, tabs, returns, and so on—is ignored. The only thing that specifies formatting in an HTML page is an HTML tag. If you spend hours carefully editing a plain text file to have nicely formatted paragraphs and columns of numbers but don't include any tags, when a web browser loads the page, all the text will flow into one paragraph. All your work will have been in vain.

NOTE

> There are two exceptions to this rule, a tag called <pre> and a CSS property. You'll learn about both of them in Lesson 6, "Formatting Text with HTML and CSS."

The advantage of having all white space (spaces, tabs, returns) ignored is that you can put your tags wherever you want. The following examples all produce the same output. Try them!

```
<h1>If music be the food of love, play on.</h1>
```

```
<h1>
If music be the food of love, play on.
</h1>
```

```
<h1>
If music be the food of love, play on.        </h1>
```

```
<h1>   If music   be   the   food  of  love,
play   on. </h1 >
```

Using Cascading Style Sheets

Earlier, I mentioned Cascading Style Sheets as a way you could control the look and feel of your pages. Styles are a way to control how the browser renders HTML tags (or elements, as they're called in standards documents). For example, in today's lesson, I've used the <h1> tag a number of times. Most browsers print text enclosed inside an <h1> tag in a large, boldface font and leave some white space after the heading before printing something else. Using Cascading Style Sheets, you can tell the browser to render the <h1> tag differently than it normally would. CSS provides a lot of flexibility in how you can alter the appearance of any type of element, and the styles can be applied in a number of different ways.

The advantage of CSS is that it can be used at varying levels of specificity. For example, you can put all your styles into a separate file, and link to that file from your web page. That way, if you want to change the appearance of your site, you can simply edit your CSS file and make changes that span every page that links to your style sheet. Or, if you prefer, you can include styles at the top of your page so that they apply only to that page. You can also include styles inside the tags themselves using the style attribute (which I'll discuss in Lesson 9, "Creating Layouts with CSS").

You can also control the specificity of the styles you create based on how you define them. For example, you can write rules that apply to all tags of a specific type, such as all `<h1>` elements. Or you can specify classes for your elements and then write rules that apply only to members of that class. For example, you could create a class called `headline` and then make all `<h1>` elements in the `headline` class red. You can also write rules that apply to specific elements by assigning them a particular identifier and writing rules that apply to that identifier.

One thing you'll find as you progress through the book is that CSS can serve as a replacement for many common tags. As I describe various tags, I'll explain how the same effects can be achieved using CSS instead. Generally, the flexibility of CSS means you should use HTML to describe the structure of pages and CSS to define their appearance. The coverage of CSS in this book culminates with Lesson 9, which explains how to use CSS to manage the entire layout of the page, or even the entire layout of a site.

Including Styles in Tags

3

You've already seen how HTML pages are created using tags. I want to stop briefly and discuss attributes as well. An attribute is an additional bit of information that somehow affects the behavior of a tag. Attributes are included inside the opening tag in a pair. Here's an example:

```
<tag attribute="value">
```

Some attributes can be used with nearly any tag; others are highly specific. One attribute that can be used with nearly any tag is `style`. By including the `style` attribute in a tag, you can include one or more style rules within a tag itself. Here's an example using the `<h1>` tag, which I introduced earlier:

```
<h1 style="font-family: Verdana, sans-serif;">Heading</h1>
```

The `style` attribute of the `<h1>` tag contains a style declaration. All style declarations follow this same basic pattern, with the property on the left and the value associated with that property on the right. The rule ends with a semicolon, and you can include more than one in a `style` attribute by placing commas between them. If you're only including one rule in the `style` attribute, the semicolon is optional, but it's a good idea to include it. In the preceding example, the property is `font-family`, and the value is `Verdana, sans-serif`. This attribute modifies the standard `<h1>` tag by changing the font to Verdana, and if the user doesn't have that font installed on his system, whichever sans-serif font the browser selects. (Sans-serif fonts are those that do not include *serifs*, the small lines at the ends of characters.)

There are many, many properties that can be used in style declarations. As I've already said, putting a declaration into a `style` attribute is just one of several ways that you can apply styles to your document.

Programs to Help You Write HTML

You might be thinking that all this tag stuff is a real pain, especially if you didn't get that small example right the first time. (Don't fret about it; I didn't get that example right the first time, and I created it.) You have to remember all the tags, and you have to type them in right and close each one. What a hassle!

Many freeware and shareware programs are available for editing HTML files. Most of these programs are essentially text editors with extra menu items or buttons that insert the appropriate HTML tags into your text. HTML-based text editors are particularly nice for two reasons: You don't have to remember all the tags, and you don't have to take the time to type them all. I've already mentioned HTML-Kit, but there are plenty of others as well. Many general-purpose text editors also include special features to make it easier to deal with HTML files these days.

Many editors on the market purport to be WYSIWYG. As you learned earlier today, there's really no such thing as WYSIWYG when you're dealing with HTML. "What You Get" can vary wildly based on the browser.

With that said, as long as you're aware that the result of working in those editors can vary, using WYSIWYG editors can be a quick way to create simple HTML pages. For professional web development and for using many of the very advanced features, however, WYSIWYG editors can fall short, and you'll need to go "under the hood" to play with the HTML code anyhow. Even if you intend to use a WYSIWYG editor for the bulk of your HTML work, bear with me for the next couple of days and try these examples in text editors so that you get a feel for what HTML really is before you decide to move on to an editor that hides the tags.

CAUTION

> WYSIWYG editors tend to work best with files they've created themselves. If you have some existing HTML files that you need to edit, opening them in a WYSIWYG editor can do more harm than good, particularly if the files were created in a different WYSIWYG editor.

In addition to HTML and WYSIWYG editors, you also can use converters, which take files from many popular word processing programs and convert them to HTML. With a simple set of templates, you can write your pages entirely in your favorite word processing program and then convert the result when you're done.

In many cases, converters can be extremely useful, particularly for putting existing documents on the Web as quickly as possible. However, converters suffer from many of the same problems as WYSIWYG editors. The results can vary from browser to browser, and many newer or advanced features aren't available in the converters. Also, most converter programs are fairly limited, not necessarily by their own features, but mostly by the limitations in HTML itself. No amount of fancy converting will make HTML do things that it can't do already. If a particular capability doesn't exist in HTML, the converter can't do anything to solve that problem. In fact, the converter might end up doing strange things to your HTML files, causing you more work than if you just did all the formatting yourself.

As previously mentioned, Appendix A lists many of the web page editors that are currently available. For now, if you have a simple HTML editor, feel free to use it for the examples in this book. If all you have is a text editor, no problem; you'll just have to do a little more typing.

3

Summary

Today, you learned some basic points about what HTML is and how you define a text document as a web page. You learned a bit about the history of HTML and the reasons why the HTML specification has changed several times since the beginning. You also learned how Cascading Style Sheets can be used to augment your HTML. You created your first web page with some basic tags. It wasn't so bad, was it? You also learned a bit about the current standard version of HTML—XHTML, and how to apply styles using Cascading Style Sheets. In tomorrow's lesson, you'll expand on this and will learn more about adding headings, text, and lists to your pages.

Workshop

Now that you've had an introduction to HTML and a taste of creating your first very simple web page, here's a workshop that will guide you toward more of what you'll learn. A couple of questions and answers that relate to HTML formatting are followed by a brief quiz and answers about HTML. The exercises prompt you to examine the code of a more advanced page in your browser.

Q&A

Q Can I do *any* formatting of text in HTML?

A You can do some formatting to strings of characters; for example, you can make a word or two bold. Pretty much all browsers support tags for formatting text (most were added in HTML 3.2), but most of these tags have given way to CSS formatting in HTML 4.01 and XHTML 1.0. You'll learn some formatting tricks in Lesson 6.

Q I'm using Windows. My word processor won't let me save a text file with an extension that's anything except .txt. If I type in index.html, **my word processor saves the file as** index.html.txt. **What can I do?**

A You can rename your files after you've saved them so that they have an html or htm extension, but having to do so can be annoying if you have a large number of files. Consider using a text editor or HTML editor for your web pages.

Quiz

1. What does HTML stand for? How about XHTML?
2. What's the primary function of HTML?
3. Why doesn't HTML control the layout of a page?
4. Which version of HTML provides the lowest common denominator of HTML tags?
5. What's the basic structure of an HTML tag?

Quiz Answers

1. HTML stands for Hypertext Markup Language. XHTML stands for Extensible HyperText Markup Language.
2. HTML defines a set of common styles for web pages (headings, paragraphs, lists, tables, character styles, and more).
3. HTML doesn't control the layout of a page because it's designed to be cross-platform. It takes the differences of many platforms into account and allows all browsers and all computer systems to be on equal ground.
4. The lowest common denominator for HTML tags is HTML 2.0, the oldest standard for HTML. This is the set of tags that *all* browsers *must* support. HTML 2.0 tags can be used anywhere.
5. Most HTML elements consist of opening and closing tags, and they surround the text that they affect. The tags are enclosed in brackets (<>). The beginning tag turns on a feature, and the ending tag, which is preceded by a forward slash (/), turns it off.

Exercises

1. Before you actually start writing a meatier HTML page, getting a feel for what an HTML page looks like certainly helps. Luckily, you can find plenty of source material to look at. Every page that comes over the wire to your browser is in HTML (or perhaps XHTML) format. (You almost never see the codes in your browser; all you see is the final result.)

   Most web browsers have a way of letting you see the HTML source of a web page. If you're using Internet Explorer 6.0, for example, navigate to the web page that you want to look at. Choose View, Source to display the source code in a text window. In Netscape, choose View, Page Source.

TIP

> In some browsers, you can't directly view the source of a web page, but you can save the current page as a file to your local disk. In a dialog box for saving the file, you might find a menu of formats—for example, Text, PostScript, or HTML. You can save the current page as HTML and then open that file in a text editor or word processor to see the HTML source.

3

   Try going to a typical home page and then viewing its source. For example, Figure 3.3 shows the home page for Craigslist, a free online classified ads service search page at http://www.craisglist.org/.

FIGURE 3.3
Craigslist home page.

The HTML source code looks something like Figure 3.4.

FIGURE 3.4
Some HTML
source code.

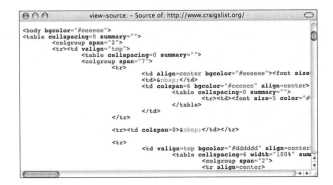

2. Try viewing the source of your own favorite web pages. You should start seeing some similarities in the way pages are organized and get a feel for the kinds of tags that HTML uses. You can learn a lot about HTML by comparing the text onscreen with the source for that text.

LESSON 4:

Learning the Basics of HTML

Over the first three days, you learned about the World Wide Web, how to organize and plan your websites, and why you need to use HTML to create a web page. Yesterday, you even created your first very simple web page.

In this Lesson

Today, you'll learn about each of the basic HTML tags in more depth, and begin writing web pages with headings, paragraphs, and several different types of lists. Today we'll focus on the following topics and HTML tags:

- Tags for overall page structure: `<html>`, `<head>`, and `<body>`

- Tags for titles, headings, and paragraphs: `<title>`, `<h1>` through `<h6>`, and `<p>`

- Tags for comments: `<!-- ...... -->`

- Tags for lists: `<ol>`, `<ul>`, `<li>`, `<dt>`, and `<dd>`

Structuring Your HTML

HTML defines three tags that are used to describe the page's overall structure and provide some simple header information. These three tags—<html>, <head>, and <body>—identify your page to browsers or HTML tools. They also provide simple information about the page (such as its title or its author) before loading the entire thing. The page structure tags don't affect what the page looks like when it's displayed; they're only there to help tools that interpret or filter HTML files.

In the strict HTML definition, these tags are optional. If your page does not contain them, browsers usually can read the page anyway. These tags, however, *are* required elements in XHTML 1.0. The most recent browsers already take advantage of XHTML. You should get into the habit of including the page structure tags now.

The DOCTYPE Identifier

Although it's not a page structure tag, the XHTML 1.0 recommendation includes one additional requirement for your web pages. The first line of each page must include a DOCTYPE identifier that defines the XHTML 1.0 version to which your page conforms, and the document type definition (DTD) that defines the specification. This is followed by the <html>, <head>, and <body> tags. In the following example, the XHTML 1.0 Strict document type appears before the page structure tags:

```
<!DOCTYPE html PUBLIC "-//W3C//DTD XHTML 1.0 Strict//EN"
  "http://www.w3.org/TR/xhtml1/DTD/strict.dtd">
<html>
<head>
<title>Page Title</title>
</head>
<body>
...your page content...
</body>
</html>
```

Three types of HTML 4.01 document types are specified in the XHTML 1.0 specification: Strict, Transitional, and Frameset. Refer to Lesson 16, "Writing Good Web Pages: Do's and Don'ts," for more information about the DOCTYPE tag, and more information about the differences between Strict, Transitional, and Frameset document types.

The <html> Tag

The first page structure tag in every HTML page is the <html> tag. It indicates that the content of this file is in the HTML language. In the XHTML 1.0 recommendation, the <html> tag should follow the DOCTYPE identifier (as mentioned in the previous note) as shown in the following example.

All the text and HTML elements in your web page should be placed within the beginning and ending HTML tags, like this:

```
<!DOCTYPE html PUBLIC "-//W3C//DTD XHTML 1.0 Transitional//EN"
 "http://www.w3.org/TR/xhtml1/DTD/transitional.dtd">
<html>
...your page...
</html>
```

Before XHTML 1.0, you could play fast and loose with the tags in your documents. In order for your HTML to be valid, you needed to include the `<html>` tag around all the other tags in your document, but none of the popular browsers cared if you really did. If you left them out, or included the beginning `<html>` tag but not the closing tag, or whatever, the browser would still display the document without complaining. With XHTML 1.0, your HTML documents must also be valid XML documents, so the rules are much more strict. XML documents require all the elements in a file to be enclosed within a root element. In XHTML 1.0 documents, the root element is the `<html>` tag.

The `<head>` Tag

The `<head>` tag specifies that the lines within the opening and closing tag are the prologue to the rest of the file. Generally, only a few tags go into the `<head>` portion of the page (most notably, the page title, described later). You should never put any of the text of your page into the header (between `<head>` tags).

Here's a typical example of how you properly use the `<head>` tag (you'll learn about `<title>` later):

```
<!DOCTYPE html PUBLIC "-//W3C//DTD XHTML 1.0 Transitional//EN"
 "http://www.w3.org/TR/xhtml1/DTD/transitional.dtd">
<html>
<head>
<title>This is the Title. It will be explained later on</title>
</head>
...your page...
</html>
```

The `<body>` Tag

The remainder of your HTML page (represented in the following example as ...*your page*...) is enclosed within a `<body>` tag. This includes all the text and other content (links, pictures, and so on). In combination with the `<html>` and `<head>` tags, your code resembles the following:

```
<!DOCTYPE html PUBLIC "-//W3C//DTD XHTML 1.0 Transitional//EN"
 "http://www.w3.org/TR/xhtml1/DTD/transitional.dtd">
<html>
```

4

```
<head>
<title>This is the Title. It will be explained later on</title>
</head>
<body>
...your page...
</body>
</html>
```

You might notice here that each HTML tag is nested. That is, both <body> and </body> tags go inside both <html> tags; the same with both <head> tags. All HTML tags work this way, forming individual nested sections of text. You should be careful never to overlap tags. That is, never do something like the following:

```
<!DOCTYPE html PUBLIC "-//W3C//DTD XHTML 1.0 Transitional//EN"
 "http://www.w3.org/TR/xhtml1/DTD/transitional.dtd">
<html>
<head>
<body>
</head>
</body>
</html>
```

Whenever you close an HTML tag, make sure that you're closing the most recent unclosed tag. (You'll learn more about closing tags as you go on.)

NOTE

In HTML 4.0 and earlier, some tags are optionally closed. In other tags, closing tags are forbidden. In the XHTML 1.0 recommendation, *all* tags *must* be closed. If you're just learning HTML, this won't be a big deal, but if you already have a passing familiarity with the language, this might surprise you. The examples shown in this book display the proper way to close tags so that older browsers will interpret XHTML 1.0 closures correctly.

The Title

Each HTML page needs a title to indicate what the page describes. It appears in the title bar of the browser when people view the web page. The title is stored in your browser's favorites (or bookmarks), and also in search engines when they index your pages. Use the <title> tag to give a page a title.

The *title* indicates what your web page is about and is used to refer to the page in the browser's list of favorites or bookmarks. Titles also appear in the title bar of graphical browsers such as Microsoft Internet Explorer.

<title> tags are placed within the page header and can be used to describe the contents of the page, as follows:

```
<!DOCTYPE html PUBLIC "-//W3C//DTD XHTML 1.0 Transitional//EN"
 "http://www.w3.org/TR/xhtml1/DTD/transitional.dtd">
<html>
<head>
<title>The Lion, The Witch, and the Wardrobe</title>
</head>
<body>
...your page...
</body>
</html>
```

You can have only one title in the page, and that title can contain only plain text; that is, no other tags should appear inside the title.

Try to choose a title that's both short and descriptive of the content. Your title should be relevant even out of context. If someone browsing on the Web follows a random link and ends up on this page, or if a person finds your title in a friend's browser history list, would he have any idea what this page is about? You might not intend the page to be used independently of the pages you specifically linked to it, but because anyone can link to any page at any time, be prepared for that consequence and pick a helpful title.

4

NOTE

When search engines index your pages, each page title is captured and listed in the search results. The more descriptive your page title, the more likely it is that someone will choose your page from all the search results.

Also, because most browsers put the title in the title bar of the window, you might have a limited number of words available. (Although the text within the <title> tag can be of any length, it might be cut off by the browser when it's displayed.) The following are some other examples of good titles:

```
<title>Poisonous Plants of North America</title>
<title>Image Editing: A Tutorial</title>
<title>Upcoming Cemetery Tours, Summer 1999</title>
<title>Installing the Software: Opening the CD Case</title>
<title>Laura Lemay's Awesome Home Page</title>
```

Here are some not-so-good titles:

```
<title>Part Two</title>
<title>An Example</title>
<title>Nigel Franklin Hobbes</title>
<title>Minutes of the Second Meeting of the Fourth Conference of the
Committee for the Preservation of English Roses, Day Four, After Lunch</title>
```

Figure 4.1 shows how a title looks in a browser.

```
<title>Poisonous Plants of North America</title>
```

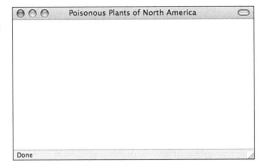

FIGURE 4.1
A page containing only header elements.

Headings

Headings are used to add titles to sections of a page. HTML defines six levels of headings. Heading tags look like the following:

```
<h1>Installing Your Safetee Lock</h1>
```

The numbers indicate heading levels (h1 through h6). The headings, when they're displayed, aren't numbered. They're displayed in larger or bolder text, are centered or underlined, or are capitalized—so that they stand out from regular text.

Think of the headings as items in an outline. If the text you're writing is structured, use the headings to express that structure, as shown in the following code:

```
<h1>Movies</h1>
    <h2>Action/Adventure</h2>
        <h3>Caper</h3>
        <h3>Sports</h3>
        <h3>Thriller</h3>
        <h3>War</h3>
    <h2>Comedy</h2>
        <h3>Romantic Comedy</h3>
        <h3>Slapstick</h3>
    <h2>Drama</h2>
        <h3>Buddy Movies</h3>
        <h3>Mystery</h3>
        <h3>Romance</h3>
    <h2>Horror</h2>
```

Notice that I've indented the headings in this example to better show the hierarchy. They don't have to be indented in your page; in fact, the browser ignores the indenting.

4

TIP

> Even though the browser ignores any indenting you include in your code, you will probably find it useful to indent your code so that it's easier to read. You'll find that any lengthy examples in this book are indented for that reason, and you'll probably want to carry that convention over to your own HTML code.

Unlike titles, headings can be any length, spanning many lines of text. Because headings are emphasized, however, having many lines of emphasized text might be tiring to read.

A common practice is to use a first-level heading at the top of your page to either duplicate the title (which usually is displayed elsewhere), or to provide a shorter or less context-specific form of the title. If you have a page that shows several examples of folding bed sheets—for example, part of a long presentation on how to fold bed sheets—the title might look something like the following:

```
<title>How to Fold Sheets: Some Examples</title>
```

The topmost heading, however, might just be as follows:

```
<h1>Examples</h1>
```

CAUTION

> Don't use headings to display text in boldface type or to make certain parts of your page stand out more. Although the result might look cool in your browser, you don't know what it'll look like when other people use their browsers to read your page. Other browsers might number headings or format them in a manner that you don't expect.

Tools to create searchable indexes of web pages might extract your headings to indicate the important parts of a page. By using headings for something other than an actual heading, you might be foiling those search programs and creating strange results.

Figure 4.2 shows the following headings as they appear in a browser.

Input ▼

```
<h1>Mythology Through the Ages</h1>
  <h2>Common Mythological Themes</h2>
  <h2>Earliest Known Myths</h2>
  <h2>Origins of Mythology</h2>
   <h3>Mesopotamian Mythology</h3>
   <h3>Egyptian Mythology</h3>
```

```
<h4>The Story of Isis and Osiris</h4>
<h4>Horus and Set: The Battle of Good vs. Evil</h4>
<h4>The Twelve Hours of the Underworld</h4>
<h4>The River Styx</h4>
   <h2>History in Myth</h2><
```

Output ▼

FIGURE 4.2
HTML heading
elements.

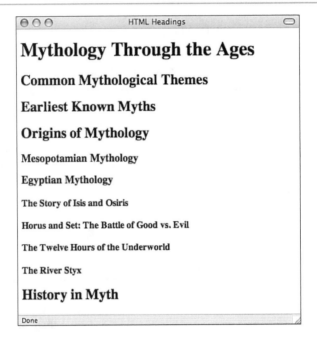

Paragraphs

Now that you have a page title and several headings, you can add some ordinary paragraphs
to the page.

The first version of HTML specified the <p> tag as a one-sided tag. There was no corresponding </p>, and the <p> tag was used to indicate the end of a paragraph (a paragraph
break), not the beginning. So, paragraphs in the first version of HTML looked like the
following:

```
Slowly and deliberately, Enigern approached the mighty dragon.
A rustle in the trees of the nearby forest distracted his attention
for a brief moment, a near fatal mistake for the brave knight.<p>
The dragon lunged at him, searing Enigern's armor with a rapid
blast of fiery breath. Enigern fell to the ground as the dragon
hovered over him. He quickly drew his sword and thrust it into the
dragon's chest.<p>
```

Most early browsers assumed that paragraphs would be formatted this way. When they came across a <p> tag, these older browsers started a new line and added some extra white space between the line that just ended and the next one.

As of the HTML 4.01 standard, paragraph tags are two-sided (<p>...</p>), and <p> indicates the beginning of the paragraph. The closing tag is no longer optional, so rather than using <p> to indicate where one paragraph ends and another begins, you enclose each paragraph within a <p> tag. So, the Enigern story should look like this:

```
<p>Slowly and deliberately, Enigern approached the mighty dragon.
A rustle in the trees of the nearby forest distracted his attention
for a brief moment, a near fatal mistake for the brave knight.</p>
<p>The dragon lunged at him, searing Enigern's armor with a rapid
blast of fiery breath. Enigern fell to the ground as the dragon
hovered over him. He quickly drew his sword and thrust it into the
dragon's chest.</p>
```

At this point, you should be wrapping your paragraphs inside opening and closing <p> tags. Older browsers accept this usage just fine, and it's up to speed with the current standards. Although at one time it was optional to use the closing </p> tag, it's required under the XHTML 1.0 recommendation because all tags must be closed.

Some people prefer to use extra <p> tags between paragraphs to spread out the text on the page. Again, here's the cardinal reminder: Design for content, not for appearance. This is also an area where browsers are inconsistent. Some of them won't add space for empty <p> tags at all. Besides, these days controlling white space is best done with CSS. Figure 4.3 shows what happens when I add another paragraph about Enigern and the dragon to the page. The paragraph breaks are added between the closing and opening <p> tags in the text.

4

Input ▼

```
<p>The dragon fell to the ground, releasing an anguished cry and
seething in pain. The thrust of Enigern's sword proved fatal as
the dragon breathed its last breath. Now Enigern was free to
release Lady Aelfleada from her imprisonment in the dragon's lair. </p>
```

Output ▼

FIGURE 4.3
An HTML
paragraph.

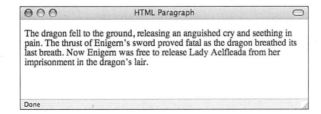

Lists, Lists, and More Lists

In addition to headings and paragraphs, probably the most common HTML element you'll use is the list. After this section, you'll not only know how to create a list in HTML, but also how to create several different types of lists—a list for every occasion!

HTML 4.01 defines these three types of lists:

- Numbered or ordered lists, which are typically labeled with numbers
- Bulleted or unordered lists, which are typically labeled with bullets or some other symbol
- Glossary lists, in which each item in the list has a term and a definition for that term, arranged so that the term is somehow highlighted or drawn out from the text

NOTE

> You'll also notice a couple of deprecated list types in the HTML 4.01 specification: menu lists (<menu>) and directory lists (<dir>). These two list types aren't frequently used and support for them varies in browsers. Instead, use the <ul> (or bulleted list) tags in place of these deprecated list types.

A *deprecated* tag or attribute is one that has been marked for removal from future specifications and products. It may still be supported for historical reasons, but when you create new pages you should not use deprecated elements or attributes, because future support for them is not guaranteed.

NOTE

> Browsers generally continue to support deprecated elements for reasons of backward compatibility. There's still a need to learn about the deprecated elements because you might run into them in existing pages.
>
> The majority of tags and attributes that are deprecated in HTML 4.01 are done so in favor of using Cascading Style Sheet (CSS) properties and values.

List Tags

All the list tags have the following common elements:

- The entire list is surrounded by the appropriate opening and closing tag for the type of list (for example, <ul> and </ul> for unordered lists, or <ol> and </ol> for ordered lists).

- Each list item within the list has its own tag: `<dt>` and `<dd>` for the glossary lists, and `<li>` for all the other lists.

> **NOTE**
> The closing tags for `<dd>`, `<dt>`, and `<li>` were optional in HTML. To comply with XHTML 1.0, use closing tags of `</dd>`, `</dt>`, `</li>`.

Although the tags and the list items can be formatted any way you like in your HTML code, I prefer to arrange the tags so that the list tags are on their own lines and each new item starts on a new line. This way, you can easily select the whole list as well as the individual elements. In other words, I find the following HTML

```
<p>Dante's Divine Comedy consists of three books:</p>
<ul>
<li>The Inferno</li>
<li>The Purgatorio</li>
<li>The Paradiso</li>
</ul>
```

easier to read than

```
<p>Dante's Divine Comedy consists of three books:</p>
<ul><li>The Inferno</li><li>The Purgatorio</li><li>The Paradiso</li></ul>
```

although both result in the same output in the browser.

Numbered Lists

Numbered lists are surrounded by the `<ol>`...`</ol>` tags (ol stands for *ordered list*), and each item within the list is included in the `<li>`...`</li>` (list item) tag.

> **NOTE**
> In HTML, the `<li>` tag is one-sided; you don't have to specify the closing tag because it's optional. The existence of the next `<li>` (or the closing `</ol>` or `</ul>` tag) indicates the end of that item in the list. However, for your documents to conform to the XHTML 1.0 specification, you must use a closing tag of `</li>`.

When the browser displays an ordered list, it numbers (and often indents) each of the elements sequentially. You don't have to perform the numbering yourself and, if you add or delete items, the browser renumbers them the next time the page is loaded.

Ordered lists are lists in which each item is numbered or labeled with a counter of some kind (like letters or roman numerals).

4

Use numbered lists only when the sequence of items on the list is relevant. Ordered lists are good for steps to follow or instructions to the readers, or when you want to rank the items in a list. If you just want to indicate that something has a number of elements that can appear in any order, use an unordered list instead.

For example, the following is an ordered list of steps that explain how to install a new operating system. You can see how the list is displayed in a browser in Figure 4.4.

Input ▼

```
<p>Installing Your New Operating System</p>
 <ol>
<li>Insert the CD-ROM into your CD-ROM drive.</li>
<li>Choose RUN.</li>
<li>Enter the drive letter of your CD-ROM (example: D:\),
followed by SETUP.EXE.</li>
<li>Follow the prompts in the setup program.</li>
<li>Reboot your computer after all files are installed.</li>
<li>Cross your fingers.</li>
</ol>
```

Output ▼

FIGURE 4.4
An ordered list
in HTML.

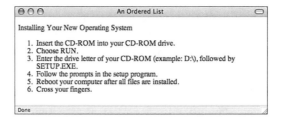

Customizing Ordered Lists

The HTML 3.2 recommendation described several attributes for ordered lists. They were used to customize ordered lists. These attributes enabled you to control several features of ordered lists including which numbering scheme to use and from which number to start counting (if you don't want to start at 1). In HTML 4.01 and XHTML 1.0, the attributes mentioned in this section are deprecated in favor of using style sheet properties and values that accomplish the same task. To support older browsers, however, you might need to use these attributes on occasion.

Attributes are extra parts of HTML tags that contain options or other information about the tag itself. To comply with the XHTML specification, you must include a value for every attribute, and enclose those values in quotation marks.

You can customize ordered lists in two main ways: how they're numbered and the number with which the list starts. HTML 3.2 provides the type attribute that can take one of five values to define which type of numbering to use on the list:

- "1"—Specifies that standard Arabic numerals should be used to number the list (that is, 1, 2, 3, 4, and so on)
- "a"—Specifies that lowercase letters should be used to number the list (that is, a, b, c, d, and so on)
- "A"—Specifies that uppercase letters should be used to number the list (that is, A, B, C, D, and so on)
- "i"—Specifies that lowercase Roman numerals should be used to number the list (that is, i, ii, iii, iv, and so on)
- "I"—Specifies that uppercase Roman numerals should be used to number the list (that is, I, II, III, IV, and so on)

You can specify types of numbering in the <ol> tag, as follows: <ol type="a">. By default, type="1" is assumed.

NOTE

The nice thing about web browsers is that they generally ignore attributes they don't understand. If a browser didn't support the type attribute of the <ol> tag, for example, it would simply ignore it when it's encountered.

4

As an example, consider the following list:

```
<p>The Days of the Week in French:</p>
<ol>
<li>Lundi</li>
<li>Mardi</li>
<li>Mercredi</li>
<li>Jeudi</li>
<li>Vendredi</li>
<li>Samedi</li>
<li>Dimanche</li>
</ol>
```

If you were to add type="I" to the <ol> tag, as follows, it would appear in a browser as shown in Figure 4.5.

Input ▼

```
<p>The Days of the Week in French:</p>
<ol type="I">
<li>Lundi</li>
<li>Mardi</li>
<li>Mercredi</li>
```

```
<li>Jeudi</li>
<li>Vendredi</li>
<li>Samedi</li>
<li>Dimanche</li>
</ol>
```

Output ▼

FIGURE 4.5

An ordered list displayed using an alternative numbering style.

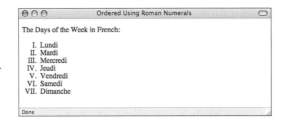

You also can apply the type attribute to the <li> tag, effectively changing the numbering type in the middle of the list. When the type attribute is used in the <li> tag, it affects the item in question and all entries following it in the list. Using the start attribute, you can specify the number or letter with which to start your list. The default starting point is 1, of course. You can change this number by using start. <ol start="4">, for example, would start the list at number 4, whereas <ol type="a" start="3"> would start the numbering with c and move through the alphabet from there.

For example, you can list the last six months of the year, and start numbering with the Roman numeral VII as follows. The results appear in Figure 4.6.

Input ▼

```
<p>The Last Six Months of the Year (and the Beginning of the NextYear):</p>
<ol type="I" start="7">
<li>July</li>
<li>August</li>
<li>September</li>
<li>October</li>
<li>November</li>
<li>December</li>
<li type="1">January</li>
</ol>
```

Output ▼

FIGURE 4.6
An ordered list with an alternative numbering style and starting number.

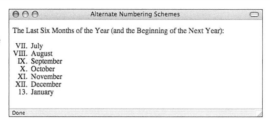

As with the `type` attribute, you can change the value of an entry's number at any point in a list. You do so by using the `value` attribute in the `<li>` tag. Assigning a `value` in an `<li>` tag restarts numbering in the list starting with the affected entry.

Suppose that you wanted the last three items in a list of ingredients to be 10, 11, and 12 rather than 6, 7, and 8. You can reset the numbering at `Eggs` using the `value` attribute, as follows:

```
<p>Cheesecake ingredients:</p>
<ol type="I">
<li>Quark Cheese</li>
<li>Honey</li>
<li>Cocoa</li>
<li>Vanilla Extract</li>
<li>Flour</li>
<li value="10">Eggs</li>
<li>Walnuts</li>
<li>Margarine</li>
</ol>
```

4

NOTE   In this section's examples, all the attribute values are enclosed in quotation marks. Most web browsers don't require you to use quotation marks this way, but XHTML 1.0 does.

Unordered Lists

In unordered lists, the elements can appear in any order. An unordered list looks just like an ordered list in HTML except that the list is created by using `<ul>...</ul>` tags rather than `ol`. The elements of the list are placed within `<li>` tags, just as with ordered lists.

Browsers usually format unordered lists by inserting bullets or some other symbol; Lynx, a text browser, inserts an asterisk (*).

The following input and output example shows an unordered list. Figure 4.7 shows the results in a browser.

Input ▼

```
<p>Things I like to do in the morning:</p>
<ul>
<li>Drink a cup of coffee</li>
<li>Watch the sunrise</li>
<li>Listen to the birds sing</li>
<li>Hear the wind rustling through the trees</li>
<li>Curse the construction noises for spoiling the peaceful mood</li>
</ul>
```

Output ▼

FIGURE 4.7
An unordered list.

Customizing Unordered Lists

As with ordered lists, unordered lists can be customized with HTML 3.2 attributes. (These are also deprecated in HTML 4.01.) By default, most browsers, including Netscape and Internet Explorer, use bullets to delineate entries on unordered lists. Text browsers such as Lynx generally opt for an asterisk.

If you use the type attribute in the <ul> tag, some browsers can display other types of markers. According to the HTML 3.2 specification, the type attribute can take three possible values:

- **"disc"**—A disc or bullet; this style is the default.
- **"square"**—Obviously, a square rather than a disc.
- **"circle"**—As compared with the disc, which most browsers render as a filled circle, this value should generate an unfilled circle.

In the following input and output example, you see a comparison of these three types as rendered in a browser (see Figure 4.8).

Input ▼

```
<ul type="disc">
  <li>DAT - Digital Audio Tapes</li>
  <li>CD - Compact Discs</li>
  <li>Cassettes</li>
</ul>
<ul type="square">
  <li>DAT - Digital Audio Tapes</li>
  <li>CD - Compact Discs</li>
```

```
  <li>Cassettes</li>
</ul>
<ul type="circle">
  <li>DAT - Digital Audio Tapes</li>
  <li>CD - Compact Discs</li>
  <li>Cassettes</li>
</ul>
```

Output ▼

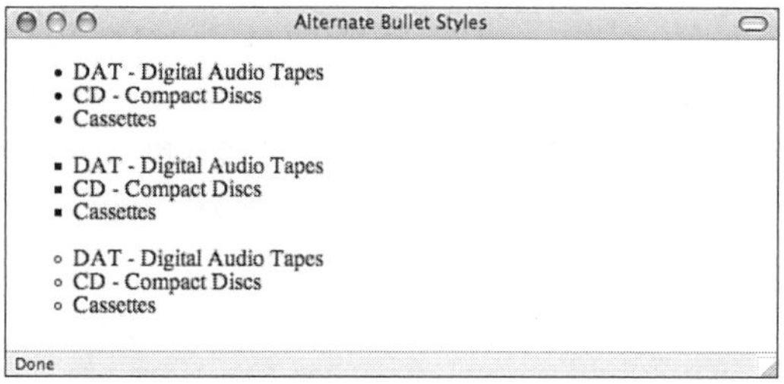

FIGURE 4.8
Unordered lists
with different
bullet types.

Just as you can change the numbering scheme in the middle of an ordered list, you can change the type of bullet midstream in a list by using the `type` attribute in the `<li>` tag. Again, this attribute is deprecated in HTML 4.01.

An alternative approach is to use style declarations to specify the bullet type for a list or list item. The property to set is `list-style-type`. To change the style from `disc` (the default) to `square`, you would use the following tag:

```
<ol style="list-style-type: square">
</ol>
```

The `list-style-type` property is also used to control the numbering style used for ordered lists. The valid values are `disc`, `circle`, `square`, `decimal`, `lower-roman`, `upper-roman`, `lower-alpha`, `upper-alpha`, and `none`. If you set it to `none`, no bullet or numbering will be shown for the list.

You can also alter this property for individual items in a list. For example, you could create a list like this:

```
<ol style="list-style-type: circle">
    <li style="list-style-type: square">One</li>
    <li style="list-style-type: disc">Two</li>
    <li>Three</li>
</ol>
```

There are a number of other properties associated with lists. The `list-style-type` property simply provides an alternative to the deprecated `type` attribute. With CSS, you can go much further. For example, using the `white-space` property, you can define how white space is handled when lists are rendered. By default, a line break follows every list item.

4

You can change that to pre, which prints the text exactly as it is formatted in the source, or nowrap, which leaves out the line breaks.

If you don't like any of the bullet styles used in unordered lists, you can substitute an image of your own choosing in place of them. To do so, use the list-style-image property. By setting this property, you can use an image of your choosing for the bullets in your list. Here's an example:

```
<ul style="list-style-image: url(/bullet.gif)">
    <li>Example</li>
</ul>
```

Don't worry much about what this all means right now. I'll discuss images later in Lesson 7, "Adding Images, Color, and Backgrounds." Right now, all you need to know is that the URL in parentheses should point to the image you want to use.

As you've seen in the screenshots so far, when items are formatted in a list and the list item spans more than one line, the lines of text that follow the first are aligned with the beginning of the text on the first line. If you prefer that they begin at the position of the bullet or list number, use the list-style-position property:

```
<ul style="list-style-position: inside">
    <li>Example</li>
</ul>
```

The default value is outside, and the only alternative is inside. Finally, if you want to modify several list-related properties at once, you can simply use the list-style property. You can specify three values for list-style: the list style type, the list style position, and the URL of the image to be used as the bullet style. This property is just a shortcut for use if you want to manipulate several of the list-related properties at once. Here's an example:

```
<ul style="list-style: circle inside URL(/bullet.gif)">
    <li>Example</li>
</ul>
```

Bear in mind that not all browsers support the manipulation of these properties—in particular, older browsers almost certainly don't.

Glossary Lists

Glossary lists are slightly different from other lists. Each list item in a glossary list has two parts:

- A term
- The term's definition

Each part of the glossary list has its own tag: <dt> for the term (*definition term*), and <dd> for its definition (*definition definition*). <dt> and <dd> usually occur in pairs, although most browsers can handle single terms or definitions. The entire glossary list is indicated by the tags <dl>...</dl> (*definition list*).

The following is a glossary list example with a set of herbs and descriptions of how they grow:

```
<dl>
<dt>Basil</dt>
<dd>Annual. Can grow four feet high; the scent of its tiny white
flowers is heavenly</dd>
<dt>Oregano</dt>
<dd>Perennial. Sends out underground runners and is difficult
to get rid of once established.</dd>
<dt>Coriander</dt>
<dd>Annual. Also called cilantro, coriander likes cooler
weather of spring and fall.</dd>
</dl>
```

Glossary lists usually are formatted in browsers with the terms and definitions on separate lines, and the left margins of the definitions are indented.

You don't have to use glossary lists for terms and definitions, of course. You can use them anywhere that the same sort of list is needed. Here's an example:

```
<dl>
<dt>Macbeth</dt>
<dd>I'll go no more. I am afraid to think of
what I have done; look on't again I dare not.</dd>
<dt>Lady Macbeth</dt>
<dd>Infirm of purpose! Give me the daggers.
The sleeping and the dead are as but pictures. 'Tis the eye
if childhood that fears a painted devil. If he do bleed, I'll
gild the faces if the grooms withal, for it must seem their
guilt. (Exit. Knocking within)</dd>
<dt>Macbeth</dt>
<dd>Whence is that knocking? How is't wit me when
every noise apalls me? What hands are here? Ha! They pluck out
mine eyes! Will all Neptune's ocean wash this blood clean from
my hand? No. This my hand will rather the multitudinous seas
incarnadine, making the green one red. (Enter Lady Macbeth)</dd>
<dt>Lady Macbeth</dt>
<dd>My hands are of your color, but I shame to
wear a heart so white.</dd>
</dl>
```

4

The following input and output example shows how a glossary list is formatted in a browser (see Figure 4.9).

Input ▼

```
<dl>
<dt>Basil</dt>
<dd>Annual. Can grow four feet high; the scent
of its tiny white flowers is heavenly.</dd>
<dt>Oregano</dt>
<dd>Perennial. Sends out underground runners
and is difficult to get rid of once established.</dd>
<dt>Coriander</dt>
<dd>Annual. Also called cilantro, coriander
likes cooler weather of spring and fall.</dd>
</dl>
```

Output ▼

FIGURE 4.9
A glossary list.

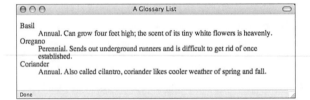

Nesting Lists

What happens if you put a list inside another list? Nesting lists is fine as far as HTML is concerned; just put the entire list structure inside another list as one of its elements. The nested list just becomes another element of the first list, and it's indented from the rest of the list. Lists like this work especially well for menu-like entities in which you want to show hierarchy (for example, in tables of contents) or as outlines.

Indenting nested lists in HTML code itself helps show their relationship to the final layout:

```
<ol>
  <ul>
  <li>WWW</li>
  <li>Organization</li>
  <li>Beginning HTML</li>
  <ul>
   <li>What HTML is</li>
   <li>How to Write HTML</li>
   <li>Doc structure</li>
   <li>Headings</li>
   <li>Paragraphs</li>
   <li>Comments</li>
  </ul>
 <li>Links</li>
 <li>More HTML</li>
</ol>
```

Many browsers format nested ordered lists and nested unordered lists differently from their enclosing lists. They might, for example, use a symbol other than a bullet for a nested list, or number the inner list with letters (a, b, c) rather than numbers. Don't assume that this will be the case, however, and refer back to "section 8, subsection b" in your text because you can't determine what the exact formatting will be in the final output. If you do need to be sure which symbols or numbering scheme will be used for a list, specify a style using CSS.

The following input and output example shows a nested list and how it appears in a browser (see Figure 4.10).

Input ▼

```
<h1>Peppers</h1>
<ul>
<li>Bell</li>
<li>Chile</li>
  <ul>
  <li>Serrano</li>
  <li>Jalapeno</li>
  <li>Habanero</li>
  <li>Anaheim</li>
  </ul>
<li>Szechuan</li>
<li>Cayenne</li>
</ul>
```

4

Output ▼

FIGURE 4.10
Nested lists.

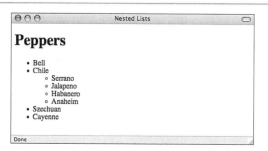

DO	DON'T
DO remember that you can change the numbering and bullet styles for lists to suit your preference. **DO** feel free to nests lists to any extent that you like.	**DON'T** use the deprecated list types; use one of the other lists instead. **DON'T** number or format lists yourself; use the list tags. **DON'T** use list tags to indent text on a page; use Cascading Style Sheets.

Comments

You can put comments into HTML pages to describe the page itself or to provide some kind of indication of the status of the page. Some source code control programs store the page status in comments, for example. Text in comments is ignored when the HTML file is parsed; comments don't ever show up onscreen—that's why they're comments. Comments look like the following:

```
<!-- This is a comment -->
```

Here are some examples:

```
<!-- Rewrite this section with less humor -->
<!-- Neil helped with this section -->
<!-- Go Tigers! -->
```

Users can view your comments using the View Source functionality in their browsers, so don't put anything in comments that you don't want them to see.

▼ Task: Exercise 4.1: Creating a Real HTML Page

At this point, you know enough to get started creating simple HTML pages. You understand what HTML is, you've been introduced to a handful of tags, and you've even opened an HTML file in your browser. You haven't created any links yet, but you'll get to that soon enough, in tomorrow's lesson.

This exercise shows you how to create an HTML file that uses the tags you've learned about up to this point. It'll give you a feel for what the tags look like when they're displayed onscreen and for the sorts of typical mistakes you're going to make. (Everyone makes them, and that's why using an HTML editor that does the typing for you is often helpful. The editor doesn't forget the closing tags, leave off the slash, or misspell the tag itself.)

So, create a simple example in your text editor. Your example doesn't have to say much of anything; in fact, all it needs to include are the structure tags, a title, a couple of headings, and a paragraph or two. Here's an example:

Input ▼

```
<!DOCTYPE html PUBLIC "-//W3C//DTD XHTML 1.0 Transitional//EN"
 "http://www.w3.org/TR/xhtml1/DTD/transitional.dtd">
<html>
<head>
<title>Camembert Incorporated</title>
</head>
<body>
<h1>Camembert Incorporated</h1>
```

```
<p>"Many's the long night I dreamed of cheese -- toasted, mostly."
-- Robert Louis Stevenson</p>
<h2>What We Do</h2>
<p>We make cheese. Lots of cheese; more than eight tons of cheese
a year.</p>
<h2>Why We Do It</h2>
<p>We are paid an awful lot of money by people who like cheese.
So we make more.</p>
<h2>Our Favorite Cheeses</h2>
<ul>
<li>Brie</li>
<li>Havarti</li>
<li>Camembert</li>
<li>Mozzarella</li>
</ul>
</body>
</html>
```

Save the example to an HTML file, open it in your browser, and see how it came out.

If you have access to another browser on your computer or, even better, one on a different kind of computer, I highly recommend opening the same HTML file there so that you can see the differences in appearance between browsers. Sometimes the differences can surprise you; lines that looked fine in one browser might look strange in another browser.

Figure 4.11 shows what the cheese factory example looks like.

Output ▼

FIGURE 4.11
The cheese factory example.

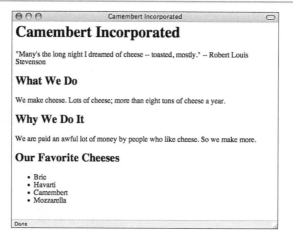

Summary

HTML, a text-only markup language used to describe hypertext pages on the World Wide Web, describes the structure of a page, not its appearance.

Today, you learned what HTML is and how to write and preview simple HTML files. You also learned about the HTML tags shown in Table 4.1, and the CSS properties shown in Table 4.2.

TABLE 4.1   HTML Tags from Lesson 4

Tag	Attribute	Use
`<html> .. </html>`		The entire HTML page.
`<head> .. </head>`		The head, or prologue, of the HTML page.
`<body> .. </body>`		All the other content in the HTML page.
`<title> .. </title>`		The title of the page.
`<h1> .. </h1>`		First-level heading.
`<h2> .. </h2>`		Second-level heading.
`<h3> .. </h3>`		Third-level heading.
`<h4> .. </h4>`		Fourth-level heading.
`<h5> .. </h5>`		Fifth-level heading.
`<h6> .. </h6>`		Sixth-level heading.
`<p> .. </p>`		A paragraph.
`<ol>...</ol>`		An ordered (numbered) list. Each of the items in the list begins with `<li>`.
	type	Specifies the numbering scheme to use in the list. This attribute is deprecated in HTML 4.01.
	start	Specifies at which number to start the list. This attribute is deprecated in HTML 4.01.
`<ul>...</ul>`		An unordered (bulleted or otherwise-marked) list. Each of the items in the list begins with `<li>`.
	type	Specifies the bulleting scheme to use in the list. This attribute is deprecated in HTML 4.01.

TABLE 4.1 continued

Tag	Attribute	Use
`<li>...</li>`		Individual list items in ordered, unordered, menu, or directory lists. The closing tag is optional in HTML, but is required in XHTML 1.0.
	`type`	Resets the numbering or bulleting scheme from the current list element. Applies only to `<ul>` and `<ol>` lists. This attribute is deprecated in HTML 4.01.
	`value`	Resets the numbering in the middle of an ordered (`<ol>`) list. This attribute is deprecated in HTML 4.01.
`<dl>...</dl>`		A glossary or definition list. Items in the list consist of pairs of elements: a term and its definition.
`<dt>...</dt>`		The term part of an item in a glossary list. Closing tag is optional in HTML, but required in XHTML 1.0.
`<dd>...</dd>`		The definition part of an item in a glossary list. Closing tag is optional in HTML, but required in XHTML 1.0.
`<!-- .. -->`		A comment.

TABLE 4.2 CSS Properties from Lesson 4

Property	Use/Values
`list-style-type`	Used to specify the bullet style or numbering style for the list. Valid values are `disc`, `circle`, `square`, `decimal`, `lower-roman`, `upper-roman`, `lower-alpha`, `upper-alpha`, and `none`.
`white-space`	Specifies how white space is handled for list items. Valid values are `pre`, `nowrap`, and `normal`.
`list-style-image`	The image to use in place of the bullets for a list. The value should be the URL of the image.
`list-style-position`	Defines the alignment of lines of text in list items after the first. Values are `inside` and `outside`.
`list-style`	Enables you to set multiple list properties at once: list style type, list style position, and the URL of the bullet style.

4

Workshop

You've learned a lot today, and the following workshop will help you remember some of the most important points. I've anticipated some of the questions you might have in the first section of the workshop.

Q&A

Q **In some web pages, I've noticed that the page structure tags (`<html>`, `<head>`, `<body>`) aren't used. Do I really need to include them if pages work just fine without them?**

A Most browsers handle plain HTML without the page structure tags. The XHTML 1.0 recommendation requires that these tags appear in your pages. It's a good idea to get into the habit of using them now. Including the tags allows your pages to be read by more general SGML tools and to take advantage of features of future browsers. And, using these tags is the correct thing to do if you want your pages to conform to true HTML format.

Q **My glossaries came out formatted really strangely! The terms are indented farther in than the definitions!**

A Did you mix up the `<dd>` and `<dt>` tags? The `<dt>` tag is always used first (the definition term), and the `<dd>` follows (the definition). I mix them up all the time. There are too many d tags in glossary lists.

Q **I've seen HTML files that use `<li>` outside a list structure, alone on the page, like this:**

```
<li>And then the duck said, "put it on my bill"</li>
```

A Most browsers at least accept this tag outside a list tag and format it either as a simple paragraph or as a nonindented bulleted item. According to the true HTML specification, however, using an `<li>` outside a list tag is illegal, so good HTML pages shouldn't do this. Enclosing list items within list tags is also required by the XHTML recommendation. Always put your list items inside lists where they belong.

Quiz

1. What three HTML tags are used to describe the overall structure of a web page, and what do each of them define?

2. Where does the <title> tag go, and what is it used for?

3. How many different levels of headings does HTML support? What are their tags?

4. Why is it a good idea to use two-sided paragraph tags, even though the closing tag </p> is optional in HTML?

5. What two list types have been deprecated? What can you use in place of the deprecated list types?

Quiz Answers

1. The <html> tag indicates that the file is in the HTML language. The <head> tag specifies that the lines within the beginning and ending points of the tag are the prologue to the rest of the file. The <body> tag encloses the remainder of your HTML page (text, links, pictures, and so on).

2. The <title> tag is used to indicate the title of a web page in a browser's bookmarks, hotlist program, or other programs that catalog web pages. This tag always goes inside the <head> tags.

3. HTML supports six levels of headings. Their tags are <h1 .. /h1> through <h6 .. /h6>.

4. The closing </p> tag becomes important when aligning text to the left, right, or center of a page (text alignment is discussed in Lesson 6, "Formatting Text with HTML and CSS"). Closing tags also are required for XHTML 1.0.

5. The <menu> and <dir> list types have been deprecated in favor of using bulleted or unordered lists, <ul>.

Exercises

1. Using the Camembert Incorporated page as an example, create a page that briefly describes topics that you would like to cover on your own website. You'll use this page to learn how to create your own links tomorrow.

2. Create a second page that provides further information about one of the topics you listed in the first exercise. Include a couple of subheadings (such as those shown in Figure 4.2). If you feel really adventurous, complete the page's content and include lists where you think they enhance the page. This exercise will also help prepare you for tomorrow's lesson.

PART II:
Creating Simple Web Pages

LESSON 5:
Adding Links to Your Web Pages

After finishing yesterday's lesson, you now have a couple of pages that have some headings, text, and lists in them. These pages are all well and good, but rather boring. The real fun starts when you learn how to create hypertext links and link your pages to the Web.

In this Lesson

Today, you'll learn just that. Specifically, you'll learn about the following:

- All about the HTML link tag (<a>) and its various parts

- How to link to other pages on your local disk by using relative and absolute pathnames

- How to link to other pages on the Web by using URLs

- How to use links and anchors to link to specific places inside pages

- All about URLs: the various parts of the URL and the kinds of URLs you can use

Creating Links

To create a link in HTML, you need two things:

- The name of the file (or the URL of the file) to which you want to link
- The text that will serve as the clickable link

Only the text included within the link tag is actually visible on your page. When your readers click on the link, the browser loads the URL associated with the link.

The Link Tag—<a>

To create a link in an HTML page, you use the HTML link tag <a>...</a>. The <a> tag often is called an *anchor* tag because it also can be used to create anchors for links. (You'll learn more about creating anchors later today.) The most common use of the link tag, however, is to create links to other pages.

Unlike the simple tags you learned about in the preceding lesson, the <a> tag has some extra features: the opening tag, <a>, includes both the name of the tag (a) and extra information about the link itself. The extra features are called *attributes* of the tag. (You first discovered attributes in Lesson 4, "Learning the Basics of HTML," when you learned about lists.) So, rather than the opening <a> tag having just a name inside brackets, it looks something like the following:

```
<a name="Up" href="menu.html" title="The Twelve Caesars">
```

The extra attributes (in this example, name, href, and title) describe the link itself. The attribute you'll probably use most often is the href attribute, which is short for *hypertext reference*. You use the href attribute to specify the name or URL of the file to which this link points.

Like most HTML tags, the link tag also has a closing tag, </a>. All the text between the opening and closing tags will become the actual link on the screen and be highlighted, underlined, or colored blue or red when the web page is displayed. That's the text you or your readers will click to follow the link to the URL in the href attribute.

Figure 5.1 shows the parts of a typical link using the <a> tag, including the href, the text of the link, and the closing tag.

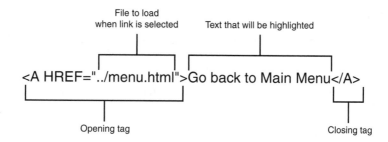

FIGURE 5.1
A link on a web page.

File to load when link is selected

Text that will be highlighted

`<A HREF="../menu.html">Go back to Main Menu</A>`

Opening tag

Closing tag

The following example shows a simple link and what it looks like (see Figure 5.2).

Input ▼

```
Go back to <a href="menu.html">Main Menu</a>
```

Output ▼

FIGURE 5.2
How a browser displays a link.

Sample Link

Go back to Main Menu

Done

Task: Exercise 5.1: Linking Two Pages ▼

5

Now you can try a simple example with two HTML pages on your local disk. You'll need your text editor and your web browser for this exercise. Because both the pages you'll work with are on your local disk, you don't need to be connected to the Internet. (Be patient; you'll get to do network stuff in the next section.)

Create two HTML pages and save them in separate files. Here's the code for the two HTML files I created for this section, which I called menu.html and claudius.html. What your two pages look like or what they're called really doesn't matter. However, make sure that you insert your own filenames if you're following along with this example.

The following is the first file, called menu.html:

```
<!DOCTYPE html PUBLIC "-//W3C//DTD XHTML 1.0 Transitional//EN"
 "http://www.w3.org/TR/xhtml1/DTD/transitional.dtd">
<html>
<head>
<title>The Twelve Caesars</title>
</head>
```

▼

```
<body>
<h1>"The Twelve Caesars" by Suetonius</h1>
<p>Seutonius (or Gaius Suetonius Tranquillus) was born circa A.D. 70
and died sometime after A.D. 130. He composed a history of the twelve
Caesars from Julius to Domitian (died A.D. 96). His work was a
significant contribution to the best-selling novel and television
series "I, Claudius." Suetonius' work includes biographies of the
following Roman emperors:</p>
<ul>
 <li>Julius Caesar</li>
 <li>Augustus</li>
 <li>Tiberius</li>
 <li>Gaius (Caligula)</li>
 <li>Claudius</li>
 <li>Nero</li>
 <li>Galba</li>
 <li>Otho</li>
 <li>Vitellius</li>
 <li>Vespasian</li>
 <li>Titus</li>
 <li>Domitian</li>
</ul>
</body>
</html>
```

The list of menu items (Julius Caesar, Augustus, and so on) will be links to other pages. For now, just type them as regular text; you'll turn them into links later.

The following is the second file, `claudius.html`:

```
<!DOCTYPE html PUBLIC "-//W3C//DTD XHTML 1.0 Transitional//EN"
 "http://www.w3.org/TR/xhtml1/DTD/transitional.dtd">
<html>
<head>
<title>The Twelve Caesars: Claudius</title>
</head>
<body>
<h2>Claudius Becomes Emperor</h2>
<p>Claudius became Emperor at the age of 50. Fearing the attack of
Caligula's assassins, Claudius hid behind some curtains. After a guardsman
discovered him, Claudius dropped to the floor, and then found himself
declared Emperor.</p>
<h2>Claudius is Poisoned</h2>
<p>Most people think that Claudius was poisoned. Some think his wife
Agrippina poisoned a dish of mushrooms (his favorite food). His death
was revealed after arrangements had been made for her son, Nero, to
succeed as Emperor.</p>
<p>Go back to Main Menu</p>
</body>
</html>
```

Make sure that both of your files are in the same directory or folder. If you haven't called
them `menu.html` and `claudius.html`, make sure that you take note of the names because
you'll need them later.

Create a link from the menu file to the feeding file. Edit the `menu.html` file, and put the
cursor at the following line:

```
<li>Claudius</li>
```

Link tags don't define the format of the text itself, so leave in the list item tags and just
add the link inside the item. First, put in the link tags themselves (the <a> and </a> tags)
around the text that you want to use as the link:

```
<li><a>Claudius</a></li>
```

Now add the name of the file that you want to link to as the `href` part of the opening link
tag. Enclose the name of the file in quotation marks (straight quotes ["], not curly or
typesetter's quotes ["]), with an equal sign between `href` and the name. Filenames in
links are case sensitive, so make sure that the filename in the link is identical to the name
of the file you created. (`Claudius.html` is not the same file as `claudius.html`; it has to
be exactly the same case.) Here I've used `claudius.html`; if you used different files, use
those filenames.

```
<li><a href="claudius.html">Claudius</a></li>
```

Now, start your browser, select Open File (or its equivalent in your browser), and open
the `menu.html` file. The paragraph you used as your link should now show up as a link
that is in a different color, underlined, or otherwise highlighted. Figure 5.3 shows how it
looked when I opened it.

5

FIGURE 5.3
The *menu.html* file
with link.

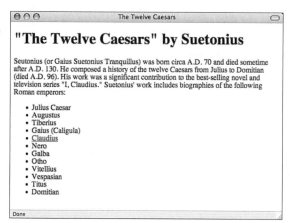

▼ Now, when you click the link, your browser should load and display the `claudius.html` page, as shown in Figure 5.4.

FIGURE 5.4
The
`claudius.html`
page.

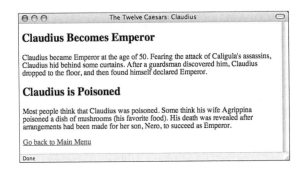

If your browser can't find the file when you click on the link, make sure that the name of the file in the `href` part of the link tag is the same as the name of the file on the disk, uppercase and lowercase match, and both files are in the same directory. Remember to close your link, using the `</a>` tag, at the end of the text that serves as the link. Also, make sure that you have quotation marks at the end of the filename (sometimes you can easily forget) and both quotation marks are ordinary straight quotes. All these things can confuse the browser and prevent it from finding the file or displaying the link properly.

CAUTION

Don't be confused by this issue of case sensitivity. Tags in HTML aren't case sensitive (although XHTML 1.0 requires that tags be lowercase). However, filenames refer to files on a web server somewhere, and because web servers often run on operating systems in which filenames are case sensitive (such as UNIX), you should make sure that the case of letters in your links' filenames is correct.

Now you can create a link from the feeding page back to the menu page. A paragraph at the end of the `claudius.html` page is intended for just this purpose:

```
<p>Go back to Main Menu</p>
```

Add the link tag with the appropriate `href` to that line, such as the following in which `menu.html` is the original menu file:

▼ `<p><a href="menu.html">Go back to Main Menu</a></p>`

▼

Nesting Tags Properly

When you include tags inside other tags, make sure that the closing tag closes the tag that you most recently opened. That is, enter

   `<p> <a> .. </a> </p>`

rather than

   `<p> <a> .. </p> </a>`

Some browsers can become confused if you overlap tags in this way, so always make sure that you close the most recently opened tag first.

Now when you reload the Claudius file, the link will be active, and you can jump between the menu and the detail page by selecting those links.

▲

Linking Local Pages Using Relative and Absolute Pathnames

The example in the preceding section shows how to link together pages that are contained in the same folder or directory on your local disk (local pages). This section continues that thread, linking pages that are still on the local disk but might be contained in different directories or folders on that disk.

5

NOTE   Folders and directories are the same thing, but they're called different names depending on whether you're on Macintosh, Windows, or UNIX. I'll simply call them *directories* from now on to make your life easier.

When you specify just the filename of a linked file within quotation marks, as you did earlier, the browser looks for that file in the same directory as the current file. This is true even if both the current file and the file being linked to are on a server somewhere else on the Internet; both files are contained in the same directory on that server. It is the simplest form of a relative pathname.

Relative pathnames point to files based on their locations relative to the current file. They can include directory names, or they can point to the path you would take to navigate to that file if you started at the current directory or folder. A pathname might, for example, include directions to go up two directory levels and then go down two other directories to get to the file.

To specify relative pathnames in links, you must use -style paths regardless of the system you actually have. You therefore separate directory or folder names with forward slashes (/), and you use two dots to refer generically to the directory above the current one (..).

Table 5.1 shows some examples of relative pathnames and where they lead.

TABLE 5.1   Relative Pathnames

Pathname	Means
href="file.html"	file.html is located in the current directory.
href="files/file.html"	file.html is located in the directory called files (and the files directory is located in the current directory).
href="files/morefiles/file.html"	file.html is located in the morefiles directory, which is located in the files directory, which is located in the current directory.
href="../file.html"	file.html is located in the directory one level up from the current directory (the parent directory).
href="../../files/file.html"	file.html is located two directory levels up, in the directory files.

If you're linking files on a personal computer (Macintosh or PC), and you want to link to a file on a different disk, use the name or letter of the disk as just another directory name in the relative path.

When you want to link to a file on a local drive on the Macintosh, the name of the disk is used just as it appears on the disk itself. Assume that you have a disk called Hard Disk 2, and your HTML files are contained in a folder called HTML Files. If you want to link to a file called jane.html in a folder called Public on a shared disk called Jane's Mac, you can use the following relative pathname:

href="../../Jane's Mac/Public/jane.html"

When linking to a file on a local drive on Windows systems, you refer to the drives by letter, just as you would expect. However, rather than using c:, d:, and so on, substitute a pipe (¦) for the colon (the colon is already used to separate the scheme from the host name in URLs). The pipe looks like two vertical dashes stacked on top of each other, and is usually found on the backslash key. Don't forget to use forward slashes as you would with UNIX. So, if the current file is located in C:\FILES\HTML\, and you want to link to D:\FILES.NEW\HTML\MORE\INDEX.HTM, the relative pathname to that file is as follows:

href="../../d¦/files.new/html/more/index.htm"

In most instances, you'll never use the name of a disk in relative pathnames, but I've included it here for completeness. After you deploy your pages to the Web, links that include drive names won't work, so it makes more sense to use relative links, which are more portable.

Absolute Pathnames

You can also specify the link to another page on your local system by using an absolute pathname.

Absolute pathnames point to files based on their absolute locations on the file system. Whereas relative pathnames point to the page to which you want to link by describing its location relative to the current page, absolute pathnames point to the page by starting at the top level of your directory hierarchy and working downward through all the intervening directories to reach the file.

Absolute pathnames always begin with a slash, which is the way they're differentiated from relative pathnames. Following the slash are all directories in the path from the top level to the file you are linking.

NOTE

Top has different meanings, depending on how you're publishing your HTML files. If you're just linking to files on your local disk, the top is the top of your file system (/ on UNIX, or the disk name on a Macintosh or PC). When you're publishing files using a web server, the top is the directory where the files served by the web server are stored, commonly referred to as the document root. You'll learn more about absolute pathnames and web servers in Lesson 18, "Putting Your Site Online."

5

Table 5.2 shows some examples of absolute pathnames and what they mean.

TABLE 5.2   Absolute Pathnames

Pathname	Means
href="/u1/lemay/file.html"	file.html is located in the directory /u1/lemay (typically on UNIX systems).
href="/d¦/files/html/file.htm"	file.htm is located on the D: disk in the directories files/html (on DOS systems).

TABLE 5.2   continued

Pathname	Means
`href="/Hard%20Disk%201/HTML Files/file.html"`	`file.html` is located on the disk `Hard Disk 1`, in the folder HTML Files (typically on Macintosh systems).

Using Relative or Absolute Pathnames?

The answer to that question is, "It depends." If you have a set of files that link only to other files within that set, using relative pathnames makes sense. On the other hand, if the links in your files point to files that aren't within the same hierarchy, you probably want to use absolute links. Generally, a mix of the two types of links makes the most sense for complex sites.

I can explain this better with an example. Let's say that your site consists of two sections, `/stuff` and `/things`. If you want to link from the file `index.html` in `/stuff` to `history.html` in `/stuff` (or any other file in `/stuff`), you use a relative link. That way, you can move the `/stuff` directory around without breaking any of the internal links. On the other hand, if you want to create a link in `/stuff/index.html` to `/things/index.html`, an absolute link is probably called for. That way, if you move `/stuff` to `/more/stuff`, your link will still work.

The rule of thumb I generally use is that if pages are part of the same collection, I use relative links, and if they're part of different collections, I use absolute links.

Links to Other Documents on the Web

So, now you have a whole set of pages on your local disk, all linked to each other. In some places in your pages, however, you want to refer to a page somewhere else on the Internet—for example, to The First Caesars page by Dr. Ellis Knox at Boise State University for more information on the early Roman emperors. You also can use the link tag to link those other pages on the Internet, which I'll call *remote* pages. *Remote pages* are contained somewhere on the Web other than the system on which you're currently working.

The HTML code you use to link pages on the Web looks exactly the same as the code you use for links between local pages. You still use the `<a>` tag with an `href` attribute, and you include some text to serve as the link on your Web page. Rather than a filename or a path in the `href`, however, you use the URL of that page on the Web, as Figure 5.5 shows.

FIGURE 5.5
Link to remote
files.

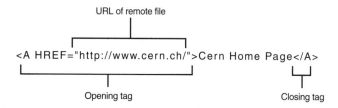

URL of remote file

`<A HREF="http://www.cern.ch/">Cern Home Page</A>`

Opening tag   Closing tag

Task: Exercise 5.2: Linking Your Caesar Pages to the Web ▼

Go back to those two pages you linked together earlier today, the ones about the Caesars. The `menu.html` file contains several links to other local pages that provide information about 12 Roman emperors.

Now suppose that you want to add a link to the bottom of the menu file to point to The First Caesars page by Dr. Ellis Knox at Boise State University, whose URL is http:// history.boisestate.edu/westciv/julio-cl/.

First, add the appropriate text for the link to your menu page, as follows:

```
<p><i>The First Caesars</i> page by Dr. Ellis Knox has more information on
these Emperors.</p>
```

What if you don't know the URL of the home page for The First Caesars page (or the page to which you want to link), but you do know how to get to it by following several links on several different people's home pages? Not a problem. Use your browser to find the home page for the page to which you want to link. Figure 5.6 shows what The First Caesars page looks like in a browser.

5

FIGURE 5.6
The First Caesars
page.

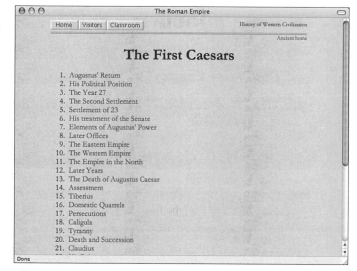

▼

NOTE   If your system isn't connected to the Internet, you might want to connect now so that you can test links to pages stored on the Web.

You can find the URL of the page you're currently viewing in your browser in the address box at the top of the browser window. To find the URL for a page you want to link to, use your browser to go to the page, copy the URL from the address field, and paste it into the `href` attribute of the link tag. No typing!

After you have the URL of the page, you can construct a link tag in your menu file and paste the appropriate URL into the link, like this:

Input ▼

```
<p>"<i><a href="http://history.boisestate.edu/westciv/julio-cl/">
The First Caesars</a></i>"page by Dr. Ellis Knox has more information
➥ on these Emperors.</p>
```

In that code I also italicized the title of the page using the `<i>` tag. You'll learn more about that tag and other text formatting tags in Lesson 6, "Formatting Text with HTML and CSS."

Of course, if you already know the URL of the page to which you want to link, you can just type it into the `href` part of the link. Keep in mind, however, that if you make a mistake, your browser won't be able to find the file on the other end. Many URLs are too complex for humans to be able to remember them; I prefer to copy and paste whenever I can to cut down on the chances of typing URLs incorrectly.

Figure 5.7 shows how the `menu.html` file, with the new link in it, looks when it is displayed.

Output ▼

FIGURE 5.7
The First Caesars link.

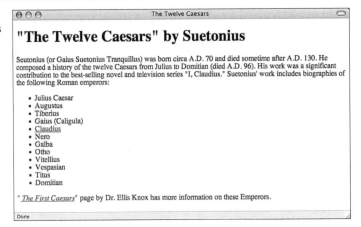

The Twelve Caesars

"The Twelve Caesars" by Suetonius

Seutonius (or Gaius Suetonius Tranquillus) was born circa A.D. 70 and died sometime after A.D. 130. He composed a history of the twelve Caesars from Julius to Domitian (died A.D. 96). His work was a significant contribution to the best-selling novel and television series "I, Claudius." Suetonius' work includes biographies of the following Roman emperors:

- Julius Caesar
- Augustus
- Tiberius
- Gaius (Caligula)
- Claudius
- Nero
- Galba
- Otho
- Vitellius
- Vespasian
- Titus
- Domitian

"*The First Caesars*" page by Dr. Ellis Knox has more information on these Emperors.

Done

▲

Task: Exercise 5.3: Creating a Link Menu ▼

Now that you've learned how to create lists and links, you can create a *link menu*. Link menus are links on your web page that are arranged in list form or in some other short, easy-to-read, and easy-to-understand format. Link menus are terrific for pages that are organized in a hierarchy, for tables of contents, or for navigation among several pages. Web pages that consist of nothing but links often organize the links in menu form.

The idea of a link menu is that you use short, descriptive terms as the links, with either no text following the link or with a further description following the link itself. Link menus look best in a bulleted or unordered list format, but you also can use glossary lists or just plain paragraphs. Link menus enable your readers to scan the list of links quickly and easily, a task that might be difficult if you bury your links in body text.

In this exercise, you'll create a web page for a set of book reviews. This page will serve as the index to the reviews, so the link menu you'll create is essentially a menu of book names.

Start with a simple page framework: a first-level heading and some basic explanatory text:

```
<!DOCTYPE html PUBLIC "-//W3C//DTD XHTML 1.0 Transitional//EN"
 "http://www.w3.org/TR/xhtml1/DTD/transitional.dtd">
<html>
<head>
<title>Really Honest Book Reviews</title>
</head>
<body>
<h1>Really Honest Book Reviews</h1>
<p>I read a lot of books about many different subjects. Though I'm not a
book critic, and I don't do this for a living, I enjoy a really good read
every now and then. Here's a list of books that I've read recently:</p>
```

Now add the list that will become the links, without the link tags themselves. It's always easier to start with link text and then attach actual links afterward. For this list, you'll use a tag to create a bulleted list of individual books. The <ol> tag wouldn't be appropriate because the numbers would imply that you were ranking the books in some way. Here's the HTML list of books; Figure 5.8 shows the page as it currently looks with the introduction and the list.

Input ▼

```
<ul>
 <li><i>The Rainbow Returns</i> by E. Smith</li>
 <li><i>Seven Steps to Immeasurable Wealth</i> by R. U. Needy</li>
 <li><i>The Food-Lovers Guide to Weight Loss</i> by L. Goode</li>
 <li><i>The Silly Person's Guide to Seriousness</i> by M. Nott</li>
</ul>
</body>
</html>
```

5

▼ Output ▼

FIGURE 5.8

A list of books.

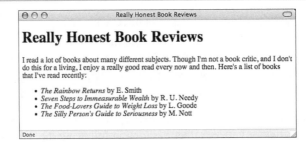

Now, modify each of the list items so that they include link tags. You'll need to keep the `<li>` tag in there because it indicates where the list items begin. Just add the `<a>` tags around the text itself. Here you'll link to filenames on the local disk in the same directory as this file, with each individual file containing the review for the particular book:

```
<ul>
 <li><a href="rainbow.html"><i>The Rainbow Returns</i> by E. Smith</a></li>
 <li><a href="wealth.html"><i>Seven Steps to Immeasurable Wealth</i> by R. U.
 Needy</a></li>
 <li><a href="food.html"><i>The Food-Lovers Guide to Weight Loss</i> by L.
 Goode</a></li>
 <li><a href="silly.html"><i>The Silly Person's Guide to Seriousness</i> by M.
 Nott</a></li>
</ul>
```

The menu of books looks fine, although it's a little sparse. Your readers don't know anything about each book (although some of the book names indicate the subject matter) or whether the review is good or bad. An improvement would be to add some short explanatory text after the links to provide hints of what is on the other side of the link:

Input ▼

```
<ul>
 <li><a href=rainbow.html"><i>The Rainbow Returns</i> by E. Smith</a>. A"
 fantasy story set in biblical times. Slow at times, but interesting.</li>
 <li><a href="wealth.html"><i>Seven Steps to Immeasurable Wealth</i> by R. U.
 Needy</a>. I'm still poor, but I'm happy! And that's the whole point.</li>
 <li><a href="food.html"><i>The Food-Lovers Guide to Weight Loss</i> by L. Goode
 </a>. At last! A diet book with recipes that taste good!</li>
 <li><a href="silly.html"><i>The Silly Person's Guide to Seriousness</i> by M.
 Nott</a>. Come on ... who wants to be serious?</li>
</ul>
```

▼ The final list looks like Figure 5.9.

Output ▼

FIGURE 5.9
The final menu listing.

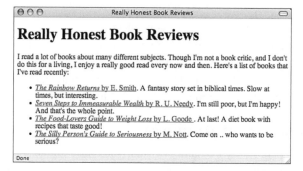

You'll use link menus similar to this one throughout this book.

Linking to Specific Places Within Documents

The links you've created so far today have been from one point in a page to another page. But what if, rather than linking to that second page in general, you want to link to a specific place within that page—for example, to the fourth major section down?

You can do so in HTML by creating an anchor within the second page. The anchor creates a special element that you can link to inside the page. The link you create in the first page will contain both the name of the file to which you're linking and the name of that anchor. Then, when you follow the link with your browser, the browser will load the second page and then scroll down to the location of the anchor (Figure 5.10 shows an example).

5

FIGURE 5.10
Links and anchors.

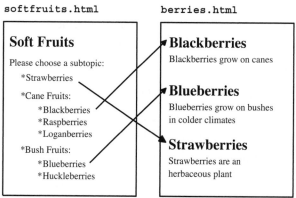

Anchors are special places that you can link to inside documents. Links can then jump to those special places inside the page as opposed to jumping just to the top of the page.

You can use links and anchors within the same page so that if you select one of those links, you jump to a different anchor within the page. For example, if you create an anchor at the top of a page, you could add links after each section of the page that return the user to the top. You could also create anchors at the beginning of each section and include a table of contents at the top of the page that has links to the sections.

Creating Links and Anchors

You create an anchor in nearly the same way that you create a link: by using the `<a>` tag. If you wondered why the link tag uses an `<a>` rather than an `<l>`, now you know: a actually stands for *anchor*.

When you specify links by using `<a>`, the link has two parts: the `href` attribute in the opening `<a>` tag and the text between the opening and closing tags that serve as a hot spot for the link.

You create anchors in much the same way, but rather than using the `href` attribute in the `<a>` tag, you use the `name` attribute. The `name` attribute takes a keyword (or words) that name the anchor. Figure 5.11 shows the parts of the `<a>` tag when used to indicate an anchor.

FIGURE 5.11
The `<a>` tag and anchors.

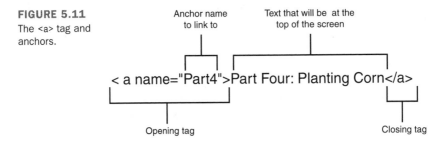

Including text between the anchor tags is optional. The actual anchor is placed at the location of the opening anchor tag, so you can just as easily write it as

```
<a name="myanchor"></a>
```

The browser scrolls the page to the location of the anchor so that it's at the top of the screen.

For example, to create an anchor at the section of a page labeled Part 4, you might add an anchor called `part4` to the heading, similar to the following:

```
<h1><a name="part4">Part Four: Grapefruit from Heaven</a></h1>
```

Unlike links, anchors don't show up in the final displayed page. They're just a marker that links can point to.

To point to an anchor in a link, use the same form of link that you would when linking to the whole page, with the filename or URL of the page in the href attribute. After the name of the page, however, include a hash sign (#) and the name of the anchor exactly as it appears in the name attribute of that anchor (including the same uppercase and lower-case characters!), like the following:

```
<a href="mybigdoc.html#part4">Go to Part 4</a>
```

This link tells the browser to load the page mybigdoc.html and then to scroll down to the anchor named part4. The text inside the anchor definition will appear at the top of the screen.

Task: Exercise 5.4: Linking Sections Between Two Pages ▼

Now let's create an example with two pages. These two pages are part of an online reference to classical music, in which each web page contains all the references for a particular letter of the alphabet (a.html, b.html, and so on). The reference could have been organized such that each section is its own page. Organizing it that way, however, would have involved several pages to manage, as well as many pages the readers would have to load if they were exploring the reference. Bunching the related sections together under lettered groupings is more efficient in this case. (Lesson 16, "Writing Good Web Pages: Do's and Don'ts," goes into more detail about the trade-offs between short and long pages.)

The first page you'll look at is for M; the first section looks like the following in HTML:

Input ▼

```
<!DOCTYPE html PUBLIC "-//W3C//DTD XHTML 1.0 Transitional//EN"
 "http://www.w3.org/TR/xhtml1/DTD/transitional.dtd">
<html>
<head>
<title>Classical Music: M</title>
</head>
<body>
<h1>M</h1>
<h2>Madrigals</h2>
<ul>
 <li>William Byrd, <em>This Sweet and Merry Month of May</em></li>
 <li>William Byrd, <em>Though Amaryllis Dance</em></li>
 <li>Orlando Gibbons, <em>The Silver Swan</em></li>
 <li>Claudio Monteverdi, <em>Lamento d'Arianna</em></li>
 <li>Thomas Morley, <em>My Bonny Lass She Smileth</em></li>
 <li>Thomas Weelkes, <em>Thule, the Period of Cosmography</em></li>
 <li>John Wilbye, <em>Sweet Honey-Sucking Bees</em></li>
</ul>
<p>Secular vocal music in four, five and six parts, usually a capella.
15th-16th centuries.</p>
```

5
▼

```
<p><em>See Also</em>
Byrd, Gibbons, Monteverdi, Morley, Weelkes, Wilbye</p>
</body>
</html>
```

Figure 5.12 shows how this section looks when it's displayed.

Output ▼

FIGURE 5.12
Part M of the
Online Music
Reference.

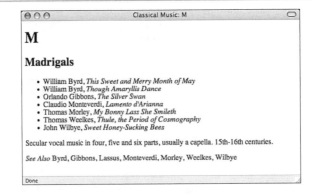

In the last line (the See Also), linking the composer names to their respective sections elsewhere in the reference would be useful. If you use the procedure you learned earlier today, you can create a link here around the word Byrd to the page b.html. When your readers select the link to b.html, the browser drops them at the top of the Bs. Those hapless readers then have to scroll down through all the composers whose names start with B (and there are many of them: Bach, Beethoven, Brahms, Bruckner) to get to Byrd—a lot of work for a system that claims to link information so that you can find what you want quickly and easily.

What you want is to be able to link the word Byrd in m.html directly to the section for Byrd in b.html. Here's the relevant part of b.html you want to link. (I've deleted all the Bs before Byrd to make the file shorter for this example. Pretend they're still there.)

NOTE

In this example, you'll see the use of the <em> tag. This tag is used to specify text that should be emphasized. The emphasis usually is done by rendering the text italic in Netscape and Internet Explorer.

```
<!DOCTYPE html PUBLIC "-//W3C//DTD XHTML 1.0 Transitional//EN"
"http://www.w3.org/TR/xhtml1/DTD/transitional.dtd">
<html>
```

```
<head>
<title>Classical Music: B</title>
</head>
<body>
<h1>B</h1>
<!-- I've deleted all the Bs before Byrd to make things shorter -->
<h2><a name="Byrd">Byrd, William, 1543-1623</a></h2>
<ul>
 <li>Madrigals
  <ul>
    <li><em>This Sweet and Merry Month of May</em></li>
    <li><em>Though Amaryllis Dance</em></li>
    <li><em>Lullabye, My Sweet Little Baby</em></li>
  </ul>
 </li>
 <li>Masses
  <ul>
    <li><em>Mass for Five Voices</em></li>
    <li><em>Mass for Four Voices</em></li>
    <li><em>Mass for Three Voices</em></li>
  </ul>
 </li>
 <li>Motets
  <ul>
    <li><em>Ave verum corpus a 4</em></li>
  </ul>
 </li>
</ul>
<p><em>See Also</em> Madrigals, Masses, Motets</p>
</body>
</html>
```

You'll need to create an anchor at the section heading for Byrd. You then can link to that anchor from the See Alsos in the file for M.

As I described earlier today, you need two elements for each anchor: an anchor name and the text inside the link to hold that anchor (which might be highlighted in some browsers). The latter is easy; the section heading itself works well because it's the element to which you're actually linking.

You can choose any name you want for the anchor, but each anchor in the page must be unique. (If you have two or more anchors with the name fred in the same page, how would the browser know which one to choose when a link to that anchor is selected?) A good, unique anchor name for this example is simply byrd because byrd can appear only one place in the file, and this is it.

After you've decided on the two parts, you can create the anchor itself in your HTML file. Add the <a> tag to the William Byrd section heading, but be careful here. If you

5

▼ were working with normal text within a paragraph, you'd just surround the whole line with <a>. But when you're adding an anchor to a big section of text that's also contained within an element—such as a heading or paragraph—always put the anchor inside the element. In other words, enter

```
<h2><a name="byrd">Byrd, William, 1543-1623</a></h2>
```

but do not enter

```
<a name="byrd"><h2>Byrd, William, 1543-1623</h2></a>
```

The second example can confuse your browser. Is it an anchor, formatted just like the text before it, with mysteriously placed heading tags? Or is it a heading that also happens to be an anchor? If you use the right code in your HTML file, with the anchor inside the heading, you avoid the confusion. The easiest answer is probably just putting the anchor ahead of the heading tag, like this:

```
<a name="byrd"></a>
<h2>Byrd, William, 1543-1623</h2>
```

> If you're still confused, refer to Appendix B, "HTML 4.01 Quick Reference," which has a summary of all the HTML tags and rules for which tags can and cannot go inside each one.

So, you've added your anchor to the heading and its name is "byrd". Now go back to the See Also line in your m.html file:

```
<p><em>See Also</em>
 Byrd, Gibbons, Lassus, Monteverdi, Morley, Weelkes, Wilbye</p>
```

You're going to create your link here around the word Byrd, just as you would for any other link. But what's the URL? As you learned previously, pathnames to anchors look similar to the following:

```
page_name#anchor_name
```

If you're creating a link to the b.html page itself, the href is as follows:

```
<a href="b.html">
```

Because you're linking to a section inside that page, add the anchor name to link that section so that it looks like this:

```
<a href="b.html#byrd">
```

Note the small b in byrd. Anchor names and links are case sensitive; if you put #Byrd in your href, the link might not work properly. Make sure that the anchor name you use in ▼ the name attribute and the anchor name in the link after the # are identical.

CAUTION

A common mistake is to put a hash sign in both the anchor name and in the link to that anchor. You use the hash sign only to separate the page and the anchor in the link. Anchor names should never have hash signs in them.

So, with the new link to the new section, the See Also line looks like this:

```
<p><em>See Also</em>
 <a href="b.html#byrd">Byrd</a>,
 Gibbons, Lassus, Monteverdi, Morley, Weelkes, Wilbye</p>
```

Of course, you can go ahead and add anchors and links to the other parts of the reference for the remaining composers.

With all your links and anchors in place, test everything. Figure 5.13 shows the Madrigals section with the link to Byrd ready to be selected.

FIGURE 5.13

The Madrigals section with a link to Byrd.

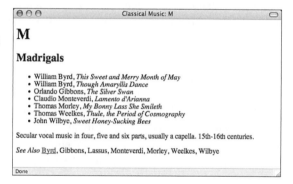

Figure 5.14 shows the screen that pops up when you select the Byrd link. You may need to reduce the size of your browser window to see how the link to the anchor takes you to the correct spot on the page.

FIGURE 5.14

The Byrd section.

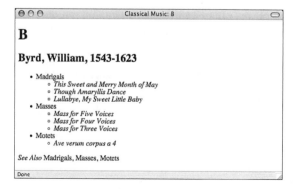

5

Linking to Anchors in the Same Document

What if you have only one large page, and you want to link to sections within that page? You can use anchors for it, too. For larger pages, using anchors can be an easy way to jump around within sections. To link to sections, you just need to set up your anchors at each section the way you usually do. Then, when you link to those anchors, leave off the name of the page itself, but include the hash sign and the name of the anchor. So, if you're linking to an anchor name called `section5` in the same page as the link, the link looks like the following:

```
Go to <a href="#section5">The Fifth Section</a>
```

When you leave off the page name, the browser assumes that you're linking with the current page and scrolls to the appropriate section. You'll get a chance to see this feature in action in Lesson 6. There, you'll create a complete web page that includes a table of contents at the beginning. From this table of contents, the reader can jump to different sections in the same web page. The table of contents includes links to each section heading. In turn, other links at the end of each section enable the user to jump back to the table of contents or to the top of the page.

Anatomy of a URL

So far in this book, you've encountered URLs twice: in Lesson 1, "Navigating the World Wide Web," as part of the introduction to the Web, and today, when you created links to remote pages. If you've ever done much exploring on the Web, you've encountered URLs as a matter of course. You couldn't start exploring without a URL.

As I mentioned in Lesson 1, URLs are uniform resource locators. In effect, URLs are street addresses for bits of information on the Internet. Most of the time, you can avoid trying to figure out which URL to put in your links by simply navigating to the bit of information you want with your browser, and then copying and pasting the long string of gobbledygook into your link. But understanding what a URL is all about and why it has to be so long and complex is often useful. Also, when you put your own information up on the Web, knowing something about URLs will be useful so that you can tell people where your web page is.

In this section, you'll learn what the parts of a URL are, how you can use them to get to information on the Web, and the kinds of URLs you can use (HTTP, FTP, Mailto, and so on).

Parts of URLs

Most URLs contain (roughly) three parts: the protocol, the hostname, and the directory or filename (see Figure 5.15).

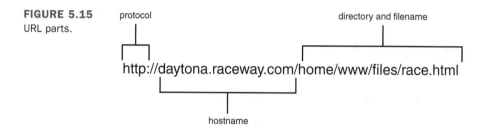

FIGURE 5.15
URL parts.

The *protocol* is the way in which the page is accessed; that is, the means of communication your browser uses to get the file. If the protocol in the URL is http, the browser will attempt to use the HTTP protocol to talk to the server. In order for a link to work, the host named in the link must be running a server that supports the protocol that's specified. So if you use an ftp URL to connect to www.example.com, the link won't work if that server isn't running FTP server software.

The *hostname* is the address of the computer on which the information is stored, like www.google.com, ftp.apple.com, or www.aol.com. The same hostname can support more than one protocol, as follows:

```
http://exammple.com
ftp://example.com
```

It's one machine that offers two different information services, and the browser will use different methods of connecting to each. As long as all three servers are installed and available on that system, you won't have a problem.

The hostname part of the URL might include a port number. The port number tells your browser to open a connection using the appropriate protocol on a specific network port. The only time you'll need a port number in a URL is if the server responding to the request has been explicitly installed on that port. If the server is listening on the default port, you can leave the port number out. This issue is covered in Day 17, "Designing for the Real World."

If a port number is necessary, it's placed after the hostname but before the directory, as follows:

```
http://my-public-access-unix.com:1550/pub/file
```

5

If the port is not included, the browser tries to connect to the default port number associated with the protocol in the URL. The default port for HTTP is 80, so a link to http://www.example.com:80/ and http://www.example.com/ are equivalent.

Finally, the *directory* is the location of the file or other form of information on the host. The directory does not necessarily point to a physical directory and file on the server. Some web applications generate content dynamically, and just use the directory information as an identifier. For the files you'll be working with while learning HTML, the directory information will point to files that exist on your computer.

Special Characters in URLs

A *special character* in a URL is anything that is not an upper- or lowercase letter, a number (0–9), or one of the following symbols: dollar sign ($), dash (-), underscore (_), or period (.). You might need to specify any other characters by using special URL escape codes to keep them from being interpreted as parts of the URL itself.

URL escape codes are indicated by a percent sign (%) and a two-character hexadecimal symbol from the ISO-Latin-1 character set (a superset of standard ASCII). For example, %20 is a space, %3f is a question mark, and %2f is a slash. (Spaces are also sometimes encoded as + signs, and + signs are encoded as %2b.)

Suppose that you have a directory named All My Files. Your first pass at a URL with this name in it might look like the following:

```
http://myhost.com/harddrive/All My Files/www/file.html
```

If you put this URL in quotation marks in a link tag, it might work (but only if you put it in quotation marks). Because the spaces are considered special characters to the URL, however, some browsers might have problems with them and not recognize the pathname correctly. For full compatibility with all browsers, use %20, as follows:

```
http://myhost.com/harddrive/A¦¦%20My%20Files/www/file.html
```

Most of the time, if you make sure that your file and directory names are short and use only alphanumeric characters, you won't need to include special characters in URLs. Keep this point in mind as you write your own pages.

HTML 4.01 and the <a> Tag

HTML 4.01 includes some additional attributes for the <a> tag that are less common. These offer the following:

- **tabindex**—Supports a tabbing order so that authors can define an order for anchors and links, and then the user can tab between them the way he does in a dialog box in Windows or the Mac OS.

- **Event handlers such as `onclick`, `onfocus`, and `onblur`**—The full list of events is listed in the section "Common Attributes and Events" of Appendix B. You'll learn how to use these events in Lesson 12, "Introducing JavaScript."

Kinds of URLs

Many kinds of URLs are defined by the Uniform Resource Locator specification. (See Appendix A, "Sources for Further Information," for a pointer to the most recent version.) This section describes some of the more popular URLs and some situations to look out for when using them.

HTTP

HTTP URLs are by far the most common type of URLs because they point to other documents on the Web. HTTP, which stands for *Hypertext Transfer Protocol*, is the protocol that World Wide Web servers use to communicate with web browsers.

HTTP URLs follow this basic URL form:

```
http://www.example.com/home/foo/
```

If the URL ends in a slash, the last part of the URL is considered a directory name. The file that you get using a URL of this type is the default file for that directory as defined by the HTTP server, usually a file called `index.html`. If the Web page you're designing is the top-level file for all a directory's files, calling it `index.html` is a good idea. Putting such a file in place will also keep users from browsing the directory where the file is located.

You also can specify the filename directly in the URL. In this case, the file at the end of the URL is the one that is loaded, as in the following examples:

```
http://www.foo.com/home/foo/index.html
```

```
http://www.foo.com/home/foo/homepage.html
```

Using HTTP URLs such as the following, where `foo` is a directory, is also usually acceptable:

```
http://www.foo.com/home/foo
```

In this case, because `foo` is a directory, this URL should have a slash at the end. Most Web servers can figure out that this is a link to a directory and redirect to the appropriate file. Some older servers, however, might have difficulties resolving this URL, so you should always identify directories and files explicitly and make sure that a default file is available if you're indicating a directory.

5

Anonymous FTP

FTP URLs are used to point to files located on FTP servers—usually anonymous FTP servers; that is, the ones that allow you to log in using anonymous as the login ID and your email address as the password. FTP URLs also follow the standard URL form, as shown in the following examples:

```
ftp://ftp.foo.com/home/foo
ftp://ftp.foo.com/home/foo/homepage.html
```

Because you can retrieve either a file or a directory list with FTP, the restrictions on whether you need a trailing slash at the end of the URL aren't the same as with HTTP. The first URL here retrieves a listing of all the files in the foo directory. The second URL retrieves and parses the file homepage.html in the foo directory.

> **NOTE**
>
> Navigating FTP servers using a web browser can often be much slower than navigating them using FTP itself because the browser doesn't hold the connection open. Instead, it opens the connection, finds the file or directory listing, displays the listing, and then closes down the FTP connection. If you select a link to open a file or another directory in that listing, the browser constructs a new FTP URL from the items you selected, reopens the FTP connection by using the new URL, gets the next directory or file, and closes it again. For this reason, FTP URLs are best for when you know exactly which file you want to retrieve rather than for when you want to browse an archive.

Although your browser uses FTP to fetch the file, if it's an HTML file, your browser will display it just as it would were it fetched using the HTTP protocol. Web browsers don't care how they get files. As long as they can recognize the file as HTML, either because the server explicitly says that the file is HTML or by the file's extension, browsers will parse and display that file as an HTML file. If they don't recognize it as an HTML file, no big deal. Browsers can either display the file if they know what kind of file it is or just save the file to disk.

Non-anonymous FTP

All the FTP URLs in the preceding section are used for anonymous FTP servers. You also can specify an FTP URL for named accounts on an FTP server, like the following:

```
ftp://username:password@ftp.foo.com/home/foo/homepage.html
```

In this form of the URL, the *username* part is your login ID on the server, and *password* is that account's password. Note that no attempt is made to hide the password in the

URL. Be very careful that no one is watching you when you're using URLs of this form—and don't put them into links that someone else can find!

Furthermore, the URLs that you request might be cached or logged somewhere, either on your local machine or on a proxy server between you and the site you're connecting to. For that reason, it's probably wise to avoid using this type of non-anonymous FTP URL altogether.

Mailto

The mailto URL is used to send electronic mail. If the browser supports mailto URLs, when a link that contains one is selected, the browser will prompt you for a subject and the body of the mail message, and send that message to the appropriate address when you're done. Depending on how the user's browser and email client are configured, mailto links might not work at all for them.

The mailto URL is different from the standard URL form. It looks like the following:

```
mailto:internet_e-mail_address
```

Here's an example:

```
mailto:lemay@lne.com
```

NOTE

> If your email address includes a percent sign (%), you'll have to use the escape character %25 instead. Percent signs are special characters to URLs.

5

Unlike the other URLs described here, the mailto URL works strictly on the client side. The mailto link just tells the browser to compose an email message to the specified address. It's up to the browser to figure out how that should happen. Most browsers will also let you add a default subject to the email by including it in the URL like this:

```
mailto:lemay@lne.com?subject=Hi there!
```

When the user clicks on the link, most browsers will automatically stick Hi there! in the subject of the message. Some even support putting body text for the email message in the link, like this:

```
mailto:lemay@lne.com?subject=Hi there!&body=Body text.
```

Usenet Newsgroups

Usenet news URLs have one of two forms:

```
news:name_of_newsgroup
news:message-id
```

The first form is used to read an entire newsgroup, such as `comp.infosystems.` `www.authoring.html` or `alt.gothic`. If your browser supports Usenet news URLs (either directly or through a newsreader), it'll provide you with a list of available articles in that newsgroup.

The second form enables you to retrieve a specific news article. Each news article has a unique ID, called a *message ID*, which usually looks something like the following:

`<lemayCt76Jq.CwG@netcom.com>`

To use a message ID in a URL, remove the angle brackets and include the `news:` part:

`news:lemayCt76Jq.CwG@netcom.com`

Be aware that news articles don't exist forever—they expire and are deleted. So, a message ID that was valid at one point can become invalid a short time later. If you want a permanent link to a news article, you should just copy the article to your web presentation and link it as you would any other file.

Both forms of URL assume that you're reading news from an NNTP server, and they can be used only if you have defined an NNTP server somewhere in an environment variable or preferences file for your browser. Therefore, news URLs are most useful simply for reading specific news articles locally, not necessarily for using in links in pages.

> **CAUTION**
> News URLs, like mailto URLs, might not be supported by all browsers.

File

File URLs are intended to reference files contained on the local disk. In other words, they refer to files located on the same system as the browser. For local files, file URLs take one of these two forms: the first with an empty hostname (three slashes rather than two) or with the hostname as `localhost`:

```
file:///dir1/dir2/file
file://localhost/dir1/dir2/file
```

Depending on your browser, one or the other will usually work. (If you're in doubt, you can open the file from within your browser and look at the address bar to see what its `file:` URL is.)

File URLs are very similar to FTP URLs. In fact, if the host part of a file URL is not empty or `localhost`, your browser will try to find the given file by using FTP. Both of the following URLs result in the same file being loaded in the same way:

```
file://somesystem.com/pub/dir/foo/file.html
ftp://somesystem.com/pub/dir/foo/file.html
```

Probably the best use of file URLs is in startup pages for your browser (which are also called *home pages*). In this instance, because you'll almost always be referring to a local file, using a file URL makes sense.

The problem with file URLs is that they reference local files, where *local* means on the same system as the browser pointing to the file—not the same system from which the page was retrieved! If you use file URLs as links in your page, and someone from elsewhere on the Internet encounters your page and tries to follow those links, that person's browser will attempt to find the file on her local disk (and generally will fail). Also, because file URLs use the absolute pathname to the file, if you use file URLs in your page, you can't move that page elsewhere on the system or to any other system.

If your intention is to refer to files that are on the same file system or directory as the current page, use relative pathnames rather than file URLs. With relative pathnames for local files and other URLs for remote files, you shouldn't need to use a file URL at all.

Summary

Today, you learned all about links. Links turn the Web from a collection of unrelated pages into an enormous, interrelated information system (there are those big words again).

To create links, you use the <a>...</a> tag pair, called the *link* or *anchor* tag. The anchor tag has attributes for creating links (the href attribute) and anchor names (the name attribute).

5

When linking pages that are all stored on the local disk, you can specify their pathnames in the href attribute as relative or absolute paths. For local links, relative pathnames are preferred because they enable you to move local pages more easily to another directory or to another system. If you use absolute pathnames, your links will break if you change anything in the hard-coded path.

If you want to link to a page on the Web (a remote page), the value of the href attribute is the URL of that page. You can easily copy the URL of the page you want to link. Just go to that page by using your favorite web browser, and then copy and paste the URL from your browser into the appropriate place in your link tag.

To create links to specific parts of a page, set an anchor at the point you want to link to, use the <a>...</a> tag as you would with a link, but rather than the href attribute, you use the name attribute to name the anchor. You then can link directly to that anchor name by using the name of the page, a hash sign (#), and the anchor name.

Finally, URLs (uniform resource locators) are used to point to pages, files, and other information on the Internet. Depending on the type of information, URLs can contain several parts, but most contain a protocol type and location or address. URLs can be used to point to many kinds of information but are most commonly used to point to web pages (`http`), FTP directories or files (`ftp`), electronic mail addresses (`mailto`), or Usenet news (`news`).

Workshop

Congratulations, you learned a lot today! Now it's time for the workshop. Many questions about links appear here. The quiz focuses on other items that are important for you to remember, followed by the quiz answers. In today's exercises, you'll take the list of items you created yesterday and link them to other pages.

Q&A

Q **My links aren't being highlighted in blue or purple at all. They're still just plain text.**

A Is the filename in a `name` attribute rather than in an `href`? Did you remember to close the quotation marks around the filename to which you're linking? Both of these errors can prevent links from showing up as links.

Q **I put a URL into a link, and it shows up as highlighted in my browser, but when I click it, the browser says "unable to access page." If it can't find the page, why did it highlight the text?**

A The browser highlights text within a link tag whether or not the link is valid. In fact, you don't even need to be online for links to show up as highlighted links, although you can't get to them. The only way you can tell whether a link is valid is to select it and try to view the page to which the link points.

As to why the browser couldn't find the page you linked to—make sure that you're connected to the network and that you entered the URL into the link correctly. Also verify that you have both opening and closing quotation marks around the filename, and that those quotation marks are straight quotes. If your browser prints link destinations in the status bar when you move the mouse cursor over a link, watch that status bar and see whether the URL that appears is actually the URL you want.

Finally, try opening the URL directly in your browser and see whether that solution works. If directly opening the link doesn't work either, there might be several reasons why. The following are two common possibilities:

- The server is overloaded or is not on the Internet.

  Machines go down, as do network connections. If a particular URL doesn't work for you, perhaps something is wrong with the machine or the network. Or maybe the site is popular, and too many people are trying to access it at once. Try again later. If you know the people who run the server, you can try sending them electronic mail or calling them.

- The URL itself is bad.

  Sometimes URLs become invalid. Because a URL is a form of absolute pathname, if the file to which it refers moves around, or if a machine or directory name gets changed, the URL won't be valid anymore. Try contacting the person or site you got the URL from in the first place. See whether that person has a more recent link.

Q Can I put any URL in a link?

A You bet. If you can get to a URL using your browser, you can put that URL in a link. Note, however, that some browsers support URLs that others don't. For example, Lynx is really good with mailto URLs (URLs that enable you to send electronic mail to a person's email address). When you select a mailto URL in Lynx, it prompts you for a subject and the body of the message. When you're done, it sends the mail.

Q Can I use images as links?

A Yup, in more ways than one, actually. You'll learn how to use images as links and define multiple links within one image using image maps in Lesson 7, "Adding Images, Color, and Backgrounds."

Q My links aren't pointing to my anchors. When I follow a link, I'm always dropped at the top of the page rather than at the anchor. What's going on here?

A Are you specifying the anchor name in the link after the hash sign the same way that it appears in the anchor itself, with all the uppercase and lowercase letters identical? Anchors are case sensitive, so if your browser can't find an anchor name with an exact match, the browser might try to select something else in the page that's closer. This is dependent on browser behavior, of course, but if your links and anchors aren't working, the problem usually is that your anchor names and your anchors don't match. Also, remember that anchor names don't contain hash signs—only the links to them do.

5

Q Is there any way to indicate a subject in a mailto URL?

A If you include `?subject=Your%20subject` in the mailto URL, it will work with most email clients. Here's what the whole link looks like:

```
<a href="mailto:someone@example.com?subject=Your%20subject">Send email</a>
```

Quiz

1. What two things do you need to create a link in HTML?
2. What's a relative pathname? Why is it advantageous to use them?
3. What's an absolute pathname?
4. What's an anchor, and what is it used for?
5. Besides HTTP (web page) URLs, what other kinds are there?

Quiz Answers

1. To create a link in HTML, you need the name or URL of the file or page to which you want to link, and the text that your readers can select to follow the link.
2. A relative pathname points to a file, based on the location that's relative to the current file. Relative pathnames are portable, meaning that if you move your files elsewhere on a disk or rename a directory, the links require little or no modification.
3. An absolute pathname points to a page by starting at the top level of a directory hierarchy and working downward through all intervening directories to reach the file.
4. An anchor marks a place that you can link to inside a web document. A link on the same page or on another page can then jump to that specific location instead of the top of the page.
5. Other types of URLs are FTP URLs (which point to files on FTP servers); file URLs (which point to a file contained on a local disk); mailto URLs (which are used to send electronic mail); and Usenet URLs (which point to newsgroups or specific news articles in a newsgroup).

Exercises

1. Remember the list of topics that you created yesterday in the first exercise? Create a link to the page you created in yesterday's second exercise (the page that described one of the topics in more detail).
2. Now, open the page that you created in yesterday's second exercise, and create a link back to the first page. Also, find some pages on the World Wide Web that discuss the same topic and create links to those pages as well. Good luck!

LESSON 6:
Formatting Text with HTML and CSS

In Lessons 4, "Learning the Basics of HTML," and 5, "Adding Links to Your Web Pages," you learned the basics of HTML, including tags used to describe page structure and create links. With that background, you're now ready to learn more about what HTML and CSS can do in terms of text formatting and layout.

In this Lesson

Today you'll learn about most of the remaining tags in HTML that you'll need to know to construct pages, including tags in HTML 2.0 through HTML 4.01, as well as HTML attributes in individual browsers. Today you'll learn how to do the following:

- Specify the appearance of individual characters (bold, italic, underlined)

- Include special characters (characters with accents, copyright marks, and so on)

- Create preformatted text (text with spaces and tabs retained)

- Align text left, right, and centered

- Change the font and font size

- Create other miscellaneous HTML text elements, including line breaks, rule lines, addresses, and quotations

In addition, you'll learn the differences between standard HTML and HTML extensions, and when to choose which tags to use in your pages. You'll also learn which of these tags have been deprecated in XHTML, and how to use CSS to achieve the same effects. Finally, you'll create a complete web page that uses many of the tags presented today, as well as the information from the preceding four days.

Today you'll cover several tags and options, so you might find it a bit overwhelming. Don't worry about remembering everything now; just get a grasp of what sort of formatting you can do in HTML, and then you can look up the specific tags later.

Character-Level Elements

When you use HTML tags for paragraphs, headings, or lists, those tags affect that block of text as a whole—changing the font, changing the spacing above and below the line, or adding characters (in the case of bulleted lists). They're referred to as *block-level* elements.

Character-level elements are tags that affect words or characters within other HTML entities and change the appearance of that text so that it's somehow different from the surrounding text—making it bold or underlined, for example.

To change the appearance of a set of characters within text, you can use one of two kinds of tags: logical styles or physical styles.

Logical Styles

Logical style tags describe the meaning of the text within the tag, not how it should be presented. They're similar to the common element tags for paragraphs or headings. For example, logical style tags might indicate a definition, a snippet of code, or an emphasized word. This can be a bit confusing because there are de facto standards that correlate each of these tags with a certain visual style. In other words, even though a tag like <strong> would mean different things to different people, in web browsers it means boldface.

Using logical style tags, the browser determines the actual presentation of the text, whether it's bold, italic, or any other change in appearance. You cannot guarantee that text that's highlighted using these tags will always be bold or italic, so you shouldn't depend on it. These days, browser makers have pretty much agreed on how each of these logical tags are rendered, but it's still important to understand that the logical tags convey more meaning than just the physical styles that they apply.

Each character style tag has both opening and closing sides and affects the text within those two tags. The following are the eight logical style tags:

<em>   This tag indicates that the characters are to be emphasized in some
                    way; that is, they're formatted differently from the rest of the text.
                    In graphical browsers, typically <em> italicizes the text. For example:

```
<p>The anteater is the <em>strangest</em> looking animal,
isn't it?</p>
```

<strong>   With this tag, the characters are to be more strongly emphasized
                    than with <em>—usually in boldface. Consider the following:

```
<p>Take a <strong>left turn</strong> at <strong>Dee's Hop
Stop</strong></p>
```

<code>   This tag indicates that the text inside is a code sample and displays
                    it in a fixed-width font such as Courier. For example:

```
<p><code>#include "trans.h"</code></p>
```

<samp>   This tag indicates sample text and is generally presented in a
                    fixed-width font, like <code>. An example of its usage follows:

```
<p>The URL for that page is <samp>http://www.cern.ch/
</samp></p>
```

<kbd>   This tag indicates text that's intended to be typed by a user. It's
                    also presented in a fixed-width font. Consider the following:

```
<p>Type the following command: <kbd>find . -name "prune"
-print</kbd></p>
```

<var>   This tag indicates the name of a variable, or some entity to be
                    replaced with an actual value. Often it's displayed as italic or
                    underline, and is used as follows:

```
<p><code>chown</code> <var>your_name for the_file
</var></p>
```

<dfn>   This tag indicates a definition. <dfn> is used to highlight a word
                    (usually in italics) that will be defined or has just been defined, as
                    in the following example:

```
<p>Styles that are named after how they are actually
used are called
<dfn>logical styles</dfn></p>
```

6

<cite>   This tag indicates a short quote or citation, as in the following:

```
<p>Eggplant has been known to cause nausea in some
people<cite> (Lemay, 1994)</cite></p>
```

NOTE   Of the tags in this list, all except <dfn> are part of the official HTML 2.0 recommendation. <dfn> was added in the HTML 3.2 recommendation. They're all still valid in the XHTML 1.0 recommendation.

HTML 4.01 introduced two additional logical style tags that are most useful for audio browsers. A graphical browser, such as Netscape or Internet Explorer, won't display them any differently. When an audio browser reads content included within one of these tags, however, each letter is spoken individually. For example, *fox* is pronounced F-O-X rather than *fox*.

These tags also use opening and closing sides and affect the text within. The following are new tags:

<abbr>   This tag indicates the abbreviation of a word, as in the following:

```
<p>Use the standard two-letter state abbreviation
(such as <abbr>CA</abbr> for California)</p>
```

<acronym>   Similar to the <abbr> tag, <acronym> designates a word formed by combining the initial letters of several words, as in the following example:

```
<p>Jonathan learned his great problem-handling skills
from <acronym>STEPS</acronym> (Simply Tackle Each Problem
Seriously)</p>
```

Got all these tags memorized now? Good! There will be a pop quiz at the end of the day. The following code snippets demonstrate each of the logical style tags, and Figure 6.1 illustrates how all the tags are displayed.

Input ▼

```
<p>The anteater is the <em>strangest</em> looking animal, isn't it?</p>
<p>Take a <strong>left turn</strong> at <strong>Dee's Hop Stop
</strong></p>
<p><code>#include "trans.h"</code></p>
<p>The URL for that page is <samp>http://www.cern.ch/</samp></p>
<p>Type the following command: <kbd>find . -name "prune" -print</kbd></p>
<p><code>chown </code><var>your_name the_file</var></p>
<p>Styles that are named after how they are used are called <dfn>logical
styles</dfn></p>
<p>Eggplant has been known to cause nausea in some
people<cite> (Lemay, 1994)</cite></p>
<p>Use the standard two-letter state abbreviation (such as
<abbr>CA</abbr> for California)</p>
<p>Jonathan learned his great problem-handling skills from
<acronym>STEPS</acronym> (Simply Tackle Each Problem Seriously)
```

Output ▼

FIGURE 6.1

Various logical styles displayed in a browser.

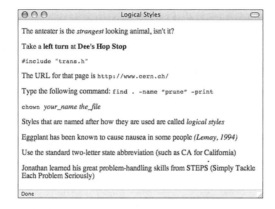

```
○ ○ ○                    Logical Styles                    ⬭

The anteater is the strangest looking animal, isn't it?

Take a left turn at Dee's Hop Stop

#include "trans.h"

The URL for that page is http://www.cern.ch/

Type the following command: find . -name "prune" -print

chown your_name the_file

Styles that are named after how they are used are called logical styles

Eggplant has been known to cause nausea in some people (Lemay, 1994)

Use the standard two-letter state abbreviation (such as CA for California)

Jonathan learned his great problem-handling skills from STEPS (Simply Tackle
Each Problem Seriously)

Done                                                                    ⌟
```

Physical Styles

In addition to these style tags, you can use a set of *physical style tags* to change the actual presentation style of the text—bold, italic, or monospace.

Like the character style tags, each formatting tag has a beginning and ending tag. Standard HTML 2.0 defined three physical style tags:

`<b>`	Bold
`<i>`	Italic
`<tt>`	Monospaced typewriter font

HTML 3.2 defined several additional physical style tags, including the following:

`<u>`	Underline (deprecated in HTML 4.0)
`<s>`	Strikethrough (deprecated in HTML 4.0)
`<big>`	Bigger print than the surrounding text
`<small>`	Smaller print
`<sub>`	Subscript
`<sup>`	Superscript

6

NOTE

Text-based browsers, such as Lynx and those associated with wireless devices, can't render bold, italic, or other styled text. They generally highlight the text in some way, but the method varies depending on the browser and platform.

You can nest character tags—for example, using both bold and italic for a set of characters—as follows:

```
<b><i>Text that is both bold and italic</i></b>
```

However, the result on the screen is browser-dependent, like all HTML tags. You won't necessarily end up with text that's both bold and italic. You might end up with one style or the other:

Input ▼

```
<p>In Dante's <i>Inferno</i>, malaboge was the eighth circle of hell,
and held the malicious and fraudulent.</p>
<p>All entries must be received by <b>September 26, 1999</b>.</p>
<p>Type <tt>lpr -Pbirch myfile.txt</tt> to print that file.</p>
<p>Sign your name in the spot marked <u>Sign Here</u>:</p>
<p>People who wear orange shirts and plaid pants <s>have no taste</s>
are fashion-challenged.</p>
<p>RCP floor mats give you <big>big</big> savings over the
competition!</p>
<p>Then, from the corner of the room, he heard a <small>tiny voice
</small>.</p>
<p>In heavy trading today. Consolidated Orange Trucking
rose <sup>1</sup>/<sub>4</sub>
points on volume of 1,457,900 shares.</p>
```

Figure 6.2 shows some of the physical tags and how they appear.

Output ▼

FIGURE 6.2
Physical styles
displayed in a
browser.

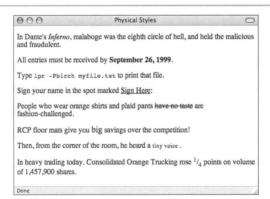

Character Formatting Using CSS

You've already seen how styles can be used to modify the appearance of various elements. Any of the effects associated with the tags introduced in today's lesson can also be created using CSS. Before I go into these properties, however, I want to talk a bit about how to use them. As I've said before, the style attribute can be used with most tags. However, most tags somehow affect the appearance of the text that they enclose. There's a tag that doesn't have any inherent effect on the text that it's wrapped around: the <span> tag. It exists solely to be associated with style sheets. It's used exactly like any of the other tags you've seen today. Simply wrap it around some text, like this:

```
<p>This is an example of the <span>usage of the span tag</span>.</p>
```

Used by itself, the <span> tag has absolutely no effect. Paired with the style attribute, it can take the place of any of the tags you've seen today and can do a lot more than that as well.

The Text Decoration Property

The text-decoration property is used to specify which, if any, decoration will be applied to the text within the affected tag. The valid values for this property are underline, overline, line-through, and blink. The application of each of them is self-explanatory. However, here's an example that demonstrates how to use each of them:

Input ▼

```
<p>Here is some <span style='text-decoration: underline">underlined
text</span>.</p>
<p>Here is some <span style="text-decoration: overline">overlined text</span>.</p>
<p>Here is some <span style="text-decoration: line-through">line-through
text</span>.</p>
<p>Here is some <span style="text-decoration: blink">blinking text</span>.</p>
```

Using <span> and the text-decoration property to underline text is no different from using the <u> tag, except that some old browsers that don't support CSS might not support it. The cool thing is that you can use this, and all the properties you'll see in today's lesson, with any tag that encloses text. Take a look at this example:

```
<h1 style="text-decoration: underline">An Underlined Heading</h1>
```

Using the style attribute, you can specify how the text of the heading appears. Choosing between this approach and the <u> tag is a wash—if you want to remove the underlining from the heading, you'd have to come back and edit the tag itself, regardless of whether you used the <u> tag or style attribute. Later, you'll see how style sheets can be used to control the appearance of many elements at once.

6

Font Properties

When you want to modify the appearance of text, the other major family of properties you can use is font properties. Font properties can be used to modify pretty much any aspect of the type used to render text in a browser. One of the particularly nice things about font properties is that they're much more specific than the tags that you've seen so far.

First, let's look at some of the direct replacements for tags you've already seen. The font-style property can be used to italicize text. It has three possible values, normal, which is the default, italic, which renders the text in the same way as the <i> tag, and oblique, which is somewhere between italic and normal, and is not as well supported by browsers as the italic style is. Here are some examples:

Input ▼

```
<p>Here's some <span style="font-style: italic">italicized text</span>.</p>
<p>Here's some <span style="font-style: oblique">oblique text</span>
(which may look like regular italics in your browser).</p>
```

Now let's look at how you use CSS to create boldfaced text. In the world of HTML, there are two options: bold and not bold. With CSS, you have (theoretically) many more options. The reason I say *theoretically* is that browser support for the wide breadth of font weights available using CSS can be spotty. To specify that text should be boldface, the font-weight property is used. Valid values are normal (the default), bold, bolder, lighter, and 100 through 900, in units of 100. Here are some examples:

Input ▼

```
<p>Here's some <span style="font-weight: bold">bold text</span>.</p>
<p>Here's some <span style="font-weight: bolder">bolder text</span>.</p>
<p>Here's some <span style="font-weight: lighter">lighter text</span>.</p>
<p>Here's some <span style="font-weight: 700">bolder text</span>.</p>
```

You can also set the typeface for text using the font-family property. You can also set the specific font for text, but I'm not going to discuss that until later today. In the meantime, let's look at how you can set the font to a member of a particular font family. The specific font will be taken from the user's preferences. The property to modify is font-family. The possible values are serif, sans-serif, cursive, fantasy, and monospace. So, if you want to specify that a monospace font should be used with CSS instead of the <tt> tag, you would use the following code:

Input ▼

```
<p><span style="font-family: monospace">This is monospaced text.</span></p>
```

Now let's look at one capability that's not available using regular HTML tags. Using the font-variant property, you can have your text rendered so that lowercase letters are replaced with larger capital letters. The two values available are normal and small-caps. Here's an example:

Input ▼

```
<p><span style='font-variant: small-caps'>This Text Uses Small Caps.</span></p>
```

The browser window in Figure 6.3 contains some text that uses the font-variant property as well as all the other properties described in this section.

Output ▼

FIGURE 6.3
Text styled using CSS.

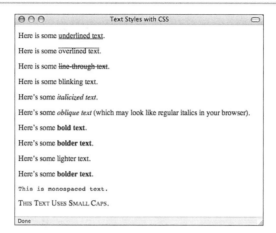

Preformatted Text

Most of the time, text in an HTML file is formatted based on the HTML tags used to mark up that text. As I mentioned in Lesson 3, "Introducing HTML and XHTML," any extra white space (spaces, tabs, returns) that you put in your text is stripped out by the browser.

The one exception to this rule is the preformatted text tag <pre>. Any white space that you put into text surrounded by the <pre> and </pre> tags is retained in the final output. With these tags, the spacing in the text in the HTML source is preserved when it's displayed on the page.

The catch is that preformatted text usually is displayed (in graphical displays, at least) in a monospaced font such as Courier. Preformatted text is excellent for displaying code examples in which you want the text formatted with exactly the indentation the author used. Because you can use the <pre> tag to align text by padding it with spaces, you can use it for simple tables. However, the fact that the tables are presented in a monospaced font might make them less than ideal. (You'll learn how to create real tables in Lesson 8, "Building Tables.") The following is an example of a table created with <pre>:

Input ▼

```
<pre>
      Diameter  Distance   Time to    Time to
      (miles)    from Sun  Orbit      Rotate
            (millions
            of miles)
------------------------------------------------------------
```

```
Mercury   3100     36    88 days     59 days
Venus    7700     67    225 days     244 days
Earth    7920     93    365 days     24 hrs
Mars     4200     141    687 days     24 hrs 24 mins
Jupiter   88640     483     11.9 years    9 hrs 50 mins
Saturn   74500     886    29.5 years    10 hrs 39 mins
Uranus   32000    1782    84 years    23 hrs
Neptune   31000     2793    165 days     15 hrs 48 mins
Pluto    1500    3670    248 years    6 days 7 hrs
</pre>
```

Figure 6.4 shows how it looks in a browser.

Output ▼

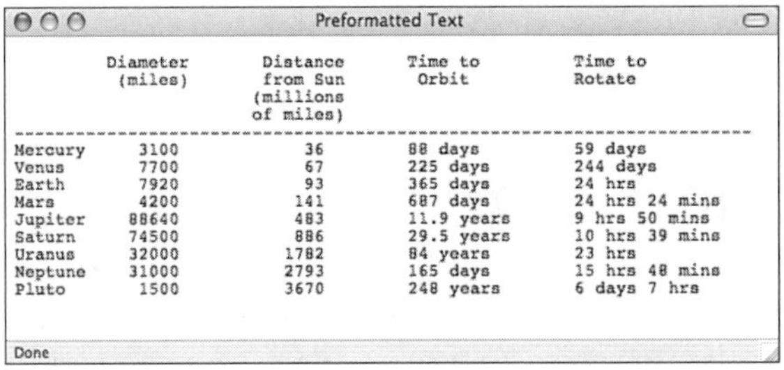

	Diameter (miles)	Distance from Sun (millions of miles)	Time to Orbit	Time to Rotate
Mercury	3100	36	88 days	59 days
Venus	7700	67	225 days	244 days
Earth	7920	93	365 days	24 hrs
Mars	4200	141	687 days	24 hrs 24 mins
Jupiter	88640	483	11.9 years	9 hrs 50 mins
Saturn	74500	886	29.5 years	10 hrs 39 mins
Uranus	32000	1782	84 years	23 hrs
Neptune	31000	2793	165 days	15 hrs 48 mins
Pluto	1500	3670	248 years	6 days 7 hrs

FIGURE 6.4 A table created using *<pre>*, shown in a browser.

When you're creating text for the <pre> tag, you can use link tags and character styles, but not element tags such as headings or paragraphs. You should break your lines with hard returns and try to keep your lines to 60 characters or fewer. Some browsers might have limited horizontal space in which to display text. Because browsers usually won't reformat preformatted text to fit that space, you should make sure that you keep your text within the boundaries to prevent your readers from having to scroll from side to side.

Be careful with tabs in preformatted text. The actual number of characters for each tab stop varies from browser to browser. One browser might have tab stops at every fourth character, whereas another may have them at every eighth character. You should convert any tabs in your preformatted text to spaces so that your formatting isn't messed up if it's viewed with different tab settings than in the program you used to enter the text.

The <pre> tag is also excellent for converting files that were originally in some sort of text-only form, such as mail messages or Usenet news postings, into HTML quickly and easily. Just surround the entire content of the article within <pre> tags and you have instant HTML, as in the following example:

```
<pre>
To: lemay@lne.com
From: jokes@lne.com
Subject: Tales of the Move From Hell, pt. 1
```

```
I spent the day on the phone today with the entire household
services division of northern California, turning off services,
turning on services, transferring services and other such fun
things you have to do when you move.

It used to be you just called these people and got put on hold for
and interminable amount of time, maybe with some nice music, and
then you got a customer representative who was surly and hard of
hearing, but with some work you could actually get your phone
turned off.
</pre>
```

One creative use of the <pre> tag is to create ASCII art for your web pages. The following HTML input and output example shows a simple ASCII-art cow:

Input ▼

```
<pre>
   ( )
Moo (oo)
   \/------\
    ||     ||  \
    ||---W|| *
    ||     ||
    ||     ||
</pre>
```

The result is displayed in Figure 6.5.

Output ▼

FIGURE 6.5
A bit of ASCII art that illustrates how preformatted text works.

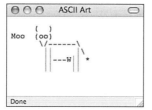

Horizontal Rules

The <hr> tag, which has no closing tag in HTML and no text associated with it, creates a horizontal line on the page. Rule lines are used to visually separate sections of a web page—just before headings, for example, or to separate body text from a list of items.

6

Closing Empty Elements

The <hr> tag has no closing tag in HTML. To convert this tag to XHTML and to ensure compatibility with HTML browsers, add a space and a forward slash to the end of the tag:

```
<hr />
```

If the horizontal line has attributes associated with it, the forward slash still appears at the end of the tag, as shown in the following examples:

```
<hr size="2" />
<hr width="75%" />
<hr align="center" size="4" width="200" />
```

The following input shows a rule line and a list as you would write it in XHTML 1.0:

Input ▼

```
<hr />
<h2>To Do on Friday</h2>
<ul>
<li>Do laundry</li>
<li>Send FedEx with pictures</li>
<li>Have lunch with Mollie</li>
<li>Read Email</li>
<li>Set up Ethernet</li>
</ul>
<hr />
```

Figure 6.6 shows how they appear in a browser.

Output ▼

FIGURE 6.6
An example of how horizontal rules are used around a list.

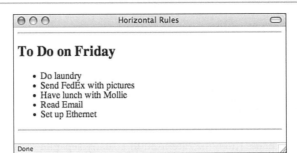

Attributes of the <hr> Tag

In HTML 2.0, the <hr> tag is just as you see it, with no closing tag or attributes. However, HTML 3.2 introduced several attributes to the <hr> tag that give you greater control over the appearance of the line drawn by <hr>. All these attributes have been deprecated in favor of style sheets in the HTML 4.01 specification.

NOTE

Although presentation attributes such as `size`, `width`, and `align` are still supported in HTML 4.01, style sheets are now the recommended way to control a page's appearance.

The `size` attribute indicates the thickness, in pixels, of the rule line. The default is 2, and this also is the smallest that you can make the rule line. Figure 6.7 shows the sample rule line thicknesses created with the following code:

Input ▼

```
<h2>2 Pixels</h2>
<hr size="2" />
<h2>4 Pixels</h2>
<hr size="4" />
<h2>8 Pixels</h2>
<hr size="8" />
<h2>16 Pixels</h2>
<hr size="16" />
```

Output ▼

FIGURE 6.7
Examples of rule
line thicknesses.

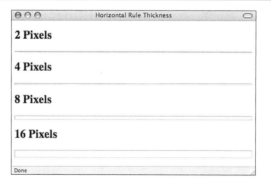

The `width` attribute specifies the horizontal width of the rule line. You can specify the exact width of the rule in pixels. You can also specify the value as a percentage of the browser width (for example, 30% or 50%). If you set the width of a horizontal rule to a percentage, the width of the rule will change to conform to the window size if the user resizes the browser window. Figure 6.8 shows the result of the following code, which displays some sample rule line widths:

Input ▼

```
<h2>100%</h2>
<hr />
<h2>75%</h2>
```

6

```
<hr width="75%" />
<h2>50%</h2>
<hr width="50%" />
<h2>25%</h2>
<hr width="25%" />
<h2>10%</h2>
<hr width="10%" />
```

Output ▼

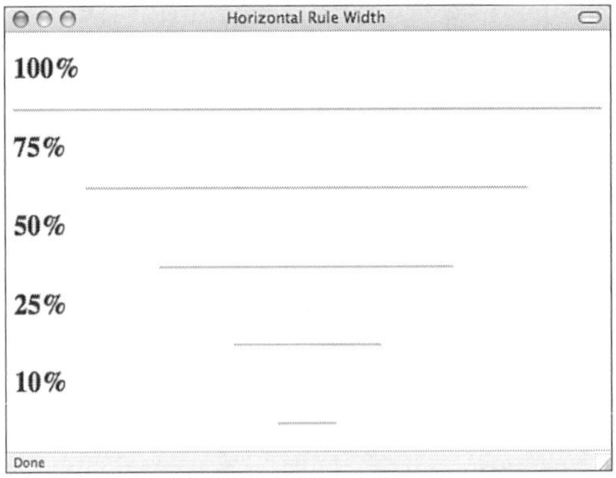

FIGURE 6.8
Examples of rule
line widths.

If you specify a width smaller than the actual width of the browser window, you can also specify the alignment of that rule with the align attribute, making it flush left (align="left"), flush right (align="right"), or centered (align="center"). By default, rule lines are centered.

Finally, in most current browsers, the noshade attribute shown in the following example causes the browser to draw the rule line as a plain line without the three-dimensional shading, as shown in Figure 6.9.

Handling Attributes Without Values

In HTML 4.0 and earlier versions, a value isn't required by the noshade attribute. The method you use to apply this attribute appears as follows:

```
<hr align="center" size="4" width="200" noshade>
```

To comply with XHTML 1.0, however, all attributes require a value. The HTML 4.01 specification requires that Boolean attributes (such as noshade) have only the name of the attribute itself as the value. The following example demonstrates how to apply the noshade attribute to the <hr> tag in compliance with the XHTML 1.0 specification.

```
<hr align="center" size="4" width="200" noshade="noshade" />
<hr align="center" size="4" width="300" noshade="noshade" />
<hr align="center" size="4" width="400" noshade="noshade" />
```

```
<h1 align="center">NorthWestern Video</h1>
<hr align="center" size="4" width="400" noshade="noshade" />
<hr align="center" size="4" width="300" noshade="noshade" />
<hr align="center" size="4" width="200" noshade="noshade" />
<h2 align="center">Presents</h2>
```

Output ▼

FIGURE 6.9
Rule lines without
shading.

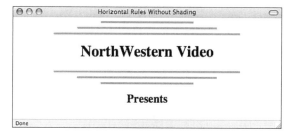

Line Break

The `<br>` tag breaks a line of text at the point where it appears. When a web browser
encounters a `<br>` tag, it restarts the text after the tag at the left margin (whatever the
current left margin happens to be for the current element). You can use `<br>` within other
elements, such as paragraphs or list items; `<br>` won't add extra space above or below
the new line or change the font or style of the current entity. All it does is restart the text
at the next line.

Closing Single Tags Properly

Like the `<hr>` tag, the `<br>` tag has no closing tag in HTML. To convert this tag to
XHTML and to ensure compatibility with HTML browsers, add a space and forward
slash to the end of the tag and its attributes, as shown in the following example:

```
And then is heard no more: it is a tale <br />
Told by an idiot, full of sound and fury, <br />
Signifying nothing.</p>
```

The following example shows a simple paragraph in which each line (except for the last,
which ends with a closing `<p>` tag) ends with a `<br>`:

Input ▼

```
<p>Tomorrow, and tomorrow, and tomorrow,<br />
Creeps in this petty pace from day to day,<br />
To the last syllable of recorded time;<br />
```

6

```
And all our yesterdays have lighted fools<br />
The way to dusty death. Out, out, brief candle!<br />
Life's but a walking shadow; a poor player,<br />
That struts and frets his hour upon the stage,<br />
And then is heard no more: it is a tale <br />
Told by an idiot, full of sound and fury, <br />
Signifying nothing.</p>
```

Figure 6.10 shows how it appears in a browser.

> **NOTE**
>
> clear is an attribute of the <br> tag. It's used with images that have text wrapped alongside them. You'll learn about this attribute in Lesson 7, "Adding Images, Color, and Backgrounds."

Output ▼

FIGURE 6.10
Line breaks.

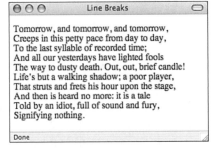

Addresses

The address tag <address> is used for signature-like entities on web pages. Address tags usually go at the bottom of each web page and are used to indicate who wrote the web page, who to contact for more information, the date, any copyright notices or other warnings, and anything else that seems appropriate. Addresses often are preceded with a rule line (<hr>), and the <br> tag can be used to separate the lines.

Without an address or some other method of signing your web pages, it's close to impossible to find out who wrote it or who to contact for more information. Signing each of your web pages by using the <address> tag is an excellent way to make sure that people can get in touch with you. <address> is a block-level tag that italicizes the text inside it.

The following input shows an address:

Input ▼

```
<hr />
<address>
Laura Lemay <a href="mailto:lemay@lne.com">lemay@lne.com</a><br />
```

```
A service of Laura Lemay, Incorporated <br />
last revised January 10, 2003 <br />
Copyright Laura Lemay 2003 all rights reserved <br />
Void where prohibited. Keep hands and feet inside the vehicle at all times.
</address>
```

Figure 6.11 shows it in a browser.

Output ▼

FIGURE 6.11
An address block.

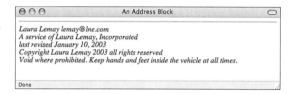

Quotations

The `<blockquote>` tag is used to create an indented block of text within a page. (Unlike the `<cite>` tag, which highlights small quotes, `<blockquote>` is used for longer quotations that shouldn't be nested inside other paragraphs.) For example, the *Macbeth* soliloquy I used in the example for line breaks would have worked better as a `<blockquote>` than as a simple paragraph. Here's an input example:

```
<blockquote>
"During the whole of a dull, dark, and soundless day in the autumn
of the year, when the clouds hung oppressively low in the heavens,
I had been passing alone, on horseback, through a singularly dreary
tract of country, and at length found myself, as the shades of evening
grew on, within view of the melancholy House of Usher."---Edgar Allen Poe
</blockquote>
```

As with paragraphs, you can split lines in a `<blockquote>` using the line break tag, `<br>`. The following input example shows an example of this use:

Input ▼

```
<blockquote>
Guns aren't lawful, <br />
nooses give.<br />
gas smells awful.<br />
You might as well live.<br />
---Dorothy Parker
</blockquote>
```

Figure 6.12 shows how the preceding input example appears in a browser.

6

Output ▼

FIGURE 6.12

A block quotation.

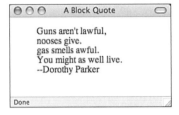

The `<blockquote>` tag is often used not to set off quotations within text, but rather to create margins on both sides of a page in order to make it more readable. This technique works, but strictly speaking, it's a misuse of the tag. These days, you should control margins with Cascading Style Sheets, as explained in Lesson 9, "Creating Layouts with CSS."

Special Characters

As you learned earlier in the week, HTML files are ASCII text and should contain no formatting or fancy characters. In fact, the only characters you should put in your HTML files are the characters that are actually printed on your keyboard. If you have to hold down any key other than Shift, or type an arcane combination of keys to produce a single character, you can't use that character in your HTML file. This includes characters you might use every day, such as em dashes and curly quotes (if your word processor is set up to do automatic curly quotes, you should turn them off when you write your HTML files).

"But wait a minute," you say. "If I can type a character like a bullet or an accented *a* on my keyboard using a special key sequence, and I can include it in an HTML file, and my browser can display it just fine when I look at that file, what's the problem?"

The problem is that the internal encoding your computer does to produce that character (which enables it to show up properly in your HTML file and in your browser's display) probably won't translate to other computers. Someone on the Internet who's reading your HTML file with that funny character in it might end up with some other character or just plain garbage. Or, depending on how your page is sent over the Internet, the character might be lost before it ever gets to the computer where the file is being viewed.

So, what can you do? HTML provides a reasonable solution. It defines a special set of codes, called *character entities*, that you can include in your HTML files to represent the characters you want to use. When interpreted by a browser, these character entities are displayed as the appropriate special characters for the given platform and font.

Some special characters don't come from the set of extended ASCII characters. For example, quotation marks and ampersands can be presented on a page using character entities even though they're found within the standard ASCII character set. These characters have a special meaning in HTML documents within certain contexts, so they can be represented with character entities in order to avoid confusing the web browsers. Modern browsers generally don't have a problem with these characters, but it's not a bad idea to use the entities anyway.

Character Entities for Special Characters

Character entities take one of two forms: named entities and numbered entities.

Named entities begin with an ampersand (&) and end with a semicolon (;). In between is the name of the character (or, more likely, a shorthand version of that name, such as `agrave` for an *a* with a grave accent, or `reg` for a registered trademark sign). Unlike other HTML tags, the names are case sensitive, so you should make sure to type them in exactly. Named entities look something like the following:

```
&agrave;
&quot;
&laquo;
&copy;
```

The numbered entities also begin with an ampersand and end with a semicolon, but rather than a name, they have a pound sign (#) and a number. The numbers correspond to character positions in the ISO-Latin-1 (ISO 8859-1) character. Every character you can type or for which you can use a named entity also has a numbered entity. Numbered entities look like the following:

```
&#130;
&#245;
```

You can use either numbers or named entities in your HTML file by including them in the same place that the character they represent would go. So, to place the word *résumé* in your HTML file, you would use either

```
r&eacute;sum&eacute;
```

or

```
r&#233;sum&#233;
```

In Appendix B, "HTML 4.01 Quick Reference," I've included a table that lists the named entities currently supported by HTML. See that table for specific characters.

6

Character Set: ISO-Latin-1 Versus Unicode

HTML's use of the ISO-Latin-1 character set allows it to display most accented characters on most platforms, but it has limitations. For example, common characters such as bullets, em dashes, and curly quotes simply aren't available in the ISO-Latin-1 character set. Therefore, you can't use these characters at all in your HTML files. (If they're absolutely necessary, you can create images representing those characters and use them on your pages. I don't recommend that option, though, because it can interfere with the layout of your page. Also, it can look odd if the user's browser is set to a nonstandard text size.) Also, many ISO-Latin-1 characters might be entirely unavailable in some browsers, depending on whether those characters exist on that platform and in the current font.

HTML 4.01 takes things a huge leap further by proposing that Unicode should be available as a character set for HTML documents. Unicode is a standard character encoding system that, although backward-compatible with our familiar ASCII encoding, offers the capability to encode characters in almost any of the world's languages, including Chinese and Japanese. This means that documents can be created easily in any language, and they also can contain multiple languages. Both Internet Explorer and Netscape support Unicode, and it can render documents in many of the scripts provided by Unicode as long as the necessary fonts are available.

This is an important step because Unicode is emerging as a new de facto standard for character encoding. Java uses Unicode as its default character encoding, for example, and Windows supports Unicode character encoding.

Character Entities for Reserved Characters

For the most part, character entities exist so that you can include special characters that aren't part of the standard ASCII character set. However, there are several exceptions for the few characters that have special meaning in HTML itself. You must use entities for these characters also.

Suppose that you want to include a line of code that looks something like the following in an HTML file:

```
<p><code>if x < 0 do print i</code></p>
```

Doesn't look unusual, does it? Unfortunately, HTML cannot display this line as written. Why? The problem is with the < (less-than) character. To an HTML browser, the less-than character means "this is the start of a tag." Because the less-than character isn't actually the start of a tag in this context, your browser might get confused. You'll have the same problem with the greater-than character (>) because it means the end of a tag in HTML, and with the ampersand (&) because it signals the beginning of a character escape. Written correctly for HTML, the preceding line of code would look like the following instead:

```
<p><code>if x &lt; 0 do print i</code></p>
```

HTML provides named escape codes for each of these characters, and one for the double quotation mark as well, as shown in Table 6.1.

TABLE 6.1 Escape Codes for Characters Used by Tags

Entity	Result
&lt;	<
&gt;	>
&amp;	&
&quot;	"

The double quotation mark escape is the mysterious one. Technically, if you want to include a double quotation mark in text, you should use the escape sequence and you shouldn't type the quotation mark character. However, I haven't noticed any browsers having problems displaying the double quotation mark character when it's typed literally in an HTML file, nor have I seen many HTML files that use it. For the most part, you're probably safe using plain old quotes (") in your HTML files rather than the escape code.

Text Alignment

Text alignment is the capability to arrange a block of text, such as a heading or a paragraph, so that it's aligned against the left margin (left justification, the default), aligned against the right margin (right justification), or centered. Standard HTML 2.0 has no mechanisms for aligning text; the browser is responsible for determining the alignment of the text (which means most of the time it's left-justified).

HTML 3.2 introduced attributes for text and element alignment, and these attributes have been incorporated into all the major browsers. HTML 4.01 still supports alignment attributes, but the preferred method of controlling text alignment now is with style sheets.

Aligning Individual Elements

To align an individual heading or paragraph, include the `align` attribute in the opening tag. `align` has four values: `left`, `right`, `center`, or `justify`. Consider the following examples in the code snippet that follows.

The following input and output example shows the simple alignment of several headings. Figure 6.13 shows the results.

6

Input ▼

```
<h1 align="center">Northridge Paints, Inc.</h1>
<p align="center">We don't just paint the town red.</p>

<h1 align="left">Serendipity Products</h1>
<h2 align="right"><a href="who.html">Who We Are</a></h2>
<h2 align="right"><a href="products.html">What We Do</a></h2>
<h2 align="right"><a href="contacts.html">How To Reach Us</a></h2>
```

Output ▼

FIGURE 6.13
Headings
with varying
alignments.

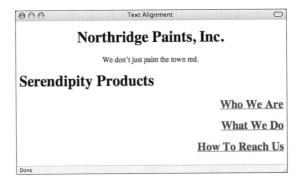

Aligning Blocks of Elements

A slightly more flexible method of aligning text elements is to use the <div> (division) tag. <div> includes several attributes, which are listed in Appendix B. Among these attributes is align (deprecated in HTML 4.01), which aligns elements to the left, right, or center just as it does for headings and paragraphs. Unlike using alignments in individual elements, however, <div> is used to surround a block of HTML tags of any kind, and it affects all the tags and text inside the opening and closing tags. Two advantages of div over the align attribute follow:

- You need to use <div> only once, rather than including align repeatedly in several different tags.

- <div> can be used to align anything (headings, paragraphs, quotes, images, tables, and so on); the align attribute is available on only a limited number of tags.

To align a block of HTML code, surround it with opening and closing <div> tags, and then include the align attribute in the opening tag. As in other tags, align can have the value left, right, or center:

```
<h1 align="left">Serendipity Products</h1>
<div align="right">
<h2><a href="who.html">Who We Are</a></h2>
<h2><a href="products.html">What We Do</a></h2>
```

```
<h2><a href="contacts.html">How To Reach Us</a></h2>
</div>
```

All the HTML between the two <div> tags will be aligned according to the value of the align attribute. If individual align attributes appear in headings or paragraphs inside the <div>, those values will override the global <div> setting.

Note that <div> itself isn't a paragraph type; it's just a container. Rather than altering the layout of the text itself, it just enables you to set off a group of text. One function of <div> is to change text alignment with the align attribute. It's also often used with CSS to apply styles to a specific block of text (much like its counterpart, <span>). In fact, to center elements within the <div> the CSS way (instead of using the deprecated align attribute), you can use the text-align property. Valid values for it are left, right, center, and justify. Figure 6.14 shows how it's used.

Input ▼

```
<div style="text-align: left">Left aligned text.</div>
<div style="text-align: right">Right aligned text.</div>
<div style="text-align: center">Centered text.</div>
<div style="text-align: justify">This text is justified. I'm adding some extra
text for padding so that you can see exactly how the justification works. As you
can see, the text is expanded so that it is aligned with both the left and right
margins.</div>
```

Output ▼

FIGURE 6.14
Various text alignments available using CSS.

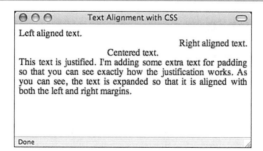

You can also include the align attribute in the <p> tag. It's most common to use the justify setting for the align attribute with the <p> and <div> tags. When you justify a paragraph, the text is spaced so that it's flush with both the left and right margins of the page.

Fonts and Font Sizes

The <font> tag, part of HTML 3.2 but deprecated in HTML 4.01 (again, in favor of style sheets), is used to control the characteristics of a given set of characters not covered by the character styles. Originally, <font> was used only to control the font size of the characters it surrounds, but it was then extended to enable you to change the font itself and the color of those characters.

In this section, I discuss fonts and font sizes. You'll learn about changing the font color in Lesson 7.

Changing the Font Size

The most common use of the <font> tag is to change the font size of a character, word, phrase, or any range of text. The <font>...</font> tags enclose the text, and the size attribute indicates the desired font size. The values of size are 1 to 7, with 3 being the default size. Consider the following example:

```
<p>Bored with your plain old font?
<font size="5">Change it.</font></p>
```

Figure 6.15 shows the typical font sizes for each value of size.

FIGURE 6.15
Font sizes.

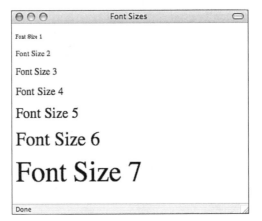

You can also specify the size in the <font> tag as a relative value by using the + or - characters in the value for size. Because the default size is 3, you can change relative font sizes in the range from -3 to +4, as in the following:

```
<p>Change the <font size="+2">Font</font> size again.</p>
```

Here, the word Font (inside the <font> tags) will be two size levels larger than the default font when you view the example in a browser that supports this feature.

Relative font sizes are actually based on a value that you can define by using the <basefont> tag, another tag that's deprecated in the HTML 4.01 specification. The <basefont> tag also has the required attribute size, which can have a value of 1 to 7. All relative font changes in the document after the <basefont> tag are relative to that value.

It's also important to note that the available font sizes—1 through 7—are completely arbitrary. They're not tied in any meaningful way to real point sizes or any other standard metric for font size. Users can choose any font size they like, and all the sizes available to <font> are applied relative to that size. Various operating systems also display fonts in different sizes on the screen, so there's little consistency from one platform to the other. You can't really count on much consistency when it comes to fonts.

Changing the Font Face

Netscape introduced the <font> tag to HTML with its 1.0 browser. Microsoft's Internet Explorer, playing the same game, extended the <font> tag to include the face attribute. The tag was made a part of HTML 3.2, but with HTML 4.01, the preferred method is to use style sheets to specify the fonts you use.

The face attribute takes as its value a set of font names, surrounded by quotation marks and separated by commas. When a browser that supports face interprets a page with face in it, it searches the system for the given font names one at a time. If it can't find the first one, it tries the second, and then the third, and so on, until it finds a font that's installed on the system. If the browser can't find any of the listed fonts, the default font is used instead. So, for example, the following text would be rendered in Futura. If Futura isn't available, the browser will try Helvetica; it will then fall back on the default if Helvetica isn't available:

```
<p><font face="Futura,Helvetica">Sans Serif fonts are fonts without
the small "ticks" on the strokes of the characters. </font></p>
```

Many fonts have different names on different systems; for example, plain old Times is Times on some systems, Times Roman on others, and Times New Roman elsewhere.

Because the names of fonts vary from system to system and because the list of installed fonts varies on a per-user basis, most browsers enable you to specify font families as well as specific font faces in your lists of fonts. The two families that are usually supported are serif and sans-serif. Usually you tack one of these two families onto your font list in case none of the other fonts you specified were there. For example, if you want to present a headline in a sans serif font, you might specify a font that's available under the Mac OS, one that's available under the X Window System, and one that's available under Microsoft Windows, and follow that up with sans-serif in case the others aren't available:

```
<font face="Geneva,Helvetica,Arial,sans-serif"><h1>Today's news</h1></font>
```

Modifying Fonts Using CSS

Earlier in this lesson, I described a few font-related properties that you can manipulate using CSS. In fact, you can use CSS as a replacement for all the features offered by the <font> tag. Earlier today, I described how the font-family property can be used to specify that text should be rendered in a font belonging to a particular general category, such as monospace or serif. You can also use the font-family property to specify a specific font, just as you can with the <font> tag.

Fonts are specified in CSS exactly the way they are in the <font> tag. You can provide a single font or a list of fonts, and the browser will search for each of the fonts until it finds one on your system that appears in the list. You can also include a generic font family in the list of fonts if you like, just as you can with the <font> tag. Here are some examples:

```
<p style="font-family: Verdana, Trebuchet, Arial, sans-serif">
This is sans-serif text.</p>
<p style="font-family: Courier New, monospace">This is
monospace text.</p>
<p style="font-family: Georgia">This text will appear in the
Georgia font, or, if that font is not installed, the browser's
default font.</p>
```

You can also use CSS to specify font size. Unfortunately, although the approach for specifying the font face itself is the same whether you're using the <font> tag or CSS, specifying font sizes under CSS is much more complicated than it is with the <font> tag. The tradeoff is that with this complexity comes a great degree more flexibility in how font sizes can be specified. Let's start with the basics. To change the font size for some text, the font-size property is used. The value is a size (relative or absolute) in any of the units of measure supported by CSS.

The catch here is that several units of measure are available. Perhaps the simplest is the percentage size, relative to the current font size being used. So, to make the font twice as large as it is currently, just use

```
<p>This text is normal sized, and this text is
<span style="font-size: 200%">twice that size</span>.</p>
```

There are also a number of length units available that you can use to specify the font size absolutely. I'll discuss the popular ones in Lesson 9. In the meantime, just know that there are two kinds of length units: relative units and absolute units. Relative units are sized based on the size of other elements on the page and based on the dots per inch setting of the user's display. Absolute units are sized based on some absolute reference. For example, the pt (point) unit is measured in absolute pixels. To set your text to be exactly 12 pixels high, the following specification is used:

```
<p style="font-size: 12px">This text is 12 pixels tall.</p>
```

CAUTION

One thing to watch out for: When you specify units in CSS, you must leave no spaces between the number of units and unit specification. In other words, 12pt and 100% are valid, and 12 pt and 100 % aren't.

There's another thing that you can do with the font-size property that's not possible with the <font> tag: specify line height. Let's say you want to use double-spaced text on your page. Before CSS, the only way to achieve the effect was to use the <br> tag inside paragraphs to skip lines, but this approach is fraught with peril. Depending on how the user has sized her browser window, pages formatted using <br> in this manner can look truly awful. To set the line height using CSS, you can include it in your font size specification, like this: font-size: 100%/200%. In this case, the size of the font is 100%—the default—and the line height is 200%, twice the standard line height.

DO	DON'T
DO specify fonts using CSS rather than the <font> tag.	**DON'T** use too many different fonts on the same page.
DO list backup fonts when specifying a font family in order to make it more likely that your users will have one of the fonts you specify.	**DON'T** use absolute font sizes with CSS if you can help it, because some browsers won't let users alter the text size if you do so.

<nobr> and <wbr>

The <nobr>...</nobr> element is the opposite of the <br> tag. The text inside the <nobr> tags always remains on one line, even if it would have wrapped to two more lines without the <nobr>. The <nobr> tag is used for words or phrases that must be kept together on one line, but be careful. Long unbreakable lines can look really strange on your page, and if they're longer than the page width, they might extend beyond the right edge of the screen.

The <wbr> tag (word break) indicates an appropriate breaking point within a line (typically inside a <nobr>...</nobr> sequence). Unlike <br>, which forces a break, <wbr> is used only where it's appropriate to do so. If the line will fit on the screen just fine, the <wbr> is ignored. In XHTML 1.0, add closure to the tag by using the syntax of <wbr />.

Neither <nobr> nor <wbr> is part of HTML 3.2 or HTML 4.01. They're extensions introduced by Netscape, and are currently supported by both Netscape and Internet Explorer.

6

Task: Exercise 6.1: Creating a Real HTML Page

Here's your chance to apply what you've learned and create a real web page. No more disjointed or overly silly examples. The web page you'll create in this section is a real one, suitable for use in the real world (or the real world of the Web, at least).

▼ Your task for this example is to design and create a home page for a bookstore called The Bookworm, which specializes in old and rare books.

Planning the Page   In lesson 2, "Preparing to Publish on the Web," I mentioned that planning your web page before writing it usually makes building and maintaining the elements easier. First, consider the content you want to include on this page. The following are some ideas for topics for this page:

- The address and phone number of the bookstore
- A short description of the bookstore and why it's unique
- Recent titles and authors
- Upcoming events

Now come up with some ideas for the content you're going to link to from this page. Each title in a list of recently acquired books seems like a logical candidate. You also can create links to more information about each book, its author and publisher, its pricing, and maybe even its availability.

The Upcoming Events section might suggest a potential series of links, depending on how much you want to say about each event. If you have only a sentence or two about each one, describing them on this page might make more sense than linking them to another page. Why make your readers wait for each new page to load for just a couple of lines of text?

Other interesting links might arise in the text itself, but for now, starting with the basic link plan is enough.

Beginning with a Framework   Next, create the framework that all HTML files must include: the document structuring commands, a title, and some initial headings. Note that the title is descriptive but short; you can save the longer title for the <h1> element in the body of the text. The four <h2> subheadings help you define the four main sections you'll have on your web page:

```
<!DOCTYPE html PUBLIC "-//W3C//DTD XHTML 1.0 Transitional//EN"
 "http://www.w3.org/TR/xhtml1/DTD/transitional.dtd">
<html>
<head>
<title>The Bookworm Bookshop</title>
</head>
<body>
<h1>The Bookworm: A Better Book Store</h1>
<h2>Contents</h2>
<h2>About the Bookworm Bookshop</h2>
<h2>Recent Titles (as of 11-Jan-2003)</h2>
<h2>Upcoming Events</h2>
</body>
▼ </html>
```

Each of the headings you've placed on your page marks the beginning of a particular section. You'll create an anchor at each of the topic headings so that you can jump from section to section with ease. The anchor names are simple: top for the main heading; contents for the table of contents; and about, recent, and upcoming for the three sub-sections on the page. The revised code looks like the following with the anchors in place:

Input ▼

```
<!DOCTYPE html PUBLIC "-//W3C//DTD XHTML 1.0 Transitional//EN"
 "http://www.w3.org/TR/xhtml1/DTD/transitional.dtd">
<html>
<head>
<title>The Bookworm Bookshop</title>
</head>
<body>
<a name="top"><h1>The Bookworm: A Better Book Store</h1></a>
<a name="contents"><h2>Contents</h2></a>
<a name="about"><h2>About the Bookworm Bookshop</h2></a>
<a name="recent"><h2>Recent Titles (as of 11-Jan-2003)</h2></a>
<a name="upcoming"><h2>Upcoming Events</h2></a>
</body>
</html>
```

Adding Content   Now begin adding the content. You're undertaking a literary endeavor, so starting the page with a nice quote about old books would be a nice touch. Because you're adding a quote, you can use the <blockquote> tag to make it stand out as such. Also, the name of the poem is a citation, so use <cite> there, too.

Insert the following code on the line after the level 1 heading:

Input ▼

```
<blockquote>
"Old books are best---how tale and rhyme<br />
Float with us down the stream of time!"<br />
- Clarence Urmy, <cite>Old Songs are Best</cite>
</blockquote>
```

Immediately following the quote, add the address for the bookstore. This is a simple paragraph with the lines separated by line breaks, like the following:

Input ▼

```
<p>The Bookworm Bookshop<br />
1345 Applewood Dr<br />
Springfield, CA 94325<br />
(415) 555-0034
</p>
```

6

▼ **Adding the Table of Contents** The page you're creating will require a lot of scrolling to get from the top to the bottom. One nice enhancement is to add a small table of contents at the beginning of the page, listing the sections in a bulleted list. If a reader clicks one of the links in the table of contents, he'll automatically jump to the section that's of most interest to him. Because you've created the anchors already, it's easy to see where the links will take you.

You already have the heading for the table of contents. You just need to add the bulleted list and a horizontal rule, and then create the links to the other sections on the page. The code looks like the following:

Input ▼

```
<a name="contents"><h2>Contents</h2></a>
<ul>
 <li><a href="#about">About the Bookworm Bookshop</a></li>
 <li><a href ="#recent">Recent Titles</a></li>
 <li><a href ="#upcoming">Upcoming Events</a></li>
</ul>
<hr />
```

Figure 6.16 shows an example of the introductory portion of the Bookworm Bookshop page as it appears in a browser.

Output ▼

FIGURE 6.16
The top section of the Bookworm Bookshop page.

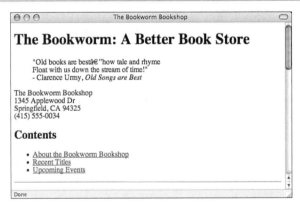

Creating the Description of the Bookstore Now you come to the first descriptive subheading on the page, which you've added already. This section gives a description of the bookstore. After the heading (shown in the first line of the following example), I've arranged the description to include a list of features to make them stand

▼ out from the text better:

Input ▼

```
<a name="about"><h2>About the Bookworm Bookshop</h2></a>
<p>Since 1933, The Bookworm Bookshop has offered
rare and hard-to-find titles for the discerning reader.
The Bookworm offers:</p>
<ul>
<li>Friendly, knowledgeable, and courteous help</li>
<li>Free coffee and juice for our customers</li>
<li>A well-lit reading room so you can "try before you buy"</li>
<li>Four friendly cats: Esmerelda, Catherine, Dulcinea and Beatrice</li>
</ul>
```

Add a note about the hours the store is open and emphasize the actual numbers:

Input ▼

```
<p>Our hours are <strong>10am to 9pm</strong> weekdays,
<strong>noon to 7</strong> on weekends.</p>
```

Then, end the section with links to the Table of Contents and the top of the page, followed by a horizontal rule to end the section:

Input ▼

```
<p><a href="#contents">Back to Contents</a> ¦ <a href="#top">Back to Top</a></p>
<hr />
```

Figure 6.17 shows you what the About the Bookworm Bookshop section looks like in a browser.

Output ▼

FIGURE 6.17
The About the Bookworm Bookshop section.

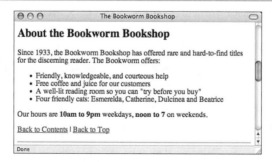

Creating the Recent Titles Section   The Recent Titles section itself is a classic link menu, as I described earlier in this section. Here you can put the list of titles in an unordered list, with the titles themselves as citations, by using the <cite> tag. End the section with another horizontal rule.

▼ After the Recent Titles heading (shown in the first line in the following example), enter the following code:

```
<a name="recent"><h2>Recent Titles (as of 11-Jan-2006)</h2></a>
<ul>
<li>Sandra Bellweather, <cite>Belladonna</cite></li>
<li>Jonathan Tin, <cite>20-Minute Meals for One</cite></li>
<li>Maxwell Burgess, <cite>Legion of Thunder</cite></li>
<li>Alison Caine, <cite>Banquo's Ghost</cite></li>
</ul>
<hr />
```

Now add the anchor tags to create the links. How far should the link extend? Should it include the whole line (author and title) or just the title of the book? This decision is a matter of preference, but I like to link only as much as necessary to make sure that the link stands out from the text. I prefer this approach to overwhelming the text. Here, I linked only the titles of the books. At the same time, I also added links to the Table of Contents and the top of the page:

Input ▼

```
<a name="recent"><h2>Recent Titles (as of 11-Jan-2006)</h2></a>
<ul>
<li>Sandra Bellweather, <a href="belladonna.html">
<cite>Belladonna</cite></a></li>
<li>Johnathan Tin, <a href="20minmeals.html">
<cite>20-Minute Meals for One</cite></a></li>
<li>Maxwell Burgess, <a href="legion.html">
<cite>Legion of Thunder</cite></a></li>
<li>Alison Caine, <a href="banquo.html">
<cite>Banquo's Ghost</cite></a></li>
</ul>
<p><a href="#contents">Back to Contents</a> ¦ <a href="#top">Back to Top</a></p>
<hr />
```

Note that I put the <cite> tag inside the link tag <a>. I could have just as easily put it outside the anchor tag; character style tags can go just about anywhere. But as I mentioned once before, be careful not to overlap tags. Your browser might not be able to understand what's going on, and it's invalid. In other words, don't do the following:

```
<a href="banquo.html"><cite>Banquo's Ghost</a></cite>
```

Take a look at how the Recent Titles section appears. An example is shown in
▼ Figure 6.18.

Output ▼

FIGURE 6.18
The Recent Titles section.

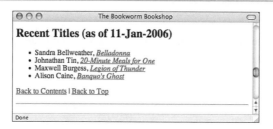

Completing the Upcoming Events Section   Next, move on to the Upcoming Events section. In the planning stages, you weren't sure whether this would be another link menu or whether the content would work better solely on this page. Again, this decision is a matter of preference. Here, because the amount of extra information is minimal, creating links for just a couple of sentences doesn't make much sense. So, for this section, create an unordered list using the <ul> tag. I've boldfaced a few phrases near the beginning of each paragraph. These phrases emphasize a summary of the event itself so that the text can be scanned quickly and ignored if the readers aren't interested.

As in the previous sections, you end the section with links to the top and to the contents, followed by a horizontal rule.

```
 <a name=upcoming"><h2>Upcoming Events</h2></a>
<ul>
<li><b>The Wednesday Evening Book Review</b> meets, appropriately, on
Wednesday evenings at 7 pm for coffee and a round-table discussion.
Call the Bookworm for information on joining the group.</li>
<li><b>The Children's Hour</b> happens every Saturday at 1 pm and includes
reading, games, and other activities. Cookies and milk are served.</li>
<li><b>Carole Fenney</b> will be at the Bookworm on Sunday, January 19,
to read from her book of poems <cite>Spiders in the Web.</cite></li>
<li><b>The Bookworm will be closed</b> March 1st to remove a family
of bats that has nested in the tower. We like the company, but not
the mess they leave behind!</li>
</ul>
<p><a href="#contents">Back to Contents</a> ¦ <a href="#top">Back to
Top</a></p>
```

Signing the Page   To finish, sign what you have so that your readers know who did the work. Here, I've separated the signature from the text with a rule line. I've also included the most recent revision date, my name as the Webmaster, and a basic copyright (with a copyright symbol indicated by the numeric escape ©):

Input ▼

```
<hr />
<address>
Last Updated: 11-Jan-2006<br />
Webmaster: Laura Lemay
```

6

```
<a href="mailto:lemay@bookworm.com">lemay@bookworm.com</a><br />
&#169; copyright 2006 the Bookworm<br />
</address>
```

Figure 6.19 shows the signature at the bottom portion of the page as well as the Upcoming Events section.

Output ▼

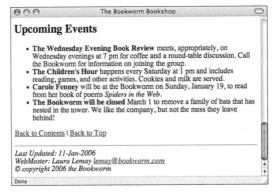

Reviewing What You've Got   Here's the HTML code for the page so far:

```
<!DOCTYPE html PUBLIC "-//W3C//DTD XHTML 1.0 Transitional//EN"
 "http://www.w3.org/TR/xhtml1/DTD/transitional.dtd">
<html>
<head>
<title>The Bookworm Bookshop</title>
</head>
<body>
<a name="top"><h1>The Bookworm: A Better Book Store</h1></a>
<blockquote>
"Old books are best---how tale and rhyme<br />
Float with us down the stream of time!"<br />
- Clarence Urmy, <cite>Old Songs are Best</cite>
</blockquote>
<p>The Bookworm Bookshop<br />
1345 Applewood Dr<br />
Springfield, CA 94325<br />
(415) 555-0034
</p>
<a name="contents"><h2>Contents</h2></a>
<ul>
 <li><a href="#about">About the Bookworm Bookshop</a></li>
 <li><a href="#recent">Recent Titles</a></li>
 <li><a href="#upcoming">Upcoming Events</a></li>
</ul>
<hr />
<a name="about"><h2>About the Bookworm Bookshop</h2></a>
<p>Since 1933, the Bookworm Bookshop has offered
```

```
rare and hard-to-find titles for the discerning reader.
The Bookworm offers:</p>
<ul>
 <li>Friendly, knowledgeable, and courteous help</li>
 <li>Free coffee and juice for our customers</li>
 <li>A well-lit reading room so you can "try before you buy"</li>
 <li>Four friendly cats: Esmerelda, Catherine, Dulcinea and Beatrice</li>
</ul>
<p>Our hours are <strong>10am to 9pm</strong> weekdays,
<strong>noon to 7</strong> on weekends.</p>
<p><a href="#contents">Back to Contents</a> ¦ <a href="#top">Back to
Top</a></p>
<hr />
<a name="recent"><h2>Recent Titles (as of 11-Jan-2003)</h2></a>
<ul>
 <li>Sandra Bellweather, <a href="belladonna.html">
  <cite>Belladonna</cite></a></li>
 <li>Johnathan Tin, <a href="20minmeals.html">
  <cite>20-Minute Meals for One</cite></a></li>
 <li>Maxwell Burgess, <a href="legion.html">
  <cite>Legion of Thunder</cite></a></li>
 <li>Alison Caine, <a href="banquo.html">
  <cite>Banquo's Ghost</cite></a></li>
</ul>
<p><a href="#contents">Back to Contents</a> ¦ <a href="#top">Back to
Top</a></p>
<hr />
<a name="upcoming"><h2>Upcoming Events</h2></a>
<ul>
 <li><b>The Wednesday Evening Book Review</b> meets, appropriately, on
   Wednesday evenings at 7 pm for coffee and a round-table discussion.
   Call the Bookworm for information on joining the group.</li>
 <li><b>The Children's Hour</b> happens every Saturday at 1 pm and includes
   reading, games, and other activities. Cookies and milk are served.</li>
 <li><b>Carole Fenney</b> will be at the Bookworm on Sunday, January 19,
   to read from her book of poems <cite>Spiders in the Web.</cite></li>
 <li><b>The Bookworm will be closed</b> March 1 to remove a family
   of bats that has nested in the tower. We like the company, but not
   the mess they leave behind!</li>
</ul>
<p><a href="#contents">Back to Contents</a> ¦ <a href="#top">Back to
Top</a></p>
<hr />
<address>
Last Updated: 11-Jan-2006<br />
WebMaster: Laura Lemay lemay@bookworm.com<br />
&#169; copyright 2006 the Bookworm<br />
</address>
</body>
</html>
```

Now you have some headings, some text, some topics, and some links, which form the basis for an excellent web page. With most of the content in place, now you need to

▼ consider what other links you might want to create or what other features you might want to add to this page.

For example, the introductory section has a note about the four cats owned by the bookstore. Although you didn't plan for them in the original organization, you could easily create web pages describing each cat (and showing pictures) and then link them back to this page, one link (and one page) per cat.

Is describing the cats important? As the designer of the page, that's up to you to decide. You could link all kinds of things from this page if you have interesting reasons to link them (and something to link to). Link the bookstore's address to an online mapping service so that people can get driving directions. Link the quote to an online encyclopedia of quotes. Link the note about free coffee to the Coffee Home Page.

I'll talk more about good things to link (and how not to get carried away when you link) in Lesson 16, "Writing Good Web Pages: Do's and Don'ts." My reason for bringing up this point here is that after you have some content in place on your web pages, there might be opportunities for extending the pages and linking to other places that you didn't think of when you created your original plan. So, when you're just about finished with a page, stop and review what you have, both in the plan and in your web page.

For the purposes of this example, stop here and stick with the links you have. You're close enough to being done, and I don't want to make this lesson any longer than it already is!

Testing the Result   Now that all the code is in place, you can preview the results in a browser. Figures 6.16 through 6.19 show how it looks in a browser. Actually, these figures show what the page looks like after you fix the spelling errors, the forgotten closing tags, and all the other strange bugs that always seem to creep into an HTML file the first time you create it. These problems always seem to happen no matter how good you are at creating web pages. If you use an HTML editor or some other help tool, your job will be easier, but you'll always seem to find mistakes. That's what previewing is for—so you can catch the problems before you actually make the document available to other people.

Getting Fancy   Everything I've included on the page up to this point has been plain-vanilla HTML 2.0, so it's readable and will look pretty much the same in all browsers. After you get the page to this point, however, you can add additional formatting tags and attributes that won't change the page for many readers, but might make it look a little fancier in browsers that do support these attributes.

So, what attributes do you want to use? I chose two:

- Centering the title of the page, the quote, and the bookstore's address
▼ - Making a slight font size change to the address itself

To center the topmost part of the page, you can use the <div> tag around the heading, the quote, and the bookshop's address, as in the following:

Input ▼

```
<div style="text-align: center">
<a name="top"><h1 style="font-variant: small-caps">The Bookworm: A Better Book
Store</h1></a>
<blockquote>
"Old books are best---how tale and rhyme<br />
Float with us down the stream of time!"<br />
- Clarence Urmy, <cite>Old Songs are Best</cite>
</blockquote>
<p>The Bookworm Bookshop<br />
1345 Applewood Dr<br />
Springfield, CA 94325<br />
(415) 555-0034
</p>
</div>
```

I've also used the style attribute to change the text in the <h1> tag to small caps. To change the font size of the address, add a style attribute to the paragraph containing the address:

Input ▼

```
<p style="font-size: 150%">The Bookworm Bookshop<br />
1345 Applewood Dr<br />
Springfield, CA 94325<br />
(415) 555-0034
</p>
```

Figure 6.20 shows the final result, with attributes. Note that neither of these changes affects the readability of the page in browsers that don't support <div> or <font>; the page still works just fine without them. It just looks different.

Output ▼

6

FIGURE 6.20
The final Bookworm home page, with additional attributes.

▼ When should you use text-formatting attributes? The general rule that I like to follow is to use these tags only when they won't interfere with other browsers, generally older ones. Similarly, although HTML 4.01 officially encourages web page authors to use style sheets rather than text formatting tags such as font and attributes such as align, support for style sheets still isn't yet universal. So, for the time being, if you want to spiff up the appearance of your text, you must continue to use these tags and attributes.

▲ You'll learn more about formatting tags and attributes, as well as how to design well with them, in Lesson 15, "Creating Applications with Dynamic HTML and AJAX."

Summary

Tags, tags, and more tags! Today you learned about most of the remaining tags in the HTML language for presenting text, and quite a few of the tags for additional text formatting and presentation. You also put together a real-life HTML home page. You could stop now and create quite presentable web pages, but more cool stuff is to come. So, don't put down the book yet.

Table 6.2 presents a quick summary of all the tags and attributes you've learned about today that are included in the HTML 4.01 specification. Table 6.3 summarizes the CSS properties that have been described in today's discussion.

TABLE 6.2   HTML Tags from Lesson 6

Tag	Attribute	Use
`<address>...</address>`		A signature for each web page; typically occurs near the bottom of each document and contains contact or copyright information.
`<b>...</b>`		Bold text.
`<big>...</big>`		Text in a larger font than the text around it.
`<blink>...</blink>`		Causes the enclosed text to blink (Netscape only).
`<blockquote>...</blockquote>`		A quotation longer than a few words.
`<cite>...</cite>`		A citation.
`<code>...</code>`		A code sample.
`<dfn>...</dfn>`		A definition, or a term about to be defined.
`<em>...</em>`		Emphasized text.

TABLE 6.2   continued

Tag	Attribute	Use
`<i>...</i>`		Italic text.
`<kbd>...</kbd>`		Text to be typed in by the user.
`<pre>...</pre>`		Preformatted text; all spaces, tabs, and returns are retained. Text is printed in a monospaced font.
`<s>...</s>`		Strikethrough text. (Deprecated in HTML 4.01.)
`<samp>...</samp>`		Sample text.
`<small>...</small>`		Text in a smaller font than the text around it.
`<strong>...</strong>`		Strongly emphasized text.
`<sub>...</sub>`		Subscript text.
`<sup>...</sup>`		Superscript text.
`<tt>...</tt>`		Text in typewriter font (a monospaced font such as Courier).
`<u>...</u>`		Underlined text.
`<var>...</var>`		A variable name.
`<span>...</span>`		A generic tag used to apply styles to a particular bit of text.
`<hr>`		A horizontal rule line at the given position in the text. There's no closing tag in HTML for `<hr>`; for XHTML, add a space and forward slash (/) at the end of the tag and its attributes (for example, `<hr size="2" width="75%" />`).
	`size`	The thickness of the rule, in pixels. (Deprecated in HTML 4.01.)
	`width`	The width of the rule, either in exact pixels or as a percentage of page width (for example, 50%). (Deprecated in HTML 4.01.)
	`align`	The alignment of the rule on the page. Possible values are `left`, `right`, and `center`. (Deprecated in HTML 4.01.)
	`noshade`	Displays the rule without three-dimensional shading. (Deprecated in HTML 4.01.)

6

TABLE 6.2   continued

Tag	Attribute	Use
` `		A line break; starts the next character on the next line, but doesn't create a new paragraph or list item. There's no closing tag in HTML for ` `; for XHTML, add a space and forward slash (/) at the end of the tag and its attributes (for example, `<br clear="left" />`).
`<nobr>...</nobr>`		Doesn't wrap the enclosed text (nonstandard; supported by Netscape and Internet Explorer).
`<wbr>`		Wraps the text at this point only if necessary (nonstandard; supported by Netscape and Internet Explorer). Adds a space and forward slash at the end of the tag for XHTML 1.0.
`<p>...</p>,` `<h1-6>...</h1-6>`	`align="left"`	Left-justifies the text within that paragraph or heading. (Deprecated in HTML 4.01.)
	`align="right"`	Right-justifies the text within that paragraph or heading. (Deprecated in HTML 4.01.)
	`align="center"`	Centers the text within that paragraph or heading. (Deprecated in HTML 4.01.)
`<div>...</div>`	`align="left"`	Left-justifies all the content between the opening and closing tags. (Deprecated in HTML 4.01.)
	`align="right"`	Right-justifies all the content between the opening and closing tags. (Deprecated in HTML 4.01.)
	`align="center"`	Centers all the content between the opening and closing tags. (Deprecated in HTML 4.01.)
`<center>...</center>`		Centers all the content between the opening and closing tags. (Deprecated in HTML 4.01.)

TABLE 6.2 continued

Tag	Attribute	Use
<font>...</font>	size	The size of the font to change to, either from 1 to 7 (default is 3) or as a relative number using +N or -N. Relative font sizes are based on the value of <basefont>. (Deprecated in HTML 4.01.)
	face	The name of the font to change to, as a list of fonts to choose from. (Deprecated in HTML 4.01.)
<basefont>	size	The default font size on which relative font size changes are based. (Deprecated in HTML 4.01.) There is no closing tag in HTML for <basefont>; for XHTML, add a space and forward slash (/) at the end of the tag and its attributes (for example, <basefont size="-1" />).

TABLE 6.3 CSS Properties from Lesson 6

Property	Use/Values
text-decoration	Specifies which sort of decoration should be applied to the text. The values are underline, overline, line-through, blink, and none.
font-style	Specifies whether text should be italicized. The three values are normal, italic, and oblique.
font-weight	Specifies the degree to which text should be emboldened. Options are normal, bold, bolder, lighter, and 100 - 900.
font-family	Enables you to specify the font used for text. You can choose families such as serif, sans serif, and monospace, or specific font names. You can specify more than one font or font family as well.
font-variant	Sets the font variant to normal or small-caps.
text-align	Specifies how text is aligned: left, right, center, or justify.
font-size	Enables you to specify the font size in any unit supported by CSS.

6

Workshop

Here you are at the close of another day (a long one!) and facing yet another workshop. Today's lesson covered a lot of ground, so I'll try to keep the questions easy. There are a couple of exercises that focus on building some additional pages for your website. Ready?

Q&A

Q If line breaks appear in HTML, can I also do page breaks?

A HTML doesn't have a page break tag. Consider what the term *page* means in a web document. If each document on the Web is a single page, the only way to produce a page break is to split your HTML document into separate files and link them.

Even within a single document, browsers have no concept of a page; each HTML document simply scrolls by continuously. If you consider a single screen a page, you still can't have what results in a page break in HTML. The screen size in each browser is different. It's based on not only the browser itself, but also the size of the monitor on which it runs, the number of lines defined, the font currently being used, and other factors that you cannot control from HTML.

When you're designing your web pages, don't get too hung up on the concept of a page the way it exists in paper documents. Remember, HTML's strength is its flexibility for multiple kinds of systems and formats. Instead, think in terms of creating small chunks of information and how they link together to form a complete presentation.

If page breaks are essential to your document, you might consider saving it in the PDF format and making it available for download.

Q How can I include em dashes or curly quotes (typesetter's quotes) in my HTML files?

A There are entities for all of these characters, but they may not be supported by all browsers or on all platforms. Most people still don't use them. To add an em dash, use `&mdash;`. The curly quote entities are `&ldquo;` for the left quote and `&rdquo;` for the right quote. Similarly, you can create curly single quotes using `&lsquo;` and `&rsquo;`.

Quiz

1. What are the differences between logical character styles and physical character styles?

2. What are some things that the `<pre>` (preformatted text) tag can be used for?

3. What's the most common use of the `<address>` tag?

4. Older versions of HTML provided ways to align and center text on a web page. What's the recommended way to accomplish these tasks in HTML 4.01?

5. Without looking at Table 6.2, list all eight logical style tags and what they're used for. Explain why you should use the logical tags instead of the physical tags.

Quiz Answers

1. Logical styles indicate how the highlighted text is used (citation, definition, code, and so on). Physical styles indicate how the highlighted text is displayed (bold, italic, or monospaced, for example).

2. Preformatted text can be used for text-based tables, code examples, ASCII art, and any other web page content that requires extra spaces to align characters.

3. The `<address>` tag is most commonly used for signature-like entities on a web page. These include the name of the author of the web page, contact information, dates, copyright notices, or warnings. Address information usually appears at the bottom of a web page.

4. Alignment and centering of text can be accomplished with style sheets, which is the recommended approach in HTML 4.01.

5. The eight logical styles are `<em>` (for emphasized text), `<strong>` (for bold text), `<code>` (for programming code), `<samp>` (similar to `<code>`), `<kbd>` (to indicate user keyboard input), `<var>` (for variable names), `<dfn>` (for definitions), and `<cite>` (for short quotes or citations). Logical tags rely on the browser to format their appearance.

6

Exercises

1. Now that you've had a taste of building your first really thorough web page, take a stab at your own home page. What can you include that would entice people to dig deeper into your pages? Don't forget to include links to other pages on your site.

2. Try out your home page in several browsers and even on multiple platforms if you have access to them. Web developers have to get used to the fact that their designs are at the mercy of their users, and it's best to see right away how different browsers and platforms treat pages.

LESSON 7:
Adding Images, Color, and Backgrounds

If you've been struggling to keep up with all the HTML tags I've been flinging at you the last couple of days, this lesson will be easier.

In this Lesson

In fact, in this lesson you won't be learning very many new HTML tags. Instead, you'll learn about how to add images to your pages and change the color of elements on a page. In particular, you'll learn the following:

- The kinds of images you can use in web pages
- How to include images on your web page, either alone or alongside text
- How to use images as clickable links
- How to set up and assign links to regions of images using client-side imagemaps
- How to provide alternatives for browsers that can't view images
- How to change the font and background colors on your web page
- How to use images for tiled page backgrounds
- How and when to use images on your web pages
- A few tips on image etiquette

After this lesson, you'll know all you need to know about adding images to your web pages.

Images on the Web

Images displayed on the Web should be converted to one of the formats supported by most browsers: GIF, JPEG, or PNG. GIF and JPEG are the popular standards, and every graphical browser supports them. PNG is a newer image format that was created in response to some patent issues with the GIF format. It's superior to GIF in almost every respect, but old browsers don't support it. Many other image formats are supported by some browsers and not others. You should avoid them.

Let's assume that you already have an image you want to put on your web page. How do you get it into GIF or JPEG format so it can be viewed on your page? Most image editing programs, such as Adobe Photoshop (http://www.adobe.com/), Paint Shop Pro (http://www.jasc.com/), and CorelDRAW (http://www.corel.com/), will convert images to most of the popular formats. You might have to look under the option for Save As or Export to find the conversion option. There are also freeware and shareware programs for most platforms that do nothing but convert between image formats. Many shareware and demo versions of image editing programs are available at http://www.download.com/ (search for "image editors" using the software platform of your choice).

TIP

> If you're a Windows user, you can download IrfanView, which allows you to view images, and convert them to various formats, at http://www.infanview.com/. It also provides a number of other image manipulation features that are useful for working with images for the Web. Best of all, it's free for non-commercial use.

To save files in GIF format, look for an option called CompuServe GIF, GIF87, GIF89a, or just plain GIF. Any of them will work. If you're saving your files as JPEG, usually the option will simply be JPEG.

Remember how your HTML files have to have an `.html` or `.htm` extension to work properly? Image files have extensions, too. For GIF files, the extension is `.gif`. For JPEG files, the extensions are `.jpg` and `.jpeg`.

NOTE

> Some image editors will try to save files with extensions in all caps (`.GIF` or `.JPEG`). Although they're the correct extensions, image names are case sensitive, so `.GIF` isn't the same extension as `.gif`. The case of the extension might not be important when you're testing on your local system, but it can be when you move your files to the server. So, use lowercase if you can.

Image Formats

As I just mentioned, three image formats are supported by every major web browser: GIF, JPEG, and PNG. JPEG and GIF are the old standbys, each useful for different purposes. PNG is designed as a replacement for the GIF format, which was necessary after Unisys invoked its patent rights on the GIF format. (The patent has since expired.) To design web pages, you must understand and be able to apply both image formats and to decide which is appropriate to use in each case.

GIF

Graphics Interchange Format, also known as GIF or CompuServe GIF, is the most widely used graphics format on the Web today. It was developed by CompuServe to fill the need for a cross-platform image format.

NOTE   GIF is pronounced *jiff*, like the peanut butter, not with a hard G as in *gift*. Really—the early documentation of GIF tools says so.

The GIF format is actually two very similar image formats: GIF87, the original format, and GIF89a, which has enhancements for transparency, interlacing, and multiframe GIF images that you can use for simple animations.

The GIF format is great for logos, icons, line art, and other simple images. It doesn't work as well for highly detailed images because it's limited to only 256 colors. For example, photographs in GIF format tend to look grainy and blotchy. The problem is that with the limited color palette, it's hard to create smooth color transitions.

JPEG

JPEG, which stands for *Joint Photographic Experts Group* (the group that developed it), is the other popular format for images on the Web. JPEG (pronounced *jay-peg*) is actually a compression type that other file formats can use. The file format for which it's known is also commonly called JPEG.

JPEG was designed for the storage of photographic images. Unlike GIF images, JPEG images can include any number of colors. The style of compression that JPEG uses (the compression algorithm) works especially well for photographs, so files compressed using the JPEG algorithm are considerably smaller than those compressed using GIF. JPEG uses a *lossy* compression algorithm, which means that some of the data used in the image is discarded to make the file smaller. Lossy compression works extremely well for photographic data, but makes JPEG unsuitable for images that contain elements with sharp

7

edges, such as logos, line art, and type. JPEG files are supported by all major web browsers.

PNG

PNG, pronounced "ping," was originally designed as a replacement for GIFs. It stands for Portable Network Graphics. Only the oldest browsers don't support PNG natively. Current browsers all support PNG, and it has some important advantages over GIF (and to a lesser extent over JPEG). Like GIF, it is a non-lossy image format. No information about the image is lost when it is compressed.

It has better support for transparency than GIF, and supports palette-based images (like GIF) as well as true-color and grayscale images (like JPEG). In other words, you don't have to worry about color usage with PNG, although limiting color usage will result in smaller files.

More and more sites are using the PNG format for images, but due mainly to inertia, GIF and JPEG are still the most used formats. For more information on PNG, see http://www.libpng.org/pub/png/.

Inline Images in HTML: The `<img>` Tag

After you have an image ready to go, you can include it on your web page. Inline images are placed in HTML documents using the `<img>` tag. This tag, like the `<hr>` and `<br>` tags, has no closing tag in HTML. For XHTML, you must add an extra space and forward slash to the end of the tag to indicate that it has no closing tag.

The `<img>` tag has many attributes that enable you to control how the image is presented on the page. Many of these attributes are part of HTML 3.2 or HTML 4.01 and might not be understood by some older browsers. Still other attributes have been deprecated in favor of style sheets with the HTML 4.01 and XHTML 1.0 specifications.

NOTE

> To use the `<img>` tag in an XHTML-compliant fashion, you need to close it, like this:
>
> `<img />`

The most important attribute of the `<img>` tag is src, which is the URL of the image you want to include. Paths to images are derived in the same way as the paths in the href attribute of links. So, to point to a GIF file named `image.gif` in the same directory as the HTML document, you can use the following XHTML tag:

```
<img src="image.gif" />
```

For an image file one directory up from the current directory, use this XHTML tag:

```
<img src="../image.gif" />
```

And so on, using the same rules as for page names in the `href` part of the `<a>` tag. You can also point to images on remote servers from the `src` attribute of an `<img>` tag, just as you can from the `href` attribute of a link. If you wanted to include the image `example.gif` from `www.example.com` on your web page, you could use the following tag:

```
<img src="http://www.example.com/example.gif" />
```

CAUTION
> Just because you can use images stored on other servers for your own web pages doesn't mean that you should. There are a lot of legal, ethical, and technical issues involved with using images on other sites. I'll discuss them later in this lesson.

Adding Alternative Text to Images

Images can turn a simple text-only web page into a glorious visual feast. But what happens if someone is reading your web page using a text-only browser? What if she has image loading turned off so that all your carefully crafted graphics appear as generic icons? All of a sudden, that visual feast doesn't look quite as glorious.

There's a simple solution to this problem. By using the `alt` attribute of the `<img>` tag, you can substitute something meaningful in place of the image on browsers that cannot display it.

In text-only browsers, such as Lynx, graphics that are specified using the `<img>` tag in the original file usually are displayed as the word IMAGE with square brackets around it, like this: [IMAGE]. If the image itself is a link to something else, that link is preserved.

The `alt` attribute in the `<img>` tag provides a more meaningful text alternative to the blank [IMAGE] for your visitors who are using text-only web browsers, or who have graphics turned off on their browsers. The `alt` attribute contains a string with the text you want to substitute for the graphic:

```
<img src="myimage.gif" alt="[a picture of a cat]" />
```

7

Most browsers interpret the string you include in the `alt` attribute as a literal string. That is, if you include any HTML tags in that string, they'll be printed as-is rather than being parsed and displayed as HTML code. Therefore, you can't use whole blocks of HTML code as a replacement for an image—just a few words or phrases.

I bring up image alternatives now for good reason. Alternatives to images are optional in earlier versions of HTML, but they're mandatory in HTML 4.01 Strict and XHTML 1.0 specifications. If there's no appropriate alternative text for an image, you can simply leave it empty, like this: `alt=""`.

▼ Task: Exercise 7.1: Adding Images to a Page

Here's the web page for a local haunted house that's open every year at Halloween. Using all the excellent advice I've given you in the preceding six lessons, you should be able to create a page like this one fairly easily. Here's the HTML code for this HTML file, and Figure 7.1 shows how it looks so far:

Input ▼

```
<!DOCTYPE html PUBLIC "-//W3C//DTD XHTML 1.0 Transitional//EN"
"http://www.w3.org/TR/xhtml1/DTD/transitional.dtd">
<html>
<head>
<title>Welcome to the Halloween House of Terror</title>
</head>
<body>
<h1>Welcome to The Halloween House of Terror!!</h1>
<hr />
<p>Voted the most frightening haunted house three years in a row,
the <strong>Halloween House of Terror</strong> provides the
ultimate in Halloween thrills. Over <strong>20 rooms of thrills
and excitement</strong> to make your blood run cold and your hair
stand on end!</p>
<p>The Halloween House of Terror is open from <em>October 20 to
November 1st</em>, with a gala celebration on Halloween night.
Our hours are:</p>
<ul>
<li>Mon-Fri 5PM-midnight</li>
<li>Sat &amp; Sun 5PM-3AM</li>
<li><strong>Halloween Night (31-Oct)</strong>: 3PM-???</li>
</ul>
<p>The Halloween House of Terror is located at:<br />
The Old Waterfall Shopping Center<br />
1020 Mirabella Ave<br />
Springfield, CA 94532</p>
</body>
</html>
```

Output ▶

FIGURE 7.1

The Halloween
House home page.

So far, so good. Now you can add an image to the page. Suppose that you happen to have an image of a haunted house lying around on your hard drive; it would look excellent at the top of this web page. The image, called house.jpg, is in JPEG format. It's located in the same directory as the halloween.html page, so adding it to the page will be easy.

Now, suppose that you want to place this image above the page heading. To do so, add an <img> tag to the file inside its own paragraph, just before the heading:

```
<p><img src="house.jpg" alt="House of Terror" /></p>
<h1>Welcome to The Halloween House of Terror!!</h1>
```

Images, like links, don't define their own text elements, so the <img> tag has to go inside a paragraph or heading element.

When you reload the halloween.html page, your browser should include the haunted house image on the page, as shown in Figure 7.2.

If the image doesn't load and your browser displays a funny-looking icon in its place, make sure that you entered the filename properly in the HTML file. Image filenames are case sensitive, so all the uppercase and lowercase letters have to be correct.

If the case isn't the problem, double-check the image file to make sure that it is indeed a GIF or JPEG image and that it has the proper file extension.

▼ **FIGURE 7.2**
The Halloween
House home page
with the haunted
house.

If one image is good, two would be really good, right? Try adding another `<img>` tag next to the first one, as follows, and see what happens:

Input ▼

```
<p><img src="house.jpg" alt="House of Terror" />
<img src="house.jpg" alt="House of Terror" /></p>
<h1>Welcome to The Halloween House of Terror!!</h1>
```

Figure 7.3 shows how the page looks in a browser. The two images are adjacent to each other, as you would expect.

Output ▶

FIGURE 7.3
Multiple images.

▲   And that's all there is to adding images!

Images and Text

In the preceding exercise, you put an inline image on a page with text below it. You also can include an image inside a line of text. In fact, this is what the phrase "inline image" actually means—it's *in a line* of text.

To include images inside a line of text, just add the `<img>` tag inside an element tag (`<h1>`, `<p>`, `<address>`, and so on), as in the following line:

```
<h2><img src="house.jpg" alt="House of Terror" />The Halloween House of
    Terror!!</h2>
```

Figure 7.4 shows the difference you can make by putting the image inline with the heading. (I've also shortened the heading itself and changed it to `<h2>` so that it all fits on one line.)

FIGURE 7.4
The Halloween House page with an image inside the heading.

The image doesn't have to be large, and it doesn't have to be at the beginning of the text. You can include an image anywhere in a block of text, as in the following:

Input ▼

```
<blockquote>
Love, from whom the world
<img src="world.gif" alt="World" />begun,<br />
Hath the secret of the sun.
<img src="sun.gif" alt="Sun" /><br />
Love can tell, and love alone, Whence the million stars
<img src="star.gif" alt="Star" /> were strewn<br />
Why each atom <img src="atom.gif" alt="Atom" />
```

```
knows its own.<br />
--Robert Bridges
</blockquote>
```

Figure 7.5 shows how this block looks.

Output ▶

FIGURE 7.5
Images can go
anywhere in text.

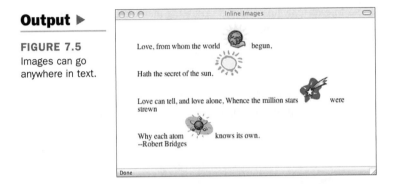

Text and Image Alignment

In these examples, the bottom of the image and the bottom of the text match up. The <img> tag also includes the align attribute, which enables you to align the top or bottom of the image with the surrounding text or other images in the line.

NOTE

The align attribute for the <img> tag is deprecated in HTML 4.01 in favor of using style sheet attributes. You'll learn more about style sheets in Lesson 9, "Creating Layouts with CSS."

Standard HTML 2.0 defines three basic values for align:

align="top"	Aligns the top of the image with the topmost part of the line (which may be the top of the text or the top of another image)
align="middle"	Aligns the center of the image with the middle of the line (usually the baseline of the line of text, not the actual middle of the line)
align="bottom"	Aligns the bottom of the image with the bottom of the line of text

HTML 3.2 provides two other values: left and right. These values are discussed in the next section, "Wrapping Text Next to Images."

Figure 7.6 shows the Robert Bridges poem from the previous section with the world image unaligned, the sun image aligned to the top of the line, the star image aligned to the middle, and the atom aligned to the bottom of the text.

Input ▼

```
<blockquote>
Love, from whom the world
<img src="world.gif" alt="World" />begun,<br />
Hath the secret of the sun.
<img src="sun.gif" alt="Sun" align="top" /><br />
Love can tell, and love alone, Whence the million stars
<img src="star.gif" alt="Star" align="middle" />
were strewn<br />
Why each atom
<img src="atom.gif" alt="Atom" align="bottom" />
knows its own.<br />
</blockquote>
```

Output ▶

FIGURE 7.6
Images unaligned,
aligned top,
aligned middle,
and aligned
bottom.

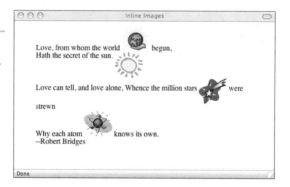

In addition to the preceding values, several other nonstandard values for align provide greater control over precisely where the image will be aligned within the line. The following values aren't part of HTML 3.2 or 4.01, and are supported unevenly by various browsers. These four attributes aren't approved in the proposed specification for XHTML 1.0, and your page won't be verified as XHTML 1.0–compliant if they're used:

align="texttop"   Aligns the top of the image with the top of the tallest text in the line (whereas align="top" aligns the image with the topmost item in the line). (Neither Netscape nor Internet Explorer handle this setting properly.)

align="absmiddle"	Aligns the middle of the image with the middle of the largest item in the line. (align="middle" usually aligns the middle of the image with the baseline of the text, not its actual middle.)
align="baseline"	Aligns the bottom of the image with the baseline of the text. align="baseline" is the same as align="bottom", but align="baseline" is a more descriptive name.
align="absbottom"	Aligns the bottom of the image with the lowest item in the line (which may be below the baseline of the text).

The following code shows these alignment options at work:

Input ▼

```
<h2>Middle of Text and Line aligned, arrow varies:</h2>
<img src="line.gif" alt="Line" />
Align: Top
<img src="uparrow.gif" alt="Up" align="top" />
Align: Text Top
<img src="uparrow.gif" alt="Up" align="texttop" />
<h2>Top of Text and Line aligned, arrow varies:</h2>
<img src="line.gif" alt="Line" />
Align: Absolute Middle
<img src="forward.gif" alt="Next" align="absmiddle" />
Align: Middle
<img src="forward.gif" alt="Next" align="middle" />
<h2>Top of Text and Line aligned, arrow varies:</h2>
<img src="line.gif" alt="Line" />
Align: Baseline / Bottom
<img src="down.gif" alt="Down" align="baseline" />
Align: Absolute Bottom
<img src="down.gif" alt="Down" align="absbottom" />
```

Figure 7.7 shows examples of all the options as they appear in a browser. In each case, the line on the left side and the text are aligned with each other, and the position of the arrow varies.

Output ▶

FIGURE 7.7
Alignment options
in Firefox.

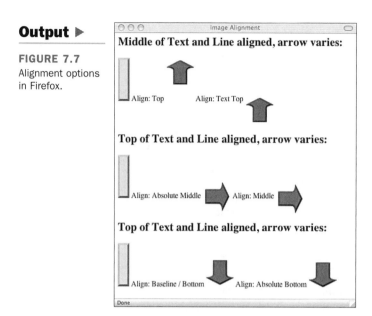

Wrapping Text Next to Images

Including an image inside a line works fine if you have only one line of text. One aspect of inline images that I've sneakily avoided mentioning so far is that in HTML 2.0, this alignment worked only with a single line of text. If you had multiple lines of text and you included an image in the middle of it, all the text around the image (except for the one line) would appear above and below that image.

What if you want text to flow around an image? Using HTML 2.0, you couldn't. You were restricted to just a single line of text on either side of the image, which limited the kinds of designs you could do.

To get around this HTML 2.0 limitation, Netscape defined two new values for the `align` attribute of the `<img>` tag: `left` and `right`. These new values were incorporated into HTML 3.2 and are now supported by all current browsers.

`align="left"` **and** `align="right"`

`align="left"` aligns an image with the left margin, and `align="right"` aligns an image with the right margin. However, these attributes also cause any text that follows the image to be displayed in the space to the right or left of that image, depending on the margin alignment:

7

Input ▼

```
<img src="tulips.gif" alt="Tulips" align="left" />
<h1>Mystery Tulip Murderer Strikes</h1>
<p>Someone, or something, is killing the tulips of New South
Haverford, Virginia. Residents of this small town are shocked and
dismayed by the senseless vandalism that has struck their tiny
town.</p>
<p>New South Haverford is known for its extravagant displays of
tulips in the springtime, and a good portion of its tourist trade
relies on the people who come from as far as New Hampshire to see
what has been estimated as up to two hundred thousand tulips that
bloom in April and May.</p>
<p>Or at least the tourists had been flocking to New South
Haverford until last week, when over the course of three days the
flower of each and every tulip in the town was neatly clipped off
while the town slept.</p>
```

Figure 7.8 shows an image with some text aligned next to it.

You can put any HTML text (paragraphs, lists, headings, other images) after an aligned image, and the text will be wrapped into the space between the image and the margin. Or you can have images on both margins and put the text between them. The browser fills in the space with text to the bottom of the image and then continues filling in the text beneath the image.

Output ▶

FIGURE 7.8
Text and images
aligned.

Stopping Text Wrapping

What if you want to stop filling in the space and start the next line underneath the image? A normal line break won't do it; it just breaks the line to the current margin alongside the image. A new paragraph also continues wrapping the text alongside the image. To stop wrapping text next to an image, use a line break tag (<br>) with the clear attribute. This enables you to break the line so that the next line of text begins after the end of the image (all the way to the margin).

The clear attribute can have one of three values:

left	Break to an empty left margin, for left-aligned images
right	Break to an empty right margin, for right-aligned images
all	Break to a line clear to both margins

NOTE
The clear attribute for the <br> tag is deprecated in HTML 4.01, in favor of using style sheet attributes.

For example, the following code snippet shows a picture of a tulip with some text wrapped next to it. A line break with clear="left" breaks the text wrapping after the heading and restarts the text after the image:

Input ▼

```
<!DOCTYPE html PUBLIC "-//W3C//DTD XHTML 1.0 Transitional//EN"
"http://www.w3.org/TR/xhtml1/DTD/transitional.dtd">
</head>
<body>
<img src="tulips.gif" alt="Tulips" align="left" />
<h1>Mystery Tulip Murderer Strikes</h1>
<br clear="left" />
<p>Someone, or something, is killing the tulips of New South
Haverford, Virginia. Residents of this small town are shocked and
dismayed by the senseless vandalism that has struck their tiny
town.</p>
<p>New South Haverford is known for its extravagant displays of
tulips in the springtime, and a good portion of its tourist trade
relies on the people who come from as far as New Hampshire to see
what has been estimated as up to two hundred thousand tulips that
bloom in April and May.</p>
<p>Or at least the tourists had been flocking to New South
Haverford until last week, when over the course of three days the
flower of each and every tulip in the town was neatly clipped off
while the town slept.</p>
```

7

Figure 7.9 shows the result in a browser.

Output ▶

FIGURE 7.9
Line break to a
clear margin.

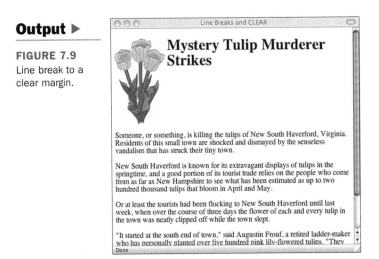

Adjusting the Space Around Images

With the capability to wrap text around an image, you also might want to add some space between the image and the text that surrounds it. The vspace and hspace attributes (introduced in HTML 3.2) enable you to make these adjustments. Both take values in pixels; vspace controls the space above and below the image, and hspace controls the space to the left and the right. Note that the amount of space you specify is added on both sides of the image. For example, if you use hspace="10", 10 pixels of space will be added on both the left and right sides of the image.

NOTE

> The vspace and hspace attributes for the <img> tag are deprecated in HTML 4.01, in favor of using style sheet attributes.

The following HTML code, displayed in Figure 7.10, illustrates two examples. The upper example shows default horizontal and vertical spacing around the image, and the lower example shows the effect produced by the hspace and vspace attributes. Both images use the align="left" attribute so that the text wraps along the left side of the image. However, in the bottom example, the text aligns with the extra space above the top of the image (added with the vspace attribute).

Input ▼

```
<img src="eggplant.gif" alt="Eggplant" align="left" />
<p>This is an eggplant. We intend to stay a good ways away from
it, because we really don't like eggplant very much.</p>
<br clear="left" />
<hr />
<img src="eggplant.gif" alt="Eggplant" vspace="50" hspace="50"
align="left" />
<p>This is an eggplant. We intend to stay a good ways away from
it, because we really don't like  eggplant very much.
```

Output ▶

FIGURE 7.10
The upper example doesn't have image spacing, and the lower example does.

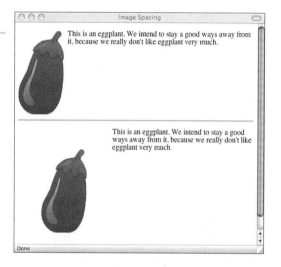

NOTE

With Cascading Style Sheets, you can control image borders, space included around images, and how text flows around images. You can also use CSS to control the properties of elements of all kinds, so I'm going to cover them in Lesson 9.

Images and Links

Can an image serve as a link? Sure it can! If you include an `<img>` tag inside a link tag (`<a>`), that image serves as a link itself:

```
<a href="index.html"><img src="uparrow.gif" alt="Up" /></a>
```

7

If you include both an image and text in the link tag, they become links to the same page:

```
<a href="index.html"><img src="uparrow.gif" alt="Up" />Up to Index</a>
```

TIP	One thing to look out for when you're placing images within links, with or without text, is white space between the `</a>` tag and the `<img>` tag or between the text and the image. Some browsers turn the white space into a link, and you get an odd "tail" on your images. To avoid this unsightly problem, don't leave spaces or line feeds between your `<img>` tags and `</a>` tags.

By default in HTML 2.0, images that are also links appear with borders around them to distinguish them from ordinary, nonclickable images. Figure 7.11 shows an example of this. The butterfly image is a nonclickable image, so it doesn't have a border around it. The up arrow, which takes the visitor back to the home page, has a border around it because it's a link.

FIGURE 7.11
Images used as links have a border around them.

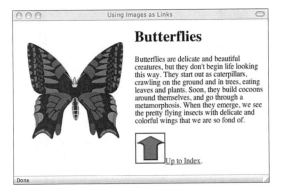

You can change the width of the border around the image by using the `border` attribute to `<img>`. The `border` attribute was a Netscape extension that became part of HTML 3.2, but it's been deprecated in HTML 4.01 in favor of style sheets. This attribute takes a number, which is the width of the border in pixels. `border="0"` hides the border entirely. This configuration is ideal for image links that actually look like clickable buttons, as shown in Figure 7.12.

NOTE	Including borders around images that are links has really fallen out of favor with most web designers. Not turning them off can make your design look very dated.

FIGURE 7.12
Images that look
like buttons.

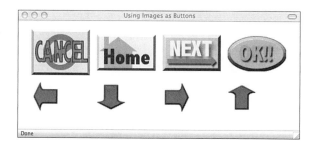

Task: Exercise 7.2: Using Navigation Icons ▼

Now you can create a simple page that uses images as links. When you have a set of
related web pages, it's usually helpful to create a consistent navigation scheme that is
used on all of the pages.

This example shows you how to create a set of icons that are used to navigate through a
linear set of pages. You have three icons in GIF format: one for forward, one for back,
and a third to enable the visitors to jump to the top-level contents page.

First, you'll write the HTML structure to support the icons. Here, the page itself isn't
very important, so you can just include a shell page:

Input ▼

```
<!DOCTYPE html PUBLIC "-//W3C//DTD XHTML 1.0 Transitional//EN"
"http://www.w3.org/TR/xhtml1/DTD/transitional.dtd">
<html>
<head>
<title>Motorcycle Maintenance: Removing Spark Plugs</title>
<h1>Removing Spark Plugs</h1>
<p>(include some info about spark plugs here)</p>
<hr />
</body>
</html>
```

Figure 7.13 shows how the page looks at the beginning.

Output ▼

At the bottom of the page, add your images using `<img>` tags:

Input ▼

```
<img src="next.gif" alt="Next" />
<img src="back.gif" alt="Back" />
<img src="uparrow.gif" alt="Up" />
```

7

Output ▼

FIGURE 7.13
The basic page, with no icons.

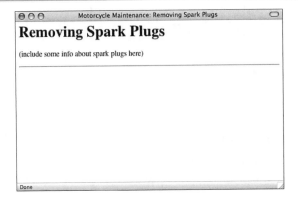

Figure 7.14 shows the result.

Output ▼

FIGURE 7.14
The basic page with icons.

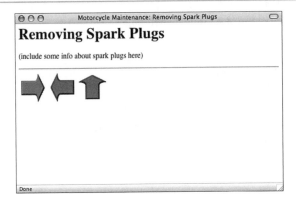

Now add the anchors to the images to activate them:

Input ▼

```
<a href="replacing.html"><img src="next.gif" alt="Next" /></a>
<a href="ready.html"><img src="back.gif" alt="Back" /></a>
<a href="index.html"><img src="uparrow.gif" alt="Up" /></a>
```

Figure 7.15 shows the result of this addition.

When you click the icons now, the browser jumps to the linked page just as it would
▼ have if you had used text links.

Output ▼

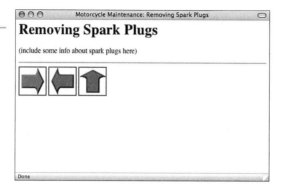

FIGURE 7.15
The basic page
with iconic links.

▼

Speaking of text, are the icons usable enough as they are? How about adding some text describing exactly what's on the other side of each link? You can add this text inside or outside the anchor, depending on whether you want the text to be a hot spot for the link as well. Here, include it outside the link so that only the icon serves as the hot spot. You also can align the bottoms of the text and the icons using the align attribute of the <img> tag. Finally, because the extra text causes the icons to move onto two lines, arrange each one on its own line instead:

Input ▼

```
<hr />
<p><a href="replacing.html"><img src="next.gif" border="0" alt="Next" /></a>
On to "Gapping the New Plugs"<br />
<a href="ready.html"><img src="back.gif" border="0" alt="Back" /></a>
Back to "When You Should Replace your Spark Plugs"<br />
<a href="index.html"><img src="uparrow.gif" border="0" alt="Up" /></a>
Up To Index
</p>
```

See Figure 7.16 for the final menu.

Output ▼

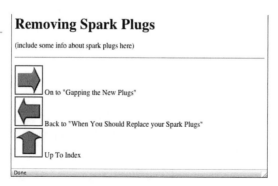

FIGURE 7.16
The basic page
with iconic links
and text.

7

What Is an Imagemap?

Earlier in this lesson, you learned how to create an image that doubles as a link simply by including the `<img>` tag inside a link tag (`<a>`). In this way, the entire image becomes a link.

In an imagemap, different parts of the image are different links. You can specify that certain areas of a map link to various pages, as in Figure 7.17. Or you can create visual metaphors for the information you're presenting, such as a set of books on a shelf or a photograph with a link from each person in the picture to a page with his or her biography on it.

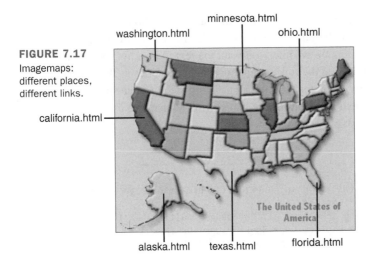

FIGURE 7.17
Imagemaps: different places, different links.

There are two kinds of imagemaps: *server-side* imagemaps and *client-side* imagemaps. Server-side imagemaps were used in the earlier days of the Web, but they posed some problems for web authors, and have fallen into disuse. In this lesson, client-side imagemaps, which are handled completely by the browser, are used almost exclusively and offer many advantages over older, server-side imagemaps.

Server-side imagemaps are implemented using an image displayed by the client and a program that runs on the server.

Client-side imagemaps work in the same ways as server-side imagemaps, except no program runs on the server. All the processing of coordinates and pointers to different locations occurs in the browser.

Every browser released since Netscape 2.0 supports client-side imagemaps, so there's not really any reason to bother with server-side imagemaps any more. In this lesson, I'm only going to talk about client-side imagemaps. To learn about server side imagemaps, check out the Apache `mod_imap` documentation at http://httpd.apache.org/docs/mod/mod_imap.html.

Client-Side Imagemaps

Although server-side imagemaps were in common use in the early days of the Web, their weaknesses led Netscape to add support for client-side imagemaps to version 2.0, which was released in March 1996. Because they were vastly superior to server-side imagemaps, soon all the other browser makers added support for them as well. Client-side imagemaps address the problems with server-side imagemaps by eliminating the need for a special imagemap program on the server. Instead, they manage all the imagemap processing locally in the web browser itself.

Later in this lesson, you'll learn how to create client-side imagemaps.

Imagemaps and Text-Only Browsers

Because of the inherently graphical nature of imagemaps, they work well only in graphical browsers. Lynx, the most popular text-based browser, provides limited support for client-side imagemaps. If you load a page in Lynx that contains a client-side imagemap, you can get a list of the links contained in the imagemap.

Creating Client-Side Imagemaps

As mentioned previously, client-side imagemaps offer several improvements over server-side imagemaps. The most significant improvement is that the link doesn't need to be processed on the server. All modern browsers process the imagemap locally on the users' computers.

Getting an Image

To create an imagemap, you'll need an image (of course). This image will be the most useful if it has several discrete visual areas that can be selected individually. For example, use an image that contains several symbolic elements or that can be easily broken down into polygons. Photographs generally don't make good imagemaps because their various elements tend to blend together or are of unusual shapes. Figures 7.18 and 7.19 show examples of good and poor images for imagemaps.

7

FIGURE 7.18
A good image for
an imagemap.

FIGURE 7.19
A not-so-good
image for an
imagemap.

Determining Your Coordinates

Client-side imagemaps consist of two parts; the first is the image used for the imagemap. The second is the set of HTML tags used to define the regions of the imagemap that serve as links. To define these tags, you must determine the exact coordinates on your image that define the regions you'll use as links.

You can determine these coordinates either by sketching regions and manually noting the coordinates or by using an imagemap creation program. The latter method is easier because the program automatically generates a map file based on the regions you draw with the mouse.

The Mapedit program for Windows, Linux, and the Mac OS can help you create client-side imagemaps. (See Appendix A, "Sources for Further Information," for a full list of related FTP sites.) In addition, many of the latest WYSIWYG editors for HTML pages and web graphics enable you to generate imagemaps. Table 7.1 lists the current tools for generating imagemaps.

TABLE 7.1   Imagemap Creation Software

Name	Platform	URL
Imaptool	Linux/X Window System	http://www.sspitzer.org/_imaptool/
Mapedit	Windows/UNIX/Mac	http://www.boutell.com/_mapedit/
Poor Person's Image Mapper	Web-based	http://www.pangloss.com/ seidel/ClrHlpr/imagemap.html

If you must create your imagemaps by hand, here's how. First, make a sketch of the regions that will be active on your image. Figure 7.20 shows the three types of shapes that you can specify in an imagemap: circles, rectangles, and polygons.

FIGURE 7.20
There are three types of shapes available for creating imagemaps.

A circular region —

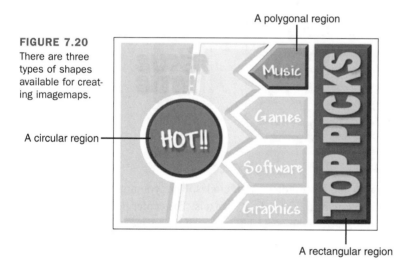

A polygonal region

A rectangular region

You next need to determine the coordinates for the endpoints of those regions. Most image-editing programs have an option that displays the coordinates of the current mouse position. Use this feature to note the appropriate coordinates. (All the mapping programs mentioned previously will create a map file for you, but for now, following the steps manually will help you better understand the processes involved.)

Defining a Polygon

Figure 7.21 shows the x,y coordinates of a polygon region. These values are based on their positions from the upper-left corner of the image, which is coordinate 0,0. The first

7

number in the coordinate pair indicates the x value and defines the number of pixels from the extreme left of the image. The second number in the pair indicates the y measurement and defines the number of pixels from the top of the image.

> **NOTE**
>
> The 0,0 origin is in the upper-left corner of the image, and positive y is down.

FIGURE 7.21
Getting the coordinates for a polygon.

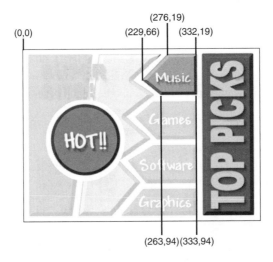

Defining a Circle

Figure 7.22 shows how to get the coordinates for circles. Here you note the coordinates for the center point of the circle and the radius, in pixels. The center point of the circle is defined as the x,y coordinate from the upper-left corner of the image.

Defining a Rectangle

Figure 7.23 shows how to obtain coordinates for rectangle regions. Note the x,y coordinates for the upper-left and lower-right corners of the rectangle.

The `<map>` and `<area>` Tags

If you're creating your imagemap manually and you've written down all of the coordinates for your regions and the URLs they'll point to, you can include this information in the client-side imagemap tags on a web page. To include a client-side imagemap inside an HTML document, use the `<map>` tag, which looks like the following:

```
<map name="mapname"> coordinates and links </map>
```

FIGURE 7.22
Getting the coordinates for a circle.

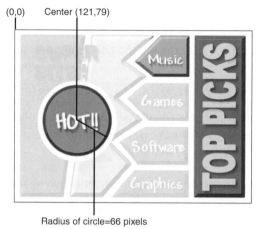

(0,0)   Center (121,79)

Radius of circle=66 pixels

FIGURE 7.23
Getting the coordinates for a rectangle.

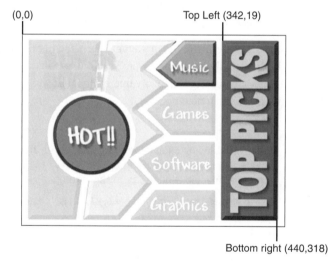

(0,0)   Top Left (342,19)

Bottom right (440,318)

The value assigned to the name attribute is the name of this map definition. This is the name that will be used later to associate the clickable image with its corresponding coordinates and hyperlink references. So, if you have multiple imagemaps on the same page, you can have multiple <map> tags with different names.

Between the <map> and the </map> tags, enter the coordinates for each area in the imagemap and the destinations of those regions. The coordinates are defined inside yet another new tag: the <area> tag. To define a rectangle, for example, you would write the following:

```
<area shape="rect" coords="41,16,101,32" href="test.html">
```

7

The type of shape to be used for the region is declared by the shape attribute, which can have the values rect, poly, circle, and default. The coordinates for each shape are noted using the coords attribute. For example, the coords attribute for a poly shape appears as follows:

```
<area shape="poly" coords="x1,y1,x2,y2,x3,y3,...,xN,yN" href="URL">
```

Each *x,y* combination represents a point on the polygon. For rect shapes, *x1,y1* is the upper-left corner of the rectangle, and *x2,y2* is the lower-right corner:

```
<area shape="rect" coords="x1,y1,x2,y2" href="URL">
```

For circle shapes, *x,y* represents the center of a circular region of size *radius*:

```
<area shape="circle" coords="x,y,radius" href="URL">
```

The default shape is different from the others—it doesn't require any coordinates to be specified. Instead, the link associated with the default shape is followed if the user clicks anywhere on the image that doesn't fall within another defined region.

Another attribute you need to define for each <area> tag is the href attribute. You can assign href any URL you usually would associate with an <a> link, including relative pathnames. In addition, you can assign href a value of "nohref" to define regions of the image that don't contain links to a new page.

NOTE

When you're using client-side imagemaps with frames, you can include the target attribute inside an <area> tag to open a new page in a specific window, as in this example:

```
<area shape="rect" coords="x1,y1,x2,y2" href="URL" target=
"window_name">
```

You need to include one more attribute in HTML 4.01. Earlier in this lesson, you learned how to specify alternate text for images. In HTML 4.01, the alt attribute is an additional requirement for the <area> tag that displays a short description of a clickable area on a client-side imagemap when you pass your cursor over it. Using the <area> example that I cited, the alt attribute appears as shown in the following example:

```
<area shape="rect" coords="41,16,101,32" href="test.html" alt="test link">
```

The usemap **Attribute**

After you've created your <map> tag and defined the regions of your image using <area> tags, the next step is to associate the map with the image. To do so, the usemap attribute of the <img> tag is used. The map name that you specified using the name attribute of the <map> tag, preceded by a #, should be used as the value of the usemap attribute, as shown in this example:

```
<img src="image.gif" usemap="#mapname">
```

NOTE

The value assigned to usemap is a standard URL. This is why *mapname* has a pound symbol (#) in front of it. As with links to anchors inside a web page, the pound symbol tells the browser to look for *mapname* in the current web page. If you have a very complex imagemap, however, you can store it in a separate HTML file and reference it using a standard URL.

Task: Exercise 7.3: A Clickable Jukebox ▼

Let's take a look at how to create a client-side imagemap for a real image. In this example, you'll define clickable regions on an image of a jukebox. The image you'll be using appears in Figure 7.24.

FIGURE 7.24
The jukebox image.

First, define the regions that will be clickable on this image. There are six rectangular buttons with musical categories on them, a center area that looks like a house, and a circle with a question mark inside it. Figure 7.25 shows regions on the image.

Now that you know where the various regions are, you need to find the exact coordinates of the areas as they appear in your image. You can use a mapping program like Mapedit, or you can do it manually. If you try it manually, it's helpful to keep in mind that most image-editing programs display the x and y coordinate of the image when you move the mouse over it.

7

▼

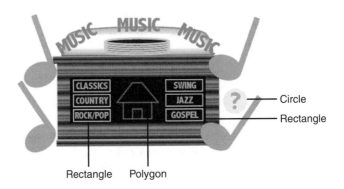

▼ FIGURE 7.25
The jukebox with
areas defined.

Getting Image Coordinates from the Browser

You don't have an image-editing program? If you use Netscape as your browser, here's a trick: Create an HTML file with the image inside a link pointing to a fake file, and include the `ismap` attribute inside the `<img>` tag. You don't need a real link; anything will do. The HTML code might look something like the following:

```
<a href="nothing"><img src="myimage.gif" ismap></a>
```

When you load this into your browser, the image is displayed as if it were an imagemap. When you move your mouse over it, the x and y coordinates appear in the status line of the browser. Using this trick, you can find the coordinates for the map file of any point on that image.

With regions and a list of coordinates, all you need are the web pages to jump to when the appropriate area is selected. These can be documents, scripts, or anything else you can call from a browser as a jump destination. For this example, I've created several documents and stored them inside the `music` directory on my web server. These are the pages you'll define as the end points when the clickable images are selected. Figure 7.26 identifies each of the eight clickable areas in the imagemap. Table 7.2 shows the coordinates of each and the URL that's called up when it's clicked.

TABLE 7.2   Clickable Areas in the Jukebox Image

Number	Type	URL	Coordinates
1	rect	music/classics.html	101,113,165,134
2	rect	music/country.html	101,139,165,159
▼ 3	rect	music/rockpop.html	101,163,165,183

TABLE 7.2 continued

Number	Type	URL	Coordinates
4	poly	music/home.html	175,152,203,118
			220,118,247,152
			237,153,237,181
			186,181,186,153
5	rect	music/swing.html	259,113,323,134
6	rect	music/jazz.html	259,139,323,159
7	rect	music/gospel.html	259,163,323,183
8	circle	music/help.html	379,152,21

FIGURE 7.26
Eight hotspots, numbered as identified in Table 7.2.

For the jukebox image, the <map> tag and its associated <area> tags and attributes look like the following:

```
<map name="jukebox">
<area shape="rect" coords="101,113, 165,134"
  href="/music/classics.html"
  alt="Classical Music and Composers" />
<area shape="rect" coords="101,139, 165,159"
  href="/music/country.html"
  alt="Country and Folk Music" />
<area shape="rect" coords="101,163, 165,183"
  href="/music/rockpop.html"
  alt="Rock and Pop from 50's On" />
<area shape="poly" coords="175,152, 203,118, 220,118, 247,152,
  237,153, 237,181, 186,181, 186,153"
  href="code/music/home.html"
  alt="Home Page for Music Section" />
<area shape="rect" coords="259,113, 323,134"
  href="/music/swing.html"
  alt="Swing and Big Band Music" />
```

7

```
<area shape="rect" coords="259,139, 323,159"
  href="/music/jazz.html"
  alt="Jazz and Free Style" />
<area shape="rect" coords="259,163, 323,183"
  href="/music/gospel.html"
  alt="Gospel and Inspirational Music" />
<area shape="circle" coords="379,152, 21"
  href="/music/help.html"
  alt="Help" />
</map>
```

The `<img>` tag that refers to the map coordinates uses usemap, as follows:

```
<img src="jukebox.gif" usemap="#jukebox">
```

Finally, put the whole thing together and test it. Here's a sample HTML file for The Really Cool Music Page with a client-side imagemap, which contains both the `<map>` tag and the image that uses it:

Input ▼

```
<!DOCTYPE html PUBLIC "-//W3C//DTD XHTML 1.0 Transitional//EN"
"http://www.w3.org/TR/xhtml1/DTD/transitional.dtd">
<html>
<head>
<title>The Really Cool Music Page</title>
</head>
<body bgcolor="#ffffff">
<div align="center">
<h1>The Really Cool Music Page</h1>
<p>Select the type of music you want to hear.<br />
 You'll go to a list of songs that you can select from.</p>
<p>
<img src="jukebox.gif" alt="Juke Box" usemap="#jukebox" />
<map name="jukebox">
<area shape="rect" coords="101,113, 165,134"
  href="/music/classics.html"
  alt="Classical Music and Composers" />
<area shape="rect" coords="101,139, 165,159"
  href="/music/country.html"
  alt="Country and Folk Music" />
<area shape="rect" coords="101,163, 165,183"
  href="/music/rockpop.html"
  alt="Rock and Pop from 50's On" />
<area shape="poly" coords="175,152, 203,118, 220,118, 247,152,
  237,153, 237,181, 186,181, 186,153"
  href="code/music/home.html"
  alt="Home Page for Music Section" />
<area shape="rect" coords="259,113, 323,134"
  href="/music/swing.html"
```

```
    alt="Swing and Big Band Music" />
<area shape="rect" coords="259,139, 323,159"
    href="/music/jazz.html"
    alt="Jazz and Free Style" />
<area shape="rect" coords="259,163, 323,183"
    href="/music/gospel.html"
    alt="Gospel and Inspirational Music" />
<area shape="circle" coords="379,152, 21"
    href="/music/help.html"
    alt="Help" />
</map></p>
<p>
<a href="code/music/home.html">Home</a> ¦
<a href="code/music/classics.html">Classics</a> ¦
<a href="code/music/country.html">Country</a> ¦
<a href="code/music/rockpop.html">Rock/Pop</a> ¦
<a href="code/music/swing.html">Swing</a> ¦
<a href="code/music/jazz.html">Jazz</a> ¦
<a href="code/music/gospel.html">Gospel</a> ¦
<a href="code/music/help.html">Help</a>
</p>
</div>
</body>
</html>
```

Figure 7.27 shows the imagemap in a browser.

Output ▼

FIGURE 7.27
The finished Really
Cool Music Page
with client-side
imagemap.

Other Neat Tricks with Images

Now that you've learned about inline images, images as links, and how to wrap text
around images, you know what *most* people do with images on web pages. But you can
play with a few newer tricks as well.

All the attributes in this section were originally Netscape extensions. They were later incorporated into HTML 3.2, but most have been deprecated in its successor, HTML 4.01.

Image Dimensions and Scaling

Two attributes of the `<img>` tag, `height` and `width`, specify the height and width of the image in pixels. Both became part of the HTML 3.2 specification, but they're deprecated in HTML 4.01 in favor of style sheets.

If you use the actual height and width of the image in these attributes (which you find by opening the image file directly in your browser), some older browsers will load and display your web pages much faster than if you don't include the values.

Why? Old browsers (Netscape 4 and Internet Explorer 3) couldn't alter the layout of pages as they were being loaded, so the size of every element on the page had to be determined before the page could be displayed. These days, browsers can resize elements on the fly so users don't have to wait for images to download before the page can be displayed. Even so, providing the proper height and width can help your pages render a bit more smoothly, so you should still include them if possible.

TIP

> Not only will browsers usually tell you the size of any image you open (in the title bar of the browser window). Just about any application that lets you view or edit image files will display the dimensions of an image as well.

If the values for `width` and `height` are different from the actual width and height of the image, your browser will resize the image to fit those dimensions. Because smaller images take up less disk space than larger images and therefore take less time to transfer over the network, you can just create a smaller version and then scale it to the dimensions you want on your web page. The downside of this technique is that the image-scaling algorithms built into browsers are not always the best. If you use the `height` and `width` attributes to change the size of an image, be prepared for it to look pretty bad, especially if the aspect ratio is not preserved (in other words, you take a 100-by-100 pixel image and expand it into a 200-by-400 pixel image).

CAUTION

Don't perform *reverse scaling*—creating a large image and then using `width` and `height` to scale it down. Smaller file sizes are better because they take less time to load. If you're going to display a small image, make it smaller to begin with.

More About Image Borders

You learned about the `border` attribute of the `<img>` tag as part of the section on links, where setting `border` to a number or to `0` determined the width of the image border (or hid it entirely).

By default, images that aren't inside links don't have borders. However, you can use the `border` attribute to include a border around any image, as follows:

```
<p><img src="eggplant.gif" alt="Eggplant" align="left" border="5"
width="102" height="178" />
This is an eggplant. We intend to stay a good ways away from it,
because we really don't like eggplant very much.</p>
```

Figure 7.28 shows an image with a border around it.

FIGURE 7.28
An image border.

Using Color

As you've seen, one way to add a splash of color to the black, gray, and white on your web pages is to add images. However, several HTML attributes enable you to change the colors of the page itself, including changing the background color, changing the color of the text and links, and adding spot color to individual characters.

In this section, you'll learn how to make all these changes in HTML 3.2. However, as is the case with most of the presentational attributes we've covered thus far, color attributes are deprecated in HTML 4.01 in favor of style sheets. You'll learn more about the style sheet approach in Lesson 9.

7

Specifying Colors

Before you can change the color of any part of an HTML page, you have to know what color you're going to change it to. You can specify colors using the color extensions to HTML in two ways:

- Using a hexadecimal number representing that color
- Using one of a set of predefined color names

The most flexible and widely supported method of specifying a color is to use the numeric identifier. Most image-editing programs have what's called a *color picker*—a tool for choosing a single color from a range of available colors. Some color pickers display the value of that color in RGB form as three numbers representing the intensity of red, green, and blue in that color. Each number is usually 0 to 255, with 0 0 0 being black and 255 255 255 being white. If you use one of these tools, you'll have to convert the decimal numbers to hexadecimal. These days, most tools with color pickers also provide the hexadecimal values for red, green, and blue, which is what web browsers require. In fact, the color picker that's built into the Mac OS includes the hexadecimal values to make things easy on web publishers.

The final hex number you need is all three numbers put together with a hash sign (#) at the beginning, as in the following:

```
#000000
#de04e4
#ffff00
```

Netscape and Internet Explorer support a much easier way of indicating colors. Rather than using arcane numbering schemes, you just choose a color name such as Black, White, Green, Maroon, Olive, Navy, Purple, Gray, Red, Yellow, Blue, Teal, Lime, Aqua, Fuchsia, or Silver.

Although color names are easier to figure out and remember than the numbers, only a few colors have names that are well supported by web browsers. After you have a color name or number in hand, you can apply that color to various parts of your HTML page.

There are also a number of websites that are designed to help web designers choose colors. One of the best is Color Schemer at http://www.colorschemer.com/online.html. It enables you to view several colors next to each other to see how they match, and will even suggest colors that match the ones you choose. The current Color Schemer interface appears in Figure 7.29.

FIGURE 7.29
Color Schemer.

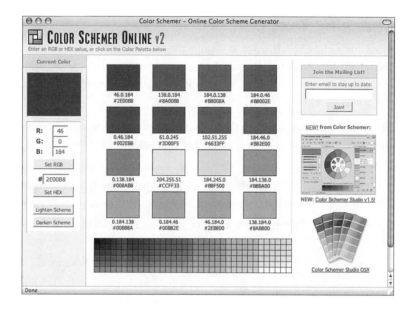

Changing Background Color of a Page

To change a page's background color, decide what color you want and then add the bgcolor attribute to the <body> tag. The <body> tag, in case you've forgotten, is the tag that surrounds all the content of your HTML file. <head> contains the title, and <body> contains almost everything else. bgcolor is an HTML extension introduced by Netscape in the 1.1 version of the browser and incorporated into HTML 3.2.

To use color numbers for backgrounds, you enter the value of the bgcolor attribute of the <body> tag (the hexadecimal number you found in the preceding section) in quotation marks. They look like the following:

```
<body bgcolor="#ffffff">
<body bgcolor="#934ce8">
```

To use color names, simply use the name of the color as the value to bgcolor:

```
<body bgcolor="white">
<body bgcolor="green">
```

NOTE

> Some browsers enable you to indicate color numbers without the leading hash sign (#). Although this method might seem more convenient, it's incompatible with many other browsers.

7

Changing Text Colors

It wouldn't make much sense to change the background color of a page if you couldn't change the text colors as well. Just as you can use the bgcolor attribute of the <body> tag to change a page's background color, there are attributes that enable you to modify text colors on a page.

Text colors are specified with the same identifiers as background colors. The following attributes can be added to the <body> tag of a page to alter the color of the page text and link colors:

text	Controls the color of all the page's body text except for link text, including headings, body text, text inside tables, and so on.
link	Controls the color of link text for links that the user has not already clicked on.
vlink	Controls the color of links that the user has already visited.
alink	Controls the color of a link while the user is clicking on it. When the user clicks on a link, it changes to this color. When he or she releases the mouse button, it switches back.

Remember the haunted house image that you inserted on a page earlier? The page would be decidedly spookier with a black background, and orange text would be so much more appropriate for the holiday. To create a page with a black background, orange text, and deep red unvisited links, you might use the following <body> tag:

```
<body bgcolor="#000000" text="#ff9933" link="#800000">
```

Using the following color names for the background and unfollowed links would produce the same effect:

```
<body bgcolor="orange" text="black" link="#800000">
```

Both these links would produce a page that looks something like the one shown in Figure 7.30.

Spot Color

When you change a page's text colors by using attributes to the <body> tag, that change affects all the text on the page. *Spot color* is the ability to change the color of individual characters on your page, which you can use instead of or in addition to a global text color.

FIGURE 7.30
Background and
text colors.

In yesterday's lesson you learned about using the HTML tag `<font>` for setting the font size and font name. A third attribute to `<font>`, `color`, enables you to change the color of individual words or phrases. The value of `color` is either a color name or number:

```
<p>When we go out tonight, we're going to paint the town
<font color="#ff0000">RED</font>.
```

Of course, you can use font spot colors in addition to font names and sizes.

Specifying Colors with CSS

Needless to say, there are ways to specify color on a page using Cascading Style Sheets. First, let's look at how colors are specified using CSS. The two methods available in HTML are also available in CSS. You can specify colors by name or by using a six-digit hexadecimal specification. There are some other options as well. You can specify colors using a three-digit hexadecimal number, which is shorthand for cases where both digits in each pair are the same. For example, if the color you're using is #FFFFFF (white), you can just specify it as #FFF. Or, if you want a light blue such as #66CCFF, you can specify it as #6CF.

You can also specify colors using decimal values or percentages. For example, #66CCFF can be specified as (102, 204, 255) using decimal notation. Or, if you prefer, using percentages, like this: (40%, 80%, 100%). If you don't want to worry about these alternative methods, that's fine. You can just use the same ones that you use when specifying colors in HTML.

7

Color-Related Properties

There are two key properties when it comes to assigning colors to elements using CSS—color and background-color. These properties are more flexible than specifying colors using the <font> tag for a number of reasons. The most obvious is that you can specify not only the text color for an element, but also the background color using CSS. For example, to indicate that a paragraph should have white text on a black background, you could use the following code:

```
<p style="color: #fff, background-color: #000">This paragraph has
white text on a black background.</p>
```

You can also use these properties to adjust the colors on the whole page by applying them to the body tag. Here's an example:

```
<body style="color: #fff; background-color: #00f">
```

This page will have white text on a blue background. That's all there is to using colors with CSS. There are other ways that color can be used, and more important, in Lesson 9, you'll see how you can apply color to elements on a page without using the style attribute, which can be cumbersome.

Image Backgrounds

The last topic in this lesson is using an image as a background for your pages, rather than simply a solid-colored background. When you use an image for a background, that image is *tiled*; that is, it's repeated in rows to fill the browser window.

To create a tiled background, you need an image to serve as the tile. Usually, when you create an image for tiling, you must make sure that the pattern flows smoothly from one tile to the next. You can do some careful adjusting of the image in your favorite image-editing program to make sure that the edges line up. The goal is for the edges to meet cleanly so that you don't have a seam between the tiles after you've laid them end to end. (See Figure 7.31 for an example of tiles that don't line up very well.) You also can try clip art packages for wallpaper or tile patterns that are designed specifically to be tiled in this fashion. Some graphics packages, such as Photoshop and Paint Shop Pro, can also modify your images so that they work as tiles. This feature works better with some kinds of images than others.

When you have an image that can be tiled smoothly, all you need to create a tiled image background is the background attribute, which is part of the <body> tag. The value of background is a filename or URL that points to your image file, as in the following example:

```
<body background="tiles.gif">
<body background="backgrounds/rosemarble.gif">
```

FIGURE 7.31
Tiled images with seams.

You can also include background images on your pages using CSS. To include a background image on a page (or under any block element), the background-image property is used. Here's an example:

```
<body style="background-image: url(backgrounds/rosemarble.gif)">
```

By default, the background image is tiled both horizontally and vertically. However, using the background-repeat property, you can control this behavior. Options include repeat (which tiles the image horizontally and vertically), repeat-x (tile horizontally only), repeat-y (tile vertically only), and no-repeat. You can also specify whether the background image scrolls along with the content of the page or remains in a fixed position using the background-attachment property. The two values there are scroll and fixed. So, if you want to put one background image in the upper-left corner of the browser window and have it stay there, you would use the following:

```
<body style="background-image: url(backgrounds/rosemarble.gif);
background-repeat: no-repeat; background-attachment: fixed">
```

What if you want the background image to appear somewhere on the page other than the upper-left corner? The background-position property enables you to position a background image anywhere you like within a page (or element). The background-position property is a bit more complex than most you'll see. You can either pass in two percentages, or the horizontal position (left, right, center), or the vertical position (top, bottom, center) or both the horizontal and vertical position. Here are some valid settings for this property:

Upper right	0% 100%
	top right
	right top
	right

7

Center	50% 50%
	center center
Bottom center	50% 100%
	bottom center
	center bottom

Here's a <body> tag that places the background in the center right of the window and does not scroll it with the page:

```
<body style="background-image: url(backgrounds/rosemarble.gif);
background-repeat: no-repeat;
background-attachment: fixed;
background-position: center right">
```

Rather than using all these different properties to specify the background, you can use the background property by itself to specify all the background properties. With the background property, you can specify the background color, image, repeat setting, attachment, and position. All the properties are optional, and the order isn't important either. To condense the preceding specification into one property, the following tag is used:

```
<body style="background: url(backgrounds/rosemarble.gif)
no-repeat fixed center right">
```

If you like, you can also include a background color as well. Here's what the new tag looks like:

```
<body style="background: #000 url(backgrounds/rosemarble.gif)
no-repeat fixed center right">
```

Image Etiquette

There are great images on sites all over the Web: cool icons, great photographs, excellent line art, and plenty of other graphics as well. You might feel the temptation to link directly to these images and include them on your own pages, or to save them to disk and then use them. There are a number of reasons why it's wrong to do so.

First of all, if you're linking directly to images on another site, you're stealing bandwidth from that site. Every time someone requests your page, they'll also be issuing a request to the site where the image is posted and downloading the image from there. If you get a lot of traffic, you can cause problems for the remote site.

The second reason is actually a problem regardless of how you use images from other sites. If you don't have permission to use an image on your site, you're violating the rights of the image's creator. Copyright law protects creative work from use without permission, and it's granted to every creative work automatically.

The best course of action is to create your own images or look for images that are explicitly offered for free use by their creators. Even if images are made available for your use, you should download them and store them with your web pages rather than linking to them directly. Doing so prevents you from abusing the bandwidth of the person providing the images.

Summary

One of the major features that makes the World Wide Web stand out from other elements of the Internet is that web pages can contain full-color images. Arguably, it was the existence of those images that helped the Web to catch on so quickly.

In this lesson you learned to place images on your Web pages. Those images are normally in GIF or JPEG format and should be small enough that they can be downloaded quickly over a slow link. You also learned that the HTML tag `<img>` enables you to put an image on a web page either inline with text or on a line by itself. The `<img>` tag has three primary attributes supported in standard HTML:

`src`	The location and filename of the image to include.
`align`	How to position the image vertically with its surrounding text. `align` can have one of three values: `top`, `middle`, or `bottom`. (Deprecated in HTML 4.01 in favor of style sheets.)
`alt`	A text string to substitute for the image in text-only browsers.

You can include images inside a link tag (`<a>`) and make them hot spots for the links.

In addition to the standard attributes, several other attributes to the `<img>` tag provide greater control over images and layout on web pages. You learned how to use these HTML 3.2 attributes in this lesson, but most of them have been deprecated in HTML 4.01 in favor of style sheets. They include the following:

`align=` `"left"`	Places the image against the appropriate margin, `align="right"`, allowing all of the following text to flow into the space alongside the image.
`clear`	An extension to ` ` that enables you to stop wrapping text alongside an image. `clear` can have three values: `left`, `right`, and `all`.

7

`align="texttop"`
`align="baseline"`
`_align="absbottom"`
	Allows greater control over the alignment of an inline `align="absmiddle"` image and the text surrounding it.

`vspace`	Defines the amount of space between an image `hspace` and the text surrounding it.
`border`	Defines the width of the border around an image (with or without a link). `border="0"` hides the border altogether.

In addition to images, you can add color to the background and the text of a page by using attributes to the <body> tag, or to individual characters by using the `color` attribute to <font>. You also learned that you can add patterned or tiled backgrounds to images by using the `background` attribute to <body> with an image for the tile. Finally, you learned the CSS properties `color`, `background-color`, and `background`, which enable you to specify colors for your page without using deprecated tags.

Workshop

Now that you know how to add images and color to your pages, you can really get creative. This workshop will help you remember some of the most important points about using images and color on your pages so that they'll be compatible with HTML 3.2 and HTML 4.01 browsers. If you want to design your pages strictly around the HTML 4.01 specification, you'll need to forego many of the presentation options you learned in this lesson in favor of style sheets.

Q&A

Q What's the difference between a GIF image and a JPEG image? Is there any rule of thumb that defines when you should use one format rather than the other?

A As a rule, you should use GIF files when images contain 256 colors or fewer. Some good examples are cartoon art, clip art, black-and-white images, and images with many solid color areas. You'll also need to use GIF files if you want your images to contain transparent areas or if you want to create an animation that doesn't require a special plug-in or browser helper. Remember to use your image-editing software to reduce the number of colors in the image palettes whenever possible, because this also reduces the size of the file.

JPEG images are best for photographic-quality or high-resolution 3D rendered graphics because they can display true-color images to great effect. Most image-editing programs enable you to specify how much to compress a JPEG image. The size of the file decreases the more an image is compressed; however, compression can also deteriorate the quality and appearance of the image if you go overboard. You have to find just the right balance between quality and file size, and that can differ from image to image.

Q My client-side imagemaps aren't working. What's wrong?

A Make sure that the pathnames or URLs in your `<area>` tags point to real files. Also, make sure the map name in the `<map>` file matches the name of the map in the `usemap` attribute in the `<img>` tag. Only the latter should have a pound sign in front of it.

Q How can I create thumbnails of my images so that I can link them to larger external images?

A You'll have to do that with some type of image-editing program (such as Adobe Photoshop or Paint Shop Pro); the Web won't do it for you. Just open up the image and scale it down to the right size.

Q What about images that are partially transparent so that they are able to display the page background? They look like they sort of float on the page. How do I create those?

A This is another task you can accomplish with an image-editing program. These types of images are known as *transparent GIFs*, and you can only achieve this effect with a GIF image. Most image-editing programs provide the capability to create these types of images.

Q Can I put HTML tags in the string for the `alt` attribute?

A That would be nice, wouldn't it? Unfortunately, you can't. All you can do is put an ordinary string in there. Keep it simple, and you should be fine.

Quiz

1. What's the most important attribute of the `<img>` tag? What does it do?
2. If you see a funny-looking icon rather than an image when you view your page, the image isn't loading. What are some of the reasons this could happen?
3. Why is it important to use the `alt` attribute to display a text alternative to an image? When is it most important to do so?
4. What is an imagemap?
5. Why is it a good idea to also provide text versions of links that you create on an imagemap?

7

6. True or false: You can use a relative URL when you specify a URL destination in an imagemap file.

Quiz Answers

1. The most important attribute of the `<img>` tag is the `src` attribute. It indicates the filename or URL of the image you want to include on your page.

2. There are several things that cause an image not to load. The URL may be incorrect; the filename might not be correct (they're case sensitive); it might have the wrong file extension; it might be the wrong type of file.

3. It's a good idea to provide text alternatives with images because some people use text-only browsers or have their graphics turned off. It's especially important to provide text alternatives for images used as links.

4. An imagemap is a special image in which different areas point to different locations on the Web.

5. It's a good idea to include text versions of imagemap links in case there are users who visit your page with text-only browsers or with images turned off. This way, they can still follow the links on the web page and visit other areas of your website.

6. False. URLs in a map file must be absolute pathnames from the top of the web root. The URLs cannot be relative from the map file.

Exercises

1. Create or find some images that you can use as navigation icons or buttons on one or more pages of your website. Remember that it's always advantageous to use images more than once. Create a simple navigation bar that you can use on the top or bottom of each page.

2. Create or find some images that you can use to enhance the appearance of your web pages. Images such as small banners (for page titles), bullets, horizontal rules, and background images are always handy to keep around. After you find some that you like, try to create background, text, and link colors that are compatible with them.

3. Create and test a simple client-side imagemap that links to pages that reside in different subdirectories in a website or to other sites on the World Wide Web.

4. Create and test a client-side imagemap for your own home page, or for the entry page in one of the main sections of your website. Remember to include alternatives for those who are using text-only browsers or browsers designed for the disabled.

PART III:
Doing More with HTML and XHTML

LESSON 8:
Building Tables

So far in this book, you've used plain vanilla HTML to build and position the elements on your pages. Although you can get your point across using paragraphs and lists, there's another way to present content on your pages. Using tables, you can lay out page content in rows and columns, with or without borders. And the content you include within your tables isn't restricted to text. Tables provide more control over the appearance of your pages because you can include *any* type of HTML content (images, links, forms, and more).

Tables were officially introduced in HTML 3.2. Since then, they've had an enormous influence on web page design and construction. HTML 4.01 includes changes that improve the way tables are loaded and displayed in browsers. Authors can specify tables that display incrementally or that are more accessible to users who browse the Web with nonvisual browsers. Additional elements create tables with fixed headers and footers that render larger tables across several pages (such as for printouts).

In this Lesson

Today, you'll learn all about tables, including the following:

- Defining tables in HTML
- Creating captions, rows, and heading and data cells
- Modifying cell alignment
- Creating cells that span multiple rows or columns
- Adding color to tables
- Using tables in web documents

Creating Tables

Creating tables in HTML is a degree more complex than anything you've seen so far in this book. Think about how many different types of tables there are. A table can be a 3-by-3 grid with labels across the top, or two side-by-side cells, or a complex Excel spreadsheet that comprises many rows and columns of various sizes. Representing tables in HTML is heavy on tags, and the tags can be hard to keep track of when you get going.

The basic approach with table creation is that you represent tabular data in a linear fashion, specifying what data goes in which table cells using HTML tags. In HTML, tables are created from left to right and top to bottom. You start by creating the upper-left cell, and finish with the bottom-right cell. This will all become clearer when you see some actual table code.

Table Parts

Before getting into the actual HTML code to create a table, let's look at the following terms so that we both know what we're talking about:

- The *caption* indicates what the table is about: for example, "Voting Statistics, 1950–1994," or "Toy Distribution Per Room at 1564 Elm St." Captions are optional.

- The *table headings* label the rows, columns, or both. Usually they're in an emphasized font that's different from the rest of the table. They're optional.

- *Table cells* are the individual squares in the table. A cell can contain normal table data or a table heading.

- *Table data* is the values in the table itself. The combination of the table headings and table data makes up the sum of the table.

Figure 8.1 shows a typical table and its parts.

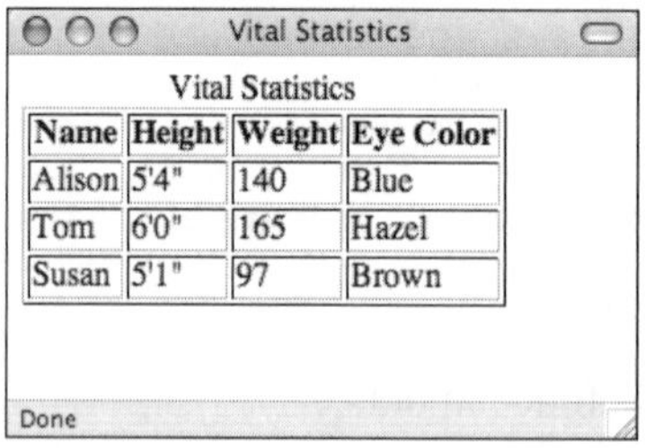

FIGURE 8.1
The elements that make up a table.

Name	Height	Weight	Eye Color
Alison	5'4"	140	Blue
Tom	6'0"	165	Hazel
Susan	5'1"	97	Brown

Vital Statistics

The `<table>` Element

To create a table in HTML, you use the `<table>`...`</table>` element to enclose the code for an optional caption, and then add the contents of the table itself:

```
<table>
...table caption (optional) and contents...
</table>
```

To demonstrate what the HTML code for a complete table looks like, here's an example of the code that created the table shown in Figure 8.1. Don't be concerned if you don't know what this all means right now. For now, notice that the table starts with a `<table>` tag and its attributes, and ends with a `</table>` tag:

```
<table border="1">
<caption>Vital Statistics</caption>
 <tr>
  <th>Name</th>
  <th>Height</th>
  <th>Weight</th>
  <th>Eye Color</th>
 </tr>
 <tr>
  <td>Alison</td>
  <td>5'4"</td>
  <td>140</td>
  <td>Blue</td>
 </tr>
 <tr>
  <td>Tom</td>
  <td>6'0"</td>
  <td>165</td>
  <td>Hazel</td>
 </tr>
 <tr>
  <td>Susan</td>
  <td>5'1"</td>
  <td>97</td>
  <td>Brown</td>
 </tr>
</table>
```

The Table Summary

If you want to play by the rules of XHTML, every time you create a table, the `<table>` element must include the `summary` attribute. The value of the summary should be a short description of the table's contents. This value isn't used by normal visual browsers; instead, it's intended for screen readers and other browsers created for users with disabilities. For example, the `<table>` tag in the previous example should include a `summary` attribute like this:

```
<table summary="vital statistics">
```

For your pages to play by the XHTML rules, you must include the summary attribute for all of your tables (just as you must include `alt` text for all of your images). You'll learn more about why accessibility features are important in Lesson 17, "Designing for the Real World."

Rows and Cells

Now that you've been introduced to the `<table>` element, we'll move on to the rows and cells. Inside the `<table>...</table>` element, you define the actual contents of the table. Tables are specified in HTML row by row, and each row definition contains definitions for all the cells in that row. So, to define a table, you start by defining a top row and each cell in turn, left to right. Then you define a second row and its cells, and so on. The number of columns is automatically calculated based on how many cells there are in each row.

Each table row starts with the `<tr>` tag and ends with the closing `</tr>`. Your table can have as many rows and columns as you like, but you should make sure that each row has the same number of cells so that the columns line up.

The cells within each row are created using one of two elements:

- `<th>...</th>` elements are used for heading cells. Generally, browsers center the contents of a `<th>` cell and render any text in the cell in boldface.
- `<td>...</td>` elements are used for data cells. td stands for *table data*.

NOTE

You might have heard somewhere that closing tags are not required for `<th>`, `<td>`, and `<tr>` tags. You might even see HTML that's written without them. However, XHTML requires that you include them, and including them makes your code much easier to follow. Don't leave them out.

In this table example, the heading cells appear in the top row and are defined with the following code:

```
<tr>
 <th>Name</th>
 <th>Height</th>
 <th>Weight</th>
 <th>Eye Color</th>
</tr>
```

The top row is followed by three rows of data cells, which are coded as follows:

```
<tr>
 <td>Alison</td>
 <td>5'4"</td>
 <td>140</td>
 <td>Blue</td>
</tr>
<tr>
 <td>Tom</td>
 <td>6'0"</td>
 <td>165</td>
 <td>Blue</td>
</tr>
<tr>
 <td>Susan</td>
 <td>5'1"</td>
 <td>97</td>
 <td>Brown</td>
</tr>
```

As you've seen, you can place the headings along the top edge by defining the <th> elements inside the first row. Let's make a slight modification to the table. You'll put the headings along the left edge of the table instead. To accomplish this, put each <th> in the first cell in each row and follow it with the data that pertains to each heading. The new code looks like the following:

Input ▼

```
<tr>
 <th>Name</th>
 <td>Alison</td>
 <td>Tom</td>
 <td>Susan</td>
</tr>
<tr>
 <th>Height</th>
 <td>5'4"</td>
 <td>6'0"</td>
 <td>5'1"</td>
```

```
</tr>
<tr>
 <th>Weight</th>
 <td>140</td>
 <td>165</td>
 <td>97</td>
</tr>
<tr>
 <th>Eye Color</th>
 <td>Blue</td>
 <td>Blue</td>
 <td>Brown</td>
</tr>
```

Figure 8.2 shows how this table is displayed in a browser.

Output ▼

FIGURE 8.2

An example of a table that includes headings in the leftmost column.

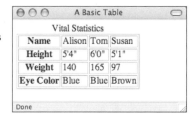

Empty Cells

Both table heading cells and data cells can contain any text, HTML code, or both, including links, lists, forms, images, and other tables. But what if you want a cell with nothing in it? That's easy. Just define a cell with a `<th>` or `<td>` element with nothing inside it:

Input ▼

```
<table border="1">
<tr>
  <td></td>
  <td>10</td>
  <td>20</td>
</tr>
</table>
```

Some browsers display empty cells of this sort as if they don't exist at all. If you want to force a *truly* empty cell, you can add a line break with no other text in that cell by itself:

Input ▼

```
<table border="1">
<tr>
```

```
  <td><br /></td>
  <td>10</td>
  <td>20</td>
</tr>
</table>
```

Figure 8.3 shows examples of both types of empty cells: the empty cell and the really empty cell with the line break added.

Output ▼

FIGURE 8.3
The difference between empty cells and really empty cells.

An empty cell

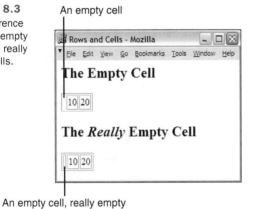

An empty cell, really empty

Captions

Table captions tell your visitor what the table is for. The <caption> element, created just for this purpose, displays the text inside the tag as the table caption (usually centered above the table). Although you could use a regular paragraph or a heading as a caption for your table, tools that process HTML files can extract <caption> elements into a separate file, automatically number them, or treat them in special ways simply because they're captions.

If you don't want a caption, it's optional. If you just want a table and don't care about a label, leave the caption off.

The <caption> element goes inside the <table> element just before the table rows, and it contains the title of the table. It closes with the </caption> tag:

```
<table>
<caption>Vital Statistics</caption>
<tr>
```

▼ Task: Exercise 8.1: Creating a Simple Table

Now that you know the basics of how to create a table, try a simple example. You'll create a table that indicates the colors you get when you mix the three primary colors together. Figure 8.4 shows the table you're going to re-create in this example.

FIGURE 8.4
A simple color table.

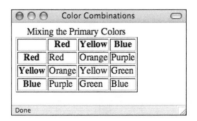

Here's a quick hint for laying out tables: Because HTML defines tables on a row-by-row basis, sometimes it can be difficult to keep track of the columns, particularly with very complex tables. Before you start actually writing HTML code, it's useful to make a sketch of your table so that you know the heads and the values of each cell. You might find that it's easiest to use a word processor with a table editor (such as Microsoft Word) or a spreadsheet to lay out your tables. Then, when you have the layout and the cell values, you can write the HTML code for that table. Eventually, if you do this enough, you'll think of these things in terms of HTML tags, whether you want to or not.

Start with a simple HTML framework for a page that contains a table. Like all HTML files, you can create this file in any text editor:

```
<html>
<head>
<title>Colors</title>
</head>
<body>
<table>
...add table rows and cells here...
</table>
</body>
</html>
```

Now start adding table rows inside the opening and closing `<table>` tags (where the line add table rows and cells here is). The first row is the three headings along the top of the table. The table row is indicated by `<tr>` and each cell by a `<th>` tag:

```
<tr>
  <th>Red</th>
  <th>Yellow</th>
  <th>Blue</th>
</tr>
```

> **NOTE**
> You can format the HTML code any way you want. As with all HTML, the browser ignores most extra spaces and returns. I like to format it like this, with the contents of the individual rows indented and the cell elements on separate lines, so that I can pick out the rows and columns more easily.

Now add the second row. The first cell in the second row is the Red heading on the left side of the table, so it will be the first cell in this row, followed by the cells for the table data:

```
<tr>
  <th>Red</th>
  <td>Red</td>
  <td>Orange</td>
  <td>Purple</td>
</tr>
```

Continue by adding the remaining two rows in the table, with the Yellow and Blue headings. Here's what you have so far for the entire table:

Input ▼

```
<table border="1" summary="color combinations">
<tr>
  <th>Red</th>
  <th>Yellow</th>
  <th>Blue</th>
</tr>
<tr>
  <th>Red</th>
  <td>Red</td>
  <td>Orange</td>
  <td>Purple</td>
</tr>
<tr>
  <th>Yellow</th>
  <td>Orange</td>
  <td>Yellow</td>
  <td>Green</td>
</tr>
<tr>
  <th>Blue</th>
  <td>Purple</td>
  <td>Green</td>
  <td>Blue</td>
</tr>
</tr>
</table>
```

▼ Finally, add a simple caption. The `<caption>` element goes just after the `<table>` tag and just before the first `<tr>` tag:

```
<table border="1">
<caption>Mixing the Primary Colors</caption>
<tr>
```

With a first draft of the code in place, test the HTML file in your favorite browser that supports tables. Figure 8.5 shows how it looks.

Output ▼

FIGURE 8.5
The not-quite-perfect color table.

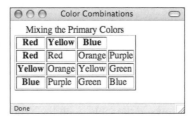

Oops! What happened with that top row? The headings are all messed up. The answer, of course, is that you need an empty cell at the beginning of that first row to space the headings out over the proper columns. HTML isn't smart enough to match it all up for you. (This is exactly the sort of error you're going to find the first time you test your tables.)

Add an empty table heading cell to that first row (here, it's the line `<th><br /></th>`):

Input ▼

```
<tr>

  <th><br /></th>
  <th>Red</th>
  <th>Yellow</th>
  <th>Blue</th>
</tr>
```

> **NOTE**
>
> I used `<th>` here, but it could be `<td>` just as easily. Because there's nothing in the cell, its formatting doesn't matter.

If you try it again, you should get the right result with all the headings over the right columns, as the original example in Figure 8.4 shows.

8

Sizing Tables, Borders, and Cells

With the basics out of the way, now you'll look at some of the attributes that can change the overall appearance of your tables. The attributes you'll learn about in this section control the width of your tables and cells, the amount of spacing between cell content and rows and columns, and the width of the borders.

Setting Table Widths

The table in the preceding example relied on the browser itself to decide how wide the table and column widths were going to be. In many cases, this is the best way to make sure that your tables are viewable on different browsers with different screen sizes and widths. Simply let the browser decide.

In other cases, however, you might want more control over how wide your tables and columns are, particularly if the defaults the browser comes up with are really strange. In this section, you'll learn a couple of ways to do just this.

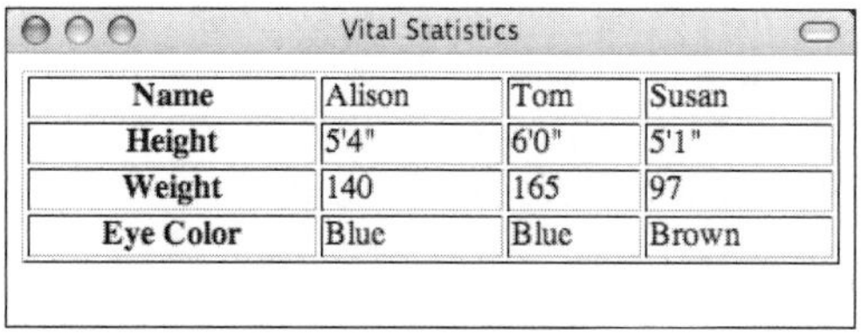

The width attribute of the <table> element defines how wide the table will be on the page. width can have a value that is either the exact width of the table (in pixels) or a percentage (such as 50% or 75%) of the current browser width, which can therefore change if the window is resized. If width is specified, the width of the columns within the table can be compressed or expanded to fit the required width.

To make a table as wide as the browser window, you add the width attribute to the table, as shown in the following line of code:

Input ▼

```
<table border="1" width="100%">
```

The result is shown in Figure 8.6.

Output ▼

FIGURE 8.6
A table set to 100% width.

Name	Alison	Tom	Susan
Height	5'4"	6'0"	5'1"
Weight	140	165	97
Eye Color	Blue	Blue	Brown

Vital Statistics

NOTE

If you make your table too narrow for whatever you put in it, the browser ignores your settings and makes the table as wide as it needs to be to display the content.

It's nearly always a better idea to specify your table widths as percentages rather than as specific pixel widths. Because you don't know how wide the browser window will be, using percentages allows your table to be reformatted to whatever width the browser is. Using specific pixel widths might cause your table to run off the page. Also, if you make your tables too wide using a pixel width, your pages might not print properly.

NOTE	Specifying column widths in percentages is illegal under the XHTML 1.0 Strict specification. If you want to specify your column widths in that manner, use Transitional DTD or specify the widths in a style sheet. I'll discuss using style sheets in this manner further along in this lesson.

Changing Table Borders

The `border` attribute, which appears immediately inside the opening `<table>` tag, is the most common attribute of the `<table>` element. With it, you specify whether border lines are displayed around the table and if so, how wide the borders should be.

The `border` attribute has undergone some changes since it first appeared in HTML:

- In HTML 2.0, you used `<table border>` to draw a border around the table. The border could be rendered as fancy in a graphical browser or just a series of dashes and pipes (¦) in a text-based browser.

- Starting with HTML 3.2 and later, the correct usage of the `border` attribute is a little different: It indicates the width of a border in pixels. `<table border="1">` creates a 1-pixel wide border, `<table border="2">` a 2-pixel wide border, and so on. HTML 3.2 and later browsers are expected to display the old HTML 2.0 form of `<table border>`, with no value, with a two-pixel border (as if you specified `<table border="1">`).

- To create a border that has no width and isn't displayed, you specify `<table border="0">`. Borderless tables are useful when you want to use the table structure for layout purposes, but you don't necessarily want the outline of an actual table on the page. Browsers that support HTML 3.2 and higher are expected not to display a border (the same as `<table border="0">`) if you leave out the `border` attribute entirely.

You can change the width of the border drawn around the table. If `border` has a numeric value, the border around the outside of the table is drawn with that pixel width. The default is `border="1"`. `border="0"` suppresses the border, just as if you had omitted the `border` attribute altogether.

Figure 8.7 shows a table that has a border width of 10 pixels. The table and border definition looks like this:

Input ▼

```
<table border="10" width="100%">
```

Output ▼

FIGURE 8.7
A table with the border width set to 10 pixels.

Figure 8.7 shows a table that has a border width of 10 pixels.

Name	Alison	Tom	Susan
Height	5'4"	6'0"	5'1"
Weight	140	165	97
Eye Color	Blue	Blue	Brown

You can also adjust the borders around your tables using CSS, with much finer control than the border attribute provides. Use of the CSS properties associated with borders isn't limited to tables, so I'm going to wait until Lesson 9, "Creating Layouts with CSS," to discuss them.

Cell Padding

The cell padding attribute defines the amount of space between the edges of the cells and the content inside a cell. By default, many browsers draw tables with a cell padding of two pixels. You can add more space by adding the cellpadding attribute to the <table> element, with a value in pixels for the amount of cell padding you want.

Here's the revised code for your <table> element, which increases the cell padding to 10 pixels. The result is shown in Figure 8.8:

Input ▼

```
<table cellpadding="10" border="1">
```

Output ▼

FIGURE 8.8
A table with the cell padding set to 10 pixels.

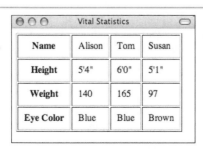

Name	Alison	Tom	Susan
Height	5'4"	6'0"	5'1"
Weight	140	165	97
Eye Color	Blue	Blue	Brown

A `cellpadding` attribute with a value of 0 causes the edges of the cells to touch the edges of the cell's contents. This doesn't look good when you're presenting text, but it can be useful in other situations.

Cell Spacing

Cell spacing is similar to cell padding except that it affects the amount of space between cells—that is, the width of the space between the inner and outer lines that make up the table border. The `cellspacing` attribute of the `<table>` element affects the spacing for the table. Cell spacing is two pixels by default.

Cell spacing also includes the outline around the table, which is just inside the table's border (as set by the `border` attribute). Experiment with it, and you can see the difference. For example, Figure 8.9 shows our table with cell spacing of 8 and a border of 4, as shown in the following code:

Input ▼

```
<table cellpadding="10" border="4" cellspacing="8">
```

Output ▼

FIGURE 8.9
How increased cell
spacing looks.

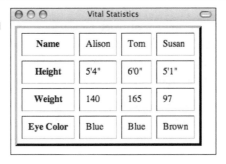

NOTE	If you want to completely eliminate any whitespace separating content in table cells, you must set the table's border, cell padding, and cell spacing to 0. Laying out your tables this way is unusual, but it can be useful if you've sliced up an image and you want to reassemble it properly on a web page.

Column Widths

You also can apply the `width` attribute to individual cells (`<th>` or `<td>`) to indicate the width of columns in a table. As with table widths, discussed earlier, you can make the `width` attribute in cells an exact pixel width or a percentage (which is taken as a percentage of the full table width). As with table widths, using percentages rather than specific pixel widths is a better idea because it allows your table to be displayed regardless of the window size.

Column widths are useful when you want to have multiple columns of identical widths, regardless of their contents (for example, for some forms of page layout).

8

Figure 8.10 shows your original table from Figure 8.1. This time, however, the table spans 100% of the screen's width. The first column is 40% of the table width and the remaining three columns are 20% each.

To accomplish this, the column widths are applied to the heading cells as follows:

Input ▼

```
<table border="1" width="100%">
<caption>Vital Statistics</caption>
<tr>
  <th width="40%">Name</th>
  <th width="20%">Height</th>
  <th width="20%">Weight</th>
  <th width="20%">Eye Color</th>
 </tr>
</table>
```

Output ▼

FIGURE 8.10
A table with manually set column widths.

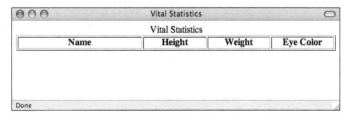

What happens if you have a table that spans 80% of the screen, and it includes the same header cells (40%, 20%, 20%, and 20%) as in the preceding example? Revise the code slightly, changing the width of the entire table to 80%, as shown in Figure 8.11. When you open the new table in your browser, you'll see that the table now spans 80% of the width of your screen. The four columns still span 40%, 20%, 20%, and 20% of the *table*. To be more specific, the columns span 32%, 16%, 16%, and 16% of the entire screen width:

Input ▼

```
<table border="1" width="80%">
<caption>Vital Statistics</caption>
<tr>
```

```
  <th width="40%">Name</th>
  <th width="20%">Height</th>
  <th width="20%">Weight</th>
  <th width="20%">Eye Color</th>
 </tr>
</table>
```

Output ▼

FIGURE 8.11
A modified table
with manually set
column widths.

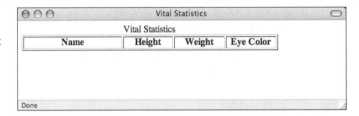

If you are going to specify cell widths, you should make sure to either specify the widths
for cells only on one row or to the same values for every row. If you specify more than
one value for the width of a column (by specifying different values on multiple rows of a
table), there's no good way to predict which one the browser will use.

Setting Breaks in Text

Often, the easiest way to make small changes to how a table is laid out is by using line
breaks (
 elements). Line breaks are particularly useful if you have a table in
which most of the cells are small and only one or two cells have longer data. As long
as the screen width can handle it, generally the browser just creates really long rows.
This looks rather funny in some tables. For example, the last row in the table shown in
Figure 8.12 is coded as follows:

Input ▼

```
<tr>
  <td>TC</td>
  <td>7</td>
  <td>Suspicious except when hungry, then friendly</td>
 </tr>
```

Output ▼

FIGURE 8.12
A table with one
long row.

Name	Age	Behavior
Whiskers	2	Friendly
Sam	3	Skittish
TC	7	Suspicious except when hungry, then friendly

By putting in line breaks, you can wrap that row in a shorter column so that it looks more like the table shown in Figure 8.13. The following shows how the revised code looks for the last row:

Input ▼

```
<tr>
  <td>TC</td>
  <td>7</td>
  <td>Suspicious except<br />
    when hungry, <br />
    then friendly</td>
 </tr>
```

Output ▼

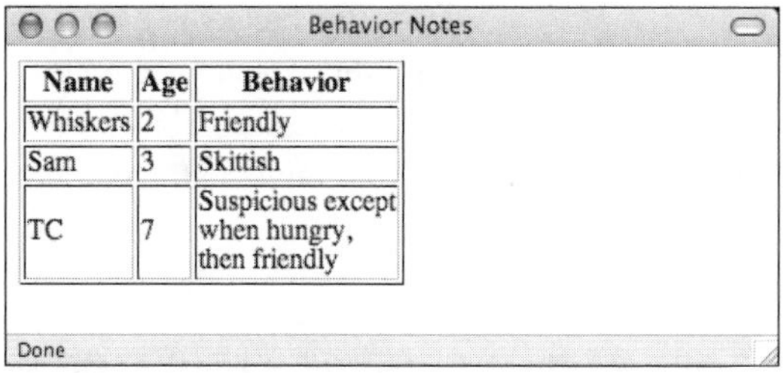

FIGURE 8.13
The long row fixed
with <br/>.

On the other hand, you might have a table in which a cell is being wrapped and you want all the data on one line. (This can be particularly important for things such as form elements within table cells, where you want the label and the input field to stay together.) In this instance, you can add the nowrap attribute to the <th> or <td> elements, and the browser keeps all the data in that cell on one line. Note that you can always add <br /> elements to that same cell by hand and get line breaks exactly where you want them.

Let's say you have a table where the column headings are wider than the data in the columns. If you want to keep them all online, use nowrap as follows:

```
<table width="50%" summary="Best Hitters of All Time">
  <tr>
    <th>Player Name</th>
    <th nowrap="nowrap">Batting Average</th>
    <th nowrap="nowrap">Home Runs</th>
    <th>RBI</th>
  </tr>
  <tr>
    <td>Babe Ruth</td>
    <td>.342</td>
    <td>714</td>
    <td>2217</td>
  </tr>
  <tr>
```

```
      <td>Ted Williams</td>
      <td>.344</td>
      <td>521</td>
      <td>1839</td>
   </tr>
</table>
```

Regardless of the width of the table, the "Batting Average" and "Home Runs" column headings will not wrap.

NOTE

> The nowrap attribute has been deprecated in HTML 4.01 in favor of using style sheet properties.

Be careful when you hard-code table cells with line breaks and nowrap attributes. Remember, your table might be viewed by users with many different screen widths. Try resizing the browser window to make sure your table still looks correct. For the most part, you should try to let the browser format your table and make minor adjustments only when necessary.

Table and Cell Color and Alignment

After you have your basic table layout with rows, headings, and data, you can start refining how that table looks. You can refine tables in a couple of ways. One way is to add color to borders and cells.

Changing Table and Cell Background Colors

There are two ways to change the background color of a table, a row, or a cell inside a row. In the pre-CSS world, you would use the bgcolor attribute of the <table>, <tr>, <th>, or <td> elements. Just as in the <body> tag, the value of bgcolor is a color specified as a hexadecimal triplet or, one of the 16 color names: Black, White, Green, Maroon, Olive, Navy, Purple, Gray, Red, Yellow, Blue, Teal, Lime, Aqua, Fuchsia, or Silver. In the style sheet world, you use the background-color property. You can use the style attribute in the <table>, <tr>, <th>, and <td> elements, just as you can in most other elements. Each background color overrides the background color of its enclosing element. For example, a table background overrides the page background, a row background overrides the table's, and any cell colors override all other colors. If you nest tables inside cells, that nested table has the background color of the cell that encloses it.

Also, if you change the color of a cell, don't forget to change the color of the text inside it so that you can still read it. If you want your pages to be compatible with antiquated browsers, use <font color...>. For browsers that support Cascading Style Sheets, use the CSS color property.

NOTE
> For table cells to show up with background colors, they must not be empty. Simply putting a `<br />` element in empty cells works fine.

Here's an example of changing the background and cell colors in a table. I've created a checkerboard using an HTML table. The table itself is white, with alternating cells in black. The checkers (here, red and black circles) are images. In the source code, I've used both bgcolor and the background-color property to set background colors for some of the cells. As you'll see in the screenshot, the appearance of both is the same when rendered in the browser.

White Space and Tables

Speaking of using images in tables, generally it doesn't matter in the final output where white space appears in your original HTML code. In Netscape, however, there's one exception to the rule, and it applies when you're placing images in table cells. Suppose that you've formatted your code with the `<img>` tag on a separate line, like the following:

```
<td>
  <img src="check.gif">
</td>
```

With this code, the return between the `<td>` tag and the `<img>` tag is significant—your image won't be placed properly within the cell (this shows up in centered cells particularly). To correct the problem, just put the `</td>` and the `<img>` on the same line like this:

```
<td><img src="check.gif"></td>
```

I've applied the rule mentioned in the "White Space and Tables" sidebar in the following example:

Input ▼

```
<html>
<head>
<title>Checkerboard</title>
</head>
<body>
<table bgcolor="#FFFFFF" width="50%" summary="checkerboard">
  <tr align="center">
    <td bgcolor="#000000" width="33%"><img src="redcircle.gif" /></td>
    <td width="33%"><img src="redcircle.gif" alt="" /></td>
    <td bgcolor="#000000" width="33%"><img src="redcircle.gif" /></td>
  </tr>
```

```
<tr align="center">
  <td><img src="blackcircle.gif" alt="" /></td>
  <td style="background-color: #000000"><br /></td>
  <td><img src="blackcircle.gif" alt="" /></td>
</tr>

<tr align="center">
  <td bgcolor="#000000"><br /></td>
  <td><img src="blackcircle.gif" alt="" /></td>
  <td bgcolor="#000000"><br /></td>
</tr>
</table>
</body>
</html>
```

The result is shown in Figure 8.14.

Output ▼

FIGURE 8.14
Table cell colors.

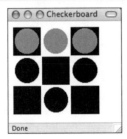

Changing Border Colors

Internet Explorer also enables you to change the colors of the table's border elements by using the bordercolor, bordercolorlight, and bordercolordark attributes. Each of these attributes takes either a color number or name and can be used in <table>, <td>, or <th>. Like background colors, the border colors each override the colors of the enclosing element. All three require the enclosing <table> tag to have the border attribute set.

Currently, these extensions are only supported in Internet Explorer, with the exception of bordercolor, which is supported in Netscape. All of these have been deprecated in favor of style sheets.

- bordercolor sets the color of the border, overriding the 3D look of the default border.
- bordercolordark sets the dark component of 3D-look borders and places the dark color on the right and bottom sides of the table border.
- bordercolorlight sets the light component of 3D-look borders and places the light color on the left and top sides of the table border.

Figure 8.15 shows an example of the table with a border of 10 pixels. To demonstrate the Internet Explorer attributes, `bordercolordark` and `bordercolorlight` have been added to give the thicker border a 3D look. The first line of the code has been changed as follows:

```
<table border="10" bordercolorlight="Red" bordercolordark="Black"
bgcolor="#ffffff" width="50%">
```

This line of code is getting a little long, isn't it? You might find it easier to read if you put each attribute on a separate line, as the following example shows. It still works the same. Just remember that the closing bracket (>) must appear only after the final attribute:

Input ▼

```
<table border="10"
  bordercolorlight="Red"
  bordercolordark="Black"
  bgcolor="#ffffff"
  width="50%">
```

> **NOTE**
>
> I've included these attributes in the book for completeness—you might see them in other people's code that you happen across sometime. I strongly urge you to avoid these vendor-specific browser extensions yourself and go down the CSS road instead. In Lesson 9, I'm going to discuss the plethora of borders you can create using CSS. After seeing them, you'll never want to use these attributes again.

Output ▼

FIGURE 8.15
Table border colors.

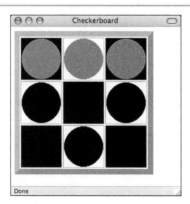

Aligning Your Table Content

Another enhancement that you can make to your tables is to adjust the alignment of their content. The `align` attribute aligns content horizontally, whereas the `valign` attribute aligns content vertically. The following sections describe how to use these attributes in tables.

DO	DON'T
DO test your tables with various sizes of browser windows to make sure they look OK. **DO** increase the `cellpadding` in your tables to make them more readable.	**DON'T** use tables just to put borders around elements on a page; use CSS. **DON'T** use tables just to apply a background color to an element; use CSS instead. **DON'T** use tables format non-tabular data if you can help it.

Table Alignment

By default, tables are displayed on a line by themselves along the left side of the page, with any text above or below the table. However, you can use the `align` attribute to align tables along the left or right margins and wrap text alongside them the same way you can with images.

`align="left"` aligns the table along the left margin, and all text following that table is wrapped in the space between that table and the right side of the page. `align="right"` does the same thing, with the table aligned to the right side of the page.

In the example shown in Figure 8.16, a table that spans 70% of the width of the page is aligned to the left with the following code:

```
<table border="1" align="left" width="70%">
```

As you can see from the screenshot, one problem with wrapping text around tables is that HTML has no provision for creating margins that keep the text and the image from jamming right up next to each other. When I discuss CSS in more detail in the next lesson, you'll see that there's a way around these problems. 

FIGURE 8.16

A table with text alongside it.

As with images, you can use the line break element with the `clear` attribute to stop wrapping text alongside an image. Centering tables is slightly more difficult. Recent browsers support the `align="center"` attribute in `table` tags. To ensure backward-compatibility with older browsers, you can use the `<center>` or `<div align="center">` elements (both of which you learned about in Lesson 6, "Formatting Text with HTML and CSS") to center tables on the page. As with other formatting attributes, however, the `align` attribute (in the `<table>` tag as well as in `<div>` and `<p>`) has been deprecated in HTML 4.01 in favor of style sheets.

Cell Alignment

After you have your rows and cells in place inside your table and the table is properly aligned on the page, you can align the data within each cell for the best effect, based on what your table contains. Several options enable you to align the data within your cells both horizontally and vertically. Figure 8.17 shows a table (a real HTML one!) of the various alignment options.

FIGURE 8.17
Aligned content within cells.

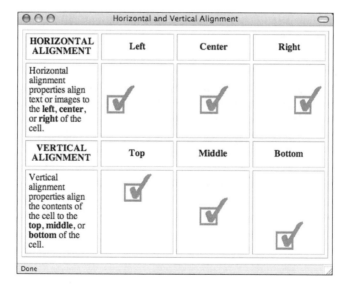

Horizontal alignment (the `align` attribute) defines whether the data within a cell is aligned with the left cell margin (`left`), the right cell margin (`right`), or centered within the two (`center`). The one place where the `align` attribute hasn't been deprecated for XHTML 1.0 is the `<td>` and `<th>` tags. It's perfectly okay to use it within your tables.

Vertical alignment (the `valign` attribute) defines the vertical alignment of the data within the cell: flush with the top of the cell (`top`), flush with the bottom of the cell (`bottom`), or vertically centered within the cell (`middle`). Newer browsers also implement `valign="baseline"`, which is similar to `valign="top"` except that it aligns the baseline of the first line of text in each cell. (Depending on the contents of the cell, this might or might not produce a different result than `align="top"`.)

By default, heading cells are centered both horizontally and vertically, and data cells are centered vertically but aligned flush left.

You can override the defaults for an entire row by adding the `align` or `valign` attributes to the `<tr>` element, as in the following:

```
<tr align="center" valign="top">
```

You can override the row alignment for individual cells by adding `align` to the `<td>` or `<th>` elements:

```
<tr align="center" valign="top">
  <td>14</td>
  <td>16</td>
  <td align=left>No Data</td>
  <td>15</td>
</tr>
```

The following input and output example shows the various cell alignments and how they look (see Figure 8.18):

Input ▼

```
<!DOCTYPE html PUBLIC "-//W3C//DTD XHTML 1.0 Transitional//EN"
  "http://www.w3.org/TR/xhtml1/DTD/xhtml1-transitional.dtd">
<html xmlns="http://www.w3.org/1999/xhtml">
<head>
<title>Cell Alignments</title>
</head>
<body>
<table border="1" cellpadding="8">
  <tr>
    <th> </th>
    <th>Left</th>
    <th>Centered</th>
    <th>Right</th>
  </tr>

  <tr>
    <th>Top</th>
    <td align="left" valign="top"><img src="button.gif" alt="" /></td>
    <td align="center" valign="top"><img src="button.gif" alt="" /></td>
    <td align="top" valign="top"><img src="button.gif" alt="" /></td>
  </tr>

  <tr>
    <th>Centered</th>
    <td align="left" valign="middle"><img src="button.gif" alt="" /></td>
    <td align="center" valign="middle"><img src="button.gif"
        alt="" /></td>
```

```
    <td align="right" valign="middle"><img src="button.gif"
        alt="" /></td>
  </tr>

  <tr>
    <th>Bottom</th>
    <td align="left" valign="bottom"><img src="button.gif" alt="" /></td>
    <td align="center" valign="bottom"><img src="button.gif"
        alt="" /></td>
    <td align="right" valign="bottom"><img src="button.gif"
        alt="" /></td>
  </tr>
</table>
</body>
</html>
```

Output ▼

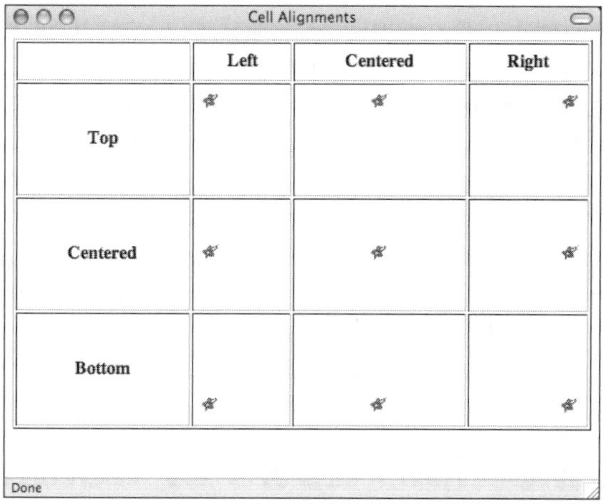

FIGURE 8.18
A matrix of cell alignment settings.

Caption Alignment

The optional align attribute of the <caption> tag determines the alignment of the caption. Depending on which browser you're using, however, you have different choices for what align means.

The HTML 4 specification names four values for the align attribute of the <caption> tag, top, bottom, left, and right. By default, the caption is placed at the top of the table (align="top"). You can use the align="bottom" attribute to the caption if you want to put the caption at the bottom of the table, like the following:

```
<table>
<caption align="bottom">Torque Limits for Various Fruits</caption>
```

Similarly, left places the caption to the left of the table, and right places it to the right.

In Internet Explorer, however, captions are handled slightly differently. The `top` and `bottom` values are treated in the standard fashion, but left and right are handled differently. Rather than placing the caption to the side of the table specified, they align the caption horizontally on the top or bottom of the table, and the placement of the caption is then left to the non-standard `valign` attribute. So, in Internet Explorer you could place a caption at the bottom of the table, aligned with the right edge like this:

```
<table>
<caption valign="bottom" align="right">Torque Limits for
    Various Fruits</caption>
```

To create the same effect in all current browsers, you can use a combination of HTML and CSS. To place the caption at the bottom right of the table, you would use the `align` attribute and `text-align` property as follows:

```
<caption align="bottom" style="text-align: right">This is a caption</caption>
```

In general, unless you have a very short table, you should leave the caption in its default position—centered at the top of the table. That way your visitors will see the caption first and know what they're about to read, instead of seeing it after they're already done reading the table (at which point they've usually figured out what it's about anyway).

TIP

> If your table contains an image, you might prefer putting the caption at the bottom. This will be more familiar to people who are used to print media.

Spanning Multiple Rows or Columns

The tables you've created up to this point all had one value per cell or the occasional empty cell. You also can create cells that span multiple rows or columns within the table. Those spanned cells then can hold headings that have subheadings in the next row or column or you can create other special effects within the table layout. Figure 8.19 shows a table with spanned columns and rows.

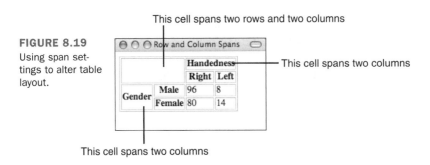

FIGURE 8.19
Using span settings to alter table layout.

This cell spans two rows and two columns

This cell spans two columns

This cell spans two columns

To create a cell that spans multiple rows or columns, you add the `rowspan` or `colspan` attribute to the `<th>` or `<td>` elements, along with the number of rows or columns you want the cell to span. The data within that cell then fills the entire width or length of the combined cells, as in the following example:

Input ▼

```
<html>
<head>
<title>Row and Column Spans</title>
</head>
<body>
<table border="1" summary="span example">
  <tr>
    <th colspan="2">Gender</th>
  </tr>

  <tr>
    <th>Male</th>
    <th>Female</th>
  </tr>

  <tr>
    <td>15</td>
    <td>23</td>
  </tr>
</table>
</body>
</html>
```

Figure 8.20 shows how this table might appear when displayed.

Output ▼

FIGURE 8.20
Using span settings to widen a column.

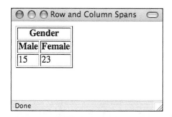

Note that if a cell spans multiple rows, you don't have to redefine it as empty in the next row or rows. Just ignore it and move to the next cell in the row. The span fills in the spot for you.

Cells always span downward and to the right. To create a cell that spans several columns, you add the `colspan` attribute to the leftmost cell in the span. For cells that span rows, you add `rowspan` to the topmost cell.

The following input and output example shows a cell that spans multiple rows (the cell with the word "Piston" in it). Figure 8.21 shows the result.

Input ▼

```
<html>
<head>
<title>Ring Clearance</title>
</head>
<body>
<table border="1" summary="ring clearance">
  <tr>
    <th colspan="2"> </th>
    <th>Ring<br />
        Clearance</th>
  </tr>

  <tr align="center">
    <th rowspan="2">Piston</th>
    <th>Upper</th>
    <td>3mm</td>
  </tr>

  <tr align="center">
    <th>Lower</th>
    <td>3.2mm</td>
  </tr>
</table>
</body>
</html>
```

Output ▼

FIGURE 8.21
Cells that span multiple rows and columns.

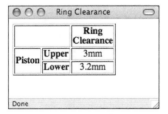

▼ Task: Exercise 8.2: A Table of Service Specifications

Had enough of tables yet? Let's do another example that takes advantage of everything you've learned here: tables that use colors, headings, normal cells, alignments, and column and row spans. This is a very complex table, so we'll go step-by-step, row by row, to build it.

Figure 8.22 shows the table, which indicates service and adjustment specifications from the service manual for a car.

Drive Belt Deflection

		Used Belt Deflection		Set deflection of new belt
		Limit	Adjust Deflection	
Alternator	Models without AC	10mm	5-7mm	5-7mm
	Models with AC	12mm	6-8mm	
Power Steering Oil Pump		12.5mm	7.9mm	6-8mm

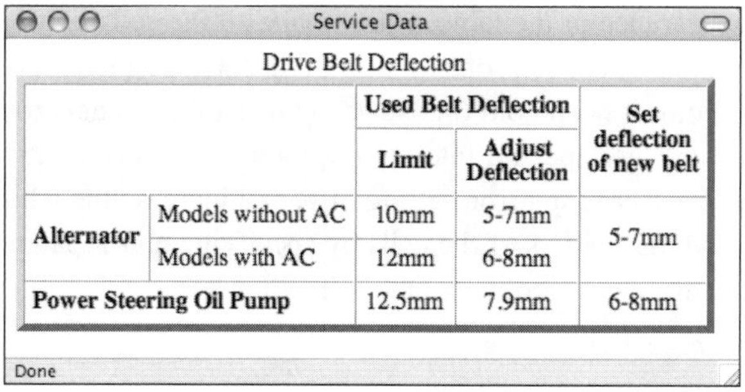

FIGURE 8.22
The really complex service specification table.

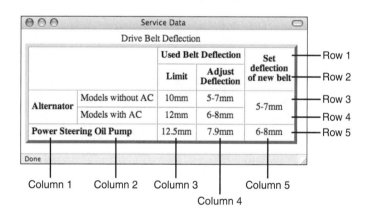

There are actually five rows and columns in this table. Do you see them? Some of them span columns and rows. Figure 8.23 shows the same table with a grid drawn over it so that you can see where the rows and columns are.

With tables such as this one that use many spans, it's helpful to draw this sort of grid to figure out where the spans are and in which row they belong. Remember, spans start at the topmost row and the leftmost column.

Drive Belt Deflection

		Used Belt Deflection		Set deflection of new belt
		Limit	Adjust Deflection	
Alternator	Models without AC	10mm	5-7mm	5-7mm
	Models with AC	12mm	6-8mm	
Power Steering Oil Pump		12.5mm	7.9mm	6-8mm

FIGURE 8.23
Five columns, five rows.

Ready? Start with the framework, just as you have for the other tables today:

```
<html>
<head>
<title>Service Data</title>
</head>
<body>
<table border="1" summary="drive belt deflection">
<caption>Drive Belt Deflection</caption>
</table>
</body>
</html>
```

▼ To enhance the appearance of the table, you'll make all the cells light yellow (#ffffcc) by using the background-color property. The border will be increased in size to 5 pixels, and you'll color it deep gold (#cc9900) by using the bordercolor attribute that's compatible with both Netscape and Internet Explorer. You'll make the rules between cells appear solid by using a cellspacing setting of 0, and increase the white space between the cell contents and the borders of the cells by specifying a cellpadding setting of 5. The new table definition now looks like the following:

```
<table summary="drive belt deflection">
  border="5"
  style="background-color: #ffffcc"
  bordercolor="#cc9900"

  cellpadding="5">
```

Now create the first row. With the grid on your picture, you can see that the first cell is empty and spans two rows and two columns (see Figure 8.24). Therefore, the HTML for that cell would be as follows:

```
<tr>
<th rowspan="2" colspan="2"></th>
```

This first cell spans two
columns and two rows

FIGURE 8.24
The first cell.

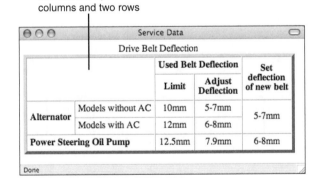

The second cell in the row is the Used Belt Deflection heading cell, which spans two columns (for the two cells beneath it). The code for that cell is as follows:

```
<th colspan="2">Used Belt Deflection</th>
```

Now that you have two cells that span two columns each, there's only one left in this row. However, this one, like the first one, spans the row beneath it:

```
<th rowspan="2">Set deflection of new belt</th>
```
▼ `</tr>`

Now go on to the second row. This isn't the one that starts with the Alternator heading. ▼
Remember that the first cell in the previous row has a rowspan and a colspan of two,
meaning that it bleeds down to this row and takes up two cells. You don't need to redefine it for this row. You just move on to the next cell in the grid. The first cell in this
row is the Limit heading cell, and the second cell is the Adjust Deflection heading cell:

```
<tr>
  <th>Limit</th>
  <th>Adjust Deflection</th>
</tr>
```

What about the last cell? Just like the first cell, the cell in the row above this one had a
rowspan of 2, which takes up the space in this row. The only values you need for this
row are the ones you already defined.

Are you with me so far? Now is a great time to try this out in your browser to make sure
that everything is lining up. It'll look kind of funny because you haven't really put anything on the left side of the table yet, but it's worth a try. Figure 8.25 shows what you've
got so far.

FIGURE 8.25
The table so far.

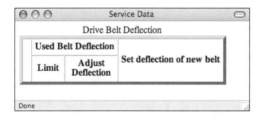

Next row! Check your grid if you need to. Here, the first cell is the heading for
Alternator, and it spans this row and the one below it:

```
<tr>
  <th rowspan="2">Alternator</th>
```

Are you getting the hang of this yet?

The next three cells are pretty easy because they don't span anything. Here are their
definitions:

```
<td>Models without AC</td>
<td>10mm</td>
<td>5-7mm</td>
```

The last cell in this row is just like the first one:

```
<td rowspan="2">5-7mm</td>
</tr>
```

▼

▼ You're up to row number four. In this one, because of the rowspans from the previous row, there are only three cells to define: the cell for Models with AC, and the two cells for the numbers:

```
<tr>
  <td>Models with AC</td>
  <td>12mm</td>
  <td>6-8mm</td>
</tr>
```

NOTE   In this table, I've made the Alternator cell a heading cell and the AC cells plain data. This is mostly an aesthetic decision on my part. I could have made all three into headings just as easily.

Now for the final row—this one should be easy. The first cell (Power Steering Oil Pump) spans two columns (the one with Alternator in it and the with/without AC column). The remaining three are just one cell each:

```
<tr>
  <th colspan="2">Power Steering Oil Pump</th>
  <td>12.5mm</td>
  <td>7.9mm</td>
  <td>6-8mm</td>
</tr>
```

That's it. You're done laying out the rows and columns. That was the hard part. The rest is just fine-tuning. Try looking at it again to make sure there are no strange errors (see Figure 8.26).

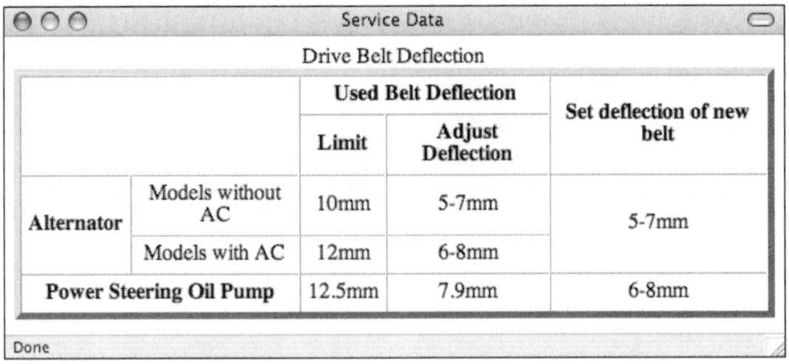

FIGURE 8.26
The table with the data rows included.

		Used Belt Deflection		Set deflection of new belt
		Limit	Adjust Deflection	
Alternator	Models without AC	10mm	5-7mm	5-7mm
	Models with AC	12mm	6-8mm	
Power Steering Oil Pump		12.5mm	7.9mm	6-8mm

Service Data — Drive Belt Deflection

Done

Now that you have all the rows and cells laid out, adjust the alignments within the cells. The numbers should be centered, at least. Because they make up the majority of the table, center the default alignment for each row:

```
<tr align="center">
```

The labels along the left side of the table (Alternator, Models with/without AC, and Power Steering Oil Pump) look funny if they're centered, however, so left-align them using the following code:

```
<th rowspan="2" align="left">Alternator</th>
<td align="left">Models without AC</td>
<td align="left">Models with AC</td>

<th colspan="2" align="left">Power Steering Oil Pump</th>
```

I've put some line breaks in the longer headings so that the columns are a little narrower. Because the text in the headings is pretty short to start with, I don't have to worry too much about the table looking funny if it gets too narrow. Here are the lines I modified:

```
<th rowspan="2">Set<br />deflection<br />of new belt</th>
<th>Adjust<br />Deflection</th>
```

For one final step, you'll align the caption to the left side of the table:

```
<caption style="text-align: left">Drive Belt Deflection</caption>
```

Voilá—the final table, with everything properly laid out and aligned! Figure 8.27 shows the final result.

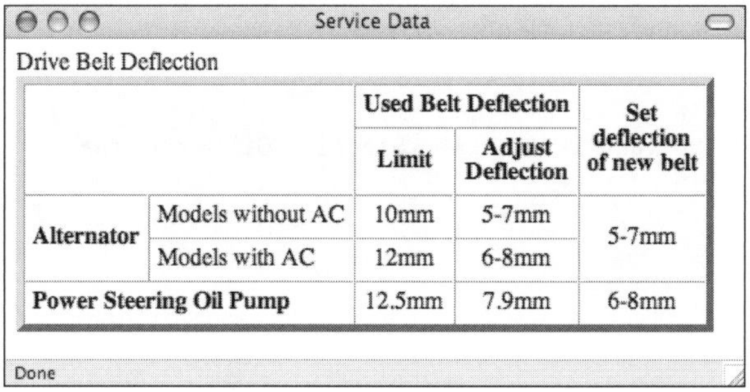

FIGURE 8.27
The final Drive Belt Deflection table.

		Used Belt Deflection		Set deflection of new belt
		Limit	Adjust Deflection	
Alternator	Models without AC	10mm	5-7mm	5-7mm
	Models with AC	12mm	6-8mm	
Power Steering Oil Pump		12.5mm	7.9mm	6-8mm

Drive Belt Deflection — Service Data

NOTE

If you got lost at any time, the best thing you can do is pull out your handy text editor and try it yourself, following along tag by tag. After you've done it a couple of times, it becomes easier.

▼ Here's the full text for the table example:

```
<html>
<head>
<title>Service Data</title>
</head>
<body>
<table border="5"
  style="background-color: #ffffcc"
  bordercolor="#cc9900"
  cellspacing="0"
  cellpadding="5">
<caption style="text-align: left">Drive Belt Deflection</caption>
<tr>
  <th rowspan="2" colspan="2"></th>
  <th colspan="2">Used Belt Deflection</th>
  <th rowspan="2">Set<br />deflection<br />of new belt</th>
</tr>
<tr>
  <th>Limit</th>
  <th>Adjust<br />Deflection</th>
</tr>
<tr align="center">
  <th rowspan="2" align="left">Alternator</th>
  <td align="left">Models without AC</td>
  <td>10mm</td>
  <td>5-7mm</td>
  <td rowspan="2">5-7mm</td>
</tr>
<tr align="center">
  <td align="left">Models with AC</td>
  <td>12mm</td>
  <td>6-8mm</td>
</tr>
<tr align="center">
  <th colspan="2" align="left">Power Steering Oil Pump</th>
  <td>12.5mm</td>
  <td>7.9mm</td>
  <td>6-8mm</td>
</tr>
</table>
</body>
</html>
```

More Advanced Table Enhancements

Believe it or not, after all the work you've done, you're *finally* getting to the table elements that were introduced in HTML 4.01. There are many improvements in the way that you define table columns and rows, which I'll cover in the following sections.

Grouping and Aligning Columns

One of the table enhancements offered in HTML 4.01 is the capability to render tables incrementally, rather than having to wait for all of the data in the table to load. This is accomplished, in part, by defining the columns of the table with the `<colgroup>` and `<col>` elements. These elements enable the web page author to create structural divisions of table columns, which then can be enhanced visually through the use of style sheet properties.

The `<colgroup>...</colgroup>` element is used to enclose one or more columns in a group. The closing `</colgroup>` tag is optional in HTML 4.01, but it's required by the XHTML 1.0 standard. This element has two attributes:

- `span` defines the number of columns in the column group. Its value must be an integer greater than `0`. If `span` isn't defined, the `<colgroup>` element defaults to a column group that contains one column. If the `<colgroup>` element contains one or more `<col>` elements (described later), however, the `span` attribute is ignored.

- `width` specifies the width of each column in the column group. Widths can be defined in pixels, percentages, and relative values. You also can specify a special width value of `"0*"` (zero followed by an asterisk). This value specifies that the width of each column in the group should be the minimum amount necessary to hold the contents of each cell in the column. If you specify the `"0*"` value, however, browsers will be unable to render the table incrementally (meaning that all of the markup for the table will have to be downloaded before the browser can start displaying it).

Suppose that you have a table that measures 450 pixels in width and contains six columns. You want each of the six columns to be 75 pixels wide. The code looks something like the following:

```
<table border="1" width="450">
<colgroup span="6" width="75">
</colgroup>
```

Now you want to change the columns. Using the same 450-pixel-wide table, you make the first two columns 25 pixels wide, and the last four columns 100 pixels wide. This requires two `<colgroup>` elements, as follows:

```
<table border="1" width="450">
<colgroup span="2" width="25">
</colgroup>
<colgroup span="4" width="100">
</colgroup>
```

What if you don't want all the columns in a column group to be the same width or have the same appearance? That's where the `<col>` element comes into play. Whereas

`<colgroup>` defines the structure of table columns, `<col>` defines their attributes. To use this element, begin the column definition with a `<col>` tag. The end tag is forbidden in this case. Instead, you should use the XHTML 1.0 construct for tags with no closing tag and write the tag as `<col />`.

Going back to your 450-pixel-wide table, you now want to make the two columns in the first column group 75 pixels wide. In the second column group, you have columns of 50, 75, 75, and 100 pixels, respectively. Here's how you format the second column group with the `<col>` tag:

```
<table border="1" width="450">
  <colgroup span="2" width="75" />
  </colgroup>
  <colgroup>
    <col span="1" width="50" />
    <col span="2" width="75" />
    <col span="1" width="100" />
  </colgroup>
```

Now apply this to some *real* code. The following example shows a table that displays science and mathematics class schedules. Start by defining a table that has a one-pixel-wide border and spans 100% of the browser window width.

Next, you define the column groups in the table. You want the first column group to display the names of the classes. The second column group consists of two columns that display the room number for the class, as well as the time that the class is held. The first column group consists of one column of cells that spans 20% of the entire width of the table. The contents of the cell are aligned vertically toward the top and centered horizontally. The second column group consists of two columns, each spanning 40% of the width of the table. Their contents are vertically aligned to the top of the cells. To further illustrate how colgroup works, I'm going to use the style attribute and background-color property to set each of the column groups to have different background colors.

Finally, you enter the table data the same way that you normally do. Here's what the complete code looks like for the class schedule, and the results are shown in Figure 8.28:

Input ▼

```
<html>
<head>
<title>Grouping Columns</title>
</head>
<body>
<table border="1" width="100%" summary="Grouping Columns">
  <caption><b>Science and Mathematic Class Schedules</b></caption>
```

```
<colgroup width="20%" align="center" valign="top"
style="background-color: #fcf"></colgroup>

<colgroup span="2" width="40%" valign="top"
style="background-color: #ccf"></colgroup>

<tr>
  <th>Class</th>
  <th>Room</th>
  <th>Time</th>
</tr>

<tr>
  <td>Biology</td>
  <td>Science Wing, Room 102</td>
  <td>8:00 AM to 9:45 AM</td>
</tr>

<tr>
  <td>Science</td>
  <td>Science Wing, Room 110</td>
  <td>9:50 AM to 11:30 AM</td>
</tr>

<tr>
  <td>Physics</td>
  <td>Science Wing, Room 107</td>
  <td>1:00 PM to 2:45 PM</td>
</tr>

<tr>
  <td>Geometry</td>
  <td>Mathematics Wing, Room 236</td>
  <td>8:00 AM to 9:45 AM</td>
</tr>

<tr>
  <td>Algebra</td>
  <td>Mathematics Wing, Room 239</td>
  <td>9:50 AM to 11:30 AM</td>
</tr>

<tr>
  <td>Trigonometry</td>
  <td>Mathematics Wing, Room 245</td>
  <td>1:00 PM to 2:45 PM</td>
</tr>
</table>
</body>
</html>
```

Output ▼

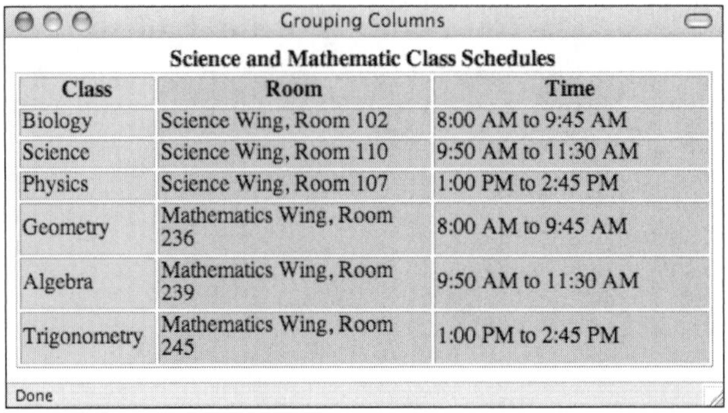

FIGURE 8.28
The class sched-
ule with formatted
column groups.

Grouping and Aligning Rows

Now that you know how to group and format columns, let's turn to the rows. You can group the rows of a table into three sections: table heading, table footer, and table body. You can apply Cascading Style Sheet properties to emphasize the table heading and table footer, and give the body of the table a different appearance.

The table header, footer, and body sections are defined by the <thead>, <tfoot>, and <tbody> elements, respectively. Each of these elements must contain the same number of columns.

The <thead>...</thead> element defines the heading of the table, which should contain information about the columns in the body of the table. Typically, this is the same type of information that you've been placing within header cells so far today. The starting <thead> tag is always required when you want to include a head section in your table, as is the closing </thead> tag under XHTML 1.0.

The head of the table appears right after the <table> element or after <colgroup> elements, as the following example shows, and must include at least one row group defined by the <tr> element. I'm including style attributes in the row grouping tags to illustrate how they are used. The table is formatted as follows:

Input ▼

```
<table border="1" width="100%" summary="Science and Mathematic Class
      Schedules">
  <caption><b>Science and Mathematic Class Schedules</b></caption>
  <colgroup width="20%" align="center" valign="top">
  <colgroup span="2" width="40%" valign="top">
  <thead style="color: red">
  <tr>
    <th>Class</th>
    <th>Room</th>
    <th>Time</th>
  </tr>
  </thead>
```

The <tfoot>...</tfoot> element defines the footer of the table. The starting <tfoot> tag is always required when defining the footer of a table. The closing <tfoot> tag was optional in HTML 4.01, but it's required for XHTML 1.0 compliance. The footer of the table appears immediately after the table heading if one is present, or after the <table> element if a table heading isn't present. It must contain at least one row group, defined by the <tr> element. A good example of information that you could place in a table footer is a row that totals columns of numbers in a table.

You must define the footer of the table before the table body because the browser has to render the footer before it receives all the data in the table body. For the purposes of this example, we'll include the same information in the table head and the table footer. The code looks like this:

Input ▼

```
<tfoot style="color: blue">
  <tr>
  <th>Class</th>
  <th>Room</th>
  <th>Time</th>
  </tr>
</tfoot>
```

After you define the heading and footer for the table, you define the rows in the table body. A table can contain more than one body element, and each body can contain one or more rows of data. This might not seem to make sense, but using multiple body sections enables you to divide up your table into logical sections. I'll show you one example of why this is rather cool in a little bit.

The <tbody>...</tbody> element defines a body section within your table. The <tbody> start tag is required if at least one of the following is true:

- The table contains head or foot sections
- The table contains more than one table body

The following example contains two table bodies, each consisting of three rows of three cells each. The body appears after the table footer, as follows:

Input ▼

```
<tbody style="color: yellow">
  <tr>
    <td>Biology</td>
    <td>Science Wing, Room 102</td>
    <td>8:00 AM to 9:45 AM</td>
  </tr>
  <tr>
    <td>Science</td>
    <td>Science Wing, Room 110</td>
```

```
      <td>9:50 AM to 11:30 AM</td>
    </tr>
    <tr>
      <td>Physics</td>
      <td>Science Wing, Room 107</td>
      <td>1:00 PM to 2:45 PM</td>
    </tr>
  </tbody>
  <tbody style="color: grey">
    <tr>
      <td>Geometry</td>
      <td>Mathematics Wing, Room 236</td>
      <td>8:00 AM to 9:45 AM</td>
    </tr>
    <tr>
      <td>Algebra</td>
      <td>Mathematics Wing, Room 239</td>
      <td>9:50 AM to 11:30 AM</td>
    </tr>
    <tr>
      <td>Trigonometry</td>
      <td>Mathematics Wing, Room 245</td>
      <td>1:00 PM to 2:45 PM</td>
    </tr>
  </tbody>
  </table>
```

Put all the preceding together and you get a table that looks like that shown in Figure 8.29.

Output ▼

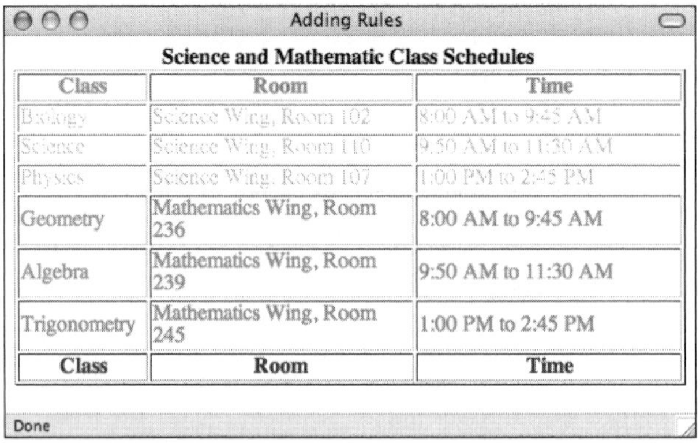

Class	Room	Time
Biology	Science Wing, Room 102	8:00 AM to 9:45 AM
Science	Science Wing, Room 110	9:50 AM to 11:30 AM
Physics	Science Wing, Room 107	1:00 PM to 2:45 PM
Geometry	Mathematics Wing, Room 236	8:00 AM to 9:45 AM
Algebra	Mathematics Wing, Room 239	9:50 AM to 11:30 AM
Trigonometry	Mathematics Wing, Room 245	1:00 PM to 2:45 PM
Class	Room	Time

FIGURE 8.29
The class schedule with a head, two bodies, and a foot.

The `frame` and `rules` Attributes

In the preceding example, it's not really clear where the column groups and row groups begin and end. You can use the `frame` and `rules` attributes of the `<table>` element to selectively control table borders.

8

The `frame` attribute affects how the external border of the table is rendered. You can specify one of several different values to define which sides of the external border are visible:

void	The default value. No sides of the external border are visible.
above	Renders only the top side of the border.
below	Renders only the bottom side of the border.
hsides	Renders the top and bottom sides of the border.
lhs	Renders the left side of the border.
rhs	Renders the right side of the border.
vsides	Renders the right and left sides of the border.
box	Renders all four sides of the border.
border	Renders all four sides of the border.

The `rules` attribute is somewhat similar to the `frame` attribute, except that it defines the rules that appear between the cells within a table. The following values apply to the `rules` attribute:

none	The default value. No rules are drawn around any of the cells.
groups	Rules appear between row groups as defined by `<thead>`, `<tfoot>`, and `<tbody>`, and between column groups as defined by `<colgroup>` and `<col>`.
rows	Rules appear only between rows.
cols	Rules appear only between columns.
all	Rules appear between all rows and columns.

Now let's alter the borders in the table so that your column groups and row groups stand out better. You'll draw a border around the Class Schedule table, but you'll place the border only along the top and bottom of the table by applying `frame="hsides"` to the `<table>` tag.

Inside the table, you'll separate the heading and footer from the two body sections (one table body for the Science subjects and one table body for the Math subjects). You'll also separate the Subject column group and the Room/Time column group. All this is accomplished by using `rules="groups"` with the `<table>` element.

You need to modify only one line in your code to accomplish all of this now. The revised table element appears as follows, and Figure 8.30 shows the results:

```
<table border="1" width="100%" frame="hsides" rules="groups">
```

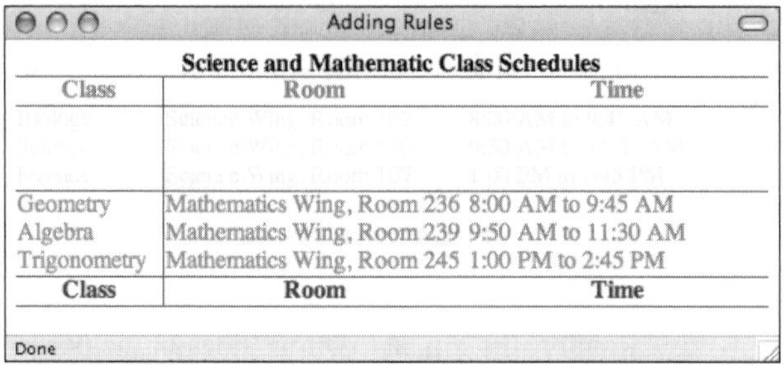

FIGURE 8.30
The class schedule with rules added.

Other Table Elements and Attributes

Table 8.1 presents some of the additional elements and attributes that pertain to tables.

TABLE 8.1   Other Table Elements and Attributes

Attribute	Applied to Element	Use
char	See "Use" column	Specifies a character to be used as an axis to align the contents of a cell. For example, you can use it to align a decimal point in numerical values. Can be applied to colgroup, col, tbody, thead, tfoot, tr, td, and th elements.
charoff	See "Use" column	Specifies the amount of offset applied to the first occurrence of the alignment character that is specified in the char attribute. Applies to colgroup, col, tbody, thead, tfoot, tr, td, and th elements.
summary	<table>	Provides a more detailed description of the contents of the table and is primarily used with nonvisual browsers.

How Tables Are Used

Today, I explained the usage of tables in publishing tabular data. That was the original purpose for HTML tables. However, Netscape 2.0 introduced the option of turning off table borders, and this, along with other limitations in HTML, changed the way tables were used.

Before style sheets were invented and implemented in most browsers, there was only one way to lay out elements on a page other than straight down the middle—tables. Every time you see a page that has navigational links running down one side or elements enclosed in boxes with a background of a different color, someone has laid things out using CSS or tables, and usually it's tables that have been used. In fact, tables were once such a huge part of web publishing that it was rare to see a page that didn't contain any.

Even though all current browsers provide solid support for Cascading Style Sheets, you'll still find that most pages are laid out using tables. Because, as you'll see tomorrow, CSS fundamentally changes the way pages are laid out, many people haven't bothered to get current and abandon tables. Furthermore, there's still some concern about making pages look the same in old browsers as they do in new browsers. Old habits die hard, so tables are still a common approach for creating complex layouts. Let's look at a page that uses tables for layout—freshmeat.net (a site that keeps track of new releases of open source software). It's a good example because it uses several clearly marked tables with nice bold borders. The page appears in Figure 8.31.

FIGURE 8.31

The freshmeat.net home page.

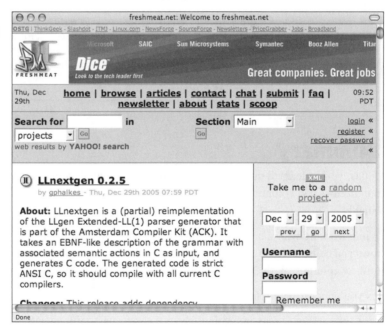

The first four rows of the page are all tables, the first containling links to related sites, then one containing an ad, one containing navigational elements, and one containing the search fields and even more navigational links.

The main content of the page is presented in a table that appears to be two columns but is actually seven columns wide. Two of the columns contain content—the list of software packages on the left and the navigation on the right—and the rest of them are used for spacing and formatting. The listings for individual software packages in the left column are also tables, and the tabular data at the bottom of each listing is yet another table.

This page illustrates the problems with laying out your page using tables. As you'll see later, using tables means including lots of tags on your pages that wouldn't be necessary if you used a CSS-based approach. You also lose the meaning of what a table is, as most of the tables aren't used to present tabular data, but rather just to make things appear on the page where you want them.

This type of layout was typical, but most new websites are being created using CSS for page layout. As you can see from the freshmeat.net page, tables can be used for a very precise layout of the elements on a page. The best way to learn how to create your own pages using these techniques is to view the source code of pages you like. It's unethical to copy someone else's code directly, but there's nothing wrong with using other people's HTML as a source of inspiration or instruction.

TIP

Before you start venturing into using nested tables to create solid borders and resorting to other such trickery, remember that Cascading Style Sheets enable you to create layouts exactly like those on the freshmeat.net page in a much simpler manner. You'll learn exactly how this is done tomorrow.

Summary

Today, you've learned quite a lot about tables. They enable you to arrange your information in rows and columns so that your visitors can get to the information they need quickly.

While working with tables today, you learned about headings and data, captions, defining rows and cells, aligning information within cells, and creating cells that span multiple rows or columns. With these features, you can create tables for most purposes.

As you're constructing tables, it's helpful to keep the following steps in mind:

- Sketch your table, indicating where the rows and columns fall. Mark which cells span multiple rows and columns.

- Start with a basic framework and lay out the rows, headings, and data row by row and cell by cell in HTML. Include row and column spans as necessary. Test frequently in a browser to make sure that it's all working correctly.

- Modify the alignment in the rows to reflect the alignment of the majority of the cells.

- Modify the alignment for individual cells.
- Adjust line breaks, if necessary.
- Make other refinements such as cell spacing, padding, or color.
- Test your table in multiple browsers. Different browsers might have different approaches to laying out your table, or might be more accepting of errors in your HTML code.

Table 8.2 presents a quick summary of the HTML elements that you learned about today, and which remain current in HTML 4.01. Attributes that apply to each element are listed in Table 8.3.

TABLE 8.2   Current HTML 4.01 Table Elements

Tag	Use
`<table>...</table>`	Indicates a table.
`<caption>...</caption>`	Creates a caption for the table (optional).
`<colgroup>...</colgroup>`	Encloses one or more columns in a group.
`<col>`	Used to define the attributes of a column in a table.
`<thead>...</thead>`	Creates a row group that defines the heading of the table. A table can contain only one heading.
`<tfoot>...</tfoot>`	Creates a row group that defines the footer of the table. A table can contain only one footer. Must be specified before the body of the table is rendered.
`<tbody>...</tbody>`	Defines one or more row groups to include in the body of the table. Tables can contain more than one body section.
`<tr>...</tr>`	Defines a table row, which can contain heading and data cells.
`<th>...</th>`	Defines a table cell that contains a heading. Heading cells are usually indicated by boldface and centered both horizontally and vertically within the cell.
`<td>...</td>`	Defines a table cell containing data. Table cells are in a regular font, and are left-aligned and vertically centered within the cell.

Because several of the table attributes apply to more than one of the preceding elements, I'm listing them separately. Table 8.3 presents a quick summary of the HTML attributes you learned about today that remain current in HTML 4.01.

TABLE 8.3 Current HTML 4.01 Table Attributes

Attribute	Applied to Element	Use
align	`<tr>`	Possible values are left, center, and right, which indicate the horizontal alignment of the cells within that row (overriding the default alignment of heading and table cells).
	`<th>` or `<td>`	Overrides both the row's alignment and any default cell alignment. Possible values are left, center, and right.
	`<thead>`, `<tbody>`, `<tfoot>`	Used to set alignment of the contents in table head, body, or foot cells. Possible values are left, center, and right.
	`<col>`	Used to set alignment of all cells in a column. Possible values are left, center, and right.
	`<colgroup>`	Used to set alignment of all cells in a column group. Possible values are left, center, and right.
	`<table>`	Deprecated in HTML 4.01. Possible values are left, center, and right. align="center" isn't supported in HTML 3.2 and older browsers. Determines the alignment of the table and indicates that text following the table will be wrapped alongside it.
	`<caption>`	Deprecated in HTML 4.01. Indicates which side of the table the caption will be placed. The possible values for most browsers are top and bottom. HTML 4.01 browsers also support left and right. In Internet Explorer, the possible values are left, right, and center, and they indicate the horizontal alignment of the caption.
bgcolor	All	(HTML 3.2, deprecated in HTML 4.01.) Changes the background color of that table element. Cell colors override row colors, which override table colors. The value can be a hexadecimal color number or a color name.
border	`<table>`	Indicates whether the table will be drawn with a border. The default is no border. If border has a value, it's the width of the shaded border around the table.

TABLE 8.3 continued

Attribute	Applied to Element	Use
bordercolor	<table>	(Internet Explorer and Netscape extension.) Can be used with any of the table elements to change the color of the border around that elements. The value can be a hexadecimal color number or a color name.
bordercolorlight	<table>	(Internet Explorer extension.) Same as bordercolor, except it affects only the light component of a 3D-look border.
bordercolordark	<table>	(Internet Explorer extension.) Same as bordercolor, except it affects only the dark component of a 3D-look border.
cellspacing	<table>	Defines the amount of space between the cells in the table.
cellpadding	<table>	Defines the amount of space between the edges of the cell and its contents.
char		Specifies a character to be used as an axis to align the contents of a cell (for example, a decimal point in numerical values). Can be applied to colgroup, col, tbody, thead, tfoot, tr, td, and th elements.
charoff		Specifies the amount of offset to be applied to the first occurrence of the alignment character specified by the char attribute. Applies to the same elements previously listed in char.
frame	<table>	Defines which sides of the frame that surrounds a table are visible. Possible values are void, above, below, hsides, lhs, rhs, vsides, box, and border.
height	<th> or <td>	Deprecated in HTML 4.01. Indicates the height of the cell in pixel or percentage values.
nowrap	<th> or <td>	Deprecated in HTML 4.01. Prevents the browser from wrapping the contents of the cell.
rules	<table>	Defines which rules (division lines) appear between cells in a table. Possible values are none, groups, rows, cols, and all.

8

TABLE 8.3   continued

Attribute	Applied to Element	Use
width	`<table>`	Indicates the width of the table, in exact pixel values or as a percentage of page width (for example, 50%).
span	`<colgroup>`	Defines the number of columns in a column group. Must be an integer greater than 0.
	`<col>`	Defines the number of columns which a cell spans. Must be an integer greater than 0.
width	`<colgroup>`	Defines the width of all cells in a column group.
	`<col>`	Defines the width of all cells in one column.
colspan	`<th>` or `<td>`	Indicates the number of cells to the right of this one that this cell will span.
rowspan	`<th>` or `<td>`	Indicates the number of cells below this one that this cell will span.
valign	`<tr>`	Indicates the vertical alignment of the cells within that row (overriding the defaults). Possible values are top, middle, and bottom.
	`<th>` or `<td>`	Overrides both the row's vertical alignment and the default cell alignment. Possible values are top, middle, and bottom. In Netscape, valign can also have the value baseline.
	`<thead>`, `<tfoot>`, `<tbody>`	Defines vertical alignment of cells in the table head, table foot, or table body.
	`<colgroup>`	Defines the vertical alignment of all cells in a column group.
	`<col>`	Defines the vertical alignment of all cells in a single column.
width	`<th>` or `<td>`	Deprecated in HTML 4.01. Indicates width of the cell, in exact pixel values or as a percentage of table width (for example, 50%).

Workshop

Today's lesson covered one of the more complex subjects in HTML—tables. Before you move on to full immersion into the world of Cascading Style Sheets, you should work through the following questions and exercises to make sure that you've really got a good grasp of how tables work.

8

Q&A

Q Tables are a real hassle to lay out, especially when you get into row and column spans. That last example was awful.

A You're right. Tables are a tremendous pain to lay out by hand like this. However, if you're using writing editors and tools to generate HTML code, having the table defined like this makes more sense because you can just write out each row in turn programmatically.

Q Can you nest tables, putting a table inside a single table cell?

A Sure! As I mentioned earlier, you can put any HTML code you want inside a table cell, and that includes other tables.

Q Why does most of the world use `align` for positioning a caption at the top or bottom of a page, but Internet Explorer does something totally different?

A I don't know. And worse, Microsoft claims it got that definition for Internet Explorer from HTML 3.0, but no version of HTML 3.0 or the tables specification in HTML 3.2 has it defined in that way. HTML 4.01 added left and right aligning to this attribute, but Internet Explorer added that alignment before HTML even mentioned the possibility.

Quiz

1. What are the basic parts of a table, and which tags identify them?

2. Which attribute is the most common attribute of the table tag, and what does it do?

3. What attributes define the amount of space between the edges of the cells and their content, and the amount of space between cells?

4. Which attributes are used to create cells that span more than one column or row?

5. Which elements are used to define the head, body, and foot of a table?

Quiz Answers

1. The basic parts of a table (the `<table>` tag) are the border (defined with the `border` attribute), the caption (defined with the `<caption>` tag), header cells (`<th>`), data cells (`<td>`), and table rows (`<tr>`).

2. The `border` attribute is the most common attribute for the table tag. It specifies whether border lines are displayed around the table, and how wide the borders should be.

3. `cellpadding` defines the amount of space between the edges of the cell and their contents. `cellspacing` defines the amount of space between the cells.

4. The `rowspan` attribute creates a cell that spans multiple rows. The `colspan` attribute creates a cell that spans multiple columns.

5. `<thead>`, `<tbody>`, and `<tfoot>` define the head, body, and foot of a table.

Exercises

1. Here's a brainteaser for you: Create a simple nested table (a table within a table) that contains three rows and four columns. Inside the cell that appears at the second column in the second row, create a second table that contains two rows and two columns.

2. Modify the table shown in Figure 8.30 so that the rules in the table only appear between columns.

LESSON 9:
Creating Layouts with CSS

In the past few lessons, I've discussed how to lay out web pages using HTML tags. Today, I'm going to describe how you can create complex pages using cascading style sheets (CSS).

In this Lesson

You've already learned about the advantages CSS can provide for formatting smaller snippets of text. In this lesson, you'll learn how to use CSS to control the appearance of an entire page.

The following topics will be covered:

- Creating style sheets and including them in a page
- Linking to external style sheets
- Using selectors to apply styles to elements on a page
- Units of measure supported by CSS
- CSS properties associated with boxes
- Positioning elements using CSS
- Applying styles to tables and the <body> tag
- Using CSS to create multicolumn layouts

Including Style Sheets in a Page

Thus far, when I've discussed style sheets, I've always applied them using the `style` attribute of tags. For example, I've shown how you can modify the font for some text using tags such as `<div>` and `<span>`, or how you can modify the appearance of a list item by applying a style within an `<li>` tag. It might have occurred to you that applying styles this way doesn't really provide much of an advantage over using things like the `<font>` tag. If you rely on the `style` attribute of tags to apply CSS, if you want to embolden every paragraph on a page, you need to put `style="font-weight: bold"` in every `<p>` tag. This is no improvement over simply using `<p><b>` and `</b></p>` instead. Fortunately, CSS provides ways to apply styles generally to a page, or even to an entire website.

Creating Page-Level Styles

First, let's look at how we can apply styles to our page at the page level. Thus far, you've seen how styles are applied, but you haven't seen any style sheets. Here's what one looks like:

```
<style type="text/css">
h1 { font-size: x-large; font-weight: bold }
h2 { font-size: large; font-weight: bold }
</style>
```

The `<style>` tag should be included within the `<head>` tag on your page. The `type` attribute indicates the MIME type of the style sheet. `text/css` is the only value you'll use. The body of the style sheet consists of a series of rules. All rules follow the same structure:

```
selector { property1: value1; property2: value2; .. }
```

Each rule consists of a selector followed by a list of properties and values associated with those properties. All the properties being set for a selector are enclosed in curly braces, as shown in the example. You can include any number of properties for each selector, and they must be separated from one another using semicolons. You can also include a semicolon following the last property/value pair in the rule, or not—it's up to you.

You should already be quite familiar with CSS properties and values because that's what you use in the `style` attribute of tags. Selectors are something new. I'll discuss selectors in detail in a bit. The ones I've used thus far have the same names as tags. If you use `h1` as a selector, the rule will apply to any `<h1>` tags on the page. By the same token, if you use `p` as your selector, it will apply to `<p>` tags.

Creating Sitewide Style Sheets

You can't capture the real efficiency of style sheets until you start creating sitewide style sheets. You can store all of your style information in a file and include it without resorting to any server trickery (which I'll discuss in Lesson 19, "Taking Advantage of the Server"). A CSS file is basically just the body of a `<style>` tag. To turn the style sheet from the previous section into a separate file, you could just save the following to a file called `style.css`:

```
h1 { font-size: x-large; font-weight: bold }
h2 { font-size: large; font-weight: bold }
```

In truth, the extension of the file is irrelevant, but the extension `.css` is the de facto standard for style sheets, so you should probably use it. Once you've created the style sheet file, you can include it in your page using the `<link>` tag, like this:

```
<link rel="stylesheet" href="style.css" type="text/css" />
```

The `type` attribute is the same as that of the `<style>` tag. The `href` tag is the same as that of the `<a>` tag. It can be a relative URL, an absolute URL, or even a fully qualified URL that points to a different server. As long as the browser can fetch the file, any URL will work. This means that you can just as easily use other people's style sheets as your own, but you probably shouldn't.

There's another attribute of the link tag as well: `media`. This enables you to specify different style sheets for different display mediums. For example, you can specify one for print, another for screen display, and others for things like aural browsers for use with screen readers. Not all browsers support the different media types, but if your style sheet is specific to a particular medium, you should include it. The options are `screen`, `print`, `projection`, `aural`, `braille`, `tty`, `tv`, and `all`.

You can also specify titles for your style sheets using the `title` attribute, as well as alternative style sheets by setting the `rel` attribute to "`alternative style sheet`". Theoretically, this means that you could specify multiple style sheets for your page (with the one set to `rel="stylesheet"` as the preferred style sheet). The browser would then enable the user to select from among them based on the title you provide. Unfortunately, none of the major browsers support this behavior.

As it is, you can include links to multiple style sheets in your pages, and all the rules will be applied. This means that you can create one general style sheet for your entire site, and then another specific to a page or to a section of the site as well.

9

As you can see, the capability to link to external style sheets provides you with a power-ful means for managing the look and feel of your site. Once you've set up a sitewide style sheet that sets up the basic look-and-feel parameters for your pages, changing things such as the headline font and background color for your pages or other such settings becomes trivial. Before CSS, making these kinds of changes required a lot of manual labor or a facility with tools that had search and replace functionality for multi-ple files. Now it requires quick edits to a single linked style sheet.

Selectors

You've already seen one type of selector for CSS—element names. Any tag can serve as a CSS selector, and the rules for that selector will be applied to all instances of that tag on the page. You can add a rule to the <b> tag that sets the font weight to normal if you choose to do so, or italicize every paragraph on your page by applying a style to the <p> tag. Applying styles to the <body> tag using the body selector enables you to apply pagewide settings. However, there are also a number of ways to apply styles on a more granular basis and to apply them across multiple types of elements using a single selector.

Let's say that you want all unordered lists, ordered lists, and paragraphs on a page to be displayed using blue text. Rather than writing individual rules for each of these elements, you can write a single rule that applies to all of them. Here's the syntax:

```
p, ol, ul { color: blue }
```

A comma-separated list indicates that the style rule should apply to all the tags listed. The preceding rule is just an easier way to write

```
p { color: blue }
ol { color: blue }
ul { color: blue }
```

Contextual Selectors

There are also contextual selectors available. These are used to apply styles to elements only when they're nested within other specified elements. Take a look at this rule:

```
p ol { color: blue }
```

The fact that I left out the comma indicates that this rule applies only to ol elements that are nested within p elements. Let's look at two slightly different rules:

```
p cite { font-style: italic; font-weight: normal }
li cite { font-style: normal; font-weight: bold }
```

In this case, `<cite>` tags that appear within `<p>` tags will be italicized. If a `<cite>` tag appears inside a list item, the contents will be rendered in boldface. Let's add in one more rule:

```
cite { color: green }
p cite { font-style: italic; font-weight: normal }
li cite { font-style: normal; font-weight: bold }
```

In this case, we have one rule that applies to all `<cite>` tags, and the two others that you've already seen. In this case, the contents of all `<cite>` tags will be green, and the appropriately nested `<cite>` tags will take on those styles as well. Here's one final example:

```
cite { color: green }
p cite { font-style: italic; font-weight: normal; color: red }
li cite { font-style: normal; font-weight: bold; color: blue }
```

In this case, the nested styles override the default style for the `<cite>` tag. The contents of `<cite>` tags that don't meet the criteria of the nested rules will appear in green. The nested rules will override the color specified in the less-specific rule, so for `<cite>` tags that are inside `<p>` tags, the contents will be red. Inside list items, the contents will be blue.

Classes and IDs

Sometimes selecting by tag (even using contextual selectors) isn't specific enough for your needs, and you must create your own classifications for use with CSS. There are two attributes supported by all HTML tags: `class` and `id`. The `class` attribute is for assigning elements to groups of tags, and the `id` attribute is for assigning identifiers to specific elements.

To differentiate between classes and regular element names in your rules, you prepend `.` to the class name. So, if you have a tag like this

```
<div class="important">Some text.</div>
```

then you write the rule like this

```
.important { color: red; font-weight: bold; }
```

Any element with its class set to `important` will appear in bold red text. If you want to give this treatment to only important `<div>`s, you can include the element name along with the class name in your rule.

```
div.important { color: red; font-weight: bold; }
p.important { color: blue; font-weight: bold; }
```

9

In this case, if a <p> tag is assigned to the important class, the text inside will be blue. If a <div> is in the important class, its text will be red. You could also rewrite the preceding two rules as follows:

```
.important { font-weight: bold; }
div.important { color: red; }
p.important { color: blue; }
```

All members of the important class will be bold and important <div>s will be red, whereas important paragraphs will be blue. If you put a list in the important class, the default color would be applied to it.

Whenever you want to specify styles for one element in a style sheet, assign it an ID. As you'll learn later in the book, assigning IDs to elements is also very useful when using JavaScript or dynamic HTML because doing so lets you write programs that reference individual items specifically. For now, though, let's look at how IDs are used with CSS. Generally, a page will have only one footer. To identify it, use the id attribute:

```
<div id="footer">
Copyright 2003, Example Industries.
</div>
```

You can then write CSS rules that apply to that element by referencing the ID. Here's an example:

```
#footer { font-size: small; }
```

As you can see, when you refer to IDs in your style sheets, you need to prepend a # on the front in order to distinguish them from class names and element names. Note that there's no additional facility for referring to IDs that are associated with particular elements. IDs are supposed to be unique, so there's no need for qualifying them further. Finally, there's nothing to say that you can't mix up all of these selectors in one rule, like so:

```
h1, #headline, .heading, div.important { font-size: large; color: green; }
```

As you can see, I've included several types of selectors in one rule. This is perfectly legal if you want to set the same properties for a number of different selectors. Classes also work with contextual selectors:

```
ul li.important { color: red }
```

In this case, list items in the important class will be red if they occur in an unordered list. If they're in an ordered list, the rule will not be applied.

Units of Measure

One of the most confusing aspects of CSS is the unit of measure it provides. Four types of units can be specified in CSS: length units, percentage units, color units, and URLs. In this lesson, we're going to deal mostly with length and percentage units.

There are two kinds of length units: absolute and relative. *Absolute* units theoretically correspond to a unit of measure in the real world, such as an inch, a centimeter, or a point. *Relative* units are based on some more arbitrary unit of measure. Table 9.1 contains a full list of length units.

TABLE 9.1   Length Units in CSS

Unit	Measurement
em	Relative; height of the element's font
ex	Relative; height of x character in the element's font
px	Relative; pixels
in	Absolute; inches
cm	Absolute; centimeters
mm	Absolute; millimeters
pt	Absolute; points
pc	Absolute; picas

The absolute measurements seem great, except that an inch isn't really an inch when it comes to measuring things on a screen. Given the variety of browser sizes and resolutions supported, the browser doesn't really know how to figure out what an inch is. For example, you might have a laptop with a 14.1" display running at 1024 by 768. I might have a 19" CRT running at that same resolution. If the browser thinks that one inch is 72 pixels, a headline set to 1in may appear as less than an inch on your monitor or more than an inch on mine. Dealing with relative units is much safer.

In this lesson, I'm going to use one length unit: px. It's my favorite for sizing most things. However, other relative units can also be useful. For example, if you want paragraphs on your page to appear as double spaced, you can specify them like this:

```
p { line-height: 2em; }
```

Percentage units are also extremely common. They're written as you'd expect: 200% (with no spaces). The thing to remember with percentages is that they're always relative to something. If you set a font size to 200%, it will be double the size of the font that's

9

currently being used. If you set a `<div>`'s width to 50%, it will be half as wide as the enclosing element (or the browser window, if there's no enclosing element). When you use percentages, always keep in mind what you're talking about a percent of.

Using Percentage Units

When you use percentages as units, bear in mind that the percentage applies not to the size of the page, but rather to the size of the box that encloses the box to which the style applies. For example, if you have a `<div>` with its width set to 50% inside a div with its width set to 500px, the inner `<div>` will be 250 pixels wide. On the other hand, if the outer `<div>` were also set to 50%, it would be half as wide as the browser window, and the inner `<div>` would be 25% of the width of the browser window.

I already discussed units of color back in Lesson 7, "Adding Images, Color, and Backgrounds," so I'll move on to URLs. Most of the time, when you use URLs, they're used in the `<a>` tag or `<img>` tag. In CSS, they're usually included to specify the location of a background image or a bullet image for a list. Generally, URLs are specified like this:

```
url(http://www.example.com/)
```

Box Properties

In previous lessons, my discussion of cascading style sheets has dealt mostly with properties that can work at a block or a character level, and are designed to change the way text looks. There are also a number of properties that pertain to blocks but not characters. These properties are used to position elements, control the white space around them, and to apply effects such as borders to them. They're referred to as *box properties*, because they work on box-shaped regions of the page.

Once you've mastered these properties, you can forget about using tables to lay out a page. CSS offers all the capabilities that tables do, with less markup and the capability to maintain the layout in one CSS file rather than on each page of your site.

When discussing box properties, I'm going to start off with a humble `<div>`. People who lay out pages using CSS love the `<div>` tag because it brings absolutely nothing to the table in terms of modifying the appearance of a page. It's just a container that you can apply styles to.

With box properties, there are general properties that enable you to set specific attributes of a more general property individually, or you can use the general property to set several attributes at once. If you want to set different values for each side of the box, you should use the properties that set individual attributes. The CSS specification says that you can set individual values for each side using the general property, but some browsers don't support that usage.

Controlling Size

There are two properties for controlling the size of a box element: `width` and `height`. They enable you to set the size of the box to an absolute size, or if you prefer, to a size relative to the browser window. For example, to make the header of your page 100 pixels high and half the width of the browser, you could use the following rule:

```
#header { width: 50%; height: 100px; }
```

Unlike tables, which, unless you say differently, are only as large as the widest bit of content, many other block-level elements are as wide as the browser window by default. For example, paragraphs and `<div>`s are both the full width of the browser window by default. If the following text were wrapped in a table, it would be very narrow. But inside a regular paragraph, the box containing the text will be as wide as possible unless you specifically indicate that it should have a particular width.

```
<p>one.<br />two.<br />three.<br /></p>
```

Of course, when you place elements side by side, you can also squeeze them down. We'll look at that a bit later.

Borders

CSS provides several properties for controlling borders around elements. When you worked with tables, you got a taste of borders. In the CSS world, you can apply them to any box. First, let's look at the border property by itself:

```
border: width style color;
```

When you use the `border` property by itself, there are three values associated with it (any of which can be eliminated). The first is the `width` of the border. You can also use any unit of measurement you like to specify the border width, or if you prefer, you can use `thin`, `medium`, or `thick`. The actual width of borders specified using the keywords is entirely dependent upon the user's browser.

The next option is `style`. The default here is `none` for most elements; the other options are `dotted`, `dashed`, `solid`, `double`, `groove`, `ridge`, `inset`, and `outset`. Not all browsers support all the border styles.

The last option is `color`. As is the case with all properties that accept multiple values, you aren't required to specify any of them. You need specify only the values that you want to change. Here are some examples that use the `border` property:

9

Input ▼

```
.one { border: thin dotted black; }
.two { border: 2px solid blue; }
.three { border: 3px groove red; }
.four { border: thick double #000; }
```

Figure 9.1 is a screenshot of the previous styles applied to some paragraphs.

Output ▼

FIGURE 9.1

Four usages of the border property.

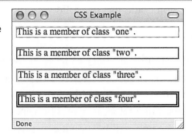

There are a number of additional properties that can be used to modify the border of the page. You can set the styles for each side's border individually using border-top, border-right, border-bottom, and border-left. That enables you to create styles like this:

```
.one { border-top: thick dotted black;
    border-right: thick solid blue;
    border-bottom: thick groove red;
    border-left: thick double #000; }
```

This is also useful if you want to create effects like marking quotes with a line down the left margin, like so:

```
blockquote { border-left: 3px solid red; }
```

You can see both of these rules in action in Figure 9.2.

FIGURE 9.2

Using directional properties to give individual borders to different sides of a box.

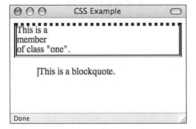

One thing that's obvious from the two previous screenshots is that there's not much space between the border and the text. I'll take care of that when I get to the padding property. Another option is to specify each specific property that's built into the composite `border` property individually. These properties are `border-style`, `border-width`, and `border-color`. Here's an example:

```
p { border-style: solid dashed;
  border-width: 2px 4px 6px;
  border-color: blue red green black; }
```

If you supply only one value for the property, it will be applied to all four sides of the box. If you supply two values, as I did for the `border-style` property, the first value will be applied to the top and bottom, and the second will be applied to the left and right side. For the `border-width` property, I supplied three values. In this case, the first value is applied to the top, the second to the left and right, and the third to the bottom. As you can see, the values are applied to the sides of the box in a clockwise fashion, and if a value isn't supplied for a particular side, the value assigned to the opposite side is used. The last property, `border-color`, has four values, so the values are applied to all four sides, clockwise. The resulting page appears in Figure 9.3.

FIGURE 9.3
A different way to apply border styles.

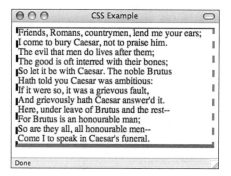

There are also four more properties: `border-top-width`, `border-right-width`, `border-left-width`, and `border-bottom-width`. These properties aren't particularly useful when you can just use `border-width` to set any or all four at the same time.

Margins and Padding

There are two sets of properties used to control white space around boxes: `margin` properties and `padding` properties. There's a reason why I discussed the `border` property before discussing `margin` and `padding`. The `padding` property controls white space inside the border, and the `margin` property controls the white space between the border and the enclosing block. Let's look at an example. The web page that follows has one `<div>` nested within another. The outer `<div>` has a solid black border; the inner `<div>` has a dotted black border. The page appears in Figure 9.4.

9

Input ▼

```
<html>
<head>
  <title>CSS Example</title>
  <style type="text/css">
    .outer { border: 2px solid black; }
    .inner { border: 2px dotted black;
        padding: 0px;
        margin: 0px; }
  </style>
</head>
<body>
<div class="outer">
Outer.
<div class="inner">
Friends, Romans, countrymen, lend me your ears;<br />
I come to bury Caesar, not to praise him.<br />
The evil that men do lives after them;<br />
The good is oft interred with their bones;<br />
So let it be with Caesar. The noble Brutus<br />
</div>
</div>

</body>
</html>
```

Output ▼

FIGURE 9.4

Nested <div>s with no margins or padding.

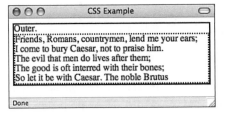

As you can see, the text in the inner <div> is jammed right up against the border, and the inner border and outer border are flush against each other. That's because I've set both the padding and margin of the inner div to 0px. The results in Figure 9.5 show what happens if I change the style sheet to this:

Input ▼

```
.outer { border: 2px solid black; }
.inner { border: 2px dotted black;
    padding: 15px;
    margin: 15px; }
```

Output ▼

FIGURE 9.5
The inner <div>
has 15 pixels of
padding and mar-
gin here.

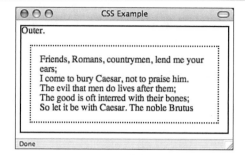

As you can see, I've created some space between the border of the inner <div> and the text inside the inner <div> using padding, and some space between the border of the inner <div> and the border of the outer <div> using margin. Now let's look at what happens when I add some margin and padding to the outer <div> as well. I'm also going to give both the inner and outer <div>s background colors so that you can see how colors are assigned to white space. The results are in Figure 9.6. Here's the new style sheet:

Input ▼

```
.outer { border: 2px solid black;
    background-color: #999;
    padding: 15px;
    margin: 40px; }
.inner { border: 2px dotted black;
    background-color: #fff;
    padding: 15px;
    margin: 15px; }
```

Output ▼

FIGURE 9.6
Both the inner
<div> and outer
<div> have margin
and padding.

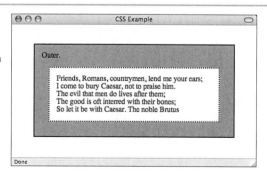

I gave the outer <div> a large 40-pixel margin so that you could see how it moves the borders away from the edges of the browser window. Note also that there's now space

9

between the text in the outer `<div>` and the border. You can also see that the padding of the outer `<div>` and the margin of the inner `<div>` are combined to provide 30 pixels of white space between the border of the outer `<div>` and the border of the inner `<div>`. Finally, it's important to understand the behavior of the background color. The background color you assign is applied to the padding, but not to the margin. So, the 15-pixel margin outside the inner `<div>` takes on the background color of the outer `<div>`, and the margin of the outer `<div>` takes on the background color of the page.

Collapsing Margins

In the CSS box model, horizontal margins are never collapsed (if you put two items with horizontal margins next to each other, both margins will appear on the page). Vertical margins, on the other hand, are collapsed. Only the larger of the two vertical margins is used when two elements with margins are next to each other. For example, if a `<div>` with a 40-pixel bottom margin is above a `<div>` with a 20-pixel top margin, the margin between the two will be 40 pixels, not 60 pixels.

At this point, it should be clicking why CSS is a nice alternative to tables, assuming that your data isn't tabular. I haven't talked at all yet about positioning, but you can see that for putting borders around things or putting them inside boxes with white space around them, CSS makes your life pretty easy.

You already know that to center text within a box, the `text-align` property is used. The question now is, how you center a box on the page. In addition to passing units of measure or a percentage to the margin property, you can also set the margin to `auto`. In theory, this means set this margin to the same value as the opposite margin. However, if you set both the left and right margins to `auto`, your element will be centered. To do so, you can use the `margin-left` and `margin-right` properties, or provide multiple values for the margin property. You can also do the same thing with `margin-top` and `margin-bottom`. So, to center a `<div>` horizontally, the following style sheet is used (the newly centered `<div>` is in Figure 9.7):

Input ▼

```
.inner { border: 2px dotted black;
    background-color: #fff;
    padding: 15px;
    width: 50%;
    margin-left: auto;
    margin-right: auto;
    }
```

Output ▼

FIGURE 9.7
Both the inner
`<div>` and outer
`<div>` have margin
and padding.

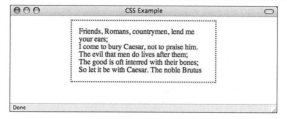

9

CAUTION

Internet Explorer cares about your document type definition (DTD) settings. If you don't indicate in your document that you're using HTML 4.01 or XHTML 1.0, Internet Explorer will not honor things such as margin: auto. If the DTD is left out, IE assumes that you're using an old version of HTML that doesn't support features like that.

TIP

If you want elements to overlap each other, you can apply negative margins to them instead of positive margins.

Another thing to remember is that the `<body>` of your page is a box as well. Let me make yet another change to my style sheet to show how you can apply styles to it. In the new style sheet, I adjust the `border`, `margin`, and `padding` properties of the `<body>` tag. I also make some changes to the outer `<div>` to better illustrate how the changes to the `<body>` tag work. The changes related to the new style sheet appear in Figure 9.8.

Input ▼

```
.outer { border: 2px solid black;
    background-color: #999;
    padding: 15px; }
.inner { border: 2px dotted black;
    background-color: #fff;
    padding: 15px;
    margin: 15px; }
body { margin: 20px;
    border: 3px solid blue;
    padding: 20px;
    background-color: #cfc;
    }
```

FIGURE 9.8
Treating the body
of a document as
a box.

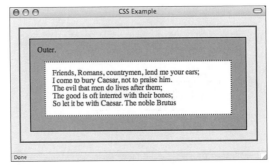

In this example, you can see that you can adjust the margin padding, and border of a document's body. In Mozilla, the margin is placed outside the border, and the padding inside it. However, unlike other boxes, the background color is applied to the margin as well as the padding. In Internet Explorer, things are a bit different. Both the margin and padding are applied, but the border appears around the edge of the window—even the scrollbars are placed inside the border, as shown in Figure 9.9.

FIGURE 9.9
Modified border
properties in
Internet Explorer.

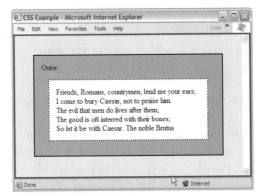

Float

Normally, elements flow down the page from left to right and top to bottom. If you want to alter the normal flow of the page, you can use absolute positioning, which I'll discuss in a bit, or you can use the `float` property. The `float` property is used to indicate that an element should be placed as far as possible to the left or right on the page, and that any other content should wrap around it. This is best illustrated with an example. First, take a look at the page in Figure 9.10.

FIGURE 9.10

A page with no floating elements.

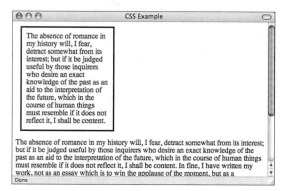

As you can see, the three boxes run straight down the page. I've added a border to the first box and reduced its width, but that's it. Here's the source code to the page, with the addition of a few additional properties to change the page layout:

Input ▼

```html
<html>
<head>
  <title>CSS Example</title>
  <style type="text/css">
.right {
  border: 3px solid black;
  padding: 10px;
  margin: 10px;
  float: right;
  width: 33%; }

.bottom { clear: both; }
  </style>
</head>
<body>
<p class="right">
The absence of romance in my history will, I fear, detract somewhat
from its interest; but if it be judged useful by those inquirers who
desire an exact knowledge of the past as an aid to the interpretation
of the future, which in the course of human things must resemble if
it does not reflect it, I shall be content.
</p>
<p class="main">
The absence of romance in my history will, I fear, detract somewhat
from its interest; but if it be judged useful by those inquirers who
desire an exact knowledge of the past as an aid to the interpretation
of the future, which in the course of human things must resemble if
it does not reflect it, I shall be content. In fine, I have written
my work, not as an essay which is to win the applause of the moment,
but as a possession for all time.
</p>
```

9

```
<p class="bottom">
The absence of romance in my history will, I fear, detract somewhat
from its interest; but if it be judged useful by those inquirers who
desire an exact knowledge of the past as an aid to the interpretation
of the future, which in the course of human things must resemble if
it does not reflect it, I shall be content. In fine, I have written
my work, not as an essay which is to win the applause of the moment,
but as a possession for all time.
</p>
</body>
</html>
```

As you can see from the style sheet, I've set up the <div> so that its width is 33% of the width of the enclosing block (in this case, the browser window), and I've added some padding, a margin, and a border for aesthetic purposes. The real key here is that I've added the `float: right` property to the style rule. I've also put the second paragraph on the page in the class `bottom`, and I've added the `clear: both` property to it. The results are in Figure 9.11.

Output ▼

FIGURE 9.11

A page with a <div> floated to the right.

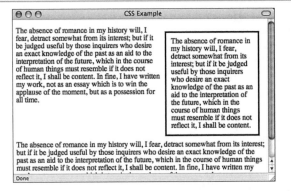

The <div> is moved over to the right side of the page, and the first paragraph appears next to it. The `float: right` property indicates that the rest of the page's content should flow around it. The bottom paragraph does not flow around the div because I've applied the `clear: both` property to it, which cancels any float that has been set. The options for `float` are easy to remember: `left`, `right`, and `none`. The options for clear are `none`, `left`, `right`, and `both`.

Using the `clear` property, you have the option of clearing either the left or right float without canceling both at the same time. This is useful if you have a long column on the right and a short one on the left and you want to maintain the float on the right even though you're canceling it on the left (or vice versa).

Now let's look at how floated elements work together. Figure 9.12 shows what happens when you have two right-floating elements together, and Figure 9.13 shows the effect with a left-floating element and a right-floating element.

FIGURE 9.12

Two right-floating elements together.

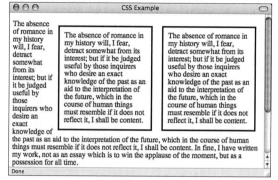

FIGURE 9.13

A left-floating and a right-floating element together.

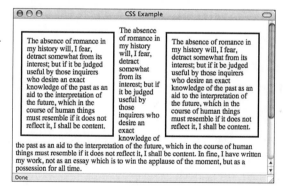

As you can see, when you put two floating elements together, they appear next to each other. If you want the second one to appear below the first, you need to use the clear property as well as the float property in the rule, as shown in this style sheet:

Input ▼

```
.right {
  border: 3px solid black;
  padding: 10px;
  margin: 10px;
  float: right;
  width: 33%; }

#second { clear: right; }

.bottom { clear: both; }
```

The additional <div> I've added has been given the ID second, so that it inherits all the styles of the class right and also the style rule associated with the ID second. The result is in Figure 9.14.

Output ▼

FIGURE 9.14
Two floating elements that are aligned vertically.

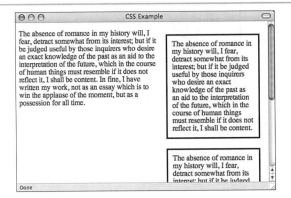

CSS Positioning

If using float to control how elements are laid out doesn't provide the measure of control you're looking for, you can use the CSS positioning attributes. To position elements yourself, you first have to choose a positioning scheme with the position property. There are four positioning schemes, three of which you'll actually use. The four are static, relative, absolute, and fixed.

The static scheme is the default. Elements flow down the page from left to right and top to bottom, unless you use the float property to change things up. The relative scheme positions the element relative to the element that precedes it. You can alter the page flow to a certain degree, but the elements will still be interdependent. The absolute and fixed schemes enable you to position elements in any location you want on the page. The fixed scheme is not well supported, so if you want to control where items appear yourself you should use absolute.

Once you've picked a positioning scheme, you can set the position for elements. There are four positioning properties: top, left, bottom, and right. The values for these properties are specified as the distance of the named side from the side of the enclosing block. Here's an example:

```
.thing {
    position: relative;
    left: 50px;
    top: 50px;
}
```

In this case, elements in the thing class will be shifted 50 pixels down and 50 pixels to the left from the element that precede them in the page layout. If I changed position to absolute, the element would appear 50 pixels from the top-left corner of the page's body.

Generally, when you're positioning elements, you pick a corner and specify where the element should be located. In other words, there's never a need to set more than two of the four positioning properties. If you set more than two, you could run into problems with how the browser renders the page because you're specifying not only where the element should be located but also the size of the element. It's much safer to use the sizing properties to size your elements and then specify the position of one corner of your element if you want to indicate where it should go on the page.

Relative Positioning

Let's look at a page that uses relative positioning. This page will illustrate both how relative positioning works and some of the problems with it. A screenshot of the page listed in the following code appears in Figure 9.15.

Input ▼

```html
<html>
<head>
  <title>CSS Example</title>
  <style type="text/css">
.two {
  border: 3px solid blue;
  padding: 10px;
  margin: 10px;
  background-color: #ffc;
  position: relative;
  top: -46px;
  left: 50px;
  width: 33%; }
  </style>
</head>
<body>
<p class="one">
The absence of romance in my history will, I fear, detract somewhat
from its interest; but if it be judged useful by those inquirers who
desire an exact knowledge of the past as an aid to the interpretation
of the future, which in the course of human things must resemble if
it does not reflect it, I shall be content.
</p>
<p class="two">
The absence of romance in my history will, I fear, detract somewhat
from its interest; but if it be judged useful by those inquirers who
desire an exact knowledge of the past as an aid to the interpretation
```

of the future, which in the course of human things must resemble if
it does not reflect it, I shall be content. In fine, I have written
my work, not as an essay which is to win the applause of the moment,
but as a possession for all time.
```
</p>
<p class="three">
```
The absence of romance in my history will, I fear, detract somewhat
from its interest; but if it be judged useful by those inquirers who
desire an exact knowledge of the past as an aid to the interpretation
of the future, which in the course of human things must resemble if
it does not reflect it, I shall be content. In fine, I have written
my work, not as an essay which is to win the applause of the moment,
but as a possession for all time.
```
</p>
</body>
</html>
```

Output ▼

FIGURE 9.15

A page that uses relative positioning for an element.

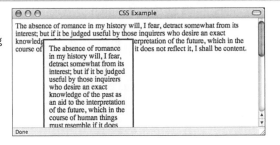

You can spot the problem right away on this page—the relatively positioned element overlaps the paragraph above it. I used a negative value for the top property to move the element up 50 pixels, and also moved it to the left 50 pixels. The hole where the content would normally be positioned if I were using static positioning remains exactly the same as it would had I not moved the element, thus creating white space before the third paragraph. However, due to the positioning, the paragraph has been moved up so that it overlaps the one above it.

Another point to note is that boxes are normally transparent. I added a background color to the relatively positioned box to more clearly illustrate how my page works. If I remove the background-color property from class two, the page looks like the one in Figure 9.16.

Needless to say, in this example, transparency is probably not the effect I'm looking for. However, taking advantage of this transparency can be a useful effect when you create text blocks that partially overlap images or other nontext boxes.

FIGURE 9.16

Transparency of overlapping elements.

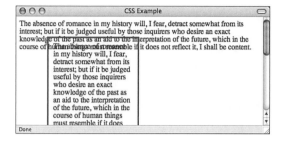

Absolute Positioning

9

Now let's look at absolute positioning. The source code for the page shown in Figure 9.17 contains four absolutely positioned elements.

Input ▼

```
<html>
<head>
  <title>CSS Example</title>
  <style type="text/css">
#topleft {
  position: absolute;
  top: 0px;
  left: 0px;
}

#topright {
  position: absolute;
  top: 0px;
  right: 0px;
}

#bottomleft {
  position: absolute;
  bottom: 0px;
  left: 0px;
}

#bottomright {
  position: absolute;
  bottom: 0px;
  right: 0px;
}

.box {
  border: 3px solid red;
  background-color: #ccf;
  padding: 10px;
  margin: 10px;
}
```

```
    </style>
</head>
<body>
<div class="box" id="topleft">
Top left corner.
</div>

<div class="box" id="topright">
Top right corner.
</div>

<div class="box" id="bottomleft">
Bottom left corner.
</div>

<div class="box" id="bottomright">
Bottom right corner.
</div>

<p class="one">
The absence of romance in my history will, I fear, detract somewhat
from its interest; but if it be judged useful by those inquirers who
desire an exact knowledge of the past as an aid to the interpretation
of the future, which in the course of human things must resemble if
it does not reflect it, I shall be content.
</p>
<p class="two">
The absence of romance in my history will, I fear, detract somewhat
from its interest; but if it be judged useful by those inquirers who
desire an exact knowledge of the past as an aid to the interpretation
of the future, which in the course of human things must resemble if
it does not reflect it, I shall be content. In fine, I have written
my work, not as an essay which is to win the applause of the moment,
but as a possession for all time.
</p>
</body>
</html>
```

Output ▼

FIGURE 9.17
A page that uses absolute positioning.

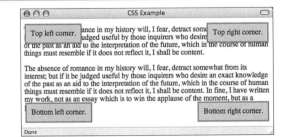

Aside from the fact that there are now four absolutely positioned <div>s on the page exactly where I indicated they should be placed, a couple of other things should stand out here. The first item to notice is that when you absolutely position elements, there's no placeholder for them in the normal flow of the page. My four <div>s are defined right at the top, and yet the first paragraph of the text starts at the beginning of the page body. Unlike relative positioning, absolute positioning completely removes an element from the regular page layout. The second interesting fact is that absolutely positioned elements overlap the existing content without any regard for it. If I wanted the text in the paragraphs to flow around the positioned elements, I would have had to use float rather than position.

Not only can I use any unit of measurement when positioning elements, I can also use negative numbers if I choose. You already saw how I applied a negative value to the top of the relatively positioned element to move it up some; I can do the same thing with these absolutely positioned elements. The result of changing the rule for the topleft class in the earlier example to

Input ▼

```
#topleft {
    position: absolute;
    top: -30px;
    left: -30px;
}
```

is that it actually pulls the element partially off of the page, where it is inaccessible even using the scroll bars, as shown in Figure 9.18.

Output ▼

FIGURE 9.18
Use of negative
absolute positioning.

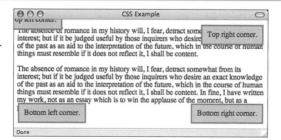

Controlling Stacking

If overlap isn't the effect you're looking for, relative and absolute positioning probably aren't for you. However, there is a way to control overlap as well. The z-index property defines stacking order for a page. By default, elements that appear in the same layer of a document are stacked sequentially. In other words, an element that appears after another will generally be stacked above it.

By assigning z-index values to elements, though, you can put elements in specific stack-ing layers. If all elements appear in stacking layer 0 by default, any element in stacking layer 1 (z-index: 1) will appear above all elements in layer 0. The catch here is that z-index can be applied only to elements that are placed using absolute or relative posi-tioning. Elements that are placed using static positioning always appear below relatively or absolutely positioned elements. The stacking layers below 0 are considered beneath the body element, and so they don't show up at all.

TIP

If you want to have an element positioned as though it were part of the static positioning scheme but you want to control its stack-ing layer, assign it the relative positioning scheme and don't spec-ify a position. It will appear on the page normally but you will be able to apply a z-index to it.

Let's look at another page. This one contains two paragraphs, both part of the same (default) stacking layer. As you can see in Figure 9.19, the second overlaps the first.

Input ▼

```
<html>
<head>
  <title>CSS Example</title>
  <style type="text/css">
.one {
  position: relative;
  width: 50%;
  padding: 15px;
  background-color: #ffc;
}

.two {
  position: absolute;
  top: 15%;
  left: 15%;
  padding: 15px;
  width: 50%;
  background-color: #060;
  color: #fff;
}
  </style>
</head>
<body>
<p class="one">
The absence of romance in my history will, I fear, detract somewhat
from its interest; but if it be judged useful by those inquirers who
desire an exact knowledge of the past as an aid to the interpretation
of the future, which in the course of human things must resemble if
```

```
it does not reflect it, I shall be content.
</p>
<p class="two">
The absence of romance in my history will, I fear, detract somewhat
from its interest; but if it be judged useful by those inquirers who
desire an exact knowledge of the past as an aid to the interpretation
of the future, which in the course of human things must resemble if
it does not reflect it, I shall be content. In fine, I have written
my work, not as an essay which is to win the applause of the moment,
but as a possession for all time.
</p>

</body>
</html>
```

9

Output ▼

FIGURE 9.19
Two normally
stacked elements.

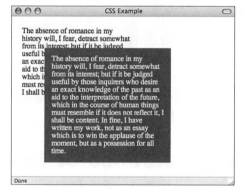

So, how do I cause the first element to overlap the second? Because I've assigned the first element the relative positioning scheme (even though I haven't positioned it), I can assign it a z-index of 1 (or higher) to move it into a stacking layer above the second paragraph. The new style sheet for the page, which appears in Figure 9.20, is as follows:

Input ▼

```
.one {
  position: relative;
  z-index: 1;
  width: 50%;
  padding: 15px;
  background-color: #ffc;
}

.two {
  position: absolute;
  top: 15%;
  left: 15%;
```

```
    padding: 15px;
    width: 50%;
    background-color: #060;
    color: #fff;
}
```

Output ▼

FIGURE 9.20

A page that uses z-index to control positioning.

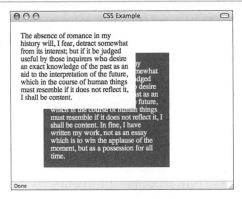

Needless to say, using a combination of absolute and relative positioning, you can create very complex pages with many stacked layers.

Modifying the Appearance of Tables

In Lesson 8, "Building Tables," I discussed the creation of tables. In it, I touched on ways that you can use CSS to improve how your tables look. Now I'm going to explain how you can use the CSS properties I've discussed to really spruce up your tables. Ironically, the main goal of today's lesson is to show you that there are alternatives to using tables to lay out complex pages. Right now, I'm going to also demonstrate how to use CSS to improve the presentation of tabular data. As a refresher, take a look at one of the tables I created in Lesson 8 in Figure 9.21.

FIGURE 9.21

One of the tables from Lesson 8.

Service Data

Drive Belt Deflection

		Used Belt Deflection		Set deflection of new belt
		Limit	Adjust Deflection	
Alternator	Models without AC	10mm	5-7mm	5-7mm
	Models with AC	12mm	6-8mm	
Power Steering Oil Pump		12.5mm	7.9mm	6-8mm

Now I'm going to replace many of the formatting changes made to the table using HTML with CSS. The source code for the new page (see Figure 9.22 for the result) follows:

Input ▼

```
<!DOCTYPE html PUBLIC "-//W3C//DTD XHTML 1.0 Strict//EN"
  "http://www.w3.org/TR/xhtml1/DTD/xhtml1-strict.dtd">
<html xmlns="http://www.w3.org/1999/xhtml">
<head>
<title>Service Data</title>
<style type="text/css">
td, th { padding: 5px;
    border: 1px solid #c90;
    background-color: #ffc;
    text-align: center;
    margin: 0px; }

th.emtpy { background-color: #fff;
    border-left: none;
    border-top: none; }

.left { text-align: left; }

table { border: 5px groove #c90; }

caption { font: bold 18px Verdana; margin: 10px; }
</style>
</head>
<body>
<table cellspacing="0">
<caption>Drive Belt Deflection</caption>

<tr>
<th rowspan="2" colspan="2" class="emtpy"></th>
<th colspan="2">Used Belt Deflection</th>
<th rowspan="2">Set<br />
deflection<br />
of new belt</th>
</tr>

<tr>
<th>Limit</th>
<th>Adjust<br />
Deflection</th>
</tr>

<tr>
<th rowspan="2" class="left">Alternator</th>
<td class="left">Models without AC</td>
<td>10mm</td>
<td>5-7mm</td>
<td rowspan="2">5-7mm</td>
</tr>
```

```
<tr>
<td class="left">Models with AC</td>
<td>12mm</td>
<td>6-8mm</td>
</tr>

<tr>
<th colspan="2" class="left">Power Steering Oil Pump</th>
<td>12.5mm</td>
<td>7.9mm</td>
<td>6-8mm</td>
</tr>
</table>
</body>
</html>
```

Output ▼

FIGURE 9.22

The table from Figure 9.21 for-matted using CSS.

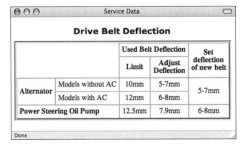

Given the size of the style sheet, we haven't gained a whole lot in terms of efficiency by using CSS for formatting. However, there are some things that can be accomplished using CSS that cannot be accomplished using regular table formatting attributes. First, though, as you can see, I used CSS to set the background colors for my table cells and to handle the alignment tasks for the table. Because nearly everything in the table is cen-tered, I made that the default for all <td> and <th> tags. I put the cells that need to be left aligned in the class left and changed its alignment to left.

One thing I could accomplish using CSS that isn't possible without it is to use a different border for the outside of the table than I used inside. For the border between the cells, I used a thin 1-pixel border. Around the table, I used a 5-pixel grooved border. I also turned off the top and left borders for the empty cell, along with setting its background color to white. You should note that one thing I didn't change was the cellspacing attribute of the <table> tag. If you want to modify cell spacing, you must use this attribute because there's no CSS equivalent.

The <body> Tag

I've already mentioned that you can adjust the margin, padding, and border of a page by applying styles to the <body> tag. More importantly, any styles that you want to apply on a pagewide basis can be assigned to the page's body. You already know about setting the background color for the page by using `style="background-color: black"` in your <body> tag. That's really just the beginning. If you want the default font for all the text on your page to appear in the Georgia font, you can use the following style:

```
body { font-family: Georgia; }
```

That's a lot easier than changing the `font-family` property for every tag that contains text on your page. A common <body> tag you often see looks something like

```
<body bgcolor="#000000" text="#ffffff" alink="blue" vlink="yellow" alink="purple">
```

You can modify the background and text colors like this:

```
body { color: white;
    background-color: black; }
```

I'll explain how to alter the link colors shortly. One of the main advantages of taking this approach, aside from the fact that it's how the standard says you should do things, is that then you can put the style into a linked style sheet and set the background color for your whole site on one page.

Many layouts require that elements be flush with the edge of the browser. In these cases, you need to set the margin to 0 for your <body> tag. Some browsers enabled you to do this with proprietary attributes of the <body> tag, but they're not reliable. To turn off margins, just use this rule:

```
body { margin: 0px; }
```

Links

You already know how to adjust the colors of elements on a page, but links are a bit different. They're more complicated than other types of elements because they can exist in multiple states: an unvisited link, a visited link, an active link, and a link that the user currently has the pointer over. As you can see, there's one more state here than has been traditionally reflected in the <body> tag. Using CSS, you can change the color of a link when the user mouses over it (referred to as the *hover* state) as opposed to when he's currently clicking on it (the *active* state).

Another advantage of CSS is that you can change the color schemes for links on the same page, rather than being forced to use one scheme throughout. Finally, you can turn off link underlining if you want. For example, here's a style sheet that turns off link

9

underlining for navigation links, renders them in boldface, and keeps the same color for visited and unvisited links.

```
a:link   { color: blue; }
a:active { color: red; }
a:visited { color: purple; }
a:hover  { color: red; }
a.nav    { font-weight: bold;
      text-decoration: none; }
a.nav:hover, a.nav: active { background-color: yellow;
                color: red; }
a.nav:link, a.nav:visited { color: green; }
```

From the style sheet, you can see that for all <a> tags in the class nav, the text-decoration property is set to none, which turns off underlining, and font-weight is set to bold. For <a> tags on the rest of the page, the underlining remains on, but I've set it up so that when the mouse is over the links, they turn red. For navigation links, when the mouse is over the links, the background of the element turns yellow and the text turns red.

You can use pretty much any property you like with these selectors, and browsers that support them will dynamically reflow the page to accommodate the change. However, changes that affect the size of the element (such as boldfacing the text dynamically or increasing the font size) can be very jarring to users, so use them cautiously.

Creating Layouts with Multiple Columns

Over the course of this lesson, you've seen how to modify many aspects of a page's design using cascading style sheets. Now let's look at an example that kind of ties everything together. In this case, we're going to see the sort of effect that might normally be accomplished using a table that encompasses the whole page implemented using CSS instead.

This page uses a two-column layout with a header across the top. One thing you'll be impressed by is the small amount of markup within the HTML. All the formatting is contained in the style sheet. Here's the source code for the page, which appears in Figure 9.23:

Input ▼

```
<!DOCTYPE html PUBLIC "-//W3C//DTD XHTML 1.0 Strict//EN"
  "http://www.w3.org/TR/xhtml1/DTD/xhtml1-strict.dtd">
<html xmlns="http://www.w3.org/1999/xhtml">
<head>
<title>The Star</title>
<style type="text/css">
body { font-family: Georgia;
    margin: 0px;
    background-color: #f90; }
```

```
#header { font: bold 48px Trebuchet MS;
     padding-left: 30px;
     border-bottom: 3px solid black;
     background-color: #c00;
     margin-bottom: 0px; }

#content { float: right;
      padding: 1px 20px 1px 10px;
      width: 70%;
      margin: 0px;
      border: none;
      background-color: #fff; }

#nav { float: left;
    width: 20%;
    margin-top: 0px;
    font-weight: bold;
    padding: 10px;
    border: none;
    font-family: Trebuchet MS; }

#nav a { text-decoration: none;
     color: #006; }

#nav a:hover { color: #c00; }

h2 { margin-top: 10px; }

</style>
</head>
<body>
<div id="header">The Star</div>

<div id="content">
<h2>Curly Bill</h2>

<h3>The Noted Desperado, Gets it in the Neck at Galeyville</h3>

<p>May 26, 1881 - The notorious Curly Bill, the man who murdered
Marshal White at Tombstone last fall and who has been concerned in
several other desperate and lawless affrays in South Eastern
Arizona, has at last been brought to grief and there is likely to
be a vacancy in the ranks of out border desperados. The affair
occurred at Galeyville Thursday. A party of 8 or 9 cowboys, Curly
Bill and his partner Jim Wallace among the number, were enjoying
themselves in their usual manner, when deputy Sheriff Breakenridge
of Tombstone, who was at Galeyville on business, happened
along.</p>

<p>Wallace made some insulting remark to the deputy at the same
time flourishing his revolver in an aggressive manner. Breakenridge
did not pay much attention to this "break" of Wallace but quietly
```

9

turned around and left the party. Shortly after this, Curly Bill, who it would seem had a friendly feeling for Breakenridge, insisted that Wallace should go and find him and apologize for the insult given. This Wallace was induced to do after finding Breakenridge he made the apology and the latter accompanied him back to the saloon where the cowboys were drinking. By this time Curly Bill who had drank just enough to make him quarrelsome, was in one of his most dangerous moods and evidently desirous of increasing his record as a man killer. He commenced to abuse Wallace, who, by the way, had some pretensions himself as a desperado and bad man generally and finally said, "You g-d Lincoln county s-of a b---, I'll kill you anyhow." Wallace immediately went outside the door of the saloon, Curly Bill following close behind him. Just as the latter stepped outside, Wallace, who had meanwhile drawn his revolver, fired, the ball entering penetrating the left side of Curly Bill's neck and passing through, came out the right cheek, not breaking the jawbone. A scene of the wildest excitement ensued in the town.</p>

<p>The other members of the cowboy party surrounded Wallace and threats of lynching him were made. The law abiding citizens were in doubt what course to pursue. They did not wish any more blood shed but were in favor of allowing the lawless element to "have it out" among themselves. But Deputy Breakenridge decided to arrest Wallace, which he succeeded in doing without meeting any resistance. The prisoner was taken before Justice Ellinwood and after examination into the facts of the shooting he was discharged.</p>

<p>The wounded and apparently dying desperado was taken into an adjoining building, and a doctor summoned to dress his wounds. After examining the course of the bullet, the doctor pronounced the wound dangerous but not necessarily fatal, the chances for and against recovery being about equal. Wallace and Curly Bill have been Partners and fast friends for the past 4 or 6 months and so far is known, there was no cause for the quarrel, it being simply a drunken brawl.</p>
</div>

<div id="nav">
<a href="">News</a>
<a href="">Sports</a>
<a href="">Weather</a>
<a href="">Business</a>
<a href="">Classified</a>
</div>

</body>
</html>

Output ▼

FIGURE 9.23
A page laid out
entirely using CSS.

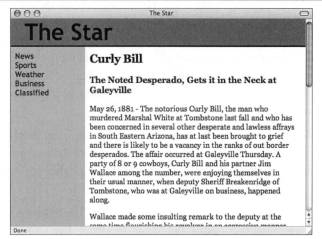

As you can see, the page I created uses a two-column layout with a header across the top. If you take a look at the source code, you'll see that there are three <div>s that are used to lay out the page. One contains the heading (with the ID "header"), one is for the main content (with the ID "content"), and one is for the navigation elements (with the ID "nav"). Note that the navigation <div> actually comes after the content in the source file. I didn't have to do it this way, but there are good reasons to do so, as I'll describe in Lesson 17, "Designing for the Real World."

Let's go through the style sheet rule by rule. First of all, I set the font for the document to Georgia in the <body> tag. I also set the margins for the page to 0px and set the page's background color to the same background color that I'm going to use in the navigation div. I'll explain why in a bit.

Next, I set up the header. I set the font size to a nice, large, bold font, befitting the header for a page. Then I add some padding to the left side of the <div> to give myself a margin because I turned off margins for the page as a whole. I add some accents to the header by putting a 3-pixel border across the bottom and setting the background of the header to a dark red color. I also turn off the margin on the bottom to get things to fit together nicely.

The next rule is for the content section. This is the most important part of the page, so I set its width to 70%. I turn off its margin completely, and give it some padding on the left and right to create some white space around the text and a 1-pixel margin on the top and bottom because there's plenty of white space there already. The background color of this <div> is white and the borders are turned off.

Now let's look at the rules for the navigation <div>. I've this one set to float: left. One thing you may be wondering is why I have float turned on for both the content

`<div>` and the navigation `<div>`. Things are set up this way so that the `<div>`s run down opposite sides of the page no matter what. I don't want one of them to wrap around the other, and I also wanted to be able to put the navigation `<div>` under the content `<div>` and have them both pushed all the way up against the header. If there were some unfloated text content for this page that was extremely skinny, or I made both of these `<div>`s narrower, I could run some content right down the middle of the page between them. If I did want to put some content on the page below the two `<div>`s, I'd need to make sure to use `clear: both` to eliminate the floats.

When you have two `<div>`s side by side on a page and you want them to appear as columns, you must set the page background color to match the background of the smaller `<div>`. That way, the background of the space below the smaller `<div>` will match that `<div>`.

The next two rules affect the links in the navigation bar. The links are set to be navy blue and to turn red when the user passes the mouse over them. I've also turned off underlining. The links were set to boldface in the larger rule for the navigation `<div>`. The last rule adjusts the white space for `<h2>` tags slightly to make it consistent between Netscape and Internet Explorer.

Summary

In the earlier days of this book, I've given you a taste of how to use cascading style sheets. You didn't get the full flavor because I used them only within the context of the `style` attribute of tags. Today, I discussed how you can create actual style sheets either as part of a page or as a standalone file that can be included by any page. I also moved beyond properties that discuss text formatting to explain how to use CSS to lay out an entire page.

CSS provides a better alternative to tables, transparent single-pixel GIFs, and other old techniques that have been relied on to gain control over how pages are laid out. By understanding how browsers render pages and how you can affect that process using CSS, you can achieve the effects you want without writing loads of markup that's difficult to understand and maintain.

As cool as cascading style sheets are, they're only half the fun. In Lesson 15, "Creating Applications with Dynamic HTML and AJAX," you'll learn how to modify styles from within your pages using JavaScript, adding an amazing degree of flexibility to how you create your web pages. Any styles you learned about today can be manipulated in the world of dynamic HTML—it's exciting stuff.

Workshop

In this lesson, you learned about cascading style sheets, the wonderful supplement to HTML that makes formatting your pages less painful. Throughout the rest of this book, I'll be using cascading style sheets where appropriate, so please review this workshop material before continuing.

Q&A

Q My CSS isn't working like I'd expect. What should I do?

A CSS probably doesn't seem that clear in the first place, and things can only get messier when you actually start applying styles to your pages. You should be sure to test your pages in every browser you can find, and don't be afraid to experiment. Just because something seems like it should work doesn't mean it will. The W3C also provides a CSS Validator (http://jigsaw.w3.org/css-validator/) that you can use to make sure that your CSS syntax is correct. You should probably use it all the time, but even if you don't, it can still help out if you get stuck.

Q Are there naming rules for classes and IDs?

A Yes, there are. A name must start with a letter, and can contain only letters, numbers, or dashes (-). Some browsers may not enforce these rules, but to be safe, you should adhere to them.

Q What are the relevant CSS standards?

A There are two CSS recommendations from the W3C: CSS1 and CSS2. Most modern browsers support a large part of CSS1 and some of CSS2, specifically the sections on positioning elements that I discussed today. You can find out more at http://www.w3.org/Style/CSS/. If you're curious about how well your browser supports CSS or the effect that properties have in real browsers, you can check out the CSS test suites at http://www.w3.org/Style/CSS/Test/.

Quiz

1. Why can't absolute units be used reliably in CSS?
2. True or False: Including style sheets on your page requires features provided by a web server.
3. How do the absolute and relative positioning schemes differ?
4. Is the margin or padding of an element inside the border?
5. How do you lay out your page so that elements positioned statically appear above elements that are positioned absolutely?

9

Quiz Answers

1. Absolute units have problems in CSS because there's no way to know exactly what sort of display medium the user has. An inch on one monitor may be completely different than an inch on another.

2. The answer is false; you can use the `<link>` tag to load external style sheets without involving the web server in any way.

3. The relative positioning scheme places elements relative to the previous element on the page, whereas the absolute positioning scheme places the element exactly where you tell it to on the page.

4. The padding of an element is inside the border of an element, and the margin is outside.

5. This is a trick question. You cannot put statically positioned elements above absolutely positioned elements. However, if you change the statically positioned elements so that they use the relative positioning scheme, you can alter their stacking layer using the `z-index` property.

Exercises

1. If you've already created some web pages, go back and try to figure out how you could apply CSS to them.

2. Take a look at some of your favorite websites and think about how the webmasters could achieve the effects on their sites using CSS.

3. Adapt today's sample page so that it has three columns of content instead of two.

LESSON 10:
Designing Forms

Up to this point, you've learned almost everything you need to know to create functional, attractive, and somewhat interactive web pages. If you think about it, however, the pages you've created thus far have a one-way information flow. Your HTML documents, images, sounds, and video have been traveling to web browsers with no return ticket.

Today's lesson is about creating HTML forms to collect information from people visiting your website. Forms enable you to gather just about any kind of information for immediate processing by a server-side script or for later analysis using other applications. If you've spent much time browsing the Web, you've undoubtedly run across forms of various flavors. Many forms exist: simple forms that perform searches, forms that log you in to websites, forms that enable you to order products online, online polls, and so on. They all share one thing in common: accepting input from a web page visitor.

If you're one to worry about compatibility, you can set your mind at ease. HTML forms have been around since the beginning of the HTML language and are supported by every web browser in common use. I'll make sure to point out any possible compatibility problems along the way.

In this Lesson

Don't be intimidated by forms! Although they might look complex, they're actually very easy to code. The hardest part is formatting them. Today's lesson covers the following topics, which enable you to create any type of form possible with HTML:

- Discovering how HTML forms interact with server-side scripts to provide interactivity
- Creating simple forms to get the hang of it

- Learning all the types of form controls you can use to create radio buttons, check boxes, and more

- Using more advanced form controls to amaze your friends and co-workers

- Planning forms so that your data matches any server-side scripts you use

Understanding Form and Function

Right off the bat, you need to understand a few things about forms. First, a form is part of a web page that you create using HTML elements. Each form contains a `form` element that has special controls, such as buttons, text fields, check boxes, Submit buttons, and menus. These controls make up the user interface for the form (that is, the pieces of the form users see on the web page). When people fill out forms, they're interacting with the controls of the forms. In addition, you can use many other HTML elements within forms to create labels, provide additional information, add structure, and so on. These elements aren't part of the form itself, but they can enhance your form's look and improve its usability.

When someone fills out an HTML form, he enters information or makes choices using the form controls. When the user submits the form, the browser collects all the data from the form and sends it to the URL specified as the form's action. It's up to the program residing at that URL to process the form input and create a response for the user.

It's very important that you understand the implications of this final step. The data is what you want, after all! This is the reason you've chosen to create a form in the first place. After a user clicks the Submit button, the process ceases to be one of pure HTML and becomes reliant on applications that reside on the web server. In other words, for your form to work, you must already have a program on the server that will store or manipulate the data in some manner.

There are some cases in which forms aren't necessarily submitted to programs. Using JavaScript and dynamic HTML, you can take action based on form input. For example, you can open a new window when a user clicks on a form button. You can also submit forms via email, which is okay for testing, but isn't reliable enough for real applications.

Okay, let's get right to it and create a simple form that illustrates the concepts just presented. It's a web page that prompts the user to enter a name and a password to continue.

Start by opening your favorite HTML editor and creating a web page template. Enter the standard HTML header information, include the body element, and then close the body and html elements to form a template from which to work. If you already have a template similar to this, just load it into your HTML editor:

```
<!DOCTYPE html PUBLIC "-//W3C//DTD XHTML 1.0 Transitional//EN"
"http://www.w3.org/TR/xhtml1/DTD/transitional.dtd">
<html>
<head>
<title>Page Title</title>
</head>
<body>

</body>
</html>
```

10

NOTE

> I tend to use Transitional HTML and note it in the <!doctype> declaration. This gives me the flexibility of adding deprecated HTML elements if I choose, without worrying about validation errors.

Next, add your title so that people will understand the purpose of the web page:

```
<title>Please Log In</title>
```

Within the body of the web page, add a form element. I've added both the opening and closing tags, with an empty line between them, so that I don't forget to close the form when I'm finished:

```
<form action="http://www.example.com/cgi-bin/entrance.cgi" method="post">

</form>
```

Before continuing, you need to know more about the form element and the attributes you see within the opening tag. Obviously, form begins the element and indicates that you're creating an HTML form. The action attribute specifies the URL to the server-side script (including the filename) that will process the form when it's submitted. It's very important that the script with the name you've entered is present on your web server at the ▼

▼ location the URL specifies. In this example, I use the full URL for the script, but you can just as easily use a relative URL if it makes more sense.

NOTE Prior to going live with forms, you should contact your web hosting provider and ask whether you can use the ISP's scripts or add your own. You must also determine the URL that points to the directory on the server that contains the scripts. Some ISPs rigidly control scripts for security purposes and won't allow you to create or add scripts to the server. If that's the case, and you really need to implement forms on your web pages, you should consider searching for a new ISP.

The next attribute is method, which can accept one of two possible values: post or get. These values define how form data is submitted to your web server. The post method includes the form data in the body of the form and sends it to the web server. The get method appends the data to the URL specified in the action attribute and most often is used in searches. I chose the post method here because I don't want to send the user's password back in plain sight as part of the URL. Now add some form controls and information to make it easy for a visitor to understand how to fill out the form. Within the form element, begin by adding a helpful description of the data to be entered by the user, and then add a text form control. This prompts the user to enter her name in a text-entry field. Don't worry about positioning just yet because you'll put all the form controls into a table later:

```
<form action="http://www.example.com/cgi-bin/entrance.cgi" method=post>
   Username: <input type="text" name="username" />
</form>
```

Next, add another bit of helpful text and a password control:

```
<form action="http://www.example.com/cgi-bin/entrance.cgi" method="post">
   Username: <input type="text" name="username" />

   Password: <input type="password" name="password" />
</form>
```

Notice that both these form controls are created using the input element. The type attribute defines which type of control will be created. In this case, you have a text control and a password control. Each type of control has a distinct appearance, accepts a different type of user input, and is suitable for different purposes. Each control is also assigned a name that distinguishes it and its data from the other form controls. Finally, add a Submit button so that the user can send the information she entered into the form.

▼ Here's the form so far:

Input ▼

```
<form action="http://www.example.com/cgi-bin/entrance.cgi" method="post">
  Username: <input type="text" name="username" /><br />
  Password: <input type="password" name="password" /><br />
  <input type="submit" value="Log In" />
</form>
```

The Submit button is another type of `input` field. The `value` attribute is used as the label for the Submit button. If you leave it out, the default label will be displayed by the browser.

TIP   When you're naming form controls and labeling buttons, you should strive for clarity and meaning. If a form is frustrating or hard to figure out, visitors will leave your site for greener pastures!

10

Figure 10.1 contains a screenshot of the form with all the form elements in place.

Output ▼

FIGURE 10.1
The form with all the input elements in place.

At this point, you've created the form and it's ready to rumble. However, if you load it into your web browser, you'll see that it doesn't look all that appealing. Placing the form controls in the table should clean things up a bit. You can put the `<table>` tags inside your form. The table should be two columns wide, with the labels in the left column and the input fields in the right column. The Submit button will be in the left column on the third row. Here's the code:

```
form action="http://www.example.com/cgi-bin/entrance.cgi" method="post">
  <table border="0">
    <tr>
      <td align="right">Username:</td>
      <td><input type="text" name="username" /></td>
    </tr>

    <tr>
      <td align="right">Password:</td>
      <td><input type="password" name="password" /></td>
    </tr>
```

```
    <tr>
      <td align="center">
        <input type="submit" value="Log In" style="margin-top: 20px"/>
      </td>
      <td><br /></td>
    </tr>
  </table>
</form>
```

Notice that we added 20 pixels of white space above the Submit button using the margin-top property in the style attribute of the <input> tag. We also aligned the two labels to the right and the button to the center, just to spiff things up a bit more.

A few final notes are warranted: First, we used the margin property to center the table. Second, we included an <h1> element on the page to give the user some idea what to do. Here's the full code for the page:

Input ▼

```
<!DOCTYPE html PUBLIC "-//W3C//DTD XHTML 1.0 Transitional//EN"
  "http://www.w3.org/TR/xhtml1/DTD/xhtml1-transitional.dtd">
<html xmlns="http://www.w3.org/1999/xhtml">
<head>
<title>Please Log In</title>
</head>
<body>
<h1 style="text-align: center">Please Log In</h1>

<form action="http://www.example.com/cgi-bin/entrance.cgi" method="get">
  <table border="0" style="margin: auto">
    <tr>
      <td align="right">Username:</td>
      <td><input type="text" name="username" /></td>
    </tr>

    <tr>
      <td align="right">Password:</td>
      <td><input type="password" name="password" /></td>
    </tr>

    <tr>
      <td align="center">
        <input type="submi" value="Log In" style="margin-top: 20px" />
      </td>
      <td><br /></td>
    </tr>
  </table>
</form>
</body>
</html>
```

That took a little work, but I think the final page shown in Figure 10.2 looks good.   ▼

Output ▼

FIGURE 10.2
A simple form.

To complete the exercise, let's test the form to see whether the form produces the data we expect. Here's what the data that's sent to the server looks like:

```
username=someone&password=somepassword
```

It's pretty measly, but you can see that the names assigned to each field are tied to the values entered in those fields. You can then use a program to use this data to process the user's request.   ▲

10

Using the <form> Tag

To accept input from a user, you must wrap all of your input fields inside a <form> tag. The purpose of the <form> tag is to indicate where and how the user's input should be sent. First, let's look at how the <form> tag affects page layout. Forms are block-level elements. That means when you start a form, a new line is inserted (unless you apply the display: inline CSS property to the form tag).

NOTE

Form controls must appear inside another block level element inside the <form> element in order to be considered valid. A <div>, <p>, or <table> will all do the trick, as will other block level elements.

Take a look at the following code fragment:

Input ▼

```
<p>Please enter your username <form><input /> and password
<input /></form> to log in.</p>
```

You might think that your entire form would appear on a single line based on the preceding markup. As shown in Figure 10.3, the opening and closing <form> tags act like opening and closing paragraph tags.

Output ▼

FIGURE 10.3
A line break inserted by an opening <form> tag.

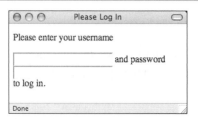

The two most commonly used attributes of the <form> tag are action and method. Both of these attributes are optional. The following example shows how the <form> tag is typically used:

```
<form action="someaction" method="get or post">
content, form controls, and other HTML elements
</form>
```

action specifies the URL to which the form is submitted. Again, remember that for the form to be submitted successfully, the script must be in the exact location you specify and must work properly.

If you leave out the action attribute, the form is submitted to the current URL. In other words, if the form appears on the page http://www.example.com/form.html and you leave off the action attribute, the form will be submitted to that URL by default. This probably doesn't seem very useful, but it is if your form is generated by a program instead of residing in an HTML file. In that case, the form is submitted back to that program for processing. One advantage of doing so is that if you move the program on the server, you don't have to edit the HTML to point the form at the new location.

Although most forms send their data to scripts, you also can make the action link to another web page or a mailto link. The latter is formed as follows:

```
<form action="mailto:somebody@isp.com" method="post">
```

This attaches the form data set to an email, which then is sent to the email address listed in the action attribute.

TIP

> To test your forms, I recommend using the get method and leaving out the action attribute of the form tag. When you submit the form, the values you entered will appear in the URL for the page so that you can inspect them and make sure that the results are what you expected.

The method attribute supports two values: get or post. The method indicates how the form data should be packaged in the request that's sent back to the server. The get method appends the form data to the URL in the request. The form data is separated from the URL in the request by a question mark and is referred to as the query string. If I have a text input field named searchstring and enter Orangutans in the field, the resulting would look like the following:

```
http://www.example.com/cgi-bin/search?searchstring=Orangutans
```

10

The method attribute is not required; if you leave it out, the get method will be used. The other method is post. Rather than appending the form data to the URL and sending the combined URL-data string to the server, post sends the form data to the location specified by the action attribute in the body of the request.

DO	DON'T
DO use the POST method when data on the server will be changed in any way.	**DON'T** use the GET method if you do not want the form parameters to be visible in a URL.
DO use the GET method if the form just requests data. (Like search forms, for example.)	**DON'T** use the GET method if the form is used to delete information.
DO use the GET method if you want to bookmark the results of the form submission.	

The general rule when it comes to choosing between post and get is that if the form will change any data on the server, you should use post. If the form is used to retrieve information, using get is fine. For example, let's say that you're writing a message board program. The registration form for new users and the form used to publish messages should use the post method. If you have a form that enables the user to show all the posts entered on a certain date, it could use the get method.

That about does it for the <form> tag, but you've really only just begun. The <form> tag alone is just a container for the input fields that are used to gather data from users. It simply indicates where the data should go and how it should be packaged. To actually gather information, you're going to need items called form controls.

One other less frequently used attribute of the `<form>` tag is `enctype`. It defines how form data is encoded when it's sent to the server. The default is `application/x-www-form-urlencoded`. The only time you ever need to use `enctype` is when your form includes a file upload field (which I'll discuss a bit later). In that case, you need to specify that the `enctype` is `multipart/form-data`. Otherwise, it's fine to leave it out.

Creating Form Controls with the `<input>` Tag

Now it's time to learn how to create the data entry fields form. The `<input>` tag enables you to create many different types of form controls.

Form controls are special HTML tags used in a form that enable you to gather information from visitors to your web page. The information is packaged into a request sent to the URL in the form's `action` attribute.

The `input` element consists of an opening tag with attributes, no other content, and no closing tag:

```
<input attributes />
```

The key point here is using the attributes that will create the form control you need. The most important of these is `type`, which specifies what kind of form control to display. For all controls, except Submit and Reset buttons, the `name` attribute is required. It associates a name with the data entered in that field when the data is sent to the server. The rest of this section describes the different types of controls you can create using the `input` element.

Creating Text Controls

Text controls enable you to gather information from a user in small quantities. This control type creates a single-line text input field in which users can type information, such as their name or a search term.

To create a text input field, create an `input` element and choose `text` as the value for the `type` attribute. Make sure to name your control so that the server script will be able to process the value:

Input ▼

```
<p>Enter your pet's name:
<input type="text" name="petname" /></p>
```

Figure 10.4 shows this text control, which tells the user what to type in.

Output ▼

FIGURE 10.4
A text entry field.

You can modify the appearance of text controls by using the size attribute. Entering a number sets the width of the text control in characters:

```
<input type="text" name="petname" size="15" />
```

To limit the number of characters a user can enter, add the maxlength attribute to the text control. This doesn't affect the appearance of the field; it just prevents the user from entering more characters than specified by this attribute. If users attempt to enter more text, their web browsers will stop accepting input for that particular control.

```
<input type="text" name="petname" size="15" maxlength="15" />
```

To display text in the text control before the user enters any information, use the value attribute. If the user is updating data that already exists, you can specify the current or default value using value, or you can prompt the user with a value:

```
<input type="text" name="petname" size="15" maxlength="15" value="Enter Pet Name" />
```

In this case, Enter Pet Name appears in the field when the form is rendered in the web browser. It remains there until the user modifies it.

CAUTION   When you're using the value attribute, using a value that's larger than the size of the text control can confuse the user because the text will appear to be cut off. Try to use only enough information to make your point. Ensure that any value is less than or equal to the number of characters you specified in size.

Creating Password Controls

The password and text field types are identical in every way except that the data entered in a password field is masked so that someone looking over the shoulder of the person entering information can't see the value that was typed into the field.

10

TIP

You don't have to limit your use of the password control to just passwords. You can use it for any sensitive material that you feel needs to be hidden when the user enters it into the form.

To create a password control, create an input element with the type set to password. To limit the size of the password control and the maximum number of characters a user can enter, you can use the size and maxlength attributes just as you would in a text control. Here's an example:

Input ▼

```
<p>Enter your password: <input type="password" name="userpassword"
  size="8" maxlength="8" /></p>
```

Figure 10.5 shows a password control.

Output ▼

FIGURE 10.5
A password form field.

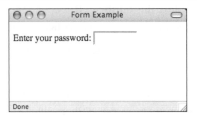

CAUTION

When data entered in a password field is sent to the server, it is not encrypted in any way. Therefore, this is not a secure means of transmitting sensitive information. Although the users can't read what they are typing, the password control provides no other security measures.

Creating Submit Buttons

Submit buttons are used to indicate that the user is finished filling out the form. Setting the type attribute of the form to submit places a Submit button on the page with the default label determined by the browser, usually Submit Query. To change the button text, use the value attribute and enter your own label, as follows:

```
<input type="submit" value="Send Form Data" />
```

NOTE

Your forms can contain more than one Submit button.

If you include a name attribute for a Submit button, the value that you assign to the field is sent to the server if the user clicks on that Submit button. This enables you to take different actions based on which Submit button the user clicks, if you have more than one. For example, you could create two Submit buttons, both with the name attribute set to "action". The first might have a value of "edit" and the second a value of "delete". In your script, you could test the value associated with that field to determine what the user wanted to do when he submitted the form.

Creating Reset Buttons

Reset buttons set all the form controls to their default values. These are the values included in the value attributes of each field in the form (or in the case of selectable fields, the values that are preselected). As with the Submit button, you can change the label of a Reset button to one of your own choosing by using the value attribute, like this:

```
<input type="reset" value="Clear Form" />
```

10

CAUTION	Reset buttons can be a source of some confusion for users. Unless you have a really good reason to include them on your forms, you should probably just avoid using them. If your form is large and the user clicks the Reset button when he means to click the Submit button, he isn't going to be very pleased with having to go back and re-enter all of his data.

Creating Check Box Controls

Check boxes are fields that can be set to two states: on and off (see Figure 10.6). To create a check box, set the input tag's type attribute to checkbox. The name attribute is also required, as shown in the following example:

Input ▼

```
<p>Check to receive SPAM email <input type="checkbox" name="spam" /></p>
```

Output ▼

FIGURE 10.6
A check box field.

To display the check box as checked, include the `checked` attribute, as follows:

```
<input type="checkbox" name="year" checked="checked" />
```

You can group check boxes together and assign them the same control name. This allows multiple values associated with the same name to be chosen:

```
<p>Check all symptoms that you are experiencing:<br />
<input type="checkbox" name="symptoms" value="nausea" /> Nausea<br />
<input type="checkbox" name="symptoms" value="lightheadedness" />
Light-headedness<br />
<input type="checkbox" name="symptoms" value="fever" /> Fever<br />
<input type="checkbox" name="symptoms" value="headache" /> Headache
</p>
```

When this form is submitted to a script for processing, each check box that's checked returns a value associated with the name of the check box. If a check box isn't checked, neither the field name nor value will be returned to the server—it's as if the field didn't exist at all.

Creating Radio Buttons

Radio buttons, which generally appear in groups, are designed so that when one button in the group is selected, the other buttons in the group are automatically unselected. They enable you to provide users with a list of options from which only one option can be selected. To create a radio button, set the `type` attribute of an `<input>` tag to `radio`. To create a radio button group, set the `name` attributes of all the fields in the group to the same value, as shown in Figure 10.7. To create a radio button group with three options, the following code is used:

Input ▼

```
<p>Select a color:<br />
<input type="radio" name="color" value="red" /> Red<br />
<input type="radio" name="color" value="blue" /> Blue<br />
<input type="radio" name="color" value="green" /> Green<br />
</p>
```

Output ▼

FIGURE 10.7
A group of radio buttons.

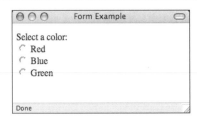

As with check boxes, if you want a radio button to be selected by default when the form is displayed, use the `checked` attribute. One point of confusion is that even though browsers prevent users from having more than one member of a radio button group selected at once, they don't prevent you from setting more than one member of a group as checked by default. You should avoid doing so yourself.

Using Images As Submit Buttons

Using `image` as the `type` of `input` control enables you to use an image as a Submit button:

Input ▼

```
<input type="image" src="submit.gif" name="submitformbtn" />_
```

Figure 10.8 shows a custom button created with an image.

Output ▼

10

FIGURE 10.8
The image input type.

When the user clicks on an image field, the x and y coordinates of the point where the user clicked are submitted to the server. The data is submitted as `name.x = x coord` and `name.y = y coord`, where `name` is the name assigned to the control. Using the preceding code, the result might look like the following:

```
submitoformbtn.x=150&submitformbtn.y=200
```

You can omit the name if you choose. If you do so, the coordinates returned would just be x = and y =. Form controls with the type `image` support all the attributes of the `<img>` tag. You can remove the border from the image by using `border="0"`, or add a horizontal buffer around it using `hspace="10"`. To refresh your memory on the attributes supported by the `<img>` tag, go back to Lesson 7, "Adding Images, Color, and Backgrounds."

Creating Generic Buttons

In addition to creating Submit, Reset, and Image buttons, you also can create buttons that generate events within the browser that can be tied to client-side scripts. To create such a button, set the `type` attribute to `button`. Figure 10.9 shows a button that calls a function when it is pressed. Use the following code to create a button:

Input ▼

```
<input type="button" name="verify" value="verify" onclick="verifydata()" />
```

Output ▼

FIGURE 10.9
A button element on a web page.

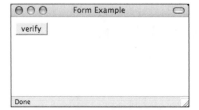

This example creates a button that runs a function called `verifydata` when it's clicked. You provide the label that appears on the button with the `value` attribute of `Verify Data`.

Unlike Submit buttons, regular buttons don't submit the form when they're clicked.

Hidden Form Fields

Hidden form fields are used when you want to embed data in a page that shouldn't be seen or modified by the user. The name and value pair associated with a hidden form field will be submitted along with the rest of the contents of the form when the form is submitted. To create such a field, set the field's type to `hidden` and be sure to include both the `name` and `value` attributes in your `<input>` tag. Here's an example:

```
<input type="hidden" name="id" value="1402" />
```

Hidden form fields are generally used when data identifying the user needs to be included in a form. For example, let's say you've created a form that allows a user to edit the name and address associated with her bank account. Because the user can change her name and address, the data she submits can't be used to look up her account after she submits the form, plus there might be multiple accounts associated with one name and address. You can include the account number as a hidden field on the form so that the program on the server knows which account to update when the form is submitted.

The File Upload Control

The file control enables a user to upload a file when he submits the form. As you can see in the following code, the `type` for the input element is set to `file`:

Input ▼

```
<p>Please select a file for upload: <input type="file" name="fileupload" /></p>
```

Figure 10.10 shows a file upload control.

Output ▼

FIGURE 10.10
The file upload
control.

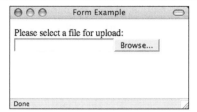

If you want to use a file upload field on your form, you have to do a lot of behind-the-scenes work to get everything working. For one thing, the program specified in the `action` attribute of your form must be able to accept the file being uploaded. Second, you have to use the `post` method for the form. Third, you must set the `enctype` attribute of the `<form>` tag to `multipart/form-data`. I haven't discussed the `enctype` attribute because this is the only case where you'll have to use it. Ordinarily, the default behavior is fine, but you must change the `enctype` in this particular case.

Let's look at a simple form that supports file uploads:

```
<form action="/cgi-bin/upload.cgi" enctype="multipart/form-data" method="post">
<input type="file" name="new_file" />
<input type="submit" />
</form>
```

After you've created a form for uploading a file, you need a program that can process the file submission. Creating such a program is beyond the scope of this book, but all popular web programming environments support file uploads.

Using Other Form Controls

In addition to form controls you can create using the `input` element, there are three that are elements in and of themselves.

Using the `button` Element

A button you create using the `button` element is similar to the buttons you create with the `input` element, except that content included between the opening and closing button tags appears on the button.

NOTE	The `button` element (as opposed to the `input` element of `type="button"`) is not supported by versions of Netscape prior to version 6.

You can create three different types of buttons: Submit, Reset, and Custom. The `<button>` tag is used to create buttons. As with other form fields, you can use the `name` attribute to specify the parameter sent to the server, and the `value` attribute to indicate which value is sent to the server. Unlike buttons created with the `<input>` tag, the button's label is specified by the content within the `<button>` tag, as seen in this code:

Input ▼

```
<button type="submit"><b><i>Submit button</i></b></button>
<button type="custom"><img src="recycle.gif"></button>
```

The button element is shown in a browser in Figure 10.11.

Output ▼

FIGURE 10.11
The button ele-
ment provides a
more flexible way
to create form
buttons.

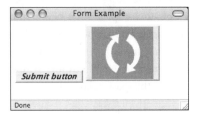

With the `<button>` tag, white space counts. If you include white space between the opening or closing `<button>` tags and the content inside the tag, it might make your button look a bit odd. The best bet is to just leave out that white space.

Creating Large Text-Entry Fields with `textarea`

The `textarea` element creates a large text entry field where people can enter as much information as they like. To create a `textarea`, use the `<textarea>` tag. To set the size of the field, use the `rows` and `cols` attributes. These attributes specify the height and width of the text area in characters. A text area with `cols` set to 5 and `rows` set to 40 creates a field that's 5 lines of text high and 40 characters wide. If you leave out the `rows` and `cols` attributes, the browser default will be used. This can vary, so you should make sure to include those attributes to maintain the form's appearance across browsers. The closing `textarea` tag is required and any text you place inside the `textarea` tag is displayed inside the field as the default value:

Input ▼

```
<p>Please comment on our customer service.<br />
<textarea name="question4" rows="10" cols="60">Enter your answer here
</textarea>
</p>
```

Figure 10.12 shows a `textarea` element in action.

Output ▼

FIGURE 10.12

Use textarea to create large text-entry areas.

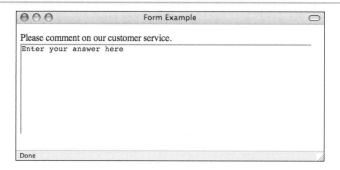

> You can also change the size of a `textarea` with the `height` and `width` CSS properties. (You can also alter the font using the CSS font properties as well.)

10

Creating Menus with `select` and `option`

The `select` element creates a menu that can be configured to enable users to select one or more options from a pull-down menu or a scrollable menu that shows several options at once. The `<select>` tag defines how the menu will be displayed and the name of the parameter associated with the field. The `<option>` tag is used to add selections to the menu. The default appearance of select lists is to display a pull-down list that enables the user to select one of the options. Here's an example of how one is created:

Input ▼

```
<p>Please pick a travel destination:
<select name="location">
  <option>Indiana</option>
  <option>Fuji</option>
  <option>Timbuktu</option>
  <option>Alaska</option>
</select>
</p>
```

As you can see in the code, the field name is assigned using the `name` attribute of the `<select>` tag. The field created using that code appears in Figure 10.13.

Output ▼

FIGURE 10.13
You can use select form controls to create pull-down menus.

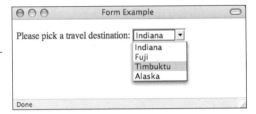

To create a scrollable list of items, just include the `size` attribute in the opening `select` tag, like this:

Input ▼

```
<select name="location" size="3">
```

Figure 10.14 shows the same `select` element as Figure 10.13, except that the `size` attribute is set to 3. Setting the size to 3 indicates that the browser should display three options at once.

Output ▼

FIGURE 10.14
You also can create scrollable lists using the `select` element.

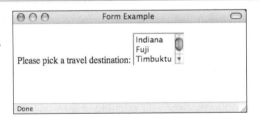

To see the fourth item, the user would have to use the scrollbar built into the select list. By default, the value inside the `<option>` tag specifies both what is displayed in the form and what's sent back to the server. To send a value other than the display value to the server, use the `value` attribute. The following code, for example, causes bw499 to be submitted to the server as the value associated with the `Courses` field instead of `Basket Weaving 499`:

```
<select name="courses">
  <option value="p101">Programming 101</option>
  <option value="e312">Ecomomics 312</option>
  <option value="pe221">Physical Education 221</option>
  <option value="bw499">Basket Weaving 499</option>
</select>
```

To select an option by default, include the `selected` attribute in an `option` element, as in the following:

```
<select name="courses">
  <option value="p101">Programming 101</option>
  <option value="e312">Ecomomics 312</option>
  <option value="pe221" selected="selected">Physical Education 221</option>
  <option value="bw499">Basket Weaving 499</option>
</select>
```

Thus far, you've created menus from which a user can select only one choice. To enable users to select more than one option, use the `multiple` attribute:

```
<select name="courses" multiple="multiple">
```

> **NOTE**
>
> A user can choose multiple options by Shift+clicking for Windows, or Ctrl–clicking or Command–clicking for Macintosh.

10

There are some usability issues associated with select lists. When you think about it, select lists that enable users to choose one option are basically the equivalent of radio button groups, and select lists that allow multiple selections are the same as check box groups. It's up to you to decide which tag to use in a given circumstance. If you need to present the user with a lot of options, select lists are generally the proper choice. A select list with a list of states is a lot more concise and usable than a group of 50 radio buttons. By the same token, if there are four options, radio buttons probably make more sense. The same rules basically hold with check box groups versus multiple select lists.

The other usability issue with select lists is specific to multiple select lists. The bottom line is that they're hard to use. Most users don't know how to select more than one item, and if the list is long enough, as they move through the list they'll have problems keeping track of the items they already selected when they scroll through to select new ones. Sometimes there's no way around using a multiple select list, but you should be careful about it.

Task: Exercise 10.2: Using Several Types of Form Controls ▼

Form controls often come in bunches. Although there are plenty of forms out there that consist of a text input field and a Submit button (like search forms), a lot of the time forms consist of many fields. For example, many websites require that you register in order to see restricted content, download demo programs, or participate in an online community. In this example, we'll look at a perhaps slightly atypical registration form for a website.

▼

▼ The purpose of this exercise is to show you how to create forms that incorporate a number of different types of form controls. In this case, the form will include a text field, a radio button group, a select list, a check box group, a file upload field, and a text area. The form is laid out using a table. Even though CSS is superior to tables for laying out most kinds of pages, forms are still well suited to being laid out using tables. The form, rendered in a browser, appears in Figure 10.15.

FIGURE 10.15
A registration form for a website.

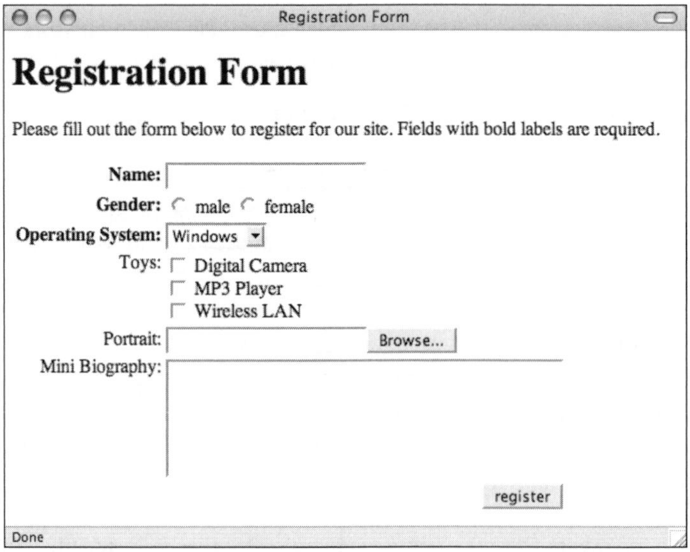

Let's look at the components used to build the form. The page's header and body tag are what you would expect—nothing interesting. After some introductory text, we open the form like this:

```
<form action="/cgi-bin/register.cgi" method="post"
enctype="multipart/form-data">
```

Because this form contains a file upload field, we have to use the post method and the multipart/form-data enctype in the <form> tag. The action attribute points to a CGI script that lives on my server. Next, we open the table that will be used to format the controls in my form. The first row of the table contains the first row in the form:

```
<tr>
<td align="right"><b>Name:</b></td>
<td><input name="name" /></td>
</tr>
```

As you can see, the table has two columns. We use the left column for labels and the
▼ right column for the form controls themselves. The first field is a text field. The only

attribute included is name because the default values for the rest of the attributes are fine. ▼
The next row includes two radio buttons:

```
<tr>
<td align="right"><b>Gender:</b></td>
<td>
<input type="radio" name="gender" value="male" /> male
<input type="radio" name="gender" value="female" /> female
</td>
</tr>
```

As you can see, the radio button group includes two controls (both with the same name, establishing the group). Because we didn't include line breaks between the two fields, they appear side by side in the form. The next field is a select list that enables the user to indicate which operating system he runs on his computer:

```
<tr>
<td align="right">Operating System:</td>
<td><select name="os">
<option value="windows">Windows</option>
<option value="macos">Mac OS</option>
<option value="linux">Linux</option>
<option value="other">Other ...</option>
</select></td>
</tr>
```

10

This select list is a single-line, single-select field with four options. Rather than using the display values as the values that will be sent back to the server, we instead opt to set them specifically using the value attribute of the <option> tag. The next form field is a check box group:

```
<tr>
<td valign="top" align="right">Toys:</td>
<td><input type="checkbox" name="toy" value="digicam" /> Digital Camera<br />
<input type="checkbox" name="toy" value="mp3" /> MP3 Player<br />
<input type="checkbox" name="toy" value="wlan" /> Wireless LAN</td>
</tr>
```

The next field is a file upload field:

```
<tr>
<td align="right">Portrait:</td>
<td><input type="file" name="portrait" /></td>
</tr>
```

The use of the post method and the multipart/form-data enctype are necessitated by the file upload field. The last input field on the form is a text area intended for the user's bio.   ▼

```
▼ <tr>
  <td valign="top" align="right">Mini Biography:</td>
  <td><textarea name="bio" rows="6" cols="40"></textarea></td>
  </tr>
```

After the text area, there's just the Submit button for the form. After that, it's all closing tags for the <table> tag, <form> tag, <body> tag, and the <html> tag. The full source code for the page follows, along with a screenshot of the form as shown earlier in Figure 10.15.

Input ▼

```
<html xmlns="http://www.w3.org/1999/xhtml">
<head>
<title>Registration Form</title>
</head>
<body>
<h1>Registration Form</h1>

<p>Please fill out the form below to register for our site. Fields
with bold labels are required.</p>

<form action="/cgi-bin/register.cgi" method="post"
enctype="multipart/form-data">
<table>
<tr>
<td align="right"><b>Name:</b></td>
<td><input name="name" /></td>
</tr>

<tr>
<td align="right"><b>Gender:</b></td>
<td>
<input type="radio" name="gender" value="male" /> male
<input type="radio" name="gender" value="female" /> female
</td>
</tr>

<tr>
<td align="right"><b>Operating System:</b></td>
<td><select name="os">
<option value="windows">Windows</option>
<option value="macos">Mac OS</option>
<option value="linux">Linux</option>
<option value="other">Other ...</option>
</select></td>
</tr>

<tr>
<td valign="top" align="right">Toys:</td>
▼ <td><input type="checkbox" name="toy" value="digicam" /> Digital Camera<br />
```

```
<input type="checkbox" name="toy" value="mp3" /> MP3 Player<br />
<input type="checkbox" name="toy" value="wlan" /> Wireless LAN</td>
</tr>

<tr>
<td align="right">Portrait:</td>
<td><input type="file" name="portrait" /></td>
</tr>

<tr>
<td valign="top" align="right">Mini Biography:</td>
<td><textarea name="bio" rows="6" cols="40"></textarea></td>
</tr>

<tr>
<td colspan="2" align="right"><input type="submit"
value="register" /></td>
</tr>
</table>
</form>
</body>
</html>
```

10

Adding Extras

You've created all the form controls that will accept user input. Now it's time to add functionality and make the controls a bit friendlier.

Displaying Control `label` Elements

The `label` element displays helpful information for a form control. You should tie the `for` attribute to the control it labels. To create a label, begin with the opening `label` tag and then enter the `for` attribute. The value for this attribute, when present, must match the `id` attribute for the control it's labeling. Next, enter text that will serve as the label and then close the element with the end `label` tag, as in the following:

Input ▼

```
<label for="control4">Who is your favorite NFL Quarterback?</label>
<input type="text" name="favqb" id="control4" />
```

Figure 10.16 shows this text control with a label assigned to it.

Output ▼

FIGURE 10.16
You can assign labels to any form control. Note that they're displayed with the control.

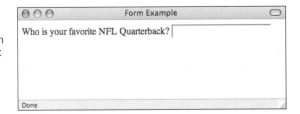

If you define your form control within the label element, as shown in the following code, you can omit the for attribute:

```
<label>User name: <input type="text" name="username" /></label>
```

The <label> tag doesn't cause any visible changes to the page, but you can always apply styles to it if you want.

Grouping Controls with `fieldset` and `legend`

The `fieldset` element organizes form controls into groupings that appear in the web browser. The `legend` element displays a caption for the `fieldset`. To create a `fieldset` element, start with the opening `fieldset` tag, followed by the `legend` element.

Next, enter your form controls and finish things off with the closing `fieldset` tag:

Input ▼

```
<fieldset>
  <legend>Oatmeal Varieties</legend>
  <label>Apple Cinnamon<input type="radio" name="applecinnamon" />
  </label><br />
  <label>Nutty Crunch<input type="radio" name="nuttycrunch" />
  </label><br />
  <label>Brown Sugar<input type="radio" name="brownsugar" /></label>
</fieldset>
```

Figure 10.17 shows the result.

Output ▼

FIGURE 10.17
The fieldset and legend elements enable you to organize your forms.

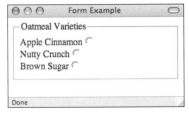

Changing the Default Form Navigation

In most browsers, you can use the Tab key to step through the form fields and links on a page. When filling out long forms, it's often much easier to use the Tab key to move from one field to the next than to use the mouse to change fields. If you have a mix of form fields and links on your page, setting things up so that using Tab skips past the links and moves directly from one form field to the next can improve the usability of your applications greatly. To set the tab order for your page, use the `tabindex` attribute. You should number your form fields sequentially to set the order that the browser will use when the user tabs through them. Here's an example:

```
<p>Enter your <a href="/">name</a>: <input type="text" name="username"
    tabindex="1" /></p>
<p>Enter your <a href="/">age</a>: <input type="text" name="age"
    tabindex="2" /></p>
<p><input type="submit" tabindex="3" /></p>
```

When you tab through this page, the browser will skip past the links and move directly to the form fields.

Using Access Keys

Access keys also make your forms easier to navigate. They assign a character to an element that moves the focus to that element when the user presses a key. To add an access key to a check box, use the following code:

```
<p>What are your interests?</p>
<p>Sports <input type="checkbox" name="sports" accesskey="S" /></p>
<p>Music <input type=""checkbox" name="music" accesskey="M" /></p>
<p>Television <input type=""checkbox" name="tv" accesskey="T" /></p>
```

Most browsers require you to hold down a modifier key and the key specified using `accesskey` to select the field. On Windows, both Netscape and Internet Explorer require you to use the Alt key along with the access key to select a field. Access keys are mostly useful for forms that will be used frequently by the same users. A user who is going to use a form only once won't bother to learn the access keys, but if you've written a form for data entry, the people who use it hundreds of times a day might really appreciate the shortcuts.

Creating `disabled` and `readonly` Controls

Sometimes you might want to display a form control without enabling your visitors to use the control or enter new information. To disable a control, add the `disabled` attribute to the form control:

```
<p>What is the meaning of life?
<textarea name="question42" disabled="disabled">
Enter your answer here.
</textarea>
</p>
```

10

When displayed in a web browser, the control will be dimmed (a light shade of gray) to indicate that it's unavailable.

To create a read-only control, use the `readonly` attribute:

Input ▼

```
<p>This month: <input type="text" name="month" value="September"
readonly="readonly" /></p>
```

The read-only control is not distinguished in any way from a normal form control. However, when visitors attempt to enter new information (or, in the case of buttons or check boxes, select them), they'll find that they cannot change the value. Figure 10.18 shows both a disabled control and a read-only control. You'll generally find `disabled` to be more useful because it's less confusing to your users.

Output ▼

FIGURE 10.18
Disabled controls are dimmed. Read-only controls appear normally—they just can't be changed.

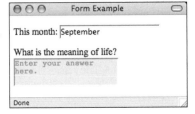

Form Security

It's important to remember that regardless of what you do with your form controls, what gets sent back to the server when the form is submitted is really up to your user. There's nothing to stop her from copying the source to your form, creating a similar page on her own, and submitting that to your server. If the form uses the `get` method, the user can just edit the URL once the form has been submitted.

The point here is that there is no form security. In Lesson 13, "Using JavaScript in Your Pages," you'll learn how to validate your forms with JavaScript. Even in that case, you can't guarantee that users will supply the input that you intend. What this means is that you must always validate the data entered by your users on the server before you use it.

Applying Cascading Style Sheet Properties to Forms

In the previous lesson, I talked about how you can apply style sheets to your pages to jazz up the look and feel or to completely control their structure. All the properties that you can apply to paragraphs, divs, and tables can just as easily be applied to forms. I'm going to talk about some ways that you can enhance the look and feel of your forms using CSS.

As you can see from the screenshots so far today, regular form controls might not blend in too well with your pages. The default look and feel of form controls can be altered in just about any way using CSS. For example, in most browsers, by default, text input fields use Courier as their font, have white backgrounds, and beveled borders. As you know, `border`, `font`, and `background-color` are all properties that you can modify using CSS. In fact, the following example uses all those properties:

10

Input ▼

```
<html xmlns="http://www.w3.org/1999/xhtml">
<head>
<title>Style Sheet Example</title>
<style type="text/css">
/*<![CDATA[*/
input.styled
{
  border: 2px solid #000;
  background-color: #aaa;
  font: bold 18px Verdana;
  padding: 4px;
}
/*]]>*/
</style>
</head>
<body>
<form>
<p>Default: <input value="value" /></p>
<p>Styled: <input value="value" class="styled" /></p>
</form>
</body>
</html>
```

The page contains two text input fields: one with the default look and feel, and another that's modified using CSS. The page containing the form appears in Figure 10.19.

Output ▼

FIGURE 10.19
A regular text input field and a styled text input field.

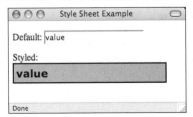

As you can see, the field that we applied styles to is radically different from the one that uses the default decoration. You can do anything to regular form fields that you can do to other block-level elements. In fact, you can make form fields look just like the rest of your page, with no borders and the same fonts as your page text if you like. Of course, that will make your forms extremely confusing to use, so you probably don't want to do it, but you could.

It's also fairly common to modify the buttons on your pages. Normally, Submit buttons on forms are gray with beveled edges, or they have the look and feel provided by the user's operating system. By applying styles to your buttons, you can better integrate them into your designs. This is especially useful if you need to make your buttons smaller than they are by default. I'll provide more examples of style usage in forms in Exercise 10.3.

Bear in mind that some browsers support CSS more fully than others. So some users won't see the styles that you've applied. The nice thing about CSS though is that they'll still see the form fields with the browser's default appearance.

▼ Task: Exercise 10.3: Applying Styles to a Form

Let's take another look at the form from Exercise 10.2. The form can easily be spruced up by tweaking its appearance using CSS. The main objectives are to make the appearance of the controls more consistent, and to make it clear to users which form fields are required and which are not. In the original version of the form, the labels for the required fields were bold. We'll keep with that convention here, and also change the border appearance of the fields to indicate which fields are required and which aren't.

Let's look at the style sheet first. We use three classes on the page: `required`, `optional`, and `submit`. First, the required styles. Here's that portion of the style sheet:

```
input.required
{
  width: 300px;
  font: bold 12px Verdana;
  background-color: #6a6;
  border: solid 2px #000;
}
```

```
select.required
{
  width: 300px;
  font: bold 12px Verdana;
  background-color: #6a6;
  border: solid 2px #000;
}

td.required
{
  font: bold 12px Verdana;
}
```

Any <input> tags that have their class attribute set to required will be set to 300 pixels of width, and the field will have a 2-pixel black border and a darker green background than is used on the page itself. Finally, we set the font to bold 12-pixel Verdana. Using the select.required selector (for required <select> tags), we set its style to match the required <input> tags as well. The td.required selector is for table cells that contain labels for required fields.

Now let's look at the styles for optional fields. Here are the style declarations:

```
input.optional
{
  width: 300px;
  font: 12px Verdana;
  background-color: #6a6;
  border: solid 2px #999;
}

textarea.optional
{
  width: 300px;
  font: 12px Verdana;
  background-color: #6a6;
  border: solid 2px #666;
}

td.optional
{
  font: 12px Verdana;
}
```

These styles are almost identical to the styles for the required class. The only differences are that the text inside the fields isn't bold and the border is dark gray instead of black. Other than those changes, the styles are the same. The other style alters the appearance of the submit button:

```
input.submit
{
  background-color: #6a6;
  border: solid 2px #000;
}
```

10

▼   `font: bold 12px Verdana;`
`}`

After the style sheet is set up, all we have to do is make sure that the `class` attributes of our tags are correct. The full source code for the page, including the form updated with classes, follows:

Input ▼

```
<!DOCTYPE html PUBLIC "-//W3C//DTD XHTML 1.0 Transitional//EN"
  "http://www.w3.org/TR/xhtml1/DTD/xhtml1-transitional.dtd">
<html xmlns="http://www.w3.org/1999/xhtml">
<head>
<title>Registration Form</title>

<style type="text/css">
/*<![CDATA[*/
body
{
  background-color: #9c9;
}

input.required
{
  width: 300px;
  font: bold 12px Verdana;
  background-color: #6a6;
  border: solid 2px #000;
}

select.required
{
  width: 300px;
  font: bold 12px Verdana;
  background-color: #6a6;
  border: solid 2px #000;
}

td.required
{
  font: bold 12px Verdana;
}

input.optional
{
  width: 300px;
  font: 12px Verdana;
  background-color: #6a6;
  border: solid 2px #999;
▼ }
```

```
textarea.optional
{
  width: 300px;
  font: 12px Verdana;
  background-color: #6a6;
  border: solid 2px #666;
}

td.optional
{
  font: 12px Verdana;
}

input.submit
{
  background-color: #6a6;
  border: solid 2px #000;
  font: bold 12px Verdana;
}
/*]]>*/
</style>
</head>
<body>
<h1>Registration Form</h1>

<p>Please fill out the form below to register for our site. Fields
with bold labels are required.</p>

<form action="/cgi-bin/register.cgi" method="post"
enctype="multipart/form-data">
<table>
<tr>
<td align="right" class="required"><b>Name:</b></td>
<td><input name="name" class="required" /></td>
</tr>

<tr>
<td align="right" class="required"><b>Gender:</b></td>
<td class="required"><input type="radio" name="gender"
value="male" /> male <input type="radio" name="gender"
value="female" /> female</td>
</tr>

<tr>
<td align="right" class="required"><b>Operating System:</b></td>
<td><select name="os" class="required">
<option value="windows">Windows</option>
<option value="macos">Mac OS</option>
<option value="linux">Linux</option>
<option value="other">Other ...</option>
</select></td>
</tr>
```

10

```
▼ <tr>
  <td valign="top" align="right" class="optional">Toys:</td>
  <td class="optional"><input type="checkbox" name="toy"
  value="digicam" /> Digital Camera<br />
  <input type="checkbox" name="toy" value="mp3" /> MP3 Player<br />
  <input type="checkbox" name="toy" value="wlan" /> Wireless LAN</td>
  </tr>

  <tr>
  <td align="right" class="optional">Portrait:</td>
  <td><input type="file" name="portrait" /></td>
  </tr>

  <tr>
  <td valign="top" align="right" class="optional">Mini
  Biography:</td>
  <td><textarea name="bio" rows="6" cols="40"
  class="optional"></textarea></td>
  </tr>

  <tr>
  <td colspan="2" align="right"><input type="submit" value="register"
  class="submit" /></td>
  </tr>
  </table>
  </form>
  </body>
  </html>
```

The page containing this form appears in Figure 10.20.

Output ▼

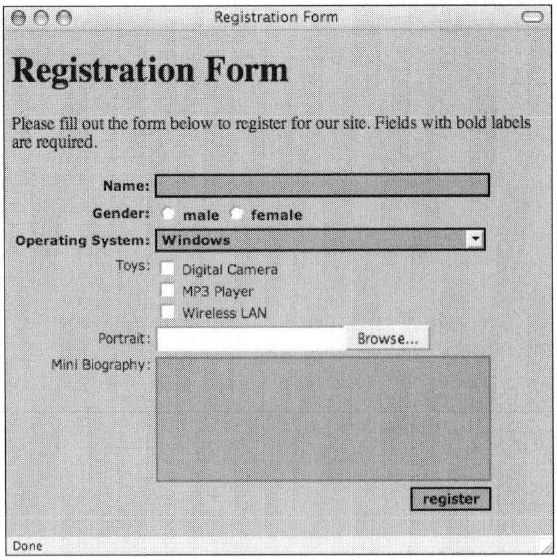

FIGURE 10.20
A form that uses
Cascading Style
Sheets.

Registration Form

Registration Form

Please fill out the form below to register for our site. Fields with bold labels are required.

Name:

Gender: ○ male ○ female

Operating System: Windows

Toys: ☐ Digital Camera
☐ MP3 Player
☐ Wireless LAN

Portrait: Browse...

Mini Biography:

register

Done

Planning Your Forms

Before you start creating complex forms for your web pages, you should do some planning that will save you time and trouble in the long run.

First, decide what information you need to collect. That might sound obvious, but you need to think about this before you start worrying about the mechanics of creating the form.

Next, review this information and match each item with a type of form control. Ask yourself which type of control is most suited to the type of questions you're asking. If you need a yes or no answer, radio buttons or check boxes work great, but the textarea element is overkill. Try to make life easier for the users by making the type of control fit the question. This way, analyzing the information using a script, if necessary, will be much easier.

You also need to coordinate with the person writing the CGI script to match variables in the script with the names you're assigning to each control. There isn't much point in naming every control before collaborating with the script author—after all, you'll need all the names to match. You also can create lookup tables that contain expansive descriptions and allowable values of each form control.

Finally, you might want to consider validating form input through scripting. Using JavaScript, you can embed small programs in your web pages. One common use for JavaScript is writing programs that verify a user's input is correct before she submits a form. I'll discuss JavaScript in more detail in Lesson 12, "Introducing JavaScript."

Summary

As you can see, the wonderful world of forms is full of different types of form controls for your visitors. This truly is a way to make your web pages interactive.

Be cautious, however. Web surfers who are constantly bombarded with forms are likely to get tired of all that typing and move on to another site. You need to give them a reason for playing!

Table 10.1 summarizes the HTML tags used today. Remember these points and you can't go wrong:

- Use the form element to create your forms.
- Always assign an action to a form.
- Create form controls with the input element or the other form control elements.
- Test your forms extensively.

TABLE 10.1 Today's HTML Tags

Tag	Use
`<form>`	Creates an HTML form. You can have multiple forms within a document, but you cannot nest the forms.
`action`	An attribute of `<form>` that indicates the server-side script (with a URL path) that processes the form data.
`enctype`	An attribute of the `<form>` tag that specifies how form data is encoded before being sent to the server.
`method`	An attribute of `<form>` that defines how the form data is sent to the server. Possible values are `get` and `post`.
`<input>`	A `<form>` element that creates controls for user input.
`type`	An attribute of `<input>` that indicates the type of form control. Possible values are shown in the following list:
`text`	Creates a single-line text entry field.
`password`	Creates a single-line text entry field that masks user input.
`submit`	Creates a Submit button that sends the form data to a server-side script.
`reset`	Creates a Reset button that resets all form controls to their initial values.
`checkbox`	Creates a check box.
`radio`	Creates a radio button.
`image`	Creates a button from an image.
`button`	Creates a pushbutton. The three types are Submit, Reset, and Push, with no default.
`hidden`	Creates a hidden form control that cannot be seen by the user.
`file`	Creates a file upload control that enables users to select a file with the form data to upload to the server.
`<button>`	Creates a button that can have HTML content.
`<textarea>`	A text-entry field with multiple lines.
`<select>`	A menu or scrolling list of items. Individual items are indicated by the `<option>` tag.
`<option>`	Individual items within a `<select>` element.
`<label>`	Creates a label associated with a form control.
`<fieldset>`	Organizes form controls into groups.
`<legend>`	Displays a caption for a `<fieldset>` element.

Workshop

If you've made it this far, I'm sure that you still have a few questions. I've included a few that I think are interesting. Afterwards, test your retention by taking the quiz, and then expand your knowledge by tackling the exercises.

Q&A

Q I want to create a form and test it, but I don't have the script ready. Is there any way I can make sure that the form is sending the right information with a working script?

A I run into this situation all the time! Fortunately, getting around it is very easy.

Within the opening `<form>` tag, modify the `action` attribute and make it a `mailto` link to your email address, as in the following:

```
<form action="mailto:youremailaddress@isp.com" method="post">
```

Now you can complete your test form and submit it without having a script ready. When you submit your form, it will be emailed to you as an attachment. Simply open the attachment in a text editor, and presto! Your form data is present.

Quiz

1. How many forms can you have on a web page?
2. How do you create form controls such as radio buttons and check boxes?
3. Are passwords sent using a `password` control secure?
4. Explain the benefit of using hidden form controls.
5. What other technology do forms rely on?

Quiz Answers

1. You can have any number of forms on a web page.
2. These form controls are created with the `input` element. Radio buttons have the `type` attribute set to `radio`, and check boxes are created using the type `checkbox`.
3. No! Passwords sent using a `password` control are not secure.
4. Hidden form controls are intended more for you than for the person filling out the form. By using unique `value` attributes, you can distinguish between different forms that may be sent to the same script or sent at different times.
5. In order for you to process the data submitted via forms, they must be paired with a server-side script through the `action` attribute.

10

Exercises

1. Ask your ISP for scripts that you can use to process your forms. If you can use them, ask how the data is processed and which names you should use in your form controls. If you need to use forms and your ISP won't allow you to use its scripts, you should start looking elsewhere for a place to host your website.

2. Visit some sites that might use forms, such as www.fedex.com. Look at which form controls they use and how they arrange them, and peek at the source to see the HTML code.

LESSON 11:

Integrating Multimedia: Sound, Video, and More

Learning how to integrate multimedia into your web pages is as simple as creating hyperlinks to sound or video files. Presto! You've added multimedia to your website. That's not the whole story, of course. You also can embed multimedia files in your web pages. Unfortunately, embedding them can be a little tricky.

Although you need to learn only a few new HTML tags, the multimedia-related HTML elements suffer from what seems like schizophrenia. They're implemented differently in Microsoft Internet Explorer and Firefox, and not supported at all in some cases. One of the elements has never been added to any HTML standard. In addition, there are a number of competing audio and video formats available today. It's almost impossible to learn the ins and outs of each one before more appear with the promise of being the "be all and end all" of multimedia.

Even with recent advances in communications speed (more and more people have broadband connections every day), improved sound and video compression/decompression technologies (MP3 audio files come to mind), and powerful audio and video adapter cards, the Web isn't the sound and video showcase that multimedia proponents dream of—not yet anyway.

Part of the problem is the incongruity between what we know today's computers are capable of and what we think the Web should deliver. Pop a CD or DVD into your drive and blammo! 3D graphics, stereo surround sound, and full-screen, 30-frames-per-second digital video jump out and assault your auditory and visual senses. Contrast that with most multimedia on the Web, and you will be sorely disappointed. Low-quality sound, small video sizes, and long download times are par for the course.

In this Lesson

Things have gotten a lot better. Macromedia Flash animations are so common that they're being used to create entire sites, and are also commonly used to deliver advertising. MP3 audio files have become so common and widespread that everybody seems to know what *ripping a CD* means. The downside is that it seems like you're always being asked to download some kind of browser plug-in, and applications on your computer are constantly fighting over which gets to display what kind of multi-media file. Having said all this, I'll try to strike a balance in this lesson between show-ing you the techniques you can use immediately and the technologies that require you to devote a significant amount of time and energy to apply what you've learned. You'll learn to accomplish the following:

- Create links to audio and video files so that visitors can download or play them

- Use the `object` and `embed` elements to include sound and video files in web pages

- Learn how to embed QuickTime, Flash, and RealAudio or RealVideo files into your web pages

- Use some of the unique multimedia capabilities of Microsoft Internet Explorer

- Recognize the most popular multimedia file types and the plug-ins or helper applications they require

Understanding How to Present Sound and Video

When you want to add multimedia to your site, there are two decisions you have to make. You have to decide which format to use for the data, and how you plan to integrate the multimedia features with the rest of your content. Before discussing the multitude of formats available, I'll talk about how to present multimedia files. The two options there are linking and embedding. When you link to a multimedia file, it's up to the browser (and user preference) to determine how best to handle it. If the browser can handle the data itself or the user has installed a plug-in compatible with the file type, sometimes the media will play within the browser window. If the browser has no idea how to handle the file, it will generally offer to let you download the file. In other cases, the browser will launch an external application like Windows Media Player or RealPlayer to handle the file. The other option is to embed the media within a page. In that case, you include tags in your page that indicate how the media should be presented within that page. The upside of this approach is that it enables you to seamlessly integrate multimedia into a website. The downside is that if your user doesn't have the right software, the experience won't turn out to be seamless. They'll see a broken file, be prompted to download additional software, or otherwise be distracted from what they were trying to accomplish. The key when embedding multimedia files is to make sure that this happens to as few users as possible.

The Old Standby: Linking

The sure-fire way to include multimedia files on your website is to provide a hyperlink to them. Hyperlinks are supported by all versions of all browsers. The browser will handle the file appropriately if the right supporting applications are installed, or users will be able to decide for themselves what they want to do with the file. A common technique is to link to the multimedia file and provide a thumbnail preview of the multimedia clip, a description, and the file size. This is considered common courtesy so that people can estimate the download time. You also should provide links to any players required so that people can download the appropriate player, should they need it.

11

For example, if I have a QuickTime video that I want to share, I might use the following code:

Input ▼

```
<div align="center">
<h1>Apollo 17 Videos</h1>

<p><a href="Apollo_17_Flag.qt">Astronauts placing the flag on the
Moon</a><br />
 [2.75Mb]</p>

<p><img src="Apollo_17_Flag.gif" width="160" height="120"
alt="Apollo 17 flag" /></p>

<p>Apple <a href="http://www.apple.com/quicktime">QuickTime</a> is
required to view this movie.
<a href="http://www.apple.com/quicktime"><img src="getquicktime4.gif"
border="0" width="88" alt="Get QuickTime 4" /></a></p>
</div>
```

Figure 11.1 shows the resulting web page.

Output ▶

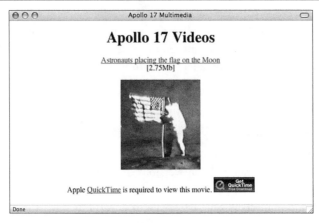

It's also considered good form to provide multiple types of multimedia to download because not all media types are usable on all platforms:

Input ▼

```
<!DOCTYPE html PUBLIC "-//W3C//DTD XHTML 1.0 Transitional//EN"
  "http://www.w3.org/TR/xhtml1/DTD/xhtml1-transitional.dtd">
<html xmlns="http://www.w3.org/1999/xhtml">
<head>
<title>Apollo Multimedia Archive</title>
</head>
<body>
<div align="center">
<h1>Apollo 17 Videos</h1>

<p>Astronauts placing the flag on the Moon</p>

<table border="0">
<tr>
<td rowspan="3"><img src="Apollo_17_Flag.gif" width="160"
height="120" alt="Apollo 17 flag"/></td>
<td><a href="Apollo_17_Flag.qt">QuickTime</a> [2.75Mb]</td>
</tr>

<tr>
<td><a href="Apollo_17_Flag.mpg">MPEG</a> [2.45Mb]</td>
</tr>

<tr>
<td><a href="Apollo_17_Flag.avi">AVI</a> [3.11Mb]</td>
```

```
</tr>
</table>

<br />
<a href="http://www.apple.com/quicktime"><img
src="getquicktime4.gif" width="88" border="0" alt="Get QuickTime"
vspace="7" /></a><br />
<a href="http://microsoft.com/windows/mediaplayer/download/default.asp">
<img src="getmedia_white.gif" width="65" height="57" border="0"
alt="Get Windows Media Player" vspace="7" /></a>
</div>
</body>
</html>
```

Figure 11.2 shows the resulting web page.

Output ▶

FIGURE 11.2
When linking
sound and video,
provide multiple
formats if
possible.

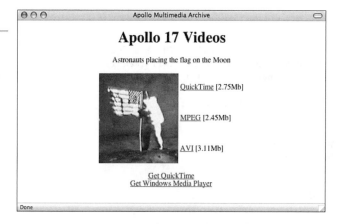

11

Task: Exercise 11.1: Creating a Family History Multimedia ▼
Archive

One of the common types of pages available on the Web is a media archive. A *media archive* is a web page that serves no purpose other than to provide quick access to images or other multimedia files for viewing and downloading.

It seems like everybody who knows the first thing about publishing on the Web sets up a media archive when they have a child. People oftentimes have family members flung all over the country, and with minimal HTML skills and a digital camera, you can quickly set up an online photo album or multimedia archive that enables everyone to see the new bundle of joy. If you're one of those people who's always emailing out photos of the kids to a huge list of people, putting up a media archive might be a smart choice. (And if you ▼

▼ want to keep strangers from peeking in, skip ahead to Lesson 19, "Taking Advantage of the Server," where I explain how to protect your web pages with a password.)

By using inline images as thumbnails and splitting up sound and video files into small sample clips with larger files, you can create a multimedia archive on the Web that is far easy to use and enables users to download exactly what they want, without wasting time.

In this exercise, you'll create a simple multimedia archive with several GIF and JPEG images, WAV sounds, and a mixture of MPEG and AVI video.

Using your favorite image editor, you can create thumbnails of each of your pictures to represent them in the archive.

First, start with the framework for the archive and then add a table for the thumbnail images, as follows:

Input ▼

```
<!DOCTYPE html PUBLIC "-//W3C//DTD XHTML 1.0 Transitional//EN"
  "http://www.w3.org/TR/xhtml1/DTD/xhtml1-transitional.dtd">
<html xmlns="http://www.w3.org/1999/xhtml">
<head>
<title>Family Multimedia Archive</title>
</head>
<body>
<div align="center">
<table border="0">
<tr>
<td width="80">
<h2>Images</h2>
</td>
<td>
<p>Select an image to view it in a larger size.</p>
</td>
</tr>

<tr>
<td width="80">Nephew opening a present.</td>
<td><img src="present.gif" height="150" width="200"
  alt="Opening presents" /></td>
</tr>

<tr>
<td width="80">Mother holding child.</td>
<td><img src="with_baby.gif" height=""150 width="200"
alt="Mother and child" /></td>
</tr>

▼  <tr>
```

```
<td width="80">House in the snow.</td>
<td><img src="snowy_house.gif" height="150" width="200"
alt="House in the snow" /></td>
</tr>
</table>
</div>
</body>
</html>
```

Figure 11.3 shows how the page looks so far.

Output ▶

FIGURE 11.3
The web page with the image archive almost completed.

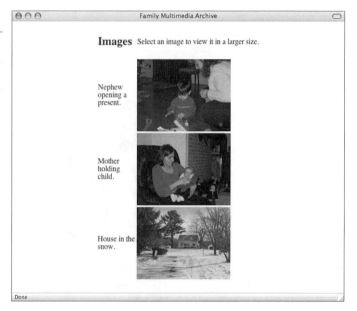

The next step is to create the hyperlinks to each image that point to the larger file. Here's the HTML code that links to the images:

Input ▼

```
...
<tr>
<td width="80">Nephew opening a present.</td>
<td><a href="present_big.gif"><img src="present.gif" height="150" width="200"
    alt="Opening presents" /></a></td>
</tr>

<tr>
<td width="80">Mother holding child.</td>
<td><a href="with_baby_big.jpg">
```

11

```
        <img src="with_baby.gif" height=""150 width="200"
        alt="Mother and child" /></a></td>
</tr>

<tr>
<td width="80">House in the snow.</td>
<td><a href="snowy_house_big.jpg">
        <img src="snowy_house.gif" height="150" width="200"
        alt="House in the snow" /></a></td>
</tr>
...
```

Figure 11.4 shows the result.

Output ▶

FIGURE 11.4
The image now
linked to larger
images.

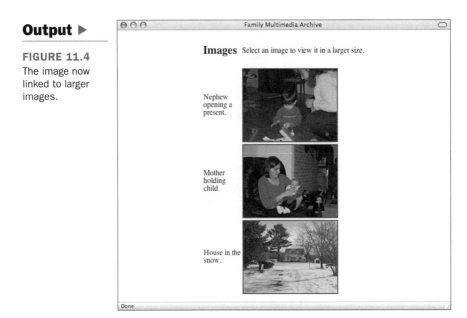

If I leave the archive like this, it looks nice, but I'm breaking one of my own rules: I
haven't noted how large each file is. Here, you have several choices for formatting, but
the easiest is to simply add the file size after the description of each picture, as follows:

Input ▼

```
<tr>
  <td width="80">Nephew opening a present. [105k]</td>
  <td><a href="present_big.gif">
    <img src="present.gif" height="150" width="200"
    alt="Opening presents" /></a>
  </td>
```

```
</tr>

<tr>
  <td width="80">Mother holding child. [211k]</td>
  <td><a href="with_baby_big.jpg">
    <img src="with_baby.gif" height=""150 width="200"
    alt="Mother and child" /></a>
  </td>
</tr>

<tr>
  <td width="80">House in the snow. [158k]</td>
  <td><a href="snowy_house_big.jpg">
    <img src="snowy_house.gif" height="150" width="200"
    alt="House in the snow" /></a>
  </td>
</tr>
```

Figure 11.5 shows this result.

Output ▶

FIGURE 11.5
Adding file sizes to the description of each image enables people to determine how long it will take to load the image.

11

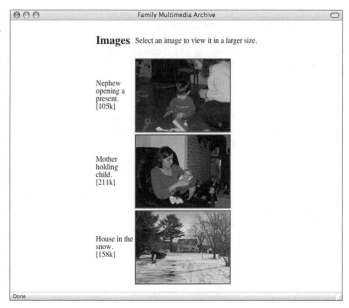

Now, let's move on to the sound and video sections. There are two approaches to formatting these sections. You can add the material in the same table that contains the images or you can create two new tables—either way is fine. For this exercise, you're going to create new tables that are virtually identical to the table that held the images.

▼ Start by adding three sound and two video files. Because the sound files can't be reduced to a simple thumbnail image, you should provide a good description. With video files, you can often use your video player to copy one frame of the clip and provide that as a thumbnail. I've included icons with the links to the sound files. Following is the code for the sound portion of your archive:

Input ▼

```
<div align="center">
<table border="0" summary="Sound files for download.">
<tr>
<td>
<h2>Sound Bites</h2>
</td>
<td>
<p>Select a sound bite to download or listen to it.</p>
</td>
</tr>

<tr>
  <td>An oral family history describing how we survived the
    tornado of 1903. [1192k]</td>
  <td><a href="tornado.wav"><img src="audio.jpg"
      alt="download tornado.wav"></a></td>
</tr>

<tr>
  <td>Don describing his first job. [1004k]</td>
  <td><a href="donjob.wav"><img src="audio.jpg"
      alt="download donjob.wav"></a></td>
</tr>

<tr>
  <td>Grandma Jo telling how she came to America. [2459k]</td>
  <td><a href="jo.wav"><img src="audio.jpg"
      alt="download jo.wav"></a></td>
</tr>
</table>
```

▼ `</div>`

Figure 11.6 shows how the linked sounds look on the web page.

Output ▶

FIGURE 11.6
Linked sound files in a family history archive.

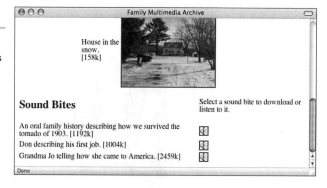

Finally, add the video clip section just as you have for the previous two. It's getting easier!

Input ▼

```
<div align="center">
<table border="0">
<tr>
<td width="100">
<h2>Video Clips</h2>
</td>
<td>
<p>Select a video clip to download it.</p>
</td>
</tr>

<tr>
  <td width="100">A video of a Christmas gathering. [2492k]</td>

  <td><a href="presents.mpeg"><img src="present.gif" height="150"
      width="200" alt="Opening presents" /></a></td>
</tr>

<tr>
  <td width="100">Massachussetts in winter. [3614k]</td>

  <td><a href="winter.mpeg"><img src="snowy_house.gif"
      height="120" width="180"
      alt="Winter snow" /></a></td>
</tr>
</table>
</div>
```

11

▼ Figure 11.7 shows how the linked videos with thumbnails look on the web page.

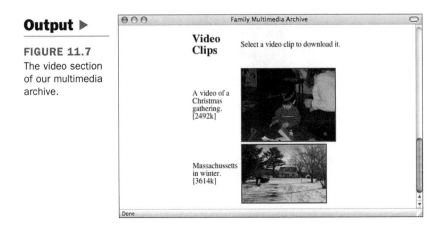

Your multimedia archive is finished. Creating one is simple with the combination of
inline images and external files. With the use of the `alt` attribute, you can even use it
reasonably well in text-only browsers.

Embedding Sound and Video

There are two tags that are used to embed multimedia files in web pages—`<object>`
and `<embed>`. The `<embed>` tag was introduced by Netscape to enable files that require
plug-ins to view within a web page. The `<embed>` tag indicates that Netscape-style
plug-ins (multimedia primarily) should be used to view embedded media. Unfortunately,
`<embed>` isn't sanctioned by the World Wide Web Consortium (W3C) and can't be found
in the official HTML standard.

The other tag, `<object>`, is officially sanctioned by the W3C. It was originally used by
Internet Explorer to allow users to load ActiveX controls within a page. I'll talk about
them more a bit later. Since then, browsers that use Netscape-style plug-ins have also
added support for the `<object>` tag. The `<embed>` tag is only necessary for older
browsers that use Netscape-style plug-ins (like old versions of Netscape).

Using the `<embed>` Element

Despite the fact that `<embed>` isn't in the HTML standard, Microsoft and Netscape continue to support it, mainly because many pages out there that still use it. The `<embed>` tag
has no closing tag; however, it does support a number of attributes.

Unfortunately, despite the fact that most browsers support <embed>, they only have a handful of attributes in common. The good news is that each web browser ignores the attributes it doesn't understand, enabling you to include as many different attributes as you like. Because of this, it's best to rely on a set of attributes that will work in all cases, and use them religiously, including the others for added value. And, because the <embed> tag won't validate anyway, you don't have to worry about complying with standards with regard to the attributes either.

Let's explore the attributes you absolutely need to use the <embed> element.

```
<embed src="a01607av.avi" height="120" width="160" />
```

The src attribute contains the location of the multimedia file you want to embed in the web page. The height and width attributes specify the dimensions of the embedded file in pixels.

There are some tricks to setting the height and width properties properly. If you're presenting video, setting the height and width to the actual resolution of the movie causes the video to become crunched because the controls are displayed in that space as well.

Figures 11.8 and 11.9 demonstrate the problem using the <embed> tags that follow:

Input ▼

```
<embed src="a01607av.avi" type="video/x-msvideo" height="120" width="180" />
```

Output ▶

FIGURE 11.8
An embedded movie that does not include space for the plug-in's controls.

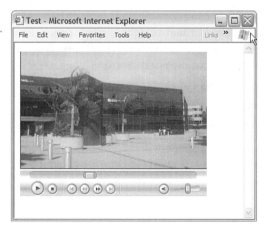

Input ▼

```
<embed src="a01607av.avi" type="video/x-msvideo" height="136" width="160" />
```

Output ▶

FIGURE 11.9
An embedded
movie with
the proper
proportions.

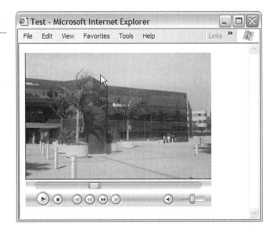

If you leave out the `height` and `width` attributes, the browser will determine how much space to reserve for the file. Unfortunately, this causes problems because each browser behaves differently. Internet Explorer 6 will provide too small a space, and only part of the movie will be shown. Mozilla Firefox provides too much space, leaving lots of padding around the movie. In other words, you need to specify a `height` and `width`.

Table 11.1 summarizes the `<embed>` attributes supported by Internet Explorer.

TABLE 11.1   `<embed>` Attributes Used in Internet Explorer

Attribute	Description
`align`	Aligns the element in relation to the web page. Allowable values are `absbottom`, `absmiddle`, `baseline`, `bottom`, `left`, `middle`, `right`, `texttop`, and `top`. This is the equivalent of the `<img>` tag's `align` attribute.
`class`	Sets or retrieves the class of the element. Used with CSS.
`height`	The height of the element.
`id`	The ID of the element. Used with JavaScript or CSS.
`name`	The name of the element. Used with JavaScript.
`pluginspage`	The URL of the page where you can download the plug-in used to view this object.
`src`	The URL of the multimedia file.
`style`	Style sheet declaration.
`title`	The title of the element.
`units`	Sets or retrieves the `height` or `width` units. Pixels are the default unit of measurement.

TABLE 11.1 continued

Attribute	Description
unselectable	Specifies that the object cannot be selected. Valid values are on and off (the default is off).
width	The width of the element.

Table 11.2 summarizes the <embed> attributes supported by Mozilla Firefox.

TABLE 11.2 <embed> Attributes Used in Mozilla Firefox

Attribute	Description
src	The URL file location.
type	The MIME type of the multimedia file indicated by the src attribute.
pluginspage	A URL pointing to a web page that has instructions for installing the required plug-in.
pluginurl	A URL to a Java Archive (JAR) file.
align	Aligns the element in relation to the web page. Allowable values are left, right, top, and bottom.
border	The width of a border drawn around the element.
frameborder	Does not draw a border around the element when set to no.
height	The height of the element.
width	The width of the element.
units	The units used to measure the height and width. Pixels are the default unit of measurement.
hidden	Hides the element when set to true and displays it when set to false, which is the default value.
hspace	The horizontal margin around the element.
vspace	The vertical margin around the element.
name	The name of the plug-in required to play the file.
palette	For use in Windows only. foreground makes the plug-in use the foreground palette, whereas background (the default) makes the plug-in use the background palette.

11

In addition to these attributes, additional attributes might be available for specific plug-ins, such as the Macromedia Flash Player.

Finally, you can include the noembed element to provide support for visitors who do not have a web browser that can display plug-ins:

```
<noembed>This Web page requires a browser that can display objects.</noembed>
<embed src="a01607av.avi" height="120" width="160" />
```

The bottom line on <embed> is that these days it makes no sense to use it alone to embed a multimedia file in a page. It is still used in conjunction with <object> in order to support the widest range of browsers. I'll discuss that technique a bit further on.

Using the <object> Element

According to the World Wide Web consortium, you should use the <object> element when embedding sound and video (among other things) in web pages. The only catch is you may run into problems if your user is running Netscape Navigator 4 (or an even older browser). If you must support these users, you need to use the <embed> tag along with <object>.

To use the <object> element, start with the opening <object> tag and attributes, as follows:

```
<object data="movie.mpeg" type="application/mpeg">
```

The data attribute is the URL for the source file for your sound or video, and type is the MIME type of the file.

Next, include any content you want to display, such as a caption, and close the <object> element with the closing tag, as follows:

```
<object data="movie.mpeg" type="video/mpeg">
My homemade movie.
</object>
```

You also can cascade objects so that if one cannot be displayed, the browser keeps trying down the list.

```
<object data="movie.mpeg" type="video/mpeg">
  <object data="moviesplash.gif" type="image/gif">
  </object>
My homemade movie.
</object>
```

<object> also uses the param element to initialize any parameters the embedded file might require. The param element is included in the body of the <object> element and does not require a closing tag:

```
<object data="movie.mpeg" type="video/mpeg">
  <param name="height" value="120" valuetype="data" />
  <param name="width" value="160" valuetype="data" />
My homemade movie.
</object>
```

The preceding code sets the height and width of the embedded object to 120 by 160 pixels. The parameters you supply via the <param> tag depend on the type of object you're embedding. For example, an audio file wouldn't have a height and width. For example, if you use the <object> tag to place a Flash movie on a page, the param elements will be used to specify the movie's URL, whether to play the movie when the page loads, and whether to loop through the movie continually or just play it once. I'll explain which parameters are required by some popular media types later in this lesson.

Combining <embed> and <object>

As you'll see in the next few sections, you can use <embed> and <object> simultaneously to make sure your page works for the widest possible audience. The key to this approach is to include the <embed> tag within the <object> tag.Here's an example:

```
<object classid="value" codebase="value" height="480" width="512"
 name="myname">
<param name="src" value="source location" />
<embed src="filename" height="480" width="512" name="myname" />
</object>
```

Browsers that support <object> will ignore the <embed> tag if it's inside the <object> tag. Browsers that don't support <object> will ignore that tag and use the <embed> tag instead.

11

When you're embedding video or other multimedia content in your pages, you have to decide whether you care more about your pages being standards compliant or reaching the widest possible audience. The <object> tag works Microsoft Internet Explorer, Mozilla Firefox, and other current browsers, but not some old browsers. The <embed> tag fills in the gaps in browser coverage, but if you use it, your pages will not be considered valid.

Embedding Flash Movies

The Flash author tool can produce the HTML to embed your movies within a page for you, but I want to explain how to create it manually as well. Here's a template for embedding a Flash movie:

```
<object classid="clsid:D27CDB6E-AE6D-11cf-96B8-444553540000"
codebase="http://download.macromedia.com/pub/shockwave/cabs/flash/swflash.
    cab#version=6,0,40,0"
width="550" height="400" id="myMovieName">
    <param name="movie" value="myFlashMovie.swf" />
    <param name="quality" value="high" />
    <param name="bgcolor" value="#FFFFFF" />
    <embed src="myFlashMovie.swf" quality="high"
      bgcolor="#FFFFFF" width="550" height="400" name="myMovieName" align=""
```

```
      type="application/x-shockwave-flash"
      pluginspage="http://www.macromedia.com/go/getflashplayer" />
</object>
```

Notice that Flash uses both the <object> and <embed> elements to embed the animation in a web page. To use this template, you need to set the height and width attributes of the <object> and the <embed> tag to the appropriate size for your movie. You also have to set the value attribute of the movie parameter to the URL for your movie. Finally, you have to set the src in the <embed> tag to that URL, and optionally update the name of the movie in the <embed> tag as well.

Table 11.3 contains a full list of <embed> attributes. Table 11.4 contains a list of <object> parameters. Table 11.5 contains a list of attributes that work with both <embed> and <object>.

TABLE 11.3 <embed> Attributes Supported by Flash

Attribute	Description
src	The URL file location. Required.
pluginspage	The URL for the Flash download page. Required.
name	The name of the movie. You can use this name to access the movie via JavaScript.

TABLE 11.4 <object> Attributes Supported by the Flash Player

Attribute	Description
classid	Identifies the ActiveX control (always the same value). Required.
codebase	Download location for the Flash player (always the same value). Required.
movie	The URL for the movie. Required.
id	An identifier for the element that can be used to access it via JavaScript.

TABLE 11.5 Attributes of Both <embed> and <object> Supported by the Flash Player

Attribute	Description
height	The height of the movie (in pixels or percentage of window size). Required.
width	The width of the movie (in pixels or percentage of the window size). Required.

TABLE 11.5 continued

`align`	Aligns the element in relation to the web page. Allowable values are `left`, `right`, `top`, and `bottom`.
`swliveconnect`	True or false value that indicates whether or not to start Java when the plug-in is loaded. (This should be set to false unless you are using FSCommand features.)
`play`	True or false value that indicates whether the movie should start playing as soon as the page is loaded. The default is true.
`loop`	True or false value that indicates whether the movie should loop (start playing again when it finishes). Defaults to true.
`menu`	True or false value that specifies whether the user can access all of the Flash player's contextual menu options when playing a movie. Defaults to false.
`quality`	Settings are `low`, `autolow`, `autohigh`, `medium`, `high`, and `best`. For more information, see the Flash documentation.
`scale`	Specifies how to handle cases where the movie is a different size than the `height` and `width` attributes. `showall` (the default) preserves the aspect ratio of the movie but sizes it as best it can in the space provided. `noborder` fills the entire space specified, preserving the movie's aspect ratio and cropping if necessary. `exactfit` stretches the movie to fit in the space provided, ignoring the aspect ratio.
`salign`	Specifies how the movie is aligned in a browser window, typically used with pop-up windows. For more information, see the Flash documentation.
`wmode`	Specifies how transparent portions of a Flash movie are handled. Values are `window`, `opaque`, and `transparent`.
`bgcolor`	Sets the background color of the Flash movie, overriding the setting in the movie.
`base`	Specifies the base URL for the Flash movie. Used by Flash movies that contain references to external files.
`flashvars`	Variables passed to the Flash player from the page.

11

Embedding RealAudio and RealVideo

Integrating RealAudio and RealVideo files into pages is a bit different than integrating Flash because RealAudio files do not necessarily require any space on the screen. That said, you can write your HTML so that RealAudio controls are integrated into your web page.

```
<object id="RVOCX" classid="clsid:CFCDAA03-8BE4-11cf-B84B-0020AFBBCCFA"
    width="320" height="240">
  <param name="SRC" value="plugin.rpm" />
  <param name="CONTROLS" value="ImageWindow" />
  <param name="CONSOLE" value="one" />
  <embed src="plugin.rpm" width="320" height="240" nojava="true"
      controls="ImageWindow" console="one" />
</object>
```

As you can see, unlike Flash, RealPlayer uses the src parameter to specify the location of the file to be displayed. The code above will show the video with no controls displayed at all. If you only wanted to show the controls for an audio file (or video file), you would use the following HTML:

```
<object id="RVOCX"
  classid="clsid:CFCDAA03-8BE4-11cf-B84B-0020AFBBCCFA"
  width="350" height="36">
  <param name="CONTROLS" value="ControlPanel" />
  <param name="CONSOLE" value="one" />
  <embed src="plugin.rpm" width="350" height="36"
  nojava="true" controls="ControlPanel" console="one" />
</object>
```

Table 11.6 lists the available attributes for <object> and the parameters (<param name="*name*" value="*value*" />) for the <object> element.

TABLE 11.6   <embed> Attributes and <object> Parameters

Attribute/Parameter	Description
autostart	Sets automatic playback (true or false).
backgroundcolor	Sets background color (hexadecimal color value or name).
center	Centers clip in window (true or false).
console	Links multiple controls (yes, name, master, or unique).
controls	Adds RealPlayer controls (control name).
height	Sets window or control height (in pixels or percentage).
loop	Loops clips indefinitely (true or false).
maintainaspect	Preserves image aspect ratio (true or false).
nojava	Prevents the Java Virtual Machine from starting (true or false).
nolabels	Suppresses presentation information (true or false).
nologo	Suppresses Real logo (true or false).
numloop	Loops clip a given number of times (*number*).
region	Ties clip to SMIL region (SMIL region).
shuffle	Randomizes playback (true or false).
src	Specifies source clip (URL).
width	Sets window or control width (in pixels or percentage).

Multimedia Techniques

Microsoft Internet Explorer offers a few unique capabilities worth mentioning: background sounds and inline video. Note, however, that neither of these techniques is part of the HTML standard. You can use style sheets to hide `<object>` elements on your pages, so there's no need to use this technique to include background audio on a page. You can also include inline video on a page using `<object>`. I'm just describing these elements so that you know what they are if you see them.

Including Background Sounds

Internet Explorer supports an element that loads and plays audio files in the background. These sound files load when the page loads, and they play automatically. Because no visual effect is created, there will be no indication that a sound is playing unless the users have speakers and they're not muted. The `<bgsound>` element is used as follows:

```
<bgsound src="ElevatorMusic.wav" />
```

Use the `loop` attribute to repeat the sound multiple times. If the value of loop is a number, the sound is played that number of times. If `loop` is –1 or `infinite`, the sound will repeat continually until the visitor leaves the page.

```
<bgsound src="ElevatorMusic.wav" loop="-1" />
```

11

Explorer supports three different formats for inline sounds: Sun's popular AU format, Windows WAV files, and MIDI files with a `MID` extension.

TIP	If you include sound on a page, be sure to provide a way for users to turn it off. If they spend any time at all on your page, the sound might start to irritate them. Even better, don't use auto play to start it without permission. Let them control the audio themselves.

Inline Video with dynsrc

You can integrate video clips (`AVI` or `MPEG`) into web pages displayed in Microsoft Internet Explorer 4 and above by using the `dynsrc` attribute in the `<img>` element, as in the following simple syntax:

```
<img dynsrc="a01607av.avi" loop="2" start="fileopen" />
```

In the previous line of code, Internet Explorer will play the video clip, indicated by the `dynsrc` attribute, two times after the web page finishes loading. The `loop` attribute specifies the number of times to play the video clip, with one time being the default value. To play the clip indefinitely, use –1 instead. The `start` attribute defines when the video clip starts playing. You can choose from `fileopen`, which is the default, or `mouseover`, which plays the video when a person moves her mouse over the video.

Because you're using the `<img>` element, you can use other `<img>` attributes, such as `alt`, `align`, `border`, `height`, `width`, and so on, to format the video clip.

To make this compatible with other browsers, you should use the `src` attribute to designate a static `GIF` or `JPG` image that will be displayed in place of the video. The code would resemble the following:

```
<img src="a01607av.gif" dynsrc="a01607av.avi" loop="2" start="fileopen" />
```

Internet Explorer will ignore the value of the `src` attribute as long as the video supplied by `dynsrc` is valid.

▼ Task: Exercise 11.2: Embedding a QuickTime Movie

For your second exercise, you'll try your hand at embedding a QuickTime movie in a web page. QuickTime is a video format created by Apple. Apple recommends that you use the combination of the `<object>` and `<embed>` tags that I've discussed in this lesson.

For starters, create or open a web page template similar to the following:

```
<!DOCTYPE html PUBLIC "-//W3C//DTD XHTML 1.0 Transitional//EN"
"http://www.w3.org/TR/xhtml1/DTD/transitional.dtd">

<html>
<head>
<title></title>
</head>
<body>

</body>
</html>
```

From here, title the page and add a `<div>` element that you will use to center everything on the page.

Next, add a heading that appropriately describes the video and a title for the video:

```
<div align="center">
<h1>Apollo 17 Videos</h1>
<p>Astronauts placing the flag on the Moon</p>

</div>
```

Now it's time to add the video itself. Start with the `<object>` tag. Here's the code:

```
<object classid="clsid:02BF25D5-8C17-4B23-BC80-D3488ABDDC6B"
codebase="http://www.apple.com/qtactivex/qtplugin.cab"
height="136" width="160">
```

```
      <param name="src" value="Apollo_17_Flag.mov" />
      <param name="autoplay" value="true" />
      <param name="controller" value="true" />
      <embed src="Apollo_17_Flag.mov" height="136" width="160"
        type="video/quicktime"
        pluginspage="http://www.apple.com/quicktime/download/" />
  </object>
```

You should recognize this code from what you've seen previously in this lesson. The classid and codebase for QuickTime are unique to that plug-in, as is the plugins page specified in the <embed> tag. You should also note that I set the height of the movie to 136. The movie is actually 120 pixels high, but the QuickTime player includes controls that are 16 pixels tall, so I added 16 pixels to the height of my movie. If I hadn't done so the controls would be cut off.

I used two parameters that are specific to QuickTime—autoplay and controller. I set the autoplay parameter to true so that the movie would start playing as soon as the page is displayed, and I set controller to true so that the video controls would be shown (this is the default). Had I set controller to false, the controls would not appear and I could have set the height attributes to 120. To see whether this works, test the page using your web browser. When you're satisfied, add a final piece to the page that will show people where to get the QuickTime plug-in if they need it. Because this is the last element on the page, remember to close the <div> with the end tag.

11

```
<p>Apple <a href="http://www.apple.com/quicktime">QuickTime</a> is
required to view this movie.
<a href="http://www.apple.com/quicktime">
     <img src=" qt7badge_getQTfreeDownload.gif"
border="0" align="absmiddle" width="88" height="31" /></a></p>
```

When it's all put together, the source code for your web page (shown in Figure 11.10) should look like this:

Input ▼

```
<html xmlns="http://www.w3.org/1999/xhtml">
<head>
<title>Apollo Multimedia Archive</title>
</head>
<body>
<div align="center">
<h1>Apollo 17 Videos</h1>

<p>Astronauts placing the flag on the Moon</p>

<object classid="clsid:02BF25D5-8C17-4B23-BC80-D3488ABDDC6B"
codebase="http://www.apple.com/qtactivex/qtplugin.cab"
```

▼
```
height="136" width="160">
    <param name="src" value="Apollo_17_Flag.mov" />
    <param name="autoplay" value="true" />
    <param name="controller" value="true" />
    <embed src="Apollo_17_Flag.mov" height="136" width="160"
      type="video/quicktime"
      pluginspage="http://www.apple.com/quicktime/download/" />
  </object>

<p>Apple <a href="http://www.apple.com/quicktime">QuickTime</a> is
required to view this movie.
<a href="http://www.apple.com/quicktime">
    <img src=" qt7badge_getQTfreeDownload.gif"
border="0" align="absmiddle" width="88" height="31" /></a></p>
</div>
</body>
</html>
```

Output ▶

FIGURE 11.10
Embedded
QuickTime movies
use special attrib-
utes created by
Apple.

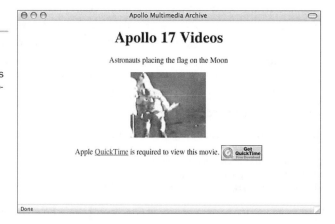

Table 11.7 summarizes the attributes that QuickTime supports.

TABLE 11.7   Attributes/Parameters Supported by QuickTime

Attribute	Description
autohref	Can be set to true or false (default false). Starts loading the URL specified in the href attribute immediately if true.
autoplay	When true, plays the movie when the plug-in estimates the clip can be played without waiting for more data (true or false).
bgcolor	Specifies the background color of any space not taken up by the movie. QuickTime 6 accepts colors specified using hexadecimal notation or a color name.

▼

TABLE 11.7   continued

Attribute	Description
cache	When `true`, the browser caches movies, resulting in the browser replaying a movie from its cache rather than downloading again. Supported by Netscape Navigator 3 and later only (`true` or `false`).
controller	When `true`, makes the movie controller visible. Sixteen pixels should be added to the height of the movie when the controller is shown and the `height` attribute is used (`true` or `false`).
correction	Applicable to QuickTime VR only (`none` or `full`).
dontflattenwhensaving	Saves the movie without flattening (no value).
enablejavascript	If this is set to true, you'll be able to control the QuickTime plug-in using JavaScript on the page.
endtime	Defines the last frame of the movie (*time in hours:minutes:_ seconds:frames*).
fov	The initial field-of-view angle for QuickTime VR movies (integer between 8 and 64).
goto	Same as `qtnext`.
height	Required. Defines the height of the region in which to display the movie. If the movie controller is visible, add 16 to the movie height to reach the total height required (in pixels).
hidden	Hides the movie, and really is only useful for background sound (no value).
hotspot*n*	Enables hotspots in a VR panorama where *n* is the hotspot ID (*URL*).
href	Links to another web page or movie (*URL*). (See the `target` attribute.)
kioskmode	When `true`, no pop-up menu is available for the movie and you cannot save it by dragging and dropping it (`true` or `false`).
loop	When `true`, the movie plays in an infinite loop. When set to `palindrome`, the movie will play alternately forward and backward (`true`, `false`, or `palindrome`).
movieid	A numeric ID (*integer*).
moviename	The movie name (*text*).
node	Sets the initial node for multinode QuickTime VR movies (*integer*).
pan	Sets the initial pan angle for QuickTime VR movies (integer from 0 to 360 degrees).

11

▼ **TABLE 11.7** continued

Attribute	Description
playeveryframe	When set to `true`, audio tracks are turned off and every frame of the movie is required to play, even if that forces a slower frame rate (`true` or `false`).
pluginspage	The URL to the QuickTime download page. You should set this to http://www.apple.com/quicktime/download/.
qtnext*n*	Identifies the URL for a movie to load and play when the current movie finishes. The number *n* can be an integer from 1 to 255 and defines the index of the URL in the playlist. The number *n* is the index of the next `qtnext` URL to load (*URL* or `goton`).
qtsrc	Forces a web browser to use the QuickTime plug-in. The URL overrides any value in the `src` attribute (*URL*).
qtsrcchokespeed	Specifies the data rate of a movie, regardless of the actual connection speed (*number*).
qtsrcdontusebrowser	Instructs the plug-in to load the movie using its own internal methods rather than using the browser, thus preventing caching.
scale	`tofit` scales the movie to the dimensions set by the `height` and `width` attributes. `aspect` scales it to fit this box while maintaining the original aspect ratio of the movie. A number scales the movie by that ratio (`tofit`, `aspect`, or a number).
src	Sets the URL of the movie (*URL*).
starttime	Sets the first frame of the movie (*time in hours:minutes:_ seconds:frames*).
target	If set to `quicktimeplayer`, launches the QuickTime Player to play the movie specified in the `href` attribute. If set to `myself`, plays the movie specified in the `href` attribute in the player embedded in the page.
target*n*	Used with `hotspot` and `href`. Sets the target for links that use the `hotspot` or `href` attribute. The number *n* corresponds to the `hotspot` number (name of a valid HTML frame).
targetcache	Caches the movie that is targeted by another movie (`true` or `false`).
tilt	Sets the initial tilt angle for QuickTime VR movies (*integer*).
type	Defines the MIME type of the movie. If the movie is visible and has `width` and `height` values, `type` must be included. This attribute is supported by Netscape Navigator 2 or later only (*MIME type*).

▼

TABLE 11.7   continued

Attribute	Description
volume	Sets the initial audio volume. The default is 100 (integer from 0 to 100).
urlsubstitute	Accepts two strings separated by a colon. In all URLs specified in the href attribute, or sprite or hotspot URLs, it replaces the first string with the second. So, "foo:bar" would replace any instance of foo in a URL with bar.
width	Sets the width of the display area for the movie (in pixels).

NOTE

> QuickTime VR enables the author to create movies with a 360-degree view of an object that the user can pan through using the QuickTime viewer.

Sound and Video File Types

11

I challenge anyone to come up with a complete list of the audio and video formats currently in use today! There are so many that it's not productive to survey all of the different multimedia file types, their extensions, and MIME types. So, I'll just cover the most popular ones, or at least the ones you might be inclined to include in your web pages.

Before I list them, however, it would be useful for you to understand what factors to consider when choosing a multimedia format. By this, I mean sound or video quality, the size of the final file, how many plug-ins or players are compatible with the format, and how readily available the file format is.

The quality of sound and video files depends primarily on the original sampling rate, number of bits used per sample, and the number of channels.

The *sampling rate* is the number of times per second the sound or video is sampled or measured. This value is represented in thousands of cycles per second or kilohertz (KHz). Imagine yourself walking through a room and being able to open your eyes only once every five seconds. Do you see how that might be dangerous? Now imagine yourself opening and closing your eyes every second. You get a much better picture of what is around you and a closer approximation of reality. It's the same with sampling rates: The faster the sample, the closer the sound or video will represent the original recording. The only problem with this is that when you increase the number of times you sample per second, the amount of data quickly becomes voluminous.

The number of bits you use determines the fidelity of the sound. An 8-bit sample, for example, can measure 256 discrete values, whereas 16-bit samples measure more than 65,000 values. The more bits you use, the closer you come to the actual pitch of a sound or the color in a video clip.

The number of channels refers primarily to audio files, where you can have mono (one channel) recordings, stereo (two channel), and even more. Having more channels enriches the sound and makes for a more enjoyable experience, but again, at the price of file size.

Six audio file types are in common use on the Web today, each with its own unique advantages and drawbacks.

- Musical Instrument Digital Interface (MIDI) files are synthesized rather than recorded sound. The file sizes are small; however, because you can't play back recorded sound, MIDI plays a niche role. (In fact, MIDI files can be so grating to listen to that you should probably never use them in a web page at all.)

- MP3 audio offers four types (or layers) of sound files and is very popular because of MPEG's widespread acceptance as an audio and video format. MP3 audio is by far the most popular and common format for MPEG audio because it can compress audio files very efficiently. MP3 remains the more popular format, and is supported by devices ranging from portable audio players like the iPod, to DVD players, to car stereos. MP3 files can also be streamed, which means that they can be played as they're being downloaded, and sites can provide a constant stream of MP3-encoded audio to act as an Internet radio station.

- Waveform (WAV) files originally were created by Microsoft and IBM, but can be played by nearly any audio program. WAV files are popular for small sound clips. Larger files are generally stored in MP3 or another format.

- Windows Media Audio (WMA) files are supported by Microsoft's Windows Media Player and anyone who licenses the formats. WMA is a format that's designed to compete with MP3, and offers both quality and compression better than MP3. There are actually a number of different formats that live under the WMA banner, including a straight MP3 competitor, a lossless audio format for distributing music purchases, and a compression scheme that's designed for speech rather than music. WMA files can be protected using a DRM scheme created by Microsoft that prevents the files from being shared freely.

- AAC audio files are compressed using the Advanced Audio Coding format. AAC is another MP3 competitor, and is the default audio format for Apple's iTunes music player. Audio tracks purchased through the iTunes Music Store are encoded using AAC, and are protected by a DRM scheme that prevents them from being shared freely. AAC is the encoding format behind the MPEG 4 audio format.

- RealAudio is an audio format designed for streaming. It's generally associated with Real Networks's line of media players. Unlike the other formats listed here, it sacrifices quality for compression so that even users with low bandwidth can receive live audio feeds over the Internet.

Table 11.8 summarizes the popular audio formats.

TABLE 11.8 Common Audio File Formats

Name	Extension(s)	MIME Type
MIDI	MID, RMI	audio/mid
Waveform (WAV)	WAV	audio/wav
MPEG Audio	MP2, MP3	audio/x-mpeg
RealAudio	RA, RAM	audio/vnd.rn-realaudio
Windows Media	WAM	audio/x-ms-wma
AAC	M4, AAC	audio/aac

The common video types available are AVI, MPEG, and QuickTime, and are described in the following list:

- AVI, which stands for *audio/video interleaved*, is a very popular Microsoft Windows video format. It's very widely supported. AVI files can be encoded using any one of a number of formats, so users must not only have an AVI player on their computer, but they must also have the codec necessary to view a file installed a well.

- MPEG video is used by things such as satellite television and digital cable. It's also a popular format for distributing video over the Internet.

- QuickTime video is proprietary to Apple. However, there are QuickTime players available for both the Mac OS X and Windows.

- Windows Media Video is the counterpart to Windows Media Audio. There are two Windows Media Video schemes. The first is a format designed for streaming and distributing video over the Internet; the second is a professional format designed for storing high-quality video for broadcast or archival.

- RealVideo is a format designed for high compression and streaming to Real Networks's media players.

- Flash Video is video that's embedded in Flash movies. The advantage of this approach is that the only dependency is the Flash player, which is already included with most browsers. The controls for video playback are also built into the Flash movie, so there's less confusion when it comes to figuring out what sizes to use when embedding the movie in a web page.

11

Table 11.9 summarizes these video formats.

TABLE 11.9   Common Video File Formats

Name	Extension(s)	MIME Type
Audio/Video Interleaved	AVI	video/x-msvideo
MPEG	MPEG, MPG	video/mpeg
QuickTime	MOV, QT	video/quicktime
Windows Media	WMV	video/x-ms-wmv
RealVideo	RV	video/vnd.m-realvideo
Flash Video	SWF	application/x-shockwave-flash

Another factor you might want to consider is whether a particular file type is *streamable*. This means it can be played as it's being downloaded. At one time, RealAudio and RealVideo were the two main streamable audio and video formats. These days, though, there are players for many file types that allow the files to be streamed. For example, many MP3 players allow MP3s to be played as they're downloaded, and QuickTime files are also streamed to the player. When you're choosing a multimedia format, you should strongly consider one that supports streaming.

Of Plug-Ins and Players

Plug-ins are external programs that can be launched within your browser. They enable you to add capabilities to your browser without adding new functionality to the browser software itself. Plug-ins are often installed as part of a larger standalone application. For example, the QuickTime Player is a standalone application used to play videos, listen to audio files, and view images, but it also installs plug-ins that enable you to view QuickTime files in your browser. On the other hand, Macromedia's Flash Player exists only as a browser plug-in. It simply enables you to view Flash animations within web pages.

Plug-ins originated with Netscape 2.0. Internet Explorer uses ActiveX controls, which provide similar functionality, but work differently. The advantage of the Internet Explorer approach is that new ActiveX controls can be downloaded and installed without closing the browser when you encounter a file that requires a control in order to be viewed. I'm lumping all of these under the general-purpose label of *plug-ins*, but the approach differs between the two browsers. Mozilla Firefox uses plug-ins just like its ancestor, Netscape Navigator.

As you learned earlier today, the problem with multimedia files that require plug-ins is that if you use them in your web pages, your visitors must have the correct plug-in installed in order to view them. Visitors who don't have your plug-in will get empty space or broken icons on your page where the multimedia should be or, in the case of Internet Explorer, be prompted to install the appropriate control. To further complicate the matter, some plug-ins are available only for some platforms.

The big four plug-ins are Windows Media Player, which is bundled with the latest versions of Windows; QuickTime, which is native to Macintosh but is available for Windows as well; RealPlayer, which is also available for Windows and Mac OS, and Flash Player, which is installed with Microsoft Internet Explorer. They each support their own proprietary formats, which generally only they can play, and except for Flash, they can also all play the common audio and video formats. When you have more than one of these applications installed, they sometimes fight over which of them gets to play the types of files that they have in common.

Windows Media Player

The Windows Media Player, available at www.microsoft.com/windows/mediaplayer, is included as part of the Windows operating system and can play many multimedia file types. It also offers a number of other features, such as the capability to copy songs from CDs, burn them to CDs, and maintain a media library. Version 10, shown in Figure 11.11, is currently available, but only for users of Windows XP. Users of Windows 2000, Windows Me, Windows 98 SE, and Mac OS X can use version 9. Windows 98 users can install version 7.1. If you're using Windows NT 4.0 or Windows 95, you must stick with Windows Media Player 6.4.

11

FIGURE 11.11
The Windows Media Player can play MP3s and other popular multimedia formats.

Version 10 of Windows Media Player can play the following file types:

- `WMF`—Windows Media Format
- `WMA`—Windows Media Audio
- `MP3`—MPEG Layer 3 audio format
- `MPG, MPEG`—Standard MPEG Layer 1 video and Layer 2 audio formats
- `WAV, AU, AIFF`—Legacy sound files
- `AVI`—Audio/Video Interleaved video (Microsoft)
- `ASF`—Advanced Systems Format (Microsoft)
- `MID`—MIDI sound files
- `RMI`—Remote Method Invocation

Macromedia Flash

Developed by Macromedia, the Flash Player is a popular plug-in that was originally designed to allow publishers to include low-bandwidth animations (created using Macromedia Flash) into web pages. Flash animations are extremely compact in comparison to traditional bitmap animations. The Flash Player offers the advantage of streaming the animations as your browser receives them rather than having to wait for the entire animation to download.

Flash is becoming a platform for deploying all sorts of web content. Not only can users create animations, but they can also create application interfaces because Flash is scriptable using JavaScript. You can also stream audio and video files to the browser through Flash. In fact, if you are publishing audio or video on the Web and are willing to buy the Flash tools, this may be the best option, because Flash is almost as common as web browsers themselves. For further information, visit the Macromedia Flash website at http://www.macromedia.com/_flash.

Macromedia Shockwave

Shockwave is a plug-in that enables Macromedia Director movies to be played as inline multimedia on a web page. Macromedia Director is a popular tool among professional multimedia developers for creating presentations that include sound, video, and 3D graphics. It is also a popular choice for creating games that can be embedded within web pages. If you're used to working with Director, Shockwave provides an easy way to put Director presentations on the Web. Or, if you're looking to do serious multimedia work on the Web or anywhere else, Director is definitely a tool to check out. You can find additional information on Macromedia Shockwave at http://www.macromedia.com/shockwave.

CAUTION | Flash is sometimes referred to as Shockwave Flash, but they are separate formats, and Shockwave requires additional software beyond the Flash Player.

Apple QuickTime

Apple QuickTime is both a file format and a player. The player, available from Apple at www.apple.com/quicktime, plays Apple's QuickTime movies (QT, MOV) along with audio and video files in a number of other formats, and is available for both Macintosh and Windows platforms (see Figure 11.12).

FIGURE 11.12
Use the QuickTime player to play saved or streaming QuickTime movies.

When you install QuickTime, it automatically installs plug-ins for your browsers.

In addition to playing QuickTime movies, QuickTime VR (for *virtual reality*) is also supported. These aren't movies per se, but rather interactive images that provide a three-dimensional view of a scene. For example, using QuickTime VR, you can provide an image of a car that allows the user to view it from any angle.

Apple also offers the iTunes music player, an application for organizing and playing music stored on your computer. It supports MP3 and AAC files, and can play audio streamed over the Internet as well.

RealPlayer

RealNetworks started out by specializing in steaming audio that you could listen to over a low bandwidth connection. They have since expanded to cover the same ground as the other major media players with support for streaming video, playing audio from CDs, and ripping songs to your computer and burning new CDs. There's a free version that

11

you can use if you just want to view RealAudio and RealVideo streams over the Internet (see Figure 11.13).

FIGURE 11.13
Use RealPlayer to check out streaming audio and video.

RealPlayer plays streaming RealAudio and RealVideo files of the following variety:

- RM, RA, RAM—RealAudio/RealVideo streamed content
- RT—Real Text streamed text formats
- RP—RealPix streamed GIF and JPG images
- GIF, JPG—Standalone JPG and GIF images
- MP3—MPEG Layer 3 audio format
- SWF—RealFlash and Shockwave Flash animation
- SMIL, SMI—SMIL-formatted (multiple data type layout) files
- .VIV, .VIVO—Vivo video files
- .MPG, .MPEG—Standard MPEG Layer 1 video and Layer 2 audio formats
- WAV, AU, AIFF—Legacy sound files
- QT, MOV—QuickTime video (uncompressed)
- AVI—Audio/Video Interleave video (Microsoft)
- ASF—Active Streaming Format (Microsoft)
- MID—MIDI sound files

WinAmp

WinAmp is the quintessential MP3 player. It was one of the first popular MP3 players, and it has remained very popular even as nearly every other audio application has added support for MP3 files. Not only can WinAmp play MP3 files that you create yourself or download over the Internet, but it can tune into Internet radio stations that stream MP3 audio and can play other popular audio formats, such as WAV. WinAmp appears in Figure 11.14.

FIGURE 11.14
The WinAmp
interface.

Summary

Well, today's lesson was certainly an eye- and earful! You learned that there are only two ways to include audio and video files in your web pages: linking to them and embedding them.

External multimedia files are files that are linked to directly rather than being embedded inside web pages. When you link to these files, your browser will launch the appropriate plug-in or external application for the file or, in some cases, ask you to save it. You also learned how external multimedia works, how to use sound and video files as external multimedia, and some hints for designing by using external multimedia files.

Much of this lesson focuses on examples of embedding multimedia files directly into the web browser. You can use the <embed> element, or a combination of <embed> and <object>.

11

Table 11.10 shows a summary of the tags you learned about in this lesson.

TABLE 11.10   Tags for Inline Multimedia

Tag	Attribute	Use
<a>	href	Links to a sound or video file exactly as you link to any other type of file.
<embed>		Embeds objects into web pages.
<object>...<object>		Embeds objects into web pages.
<param>...</param>		Specifies parameters to be passed to the embedded object. Used in the object element.
<img>	dynsrc	Includes a sound or video file instead of an image. If the file cannot be found or played, the normal image (in src) is shown. Used by Internet Explorer only.
<bgsound>		Plays a background sound. Used by Internet Explorer only.

Workshop

The following workshop includes questions you might ask about including sound and video in web pages, quizzes to test your knowledge, and two quick exercises.

Q&A

Q What's the quickest way to get started adding multimedia to my site?

A Remember that you can use at least one absolutely sure-fire method to include sound and video in your web pages: Link to them. Although that might not be as exciting as embedding them in the web browser window, you know the web page will work. Of course, the person visiting your site must have the appropriate application to play the file, but you can help her out by providing links to any required players or plug-ins.

Q Should I be worried about web browser and HTML compatibility when it comes to audio and video?

A Unfortunately, yes. Most other HTML elements and techniques are standardized to the point that you can be confident that your code will work across most popular web browsers. Embedding audio and video is a completely different ballgame. Generally if you stick with the guidelines provided by whoever created the plug-in used to listen to or view your files, you'll be OK.

Q What are the differences between AVI, MPEG, and QuickTime movies?

A The underlying differences are beyond the scope of this lesson, but it has to do with how the audio and video data is encoded, compressed, and stored in the resulting files. Each file type uses different methods that are all unique. The practical difference is that each one might require a different player to be heard/viewed properly.

Q Should I bother using the techniques solely compatible with Internet Explorer, such as `dynsrc`?

A My advice is not to bother with them because you might be ignoring (and hence alienating) a good portion of your audience. If you're in an environment that's IE-only, you can feel free to use them. Ultimately, the choice is up to you.

Quiz

1. What are the differences between a helper application (also called a *player*) and a plug-in?
2. In what ways can you insert multimedia into your web pages?
3. What are the advantages and disadvantages of using plug-ins?
4. What is streaming multimedia?

Quiz Answers

1. Helper applications run externally to your web browser and open files that your browser does not support. The browser downloads a file and then passes it on to an external helper application that reads and plays the file. Plug-ins work within the browser to read and play files.

2. You can link to them or embed them.

3. The advantage to using plug-ins is that they enable you to insert many different types of content into your pages. The disadvantage to using them is that you can't guarantee that everyone will have them or will want to take the time to download them to experience your site. Some people use browsers that don't support them, and not all plug-ins are universally supported across web browsers and operating systems.

4. Streaming multimedia plays as it's transmitted to the client, unlike media types that send an entire file to the client before it can be played. In fact, with streaming media, you don't even have to start at the beginning of a file—you can jump in anywhere on the stream or listen to a live feed.

Exercises

1. Tour the Web and visit sites that use multimedia. You might start out at http://www. youtube.com for an example of video, and http://www.live365.com for streaming audio. Macromedia's Showcase at http://shockwave.com/ always features sites that create multimedia content. See how others include it in their websites. Try visiting the same site using Internet Explorer and Netscape Navigator. Is there a difference? What prompts you to download a plug-in?

2. View the source for some pages that present multimedia files and see whether they use <embed>, <object>, or both.

11

PART IV:
JavaScript and Dynamic HTML

LESSON 12:
Introducing JavaScript

JavaScript is a scripting language for adding functionality to HTML pages. Its scripts are embedded in HTML files and run completely within the browser. JavaScript turns the browser into an application that runs other applications, rather than one that just displays documents. Support for JavaScript is included in Netscape, Internet Explorer, Mozilla Firefox, and Opera. The ongoing evolution of JavaScript is being managed by ECMA, a European standards body.

As with most technologies in use on the Internet, and especially the World Wide Web, JavaScript is under constant development. It moved rapidly from version 1.0 in Netscape Navigator 2 to version 1.1 in Navigator 3, version 1.2 in Navigator 4, version 1.3 in Navigator 4.5, and version 1.5 in Netscape 6. Meanwhile, Microsoft introduced JScript, its own variation on JavaScript that was first supported in Internet Explorer 3.0. Each of these variations and versions has subtle differences and inconsistencies. Instead of dealing with these differences, this discussion of JavaScript looks at the basic features that are common to all implementations of JavaScript.

In this Lesson

Today, you learn about the basics of JavaScript by exploring the following topics:

- What JavaScript is

- Why you would want to use JavaScript

- The <script> tag

- Basic commands and language structure

- Basic JavaScript programming

Introducing JavaScript

JavaScript was initially introduced with Netscape Navigator 2.0. Before its introduction, there was no way to add interactive content to web pages. If you wanted to create an interactive application, you had to do everything on the server using CGI scripts or other server-side techniques. Netscape embedded a JavaScript interpreter within its browser so that web designers could add programs to their pages to provide interactive content.

JavaScript is useful because it's deeply integrated with the browser. This integration allows it to manipulate various aspects of the browser behavior, as well as objects included on an HMTL page. JavaScript uses what's referred to as an *event-driven model* of execution. When you embed JavaScript code in a web page, it isn't run until the event it's associated with is triggered.

The types of events that can call JavaScript include loading the page, leaving the page, interacting with a form element in some way, or clicking a link. Plenty of other events are available as well. Many of these events are taken advantage of in what most users would consider to be annoying ways. For example, many sites open an additional window containing an advertisement when you navigate to one of their pages. This is accomplished using JavaScript and the page load event. Other sites open additional windows when you leave them; this is also accomplished using JavaScript triggered on an event. Less annoying applications include displaying a custom message in the status bar when a user holds the mouse over a link, and swapping out images when the user moves the mouse over them.

Why Would You Want to Use JavaScript?

JavaScript enables you to manipulate web pages without sending a request back to the server. Using this capability, you can alter elements on a page, validate user input before a user submits a form, and modify the behavior of the browser—all by using scripts embedded within your web pages. Let's look at some of the advantages of using JavaScript to enhance your web pages.

Ease of Use

Unlike Java, JavaScript is designed for nonprogrammers. As such, it's relatively easy to use and is far less pedantic about details such as the declaration of variable types. In addition, you don't need to compile JavaScript code before it can be used, unlike most other languages, including Java. Still, JavaScript is a scripting language, which gives it a steeper learning curve than HTML (although JavaScript's curve isn't as steep as Java's). Without any programming background, however, you can use JavaScript for very simple tasks such as the ones presented later in this lesson. More complex jobs require learning key programming concepts and techniques.

Increasing Server Efficiency

Some JavaScript applications can save round trips to the server, and prevent the user from waiting for a form submission to be processed. In other cases, you can use advanced JavaScript applications along with programs on the server to update parts of a page rather than reloading the entire thing. I'll discuss that in Lesson 15, "Creating Applications with Dynamic HTML and AJAX." Traffic on the Internet is only going up, and you never know when a website is going to be the next hot thing. Reducing server traffic through the use of JavaScript can help ensure that your website remains responsive even as traffic goes up. Let's say that you've created a form that people use to enter their billing details into your online ordering system. When this form is submitted, your CGI script first needs to validate the information provided and make sure that all the appropriate fields have been filled out correctly. It needs to check that a name and address have been entered, that a billing method has been selected, that credit card details have been completed—and the list goes on.

But what happens if your CGI script discovers that some information is missing? You need to alert the visitor that there are problems with the submission and then ask the user to edit the details and resubmit the completed form. This process involves sending the form back to the browser, having the visitor resubmit it with the right information, revalidating it, and repeating the process until everything is current. This process is very resource-intensive, both on the server side (each CGI program takes up CPU and memory time) and in the repeated network connections back and forth between the browser and the server.

By adding validation and checking procedures to the web browser with JavaScript, you can reduce the number of transactions because many errors will be caught before forms are ever submitted to the server. And, because the web server doesn't need to perform as many validations of its own, fewer server hardware and processor resources are required to process form submissions. The side benefit is that users will find your application more responsive because the trip back to the server isn't required for validation.

12

Integration with the Browser

You can add interactive features to your pages using Java applets or plug-ins such as Macromedia Flash and Macromedia Shockwave. However, these technologies are separate from the pages that they're embedded within. JavaScript, on the other hand, enables you to manipulate objects on the page such as links, images, and form elements. You can also use JavaScript to control the browser itself by changing the size of the browser window, moving the browser window around the screen, and activating or deactivating elements of the interface. None of these options is available with Java or plug-ins.

The `<script>` Tag

To accommodate the inclusion of JavaScript programs in a normal HTML document, Netscape introduced the `<script>` tag. By placing a `<script>` tag in a document, you tell the web browser to treat any lines of text following the tag as script rather than as content for the web page. This continues until a corresponding `</script>` tag is encountered, at which point the browser reverts to treating text as web content.

When used in a document, every script tag must include a `language` attribute to declare the scripting language to be used. If you're writing a script in JavaScript, you should use the attribute `language="JavaScript"`.

> **NOTE**
>
> JavaScript has now appeared in five versions of Netscape Navigator and two versions of Microsoft Internet Explorer, plus Mozilla Firefox and Opera. This means that there are now several possible values for the `language` attribute. With Navigator 3, Netscape extended JavaScript to JavaScript 1.1. Netscape Navigator 4.0 added even more to JavaScript and called it JavaScript 1.2. Navigator 4.5 introduced JavaScript 1.3. Even though many browsers have been released since Netscape Navigator 4.5, the version number for JavaScript remains the same.

The Structure of a JavaScript Script

When you include any JavaScript code in an HTML document (apart from using the `<script>` tag), you should also follow a few other conventions:

- As a rule, the `<script>` tag should be placed between the `<head>` and `</head>` tags at the start of your document, not between the `<body>` tags. This isn't a hard-and-fast requirement (as you'll learn later), but it's a standard that you should adopt whenever possible. Because the code for your scripts won't be displayed on the web page itself, it should be included in the `<head>` section with all the other control and information tags, such as `<title>` and `<meta>`.

- Unlike HTML, which uses the `<!-- comment tag -->`, comments inside JavaScript code use the `//` symbol at the start of a line. Any line of JavaScript code that starts with this symbol will be treated as a comment and ignored.

Taking these three points into consideration, the basic structure for including JavaScript code inside an HTML document looks like this:

```html
<html>
<head>
<title>Test script</title>
<script language="JavaScript">
// Your JavaScript code goes here
</script>
</head>
<body>
  Your Web document goes here
</body>
</html>
```

The src Attribute

Besides the language attribute, the <script> tag can also include an src attribute, which allows a JavaScript script stored in a separate file to be included as part of the current web page. This option is handy if you have several web pages that use the same JavaScript code and you don't want to copy and paste the scripts into each page's code.

When used this way, the <script> tag takes the following form:

```html
<script language="JavaScript" src="http://www.myserver.com/script.js">
```

In this form, script can be any relative or absolute URL, and .js is the file extension for a JavaScript file.

Basic Commands and Language Structure

12

JavaScript is an object-based language. It accesses the browser and elements on the page in an object-oriented fashion. All the objects are stored in a hierarchy, and you can specify specific elements in the hierarchy using a dot-based notation that I'll explain in a bit.

Using this structure, all the elements of a single web page are contained within a base object container called window. Inside the window object is a set of smaller containers (or objects) that hold information about the various elements of a web page. The following are some of the main objects:

location   Contains information about the location of the current web document, including its URL and separate components such as the protocol, domain name, path, and port.

history	Holds a record of all the sites that a web browser has visited during the current session, and also gives you access to built-in functions that enable you to change the contents of the current window.
document	Contains the complete details of the current web page. This information includes all the forms, form elements, images, links, and anchors. It also provides many functions that enable you to programmatically alter the contents of items such as text boxes, radio buttons, and other form elements.

You can find a complete list of the available objects in JavaScript in Microsoft's JScript reference at http://msdn.microsoft.com, and in the Mozilla JavaScript documentation at http://developer.mozilla.org/en/docs/JavaScript.

Objects are accessed using a dot-based notation. To refer to a specific object, you need to locate it within the object hierarchy. For example, to refer to a form field called quantity in the first form on a page, you'd refer to it as document.forms[0].quantity. When multiple objects of the same type appear at the same location in a hierarchy, you have to refer to them by position in a list or by name. In this case, I'm referring to the first form on the document, so it's in the first position in the list—thus, forms[0]. JavaScript, like most programming languages, starts counting at zero.

Properties and Methods

Within each object container, you can access two main types of resources: properties and methods.

Properties are variables that hold a value associated with the object you're interested in. For example, within the document object is a property called title that contains the title of the current document as described by the <title> tag.

In JavaScript, you obtain the value of this property by using the command document.title. Properties are accessed using the dot notation I mentioned earlier. The item after the final dot is the property that you want to reference.

Some examples of properties that you can use include the following:

document.bgcolor	The color of the page's background
document.fgcolor	The color of the page's text
document.lastModified	The date the page was last modified
document.title	The title of the current web page

`form.action`	The URL of the CGI script to which the form will be submitted
`location.hostname`	The hostname of the current web page's URL

See the JavaScript documentation at http://developer.mozilla.org/en/docs/JavaScript for all the properties of each built-in object.

Methods are actions associated with a particular object. For example, the `document` object has a method called `write` associated with it that enables you to write text directly onto a web page. It takes the following form:

```
document.write("Hello world");
```

As was the case with properties, you execute, or *call*, a method by referencing the object that it's associated with, followed by a dot, and then the name of the method itself. Method names are followed by parentheses (`()`). The parentheses surround any arguments to that method. For example, if the method operates on numbers, the parentheses will contain those numbers. In the `"Hello World"` example, the `write()` method takes a string to write as an argument.

Note that even if a method accepts no arguments, you still have to include the parentheses. For example, the `toString()` method, which belongs to the `location` object, is used to convert the current document's URL into a string suitable for use with other methods such as `document.write()`. This method has no arguments. You just call it with empty parentheses, like this: `location.toString()`. The parentheses are necessary to distinguish between methods and properties.

As with properties, each object has a set of methods that you can use in your JavaScript scripts. The full list is at the same URL as the list of objects and properties mentioned earlier. Here are a few choice methods:

`document.write(`*`string`*`)`	Writes HTML or text to the current page. `string` is the text to write.
`form.submit()`	Submits the form.
`window.alert(`*`string`*`)`	Pops up an alert box. `string` is the message to display in the alert.
`window.open(`*`URL, name`*`)`	Opens a new browser window. `URL` is the URL of the page to open, and `name` is the window name for frame or link targets.

By combining the `document.write()` and `location.toString()` methods and the `document.title` property mentioned previously into an HTML document, you can create a simple JavaScript script such as the one shown here:

12

Input ▼

```
<html>
<head>
<title>Test JavaScript</title>
<script language="JavaScript">
<!-- hide from old browsers
document.write(document.title + "<br />");
document.write(location.toString());
// done hiding -->
</script>
</head>
 </html>
```

The results are shown in Figure 12.1.

Output ▼

FIGURE 12.1
The results of your
first JavaScript
script.

```
Test JavaScript
file:///Users/rafeco/Documents/tywebpub/code/12/figure01.html
```

CAUTION

> Method, property, function, and variable names in JavaScript are
> all case sensitive. That is, uppercase and lowercase are different.
> If you're having problems getting the script for Figure 12.1 to
> work, make sure that you've written `location.toString()` and not
> `location.tostring()`.

Events and JavaScript

Although implementing methods such as `document.write()` to create web pages might
be useful, the real power behind JavaScript lies in its capability to respond to events.

As I mentioned earlier, *events* are actions that occur on a web page, normally when a visitor interacts with the page in some way. For example, when someone enters a value into
a text box on a form or clicks a Submit button, a series of events is triggered inside the
web browser. All these events can be intercepted by JavaScript programs.

Functions

Functions are similar to methods. The difference is that whereas methods are associated
with built-in objects, functions are standalone routines that are embedded in the page. To
define a function for the current web page, you would write something like this:

```
<script language="JavaScript">

function functionName(arguments) {
 The actions to be performed by your function go here
}
</script>
```

In this code, `functionName` is just about any unique name that you choose, and `arguments` is a list of any values that you want to be sent to the function. The only function names you can't choose are those that are already part of JavaScript. Following the function definition and inside the set of braces ({}), you include the list of instructions that you want the function to perform. It could be a set of calculations, validation routines for a form, or just about anything else you can think of.

NOTE

JavaScript also includes a set of built-in objects and functions that enable you to perform mathematical operations, string manipulation, and date and time calculations. For a full list of built-in functions, refer to the online JavaScript documentation.

Functions are the core unit of reuse in JavaScript. If you want to do something more than once, you put the code to do it in a function, and then call the function wherever you want to do that thing. For example, let's say you had two values, a first name and a last name, and you wanted to turn them into one value. You could use the following code every time you wanted to do that:

```
fullName = firstName + " " + lastName;
```

Or you could write a function to take care of it, like this:

```
function makeFullName(firstName, lastName) {
   return firstName + " " + lastName;
}
```

The name of the function is `makeFullName`, and it has two arguments, `firstName` and `lastName`. It combines the two names using the + operator and returns the result. This code is pretty simple, and putting it in a function doesn't save much work. For more complex operations, creating a function makes more sense.

Later in this lesson, you'll learn how to include external JavaScript files on your page, much like you learned to link to external style sheets in Lesson 9, "Creating Layouts with CSS." You can put functions you commonly use in an external JavaScript file and link to that file from all of the pages that use the functions, saving yourself a lot of maintenance work if any of the functions need to be updated later on.

12

Assigning Functions to Events

After you define your functions, your next step is to assign them to the various events that you want to act on. You do so by assigning event handlers to the various elements of a web page or form. Currently, you can set the event handlers shown in Table 12.1.

TABLE 12.1   JavaScript Event Handlers

Event Handler	When It's Called
onblur	Whenever a visitor leaves a specified form field
onchange	Whenever a visitor changes the contents of a specified form field
onclick	Whenever a visitor clicks a specified element
onfocus	Whenever a visitor enters a specified form field
onload	Whenever a web page is loaded or reloaded
onmouseover	Whenever a visitor places the mouse cursor over a specified object
onselect	Whenever a visitor selects the contents of a specified field
onsubmit	Whenever a visitor submits a specified form
onunload	Whenever the current web page is changed

To specify functions that should be associated with any of these events, you just need to include the appropriate event handler as an attribute of the tag associated with that event. For example, consider a standard form with a couple of text fields and a Submit button, as shown here:

```
<form method="post" src="/cgi-bin/form">
<input type="text" name="username">
<input type="text" name="emailAddress">
<input type="submit">
</form>
```

Adding onsubmit="return checkform(this)" to the <form> tag causes the function called checkform() to be executed before the browser submits the form. In checkform(), you can perform any checks that you want and, if any problems occur, halt the form submission and ask the user to fix them. The this parameter inside the parentheses is used to tell the checkform() function which form object is associated with the <form> tag.

The Meaning of this

You might be a bit puzzled by the use of this as an argument passed to a function. Here, this is shorthand for the current object. When you're using an event handler in a tag, this refers to the object represented by that tag. In the previous example, it refers

> to the form associated with the `<form>` tag in which it appears. Why use an argument at all? So that one function can be used with many objects. In this case, we might have four forms on the page that can all be validated using `checkform()`; we can distinguish between those forms by passing a reference to the form using `this`.

In addition, you can do field-by-field checking by including either `onchange` or `onblur` event handlers in each `<input>` tag. Because the `onblur` handler is called each time a person leaves a field, it's ideal for input validation.

Buttons such as the Submit button trigger the `onclick` event. For example, `<input type="submit" onclick="processclick()">` calls the function `processclick()` whenever the Submit button is clicked.

Variables

In addition to properties, JavaScript also enables you to assign or retrieve values from variables. A *variable* is a user-defined container that can hold a number, some text, or an object. But unlike most high-level languages that force you to limit the contents of each variable to a specific type, JavaScript is a *loosely typed language*. This means that you don't need to specify the type of information that a variable can contain when you create it. In fact, data of different types can be assigned to the same variable, depending on your requirements.

To declare a variable for a JavaScript program, you would write the following:

```
var variablename = value ;
```

12

In this form, *variablename* is a name that you choose. You can choose any name you like, as long as it's not already reserved as part of the JavaScript language. The equal sign (=) following the *variablename* is called an *assignment operator*. It tells JavaScript to assign whatever is on the right side of the = sign—*value*—as the contents of the variable. This *value* can be a text string, a number, a property, the results of a function, an array, a date, or even another variable. Here's an example:

```
var name = "Laura Lemay";
var age = 28;
var title = document.title;
var documenturl = location.toString();var myarray = new Array(10);
var todaysdate = new Date();
var myname = anothername;
```

> **NOTE**
>
> Variable names (and function names) can consist of the letters *a* through *z*, the numbers 0 through 9, and the underscore (_) symbol. A variable name cannot start with a number.

> **TIP**
>
> If you declare a variable inside a function, you can access the contents of that variable only from inside the function itself. This is said to be the *scope* of the variable. On the other hand, if you declare a variable inside a `<script>` block outside your functions, you can access the contents of that variable from any JavaScript code on the web page. This is referred to as global scope.

Operators and Expressions

After you define a variable, you can work with its contents or alter them using operators. Table 12.2 lists some of the more popular operators provided by JavaScript and examples of each. (As before, for a full list of all the supported operators, refer to the online JavaScript documentation.)

> **NOTE**
>
> The examples shown in the second column of Table 12.2 are called *expressions*. An expression is any valid set of variables, operators, and other expressions that evaluate to a single value. For example, `b + c` evaluates to a single value, which is assigned to a.

TABLE 12.2   JavaScript Operators and Expressions

Operator	Example	Description
+	a = b + c	Adds variables b and c and assigns the result to variable a.
-	a = b - c	Subtracts the value of variable c from variable b and assigns the result to variable a.
*	a = b * c	Multiplies variable b by variable c and assigns the result to variable a.
/	a = b / c	Divides variable b by variable c and assigns the result to variable a.
%	a = b % c	Obtains the modulus of variable b when it's divided by variable c, and assigns the result to variable a. (Note: A *modulus* is a function that returns the remainder.)

TABLE 12.2 continued

Operator	Example	Description
++	a = ++b	Increments variable b by 1 and assigns the result to variable a.
- -	a = - -b	Decrements variable b by 1 and assigns the result to variable a.

You also can use a special set of operators, called *assignment operators*, that combine the assignment function (=) and an operator into a single function. Table 12.3 lists the assignment operators provided by JavaScript.

TABLE 12.3 JavaScript Assignment Operators

Assignment Operator	Example	Description
+=	a += b	This example is equivalent to the statement a = a + b.
-=	a -= b	This example is equivalent to the statement a = a - b.
*=	a *= b	This example is equivalent to the statement a = a * b.
/=	a /= b	This example is equivalent to the statement a = a / b.
/=	a %= b	This example is equivalent to the statement a = a % b.

NOTE

The + and += operators can be used with string variables as well as numeric variables. When you use them with strings, the result of a = "text" + " and more text" is a variable containing "text and more text".

12

Basic JavaScript Programming

To tie together all the event handlers, methods, parameters, functions, variables, and operators, JavaScript includes a simple set of programming statements that are similar to those provided in most other programming languages.

If you have any programming experience at all, spending a few minutes browsing the list of supported statements discussed in Netscape's online documentation will set you well on your way toward creating your first JavaScript programs. If you don't have the experience, the following section includes a quick crash course in basic programming.

What Is a Script?

Regardless of which programming language you use, a *script* is simply a set of instructions that describes some action, or group of actions, that you want the computer to perform. In the most basic case, a script starts at the beginning of a list of code and works through each instruction in the list one at a time until it reaches the end, as follows:

```
<script language="JavaScript">
// Start of program - NOTE: lines that start with '//' are treated as comments.
document.write("step one") ;
document.write("step two") ;
// End of program.
</script>
```

However, you'll rarely ever want a script to proceed straight through a list of steps—especially in JavaScript—because writing the messages on the screen using HTML would be easier than coding them with JavaScript. For this reason, most scripting languages include a basic set of statements that enable you to control the flow of execution.

The `if` Statement

The first instruction that enables you to control the flow is the `if` statement. It enables you to create blocks of code that will be executed only if a particular condition is satisfied. For example, if you have a web form that asks whether a person is male or female, you might want to respond to the person using a gender-specific response:

```
if (form.theSex.value == "male") {
  document.write("Thank you for your response, Sir" ) ;
}
if (form.theSex.value == "female") {
  document.write("Thank you for your response, Madam" ) ;
}
```

If this piece of code is run and the property `form.theSex.value` is assigned a value of `"male"`, the first `document.write()` method is called. If it's assigned a value of `"female"`, the second statement is displayed. The block of code next to the `if` statement performs a comparison between the property `form.theSex.value` and the word `"male"`. This comparison is made using comparison operators. In this case, a test for equivalence was performed, as signified by the `==` symbol. Table 12.4 lists the comparison operators currently recognized by JavaScript.

TABLE 12.4   JavaScript Comparison Operators

Operator	Operator Description	Notes
==	Equal to	a == b tests to see whether a equals b.
!=	Not equal to	a != b tests to see whether a does not equal b.

TABLE 12.4   continued

Operator	Operator Description	Notes
<	Less than	a < b tests to see whether a is less than b.
<=	Less than or equal to	-a <= b tests to see whether a is less than or equal to b.
>=	Greater than or equal to	-a >= b tests to see whether a is greater than or equal to b.
>	Greater than	a > b tests to see whether a is greater than b.

The if...else Statement

You also can write the preceding example using a different version of the if statement that incorporates an else statement:

```
if (form.theSex.value == "male") {
  document.write("Thank you for your response, Sir") ;
}
else {
  document.write("Thank you for your response, Madam") ;
}
```

In this example, you don't need a second if test—a person can be only male or female—so you use the else statement to tell the program to display the second message if the first test fails.

> **NOTE**
>
> In both the preceding examples, any number of statements could be assigned to each outcome by including them inside the appropriate set of braces.

12

Looping Statements

You'll occasionally want a group of statements to be executed repeatedly. Two looping statements are supported by JavaScript. The first, the for loop, is ideal for situations in which you want a group of instructions to occur a specific number of times. The second, the while loop, is useful when you want a set of statements to be completed until a condition is satisfied.

for Loops   The basic structure of a for loop looks like this:

```
for (var count = 1; count <= 10; ++count ) {
 your statements go here
}
```

In this example, a variable called count is declared and set to a value of 1. Then a test is run to see whether the value of count is less than or equal to 10. If it is, all the statements inside the braces ({}) following the for statement are executed once. The value of count is then incremented by 1 by the ++count statement, and the count <= 10 test is performed again. If the result is still true, all the instructions inside the braces are executed again. This process proceeds until the value of count is greater than 10, at which point the for loop ends. In the preceding example, the variable count is incremented using the increment operator, ++. The ++ appears before the variable name, which means that the variable is pre-incremented. You could also write the expression as count++, which would post-increment the variable. In this case, the results are the same, but if the expression were nested in a larger expression, like the one that follows, the results would differ. Here's the example:

```
count++ <= 10
```

In that case, I post-increment the variable, so the variable of count before it is incremented would be compared to 10. Let's say I changed the expression to look like this:

```
++count <= 10
```

In that case, the value of count would be incremented before the comparison. Check out the comments in the example that follows to see what I'm talking about.

```
count = 9;
return ++count <= 10; // returns true
count = 9;
return count++ <= 10; // returns false
```

CAUTION

As you can see, the for statement is self-contained. The count variable is declared, tested, and incremented within that statement. You shouldn't modify the value of count within the body of your loop unless you're absolutely sure of what you're doing. If you modify count so that it never has a value greater than 10, your loop will never stop running and your program won't work. Anytime you use a for loop, you should avoid manipulating your counter inside the loop; it's not a good programming practice.

while Loops   The basic structure of a while loop looks like this:

```
while ( condition ) {
 your statements go here
}
```

Unlike the for loop, which has a built-in increment mechanism, the only test required for a while loop is a true result from the condition test following the while statement. This test could be an equivalence test, as in a == b, or any of the other tests mentioned previously with the if statement. It might help you to think of a while loop as an if statement that's executed repeatedly until a condition is satisfied.

As long as this expression is true, the statements inside the braces following the while loop continue to run forever—or at least until you close your web browser.

If you prefer, you can write while loops with the condition at the end, which ensures that they always run once. These are called do ... while loops, and look like this:

```
var color = "blue";
do {
  // some stuff
}
while (color != "blue");
```

Even though the test in the loop will not pass, it will still run once because the condition is checked after the first time the body of the loop runs.

CAUTION

When you're using while loops, you need to avoid creating infinite loops. This means that you must manipulate one of the values in the looping condition within the body of your loop. If you do manage to create an endless loop, about the only option you have is to shut down the web browser. If you're going to iterate a specific number of times using a counter, it's usually best to just use a for loop.

12

Learning More About JavaScript

The list of statements, functions, and options included in this lesson represents only part of the potential offered by JavaScript.

For this reason, I cannot overemphasize the importance of the online documentation provided by Netscape. All the latest JavaScript enhancements and features will be documented first at http://developer.mozilla.org/en/docs/JavaScript.

Summary

JavaScript enables HTML publishers to include simple programs or scripts within a web page without having to deal with the many difficulties associated with programming in high-level languages such as Java or C++.

In this lesson, you learned about the `<script>` tag and how it's used to embed JavaScript programs into an HTML document. In addition, you explored the basic structure of the JavaScript language and some of the statements and functions that it offers.

With this basic knowledge behind you, in the next lesson, you'll explore some real-world examples of JavaScript and learn more about the concepts involved in JavaScript programming.

Workshop

The following workshop includes questions, a quiz, and exercises related to JavaScript.

Q&A

Q Don't I need a development environment to work with JavaScript?

A Nope. As with HTML, all you need is a text editor and a browser that supports JavaScript. You might be confusing JavaScript with Java, a more comprehensive programming language that needs at least a compiler for its programs to run.

Q Are Java and JavaScript compatible?

A The answer depends on what you mean by *compatible*. Some of the syntax is similar between Java and JavaScript, but the connection doesn't go much further than that. JavaScript scripts won't compile using a Java compiler, nor can Java programs be included in an HTML file the way JavaScript scripts can. Java programs require a Java compiler and are then included as executable programs in web pages, whereas JavaScript scripts are interpreted in code form as the HTML page is being downloaded.

Q In Java and C++, I previously defined variables with statements such as int, char, and String. Why can't I do this in JavaScript?

A As I mentioned previously, JavaScript is a loosely typed language. This means that all variables can take any form and can even be changed on the fly. As a result, the type of value assigned to a variable automatically determines its type.

Quiz

1. How is JavaScript different from Java?
2. How is JavaScript *similar* to Java (other than in name)?
3. What HTML tag did Netscape introduce to identify JavaScript scripts?
4. What are *events*? What can JavaScript do with them?
5. How are functions different from methods?

Quiz Answers

1. JavaScript is a simple language that works only in web browsers; Java is a more comprehensive programming language that can be used just about anywhere.
2. Because JavaScript scripts are run by the web browser itself, they're portable across any browser that includes JavaScript support, regardless of the computer type or operating system (like Java).
3. To accommodate the inclusion of JavaScript programs in a normal HTML document, Netscape introduced the `<script>` tag. By placing a `<script>` tag in a document, you tell the web browser to treat any lines of text following the tag as script rather than as content for the web page.
4. Events are special actions triggered by things happening in the system (windows opening, pages being loaded, forms being submitted) or by reader input (text being entered, links being followed, check boxes being selected). Using JavaScript, you can perform different operations in response to these events.
5. Methods are associated with a specific object, and functions are standalone routines that operate outside the bounds of an object.

12

Exercises

1. If you haven't done so already, take a few minutes to explore Netscape's online documentation for JavaScript at http://devedge.netscape.com/central/javascript/. See whether you can find out what enhancements were included in JavaScript 1.5 that weren't included in earlier versions.
2. Find a simple JavaScript script somewhere on the Web—either in use in a web page or in an archive of scripts. Look at the source code and see whether you can decode its logic and how it works.

LESSON 13:
Using JavaScript in Your Pages

Now that you have some understanding of what JavaScript is all about, you're ready to look at some practical applications of JavaScript.

In this Lesson

Today, you'll learn how to complete the following tasks:

- Create a random link generator
- Validate the contents of a form
- Create an image rollover

Creating a Random Link Generator

A random link generator is basically a link that takes you to a different location every time you click it. In the past, the only way to implement such a link was to use a CGI script. With JavaScript, you can move the process of choosing a link from a script on the server to a script running in the browser.

In the following sections, you'll learn how to create three different random link generators. The first uses an inline `<script>` tag and a single function, the second uses event handlers, and the third uses arrays within a script.

NOTE

An *inline* `<script>` tag is one that is embedded in the `<body>` section of an HTML document rather than in the `<head>` section, as is more common.

▼ Task: Exercise 13.1: The Inline Random Link Generator

Because the JavaScript code for this generator will be incorporated into a standard HTML document, open the text editor or HTML editor that you normally use for designing web pages and create a new file called `random.html`.

In this new file, create a basic document framework like the following one. You should recognize all the elements of this document from preceding lessons, including the `<a>...</a>` tag combination on the third-from-last line:

Input ▼

```
<html>
<head>
<title>Random Link Generator</title>
</head>
<body>
<h1>My random link generator</h1>
<p>Visit a <a href="dummy.html">randomly selected</a>
site from my list of favorites.</p>
</body>
</html>
```

▼ If you ran this document as it is, you would see a result like the one shown in Figure 13.1.

Output ▼

FIGURE 13.1
The Random Link Generator page.

Now you can add some JavaScript code to turn the link into a random link generator. First, add a `<script>` tag to the `<head>` section immediately after the `<title>` tag block:

```
<title>Random Link Generator</title>
<script language="JavaScript">
<!-- the contents of the script need to be hidden from other browsers
 the JavaScript code goes here.
// End of script -->
</script>
</head>
```

The next step involves adding the code that generates the random links based on a list of your favorite sites. Inside the `<script>` tag—and comment tag—you'll create a function called `picklink()`. First, you need to define the function:

```
function picklink() {
 your JavaScript code goes here.
}
```

The code that follows actually makes the `picklink()` function work, with a list of four sites to choose from.

```
function picklink()
{

  var linknumber = 4;
  var linktext = "nolink.html";

  var linkselect = Math.floor(linknumber * Math.random()) + 1;

  if (linkselect == 1)
  {
   linktext = "http://www.netscape.com/"
  }
  if (linkselect == 2)
  {
   linktext = "http://www.lne.com/Web/"
  }
```

13

```
▼  if (linkselect == 3 )
   {
     linktext = "http://java.sun.com/"
   }
   if (linkselect == 4)
   {
     linktext="http://www.realaudio.com/"
   }

     document.write('<a href="' + linktext + '">randomly selected</a>');
   }
```

To help you understand what this code is doing, I'll explain it section by section. The first two lines following the function definition declare some work variables used inside the function: `linknumber` tells the function how many links it has to choose from, and `linktext` is a work variable that holds the value of the URL for the selected random link.

The next line creates a number called `linkselect`, which contains an integer between 1 and the value set in `linknumber`. It does so by multiplying the number of links available with a random number between 0 and 1, obtained using `Math.random()` (`random()` is a method built into the `Math` object). This returns a number such as 2.138413 or 0.13451. The `Math.floor()` method then returns the highest integer less than that number. That leaves us with a number between 0 and 3. Adding 1 to that result gives us a number between 1 and 4, which is what we need.

The set of `if` statements that follows checks the randomly selected value assigned to `linkselect`. When a match is found, it assigns a URL to the variable `linktext`. You can add as many URLs as you want here, but remember that you need to alter the value of `linknumber` so that it reflects how many links you've defined.

After you assign a URL to `linktext`, the next step is to create the physical link by using a `document.write()` method:

```
document.write('<a href="' + linktext + '">randomly selected</a>');
```

The value inside the parentheses takes advantage of JavaScript's capability to add strings of text together. In this case, `'<a href="'`, the values of `linktext`, and `'">randomly selected</a>'` are added together to create a properly formed link tag.

Now that you've defined `picklink()` in the `<script>` definition, all that remains is to replace the original anchor tag from the original page with the new link created by `picklink()`. You can do so in various ways, but the simplest method is to embed a call to `picklink()` inside the body of your document, as shown here:

```
   <p>Visit a <script language="JavaScript">picklink()</script>
▼  site from my list of favorites.</p>
```

Some JavaScript purists might argue that you should include `<script>` blocks only in the `<head>` section of an HTML document, and for the most part they're correct. But you'll break this rule in this exercise to see how inline script calls work. In the following exercise, you'll learn about a mechanism that enables you to create a random link generator without the use of inline `<script>` tags.

The Completed Document   Here's the final random number HTML page with all the JavaScript intact.

Input ▼

```
<html>
<head>
<title>Random Link Generator</title>
<script language="JavaScript">
function picklink()
{

 var linknumber = 4;
 var linktext = "nolink.html";

 var linkselect = Math.round((linknumber - 1) * Math.random()) + 1;

 if (linkselect == 1)
 {
  linktext = "http://www.netscape.com/"
 }
 if (linkselect == 2)
 {
  linktext = "http://www.lne.com/Web/"
 }
 if (linkselect == 3 )
 {
  linktext = "http://java.sun.com/"
 }
 if (linkselect == 4)
 {
  linktext="http://www.realaudio.com/"
 }

 document.write('<a href="' + linktext + '">randomly selected</a>');
}

</script>
</head>
<body>
```

13

```
<h1>My random link generator</h1>
<p>Visit a <script language="JavaScript">picklink()</script>
site from my list of favorites.</p>
</body>
</html>
```

▼ Task: Exercise 13.2: A Random Link Generator Using an Event Handler

Besides being bad style-wise, using inline <script> tags can cause unpredictable problems when images are displayed on a page. If you want to avoid such difficulties, it's safest to use scripts only in the <head> block, when practical.

However, this poses a problem for your random link generator, which needs to alter the value of a link each time it's used. If you can't include <script> tags in the <body> of a document, how can the link be randomly selected?

Whenever you click a link, a button, or any form element, the browser generates an event signal that can be trapped by one of the event handlers mentioned in Lesson 12, "Introducing JavaScript." If you take advantage of this fact, as well as the fact that each link in a document is actually stored as an object that can be referenced by JavaScript, you'll find it surprisingly easy to alter your existing script to avoid the need for an inline <script> tag.

First, look at the changes that you need to make in the body of the document to accommodate an event handler. In this exercise, the inline <script> tag is replaced by a normal <a> tag, as shown here:

```
<p>Visit a <a href="dummy.html">randomly selected</a>
site from my list of favorites.</p>
```

Next, associate an onclick event handler with the link by including the handler as an attribute of the <a> tag. When onclick is used as an attribute, the value assigned to it must represent a valid JavaScript instruction or function call. For this exercise, you want to call the picklink() function created previously and make the URL that it selects overwrite the default URL, defined in the <a> tag as href="dummy.html".

This job is easy because each link is actually stored as an object of type link, which contains the same properties as the location object mentioned in Lesson 12. As a result, all you need to do is assign a new value to the href property of the link in the onclick event handler, as shown here:

```
<p>Visit a <a href="dummy.html"
  onclick="this.href=picklink()">randomly selected</a>
site from my list of favorites.</p>
```

NOTE Earlier I explained that `this` is a reference to the current object. In this example, `this` points to the `link` object associated with the anchor tag in which it is used, and `this.href` indicates the `href` property of the object. Therefore, by assigning a new value to `this.href`, you change the destination URL of the link.

With the `onclick` handler set up, you need to alter the `picklink()` function. Because you're no longer physically writing anything onto the web page, you can remove the `document.write()` function. But in its place, you need some way for the value of `linkselect` to be sent back to the `this.href` property. Do this by using the `return` statement, which sends a value back from a function call, as shown here:

```
return linktext;
```

This `return` statement causes the function to return the value of `linktext`, which is the randomly picked URL that `picklink()` chose. Add the `return` line inside the `picklink()` function in place of the last `document.write()` line.

The Completed Exercise If you examine the completed text for this new HTML document, which follows, you'll notice that it's similar to Exercise 13.1, except for the removal of the inline `<script>` tag and the replacement of `document.write()` with a return statement.

```
<html>
<head>
<title>Random Link Generator</title>
<script language="JavaScript">
function picklink()
{

  var linknumber = 4;
  var linktext = "nolink.html";

  var linkselect = Math.floor(linknumber * Math.random()) + 1;
  if (linkselect == 1)
  {
   linktext = "http://www.netscape.com/"
  }
  if (linkselect == 2)
  {
   linktext = "http://www.lne.com/Web/"
  }
  if (linkselect == 3 )
  {
   linktext = "http://java.sun.com/"
  }
```

13

▼
```
if (linkselect == 4)
{
 linktext="http://www.realaudio.com/"
}

 return linktext;
}

</script>
</head>
<body>
<h1>My random link generator</h1>
<p>Visit a
<a href="dummy.html" onClick="this.href = picklink()">randomly selected</a>
site from my list of favorites.</p>
</body>
```
▲
```
</html>
```

▼ Task: **Exercise 13.3: A Random Link Generator Using an Array**

The only problem with the preceding example is that you need to keep adding if tests for each new link that you want to include in your list of favorites. To get around this difficulty, and to streamline the appearance of the script considerably, there's a JavaScript mechanism that enables you to create lists of variables—or arrays.

An *array* is a list of values associated with a single variable. For example, an array called mylinks[] can contain a list of all the links used by the picklink() function. The value of each link in the list is then referenced by a numeric value inside the square brackets, starting with 0: The first variable can be found with mylinks[0], the second with mylinks[1], and so on.

Before you can use an array, you must first construct it. The easiest way to do this is to just make an empty array by calling the Array constructor with no argument, like this:

```
mylinks = new Array();
```

You can then populate each of the elements individually:

```
mylinks[0] = "http://www.netscape.com/";
mylinks[1] = "http://www.lne.com/Web/";
mylinks[2] = "http://java.sun.com/";
mylinks[3] = "http://www.realaudio.com/";
mylinks[4] = "http://www.worlds.com/";
```

The elements of the array are created automatically when they're referenced. When the array is constructed, it contains no elements. You add five elements when you reference them by assigning values to them. Let's look at what happens when you skip some
▼ indexes when assigning elements in an array:

```
mylinks = new Array()
mylinks[0] = "http://www.netscape.com/";
mylinks[4] = "http://www.worlds.com/";
```

This array still contains five elements—the elements with indexes of 1, 2, and 3 are just empty. The size of an array is dictated by the highest index referenced in that array, regardless of whether you've referenced all the indexes before the highest index.

You can skip the step of assigning each of the array indexes individually by simply passing a list of elements to the array constructor when you call it, like this:

```
mylinks = new Array("http://www.netscape.com/",
        "http://www.lne.com/Web/",
        "http://java.sun.com/",
        "http://www.realaudio.com/",
        "http://www.worlds.com/");
```

When you use this method of construction, the mylinks array is prepopulated with the five elements that you passed to the Array() constructor as arguments.

You can then fill the mylinks array with values by assigning them as you would any other variable. For example, in Exercise 13.2, you can add code to the <script> section that creates an array with the number of links and then stores those link names into that array. Here's an example of an array with five elements, with a URL assigned to each:

```
mylinks = new Array("http://www.netscape.com/",
        "http://www.lne.com/Web/",
        "http://java.sun.com/",
        "http://www.realaudio.com/",
        "http://www.worlds.com/");
```

With a list of URLs defined, you can modify the original picklink() function so that it selects a link by choosing from those included in the array instead of by using a number of if tests. The following is the new code for picklink():

```
function picklink()
{
 var linkselect = Math.floor(Math.random() * mylinks.length);
 return (mylinks[linkselect]);
}
```

13

As you can see, this function is much smaller than it was previously. Obviously, the fact that we moved the list of URLs out of the function helped, but we economized in other ways as well. Arrays have a property called length that contains the number of elements in the array. Instead of creating a variable called linknumber and manually entering the number of links available, we just grab the size of the array and plug that into the random number generator. Because the size of the array is 5 and the elements are numbered ▼

▼ 0 through 4, we don't need to add 1 to the random number that we generate to get things to work properly. When I've got a random number, I return the array element with that number as its index.

We can also consolidate the `picklink()` function further by removing all the work variables and performing all the math inside the `return` statement, like this:

```
function picklink()
{
 return mylinks[(Math.floor(Math.random) * mylinks.length))];
}
```

The Completed Random Link Script with an Array   The following code shows the final version of the script, which incorporates all the changes we've made in this exercise, including the `MakeArray()` constructor function, the creation of the array of links, and the modifications to `picklink()`.

```
<html>
<head>
<title>Random Link Generator</title>
<script language="JavaScript">
var mylinks = new Array("http://www.netscape.com/",
            "http://www.lne.com/Web/",
            "http://java.sun.com/",
            "http://www.realaudio.com/",
            "http://www.worlds.com/");
function picklink()
{
 var linkselect = Math.floor(Math.random() * mylinks.length);
 return (mylinks[linkselect]);
}
</script>
</head>
<body>
<h1>My random link generator</h1>
<p>Visit a
<a href="dummy.html" onClick="this.href=picklink()">randomly selected</a>
site from my list of favorites.</p>
</body>
</html
```

▲

TIP | To add new links to your list, just add them to the list of arguments to the array constructor.

Validating Forms with JavaScript

Remember the example form that you created back in Lesson 10, "Designing Forms?" It's shown again in Figure 13.2. This form queries visitors for several pieces of information, including name, gender, and several bizarre options.

What happens when this form is submitted? In the real world, a script on the server side validates the data that the visitor entered, stores it in a database or file, and then thanks the visitor for her time.

But what happens if a visitor doesn't fill out the form correctly—for example, she doesn't enter her name or choose a value for gender? The CGI script can check all that information and return an error. But because all this checking has to be done on a different machine using a script, and because the data and the error messages have to be transmitted back and forth over the network, this process can be slow and takes up valuable resources on the server.

FIGURE 13.2
The registration form.

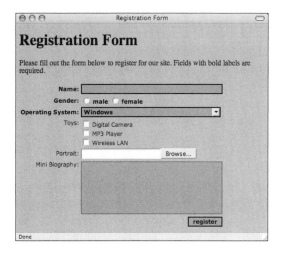

JavaScript enables you to do error checking on the browser side before the form is ever submitted to the server. This saves time for both you and your visitors because everything is corrected on the visitors' side. After the data actually gets to your script, it's more likely to be correct.

13

Task: Exercise 13.4: Form Validation

Now take a look at how the registration form is validated with JavaScript. Whenever you click the Submit button on a form, two events are triggered in the browser: `onclick` and

▼ onsubmit. You're interested in the onsubmit event. When the onsubmit event occurs, a JavaScript function will be called to validate the form data.

To call a JavaScript function when the onsubmit event occurs, you include onsubmit as an attribute of the <form> tag, like this:

```
<form method="post"
    action="http://www.example.com/cgi-bin/post-query"
    onsubmit="return checkform(this)">
```

In this example, the value assigned to onsubmit is a call to a function named checkform()—which will be defined in a bit. But first, the return statement at the beginning of the onsubmit field and the this argument inside the parentheses in the checkform() function need some further explanation.

First, let's tackle this. Whenever you call a function, you can send it a list of parameters, such as numbers, strings, or other objects, by including them in the parentheses that follow the function name. In the preceding example, the this statement passes a reference to the form object associated with the current form.

Second, the return statement transmits a value back to the internal routine that called the onsubmit event handler. For example, if the checkform() function returns a value of false after evaluating the form, the submission process will be halted as the return command transmits this false value back to the submit event. If the return statement was not included in the event handler, the false value returned by the function would not be received by the event handler, and the submission process would continue even if problems were detected by the checkform() function.

The Validation Script   As you've done before, define a <script> tag inside the <head> block and declare checkform() as a function. But this time, you also need to define a variable to hold a reference to the form object sent by the calling function, as mentioned previously. The code for the function declaration looks like this:

```
<script language="JavaScript">
<!-- start script here
function checkform(thisform)
```

The reference to the current form is given the name thisform by the function declaration. By accessing the thisform object, you can address all the fields, radio buttons, check boxes, and buttons on the current form by treating each as a property of thisform.

Having said this, you first want to test whether a name has been entered in the Name text box. In the HTML code for this form, the <input> tag for this field is assigned a name attribute of theName, like this:

▼ `<input type="text" name="theName" />`

You use this name to reference the field as a child of `thisform`. As a result, the field theName can be referenced as `thisform.theName`, and its contents can be referenced as `thisform.theName.value`.

Using this information and an `if` test, you can test the contents of `theName` to see whether a name has been entered:

```
if (thisform.theName.value == null ¦¦ thisform.theName.value == "")
  {
    alert ("Please enter your name");
    thisform.theName.focus();
    thisform.theName.select();
    return false;
  }
```

> **NOTE**
>
> The ¦¦ operator (the *or* operator) shown in the `if` expression tells JavaScript to execute the statements if either of the two tests is true.

In the first line, `thisform.theName.value` is tested to see whether it contains a `null` value or is empty (`""`). When a field is created and contains no information at all, it is said to contain a `null`; this is different from being empty or containing just spaces. If either of these situations is true, an `alert()` message is displayed (a pop-up dialog box with a warning message), the cursor is repositioned in the field by `thisform.theName.focus()`, the field is highlighted by `thisform.theName.select()`, and the function is terminated by a `return` statement that is assigned a value of `false`.

If a name has been entered, the next step is to test whether a gender has been selected by checking the value of `gender`. However, because all the elements in a radio button group have the same name, you need to treat them as an array. As a result, you can test the status value of the first radio button by using `testform.gender[0].status`, the second radio button by using `testform.gender[1].status`, and so on. If a radio button element is selected, the `status` returns a value of `true`; otherwise, it returns a value of `false`.

To test whether one of the `gender` radio buttons has been selected, declare a new variable called `selected` and give it a value of `false`. Now loop through all the elements using a `for` loop; if the `status` of any radio button is `true`, set `selected = true`. Finally, if `selected` still equals `false` after you finish the loop, display an `alert()` message and exit the function by calling `return false`. The code required to perform these tests is shown here:

```
var selected = false ;
 for (var i = 0; i <= 2 ; ++i)
  {
    if (thisform.gender[i].status == true)
```

13

```
{
  selected = true;
  }
}
if (selected == false)
{
  alert ("Please choose your gender");
  return false;
}
```

If both of the tests pass successfully, return a value of `true` to indicate that the form sub-mission should go ahead:

```
return true;
}
```

The Completed Registration Form with JavaScript Validation   When the JavaScript script that you just created is integrated with the original registration form document from Lesson 10, the result is a web form that tests its contents before they're transmitted to the CGI script for further processing. This way, no data is sent to the CGI script until everything is correct. If a problem occurs, the browser informs the user (see Figure 13.3).

FIGURE 13.3
An alert message.

So that you don't need to skip back to the exercise in Lesson 10 to obtain the HTML source used when creating the form, here's the completed form with the full JavaScript code.

```
<!DOCTYPE html PUBLIC "-//W3C//DTD XHTML 1.0 Transitional//EN"
  "http://www.w3.org/TR/xhtml1/DTD/xhtml1-transitional.dtd">
<html xmlns="http://www.w3.org/1999/xhtml">
<head>
<title>Registration Form</title>
<script language="JavaScript">
<!-- start script here
function checkform(thisform)
{
  if (thisform.name.value == null || thisform.name.value == "")
  {
  alert ("Please enter your name");
  thisform.name.focus();
  thisform.name.select();
  return false;
  }
  var selected = false ;
```

```
 for (var i = 0; i <= 2 ; ++i)
 {
  if (thisform.gender[i].status == true)
  {
   selected = true;
  }
 }
 if (selected == false)
 {
   alert ("Please choose your sex");
   return false;
 }
 return true;
}
// End of script -->
</script>

<style type="text/css">
body
{
  background-color: #9c9;
}

input.required
{
  width: 300px;
  font: bold 12px Verdana;
  background-color: #6a6;
  border: solid 2px #000;
}

select.required
{
  width: 300px;
  font: bold 12px Verdana;
  background-color: #6a6;
  border: solid 2px #000;
}

td.required
{
  font: bold 12px Verdana;
}

input.optional
{
  width: 300px;
  font: 12px Verdana;
  background-color: #6a6;
  border: solid 2px #999;
}
```

13

```
▼ textarea.optional
  {
    width: 300px;
    font: 12px Verdana;
    background-color: #6a6;
    border: solid 2px #666;
  }

  td.optional
  {
    font: 12px Verdana;
  }

  input.submit
  {
    background-color: #6a6;
    border: solid 2px #000;
    font: bold 12px Verdana;
  }
  </style>
  </head>
  <body>
  <h1>Registration Form</h1>

  <p>Please fill out the form below to register for our site. Fields
  with bold labels are required.</p>

  <form action="/cgi-bin/register.cgi" method="post"
  enctype="multipart/form-data" onsubmit="return checkform(this)">
  <table>
  <tr>
  <td align="right" class="required"><b>Name:</b></td>
  <td><input name="name" class="required" /></td>
  </tr>

  <tr>
  <td align="right" class="required"><b>Gender:</b></td>
  <td class="required">
  <input type="radio" name="gender" value="male" /> male
  <input type="radio" name="gender" value="female" /> female</td>
  </tr>

  <tr>
  <td align="right" class="required">
  <b>Operating System:</b></td>
  <td>
  <select name="os" class="required">
  <option value="windows">Windows</option>
  <option value="macos">Mac OS</option>
  <option value="linux">Linux</option>
  <option value="other">Other ...</option>
  </select>
  </td>
▼ </tr>
```

```
<tr>
<td valign="top" align="right" class="optional">Toys:</td>
<td class="optional">
<input type="checkbox" name="toy" value="digicam" /> Digital Camera<br />
<input type="checkbox" name="toy" value="mp3" /> MP3 Player<br />
<input type="checkbox" name="toy" value="wlan" /> Wireless LAN</td>
</tr>

<tr>
<td align="right" class="optional">Portrait:</td>
<td><input type="file" name="portrait" /></td>
</tr>

<tr>
<td valign="top" align="right" class="optional">
Mini Biography:</td>
<td>
<textarea name="bio" rows="6" cols="40" class="optional"></textarea>
</td>
</tr>

<tr>
<td colspan="2" align="right">
<input type="submit" value="register" class="submit" />
</td>
</tr>
</table>
</form>
</body>
</html>
```

Creating an Image Rollover

Image rollovers are one of the most popular JavaScript applications around. An *image rollover* is just an image that is replaced by a different image when someone positions the mouse pointer over it. Rollovers are often used with navigational elements to give viewers visual feedback indicating what will happen if they click on the image. This technique is particularly useful when you have a number of navigational elements positioned close together, and you want to make it easier to see which element they'll be clicking on.

13

Task: Exercise 13.5: A JavaScript Image Rollover

In this example, we're going to create a page that contains an image that will be swapped out when the pointer is moved over it. Image rollovers are generally made up of three components: an event handler associated with the image, a preload script to load the

▼ image that's not displayed when the page loads, and a function that switches between the two images. Let's take a look at each of these components.

Browser Detection   One big disadvantage of using JavaScript is that JavaScript works differently from browser to browser. A feature that exists in Firefox 1.5 might not exist in Microsoft Internet Explorer 6.0. This problem is compounded by the fact that JavaScript capabilities change from version to version of the browsers. Originally, most people handled this problem by determining which browser made the request and then turning on only those features that worked with that browser. Unfortunately, this was kind of an overly complex way to write JavaScript code. As new versions of browsers were released, all the JavaScript code with browser detection had to be changed.

Fortunately, a better technique is available. Rather than relying on the inexact technique of determining which browser the user is using, you can detect whether the actual object that you want to manipulate exists and then base your functionality on that. In this case, we need to manipulate the document.images object, which contains information about all the images used on the page. The browser detection code that we use is very simple; it consists of one statement:

```
if (document.images) {
    // manipulate image object here
}
```

Any time you want to manipulate the images on the page, you wrap the code inside this if statement. If the browser acknowledges the existence of the document.images object, you can manipulate that object.

The Preload Script   When you add an image rollover to a web page, you should pre-load the images so that the first time the user moves the mouse over the rollover, the browser won't have to download the image before it can be displayed. Preload scripts load the images into memory so that they can appear instantly when the pointer is positioned over the image that they will replace. The preload script appears in the page header and simply creates new objects for all the images involved in the rollover. This sample page contains only one image, so the preload code is very simple:

```
if (document.images) {
    buttonOn = new Image();
    buttonOn.src = "on.gif";
    buttonOff = new Image();
    buttonOff.src = "off.gif";
}
```

As you can see, the preload code is wrapped within the object detection code. Two new images are created, one containing the "on" image and the other containing the "off" image. When the page loads, both of the image files assigned to the attributes of the
▼ images will be downloaded.

The Rollover Functions   Two functions are associated with an image rollover—one ▼
that replaces the "on" image with the "off" image, and another that replaces the "off"
image with the "on" image. In this example, the two functions are called `activate` and
`deactivate`. Here's the source code:

```
function activate(image_name) {
    if (document.images) {
        document[image_name].src = eval(image_name + "On.src");
    }
}

function deactivate(image_name) {
    if (document.images) {
        document[image_name].src = eval(image_name + "Off.src");
    }
}
```

Again, note that the object-detection code is used to protect users whose browsers don't
allow the document's images to be manipulated using JavaScript. Both of these functions
accept a single parameter: the name of the image that will be swapped out. In this particular example, I could have hard-coded the image name into the script because there's
only one image on the page. However, passing the image name is more useful to you
because you'll be able to use these scripts with pages that contain multiple image
rollovers.

This is the most important code in the `activate` function:

```
document[image_name].src = eval(image_name + "On.src");
```

`document[image_name]` references the object on the page with the same name as the
argument passed to the function. This code changes the `src` property of that argument to
the "on" version of the image. The call to the `eval()` function concatenates the argument
with the string `On.src`. If the argument to the function is `button`, the function call returns
`buttonOn.src`. As you can see in the preload code, `buttonOn.src` is set to `on.gif`. So,
this line of code changes the `src` property of the referenced object to `on.gif`.

For all this to work, you have to create images in your preload code with the same name
as the images to which they correspond on the page. That way, the single argument to the
function can be used to reference both the image objects created when the page was
loaded and the image on the page itself. The code in the `deactivate` function works the
same way, except that it assigns the "off" image to the image object on the page.

Calling the Functions   After all the code used to drive the rollover functions is in
place, the next step is to place the image and event handlers on the page. Rollovers use
the `onmouseover` and `onmouseout` event handlers associated with anchor tags to fire the
image-swapping functions. In this example, we're going to place the image itself within a
link, but we could just as easily associate the image rollover with a text link elsewhere ▼

13

▼ on the page. The only thing different about the image tag in this example is that the `name` attribute is included so that we can associate the name that we used in the preload code with the image.

Here's the code that is used to place the image itself and fire the rollover functions:

```
<a href="rollover.html"
    onmouseover="activate('button')"
    onmouseout="deactivate('button')">
<img name="button" border=0 height=100 width=100 src="off.gif"></a>
```

As you can see, the link includes `onmouseover` and `onmouseout` attributes, which indicate the function that should be called when those events fire. The argument to the functions corresponds to the image name that we used.

Putting It All Together   When you've created your images and saved them in the proper folder, this code will create a dynamic page with images that turn on and off. The full source code for the page with the rollover is shown as follows:

Input ▼

```
<!DOCTYPE html PUBLIC "-//W3C//DTD HTML 4.01 Transitional//EN">
<html>
<head>
<title>JavaScript Rollover Example</title>
<script type="text/javascript" language="JavaScript">
<!--
    // Preload the images for the rollover

    if (document.images) {
        buttonOn = new Image();
        buttonOn.src = "on.gif";
        buttonOff = new Image();
        buttonOff.src = "off.gif";
    }

    // Function to replace the off images with on images.

    function activate(image_name) {
        if (document.images) {
            document[image_name].src = eval(image_name + "On.src");
        }
    }

    function deactivate(image_name) {
        if (document.images) {
            document[image_name].src = eval(image_name + "Off.src");
        }
▼   }
```

```
// -->
</script>
</head>
<body>
<a href="rollover.html" onmouseover="activate('button')"
onmouseout="deactivate('button')"><img name="button" border="0"
height="100" width="100" src="off.gif"></a>
</body>
</html>
```

Summary

JavaScript offers many exciting new possibilities for web developers. You explored several possible applications of JavaScript in this chapter, including generating bits of HTML code and verifying form data.

JavaScript isn't the only way to write code for web pages, however. Java, the big brother of JavaScript, has even greater flexibility and capabilities. In Lesson 15, "Creating Applications with Dynamic HTML and AJAX," you'll learn how JavaScript forms the foundation for a group of technologies collectively known as Dynamic HTML.

Workshop

The following workshop includes questions, a quiz, and exercises related to the uses of JavaScript.

Q&A

Q **Can you point me in the direction of more scripts that I can integrate with my pages?**

A Sure, there are lots of sites with prepackaged JavaScript programs that you can use on your pages. You might try The JavaScript Source at http://javascript.internet. com/, or JavaScript.com at http://www.javascript.com/.

Q **I've seen the source for other image rollover scripts—why are they so different from the one in this lesson?**

A Image rollovers are one of the most popular uses of JavaScript, and over the years, opinions on how to write the perfect image rollover have changed. Plus, the bottom line is that there's more than one way to do it. As long as the script works in the browsers that the person who wrote the script cares about, it works. The technique demonstrated in this lesson will work fine, but if you see a script out there that you like better, feel free to use it instead.

13

Quiz

1. What's an inline `<script>` tag?
2. What happens whenever a user clicks a link, button, or form element on a web page?
3. What's the `this` statement?
4. How can arrays streamline a script?
5. How does form validation with JavaScript conserve server resources?

Quiz Answers

1. An inline `<script>` tag is one that is embedded in the `<body>` section of an HTML document rather than in the `<head>` section, as is the more common practice.
2. Whenever a user clicks a link, a button, or any form element, the browser generates an event signal that can be trapped by one of the event handlers mentioned in Lesson 2, "Preparing to Publish on the Web."
3. The `this` statement is a special value that tells JavaScript to reference the current object without having to worry about its exact name or location.
4. With arrays, you can create a single list of variables that are all referenced by the same variable name.
5. JavaScript enables you to do error checking in forms on the browser side before the form is ever submitted to the server. A CGI script must access the server before it can determine the validity of the entries on a form. (Note that even if you use JavaScript form validation you must validate user input on the server as well, because users can bypass the JavaScript if they choose.)

Exercises

1. Add new links to your list of random links in Exercise 13.3 by increasing the value assigned by `new MakeArray( value )` and adding the new links to the list following the array elements already defined.
2. Take the registration form example used in Exercise 13.4 and see whether you can adapt it to a form of your own on your own website.

LESSON 14:

Working with Frames and Linked Windows

In the early days of the Web, two significant limitations of web browsers were that they could only display one document in a browser window at a time and that sites couldn't open more browser windows if needed. Frames enable you to divide the browser window into sections, each containing a different document, and linked windows enable you to create links that open pages in new browser windows. Used properly, these two techniques can make your website easier to navigate. Unfortunately, they can also be misused to make your site confusing, difficult to use, and annoying to your users. In this lesson, you'll learn how to apply these techniques to make your site more usable.

In this Lesson

Today, you'll learn all about the following topics:

- What frames are, how they can affect your layout, and who supports them
- How to work with linked windows
- How to work with frames
- How to create complex framesets
- Floating frames

What Are Frames and Who Supports Them?

Today you'll learn about the tags that you can use to create frames. Simply put, *frames* enable you to divide a browser window and load a different document in each section of the window that you define. Due to the nature of these tags, web pages that use frames simply can't be displayed in really old browsers. They were introduced as a new feature with Netscape Navigator 2.0, which is several years old. Frames rapidly became popular, and they were included in the HTML 4.01 standard. Every popular web browser supports them these days.

With version 3.0 of Internet Explorer, Microsoft introduced floating frames. Instead of dividing the browser window into sections, floating frames enable you to include frames inline in your documents, the same way you can with images. Floating frames were also included in the HTML 4.01 standard, and they're supported by all versions of Netscape since 2.0 as well as every version of Internet Explorer since 3.0.

Frames give you an entirely different level of layout control than you've had so far in this book. For example, take a look at the example in Figure 14.1.

FIGURE 14.1
A sample web page with frames.

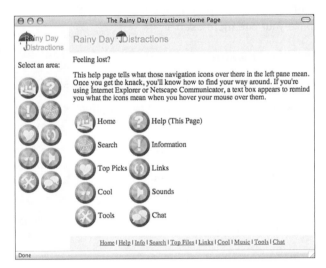

On this screen, you see four frames displayed within one browser window. The left frame contains graphical navigation elements, the lower-right frame contains text navigational links, the upper-right frame contains the page header, and the middle-right frame contains the main content of the site. This screenshot also illustrates one of the disadvantages of using frames. The frame that contains the actual page content actually uses a fairly small section of the browser window; the rest of the window is consumed by the other frames. When you separate your layout using frames, you can detract from the important content on your site.

Because the information displayed on the page is separated into individual frames, the contents of a single frame can be updated without affecting the contents of any other frame. If you click on one of the linked images in the left frame, for example, the contents of the large frame on the right are automatically updated to display the details about the subject you've selected. When this update occurs, the contents of the left frame and the bottom frame aren't affected.

Working with Linked Windows

Before you learn how to use frames, you need to learn about the `target` attribute of the `<a>` tag. This attribute takes the following form:

`target="window_name"`

Usually, when you click a hyperlink, the page to which you're linking replaces the current page in the browser window. When you use the `target` attribute, you can open links in new windows, or in existing windows other than the one that the link is in. With frames, you can use the `target` attribute to display the linked page in a different frame. A *frameset* is a group of frames that's defined within a framed document through the use of the `<frameset>` tags. The `target` attribute tells the web browser to display the information pointed to by a hyperlink in a window called *window_name*. Basically, you can call the new window anything you want, except that you can't use names that start with an underscore (_). These names are reserved for a set of special `target` values that you'll learn about later in the "Magic `target` Names" section.

When you use the `target` attribute inside an `<a>` tag, a frames-compatible browser first checks whether a window with the name *window_name* exists. If it does, the document pointed to by the hyperlink replaces the current contents of *window_name*. On the other hand, if no window called *window_name* currently exists, a new browser window opens with that name. Then the document pointed to by the hyperlink is loaded into the newly created window.

14

▼ **Task: Exercise 14.1: Working with Windows**

Framesets rely on the `target` attribute to load pages into specific frames in a frameset. Each of the hyperlinks in the following exercise uses the `target` attribute to open a web page in a different browser window. The concepts you'll learn here will help you understand later how targeted hyperlinks work in a frameset.

In this exercise, you'll create four separate HTML documents that use hyperlinks, including the `target` attribute. You'll use these hyperlinks to open two new windows called `yellow_page` and `blue_page`, as shown in Figure 14.2. The top window is the original web browser window (the red page), `yellow_page` is at the bottom left, and `blue_page` is at the bottom right.

FIGURE 14.2

Using the target attribute indicates that links should open new windows.

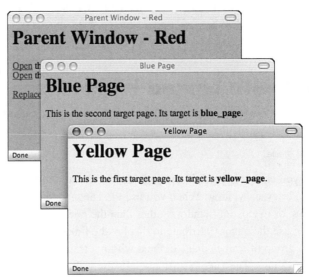

First, create the document to be displayed by the main web browser window, shown in Figure 14.3, by opening your text editor of choice and entering the following lines of code:

Input ▼

```
<html>
<head>
<title>Parent Window - Red</title>
</head>
<body bgcolor="#ff9999">
<h1>Parent Window - Red</h1>
<p><a href="yellow.html" target="yellow_page">Open</a> the Yellow Page in a new
▼ window. <br />
```

```
 <a href="blue.html" target="blue_page">Open</a> the Blue Page in a new
 window. </p>
<p><a href="green.html" target="yellow_page">Replace</a> the yellow page with
the Green Page.</p>
</body>
</html>
```

Output ▼

FIGURE 14.3
The parent window
(the red page).

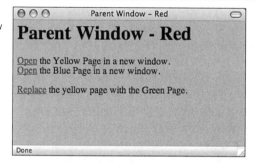

This creates a light-red page that links to the other three pages. Save this HTML source as parent.html.

Next, create a document called yellow.html (see Figure 14.4) by entering the following code:

Input ▼

```
<html>
<head>
<title>Yellow Page</title>
</head>
<body bgcolor="#ffffcc">
<h1>Yellow Page</h1>
<p>This is the first target page. Its target is <b>yellow_page</b></p>
</body>
</html>
```

Output ▼

FIGURE 14.4
yellow.html
web browser
window named
yellow_page.

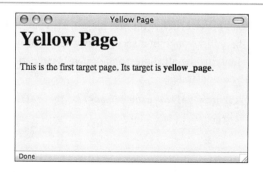

14

▼ After saving `yellow.html`, create another document called `blue.html` (see Figure 14.5) by entering the following code:

Input ▼

```
<html>
<head>
<title>Blue Page</title>
</head>
<body bgcolor="#99ccff">
<h1>Blue Page</h1>
<p>This is the second target page. Its target is <b>blue_page</b>.</p>
</body>
</html>
```

Output ▼

FIGURE 14.5
blue.html dis-
played in the web
browser window
named blue_
window.

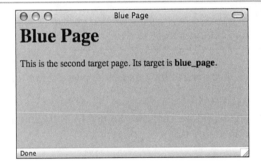

Next, create a fourth document called `green.html`, which looks like the following:

```
<html>
<head>
<title>Green Page</title>
</head>
<body bgcolor="#ccffcc">
<h1>Green Page</h1>
<p>This is the third target page. Its target is <b>yellow_page</b>.
It should replace the yellow page in the browser.</p>
</body>
</html>
```

To complete the exercise, load `parent.html` (the red page) into your web browser. Click the first hyperlink to open the yellow page in a second browser window. This happens because the first hyperlink contains the attribute `target="yellow_page"`, as the following code from `parent.html` demonstrates:

```
<p><a href="yellow.html" target="yellow_page">Open</a> the Yellow Page in a
  new window.<br />
```

Now return to the red page and click the second link. The blue page opens in a third browser window. Note that the new windows probably won't be laid out like the ones shown in Figure 14.2; they usually overlap each other. The following `target="blue_page"` statement in the `parent.html` page is what causes the new window to open:

```
<a href="blue.html" target="blue_page">Open</a> the Blue Page in a new
window.</p>
```

The previous two examples opened each of the web pages in a new browser window. The third link, however, uses the `target="yellow_page"` statement to open the green page in the window named `yellow_page`. You accomplish this using the following code in `parent.html`:

```
<p><a href="green.html" target="yellow_page">Replace</a> the yellow page
with the Green Page.</p>
```

Because you already opened the `yellow_page` window when you clicked the link for the yellow page, the green page should replace the page that's already in it. To verify this, click the third hyperlink on the red page. This replaces the contents of the yellow page (with the `yellow_page` target name) with the green page (`green.html`), as shown in Figure 14.6.

FIGURE 14.6

green.html displayed in the web browser window named green_page.

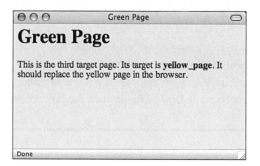

Green Page

This is the third target page. Its target is **yellow_page**. It should replace the yellow page in the browser.

The `<base>` Tag

When you're using the `target` attribute with links, you'll sometimes find that all or most of the hyperlinks on a web page point to the same window. This is especially true when you're using frames, as you'll discover in the following section.

In such cases, rather than including a `target` attribute for each `<a>` tag, you can use another tag, `<base>`, to define a global target for all the links on a web page. The `<base>` tag is used as follows:

```
<base target="window_name">
```

14

▼ If you include the <base> tag in the <head>...</head> block of a document, every <a> tag that doesn't have a target attribute will be directed to the window indicated by the base tag. For example, if you had included the tag <base target="yellow_page"> in the HTML source for parent.html, the three hyperlinks could have been written the following way:

```
<html>
<head>
<title>Parent Window - Red</title>
<base target="yellow_page"> <!-- add base target="value" here -->
</head>
<body bgcolor="#ff9999">
<h1>Parent Window - Red</h1>
<p>
<a href="yellow.html">Open</a> <!-- no need to include a target -->
 the Yellow Page in a new window.<br />
<a href="blue.html" target="blue_page">Open</a> the Blue Page in a new
 window. </p>
<p><a href="green.html">Replace</a> <!-- no need to include a target -->
the yellow page with the Green Page.</p>
</body>
</html>
```

In this case, yellow.html and green.html load into the default window assigned by the <base> tag (yellow_page); blue.html overrides the default by defining its own target window of blue_page.

You also can override the window assigned with the <base> tag by using one of two special window names. If you use target="_blank" in a hyperlink, it opens a new browser window that doesn't have a name associated with it. Alternatively, if you use target="_self", the current window is used rather than the one defined by the ▲ <base> tag.

NOTE

If you don't provide a target using the <base> tag and you don't indicate a target in a link's <a> tag, the link will load the new document in the same frame as the link.

Working with Frames

The introduction of frames in Netscape 2.0 heralded a new era for web publishers. With frames, you can create web pages that look and feel entirely different from other pages. You can have tables of contents, banners, footnotes, and sidebars, just to name a few common features.

At the same time, frames change what a "page" means to the browser and to your visitors. Unlike all the preceding examples, which use a single HTML page to display a screen of information, a single screen actually consists of a number of separate HTML documents that interact with each other. Figure 14.7 shows how a minimum of five separate documents is needed to create the screen shown earlier in Figure 14.1.

FIGURE 14.7
You must create a separate HTML document for each frame.

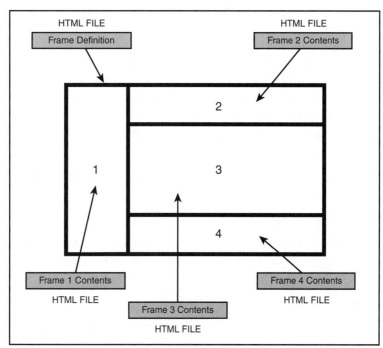

The first HTML document you need to create is called the *frameset document*. In this document, you define the layout of your frames, and the locations of the documents to be initially loaded in each frame. The document in Figure 14.7 has three frames.

Each of the three HTML documents other than the frameset document, the ones that load in the frames, contain normal HTML tags that define the contents of each separate frame area. These documents are referenced by the frameset document.

The `<frameset>` Tag

14

To create a frameset document, you begin with the `<frameset>` tag. When used in an HTML document, the `<frameset>` tag replaces the `<body>` tag, as shown in the following code:

```
<html>
<head>
<title>Page Title</title>
</head>
<frameset>
  .. your frameset goes here ...
</frameset>
</html>
```

It's important that you understand up front how a frameset document differs from a normal HTML document. If you include a <frameset> tag in an HTML document, you cannot include a <body> tag also. The two tags are mutually exclusive. In addition, no other formatting tags, hyperlinks, or document text should be included in a frameset document. (The exception to this is the <noframes> tag, which you'll learn about later today in the section called, appropriately enough, "The <noframes> Tag.") The <frameset> tags contain only the definitions for the frames in this document—what's called the page's *frameset*.

The HTML 4.01 specification supports the <frameset> tag along with two possible attributes: cols and rows.

The cols **Attribute**

When you define a <frameset> tag, you must include one of two attributes as part of the tag definition. The first of these attributes is the cols attribute, which takes the following form:

```
<frameset cols="column width, column width, ...">
```

The cols attribute tells the browser to split the screen into a number of vertical frames whose widths are defined by *column width* values separated by commas. You define the width of each frame in one of three ways: explicitly in pixels, as a percentage of the total width of the <frameset>, or with an asterisk (*). When you use the asterisk, the frames-compatible browser uses as much space as possible for the specified frame.

When included in a complete frame definition, the following <frameset> tag creates a screen with three vertical frames, as shown in Figure 14.8. The fifth line in the following code example creates a left frame 100 pixels wide, a middle column that's 50% of the width of the screen, and a right column that uses all the remaining space:

Input ▼

```
<html>
<head>
<title>Three Columns</title>
</head>
<frameset cols="100,50%,*">
  <frame src="leftcol.html">
```

```
   <frame src="midcol.html">
   <frame src="rightcol.html">
</frameset>
</html>
```

Output ▼

FIGURE 14.8
The cols attribute defines the number of vertical frames or columns in a frameset.

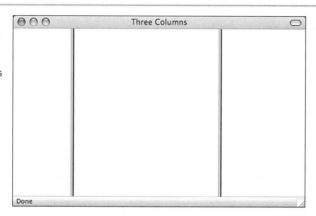

NOTE

Because you're designing web pages for users with various screen sizes, you should use absolute frame sizes sparingly. Whenever you do use an absolute size, ensure that one of the other frames is defined using an * to take up all the remaining screen space.

TIP

To define a frameset with three columns of equal width, use cols="*,*,*". This way, you won't have to mess around with percentages because frames-compatible browsers automatically assign an equal amount of space to each frame assigned a width of *.

The rows Attribute

The rows attribute works the same as the cols attribute, except that it splits the screen into horizontal frames rather than vertical ones. To split the screen into two frames of equal height, as shown in Figure 14.9, you would write the following:

14

Input ▼

```
<html>
<head>
<title>Two Rows</title>
</head>
```

```
<frameset rows="50%,50%">
  <frame src="toprow.html">
  <frame src="botrow.html">
</frameset>
</html>
```

Alternatively, you could use the following line:

```
<frameset rows="*,*">
```

Output ▼

FIGURE 14.9
The rows attribute defines the number of horizontal frames or rows in a frameset.

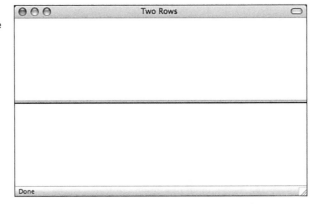

| NOTE | If you try either of the preceding examples for yourself, you'll find that the `<frameset>` tag doesn't appear to work. You get this result because there are no contents defined for the rows or columns in the frameset. To define the contents, you need to use the `<frame>` tag, which is discussed in the next section. |

The `<frame>` Tag

After you have your basic frameset laid out, you need to associate an HTML document with each frame by using the `<frame>` tag, which takes the following form:

```
<frame src="document URL">
```

For each frame defined in the `<frameset>` tag, you must include a corresponding `<frame>` tag, as shown in the following:

Input ▼

```
<html>
<head>
<title>The FRAME Tag</title>
```

```
</head>
<frameset rows="*,*,*">
  <frame src="document1.html" />
  <frame src="document2.html" />
  <frame src="document3.html" />
</frameset>
</html>
```

This example defines a frameset with three horizontal frames of equal height (see Figure 14.10). The contents of document1.html are displayed in the first frame, the contents of document2.html in the second frame, and the contents of document3.html in the third frame.

Output ▼

FIGURE 14.10
You use the <frame> tag to define the contents of each frame.

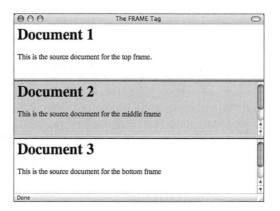

TIP

When you're creating frameset documents, you might find it helpful to indent the <frame> tags so that they're separated from the <frameset> tags in your HTML document. This has no effect on the appearance of the resulting web pages, but it does tend to make the HTML source easier to read.

The <noframes> Tag

What happens if a browser that doesn't support frames navigates to a frameset document? Nothing. You get a blank page. Fortunately, there's a way around this problem.

A special tag block called <noframes> enables you to include additional HTML code as part of the frameset document. The code you enclose within the <noframes> element isn't displayed in frames-compatible browsers, but it's displayed in browsers that don't support frames. The <noframes> tag takes the following form:

```
<html>
<head>
<title>Frameset with No Frames Content</title>
</head>
<frameset>
 your frameset goes here.
<noframes>
 Include any text, hyperlinks, and tags you want to here.
</noframes>
</frameset>
</html>
```

Using the frames' content and tags inside <noframes>, you can create pages that work well with both kinds of browsers. Later today, you'll add some <noframes> content to a frameset.

> **NOTE**
>
> The way the <noframes> tag works is actually kind of interesting. It works because web browsers are designed to ignore tags that they don't understand. So, browsers that don't support frames ignore the <frameset> and <frame> tags. They also ignore the <noframes> tag and just display whatever is inside it. Browsers that do support frames know to render the frames and ignore the text inside the <noframes> tag.

Changing Frame Borders

Notice that all the frames in today's lesson have thick borders separating them. There are a number of attributes that can be set to control the appearance of frame borders or prevent them from appearing altogether.

Start with the <frame> tag. By using two attributes, bordercolor and frameborder, you can turn borders on and off and specify their color. You can assign bordercolor any valid color value, either as a name or a hexadecimal triplet. frameborder takes two possible values: 1 (to display borders) or 0 (to turn off the display of borders).

> **NOTE**
>
> If you turn off the border, frames-compatible browsers won't display its default three-dimensional border. However, a space will still be left for the border.
>
> HTML 4.01 currently lists only the frameborder attribute. The bordercolor attribute qualifies as an extension.

For example, the following code adds a deep red border (defined by #cc3333) around the middle frame in the frameset:

```
<html>
<head>
<title>The frame Tag</title>
</head>
<frameset rows="*,*,*">
  <frame src="document1.html">
  <frame frameborder="1" bordercolor="#cc3333" src="document2.html">
  <frame src="document3.html">
</frameset>
</html>
```

Although HTML 4.01 doesn't provide either of these attributes for the <frameset> tag, you can use both of them to define default values for the entire frameset in current browsers.

Of course, there's room for confusion when colored borders are defined. In the following frameset definition, a conflict arises because the two frames share a single common border, but each frame is defined to have a different border color with the bordercolor attribute:

```
<html>
<head>
<title>Conflicting Borders</title>
</head>
<frameset frameborder="0" rows="*,*,*">
  <frame frameborder="1" bordercolor="yellow" src="document1.html">
  <frame bordercolor="#cc3333" src="document2.html">
  <frame src="document3.html">
</frameset>
</html>
```

In addition, the frameset is defined as having no borders, but the first frame is supposed to have a border. How do you resolve this problem? You can apply three simple rules:

- Attributes in the outermost frameset have the lowest priority.
- Attributes are overridden by attributes in a nested <frameset> tag.
- Any bordercolor attribute in the current frame overrides previous ones in <frameset> tags.

Additional Attributes

14

Table 14.1 shows a few extra attributes for the <frame> tag. These attributes can give you additional control over how the user interacts with your frames. Other attributes control margins or spacing between frames and whether scrollbars appear when required.

TABLE 14.1 Control Attributes for the <frame> Tag

Attribute	Value	Description
frameborder	1	Displays borders around each frame (default).
frameborder	0	Creates borderless frames.
longdesc	URL	Specifies a URL that provides a longer description of the contents of the frameset. Primarily used with nonvisual browsers.
marginheight	pixels	To adjust the margin that appears above and below a document within a frame, set marginheight to the number indicated by pixels.
marginwidth	pixels	The marginwidth attribute enables you to adjust the margin on the left and right sides of a frame to the number indicated by pixels.
name	string	Assigns a name to the frame for targeting purposes.
noresize		By default, the users can move the position of borders around each frame on the current screen by grabbing the borders and moving them with the mouse. To lock the borders of a frame and prevent them from being moved, use the noresize attribute.
scrolling	auto	(Default) If the content of a frame takes up more space than the area available, frames-compatible browsers automatically add scrollbars to either the right side or the bottom of the frame so that the users can scroll through the document.
scrolling	no	Setting the value of scrolling to no disables the use of scrollbars for the current frame. (Note that if you do this but the document contains more text than can fit inside the frame, users won't be able to scroll the additional text into view.)
scrolling	yes	If you set scrolling to yes, scrollbars are included in the frame even if they aren't required.
src	URL	Specifies the URL of the initial source document that appears in a frame when the frameset first opens in the browser.

Creating Complex Framesets

The framesets you've learned about so far are the most basic types of frames that can be displayed. In day-to-day use, however, you'll rarely use these basic frame designs. On all but the simplest sites, you'll most likely want to use more complex framesets.

Therefore, to help you understand the possible combinations of frames, links, images, and documents that can be used by a website, this section will explore complex framesets.

Task: Exercise 14.2: Creating the Content Pages for Your Frameset ▼

Most commonly, framesets provide navigation bars that keep navigational elements in view as the user scrolls through the contents of the document. By far, the most common place to present the navigation bars is on the left side of the browser window. Each time the visitor clicks a link in the left navigation frame, the content in the main frame displays the selected page. The (very silly) frameset that you'll create in this exercise demonstrates this technique. Although it's not a really practical example, it's simple, fun, and demonstrates the very same techniques you would use for a navigation bar.

When you design a web page that uses frames, you normally design the frameset before you go through all the trouble of designing the content that goes into it. That's because you'll want to know how big your frames are going to be before you start designing graphics and other page content to put into them.

I'm doing things a little backward here, but for good reason. It may help you to better understand how things fit together if you see real content in the frames as you design the frameset. For this reason, I'll have you design the content first.

The following content pages don't include any of the frameset tags discussed so far. There are eight pages in all, but I promise that I'll keep the code for these pages really brief. Ready?

TIP

> When you lay out the basic structure of a frameset, you don't normally want to be bothered with details such as the actual contents of the frames. However, your frameset won't be displayed properly when it's loaded into a frames-compatible browser for testing unless you define `<frame>` tags that include valid documents. If you want to design a frameset before you create the content, you can create a small empty HTML document called `dummy.html` and use it for all your frame testing.

14

The frameset that you'll create in Exercises 14.3 through 14.7 consists of three frames. The layout of the frameset will be as shown in Figure 14.11. The frameset page loads first and instructs the browser to divide the browser window into three frames. Next, it loads the three pages that appear in the top, left, and main frames. Finally, if a user browses to the frameset without a frames-compatible browser, an alternative page will appear. ▼

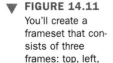

FIGURE 14.11

You'll create a frameset that consists of three frames: top, left, and main.

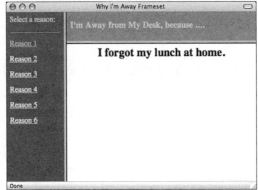

The top frame always displays the same web page—away.html. The choices.html page that appears in the frame on the left side contains a list of links to six different pages named reason1.html through reason6.html. Each of these six pages will load into the main frame on the bottom-right portion of the frameset.

Start with the page displayed in the top frame. This page will always appear in the frameset. Here you can include any information you want to display permanently as visitors browse through your site. Real-world examples for the content of this frame include the name of your website, a site logo, a link to your email address, or other similar content. Type in the following code and save it to your hard drive as away.html:

```
<html>
<head>
<title>I'm Away from My Desk Because</title>
</head>
<body bgcolor="#cc6600" text="#000000">
<h3>I'm Away from My Desk, because ... </h3>
</body>
</html>
```

Figure 14.12 shows this page.

Next, you'll create the left frame in the frameset. On real websites, this is typically the frame used for text or image navigation links that take your visitors to several different key pages on your site. For example, a personal site might have a navigation bar that takes its visitors to a home page, a guest book, a links page, and other sections of interest. A corporate or business site could contain links for products, customer support, frequently asked questions, employment opportunities, and so on.

FIGURE 14.12
The top frame in the frameset.

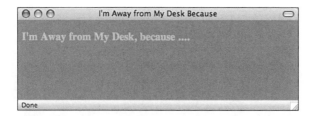

The contents page in the following example works exactly the same way that a real-world navigation bar does. When the appropriate link is selected, it displays one of the six pages in the main frame of the frameset. The contents page contains links to six pages, reason1.html through reason6.html, which you'll create next.

After you enter the following code into a new page, save it to your hard drive in the same directory as the first page and name it choice.html:

Input ▼

```html
<html>
<head>
<title>Reason I'm Out</title>
</head>
<body bgcolor="#006699" text="#ffcc66" link="#ffffff" vlink="#66ccff"
alink="#ff6666">
<p>Select a reason:</p>
<hr />
<p><a href="reason1.html">Reason 1</a></p>
<p><a href="reason2.html">Reason 2</a></p>
<p><a href="reason3.html">Reason 3</a></p>
<p><a href="reason4.html">Reason 4</a></p>
<p><a href="reason5.html">Reason 5</a></p>
<p><a href="reason6.html">Reason 6</a></p>
</body>
</html>
```

Your page should look as shown in Figure 14.13 when you open it in a browser.

Now you need to create the six pages that will appear in the main frame when the visitor selects one of the links in the contents frame. The main frame is designed to display pages that normally you would display in a full browser window. However, if you're going to display your pages in a frameset that has a left navigation bar, you'll have to account for the reduced size of the frame in your design.

▼ 14

▼ **FIGURE 14.13**
The left frame in
the frameset.

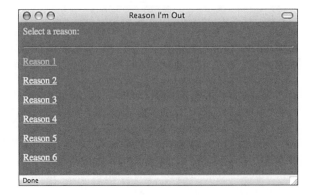

To keep the page examples relatively easy, I've given them all the same basic appearance. This means that the code for all of these pages is pretty much the same. The only items that change from page to page are the following:

- The title of the page.
- The description of my current mood.
- The text that describes what each image means.

To create the first of the six pages that will appear in the main frame, type the following code into a new page and save it as reason1.html:

Input ▼

```
<html>
<head>
<title>Reason 1 - Forgot My Lunch</title>
</head>
<body bgcolor="#ffffff">
<h2><img src="uhoh.jpg" width="275" height="275" align="left">I forgot my lunch
at home.</h2>
</body>
</html>
```

Figure 14.14 shows what this page should look like in a browser.

Output ▼

FIGURE 14.14
The first of the six
pages that appear
in the main frame.

▼

You code the remaining five pages for the main frame similarly. Modify the code you just created to build the second of the six main pages. The only differences from the previous code (reason1.html) are shown with a gray background. Save the new page as reason2.html. The complete code appears as follows:

```
<html>
<head>
<title>Reason 2 - By the Water Cooler</title>
</head>
<body bgcolor="#ffffff">
<h2><img src="flirty.jpg" width="275" height="275" align="left">I'm flirting by
 the water cooler.</h2>
</body>
</html>
```

For the third page, modify the code again and save it as reason3.html. The complete code appears as follows:

```
<html>
<head>
<title>Reason 3 - Don't Ask!</title>
</head>
<body bgcolor="#ffffff">
<h2><img src="grumpy.jpg" width="275" height="275" align="left">None of
 your business!</h2>
</body>
</html>
```

Here's the fourth page (reason4.html):

```
<head>
<title>Reason 4 - Out to Lunch</title>
</head>
<body bgcolor="#ffffff">
<h2><img src="happy.jpg" width="275" height="275" align="left">I'm out
 to lunch.</h2>
</body>
</html>
```

The fifth page (reason5.html) looks like the following:

```
<head>
<title>Reason 5 - Boss's Office</title>
</head>
<body bgcolor="#ffffff">
<h2><img src="scared.jpg" width="275" height="275" align="left">The boss
 called me into his office.</h2>
</body>
</html>
```

14

▼ The last main page (`reason6.html`) appears as follows:

```
<head>
<title>Reason 6 - I Don't Work Here Anymore</title>
</head>
<body bgcolor="#ffffff">
<h2><img src="duh.jpg" width="275" height="275" align="left">I just
 got fired.</h2>
</body>
</html>
```

Now you have the six pages that will appear in the main frame of the frameset. You're
▲ finally ready to build the frameset itself.

▼ Task: **Exercise 14.3: Combining** rows **and** cols

To remind you of the basic layout of the frameset that you'll create, Figure 14.15 is
another look at the complete page. It provides a simple example of how you can combine
framesets to create complex designs.

Output ▼

FIGURE 14.15
The frameset with
three frames: top,
left, and main.

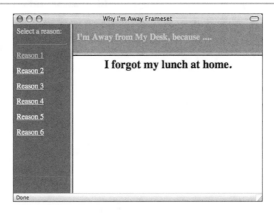

TIP	When you're designing complex frame layouts, a storyboard is an invaluable tool. It helps you block out the structure of a frameset, and it can be invaluable when you're adding hyperlinks (as you'll see in Exercise 14.5, "Using Named Frames and Hyperlinks").

In Figure 14.15, the right section of the screen is split into two horizontal frames, and
▼ the third frame at the left of the page spans the entire height of the screen. To create a

frameset document that describes this layout, open your text editor and enter the follow- ▼
ing basic HTML structural details:

```
<html>
<head>
<title>Why I'm Away Frameset</title>
</head>
<frameset>
</frameset>
</html>
```

Next, you must decide whether you need to use a `rows` or `cols` attribute in your base
`<frameset>`. Look at your storyboard—in this case Figure 14.15—and work out whether
any frame areas extend right across the screen or from the top to the bottom. If any
frames extend from the top to the bottom, as in this example, you need to start with a
`cols` frameset; otherwise, you need to start with a `rows` frameset. On the other hand, if
no frames extend completely across the screen either vertically or horizontally, you
should start with a `cols` frameset.

To put it more simply, here are three easy-to-remember rules:

- Left to right, use `rows`
- Top to bottom, use `cols`
- Can't decide, use `cols`

NOTE

The reasoning behind the use of the "left to right, use `rows`" rule
relates to how frames-compatible browsers create frames. Each
separate `<frameset>` definition can split the screen (or a frame)
either vertically or horizontally, but not both ways. For this reason,
you need to define your framesets in a logical order to ensure that
you achieve the layout you want.

In Figure 14.15, the left frame extends across the screen from top to bottom. As a result,
you need to start with a `cols` frameset by using the rules mentioned previously. To define
the base frameset, enter the following:

```
<frameset cols="125,*">
 <frame src="choice.html"> <!-- loads the choices page into the left frame -->
 <frame src="dummy.html"> <!-- this line is only temporary -->
</frameset>
```

14

Writing this code splits the screen into two sections. The first line defines a small frame
at the left of the screen that is 125 pixels wide, and a large frame at the right of the ▼
screen that uses the rest of the available space.

▼ As mentioned earlier today, the frameset document itself doesn't describe the contents of each frame. The documents specified in the src attribute of the <frame> actually contain the text, images, and tags displayed by the frameset. You can see an example of this tag in the second and third lines of the preceding code. The second line specifies the URL of the web page in the left frame (the choice.html page that you created earlier). The third line would display a web page named dummy.html (if you created one, that is), but we're
▲ just using this as a placeholder for the next exercise.

▼ Task: Exercise 14.4: Nesting Framesets

The next step in the process is to split the right frame area into two horizontal frames. You achieve this effect by placing a second <frameset> block inside the base <frameset> block. When one <frameset> block is nested inside another, the nested block must replace one of the <frame> tags in the outside frameset. In this case, you'll replace the line that loads the temporary dummy.html page (which doesn't really exist).

To split the right frame into two frame areas, you replace the dummy <frame> tag with an embedded <frameset> block. This embeds the new frameset inside the area defined for the <frame> tag it replaces. Inside the <frameset> tag for this new block, you need to define a rows attribute, as shown in the complete code:

```
<html>
<head>
<title>Why I'm Away Frameset</title>
</head>
<frameset cols="125,*">
 <frame src="choice.html" <!-- this loads the choices page_into the left frame
   -->
 <frameset rows="60,*">    <!-- the frame for column 2 -->
  <frame src="away.html">  <!-- has been replaced -->
  <frame src="reason1.html"> <!-- with an embedded -->
 </frameset>            <!-- frameset block -->
</frameset>
```

The embedded rows frameset defines two rows, the first being 60% of the height of the embedded frame area and the second taking up all the remaining space in the embedded frame area. In addition, two <frame> tags are embedded inside the <frameset> block to define the contents of each column. The top frame loads away.html, and the bottom frame loads reason1.html.

NOTE | When used inside an embedded frameset, any percentage sizes are based on a percentage of the total area of the embedded frame, not on a percentage of the total screen.

▼

Save the finished HTML document to your hard drive as `frameset.html`. Test it using a ▼
frames-compliant browser. Also, if you happen to have a copy of a web browser that isn't
frames-compliant, try loading the document into it. You shouldn't see anything onscreen. ▲

Task: Exercise 14.5: Using Named Frames and Hyperlinks ▼

If you were to load your `frameset.html` page into a frames-compatible browser at this
stage, you would see a screen similar to the one shown in Figure 14.15. Some of the text
sizes and spacing might be slightly different, but the general picture would be the same.

Although it looks right, it doesn't *work* right yet. If you click any of the hyperlinks in the
left frame, the frames-compatible browser will attempt to load the contents of the file
you select into the left frame. What you really want it to do is to load each document into
the larger right frame.

Earlier today, you learned about the `target` attribute, which loads different pages into a
different browser window. To make the frameset work the way it should, you need to use
a slight variation on the `target` attribute. Rather than the `target` pointing to a new window, you want it to point to one of the frames in the current frameset.

You can achieve this by first giving each frame in your frameset a frame name or window name. To do so, include a `name` attribute inside the `<frame>` tag, which takes the following form:

```
<frame src="document URL" name="frame name">
```

Therefore, to assign a name to each of the frames in the `frameset.html` document, you
add the `name` attribute to each of the `<frame>` tags. Your frameset page now looks like the
following, with the additions indicated with the shaded background:

```
<html>
<head>
<title>Why I'm Away Frameset</title>
</head>
<frameset cols="125,*">
 <frame src="choice.html" name="left">
 <!-- this loads the choices page into the left frame -->
 <frameset rows="60,*">    <!-- the frame for column 2 -->
  <frame src="away.html" name="top">  <!-- has been replaced -->
  <frame src="reason1.html" name="main"> <!-- with an embedded -->
 </frameset>          <!-- frameset block -->
</frameset>
```

14

This source code names the left frame `"left"`, the top-right frame `"top"`, and the
bottom-right frame `"main"`. Next, resave the updated `frameset.html` file, and you're just
about finished with the example. ▲

▼ Task: Exercise 14.6: Linking Documents to Individual Frames

Once you've named the frames, you have to fix the links in the choice.html page so that they load the target pages in the main frame rather than the left frame.

You might recall that the target attribute was used with the <a> tag to force a document to load into a specific window. You'll use the same attribute to control into which frame a document is loaded.

In this exercise, you want to load a page in the main (bottom-right) frame whenever you click a hyperlink in the left frame. Because you've already named the bottom-right frame "main", all you need to do is add target="main" to each tag in the choice.html document. The following snippet of HTML source code demonstrates how to make this change:

```
<p><a href="reason1.html" target="main">Reason 1</a></p>
<p><a href="reason2.html" target="main">Reason 2</a></p>
<p><a href="reason3.html" target="main">Reason 3</a></p>
<p><a href="reason4.html" target="main">Reason 4</a></p>
<p><a href="reason5.html" target="main">Reason 5</a></p>
<p><a href="reason6.html" target="main">Reason 6</a></p>
```

Alternatively, you could use the <base target="value"> tag because every tag in the choice.html document points to the same frame. In this case, you don't need to include target="main" inside each <a> tag. Instead, place the following inside the <head>...</head> block of the document:

```
<base target="main">
```

With all the changes and new documents created, you should now be able to load frameset.html into your frames-compatible browser and view all your HTML reference documents by selecting from the choices in the left frame.

▲

TIP

> After you get all your links working properly, you might need to go back and adjust the size of the rows and columns as defined in the <frameset> tags to get the layout exactly right. Remember, the final appearance of a frameset is still determined by the size of the screen and the visitor's operating system.

Task: **Exercise 14.7: Adding Your** noframes **Content** ▼

Although you have a frameset that works perfectly now, there's another feature you need to add to it. Remember, some people who visit your frames page won't be using frames-compatible browsers. The following addition to the frameset page creates some content that they'll see when they open the frameset.

Once again, open the frameset.html page. At this point, your code looks like the following:

```
<html>
<head>
<title>Why I'm Away Frameset</title>
</head>
<frameset cols="125,*">
 <frame src="choice.html" name="left">
 <!-- this loads the choices page into the left frame -->
 <frameset rows="60,*">    <!-- the frame for column 2 -->
  <frame src="away.html" name="top">  <!-- has been replaced -->
  <frame src="reason1.html" name="main"> <!-- with an embedded -->
 </frameset>          <!-- frameset block -->
</frameset>
</html>
```

Immediately after the last </frameset> tag and before the final </html> tag, insert the following <noframes>...</noframes> element and content:

Input ▼

```
<noframes>
  <body bgcolor="#ffffff">
<h1>I'm Away from My Desk, because ...</h1>
<ul>
 <li>Reason 1 -
 <a href="reason1.html">I forgot my lunch at home.</a></li>
 <li>Reason 2 -
 <a href="reason2.html">I'm flirting by the water cooler.</a></li>
 <li>Reason 3 - <a href="reason3.html">None of your business.</a></li>
 <li>Reason 4 - <a href="reason4.html">I'm out to lunch.</a></li>
 <li>Reason 5 -
 <a href="reason5.html">The boss just called me in his office.</a></li>
 <li>Reason 6 - <a href="reason6.html">I just got fired.</a></li>
</ul>
</body>
</noframes>
```

14

When a user who isn't using a frames-compatible browser navigates to the frameset, she'll see the page that's similar to the one shown in Figure 14.16.

▼ Output ▼

FIGURE 14.16

This page appears when users view the frameset with a browser that isn't frames-compatible.

Magic `target` Names

Now that you've learned what the `target` attribute does in a frameset, you should know that there are some special target names you can apply to a frameset.

You can assign four special values to a `target` attribute, two of which (`_blank` and `self`) you've already encountered. Netscape called these values *magic target names*. They're case sensitive. If you enter a magic target name in anything other than lowercase, the link will attempt to display the document in a window with that name, creating a new window if necessary. Table 14.2 lists the magic `target` names and describes their use.

TABLE 14.2   Magic `target` Names

`target` Name	Description
`target="_blank"`	Forces the document referenced by the `<a>` tag to be loaded into a new unnamed window.
`target="_self"`	Causes the document referenced by the `<a>` tag to be loaded into the window or frame that held the `<a>` tag. This can be useful if the `<base>` tag sets the target to another frame but a specific link needs to load in the current frame.
`target="_parent"`	Forces the link to load into the `<frameset>` parent of the current document. If the current document has no parent, however, `target="_self"` will be used.
`target="_top"`	Forces the link to load into the full web browser window, replacing the current `<frameset>` entirely. If the current document is already at the top, however, `target="_self"` will be used. More often than not, when you create links to other sites on the Web, you don't want them to open within your frameset. Adding `target="_top"` to the link will prevent this from occurring.

Floating Frames

With Internet Explorer 3.0, Microsoft introduced a novel variation on frames: floating frames. This concept, which is a part of HTML 4.01, is somewhat different from the original frames idea that was introduced in Netscape.

Floating frames have their advantages and disadvantages. One advantage is that you can position a floating frame anywhere on a web page, just as you can with an image, a table, or any other web page element.

Browser Support for Floating Frames

The authors of the HTML 4.01 frames specification included floating frames with some hesitation. According to the specification, you can use the <object> tag to achieve the same effect as floating frames, so the inclusion of this type of frame is questionable. Still, the tag is included in the HTML 4.01 specification, and all versions of Internet Explorer since version 3, Mozilla Firefox, Netscape 6 (and above), and Opera 5 (and above) all support it. Learning to use floating frames is worthwhile.

Standard framesets enable you to specify alternative content that can be viewed when someone without a frames-compatible browser navigates to a frameset. Unfortunately, you don't have this option with the <iframe> element. If you include a floating frame on your web page and a user navigates to it with a browser that doesn't support them, he'll see absolutely nothing at all in the area where the frame should be.

With that warning out of the way, here's a brief run-through of how to create floating frames. First, you define them by using the <iframe> tag. Like images, these frames appear inline in the middle of the body of an HTML document (hence the i in <iframe>). The <iframe> tag enables you to insert an HTML document in a frame anywhere in another HTML document.

Table 14.3 shows how <iframe> takes the key attributes—all of which, except for those indicated as Internet Explorer extensions, appear in HTML 4.01.

TABLE 14.3   Key Attributes

Attribute	Description
width	Specifies the width, in pixels, of the floating frame that will hold the HTML document.
height	Specifies the height, in pixels, of the floating frame that will hold the HTML document.
src	Specifies the URL of the HTML document to be displayed in the frame.

14

TABLE 14.3   continued

Attribute	Description
name	Specifies the name of the frame for the purpose of linking and targeting.
frameborder	Indicates whether the frame should display a border. A value of 1 indicates the presence of a border, and a value of 0 indicates no border should be displayed.
marginwidth	Specifies the margin size for the left and right sides of the frame in pixels.
marginheight	Specifies the size of the top and bottom margins in pixels.
noresize	Indicates that the frame should not be resizable by the user (Internet Explorer extension).
scrolling	As with the <frame> tag, indicates whether the inline frame should include scrollbars. (This attribute can take the values yes, no, or auto; the default is auto.)
vspace	Specifies the height of the margin (Internet Explorer extension).
hspace	Specifies the width of the margin (Internet Explorer extension).
align	As with the <img> tag, specifies the positioning of the frame with respect to the text line in which it occurs. Possible values include left, middle, right, top, and bottom, which is the default value. absbottom, absmiddle, baseline, and texttop are available as Internet Explorer extensions.

Because you know how to use both regular frames and inline images, using the <iframe> tag is fairly easy. The following code displays one way to use the Away from My Desk pages in conjunction with a floating frame. In this example, you begin by creating a page with a red background. The links that the user clicks appear on a single line, centered above the floating frame. For clarity, I've placed each of the links on a separate line of code.

Following the links (which target the floating frame named "reason"), the code for the floating frame appears within a centered <div> element. As the following code shows, the floating frame will be centered on the page and will measure 450 pixels wide by 315 pixels high:

Input ▼

```
<html>
<head>
<title>I'm Away From My Desk</title>
</head>
<body bgcolor="#ffcc99">
```

```
<h2>I'm away from my desk because ...</h2>
<p align="center">
  <a href="reason1.html" target="reason">Reason 1</a> |
  <a href="reason2.html" target="reason">Reason 2</a> |
  <a href="reason3.html" target="reason">Reason 3</a> |
  <a href="reason4.html" target="reason">Reason 4</a> |
  <a href="reason5.html" target="reason">Reason 5</a> |
  <a href="reason6.html" target="reason">Reason 6</a> </p>
<div align="center">
<iframe name="reason"
  src="reason1.html"
  width="450"
  height="315">
</div>
</body>
</html>
```

Figure 14.17 shows the result.

Output ▼

FIGURE 14.17
An inline (or floating) frame.

Opening Linked Windows with JavaScript

Pop-up windows are used all over the Web. They are often used to display advertisements, but they can be used for all sorts of other things as well, such as creating a separate window to show help text in an application, or to display a larger version of a graph that's embedded in a document. You've seen how you can use the target attribute to open a link in a new window, but that approach isn't very flexible. You can't control the size of the window being displayed, nor which browser interface controls are displayed.

Fortunately, with JavaScript you can take more control of the process of creating new windows. You've already learned that one of the objects supported by JavaScript is window. It refers to the window that's executing the script. To open a new window, you use the open method of the window object. Here's a JavaScript function that opens a window:

14

```
function popup(url) {
  mywindow = window.open(url, 'name', 'height=200,width=400');
  return false;
}
```

The function accepts the URL for the document to be displayed in the new window as an argument. It creates a new window using the `window.open` function, and assigns that new window to a variable named `mywindow`. (I'll explain why we assign the new window to a variable in a bit.)

The three arguments to the function are the URL to be displayed in the window, the name for the window, and a list of settings for the window. In this case, I indicate that I want the window to be 400 pixels wide and 200 pixels tall. The name is important because if other links target a window with the same name, either via the `window.open()` function or the `target` attribute, they'll appear in that window.

At the end of the function, I return `false`. That's necessary so that the event handler used to call the function is stopped. To illustrate what I mean, it's necessary to explain how this function is called. Rather than using the `target` attribute in the `<a>` tag, the `onclick` handler is utilized, as follows:

```
<a href="whatever.html" onclick="popup('whatever.html')">Pop up</a>
```

Ordinarily, when a user clicks on the link, the browser will call the function and then go right back to whatever it was doing before, navigating to the document specified in the `href` attribute. Returning `false` in the `popup()` function tells the browser not to continue what it was doing, so the new window is opened by the function, and the browser doesn't follow the link. If a user who had JavaScript turned off visited the page, she would follow the link directly to `whatever.html` because the `onclick` attribute would be ignored.

In the preceding example, I specified the `height` and `width` settings for the new window. There are several more options available as well, which are listed in Table 14.4.

TABLE 14.4   Settings for Pop-up Windows

Setting	Purpose
height	Height of the window in pixels.
width	Width of the window in pixels.
resizable	Enable window resizing.
scrollbars	Display scroll bars.
status	Display the browser status bar.
toolbar	Display the browser toolbar.
directories	Display the browser's directory buttons.
location	Display the browser's location bar.
menubar	Display the browser's menu bar. (Not applicable on Mac OS X.)
left	Left coordinate of the new window onscreen (in pixels).
top	Top coordinate of the new window onscreen (in pixels).

When you specify the settings for a window, you must include them in a comma-separated list, with no spaces anywhere. For the settings that allow you to enable or disable a browser interface component, the valid values are on or off. Here's a valid list of settings:

```
status=off,toolbar=off,location=off,left=200,top=100,width=300,height=300
```

Here's an invalid list of settings:

```
status=off, toolbar=off, location=false, top=100
```

Including spaces (or carriage returns) anywhere in your list will cause problems. It's also worth noting that when you provide settings for a new window, the browser automatically assumes a default of off for any on/off settings that you don't include. So you can leave out anything you want to turn off.

Here's a complete example that uses JavaScript to create a new window:

```html
<html>
    <head>
        <meta http-equiv="Content-type" content="text/html; charset=utf-8" />
        <title>Popup example</title>
        <script type="text/javascript" language="javascript">
        function popup(url) {
          mywindow = window.open(url, 'name', 'height=200,width=400');
          return false;
        }
        </script>
    </head>
    <body>
        <h1>Popup Example</h1>

        <p><a href="popup.html" onclick="popup('popup.html')">Launch
            popup</a></p>
    </body>
</html>
```

When a user clicks on the "Launch popup" link, a new 200 by 400 pixel window appears with the contents of popup.html.

Summary

If your head is hurting after today, you're probably not alone. Although the basic concepts behind the use of frames are relatively straightforward, their implementation is somewhat harder to come to grips with. As a result, the best way to learn about frames is by experimenting with them.

14

Today, you learned how to link a document to a new or existing window. In addition, you learned how to create framesets and link them together by using the tags listed in Table 14.5.

The Downside of Frames

In this lesson I've mentioned a few drawbacks of frames here and there. I wanted to talk about them one more time now that the discussion of frames is coming to a close. The problem with frames is that they change the concept of a web page. Unfortunately, many mechanisms that users are familiar with rely on the original concept. So when it comes to navigation, bookmarking pages, or using the browser's Back button, frames can cause confusion. There are also issues when it comes to printing, and frames can cause problems on devices with small screens, like mobile phones.

The point here isn't to say that frames should never be used, but rather that you should think about what you're trying to accomplish and decide whether another approach wouldn't work better. CSS adds enough layout options that frames can often be avoided, especially floating frames.

TABLE 14.5   New Tags Discussed in Lesson 14

Tag	Attribute	Description
`<base target="`*`window`*`">`		Sets the global link window for a document.
`<frameset>`		Defines the basic structure of a frameset.
	`cols`	Defines the number of frame columns and their width in a frameset.
	`rows`	Defines the number of frame rows and their height in a frameset.
	`frameborder`	Indicates whether the frameset displays borders between frames.
	`bordercolor`	Defines the color of borders in a frameset.
`<frame>`		Defines the contents of a frame within a frameset.
	`src`	Indicates the URL of the document to be displayed inside the frame.
	`marginwidth`	Indicates the size in pixels of the margin on each side of a frame.

TABLE 14.5 continued

Tag	Attribute	Description
	marginheight	Indicates the size in pixels of the margin above and below the contents of a frame.
	scrolling	Enables or disables the display of scrollbars for a frame. Values are yes, no, and auto.
	noresize	Prevents the users from resizing frames.
	frameborder	Indicates whether the frameset displays borders between frames.
	bordercolor	Defines the color of borders in a frameset.
	longdesc	Specifies a URL that provides a longer description of the contents of the frameset. Used with nonvisual browsers.
	name	Assigns a name to the frame for targeting purposes.
<iframe>		Defines an inline or floating frame.
	src	Indicates the URL of the document to be displayed in the frame.
	name	Indicates the name of the frame for the purpose of linking and targeting.
	width	Indicates the width of the frame in pixels.
	height	Indicates the height of the frame in pixels.
	marginwidth	Indicates the width of the margin in pixels.
	marginheight	Indicates the height of the margin in pixels.
	scrolling	Enables or disables the display of scrollbars in the frame. Values are yes, no, and auto.
	frameborder	Enables or disables the display of a border around the frame. Values are 1 and 0.
	vspace	Indicates the height of the margin in pixels.
	hspace	Indicates the width of the margin in pixels.
	align	Specifies the alignment of the frame relative to the current line of text. Values are left, right, middle, top, and bottom (also absbottom, absmiddle, texttop, and baseline in Internet Explorer).
<noframes>		Defines text to be displayed by web browsers that don't support the use of frames.

14

Workshop

As if you haven't had enough already, here's a refresher course of questions, quizzes, and exercises that will help you remember some of the most important points you learned today.

Q&A

Q Is there any limit to how many levels of `<frameset>` tags I can nest within a single screen?

A No, there isn't a limit. Practically speaking, however, the available window space starts to become too small to be usable when you get below about four levels.

Q What would happen if I included a reference to a frameset document within a `<frame>` tag?

A Netscape handles such a reference correctly by treating the nested frameset document as a nested `<frameset>`. In fact, this technique is used regularly to reduce the complexity of nested frames.

One limitation does exist, however. You cannot include a reference to the current frameset document in one of its own frames. This situation, called *recursion*, causes an infinite loop. Netscape Communications has included built-in protection to guard against this type of referencing.

Quiz

1. What are the differences between a *frameset document*, a *frameset*, a *frame*, and a *page*?

2. When you create links to pages that are supposed to load into a frameset, what attribute makes the pages appear in the right frame? (Hint: It applies to the `<a>` element.)

3. When a web page includes the `<frameset>` element, what element cannot be used at the beginning of the HTML document?

4. What two attributes of the `<frameset>` tag divide the browser window into multiple sections?

5. What attribute of the `<frame>` tag defines the HTML document that first loads into a frameset?

Quiz Answers

1. A *frameset document* is the HTML document that contains the definition of the frameset. A *frameset* is the portion of the frameset document that is defined by the `<frameset>` tag, which instructs the browser to divide the window into multiple sections. A *frame* is one of the sections, or windows, within a frameset. The *page* is the web document that loads within a frame.

2. The `target` attribute of the `<a>` tag directs linked pages to load into the appropriate frame.

3. When a web page includes the `<frameset>` element, it cannot include the `<body>` element at the beginning of the page. They're mutually exclusive.

4. The `cols` and `rows` attributes of the `<frameset>` tag divide the browser window into multiple frames.

5. The `src` attribute of the `<frame>` tag defines the HTML document that first loads into the frameset.

Exercises

1. Create a frameset that divides the browser window into three sections, as follows:

   - The left section of the frameset will be a column that spans the entire height of the browser window and will take up one-third of the width of the browser window. Name this frame `contents`.

   - Divide the right section of the frameset into two rows, each taking half the height of the browser window. Name the top section `top` and the bottom section `bottom`.

2. For the preceding frameset, create a page that you will use for a table of contents in the left frame. Create two links on this page, one that loads a page in the top frame and another that loads a page in the bottom frame.

14

LESSON 15:

Creating Applications with Dynamic HTML and AJAX

Dynamic HTML offers you something unique: the capability to make changes in web pages on the fly. Using conventional HTML, web pages are loaded by a browser and just sit there until you click a link or interact with forms. That's pretty simple, but it can be static and boring.

People have improved upon static web pages by using a variety of technologies outside the realm of HTML. Any number of platforms are available for creating server-side web applications. You can embed Shockwave and Flash in your pages to add animation and interactivity, and use Java applets to provide application-like functions. However, these methods rely on browser plug-ins or virtual machines (which can be messy), and can lead to longer download times.

Dynamic HTML is different. *DHTML*, as it is commonly known, enables you to create web pages that look, feel, and act a lot like the other programs you use on your computer—using the web browser as an interface—without having to rely on external programming solutions. AJAX takes that one step further, and allows you to actually exchange data with the server from within your web page, without submitting a form or clicking on a link.

In this Lesson

Today's lesson is a full plate of information, so let's get right to it. In this lesson, you will learn about the following:

- Defining Dynamic HTML and the technologies that make it possible

- Understanding the Document Object Model (DOM)
- Creating cross-browser routines with DHTML by testing browser capabilities
- Examples of using DHTML to manipulate elements on a page

What Exactly Is Dynamic HTML?

Simply put, Dynamic HTML uses normal HTML elements to create a web page that relies on style sheets for element formatting, and scripting to *dynamically* change HTML content, style, or positioning, without having to *re-download* the page from the server. Dynamic HTML isn't a thing by itself, but a collection of technologies working together to produce an interactive interface. So, what can you do with DHTML? The possibilities are endless! Just to whet your appetite, here are a few of them:

- Move objects around the web page
- Show or hide elements
- Dynamically alter the color and size of web content
- Provide drag-and-drop functionality similar to that used by modern graphical operating systems (such as Windows and the Mac OS)

Dynamic HTML was born with the advent of the "fours." The World Wide Web Consortium developed HTML 4.01 and released the official recommendation at about the same time Microsoft and Netscape released their competing web browsers, Internet Explorer 4 and Netscape 4. There was a flurry of activity surrounding all this. HTML 4.01 promoted several new features to better integrate itself with cascading style sheets and respond to user events. Microsoft and Netscape were competing hard for market share in the browser war, and the result of it all was a drive for something different: a level of user interactivity and "dynamism" in web pages that previously was impossible without resorting to external programming. DHTML was born.

For DHTML to work, it requires the following three key technologies supported by the web browser:

- HTML
- Cascading style sheets
- Scripting

Style sheets are wonderful after you know how to use them, and are a critical component of DHTML. Although DHTML technically isn't dependent on any one type of style sheet, the official W3C style sheet technology, *cascading style sheets (CSS)*, is the standard. CSS enables you to format elements on your web pages using properties, such as font, color, and spacing, as well as positioning items on the web page.

DHTML takes style to a new level. Rather than creating a style rule or positioning an element on the page and then forgetting about it, you can use DHTML to dynamically alter the visual style or position of your elements. As with HTML, there are inconsistencies in how various browsers implement CSS. None have *fully* implemented all of the specifications, but also browsers have implemented portions differently. Things are a lot better now than they were a few years ago. The latest versions of Internet Explorer, Netscape, and Opera offer much closer adherence to the HTML and CSS standards than they once did. That said, complex dynamic HTML applications require lots of testing and many workarounds to work on all the browsers that are still in common use.

Finally, scripting is a sort of glue that holds together everything in DHTML. Scripting is the engine that makes DHTML go. Using scripting, you can alter the content on your page when the page loads in response to any of the events discussed in Lesson 12, "Introducing JavaScript," or even when the user leaves the page.

CAUTION	If you've caught on to the "inconsistent implementation across web browsers" pattern here, you should know that official specifications may bear little resemblance to reality. You should always read any browser-specific documentation you can find to ensure that the web browsers you're targeting support what you're attempting to accomplish. Even then, some experimentation will usually be required.

The scripting *lingua franca* of today is JavaScript. JavaScript was the first scripting language to be implemented in a web browser, and currently enjoys the most widespread support across different web browsers. Although you can create DHTML using other scripting languages such as VBScript, I recommend always using JavaScript unless you are in a Microsoft-only environment (such as an intranet).

As you'll see when we get to the DHTML examples, a large part of DHTML involves creating scripts that manipulate elements on a page. You'll probably need to fall back on the discussion of JavaScript back in Lessons 12, "Introducing JavaScript," and 13,

"Using JavaScript in Your Pages," to refresh your memory of JavaScript at times. Because DHTML is really just an application of JavaScript, it might even be helpful to think about this lesson as a follow-up to those.

Two final notes about what DHTML actually is: DHTML (the scripting part of it) relies on something called a *Document Object Model (DOM)* to identify, create, and manipulate elements on a web page. For example, you have to be able to identify an element, such as an image, in order to manipulate it with a script. Likewise, you must be able to identify an element's style in order to change it. This is what the DOM does. It provides a bridge between the content of the web page and scripts.

Finally, DHTML relies on *event handling* to track the actions of the web browser and user. When the page loads, the `onload` event is triggered. Likewise, when a visitor clicks a button in a form, several events might be triggered that you, the DHTML author, can use to run scripts. Event handling is covered in more depth later on.

Using the Document Object Model

When you think of a web page, you probably think of the document that's produced when it's displayed in the browser, or the HTML codes that you see when you use your browser's View Source functionality. However, there are other ways that the same data can be represented. Modern web browsers create a representation of a page that can be accessed via scripts in a standardized fashion. This representation is called the Document Object Model, or DOM. Under the DOM, the page content is treated as a tree of objects. I'm using the word *objects* the way a software developer would. In that parlance, an *object* is a component that generally has different properties, methods, and event handlers. A *property* is data that somehow describes the object. A *method* is a function you can call to make the object do something or to manipulate the object itself. An *event handler* is a hook you can use to enable the object to respond to an action (generally an action performed by the user). If you were speaking grammatically, you'd say that properties are an object's nouns and methods are its verbs.

NOTE

Fully realizing the capabilities of the DOM requires a depth of knowledge beyond the scope of this book. But, as with other web-related code, you can learn a lot by cutting and pasting scripts and taking the time to study their results.

DOM Data Types

When a DOM representation of a web page is created, all of the objects that are used to construct the page are assigned to various categories, which are called *interfaces* in the world of object-oriented programming. If an object has a certain interface then it has the properties and methods associated with that interface. For example, all of the tags on a page have the element interface, which means that they support methods such as getAttribute and setAttribute. The generic data types that make up the DOM are listed in Table 15.1.

TABLE 15.1 Interfaces in the DOM

Data Type	Purpose
document	This is the root object in the DOM.
node	All of the other interfaces mentioned are children of the node interface, and express all of its properties and methods.
element	All the tags on a page express the element interface, and thus inherit all its properties, methods, and event handlers.
nodeList	An array (or list) of elements. Some method calls return lists of elements. For example, you can fetch all the items in a list or all the children of any element. The results are returned in a nodeList.
attribute	Attributes of tags have their own interface.
NamedNodeMap	An alternative form of list for dealing with groups of elements.

Objects in the DOM

The base of the DOM tree is the document object. The document object should look familiar to you from the examples in Lesson 13. You can call methods of the document object directly, such as document.write() to add content to the page, or you can reference children of the document object, using methods such as getElementById() or getElementsByTagName().

Even if you don't explicitly use the document object, you're still accessing the DOM any time you reference objects on the page. For example, in the form validation example in Lesson 13, I passed the form object to the validation function using the onsubmit handler and this. In that case, this referred to the form being validated. Had the form not been passed to the function using an argument, it could have been referenced by name or count using the document object.

Another object that you'll deal with frequently is window. The window object (unlike document) is not formally part of the DOM, but browsers include it in order to provide an interface to the browser itself. For example, the height and width of the browser window are properties of the `window` object rather than the `document` object.

Each element on the page is also an object unto itself and is accessible using the `document` object. Using generic methods, you can get to all the children of the `document` object, but a number of convenience methods are included to give you shortcuts to things such as the forms, images, and links on a page. Before going further, let's look at an example.

There's More to the DOM

The DOM consists of many more objects as well, but discussing each of them in detail is beyond the scope of this lesson. There are up-to-date online DOM references provided by the browser vendors online. Microsoft's DOM/DHTML reference is at http://msdn.microsoft.com/workshop/author/dhtml/_dhtml_node_entry.asp.

The DOM reference for Netscape and Mozilla is at http://www.mozilla.org/docs/dom/domref/.

Opera attempts to hew as closely to published standards as possible. Notes on their departures from the specification can be found at http://www.opera.com/docs/specs/.

Using the DOM

You should be thankful that I'm not going to discuss the DOM in detail because it would be incredibly dry and boring, and chances are whatever I put in this book would be at least somewhat out of date not a year after it is published. For reference materials on the specific properties, methods, and event handlers for each object in the DOM, you should rely on the vendor references. Generally speaking, web programmers use the DOM in a few specific ways. I'll go over those.

In this example, we're going to create a web page that enables us to manipulate elements on a page in various ways using the DOM. This example will work in any modern browser that supports the DOM. First, let's get the code listing out of the way:

Input ▼

```
<html>
<head>
<title>DOM Example</title>
<script language="JavaScript">

function changeBgColor(newColor)
{
  if (document.body)
```

```
    {
      eval('document.body.bgColor="' + newColor + '"');
    }
  }

function tackOn(headingText)
{
  if (document.body)
  {
    if (headingText)
    {
      var newHeading = document.createElement("h1");
      someText = document.createTextNode(headingText);
      newHeading.appendChild(someText);
      document.body.appendChild(newHeading);
    }
  }
}

function setHeadingColors()
{
  var headings = document.getElementsByTagName("h1");

  for (var i = 0; i < headings.length; i++)
  {
    headings.item(i).style.color = "yellow";
  }
}

</script>
</head>
<body>

<form>
  Background color:
  <select onchange="changeBgColor(this.options[this.selectedIndex].value);">
    <option value="white">white</option>
    <option value="red">red</option>
    <option value="blue">blue</option>
  </select><br />

  Add heading:
  <input type="text" value="Spam" id="newHeading" />
  <input type="button" value="tack it on"
    onclick="tackOn(document.getElementById('newHeading').value);" />
  <br />
  <input type="button" value="change colors"
    onclick="setHeadingColors();" />
</form>

</body>
</html>
```

15

Let me describe quickly how the page works. The form on the page enables you to change the page's background color, add new headings to the page, and set the color of all the headings currently on the page to yellow. We accomplish this using three JavaScript functions and five form fields. A screenshot of the page after I've manipulated it a bit appears in Figure 15.1.

Output ▼

FIGURE 15.1
A page that demonstrates how the DOM is used.

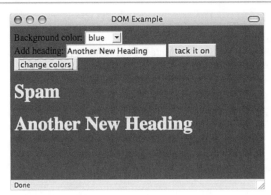

I use the DOM in both the event handlers called within the form as well as within the actual JavaScript on the page. The first form field is the select list that's used to change the page's background color. To accomplish this, we use the `onchange` handler for this field. When the value of the field is changed, the `changeBgColor()` function defined on the page is called, and the new background color is passed in as a parameter. We obtain this value by retrieving the value of the currently selected option using this reference:

```
this.options[this.selectedIndex].value
```

`this` refers to the select field. The `options` method retrieves a `nodeList` of options associated with the field. We can obtain the currently selected index of the field using the `selectedIndex` property of the select list, and use it as the index for the `nodeList`. Based on the DOM specification, I know that we could just as easily obtain the currently selected index using `options.item(this.selectedIndex)`. Both approaches are valid. Finally, the `value` property of the currently selected option is what's actually passed in to the function.

Now let's look at the `changeBgColor()` function. This function is quite short. First, it performs a simple test to verify that the `document.body` property even exists. If the function can't get a reference to the body element in this way, there's no sense in going on. Once it has it, it uses the `eval` function to create and run a bit of JavaScript that sets the `bgColor` property of the body element to the value that was passed in. `bgColor` is a property that's specific to the document body; it's not available for all elements.

Next, I enable the user to add <h1> elements to the page. This bit of manipulation is accomplished using only methods and properties that are part of the core DOM, except for document.body. This is intended to demonstrate how elements on a page can be treated in a generic fashion. This part of the form uses two form fields; the first is a text field that provides the value of the text to be added. The second part is a button that calls the function that appends the new heading to the page. The only notable thing about the text field is that we've assigned it an ID, "newHeading".

The button uses an onclick handler to call the tackOn() function. As its parameter, it passes in the value of newHeading. As you can see, it references newHeading using the getElementById method of the document object, and then referencing the value property of that element. I included a default value in the form field so that the user doesn't have to type in something every time.

As you saw back in Lesson 9, "Creating Layouts with CSS," the id attribute can be used to assign an identifier to an element so that you can apply styles to it individually. As you can see from this example, you can also access items with an id through the DOM using the getElementById() function. This one capability alone makes the entire DOM worthwhile—before the getElementById() function was supported by browsers, referencing a specific object on a page was tedious and difficult. Now all you have to do is assign an identifier to it. The only catch is that you have to make sure not to use the same identifier more than once on the same page.

Now let's look at the tackOn() function. Before we do anything else, we make sure that document.body is supported and that a value was actually passed in. There's no need to go further if we're not able to add on the heading or there's no heading to add. Once we've done that, we use the document.createElement() method to create a reference to a brand new <h1> element. Then we use document.createTextNode() to create a text node containing the header text. To associate the text node with the heading, we use appendChild() to indicate that the new text node is a child of the heading. This is how you build onto your document structure using the DOM. You generate new elements, and then add them onto existing elements as children. We could also modify any properties of the heading that we wanted at this point.

Once we have a reference to an <h1> element with some text as its child, we use appendChild() again to append the new heading onto the document body. At this point, the new heading should appear at the bottom of the page. When thinking of parent-child relationships in the DOM, just remember that, in HTML, if one object is a child of another, it just means that it's inside it. For example, take a look at this HTML:

```
<p>The quick brown fox <em>jumped over</em> the lazy dog.</p>
```

The quick brown fox is a child of the paragraph tag. So is the <em> tag. The text jumped over is a child of the <em> tag, and the lazy dog is the third child of the <p> tag. That's how the DOM tree works. To construct this text using JavaScript, you could use the following code:

```
var newParagraph = document.createElement("p");
someText = document.createTextNode("The quick brown fox ");
newParagraph.appendChild(someText);
var newElement = document.createElement("em");
someText = document.createTextNode("jumped over");
newElement.appendChild(someText);
newParagraph.appendChild(newElement);
someText = document.createTextNode(" the lazy dog.");
newParagraph.appendChild(someText);
document.body.appendChild(newParagraph);
```

Yes, it really is easier to just write the HTML. In any case, let's move on to the next part of the example. The last method of modifying the page is with a button labeled Change Colors. It uses the onclick handler to call the setHeadingColors() function. This function uses the document.getElementsByTagName() to retrieve all instances of the <h1> tag on the page. We then use a loop to iterate over the individual elements (which are stored in a nodeList), and set their color to yellow. It's worth looking at this a bit more closely.

This example demonstrated how to modify the style sheet for a page from JavaScript using the DOM. The style property provides access to all the properties associated with the element it is associated with. In this case, we use style.color to change the color to yellow. By the same token, we could use style.backgroundColor to change the background color. When you transform property names in CSS to attributes in the DOM, the hyphens are removed and the words that follow hyphens are capitalized.

Coping with Reality: Cross-Browser DHTML Techniques

The majority of the day thus far has been devoted to understanding the technologies behind DHTML and how to use them separately. It's time to start creating real DHTML web pages. As I've mentioned, the real challenge is creating DHTML so that you reach the largest possible audience within certain practical limitations. I say *practical* because true DHTML isn't possible in any web browser that doesn't implement scripting or style sheets, and impractical in those that suffer from partial or poor implementations. In other words, using DHTML, you'll never be able to reach 100% of your potential audience.

There are a number of different approaches you can take when creating Dynamic HTML, given that not all browsers are created equal when it comes to support for JavaScript and cascading style sheets. The first option is to create separate pages for separate browsers, or separate style sheets and JavaScript files for separate browsers. This requires a lot of duplicated effort, and can be extremely painful.

The second option is to try to write your code so that it will work with as many browsers as possible, no matter how poor their support for standards is. This is often what happens when Netscape Navigator 4 is in the mix, or even older versions of Internet Explorer. The version 4 generation of browsers was the furthest from standards compliance browsers have ever been. It was common for pages to include massive amounts of extra code that figured out which browser was viewing the page and accounting for how its DHTML model works. This technique is still relatively common, but I'm not going to cover it today.

The third option is to create your pages so that they work in browsers that implement the current web standards, and degrade gracefully in older browsers. Given the small percentage of users who still use older browsers, unless you're specifically required to support them, just making sure that your pages aren't broken in them should be enough.

Sniffing for Browsers

At one time, the most common technique for creating cross-browser DHTML was detecting the user's web browser (commonly called *sniffing*). After you determined which browser the user was using, you could simply execute the code tailored to that browser.

The problem is that there are many browsers out on the market, and many versions of each one. For example, there are two or three versions of both Netscape and Internet Explorer in fairly common usage even today. As you might imagine, accounting for all the available browsers and keeping your scripts up-to-date to accommodate new browsers is a daunting task.

Here's a relatively simple browser sniffer that detects only Netscape Navigator 4 and Microsoft Internet Explorer 4 and up. It doesn't distinguish between Netscape 7 and Netscape 4, which are completely different, and doesn't even take browsers like Opera (or other common browsers) into consideration. You may run into code like the sample that follows, but you shouldn't use such code yourself. The following listing creates variables that parse the appropriate objects to return `true` or `false` values for the final variables: `is_nav4up` and `is_ie4up`.

```
// Trimmed down browser sniffer that
// detects Navigator 4+ and IE 4+.
// Reference is_nav4up and is_ie4up in other
```

```
// portions of the script.
var agt = navigator.userAgent.toLowerCase();
var is_major = parseInt(navigator.appVersion);
var is_minor = parseFloat(navigator.appVersion);
var is_nav = ((agt.indexOf('mozilla')!=-1) && (agt.indexOf('spoofer')==-1)
       && (agt.indexOf('compatible') == -1) && (agt.indexOf('opera')==-1)
       && (agt.indexOf('Webtv')==-1));
var is_nav4up = (is_nav && (is_major >= 4));
var is_ie  = (agt.indexOf("msie") != -1);
var is_ie4up = (is_ie && (is_major >= 4));
```

To check for the existence of Netscape Navigator 4 and Microsoft Internet Explorer 4 and later versions, use the following script:

```
if (is_nav4up) {
  do something }
if (is_ie4up) {
  do something else }
```

You'll see that later as you perform some more scripting. The overall browser sniffer function exists solely to return the proper variables to you so that you can check in other portions of your script. By itself, it won't actually take any action.

The following example shows the browser sniffer in action. The body element of the web page calls the doSniff function, which in turn, creates a variable called sniff and assigns it a string value to display, depending on the browser version it detects.

Input ▼

```
<!DOCTYPE html PUBLIC "-//W3C//DTD XHTML 1.0 Transitional//EN"
"http://www.w3.org/TR/xhtml1/DTD/transitional.dtd">

<html>
<head>
<title>Browser Sniffing</title>
<meta http-equiv="Content-Script-Type" content="text/javascript" />

<script language="javascript" type="text/javascript">
<!-- Hide JavaScript

// Trimmed down browser sniffer that
// detects Navigator 4+ and IE 4+.
// Reference is_nav4up and is_ie4up in other
// portions of the script.
var agt = navigator.userAgent.toLowerCase();
var is_major = parseInt(navigator.appVersion);
var is_minor = parseFloat(navigator.appVersion);
var is_nav = ((agt.indexOf('mozilla')!=-1) && (agt.indexOf('spoofer')==-1)
       && (agt.indexOf('compatible') == -1) && (agt.indexOf('opera')==-1)
       && (agt.indexOf('Webtv')==-1));
```

```
var is_nav4up = (is_nav && (is_major >= 4));
var is_ie   = (agt.indexOf("msie") != -1);
var is_ie4up = (is_ie && (is_major >= 4));


// Function to display the browser version
function doSniff() {
  var sniff
  if (is_nav4up == true) {
    sniff = "Netscape Navigator 4+" }
  if (is_ie4up == true) {
    sniff = "Microsoft Internet Explorer 4+" }
  alert(sniff);
}
// end hide -->
</script>
</head>
<body onload="doSniff()">
</body>
</html>
```

Figure 15.2 shows the result in Mozilla Firefox.

Output ▼

FIGURE 15.2
Sniffing for the
web browser
detects the
browser version.

Detecting Capabilities

There are several big problems with relying on browser detection to make sure that your scripts work across multiple browsers. When new browsers are released, you have to go back through all your scripts that include browser detection and update them to account for the new browsers. Another problem is that if a browser you didn't account for supports the features included on your page, you might be denying access to people for no reason.

Rather than trying to determine the user's browser and then running the JavaScript code for it, it makes more sense to test whether the browser supports the specific feature you're going to use. Let's try an analogy: You've rented a car and you want to turn on the air conditioner. The problem is that you're not sure whether the car even *has* an air conditioner. To find this out, you could get the year, make, and model of the car and then look it up in a service manual. This is what browser detection is. On the other hand, you could just look at the dashboard of the car and see whether it has an air conditioner. This is how capability detection works.

This might seem like an oversimplification, but that's really all there is to it. Before you call a particular piece of code, you just have to test whether the browser supports the objects associated with the code you're calling. Back in Lesson 13, I gave you a sneak preview of this technique. Before I attempted to perform an image rollover, I tested whether the browser supported the `document.images` object—if it didn't, I knew that the rollover wouldn't work and moved on.

Testing for the Existence of Objects

Let me explain how this works in more detail. JavaScript is an object-oriented language, so you generally deal with objects that both contain data and have methods that can be called to perform various tasks. You can easily test for the existence of objects and, if they exist, call methods of those objects to perform the tasks you want to accomplish.

Using JavaScript to Manipulate Elements

In the world of Dynamic HTML, one of the most important tags you'll use is `<div>`. This tag is just a container into which you can put other elements. In Lesson 9, you saw that I used `<div>`s for just about everything. In Dynamic HTML, you'll see the very same thing. It's perfect because it enables you to group together some elements without any extra formatting baggage.

Once you've placed content within a `<div>` (or any other block level element), you can use JavaScript to manipulate its properties in the same way you set those properties when the page is displayed using CSS.

Back in Lesson 9, you learned how to place elements you want to apply styles to inside a `<div>`, and how to position those elements using CSS. Now we can combine that knowledge with the JavaScript you've learned and start putting the *dynamic* in Dynamic HTML.

Let's look at some basic techniques that will serve you well when you build your own DHTML applications.

Hiding and Revealing Elements

One CSS property that I haven't talked about yet is `visibility`. The two values for this attribute that you'll use are `hidden` and `visible`. Manipulating this property using JavaScript enables you to hide or reveal elements on a page.

I'm going to modify a page with the two overlapping elements so that if you click on one of the menus of links, the other is hidden. The results appear in Figure 15.3.

Input ▼

```
<!DOCTYPE html PUBLIC "-//W3C//DTD XHTML 1.0 Strict//EN"
  "http://www.w3.org/TR/xhtml1/DTD/xhtml1-strict.dtd">
<html xmlns="http://www.w3.org/1999/xhtml">
<head>
<title>DHTML Test</title>
<script language="JavaScript">

function hideMenu(idToHide)
{
  if (document.childNodes)
  {
    document.getElementById(idToHide).style.visibility = 'hidden';
  }
}

</script>

<style type="text/css">
  #menu
  {
    font-family: Verdana, sans-serif;
    padding: 10px;
    border: 1px solid black;
    background-color: #ffc;
    width: 150px;
    position: absolute;
    top: 50px;
    left: 50px;
    z-index: 5;
  }

  #menu2
  {
    font-family: Verdana, sans-serif;
    padding: 10px;
    border: 1px solid black;
    background-color: #cff;
    width: 150px;
    position: absolute;
    top: 100px;
    left: 100px;
    z-index: 1;
  }
</style>
</head>
```

```
<body>
<div onclick="hideMenu('menu2');" id="menu"><b>Links</b><br />
<a href="http://www.yahoo.com/">Yahoo</a><br />
<a href="http://www.salon.com/">Salon</a><br />
<a href="http://www.slashdot.org/">Slashdot</a><br />
</div>
<div onclick="hideMenu('menu');" id="menu2"><b>More Links</b><br />
<a href="http://www.google.com/">Google</a><br />
<a href="http://www.slate.com/">Slate</a><br />
<a href="http://www.wired.com/">Wired</a><br />
</div>
</body>
</html>
```

Output ▼

FIGURE 15.3
Overlapping
absolutely posi-
tioned elements.
Clicking on one of
the menus hides
the other.

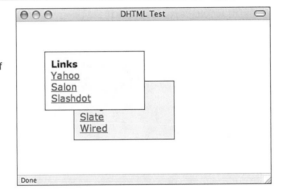

When a user clicks on one of the menus, the other menu is hidden. One thing you'll notice about this page is that as soon as you click on one of the menus, you're out of luck because the other one is hidden and you can't get it back. You could easily add a button to the page that calls a function to reveal them both again if you wanted. We'll look at some other ways to manipulate them soon.

The style sheets and <div> elements should look pretty standard. The onclick event handler included in the <div> tag for each menu calls a function called hideMenu(), and passes the ID of the menu to hide as a parameter. In the hideMenu() function, we first test for the presence of document.childNodes, which indicates that the browser has DOM support. If it does, we use document.getElementById to get a reference to the menu we want to hide, and I set the visibility property to hidden.

Moving Objects Around

As you've seen, it's possible to position elements on a page in a specific spot using style sheets. After they're positioned, you can move them around the page using JavaScript.

Here's a really simple script that keeps the menu out from under the mouse. It's not very useful if you actually want to use the links on the menu, but it's fun to play with.

Here's the source code for the page, which is shown in Figure 15.4:

Input ▼

```
<!DOCTYPE html PUBLIC "-//W3C//DTD XHTML 1.0 Strict//EN"
  "http://www.w3.org/TR/xhtml1/DTD/xhtml1-strict.dtd">
<html xmlns="http://www.w3.org/1999/xhtml">
<head>
<title>DHTML Test</title>
<script language="JavaScript">
function flee(menu)
{
  menu.style.left = ((Math.random() * 80) + 10) + '%';
  menu.style.top = ((Math.random() * 80) + 10) + '%';
}
</script>

<style type="text/css">
  #menu
  {
    font-family: Verdana, sans-serif;
    padding: 10px;
    border: 1px solid black;
    background-color: #ffc;
    width: 150px;
    position: absolute;
    top: 40%;
    left: 40%;
  }
</style>
</head>
<body>
<div onmouseover="flee(this);" id="menu"><b>Links</b><br />
<a href="http://www.yahoo.com/">Yahoo</a><br />
<a href="http://www.salon.com/">Salon</a><br />
<a href="http://www.slashdot.org/">Slashdot</a><br />
</div>
</body>
</html>
```

Output ▼

FIGURE 15.4
A page with an
element that
moves out of the
way of the user's
mouse.

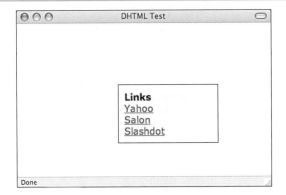

This page uses the same `<div>` and style sheet that we've used in the past few examples. In this case, though, the onmouseover event handler associated with the `<div>` calls the flee() function. We pass in a reference to the `<div>` and the function automatically sets the position of the `<div>` to a random location on the page.

Creating a DHTML Pull-Down Menu

Let's look at a common application of DHTML that you'll see on many websites: a pull-down menu implemented in Dynamic HTML. The menu that we've used in the past few examples makes yet another appearance here. In this case, we've created a navigation bar across the top of the page. When the user puts the mouse pointer over the button in the navigation bar, the menu appears (and the button is highlighted). As long as the mouse pointer is over the button or the menu, the menu is displayed. Once the user removes the pointer, the menu will disappear after a 1-second delay. The page also contains some text to show that the menu does not disrupt the page layout. This page illustrates how to create a dynamic HTML interface, and shows just how many event handlers and functions are required to do so. One of the other puzzles is how to make sure that the menu appears in the correct position. Before I explain how it all works, here's the source code:

Input ▼

```
<!DOCTYPE html PUBLIC "-//W3C//DTD XHTML 1.0 Strict//EN"
  "http://www.w3.org/TR/xhtml1/DTD/xhtml1-strict.dtd">
<html xmlns="http://www.w3.org/1999/xhtml">
<head>
<title>DHTML Test</title>
<script language="JavaScript">
function highlightAndPersist(button)
{
  button.style.backgroundColor = '#ffc';
  persist();
}
```

```
function unhighlight(button)
{
  button.style.backgroundColor = '#ccf';
}

function persist()
{
  var menu = document.getElementById('menu');
  var button = document.getElementById('linkbutton');
  menu.style.position = 'absolute';
  menu.style.top = (button.offsetTop + button.offsetHeight) + 'px';
  menu.style.left = (button.offsetLeft) + 'px';
  menu.style.visibility = 'visible';
}

function hideSoon()
{
  setTimeout("hide()", 1000);
}

function hide()
{
  var menu = document.getElementById("menu");
  menu.style.visibility = "hidden";
}
</script>

<style type="text/css">
  body { margin: 0px; }
  #menu
  {
    font-family: Verdana, sans-serif;
    padding: 10px;
    border: 1px solid black;
    background-color: #ffc;
    width: 150px;
    visibility: hidden;
    position: absolute;
    top: 0px;
    left: 0px;
  }

  #navbar
  {
    font: 18px Verdana, sans-serif;
    width: 100%;
    height: 30px;
    background-color: #ccf;
    padding: 0px;
  }
```

15

```
.button
{
  width: 80px;
  height: 30px;
  text-align: center;
}

p { margin: 10px; }
</style>
</head>
<body>
<div id="navbar">
<div id="linkbutton" class="button" onmouseover="highlightAndPersist(this);"
  onmouseout="unhighlight(this);">
<b><a href="" onmouseover="persist();" onclick="return false;">Links</a></b>
</div>
</div>
<div id="menu" onmouseout="hideSoon();" onmouseover="persist();">
<a onmouseover="persist();" href="http://www.yahoo.com/">Yahoo</a><br />
<a onmouseover="persist();" href="http://www.salon.com/">Salon</a><br />
<a onmouseover="persist();" href="http://www.slashdot.org/">Slashdot</a><br />
</div>

<p>
Friends, Romans, countrymen, lend me your ears;<br />
I come to bury Caesar, not to praise him.<br />
The evil that men do lives after them;<br />
The good is oft interred with their bones;<br />
So let it be with Caesar. The noble Brutus<br />
Hath told you Caesar was ambitious:<br />
If it were so, it was a grievous fault,<br />
And grievously hath Caesar answer'd it.<br />
Here, under leave of Brutus and the rest--<br />
For Brutus is an honourable man;<br />
So are they all, all honourable men--<br />
Come I to speak in Caesar's funeral.<br />
</p>

</body>
</html>
```

Figure 15.5 shows what the pop-up menu looks like when it appears.

Output ▼

FIGURE 15.5

A pull-down menu implemented using DHTML.

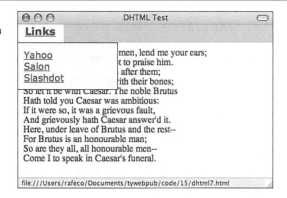

Take a look at the style sheet first. Many of the rules are required to make the page look right. I also set up specific styles for the navigation bar and buttons on the navigation bar. The style applied to the menu sets its absolute position to the upper-left corner of the page, but it's also set as invisible. We'll take care of positioning it with JavaScript a bit later.

Looking at the body of the page, you can see all the event handlers we use. The `<div>` with the ID `linkbutton` is the actual button that causes the menu to appear. It has two event handlers associated with it: `onmouseover` and `onmouseout`. When the pointer is moved over it, the `highlightAndPersist()` function is called, and when the mouse moves away, `unhighlight()` is called. The `highlightAndPersist()` function highlights the button in the navigation bar and displays the menu. The `unhighlight()` function turns off the button highlighting without hiding the menu.

The link itself that's inside the button also has two event handlers: `onmouseover` and `onclick`. The `onclick` is just used to turn off the link so the user doesn't navigate away without seeing the menu. If you wanted to set up the page so that users who don't have browsers that support DHTML can still benefit from the navigation bar, you could take out the `onclick` handler and put the URL for the links page in the link. The `onmouseover` event handler calls `persist()`, which displays the menu.

The `<div>` containing the menu also has two event handlers: `onmouseout` and `onmouseover`. The `onmouseout` handler calls `hideSoon()`, which waits 1 second and then hides the menu. The `onmouseover` handler calls `persist()`, which displays the menu. This ensures that the menu stays open as long as the mouse is over the menu. Finally, each of the links in the menu also has an `onmouseover` handler that calls `persist()` so that the menu stays open when the user moves his mouse over the links themselves.

Now let's look at the JavaScript code. You've already seen most of this stuff; it has just been put together in a different way. The `persist()` function is in charge of positioning and displaying the menu. First, I grab two references—one to the menu and the other to the menu button. Were there multiple menus, this function would take the IDs of the button and menu as parameters. Once I have the references I need, it's time to display the menu. I set the `position` property to `absolute`, just in case. Then I set the `top` and `left` properties of the menu based on the position of the button associated with the menu:

```
menu.style.top = (button.offsetTop + button.offsetHeight) + 'px';
menu.style.left = (button.offsetLeft) + 'px';
```

The `offsetTop`, `offsetLeft`, and `offsetHeight` properties are available for any visual element on a page. I determine where to put the top of the menu by adding the height of the button to the top position of the menu. That places it immediately under the button. The left side of the menu should line up with the left side of the button, so I just used `offsetLeft` for the `left` position of the menu.

The other functions are less interesting. The `highlightAndPersist()` function just changes the background color of the button and calls `persist()`. The `unhighlight()` function just changes the background color of the button back to what it was. The `hide()` function sets the visibility of the menu back to `hidden`. There's a bit more going on in `hideSoon()`. It uses the `setTimeout()` function to wait 1,000 milliseconds (one second) and then call the `hide()` function. This improves the usability of the page a bit by giving the user a chance to see the menu even if he mouses out of it by mistake.

Continuing Your DHTML Education

I encourage you to visit both the Microsoft and Netscape websites devoted to DHTML. Each offers an interesting perspective.

The Microsoft website has a ton of great information for using HTML and DHTML with Internet Explorer:

http://msdn.microsoft.com/workshop/author/dhtml/dhtml_node_entry.asp

Netscape appears to be leading the cross-browser compatibility charge and has extensive articles and technical notes at http://devedge.netscape.com/. You might also find http://www.mozilla.org/docs/dom/ interesting.

Other sites that have useful information include the following:

- **WebReference Dynamic HTML Lab (http://www.Webreference.com/dhtml/)**—Contains examples and code ranging from drag-and-drop DHTML to expandable menus and outlines
- **Brainjar (http://www.brainjar.com)**—Offers a library of JavaScript functions for adding DHTML to web pages

Connecting to a Server with AJAX

The aspect that dynamic HTML adds to regular HTML is the capability to manipulate elements on a page without sending requests back to the server to reload the entire page. You can hide or display items or even change their contents using JavaScript, Cascading Style Sheets, and the DOM. Using a JavaScript feature called XmlHttpRequest, you can take dynamic HTML one step further by requesting data from the server and incorporating it on the page without reloading the entire page. The technique is commonly referred to as AJAX, which is short for Asynchronous JavaScript + XML, and was originally described that way in an article by Jesse James Garrett of Adaptive Path.

So far, you've seen how JavaScript can be used to manipulate objects that are already present on a web page. With XmlHttpRequest, you can write JavaScript that actually makes a call back to the server, submitting and receiving data. Let's say you have a web page that displays baseball scores and you want the scores to be updated automatically to show the progress of the games. Ordinarily, you would automatically refresh the entire page every so often, or the user could reload the page using her browser to get the most recent scores. Using AJAX, you could add some JavaScript to the page that goes back to the server and gets the latest scores periodically, updating that information while leaving the rest of the page intact.

This provides users with a more seamless experience and saves bandwidth on your server, as the only parts that are downloaded are those that actually change. Dynamic HTML took web programmers most of the way toward creating web applications that work like desktop applications, and AJAX closes that gap even further.

How AJAX Works

AJAX depends on XmlHttpRequest. It was originally added to Microsoft Internet Explorer 5 as an ActiveX object, and has since been added to other browsers as a built-in JavaScript object. XmlHttpRequest will submit a request to a web server where the enclosing page is stored and return the results so that they can be used within the web page that made the XmlHttpRequest request. For security reasons, XmlHttpRequest only allows connections back to the web server where the page making the request is stored. In other words, if the page containing the XmlHttpRequest call is http://www.example.com/ajax.html, the browser could only submit requests to www.example.com.

Originally, XmlHttpRequest was intended to retrieve XML documents from the server, but in actuality it can retrieve any content as long as it's text. You can then incorporate the results into your page using the DHTML techniques you've already seen in this lesson. The first step in using XmlHttpRequest is creating the object. As I mentioned, Internet Explorer and other browsers handle XmlHttpRequest differently, so you have to use the capability detection features that I mentioned in the "Creating an Image

Rollover" section in Lesson 13, "Using JavaScript in Your Pages," to properly create the object. This also enables you to avoid running into problems with browsers that don't support XmlHttpRequest at all. Here's the code:

```
if (window.XMLHttpRequest) {
    request = new XMLHttpRequest();
}
else if (window.ActiveXObject) {
    request = new ActiveXObject("Microsoft.XMLHTTP");
}
```

First I check to see whether the browser provides XmlHttpRequest as a property of the window object. If it does (as browsers other than Internet Explorer do), I use the new keyword to create a new XmlHttpRequest object. If it does not, I check to see whether the browser supports the ActiveXObject property of window. Only Internet Explorer provides that feature, so if that check returns true, I can create an XmlHttpRequest object using ActiveX. The XmlHttpRequest object, once created, works the same in all browsers that support it. Here's how you use it to retrieve information from the server:

```
request.onreadystatechange = processReadyStateChange;
request.open("POST", "remote.cgi", true);
request.send("user=test");
```

I'll explain the first line last. The second line is used to specify the request method and URL for the connection. The first argument, "POST" in this example, is the request method to use. You can use "GET" or "POST" here, just as you can with the action attribute of the <form> element, as discussed in Lesson 10, "Designing Forms." The second argument is the URL. Since the request must go to the server where the page resides, you can just use a relative or absolute URL. There's no need to specify the server or protocol. In this case, the script would submit the request to remote.cgi in the same directory as the page containing this code. The final argument specifies whether the request should be asynchronous, and can be either true or false. You'll almost certainly want to use true here all the time. If you don't set the request to be asynchronous, the browser will wait for the request to complete before letting the user do anything.

Once you've created the connection, you need to send data over the connection using the send() method. If you use the GET method, you can just use an empty string ("") here. If you use POST, you'll include the actual data to send with the request as the argument to the send() method. Once again, think about the request as a form submission. You can gather data from form elements on the page and pass it to send() to submit the form via XmlHttpRequest rather than submitting the form itself. The data passed to send() should be encoded using URL encoding, as discussed in Lesson 10. After the data is submitted, your script has to handle the response from the server. That's where the first line comes in. In order to deal with the response, you have to register a function to handle events associated with XmlHttpRequest. You'd think that you could just write some JavaScript to handle the results and put it in your script after the line that sends the data to the server, but that's not how XmlHttpRequest works. Remember that I mentioned that XmlHttpRequest can be used asynchronously. What that means is that once the script sends the request, your code can go on and do other things while the browser deals with handling the results of the request.

The browser processes the response by generating events. If you want to do anything with the results, you have to register a function as the handler for those events. I discussed event handlers back in Lesson 12, and I showed how you can register a function to handle them by using attributes of elements using attributes such as onclick or onchange. For example, if you wanted to register a handler for an onclick event for a link, you could use this code:

```
<a href="/" id="mylink" onclick="linkClicked()">My link</a>
```

There's another way to register a handler as well, entirely within a script. If you wanted to use JavaScript to register the event handler for the link, which I helpfully gave the ID mylink, you could do it like this:

```
document.getElementById("mylink").onclick = linkClicked;
```

One thing to note is that I don't include the () after linkClicked in the JavaScript example. That's because I want to associate the function named linkClicked with that event. If I include the parentheses, the script will actually call the function and assign the results to the onclick property. I want the function itself in this case.

OK, back to XmlHttpRequest. As I mentioned, the browser handles the response by generating events. I specified the handler for those events on this line:

```
request.onreadystatechange = processReadyStateChange;
```

That line says that onreadystatechange events for the XmlHttpRequest object should be passed to a function named processReadyStateChange. When a response is being processed, it goes through multiple states before it's finished. Those states are listed in Table 15.2.

TABLE 15.2   XmlHttpRequest States

State	Description
0	The open() method has not been called.
1	The send() method has not been called.
2	The send() method has been called but the response headers have not been sent back.
3	Some response data has been received.
4	All of the response data has been received.

15

As you can probably guess, the states progress from 0 to 4. The function you associate with onreadystatechange is called every time the state advances. Here's what such a function looks like:

```
function onreadystatechange() {
    if (request.readyState == 4) {
        window.alert("Finished!");
    }
}
```

This function examines the readyState property of the XmlHttpRequest object to see what the current state of the request is. This function will be called once for every state change, but it doesn't do anything until state 4 is reached and the request is finished. At that point, it just displays an alert. Most handlers will be written like this because the only state you care about is state 4. In addition to readyState, XmlHttpRequest has other properties, which are listed in Table 15.3.

TABLE 15.3   XmlHttpRequest Properties

Property	Description
onreadystatechange	The function specified to handle state change events
readyState	The current ready state for the object
responseText	The response sent by the server
status	The HTTP status code of the response
statusText	The text message associated with the HTTP status

Once you've reached readyState 4, you can access the data passed back from the server via the responseText property and deal with it as you wish.

An AJAX Example

Now that you understand how AJAX works, here's an actual page that applies these principles. In this example, I've created a page that allows you to update the current temperature by pressing a button. I use XmlHttpRequest to retrieve the current temperature, and use JavaScript to replace a <div> on the page with data from the server. Here's the source code for the page:

Input ▼

```
<!DOCTYPE html PUBLIC "-//W3C//DTD XHTML 1.1//EN"
    "http://www.w3.org/TR/xhtml11/DTD/xhtml11.dtd">

<html xmlns="http://www.w3.org/1999/xhtml" version="-//W3C//DTD XHTML 1.1//EN"
xml:lang="en">
```

```
<head>
    <title>AJAX Example</title>
    <script language="JavaScript">
    var request = false;

    function sendAjaxRequest(toUrl) {
        if (window.XMLHttpRequest) {
            request = new XMLHttpRequest();
        }
        else if (window.ActiveXObject) {
            request = new ActiveXObject("Microsoft.XMLHTTP");
        }

        if (request) {
            request.onreadystatechange = processReadyStateChange;
            request.open('GET', toUrl, true);
            request.send("");
        }
    }

    function updateTemperature(msg) {
        var contentDiv = document.getElementById("ajaxTarget");
        contentDiv.innerHTML = msg;
    }

    function getLatestTemp() {
        sendAjaxRequest("temp.txt");
    }

    function processReadyStateChange() {
        if (request.readyState == 4) {
            if (request.status == 200) {
                updateTemperature(request.responseText);
            }
            else {
                alert("An error occurred.");
            }
        }
    }
    </script>
</head>

<body>
    <p>
        Current temperature:
        <div id="ajaxTarget" style="font-size: x-large;">90 degrees</div>
    </p>

    <p>
        <button onclick="getLatestTemp()">Update Temperature</button>
    </p>
</body>
</html>
```

15

The page appears in Figure 15.6.

Output ▼

FIGURE 15.6
A page that uses AJAX to update the current temperature.

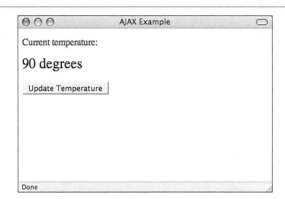

As you can see, the HTML section of the page is relatively short. All I have is a paragraph containing a `<div>` that contains the current temperature and another paragraph with a button that's used to update the temperature.

When the user clicks on the Update Temperature link, the function specified in the `onclick` handler—`getLatestTemp()`—is called. That function contains a single line of code:

```
sendAjaxRequest("temp.txt");
```

This code just calls another function I wrote called `sendAjaxRequest()`. The argument is the URL for the content on the server. Ordinarily, the URL would point to a script that looks up the current temperature and transmits it back to the user. In this case, I have a text file on the server in the same directory as this page, and `XmlHttpRequest` is happy to retrieve it. The `temp.txt` file contains only the following text:

```
55 degrees
```

The code in the `sendAjaxRequest()` function should look familiar, since I just explained how it works. I create a new `XmlHttpRequest` object, assign a handler to the `onreadystatechange` event, open the connection, and send the request data. One thing you might notice is that I declare the `request` variable at the top level of my script rather than within my function. That's so that the variable is visible to the handler function as well as to the function where it is assigned.

I also test to make sure that my attempts to create the `XmlHttpRequest` object were successful prior to calling any of its methods. That way I won't produce errors in older browsers that don't support `XmlHttpRequest`. In this script, my event handling function does a lot more than the previous one. Here's the source:

```
function processReadyStateChange() {
    if (request.readyState == 4) {
        if (request.status == 200) {
            updateTemperature(request.responseText);
        }
        else {
            alert("An error occurred.");
        }
    }
}
```

As in the preceding code, the script only cares about readyState 4. It ignores all of the state changes leading up to it. Once readyState 4 has been reached, it checks the status property of the XmlHttpRequest object. A status of 200 means that the request was successful and the script received the text it wants. If the status is anything else, an error message is displayed. If the request was successful then the script calls the updateTemperature function, passing in the response text as an argument.

In this case, temp.txt contains only the temperature to be displayed. More involved scripts could produce complex data structures represented as XML that the page has to unpack, but in this example I just want to take the result and display it. That's what updateTemperature() is for:

```
function updateTemperature(msg) {
    var contentDiv = document.getElementById("ajaxTarget");
    contentDiv.innerHTML = msg;
}
```

The code uses the getElementById() function to obtain a reference to the <div> on the page. It then replaces its current contents with the response text using the innerHTML property.

As I said before, a real-life example would be significantly more complex, but this example illustrates how AJAX is used in a simple case. Unlike the other examples you've seen in this book so far, you'd have to put both the HTML page and temp.txt file on a web server in order for the example to work. XmlHttpRequest relies on the HTTP protocol, and its security constraints require the target to be on the same server as the page making the call.

In Lesson 20, "Understanding Server-Side Processing," you'll learn how to write the kinds of scripts that are used to produce dynamic results for AJAX calls, unlike the static text file I provided for this example.

Be Careful with AJAX

AJAX is relatively new, and isn't supported in older browsers. As with dynamic HTML, you should make sure that your site is usable by people who can't take advantage of any of the features you provide using AJAX.

AJAX can also be used in such a way that it breaks well-established web browsing conventions, such as the Back button. You should use AJAX to supplement your site, and not to implement the entire thing. Your users will probably be used to the way that most other websites work, and using too much AJAX may confuse them.

Summary

Today, you learned that Dynamic HTML is comprised of three technologies: HTML, style sheets, and scripting. Each one is important to DHTML and plays a distinct role. HTML provides the foundation for the web page. Style sheets enable you to format and position elements to suit your taste. Scripting makes DHTML dynamic.

I explained how to use the DOM to manipulate elements on web pages, and some techniques for dealing with cross-browser issues. I also provided some specific examples that demonstrate how to use DHTML, including a page that includes a DHTML pull-down menu. I also explained how AJAX is used to update parts of a page that's being presented with data retrieved from the server.

Workshop

This workshop includes some questions you might have, a quiz about some of today's most important topics, and some exercises you can do to reinforce your knowledge of DHTML.

Q&A

Q Is DHTML really worth the time and effort?

A DHTML is the key to web applications taking on the functionality of desktop applications. If you use applications such as Google Mail, Yahoo! Mail, or any of the online mapping services, you'll see DHTML used in many ways to make the applications more interactive than the typical web page. If you're working on an application that would benefit from giving the user instant feedback in the user interface, then learning DHTML is for you. If you're publishing a static website, you can probably skip it.

Q There's so much information to learn. How do I do it?

A First, start with HTML. Become an expert in it!

After that, you could take either of two approaches: master everything or learn only what you need.

The "master everything" approach leads you, in succession, from HTML to CSS, and then to JavaScript, moving on only when you're competent and comfortable with the technology at hand. After you master all three technologies, study how they interrelate and try your hand at DHTML.

The "learn only what you need" approach gets you started more quickly. Find a specific technique that you want to use, such as dynamically changing the visibility of an object, and learn how to do that. After you finish, go on to the next technique that you find interesting. You'll learn a little bit about all the technologies along the way, but will have DHTML to show for it almost immediately.

You might also want to find DHTML code on sites around the Web and see how it works. Although most code is protected by copyright, there's certainly nothing wrong with reviewing it and applying the concepts to your own work.

Q What about Netscape's LAYER element and other browser-specific DHTML features?

A As far as I'm concerned, cross-browser DHTML is where it's at if you're going to bother with DHTML at all. If you want to reach the greatest number of people (and offend the fewest), you should concentrate on creating web pages that are (relatively) universal. I admit that these proprietary web browser features can be very tempting, and that some of the effects are pretty neat; however, there's nothing more frustrating than spending weeks developing a cool DHTML web page and finding out that most people can't even see it.

Quiz

1. Which three technologies make Dynamic HTML possible?
2. What is a Document Object Model?
3. Can you use VBScript or another scripting language to create DHTML?
4. What's the most important element of cross-browser DHTML?
5. Which XmlHttpRequest ready state is the most important?

Quiz Answers

1. HTML, cascading style sheets, and scripting.

2. DOM is the language you use when you refer to scriptable objects on a web page.

3. Yes, but you should know that VBScript isn't supported in Netscape Navigator without a special plug-in. Other scripting languages are even less supported. JavaScript is your best choice.

4. Undoubtedly, the capability detection. This enables you to support not only today's browsers, but also browsers that haven't been released yet.

5. State 4 is the most important, because it indicates that the request is complete and the data returned by the request is ready for you to use on your web page.

Exercises

1. Create a list and let users add items to it by entering them in a text field, and remove items from it by clicking on them. (You'll need to add an `onclick` handler to your list items.)

2. Create a `<div>` that only appears when you move the mouse over a particular element on a page.

3. Copy the pull-down menu example and add a second menu.

PART V:
Designing Effective Web Pages

LESSON 16:
Writing Good Web Pages: Do's and Don'ts

You won't learn about any HTML tags today, or how to convert files from one strange file format to another. You're mostly done with the HTML part of web page design. Next come the intangibles. These are the things that separate your pages from those of a designer who just knows the tags and flings text and graphics around and calls it a site.

Armed with the information from the previous 15 days, you could put this book down now and go off and merrily create web pages to your heart's content. However, if you stick around, you can create *better* web pages. Do you need any more incentive to continue reading?

In this Lesson

Today's lesson includes hints for creating well-written and well-designed web pages, and it highlights do's and don'ts concerning the following:

- How to decide whether to use standard XHTML 1.0 tags, a subset of HTML 4.01 tags that works with older browsers, style sheets, HTML extensions, or a combination of two or more

- How to write your web pages so that they can be easily scanned and read

- Issues concerning the design and layout of your web pages

- When and why you should create links

- How to use images effectively

- Other miscellaneous tidbits and hints

Standards Compliance

In some ways, we're through the dark ages when it comes to cross-browser issues. The generation of browsers that includes Netscape Navigator 4 and Internet Explorer 4 probably marked the low point for web developers in terms of deciding how pages should be written. In the heat of the browser wars, Netscape and Microsoft were adding new features to their browsers hand over fist, with no regard for published standards. These features tended to be at odds with each other, and for web designers to create complex pages that worked in both popular browsers, they had to use some really awful techniques to make things look okay. Worse, the differences made things like CSS and JavaScript nearly useless. Even if you could get things to work properly, the work involved was immense.

Since then, Netscape released the source code to its browser and the Mozilla foundation rewrote it to adhere as closely as possible to web standards. Internet Explorer has also been improving on the standards front with every release, although Internet Explorer 6 (the current version) still has some nagging bugs that web developers have to work around. Even so, when you look at the various generations of browsers that have been released, there are still some pitfalls that you might face. Every browser ever released is still being used by somebody; it's up to you to decide the degree to which you want to accommodate them. Here are some examples of the different generations of technology that are out there:

- HTML 2.0 tags
- HTML 3.2 features such as tables, divisions, backgrounds, and color, which are supported by most, but not all, browsers
- HTML 4.01 and related features such as cascading style sheets, Dynamic HTML, and framesets
- XHTML 1.0, the enhancement to HTML 4.0 that makes HTML markup more uniform and makes it compatible with XML
- Plug-ins and other embedded objects, which use files and data that are external to the browser
- Browser-specific tags (from Netscape or Internet Explorer) that may or may not end up as part of the official HTML specification and whose support varies from browser to browser

If you're finding all this information rather mind-boggling, you're not alone. Other authors and developers just like you are trying to sort out the mess and make decisions based on how they want their pages to look. Cascading style sheets and Dynamic HTML do give you more flexibility with layout and content in HTML 4.01 and XHTML 1.0.

However, they're not supported (or worse, supported improperly) by many older browsers. These browsers are still used by only a small percentage of users, but many high-traffic sites still take them into account.

Choosing a strategy for using HTML is one of the more significant design decisions you'll make as you start creating web pages. There are really three approaches you can take with your markup. You can refer to them as "least common denominator," "maximum compatibility," and "graceful degradation." None of the three makes a whole lot of sense just given the name, so I'll explain each of the three approaches.

The least common denominator approach basically just involves using the tags and techniques that work everywhere. Rather than worrying about advanced approaches to control look and feel, use the simplest tags possible to convey your information. Taking this approach guarantees that your pages will look fine on old browsers, new browsers, handheld devices, and just about everything else. You won't win any design awards this way, but you'll succeed in communicating with your users. This approach makes sense when you're publishing basic documents to your Intranet or basic text information on the Web. When you're writing up those instructions on how to install a CD burner in a PC, this approach works great. Sticking with paragraphs, lists, links, and basic tables makes it easy to create your pages, and ensures that your pages are viewable by the widest possible audience.

The maximum compatibility approach still dominates web design. The goal of this approach is to make sure that your design looks exactly the same for users regardless of the browser and platform that they're using. The design appears the same for Mac users with Netscape 4.5 or PC users with Internet Explorer 6—at least that's the goal. Generally this approach involves the heavy use of tables for page layout, invisible single-pixel GIFs for spacing, and lots of other trickery that creates web pages with incredible numbers of tags and brittle layouts that are full of workarounds. This approach is finally starting to fade away, even for the most popular websites. They may use some of the older techniques, but they're moving to more CSS-oriented approaches.

The last approach I'll discuss is the graceful degradation approach. It sounds bad, but in fact, it's really nice if you're a web designer. The idea here is that you use basic tags that work with just about any web browser, and you use Cascading Style Sheets to manage the look and feel of your page. Anyone using a modern web browser that offers good support for CSS will see your page in all its splendor, whereas people using older browsers will see a simple page that, although it lacks advanced formatting, at least doesn't look broken. The advantage for you as the web designer is that your pages can be written simply and cleanly without lots of browser-specific workarounds. The downside of this approach is that users with older browsers are treated as lesser citizens by your site. Fortunately, not many people are using older browsers these days, and that number is growing smaller all the time.

16

TIP

The graceful degradation approach actually makes a nice complement to the least common denominator approach. Once you've designed your pages using the least common denominator approach, you can modify their appearance using Cascading Style Sheets. That way the pages will look fine in older browsers and will take on the improved appearance you specify in browsers that support CSS.

In light of these different approaches to writing HTML, let's look at the current HTML standards. The HTML 4.01 and XHTML 1.0 definitions include three flavors of HTML, and the main differences between HTML 4.01 and XHTML 1.0 have been noted throughout this book. The three flavors are

- **HTML 4.01 or XHTML 1.0 Transitional** is geared toward the web developer who still uses deprecated tags rather than migrating to CSS. For example, if you want to write valid pages that include <font> tags, and attributes of the <body> tag like bgcolor or text, this is your best bet.
- **HTML 4.01 or XHTML 1.0 Frameset** is a strict specification that includes the frame-related tags. You should use this standard when you're writing framed pages.
- **HTML 4.01 or XHTML 1.0 Strict** is for people who don't have deprecated tags in their documents. This specification basically mandates that tags are used strictly for page structure, and that all of your look-and-feel modifications are accomplished using CSS.

Throughout this book, I've explained which tags are part of HTML 4.01 and XHTML 1.0 and which tags are available in which major browsers. For each tag, I've also noted the alternatives you can use if a browser can't view that tag. With this information in hand, you should be able to experiment with each tag in different browsers to see the effect on your design.

Regardless of the strategy you use for creating content, the key to making sure everything works is to test it as widely as possible. If you're concerned about how your page looks in Netscape 4.7 on a Macintosh, you'll need to test it in Netscape 4.7 on the Macintosh. After a while, you'll get the feel for how things are going to look, but at first you'll need to test exhaustively. Even after you've been at it for a while, more testing never hurts. Regardless of whether you go with the least common denominator approach, the graceful degradation approach, or the maximum compatibility approach, you should test your pages broadly to ensure that your users won't have problems. You may have a favorite browser, but as a web designer, you can't afford to ignore the others that aren't your favorites.

Validating Your Pages

It's all well and good to attempt to write valid pages, but how do you know whether you've succeeded? It's easy enough to determine whether your pages look okay in your browser, but verifying that they're valid is another matter. Fortunately, the W3C, which is responsible for managing the HTML recommendations, also provides a service to validate your pages. It's a web application that enables you to upload an HTML file or to validate a specific URL to any W3C recommendation. The URL is http://validator.w3.org/.

Figure 16.1 is a screenshot of the validator in action. I've sent it off to validate http://www.samspublishing.com/. The first problem I ran into was that the character set and doctype were not set, so I had to specify them myself. Once I did that, the validator determined how compliant the page was with the standard specified by the DOCTYPE identifier on the target page.

FIGURE 16.1
The W3 validator.

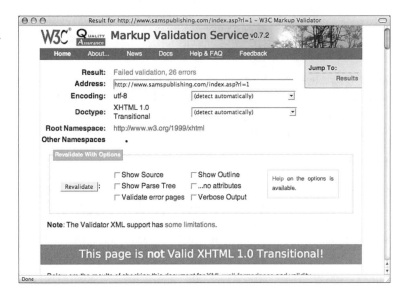

If you look closely at the screenshot, you can see that at the time I validated this page, it came out with 26 errors, all of which are violations of the XHTML 1.0 Transitional recommendation. The page looks fine in the popular browsers, but it's not really in sync with the recommendation. The errors generally fall into two categories: missing closing tags (usually for the <img> tag) and missing required attributes (mainly the alt attribute for <img> tags). Some of the errors found on the page can be seen in Figure 16.2.

FIGURE 16.2
Error messages
produced by the
W3 validator.

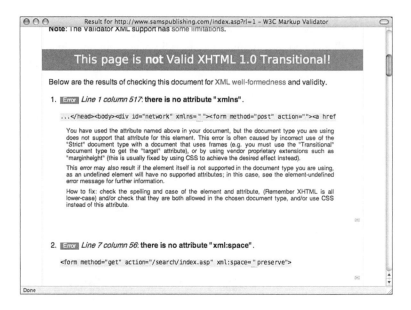

In the screenshot, you'll see that each error is accompanied by the subset of the page's source where the error appears and a link to an explanation of why it's an error at all. If you do get all the errors on your page fixed, you'll be privileged enough to see the message indicating that your page is valid, as shown in Figure 16.3.

HTML Tidy

If you have some existing pages and you're not up for the challenge of turning them into valid HTML yourself, there's a program that will not only validate your pages, but also correct them as best as it can. This program, HTML Tidy, was originally written by a staffer at the W3C named David Raggett, and has since been handed over to the community for maintenance. You can obtain it at http://tidy.sourceforge.net/.

Tidy accepts a number of command-line options that enable you to indicate how you want your page to be validated and modified. For example, if you want to convert your pages to XHTML, you can call it like this:

```
tidy -asxhtml myfile.html
```

Tidy will strip out all the deprecated <font> tags in your document, along with other tags that can be replaced by CSS properties if you pass it the -clean option, like this:

```
tidy -clean myfile.html
```

Once you've run Tidy on your files, they may still need some cleaning up, but Tidy will fix all the obvious errors.

FIGURE 16.3
The W3 validator acknowledges a job well done.

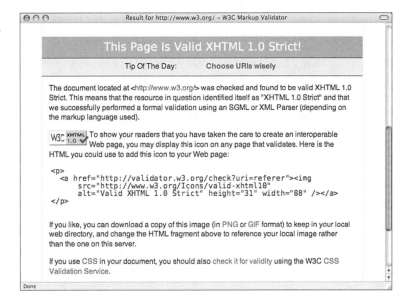

Writing for Online Publication

Writing on the Web is no different from writing in the real world. Although it's not committed to hard copy, it's still published and is still a reflection of you and your work. In fact, because your writing is online and your visitors have many other options when it comes to finding something to read, you'll have to follow the rules of good writing that much more closely.

Because of the vast quantities of information available on the Web, your visitors aren't going to have much patience if your web page is poorly organized or full of spelling errors. They're likely to give up after the first couple of sentences and move on to someone else's page. After all, there are several million pages out there. No one has time to waste on bad pages.

I don't mean that you have to go out and become a professional writer to create a good web page, but I'll give you a few hints for making your web page easier to read and understand.

Write Clearly and Be Brief

Unless you're writing the Great American Web Novel, your visitors aren't going to linger lovingly over your words. You should write as clearly and concisely as you possibly can, present your points, and then stop. Obscuring what you want to say with extra words just makes figuring out your point more difficult.

If you don't have a copy of Strunk and White's *The Elements of Style*, put down this book right now and go buy that book. Read it, reread it, memorize it, inhale it, sleep with it under your pillow, show it to all your friends, quote it at parties, and make it your life. You'll find no better guide to the art of good, clear writing than *The Elements of Style*.

Organize Your Pages for Quick Scanning

Even if you write the clearest, briefest, most scintillating prose ever seen on the Web, chances are good that your visitors won't start at the top of your Web page and carefully read every word down to the bottom.

In this context, *scanning* is the first quick look your visitors give to each page to get the general gist of the content. Depending on what your users want out of your pages, they may scan the parts that jump out at them (headings, links, other emphasized words), perhaps read a few contextual paragraphs, and then move on. By writing and organizing your pages for easy "scannability," you can help your visitors get the information they need as fast as possible.

To improve the scannability of your web pages, follow these guidelines:

- **Use headings to summarize topics**—Note that this book has headings and subheadings. You can flip through quickly and find the parts that interest you. The same concept applies to web pages.

- **Use lists**—Lists are wonderful for summarizing related items. Every time you find yourself saying something like "each widget has four elements" or "use the following steps to do this," the content after that phrase should be in an ordered or unordered list.

- **Don't forget link menus**—As a type of list, the link menu has all the same advantages of lists for scannability, and it doubles as an excellent navigation tool.

- **Don't bury important information in text**—If you have a point to make, make it close to the top of the page or at the beginning of a paragraph. Forcing readers to sift through a lot of information before they get to what's important means that many of them won't see the important stuff at all.

- **Write short, clear paragraphs**—Long paragraphs are harder to read and make gleaning the information more difficult. The further into the paragraph you put your point, the less likely it is that anybody will read it.

Figure 16.4 shows the sort of writing technique that you should avoid.

FIGURE 16.4
DON'T: A web page that is difficult to scan.

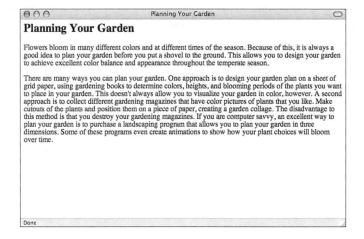

Planning Your Garden

Flowers bloom in many different colors and at different times of the season. Because of this, it is always a good idea to plan your garden before you put a shovel to the ground. This allows you to design your garden to achieve excellent color balance and appearance throughout the temperate season.

There are many ways you can plan your garden. One approach is to design your garden plan on a sheet of grid paper, using gardening books to determine colors, heights, and blooming periods of the plants you want to place in your garden. This doesn't always allow you to visualize your garden in color, however. A second approach is to collect different gardening magazines that have color pictures of plants that you like. Make cutouts of the plants and position them on a piece of paper, creating a garden collage. The disadvantage to this method is that you destroy your gardening magazines. If you are computer savvy, an excellent way to plan your garden is to purchase a landscaping program that allows you to plan your garden in three dimensions. Some of these programs even create animations to show how your plant choices will bloom over time.

Because all the information on this page is in paragraph form, your visitors have to read both paragraphs to find out what they want and where they want to go next.

How would you improve the example shown in Figure 16.4? Try rewriting this section so that visitors can better find the main points from the text. Consider the following:

- These two paragraphs actually contain three discrete topics.
- The ways to plan the garden would make an excellent nested list.

Figure 16.5 shows what an improvement might look like.

Make Each Page Stand on Its Own

As you write, keep in mind that your visitors could jump to any of your web pages from anywhere. For example, you can structure a page so that section 4 distinctly follows section 3 and has no other links to it. Then someone you don't even know might create a link to the page starting at section 4. From then on, visitors could find themselves at section 4 without even knowing that section 3 exists.

FIGURE 16.5

DO: An improvement to the difficult-to-scan web page.

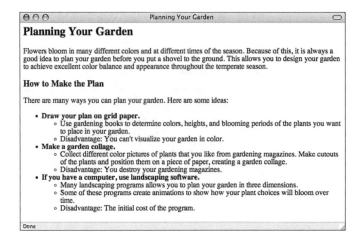

Be careful to write each page so that it stands on its own. The following guidelines will help:

- **Use descriptive titles**—The title should provide not only the direct subject of this page, but also its relationship to the rest of the pages on the site.

- **Provide a navigational link**—If a page depends on the one before it, provide a navigational link back to that page (and also a link up to the top level, preferably).

- **Avoid initial sentences such as the following**—"You can get around these problems by…", "After you're done with that, do this…", and "The advantages to this method are…". The information referred to by "these," "that," and "this" are off on some other page. If these sentences are the first words your visitors see, they're going to be confused.

Be Careful with Emphasis

Use emphasis sparingly in your text. Paragraphs with a whole lot of words in **boldface** or *italics* or ALL CAPS are hard to read, whether you use them several times in a paragraph or to emphasize long strings of text. The best emphasis is used only with small words such as "and," "this," or "but."

Link text also is a form of emphasis. Use single words or short phrases for link text. Do not use entire passages or paragraphs. Figure 16.6 illustrates a particularly bad example of too much emphasis obscuring the rest of the text.

By removing some of the boldface and using less text for your links, you can considerably reduce the amount of clutter in the paragraph, as you can see in Figure 16.7.

Be especially careful of emphasis that moves or changes, such as marquees, blinking text, or animation. Unless the animation is the primary focus of the page, use movement and sound sparingly.

FIGURE 16.6
DON'T: Too much emphasis.

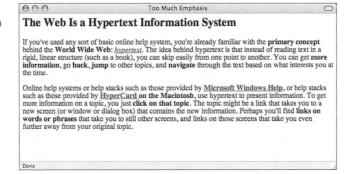

FIGURE 16.7
DO: Less emphasis.

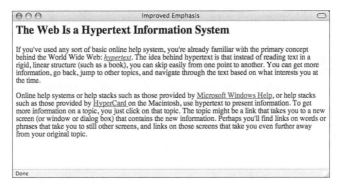

16

Don't Use Browser-Specific Terminology

Avoid references in your text to specific features of specific browsers. For example, don't use the following wording:

- **"Click here"**—What if your visitors are surfing without a mouse? A more generic phrase is "Select this link." (Of course, you should avoid the "here" syndrome in the first place, which neatly gets around this problem as well.)
- **"To save this page, pull down the File menu and select Save"**—Each browser has a different set of menus and different ways of accomplishing the same actions. If at all possible, do not refer to specifics of browser operation in your web pages.
- **"Use the Back button to return to the previous page"**—Each browser has a different set of buttons and different methods for going back. If you want your visitors to be able to go back to a previous page or to any specific page, link those pages.

Spell Check and Proofread Your Pages

Spell checking and proofreading may seem like obvious suggestions, but they bear mentioning given the number of pages I've seen on the Web that obviously haven't had either.

The process of designing a set of web pages and making them available on the Web is like publishing a book, producing a magazine, or releasing a product. Publishing web pages is considerably easier than publishing books, magazines, or other products, of course, but just because the task is easy doesn't mean your product should be sloppy.

Thousands of people may be reading and exploring the content you provide. Spelling errors and bad grammar reflect badly on you, on your work, and on the content you're describing. It may be irritating enough that your visitors won't bother to delve any deeper than your home page, even if the subject you're writing about is fascinating.

Proofread and spell check each of your web pages. If possible, have someone else read them. Often other people can pick up errors that you, the writer, can't see. Even a simple edit can greatly improve many pages and make them easier to read and navigate.

Design and Page Layout

With the introduction of technologies such as style sheets and Dynamic HTML, people without a sense of design have even more opportunities to create a site that looks simply awful.

Probably the best rule of web design to follow at all times is this: *Keep the design of each page as simple as possible*. Reduce the number of elements (images, headings, and rule lines) and make sure that visitors' eyes are drawn to the most important parts of the page first.

Keep this cardinal rule in mind as you read the next sections, which offer some other suggestions for basic design and layout of web pages.

Use Headings As Headings

Headings tend to be rendered in larger or bolder fonts in graphical browsers. Therefore, using a heading tag to provide some sort of warning, note, or emphasis in regular text can be tempting (see Figure 16.8).

FIGURE 16.8
DON'T: The wrong way to use headings.

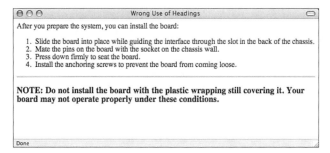

Headings stand out from the text and signal the start of new topics, so they should be used only as headings. If you really want to emphasize a particular section of text, consider using a small image, a rule line, or some other method of emphasis instead. Remember that you can use CSS to change the color, background color, font size, font face, and border for a block of text. Figure 16.9 shows an example of the text from Figure 16.8 with a different kind of visual emphasis.

FIGURE 16.9
DO: The right way to use headings.

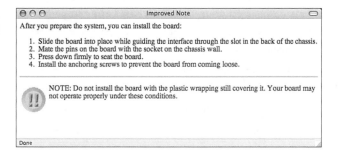

Group Related Information Visually

Grouping related information within a page is a task for both writing and design. As I suggested in the "Writing for Online Publication" section, grouping related information under headings improves the scannability of that information. Visually separating each section from the others helps to make it distinct and emphasizes the relatedness of the information.

If a web page contains several sections, find a way to separate those sections visually— for example, with a heading, a rule line, or tables, as shown in Figure 16.10.

FIGURE 16.10
DO: Separate
sections visually.

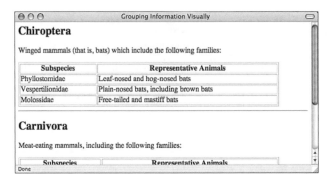

Use a Consistent Layout

When you're reading a book, each page or section usually has the same layout. The page numbers are placed where you expect them, and the first word on each page starts in the same place.

The same sort of consistent layout works equally well on web pages. Having a single look and feel for each page on your website is comforting to your visitors. After two or three pages, they'll know what the elements of each page are and where to find them. If you create a consistent design, your visitors can find the information they need and navigate through your pages without having to stop at every page and try to find where certain elements are located.

Consistent layout can include the following:

- **Consistent page elements**—If you use second-level headings (<h2>) on one page to indicate major topics, use second-level headings for major topics on all your pages. If you have a heading and a rule line at the top of your page, use that same layout on all your pages.

- **Consistent forms of navigation**—Put your navigation menus in the same place on every page (usually the top or the bottom of the page, or even both), and use the same number of them. If you're going to use navigation icons, make sure that you use the same icons in the same order for every page.

- **The use of external style sheets**—If you want to stick to pure HTML 4.01 (or XHTML 1.0), you can create a master style sheet that defines background properties, text and link colors, font selections and sizes, margins, and more. The appearance of your pages maintains consistency throughout your site.

Using Links

Without links, web pages would be really dull and finding anything interesting on the Web would be close to impossible. In many ways, the quality of your links can be as important as the writing and design of your actual pages. Here's some friendly advice on creating and using links.

Use Link Menus with Descriptive Text

As I've noted throughout this book, using link menus is a great way of organizing your content and the links on a page. If you organize your links into lists or other menu-like structures, your visitors can scan their options for the page quickly and easily.

16

Just organizing your links into menus might not be enough, however. Make sure that your descriptions aren't too short. For example, using menus of filenames or other marginally descriptive links in menus can be tempting (see Figure 16.11).

FIGURE 16.11
DON'T: A poor link menu.

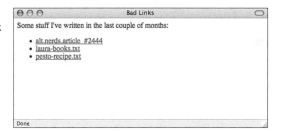

Each link describes the actual page to which it points, but it doesn't really describe the *content* of the page. How do visitors know what's on the other side of the link, and how can they decide whether they're interested in it from the limited information you've given them? Of these three links, only the last (`pesto-recipe.txt`) gives the visitors a hint about what they'll see when they jump to that file.

A better plan is either to provide some extra text describing the content of the file, as shown in Figure 16.12, or to avoid the filenames altogether. Just describe the contents of the files in the menu with the appropriate text highlighted, as shown in Figure 16.13.

Either one of these forms is better than the first. They both give your visitors more clues about what's on the other side of the link.

FIGURE 16.12

DO: A better link menu.

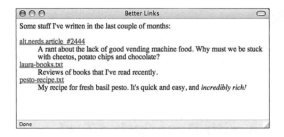

FIGURE 16.13

DO: Another better link menu.

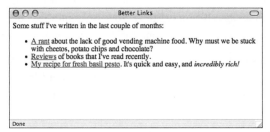

Use Links in Text

The best way to provide links in text is to first write the text as if it isn't going to have links at all—for example, as if you were writing it for hard copy. Then you can highlight the appropriate words that will link to other pages. Make sure that you don't interrupt the flow of the page when you include a link. The text should stand on its own. That way, the links provide additional or tangential information that your visitors can choose to follow or ignore at their own whim.

Figure 16.14 shows another example of using links in text. Here the text itself isn't particularly relevant; it's just there to support the links. If you're using text just to describe links, consider using a link menu instead of a paragraph. Instead of having to read the entire paragraph, your visitors can skim for the links that interest them.

FIGURE 16.14

DON'T: Links in text that don't work well.

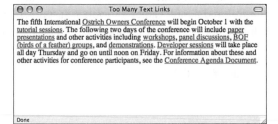

Figure 16.15 shows one way to restructure the previous example. The most important items on the page are the name of the conference, the events, and the dates on which they occur. You can restructure the page so that this information stands out. As you can see in Figure 16.15, presenting the events in a preformatted text table makes the important information stand out from the rest.

FIGURE 16.15

DO: Restructuring the links in the text.

Probably the easiest way to figure out whether you're creating links within text properly is to print out the formatted web page from your browser. In hard copy, without hypertext, does the paragraph still make sense? If the page reads funny on paper, it'll read funny online as well.

The revisions don't always have to be as different as they are in this example. Sometimes, a simple rephrasing of sentences can make the text on your pages more readable and more usable, both online and when printed.

Avoid the "Here" Syndrome

A common mistake that many web authors make when creating links in body text is using the "Here" syndrome. This is the tendency to create links with a single highlighted word (here) and to describe the links somewhere else in the text. Look at the following examples, with underlining to indicate link text:

> Information about ostrich socialization is contained here.

> Select this link for a tutorial on the internal combustion engine.

Because links are highlighted on the web page, the links visually pop out more than the surrounding text (or *draw the eye*, in graphic design lingo). Your visitors will see the link first, before reading the text. Try creating links this way.

16

Figure 16.16 shows a particularly heinous example of the "Here" syndrome. Close your eyes, open them quickly, pick a "here" in the figure at random, and then see how long it takes you to find out what the "here" is for.

FIGURE 16.16

DON'T: The "Here" syndrome.

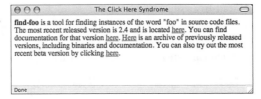

Now try the same exercise with a well-organized link menu of the same information, as shown in Figure 16.17.

FIGURE 16.17

DO: The same page reorganized.

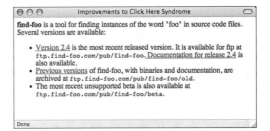

Because "here" says nothing about what the link is used for, your poor visitors have to search the text before and after the link itself to find out what's supposed to be "here." In paragraphs that have many occurrences of "here" or other nondescriptive links, matching up the links with what they're supposed to link to becomes difficult. This forces your visitors to work harder to figure out what you mean.

To Link or Not to Link

Just as with graphics, every time you create a link, consider why you're linking two pages or sections. Is the link useful? Does it give your visitors more information or bring them closer to their goal? Is the link relevant in some way to the current content?

Each link should serve a purpose. Just because you mention the word "coffee" on a page about some other topic, you don't have to link that word to the coffee home page. Creating such a link may seem cute, but if a link has no relevance to the current content, it just confuses your visitors.

The following list describes some of the categories of useful links in web pages. If your links don't fall into one of these categories, consider the reasons why you're including them in your page:

- Explicit navigation links indicate the specific paths that visitors can take through your web pages: forward, back, up, and home. These links are often indicated by navigation icons, as shown in Figure 16.18.

FIGURE 16.18
Explicit navigation links.

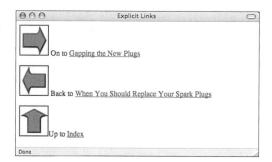

16

- Implicit navigation links (see Figure 16.19) are different from explicit navigation links because the link text implies, but does not directly indicate, navigation between pages. Link menus are the best example of this type of link. The highlighting of the link text makes it apparent that you'll get more information on this topic by selecting the link, but the text itself doesn't necessarily say so. Note the major difference between explicit and implicit navigation links: If you print a page containing both, you won't be able to pick out the implicit links.

FIGURE 16.19
Implicit navigation links.

Implicit navigation links also can include tables of contents or other overviews made up entirely of links.

- Definitions of words or concepts make excellent links, particularly if you're creating large networks of pages that include glossaries. By linking the first instance of a word to its definition, you can explain the meaning of that word to visitors who don't know what it means without distracting those who do. Figure 16.20 shows an example of this type of link. (You could also use a DHTML effect to display the definition without requiring the user to follow the link.)

FIGURE 16.20

Definition links.

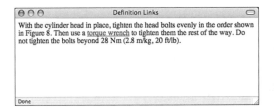

- Finally, links to tangents and related information are valuable when the text content will distract from the main purpose of the page. Think of tangent links as footnotes or endnotes in printed text (see Figure 16.21). They can refer to citations to other works or to additional information that's interesting, but isn't necessarily directly relevant to the point you're trying to make.

FIGURE 16.21

Footnote links.

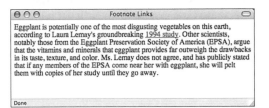

Be careful that you don't get carried away with definitions and tangent links. You might create so many tangents that your visitors spend too much time linking elsewhere to follow the point of your original text. Resist the urge to link every time you possibly can, and link only to tangents that are relevant to your own text. Also, avoid duplicating the same tangent—for example, linking every instance of the letters "WWW" on your page to the WWW Consortium's home page. If you're linking twice or more to the same location on one page, consider removing most of the extra links. Your visitors can select one of the other links if they're interested in the information.

NOTE Thanks to Nathan Torkington for his "Taxonomy of Tags," published on the www-talk mailing list, which inspired this section.

Using Images

In Lesson 7, "Adding Images, Color, and Backgrounds," you learned all about creating and using images in web pages. This section will summarize many of those hints.

16

Don't Overuse Images

Be careful about including a large number of images on your web page. Besides the fact that each image adds to the amount of time it takes to load the page, having too many images on the same page makes it look cluttered and distracts from the point you're trying to get across. Sometimes, though, people think that the more images they include on a page, the better it is. Figure 16.22 shows such an example.

FIGURE 16.22
DON'T: Images that are too large.

Remember the hints I gave you in Lesson 7. Consider how important each image really is before you put it on the page. If an image doesn't directly contribute to the content, consider leaving it out.

Use Alternatives to Images

Of course, as soon as I mention images, I also have to mention that a small minority of web users either use a web browser that doesn't support graphics or turn off image loading in their browser. Furthermore, visually impaired users need accommodation as well. To make your pages accessible to the widest possible audience, you need to take the text-only browsers into account. The following two solutions can help:

- Use the `alt` attribute of the `<img>` tag to automatically substitute appropriate text strings for the graphics in text-only browsers (a requirement in XHTML 1.0). Use a descriptive label to substitute for the default `[image]` that appears in the place of each inline image.

- If providing a single-source page for both graphical and text-only browsers becomes too much work and the result isn't acceptable, consider creating separate pages for each one: a page designed for the full-color, full-graphical browsers, and a page designed for the text-only browsers. Then allow visitors to choose one or the other from your home page.

Keep Images Small

Keep in mind that each image you use is a separate network connection and takes time to load over a network. This means that each image adds to the total time it takes to view the page. Try to reduce the number of images on the page, and keep them small both in file size and in actual dimensions. In particular, keep the following hints in mind:

- Your page should load at an average of 3KB to 4KB per second with a 56Kbps modem connection. The entire page (text and images) shouldn't take more than 20 seconds to load; otherwise, your visitors may get annoyed and move on without reading your page. This rule of thumb limits you to 60KB–80KB total for everything on your page. Strive to achieve that size by keeping your images small.

- For larger images, consider using thumbnails on your main page and then linking to the images rather than putting them inline.

- Interlace your larger GIF files or save your JPEGs as progressive JPEGs.

- Save your image in both the JPEG and GIF formats to see which creates a smaller file for the type of image you're using. You might also want to increase the level of compression for your JPEG images or reduce the number of colors in the palette of the GIF images to see whether you can save a significant amount of space without adversely affecting image quality.

- The fewer colors you use in a GIF file, the smaller the image will be. You should try to use as few colors as possible to avoid problems with system-specific color allocation.

- You can reduce the physical size of your images by cropping them (using a smaller portion of the overall image) or scaling (shrinking) them. When you scale an image, you might lose some of the detail.

CAUTION	Remember that reducing the size of your images using the `height` attributes of the `<img>` tag only makes them take up less space on the page; it doesn't affect the size of the image file or the download speed. It also has a tendency of making your images just look bad.

16

- You can use the `width` and `height` attributes to scale the image to a larger size than it actually is. These attributes originally were Netscape-only extensions, but were added to the HTML standard with version 3.2. Note that the scaled result might not be what you expect. Test this procedure before trying it.

With the preceding suggestions in mind, take a second look at the images on your page. You really have your heart set on using all these different images. How can you put the page shown in Figure 6.22 on a diet and improve its appearance?

- The graphic at the top of the page, which displays a logo for the site, could stand some size reduction. It's basically just a banner and doesn't have any links on it, so you can make it half as high. That will cut the download time for the graphic roughly in half.

- Another problem that needs to be addressed is that the title of the page (in this case, the name of the site) doesn't appear anywhere as text. Anyone who visits the site with graphics turned off won't know the name of the site! You need to add that to your improved version.

- Those horizontal rules are a *big* problem. First, there are too many of them. Second, they overpower the banner image because they're so much wider. Third, they distract from the list of items because they create separation between them. So, reduce the quantity and the size of those images for more download time savings.

- The bullets that appear before each list item are way too large. They could stand to be cut down to half their size. As a rule, most bullets are kept to 30∞30 pixels or less.

- The bullets and text were centered on the page, making the list items look very disorganized. Actually, there are several different ways to use images for bullets. You can make this an "official" bulleted list, using the `<ul>` tag, and use CSS to specify the bullet image. However, browsers running HTML 3.2 and earlier will see standard bulleted lists instead of the images. Another alternative is to lay out the images and the list items in a borderless table.

All the improvements I've suggested here are shown in Figure 16.23.

FIGURE 16.23
DO: Better use of images.

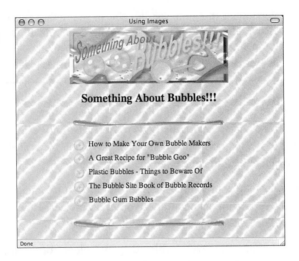

Watch Out for Assumptions About Your Visitors' Hardware

Many web designers create problems for their visitors by making a couple of careless assumptions about their hardware. When you're developing web pages, be kind and remember that not everyone has the same screen and browser dimensions as you do.

Just because that huge GIF you created is narrow enough to fit in your browser doesn't mean that it'll fit in someone else's. An image that's too wide is annoying because the visitors need to resize their windows or scroll sideways.

To fit within a majority of browsers, try to keep the width of your images to fewer than 600 pixels or, even better, don't set the page width to a specific amount.

Be Careful with Backgrounds and Link Colors

Using HTML extensions, you can use background colors and patterns on your pages and change the color of the text. This can be very tempting, but be very careful. Changing the page and font colors and providing fancy backdrops can quickly and easily make your pages entirely unreadable. The following are some hints for avoiding these problems:

- **Make sure you have enough contrast between the background and foreground (text) colors**—Low contrast can be hard to read. Also, light-colored text on a dark background is harder to read than dark text on a light background.

- **Increasing the font size of all the text on your page can sometimes make it more readable on a low-contrast background**—You can use the `<basefont>` tag or Cascading Style Sheets to increase the default font size for your page.

- **If you're using a background image, make sure that it doesn't interfere with the text**—Some images may look interesting on their own but can make text difficult to read when you put it on top of them. Keep in mind that backgrounds are supposed to be in the *background*. Subtle patterns are always better than wild patterns. Your visitors are visiting your pages for their content, not to marvel at your ability to create faux marble in your favorite image editor.

When in doubt, try asking a friend to look at your pages. Because you're already familiar with the content, you may not realize how hard your pages are to read. Someone who hasn't read them before will be able to tell you that your text colors are too close to your background color, or that the background image is interfering with the text. Of course, you'll have to find a friend who will be honest with you.

Other Good Habits and Hints

In this section, I've gathered several other miscellaneous hints and advice about working with groups of web pages. This includes notes on how big to make each page and how to sign your pages.

Link Back to Home

Consider linking back to the top level or home page on every page of your site. This link will give visitors a quick escape from the depths of your site. Using a home link is much easier than trying to navigate backward through a hierarchy or repeatedly clicking the Back button. This is especially important since the visitors to most sites are directed there by search engines. If a search engine leads users to an internal page on your site, you'll want to give them a way to find their way to the top.

Don't Split Topics Across Pages

Each web page works best if it covers a single topic in its entirety. Don't split topics across pages; even if you link between them, the transition can be confusing. It will be even more confusing if someone jumps in on the second or third page and wonders what's going on.

If you think that one topic is becoming too large for a single page, consider reorganizing the page so that you can break up the topic into subtopics. This tip works especially well in hierarchical organizations. It enables you to determine the exact level of detail that each level of the hierarchy should go and exactly how big and complete each page should be.

Don't Create Too Many or Too Few Pages

There are no rules for how many pages your website must have, nor for how large each page should be. You can have one page or several thousand, depending on the amount of content you have and how you've organized it.

With this point in mind, you might decide to go to one extreme or another. Each one has advantages and disadvantages. For example, let's say that you put all your content on one big page and create links to sections within that page, as illustrated in Figure 16.24.

FIGURE 16.24
One big page.

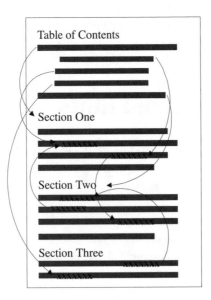

Advantages:

- One file is easier to maintain, and links within that file won't ever break if you move elements around or rename files.
- This file mirrors real-world document structure. If you're distributing documents both online and in hard copy, having a single document for both makes producing them easier.

Disadvantages:

- A large file can take a long time to download, particularly if the visitor has a slow network connection and the page includes a large number of images.
- Visitors must scroll a lot to find what they want, and accessing particular bits of information can become tedious. Navigating anywhere other than at the top or bottom becomes close to impossible.
- The structure is overly rigid. A single page is inherently linear. Although visitors can skip around within the page, the structure still mirrors that of the printed page and doesn't take advantage of the flexibility of smaller pages linked in a nonlinear fashion.

At the other extreme, you could create a whole bunch of little pages with links between them, as illustrated in Figure 16.25.

FIGURE 16.25
Many little pages.

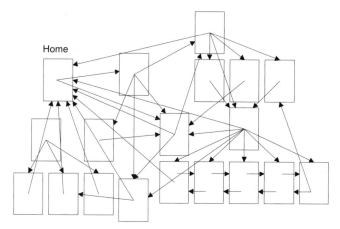

Advantages:

- Smaller pages load very quickly.
- You can often fit the entire page on one screen, so the information can be scanned very easily.

Disadvantages:

- Maintaining all those links will be a nightmare. Just adding some sort of navigational structure to that many pages may create thousands of links.
- If you have too many links between pages, the links may seem jarring. Continuity is difficult when your visitors spend more time moving from page to page than actually reading.

What's the solution? The content you're describing will often determine the size and number of pages you need, especially if you follow the one-topic-per-page suggestion. Testing your web pages on a variety of platforms at different network speeds will tell you whether a single page is too large. If you spend a lot of time scrolling around in your page, or if it takes more time to load than you expected, it may be too large.

Sign Your Pages

Each page should contain some sort of information at the bottom to act as the signature. I mentioned this tip briefly in Lesson 6, "Formatting Text with HTML and CSS," as part of the description of the `<address>` tag. That particular tag was intended for just this purpose.

Consider putting the following useful information in the `<address>` tag on each page:

- Contact information for the person who created this web page or who is responsible for it, colloquially known as the *webmaster*. This information should include the person's name and an email address, at the least.

- The status of the page. Is it complete? Is it a work in progress? Is it intentionally left blank?

- The date this page was most recently revised. This information is particularly important for pages that change often. Include a date on each page so that people know how old it is.

- Copyright or trademark information, if it applies.

Figure 16.26 shows a nice example of an address block.

FIGURE 16.26
A sample address.

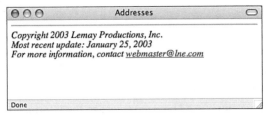

Another nice touch is to link a Mailto URL to the text containing the email address of the Webmaster, as in the following:

```
<address>
Laura Lemay <a href="mailto:lemay@lne.com">lemay@lne.com</a>
</address>
```

This way, the visitors who have browsers that support the Mailto URL can simply select the link and send mail to the person responsible for the page without having to retype the address into their mail programs.

> **NOTE**
>
> One downside of putting your email address on your web page is that there are programs that search websites for email addresses and add them to lists that are sold to spammers. You'll want to consider that risk before posting your email address on a public web page.

Finally, if you don't want to clutter each page with a lot of personal contact information or boilerplate copyright info, a simple solution is to create a separate page for the extra information and then link the signature to that page. Here's an example:

```
<address>
<a href="copyright.html">Copyright</a> and
<a href="webmaster.html">contact</a> information is available.
</address>
```

Provide Nonhypertext Versions of Hypertext Pages

Although the Web provides a way to publish information in new and exciting ways, some visitors still like to print things off to read on the bus or at the breakfast table. These kinds of visitors have real problems with web pages because it's difficult to tell your browser to print the whole thing. The browser knows only the boundaries of individual pages.

If you're using the Web to publish anything that might be readable and usable offline, consider creating a text or PDF version that's available as an external document for downloading, or even just publishing your information on one page without navigational elements or excessive layout. This way, your visitors can both browse the document online, print it out for reading offline, or even just save it to their local drive so that they can read it on their computer when it's not connected to the network. You can link the location of the hard-copy document to the start of the hypertext version, like the following:

```
A <a href="ftp://myhome.com/pub/mydir/myfile.pdf">PDF version</a> of
this document is available via ftp at myhome.com in the directory /pub/mydir/
myfile.pdf.
```

Of course, a handy cross-reference for the hard-copy version would be to provide the URL for the hypertext version, as follows:

```
This document is also available on hypertext form on
the World Wide Web at the URL:
http://myhome.com/pub/mydir/myfile.index.html.
```

Summary

The main do's and don'ts for web page design are as follows:

- Do understand the differences between HTML 2.0, HTML 3.2, and the different flavors of HTML 4.01 and XHTML 1.0. Decide which design strategy to follow while using them.
- Do provide alternatives if at all possible if you use nonstandard HTML tags.
- Do test your pages in multiple browsers.
- Do write your pages clearly and concisely.
- Do organize the text of your page so that your visitors can scan for important information.
- Do spell check and proofread your pages.
- Do group related information both semantically (through the organization of the content) and visually (by using headings or separating sections with rule lines).
- Do use a consistent layout across all your pages.
- Do use link menus to organize your links for quick scanning, and do use descriptive links.
- Do have good reasons for using links.
- Do keep your layout simple.
- Do provide alternatives to images for text-only browsers.
- Do try to keep your images small so that they load faster over the network.
- Do be careful with backgrounds and colored text to avoid making your pages flashy but unreadable.
- Do always provide a link back to your home page.
- Do match topics with pages.
- Do provide a signature block or link to contact information at the bottom of each page.
- Do provide single-page, nonhypertext versions of linear documents.
- Do write context-independent pages.
- Don't link to irrelevant material.
- Don't write web pages that are dependent on pages before or after them in the structure.
- Don't overuse emphasis (such as boldface, italic, all caps, link text, blink, or marquees).

- Don't use terminology that's specific to any one browser ("click here," "use the Back button," and so on).
- Don't use heading tags to provide emphasis.
- Don't fall victim to the "Here" syndrome with your links.
- Don't link repeatedly to the same site on the same page.
- Don't clutter the page with a large number of pretty but unnecessary images.
- Don't split individual topics across pages.

Workshop

16

Put on your thinking cap again because it's time for another review. These questions, quizzes, and exercises will remind you about the items that you should (or should not) include on your pages.

Q&A

Q **I've seen statistics that say the majority of people on the Web are using Internet Explorer. Why should I continue designing and testing my pages for other browsers when most of the world is using one browser?**

A You can design your pages explicitly for Internet Explorer. Your pages are your pages, and the decision is yours. *But*, given how easy it is to make small modifications so your pages can be viewed and read in other browsers without losing much of the design, why lock out the remainder of your audience for the sake of a few tags? Remember, the Web is growing all the time, and that "small" minority of visitors could very well be a million people or more.

Q **I'm converting existing documents into web pages. These documents are very text-heavy and are intended to be read from start to finish instead of being scanned quickly. I can't restructure or redesign the content to better follow the guidelines you've suggested—that's not my job. What can I do?**

A All is not lost. You can still improve the overall presentation of these documents by providing reasonable indexes to the content (summaries, tables of contents pages, subject indexes, and so on) and including standard navigation links. In other words, you can create an easily navigable framework around the documents themselves. This can go a long way toward improving content that's otherwise difficult to read online.

Q **I have a standard signature block that contains my name and email address, revision information for the page, and a couple of lines of copyright information that my company's lawyers insisted on. It's a little imposing, particularly on small pages. Sometimes the signature is bigger than the page itself! How do I integrate it into my site so that it isn't so obtrusive?**

A If your company's lawyers agree, consider putting all your contact and copyright information on a separate page and then linking to it on every page rather than duplicating it every time. This way, your pages won't be overwhelmed by the legal stuff. Also, if the signature changes, you won't have to change it on every single page. Failing that, you can always just reduce the font size for that block and perhaps change the font color to something with less contrast to the background of the page. This indicates to users that they're looking at fine print.

Quiz

1. What are the three flavors of XHTML 1.0, and which of these three accommodates the widest range of markup?

2. What are some ways you can organize your pages so that visitors can scan them more easily?

3. True or false: Headings are useful when you want information to stand out because they make the text large and bold.

4. True or false: You can reduce the download time of an image by using the `width` and `height` attributes of the `<img>` tag to scale down the image.

5. What are the advantages and disadvantages of creating one big web page versus several smaller ones?

Quiz Answers

1. The three flavors of XHTML 1.0 are Transitional (designed for the widest range of markup, including tags that are deprecated in the standard), Frameset (which includes all tags in the Transitional specification, plus those for framesets), and Strict (for those who want to stick to pure XHTML 1.0 tags and attributes).

2. You can use headings to summarize topics, lists to organize and display information, and link menus for navigation, and you can separate long paragraphs with important information into shorter paragraphs.

3. False. You should use headings as headings and nothing else. You can emphasize text in other ways, or use a graphic to draw attention to an important point.

4. False. When you use the width and height attributes to make a large image appear smaller on your page, it may reduce the dimensions of the file, but it won't decrease the download time. The visitor still downloads the same image, but the browser just fits it into a smaller space.

5. The advantages of creating one large page are that one file is easier to maintain, the links don't break, and it mirrors real-world document structure. The disadvantages are that it has a longer download time, visitors have to scroll a lot, and the structure is rigid and too linear.

Exercises

16

1. Try your hand at reworking the example shown in Figure 16.5. Organize the information into a definition list or a table. Make it easy for the visitor to scan for the important points on the page.

2. Try the same with the example shown in Figure 16.7. How can you arrange the information so that it's easier to find the important points and links on the page?

LESSON 17:
Designing for the Real World

In previous lessons, you learned about what you should and shouldn't do when you plan your website and design your pages. You also learned about what makes a good or bad website. There's another important factor that you should take into consideration, and that's how to design your pages for the real world.

You've already learned that the real world consists of many different users with many different computer systems who use many different browsers. Some of the things we haven't yet addressed, however, are the many different preferences and experience levels that the visitors to your site will have. By anticipating these real-world needs, you can better judge how you should design your pages. I'll also explain how you can make sure that your websites are usable people who are disabled and must use accessibility technologies to browse the Web.

In this Lesson

In today's lesson, you'll learn some ways that you can anticipate these needs, as well as the following:

- Things to consider when you're trying to determine the preferences of your audience

- Various ways of helping users find their way around your site

- HTML code that displays the same web page in each of the XHTML 1.0 specifications (Transitional, Frameset, and Strict)

- What accessibility is, and how to design accessible sites

- Using an accessibility validator

What Is the Real World, Anyway?

You're probably most familiar with surfing the Internet on a computer that runs a specific operating system, such as Windows, Mac OS X, or something similar. You may think you have a pretty good idea of what web pages look like to everyone.

Throughout this book, you've learned that the view you typically see on the Web isn't the view that everyone else sees. The real world has many different computers with many different operating systems. Even if you try to design your pages for the most common operating system and the most common browsers, there's another factor that you can't anticipate: *user preference*. Consider the following family, for example:

- Bill is a top-level executive at a Fortune 100 company that has its own intranet. Almost everyone in the company uses the same operating system and the same browser. Bill is used to seeing the Internet as mostly text, with a smattering of images here and there to stress informational points—a lean and mean Web with very little multimedia and a lot of information. He finds all the extra glitz annoying and inconvenient to download, so he turns off JavaScript and Flash.

- Bill's wife, Susan, has never used a computer before, but she has always wanted to learn. She's a genealogist by hobby and has learned that the Internet has many resources in that field. She also wants to publish her family history on the Web. When she and her husband got their cable modem hooked up, she was thrilled. But soon she was asking questions such as, "Can we fit more on the screen? Those letters are a bit too small…can we make them larger? Where are the pictures? How come you have the music turned off? It says that there's sound on this page!" She already wanted to see the Internet much differently than what her husband was used to seeing.

- Bill and Susan have a son, Tom, who's in high school. He's an avid gamer and wants to see special effects—*glitz, multimedia*! He pumps up the volume as loud as he can and pushes the capacities of their new computer to the max. He also thinks "Browser X" is better than "Browser Y" because it supports lots of cutting-edge features. He wants to design a website that provides hints, tips, and tricks for one of his favorite online games.

- Tom's older sister, Jill, is an art major in college, studying to be a commercial artist. She has a keen interest in sculpture and photography. She plans to use her new computer for homework assignments, so she'll be looking at the Web with a keen visual interest. She wants to view her pages in true color, in the highest resolution possible.

- Then there are the senior members 533 the family, Susan's aging parents, who have recently moved in with the family after years of living in a rural town. Their experience with computers is minimal—they've only seen them in stores. They're interested in learning so that they can view family photos online and exchange email with out of town relatives, but Dad's eyes aren't quite as sharp as they used to be. He needs a special browser so that he can hear the text as well as see it.

All these people are using the same computer and operating system to view the Web. In all cases but one (young Tom), they're also using the same browser. This example illustrates one of the other things that you need to think about when you design your website: the needs of the users themselves. Some of these needs are easier to accommodate than others. The following section describes some of the considerations you saw in the previous example.

Considering User Experience Level

There are varied levels of experience in our fictitious family. Although everyone is keenly interested in the Web, some of them have never even seen a Web browser before. When you design your site, you should consider that the people who visit it might have varying levels of experience and browsing requirements.

17

Will the topics that you discuss on your site be of interest to people with different levels of experience? If so, you might want to build in some features that help them find their way around more easily. The key, of course, is to make your navigation as intuitive as possible. By keeping your navigation scheme consistent from page to page throughout the site, you'll do a favor for users of all experience levels. There are a number of features you can add to your site that will improve its usability for everyone.

Add a Search Engine

Many users go straight to the search engine when they want to find something on a site. No matter how much time and effort you put into building a clear, obvious navigation scheme, someone looking for information about Frisbees is going to look for a box on your page where they can type in the word "Frisbee" and get back a list of the pages where you talk about them.

Unfortunately, locating a good search engine package and setting it up can be an awful lot of work, and difficult to maintain. On the other hand, there are some alternatives. Some search engines enable you to search a specific site for information. You can add a link to them from your site. Some search engines even allow you to set things up so that you can add their search engine to your site, such as Google:

http://www.google.com/services/free.html

By signing up, you can add a search box to your site that enables your users to search only pages on your own site for information. For a list of other ways to add search functionality to your site, see the following page in the Mozilla Directory:

http://dmoz.org/Computers/Software/Internet/Servers/Search/

Use Frames Wisely

One failing of some HTML books is that they tell you about all the different techniques you can use to create Web pages, but they don't offer any comparative information that explains when and how these techniques ought to be used. For example, I've devoted a number of pages to discussing frames, but the fact is that they should really be used only when nothing else will work. For example, putting all of your navigation in one frame and your content in another just because you can is generally a poor idea.

Frames have a couple of specific disadvantages that make them unsuitable for use in many cases. The first is that they make it hard for users to bookmark inner pages on sites. If your entire site is a frameset, the URL in the user's location bar never changes as the user navigates within the site. When the user gets to your inner page that has a wonderful recipe for chocolate chip cookies that your grandmother gave you, he'll have a hard time bookmarking it because his browser wants to bookmark the top-level frameset itself. When he returns on future visits, he'll be taken back to your home page.

The second issue that's common with framesets is that they can interfere with search engines. Again, if your entire site is inside a frameset, when a search engine fetches your home page, it's probably going to get a page with no real content to speak of. Then, it will download, say, the navigation frame, which lacks context, the content frame, which may lack header and footer information, and on and on. If you want people to be able to find your site using search engines, frames can get in your way.

There are also other issues people have had with framesets in the past, like problems printing and problems with the back button. Browsers mostly compensate for these issues today, but even so, frames can confuse your users. In some cases, there's just no other good way to attack a problem, but you should always make sure that there's not a better way before going the frames route.

Use Concise, Sensible URLs

One common mistake made by web designers is not considering how users share URLs. If your site is interesting at all, people are going to email the URL to their friends, paste it into instant messaging conversations, and talk about it around the water cooler. Making your URLs short and easy to remember makes them that much easier for people to share.

There's a reason why people have paid huge sums for domain names like business.com and computers.com in the past. They're easy to remember and you don't have to spell them out when you tell them to people.

You may not have any control over your domain name, but you can exercise control over the rest of your URLs. Say that you have a section of your site called "Products and Services." All the pages in that section are stored in their own directory. You could call it any one of the following:

```
/ps
/prdsvcs
/products
/products_services
/products_and_services
```

There are plenty of other options as well (you could call it /massapequa if you wanted to), but the preceding list seems like a reasonable group of options. Of the list, a few stand out to me as being poor choices. /products_service and /products_and_ services just seem too verbose. If the pages under those directories have long names at all, you're suddenly in very long URL territory, which isn't conducive to sharing. On the other hand /prdsvcs may be short, but it's also difficult to remember, and almost certainly has to be spelled out if you tell it to anyone. It's probably no good. That leaves two remaining choices: /ps and /products. The first, /ps, is nice and short, and probably easy to remember. Using it would be fine. However, there's one other principle of URLs that I want to talk about—guessability.

17

Chances are that most of the people who visit your website have been using the Web for awhile. There's some chance that they might just assume that they know where to go on your site based on experience. If they want to read about your products, they may guess—based on their experience with other sites they've visited—that your products will be listed at http://www.your-url.com/products. Any time you can put your content where your users will assume it to be, you're doing them a favor. Using standard directory names such as /about, /contact, and /products can make things ever so slightly easier for your users at no cost to you.

My final bit of advice on URLs is to make sure that they reflect the structure of your site. One time, I worked on a site that consisted of hundreds of files, all in a single directory. The site itself had structure, but the files were not organized based on that structure. Whether the user was on the home page or five levels deep within the site, the URL was still just a filename tagged onto the hostname of the server. Not only did this make the site hard to work on, but it also kept some useful information away from users. Let's say you have a site about cars. What's more useful to your users? This:

http://www.example.com/camry.html

or

http://www.example.com/cars/toyota/2003/camry.html

The second URL provides a lot more information to the user than the first one does. As an added bonus, you can set up your site so that the user can take `camry.html` off the end and get a list of all Toyota models for 2003, or take `toyota/2003/camry.html` off the end and get a list of all car makes discussed on the site. Veteran web users are accustomed to dealing with URLs; you should help them out as much as you can by using URLs responsibly.

Navigation Provides Context

The key purpose of navigation is obviously to enable your users to get from one place to another within your site. However, its secondary purpose is to let your users know where they are within the site. This was the stroke of genius behind Yahoo!'s introduction of "breadcrumb" navigation in its directory. Take a look at the screenshot from Yahoo!'s directory in Figure 17.1.

FIGURE 17.1
A page from Yahoo!'s directory.

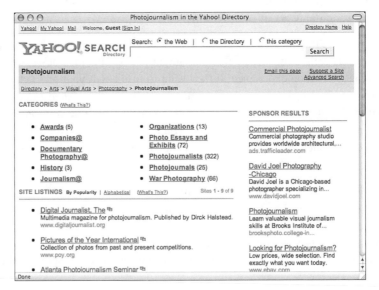

Near the top, you can see a list of links that start at the top of the directory and lead down to the page that I'm actually on. The first thing it does is give me the ability to go back to any level of the directory between the home page and the Photojournalism page that I'm actually on. The second thing it does is let me know that I'm six levels into the directory, and that the page I'm on is part of the Arts category of the directory, and all the subcategories between that category and the page that I'm on. That's a lot of utility packed into a small feature.

Not all sites have as large and complex a structure as Yahoo!, but you can still provide context for your users through your navigation scheme. By altering your navigational elements based on the page that the user is on, you can indicate to them not only where she can go but also where she is. This is also particularly helpful to users who arrive at your site not via the home page, but from an external link. Enabling users to immediately deduce where they are in the larger scheme of things makes it more likely that they'll take in more of your site.

Are Your Users Tourists or Regulars?

17

When you're designing a site, especially one that uses forms, one of the key questions you have to ask yourself is whether your users are tourists or regulars. If your users are tourists, which means that they don't use your site very often, or will probably only ever use it one time, you should design your site so that the first-timer can easily figure out what he should be doing and where he needs to go. This may annoy regular users who already know where they're going, but in some cases you have to cater to tourists.

On the other hand, if your site is normally used by the same existing group of users who come back once a day or once a week, your emphasis should be on providing shortcuts and conveniences that enable them to use your site as efficiently as possible. It's okay if it takes a bit of work to learn about the conveniences, because it's worth your users' time.

Clearly, the secret is to strike a balance here. The holy grail is a site that's obvious and clear to new users but also provides the features that repeat users crave. However, understanding what sort of audience you have can help you determine how to assign your resources.

All of this is doubly true with forms. The forms that are part of a discussion board used by the same people day after day will be designed much differently from those that are part of a request-more-information form on a product page. When you design a form, always think about the type of user who'll be using it.

Determining User Preference

In addition to the various levels of experience that visitors have, everyone has his own preferences for how he wants to view your web pages. How do you please them all? The truth is, you can't. But you *can* give it your best shot. Part of good web design is anticipating what visitors want to see on your site. This becomes more difficult if the topics you discuss on your site are of interest to a wider audience.

You'll notice that each person in our fictitious family needs to see the Web differently. Sometimes this is due to his or her interests, but other times it's because of special needs. Therein lies the key to anticipating what you'll need on your web pages.

A topic such as "Timing the Sparkplugs on Your 300cc Motorcycle Engine" is of interest to a more select audience. It will attract only those who are interested in motorcycles—more specifically, those who want to repair their own motorcycles. It should be relatively easy to anticipate the types of things these visitors would like to see on your site. Step-by-step instructions can guide them through each process, while images or multimedia can display techniques that are difficult to describe using text alone.

"The Seven Wonders of the Ancient World," on the other hand, will attract students of all ages as well as their teachers. Archaeologists, historians, and others with an interest in ancient history also might visit the site. Now you have a wider audience, a wider age range, and a wider range of educational levels. It won't be quite as easy to build a site that will please them all.

In cases such as this, it might help to narrow your focus a bit. One way is to design your site for a specific user group, such as the following:

- **Elementary school students and their teachers**—This site requires a very basic navigation system that's easy to follow. Content should be basic and very easy to read. Bright, colorful images and animations can help keep the attention of young visitors.

- **High school students and their teachers**—You can use a slightly more advanced navigation system. Multimedia and the latest in web technology will keep these students coming back for more.

- **College students and their professors**—A higher level of content is necessary, whereas multimedia may be less important. An online encyclopedia format might be a good approach here.

- **Professional researchers and historians**—This type of site probably requires pages that are heavier in text content than multimedia.

It's not always possible to define user groups for your website, so you'll need to start with your *own* preferences. Survey other sites that include similar content. As you browse through them, ask yourself what you hope to see there. Is the information displayed well? Is there enough help on the site? Does the site have too much or too little multimedia? If you can get a friend or two to do the survey along with you, it helps you get additional feedback before you start your own site. Take notes and incorporate those ideas into your own web pages.

After you design some initial pages, ask your friends, family members, and associates to browse through your site and pick it apart. Keep in mind that when you ask others for constructive criticism, you might hear some things that you don't want to hear. However, this process is important because you'll often get many new ideas on how to improve your site even more.

Deciding on an HTML 4.01 or XHTML 1.0 Approach

17

First, let me explain the difference between HTML 4.01 and XHTML 1.0. The HTML specification dictates which HTML tags are valid. XHTML describes how to write HTML so that it conforms to the XML specification. When you want to know whether a particular tag or attribute is valid, check out the HTML specification. When you want to know how to close a tag that has no closing tag, such as <br>, consult with the XHTML spec. In earlier lessons, you learned about the various flavors of HTML 4.01 and XHTML 1.0 and how each of them is geared toward users of older or newer browsers:

- **HTML 4.01 or XHTML 1.0 Transitional**—For those who want to provide support for older browsers
- **HTML 4.01 or XHTML 1.0 Frameset**—For sites that want to use frames in a standards-compliant manner
- **HTML 4.01 or XHTML 1.0 Strict**—For those who want to develop pages that strictly adhere to the HTML 4.0 or XHTML 1.0 specification by not using deprecated elements or attributes

HTML 4.01 and XHTML 1.0 Transitional

If you expect your visitors to use a wide variety of different browsers, it's probably to your advantage to design your web pages around the HTML 4.01 or XHTML 1.0 Transitional specification. By doing so, you provide backward compatibility with older browsers. The Transitional specification provides the flexibility to use tags that are deprecated in the strict HTML 4.01 specification. Therefore, you can use presentation attributes that were introduced in HTML 3.2, such as the center or align attribute for alignment or bgcolor and color attributes for background and foreground colors.

For example, look at the Halloween House of Terror page that you created in Lesson 7, "Adding Images, Color, and Backgrounds." Here, the page has undergone yet another facelift, as shown in the following code. This page uses HTML 3.2-compatible tags to display the page. Fonts, colors, and alignment are formatted with tags that have been deprecated in the Strict specification.

The deprecated tags and attributes are shown in italics in the following code example. In addition, a table is used to create a staggered layout of links, descriptions, and images on the page.

Input ▼

```
<!DOCTYPE html PUBLIC "-//W3C//DTD XHTML 1.0 Transitional//EN"
"http://www.w3.org/TR/xhtml1/DTD/transitional.dtd">
<html>
<head>
<title>Welcome to the Halloween House of Terror</title>
</head>
<body bgcolor="#ff9933" link="#990000">
<h1 align="center">
  <font face="Arial, sans-serif">
  The Halloween House of Terror!!</font></h1>
<div align="center">
  <p>
    <img src="skel05.gif" alt="skel05.gif" width="140" height="100" />
    <img src="skel07.gif" alt="skel07.gif" width="140" height="100" />
    <img src="skel06.gif" alt="skel06.gif" width="140" height="100" />
  </p>
</div>
<hr />
<p>
  <font face="Arial, sans-serif">
  Voted the most frightening haunted house three years in a row, the
  <font color="#cc0000"><b>Halloween House of Terror</b></font>
  provides the ultimate in Halloween thrills. Over 20 rooms of thrills and
  excitement to make your blood run cold and your
  hair stand on end!
  </font>
</p>
<hr />
<p><font face="Arial, sans-serif">
  Don't take our word for it .. preview some images of what awaits!
  </font>
</p>
<div align="center">
  <table border="0" width="75%" cellspacing="5" cellpadding="5">
```

```
<tr>
  <td width="30%">
   <font face="Arial, sans-serif">
   <img src="skel01.gif" alt="skel01.gif" width="140" height="100" />
   </font>
  </td>
 <td width="40%" bgcolor="#CC0000"> <font face="Arial, sans-serif">
  Watch out for Esmerelda. You never know what she has in her cauldron.
  </font> </td>
 <th width="30%" bgcolor="#FF6600"> <b><font face="Arial, sans-serif">
  <a href="entry.gif">The Entry Way</a> </font></b> </th>
 </tr>
 <tr>
 <th width="30%" bgcolor="#FF6600"> <b><font face="Arial, sans-serif">
  <a href="bedroom.gif">The Master Bedroom</a> </font></b> </th>
 <td width="40%" bgcolor="#CC0000"> <font face="Arial, sans-serif">
  Don't open the closet door, whatever you do!</font></td>
   <td width="30%">
    <font face="Arial, sans-serif">
    <img src="skel02.gif" alt="skel02.gif" width="140" height="100" />
    </font>
   </td>
 </tr>
 <tr>     <td width="30%">
    <font face="Arial, sans-serif">
    <img src="skel03.gif" alt="skel03.gif" width="140" height="100" />
    </font></td>
 <td width="40%" bgcolor="#CC0000"> <font face="Arial, sans-serif">
  More than a few innocents have been cast in chains for eons. They just
  aren't the same anymore.</font></td>
 <th width="30%" bgcolor="#FF6600"><b> <font face="Arial, sans-serif">
  <a href="galley.gif">The Galley</a></font></b></th>
 </tr>
 <tr>
 <th width="30%" bgcolor="#FF6600"> <b><font face="Arial, sans-serif">
  <a href="dungeon.gif">The Dungeon</a> </font> </b></th>
 <td width="40%" bgcolor="#CC0000"> <font face="Arial, sans-serif">
  Better listen to the tour guides, or you'll get lost! </font> </td>
   <td width="30%">
   <font face="Arial, sans-serif">
   <img src="skel04.gif" alt="skel04.gif" width="140" height="100" />
   </font></td>
 </tr>
 </table>
</div>
<hr />
<p><font face="Arial, sans-serif"> The
  <font color="#cc0000">Halloween House of Terror</font>
  is open from October 20 to November 1st, with a gala celebration
  on Halloween night. Our hours are: </font></p>
<ul>
```

17

```
<li>
 <font face="Arial, sans-serif">
 Mon-Fri 5PM-midnight</font>
</li>
<li>
 <font face="Arial, sans-serif">
 Sat &amp; Sun 5PM-3AM</font>
</li>
<li>
   <font face="Arial, sans-serif">
   Halloween Night (31-Oct): 3PM-???</font></li>
</ul>
<p align="center">
<font face="Arial, sans-serif"> The
  <font color="#cc0000">Halloween House of Terror</font>
  is located at:<br />
  The Old Waterfall Shopping Center<br />
  1020 Mirabella Ave<br />
  Springfield, CA 94532</font></p>
</body>
</html>
```

Figure 17.2 shows the result of the preceding code as it's displayed in a browser.

Output ▶

FIGURE 17.2
An example of
HTML 4.01
Transitional code.

HTML 4.01 and XHTML 1.0 Frameset

If your site uses frames and you want to adhere to standards, the specification of choice is HTML 4.01 or XHTML 1.0 Frameset. It includes all the tags and attributes that are "legal" in the HTML 4.01 or XHTML 1.0 Transitional specification. In addition, you can use all tags and attributes that pertain to framesets and frames.

The key to good frameset design is to create as few frames as possible, while making the navigation system easy to understand. The hard decision, however, is which resolution to use for your frameset, because the browser is divided into multiple sections. The more frames you create in the frameset, the smaller each page will be in each frame.

In Figure 17.3, the Halloween House of Terror web page has been converted to a frameset. The main frame displays exactly the same page you saw in Figure 17.2, but the links in the left frame take the visitor to the pictures and descriptions of each room in the haunted house. When you add the links in the left frame, the visitor no longer has to use his Browse button to take a small virtual tour through the haunted house. This simplifies the navigation greatly.

FIGURE 17.3
An example of HTML 4.01 Frameset code.

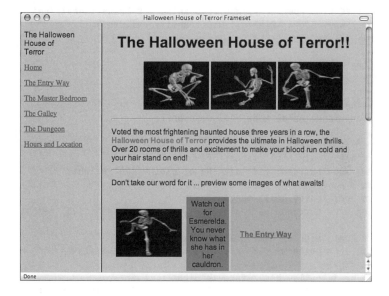

17

The code for the frameset divides the browser window into two frames: left and right. The `navigation.html` page loads into the left frame, and the main page (`main.html`) loads into the right frame. The code for the frameset looks like the following:

```
<!DOCTYPE html PUBLIC "-//W3C//DTD XHTML 1.0 Frameset//EN"
"http://www.w3.org/TR/xhtml1/DTD/frameset.dtd">
<html>
<head>
<title>Halloween House of Terror Frameset</title>
</head>
```

```
<frameset cols="170,*">
 <frame name="left" src="navigation.html" />
 <frame name="right" src="main.html" />
 <noframes>
 <body>
 <p> .. insert noframes content here .. </p>
 </body>
 </noframes>
</frameset>
</html>
```

The code for the left frame in the frameset (navigation.html) displays each page in
the right frame when the user selects one of the image links (as defined by the
<target="right"> tag). Each image link displays alternative text when the user hovers
his mouse over the button or when images are turned off in the browser. The code for the
left frame looks like the following:

```
<!DOCTYPE html PUBLIC "-//W3C//DTD XHTML 1.0 Transitional//EN"
"http://www.w3.org/TR/xhtml1/DTD/transitional.dtd">
<html>
<head>
<title>The Halloween House of Terror</title>
<base target="right" />
</head>
<body bgcolor="#ff9933" text="#000000">
<p><font face="Arial">The Halloween<br />
House of<br />
Terror</font></p>
<p><a href="main.html" target="right">
  <img src="button01.gif" alt="Home" width="125" height="50" />
  </a></p>
<p><a href="entry.html" target="right">
  <img src="button02.gif" alt="The Entry Way" width="125" height="50" />
  </a></p>
<p><a href="bedroom.html" target="right">
  <img src="button03.gif" alt="The Master Bedroom" width="125" height="50" />
  </a></p>
<p><a href="galley.html" target="right">
  <img src="button04.gif" alt="The Galley" width="125" height="50" />
  </a></p>
<p><a href="dungeon.html" target="right">
  <img src="button05.gif" alt="The Dungeon" width="125" height="50" />
  </a></p>
<p><a href="location.html" target="right">
  <img src="button06.gif" alt="Hours and Location" width="125" height="50" />
  </a></p>
</body>
</html>
```

HTML 4.01 and XHTML 1.0 Strict

The Transitional and Frameset specifications enable you to provide support for Netscape Navigator 4.0 or Microsoft Internet Explorer 4.0, and older browsers. The HTML 4.01 or XHTML 1.0 Strict specification, however, is designed for people who want to abandon the idea of making pages look the same in old browsers as they do in new ones in favor of using modern layout techniques, such as building page layout using CSS exclusively. To comply with the HTML 4.01 or XHTML 1.0 Strict specification, you must avoid using any HTML tags and attributes that are marked as *deprecated*. Instead, use cascading style sheets in place of the deprecated tags.

If you're willing to abandon the idea of presenting your page identically to all users, there are several advantages to using the HTML 4.01 or XHTML 1.0 Strict specification. As you learned in Lesson 9, "Creating Layouts with CSS," CSS technology gives you greater control over page layout and appearance. In many ways, you can lay out your pages as if you were using a page layout or word processing program. Another advantage is that cascading style sheets level 2, or CSS2 for short, incorporates additional features for nonvisual browsers. This means that you can design pages for people who are visually impaired or have other special needs.

The following code example illustrates how you can implement the page shown in Figure 17.2 into the XHTML 1.0 Strict specification. In this example, the Halloween House of Terror uses embedded style sheet properties and values to format the text and images on the page. The colors for the text, links, and table cells are defined in the style section at the beginning of the page. Margins are added to the top, bottom, left, and right of the page. Also, rather than using standard bullets, the bulleted list at the bottom of the page displays image bullets as defined by the style sheet.

Input ▼

```
<!DOCTYPE html PUBLIC "-//W3C//DTD XHTML 1.0 Strict//EN"
"http://www.w3.org/TR/xhtml1/DTD/strict.dtd">
<html>
<head>
<title>Welcome to the Halloween House of Terror</title>
<meta http-equiv="Content-Type" content="text/html; charset=ISO-8859-1" />
<style type="text/css">
body { background-color: #ff9933;
    color: #000000;
    font-family: Arial, sans-serif;
    font-size: 12pt;
    margin-left: 20px;
    margin-right: 20px;
    margin-top: 10px;
    margin-bottom: 10px }
```

17

```
a:link{ color: #990000 }
a:visited{ color: #CC00CC }
a:active{ color: #CC0000 }
h1{ font-family: Arial, sans-serif;
    font-size: 24pt }
table { text-align: center }
th { background-color: #ff6600;
   color: #000000;
   font-family: Arial, sans-serif;
   font-size: 12pt;
   font-weight: bold }
td { color: #000000;
   font-family: Arial, sans-serif;
   font-size: 12pt }
td.red { background-color: #cc0000 }
ul { list-style-image: url("bullet.gif") }
.bloodred { color:#CC0000 }
.bloodredbold { color: #CC0000; font-weight: bold }
.center { text-align: center }
</style>
</head>
<body>
<h1 class="center">The Halloween House of Terror!!</h1>
<div class="center">
<dl>
<dd>
<img src="skel05.gif" alt="skel05.gif" width="140" height="100" />
<img src="skel07.gif" alt="skel07.gif" width="140" height="100" />
<img src="skel06.gif" alt="skel06.gif" width="140" height="100" />
</dd>
</dl>
</div>
<hr />
<p>Voted the most frightening haunted house three years in a row,
the <span class="bloodredbold">Halloween House of Terror</span>
provides the ultimate in Halloween thrills. Over 20 rooms of
thrills and excitement to make your blood run cold and your hair
stand on end!</p>
<hr />
<p>Don't take our word for it .. preview some images of what
awaits!</p>
<table border="0" summary="House of Terror" width="75%" cellspacing="5"
    cellpadding="5">
<tr>
```

```
<td>
<img src="skel01.gif" alt="skel01.gif" width="140" height="100" />
</td>
<td class="red">Watch out for Esmerelda. You never
know what she has in her cauldron.</td>
<th><a href="code/entry.gif">The Entry Way</a></th>
</tr>
<tr>
<th><a href="code/bedroom.gif">The Master Bedroom</a></th>
<td class="red">Don't open the closet door, whatever
you do!</td>
   <td>
   <img src="skel02.gif" alt="skel02.gif" width="140" height="100" /></td>
</tr>
<tr>
   <td><img src="skel03.gif" alt="skel03.gif" width="140" height="100" /></td>
<td class="red">More than a few innocents have been
cast in chains for eons. They just aren't the same anymore.</td>
<th><a href="code/galley.gif">The Galley</a></th>
</tr>
<tr>
<th><a href="code/dungeon.gif">The Dungeon</a></th>
<td class="red">Better listen to the tour guides, or
you'll get lost!</td>
   <td><img src="skel04.gif" alt="skel04.gif" width="140" height="100" /></td>
</tr>
</table>
<hr />
<p>The <span class="bloodred">Halloween House of Terror</span> is
open from October 20 to November 1st, with a gala celebration on
Halloween night. Our hours are:</p>
<ul>
<li>Mon-Fri 5PM-midnight</li>
<li>Sat &amp; Sun 5PM-3AM</li>
<li>Halloween Night (31-Oct): 3PM-???</li>
</ul>
<p class="center">The <span class="bloodred">Halloween House of
Terror</span> is located at:<br />
The Old Waterfall Shopping Center<br />
1020 Mirabella Ave<br />
Springfield, CA 94532</p>
</body>
</html>
```

17

Figure 17.4 shows the result of the preceding code in a browser.

Output ▶

FIGURE 17.4
An example of
XHTML 1.0 Strict
code.

What Is Accessibility?

Accessibility is basically the effort to make websites as usable as possible for people with disabilities. This involves the creation of software and hardware that enables people with various disabilities to use computers and the Web. It also means addressing accessibility concerns in the design of HTML as a markup language and efforts on the part of web designers to incorporate accessibility into their websites. When a person with impaired vision uses a screen reader to visit a website, there are things the site's author can do to make that experience as rich and fulfilling as possible given the user's disability.

Common Myths Regarding Accessibility

Historically, there has been some resistance among web designers toward building websites in an accessible manner. This resistance has arisen not due to a wish to discriminate against people who might benefit from accessible design, but rather from a fear that accessibility will limit designers' options in how they create their sites. There's also the fact that accessibility seems like it will add additional work, and most people have too much to do already.

For a long time, many people thought that *accessible* was a code word for *all text*. It was believed that adding accessibility meant putting all of your content in a single column running straight down the page, and avoiding the bells and whistles that many people believe are necessary for an attractive website. The fact is that this couldn't be further from the truth. Although some common techniques can interfere with accessibility, that doesn't mean that you must remove any images, sounds, or multimedia from your website. Nor does it dictate that your layout be simplified.

The demand that accessibility places on designers is that they write clean, standards-compliant markup, take advantage of HTML features that improve accessibility, and that they use tags as they are intended to be used in the specification rather than based on how they make your pages look in the browser. The best example here is tables. At one time, nearly all websites used tables not only for showing things like tables of statistics, but also for controlling the layout of entire pages. These types of approaches run counter to how HTML was intended to be used, and make things much more difficult for users with alternative browsers.

Needless to say, to continue to use complex layouts in an accessible world, you have to upgrade to current techniques—in other words, create your layouts using cascading style sheets (CSS). Just as this approach provides cutting-edge look and feel in the latest browsers and yet gracefully degrades to still display information adequately in older browsers, it provides the same benefits in alternative browsers. Because the markup is so simple and is properly used when you use CSS to handle layout, alternative browsers for the disabled can handle the markup just fine. That's not the case when you use eight levels of nested tables to make your page look the way you want it to.

17

The other common misapprehension with regard to accessibility is that it will require a lot of extra work on your part. The fact is that it does require some extra work—creating your pages so that they take advantage of accessibility features in HTML is more work than leaving them out. However, in many cases, coding for accessibility will help all of your users, not just those using alternative browsers.

Section 508

Section 508 is a government regulation specifying that United States federal government agencies must provide access for all users, including those with disabilities, to electronic and information technology resources. It requires that federal agencies consider the needs of disabled users when they spend money on computer equipment or other computer resources. What this boils down to is that federal websites must be designed in an accessible fashion.

Not only did Section 508 change the rules of the game for many web designers (anyone involved with federal websites), but it also raised the profile of accessibility in general.

Thanks in part to the fact that people didn't really understand the implications of Section 508 at first, people started thinking a lot about accessibility and what it meant for the Web.

NOTE	For more information on Section 508, see http://www.section508. gov/.

Alternative Browsers

Just as there are a number of disabilities that can make it more challenging for people to use the Web, there are a number of browsers and assistive technologies that are designed to level the playing field to a certain degree. I'm going to discuss some common types of assistive technologies here so that when you design your web pages you can consider how they'll be used by people with disabilities.

Disabled users access the Web in a variety of ways, depending on their degree and type of disability. For example, some users just need to use extra large fonts on their computer, whereas others require a completely different interface from the standard used by most people.

Let's look at some of the kinds of browsers specifically designed for disabled users. For users who read Braille, there are a number of browsers available that provide Braille output. Screen readers are also common. Rather than displaying the page on the screen (or in addition to displaying it), screen readers attempt to organize the contents of a page in a linear fashion and use a voice synthesizer to speak the page's contents. Some browsers also accept audio input—users who are uncomfortable using a mouse and keyboard can use speech recognition to navigate the Web.

Another common type of assistive technology is a screen magnifier. Screen magnifiers enlarge the section of the screen where the user is working to make it easier for users with vision problems to use the computer.

Writing Accessible HTML

When it comes to writing accessible HTML, there are two steps to follow. The first step is to use the same tags you normally use as they were intended. The second step is to take advantage of HTML features specifically designed to improve accessibility. I've already mentioned a number of times that tags should be used based on their semantic meaning rather than how they're rendered in browsers. For example, if you want to print some bold text in a standard size font, <h4> will work, except that it not only boldfaces the text, it also indicates that it's a level 4 heading. In screen readers or other alternative browsers, that might cause confusion for your users.

Tables

This problem is particularly acute when it comes to tables. I've already mentioned that it's not a good idea to use tables for page layout when you're designing for accessibility. Alternative browsers must generally indicate to users that a table has been encountered, and then unwind the tables so that the information can be presented to the user in a linear fashion. To make things easier on these users, you should use tables as intended where you can. Even if you can't avoid using tables to lay out your page, be aware of how the table will be presented to users. If possible, try to avoid putting lots of navigation text and other supplemental text between the beginning of the page and the content the user is actually looking for.

When you're presenting real tabular data, it's worthwhile to use all of the supplemental tags for tables that are all too often ignored. When you're inserting row and column headings, use the <th> tag. If the default alignment or text presentation is not to your liking, use CSS to modify it. Some browsers will indicate to users that the table headings are distinct from the table data. Furthermore, if you label your table, using the <caption> tag is a better choice than simply inserting a paragraph of text before or after the table. Some browsers indicate that the text is a table caption.

Finally, using the summary attribute of the <table> tag can be a great aid to users with alternative browsers. How you use the summary and caption are up to you. The caption can explain what the table contains, and the summary can explain how the data in the table is used if it's not obvious from the row and/or column headings. Here's an example of a table that's designed for accessibility:

```
<table summary="This is the famous Boston Consulting Group Product
Portfolio Matrix. It's a two by two matrix with labels." border="1"
cellpadding="12">
  <caption>Boston Consulting Group Product Portfolio Matrix</caption>
  <tr>
    <td colspan="2" rowspan="2"><br /></td>
    <th colspan="2">Market Share</th>
  </tr>
  <tr>
    <th>High</th>
    <th>Low</th>
  </tr>
  <tr>
    <th rowspan="2">Market Growth</th>
    <th>High</th>
```

17

```
      <td align="center">Star</td>
      <td align="center">Problem Child</td>
    </tr>
    <tr>
      <th>Low</th>
      <td align="center">Cash Cow</td>
      <td align="center">Dog</td>
    </tr>
</table>
```

Links

As mentioned in Lesson 16, "Writing Good Web Pages: Do's and Don'ts," avoiding the "here" syndrome is imperative, particularly when it comes to accessibility. Having all the links on your page described as "click here" or "here" isn't very helpful to disabled users (or any others). Just thinking carefully about the text you place inside a link to make it descriptive of the link destination is a good start.

To make your links even more usable, you can employ the `title` attribute. The `title` attribute is used to associate some descriptive text with a link. It is used not only by alternative browsers, but many standard browsers will display a tool tip with the link title when the user holds her mouse pointer over it. Here are some examples:

```
<a href="http://www.dmoz.org/"
title="The volunteer maintained directory.">dmoz</a>

<a href="document.pdf" title="1.5 meg PDF document">Special Report</a>
```

Navigational links are a special case because they usually come in sizable groups. Many pages have a nice navigation bar right across the top that's useful to regular users who are able to skim the page and go directly to the content that they want. Users who use screen readers with their browsers and other assistive technologies aren't so lucky. You can imagine what it would be like to visit a site that has 10 navigational links across the top of the page if you relied on every page being read to you. Every time you move from one page to the next, the navigation links would have to be read over again.

There are a few ways around this that vary in elegance. If you're using CSS to position elements on your page, it can make sense to place the navigational elements after your main content in your HTML file, but use CSS to position them wherever you like. When a user with a screen reader visits the site, he'll get the content before getting the navigation. Another option is to include a link on your page that enables the user to skip past the navigation—you can use CSS to hide this link from users who can see the page, leaving it in place for disabled users who can benefit from it.

TIP

It's worth remembering that many disabled users rely on keyboards to access the Web. You can make things easier on them by using the `accesskey` and `tabindex` attributes of the `<a>` tag to enable them to step through the links on your page in a logical order. This is particularly useful if you also include forms on your page. For example, if you have a form that has links interspersed in the form, setting up the `tabindex` order so that the user can tab through the form completely before he runs into any links can save him a lot of aggravation. This is the sort of convenience that all of your users will appreciate as well.

Images

Needless to say, images are a sticky point when it comes to accessibility. Users with impaired vision may not be able to appreciate your images at all. However, clever design and usage of the tools provided by HTML can, to a certain degree, minimize the problem of image usage.

17

Images are known for having probably the best-known accessibility feature of any HTML element. The alt attribute has been around as long as the `<img>` tag and provides text that can stand in for an image if the user has a text-only browser or the image wasn't downloaded for some reason. Back when everybody used slow dialup connections to the Internet, it was easy to become intimately familiar with alt text because it displayed while the images on a page downloaded. Later, some browsers started showing alt text as a tool tip when the user let her mouse pointer hover over an image.

Despite the fact that alt text is useful, easy to add, and required by the XHTML 1.0 specification, many pages on the Internet still lack meaningful alternative text for most (if not all) of their images. Taking a few extra minutes to enter alt text for your images is a must for anyone who uses HTML that includes images. Also bear in mind that using `alt=""` is perfectly valid and is sometimes appropriate. In particular, some sites use very small images to help position elements on a page. Although this practice is strongly discouraged, it's still used. Text-based browsers will, in the absence of alt text, generally display something like [IMAGE] on the page. If you include the alt attribute but leave it empty, the label IMAGE will be left out, making things easier on your users.

HTML also provides an another way of describing images that's meant to improve accessibility: the longdesc attribute of the `<img>` tag. The longdesc attribute is intended to be used as a place to enter long descriptions of images. For example, if an image is a chart or graph, you can explain how it is used and what information it is intended to convey. If the picture is a nice photo of a waterfall, you can describe the waterfall. In many cases, images are used simply to make web pages flashier or aesthetically pleasing, and nothing more than `alt` text is required. However, when the actual meaning of a page is conveyed through the use of images, providing descriptions of those images is a key to accessibility. For example, let's say that you're working for a financial publication, and a story on the declining stock market includes a graph showing the consistent decline of the major indexes over the past few years. In print, that image would probably include a caption explaining what's in the image. On the Web, you could put that caption in the image's `longdesc` attribute. Or, if you prefer, you could put it on the page as a caption, as long as your layout indicates in some way that the caption refers to the image in question.

Here's an example of what I'm talking about:

```
<img src="graph1.gif" longdesc="Graph showing that the S&P
500 and Dow Jones Industrial Average have dropped an average of 20%
annually over the last 3 years." />
```

There's one final area to discuss when it comes to images—the marriage of images and links in the form of image maps. As you might imagine, image maps can be a major accessibility issue. The only way around this is to provide users with an alternative to imagemaps in the form of text links. Whenever you use an image map, you should make sure to include text equivalents of the links somewhere on the page.

Designing for Accessibility

Just as important as taking advantage of the HTML features provided specifically for accessibility is taking care to design your pages in a manner that's as accommodating as possible for users who are in need of assistance. Most of these techniques are relevant to all users, not just those using alternative browsers or assistive technologies.

Use Color

A common pitfall designers fall into is using color to confer meaning to users. For example, they print an error on the page and change the font color to red to indicate that something went wrong. Unfortunately, visually impaired users won't be able to distinguish your error message from the rest of the text on the page without reading it. Needless to say, putting two elements on the page that are the same except for color (such as using colors to indicate the status of something) is not accessible. You can add borders to elements that need to stand out, or you can label them with text. For example, you might display an error message this way:

```
<p class="error">ERROR: You must enter your full name.</p>
```

Fonts

When you specify fonts on your pages, you can cause accessibility problems if you're not careful. In some cases, font specification doesn't matter at all because the user accesses your site with a screen reader or alternative browser that completely ignores your font settings. However, users who simply see poorly can have an unpleasant experience if you set your fonts to an absolute size—particularly if you choose a small size. If a user has set his browser's default font to be larger than normal, and your pages are hard coded to use 9-point text, that user will probably dump your site altogether.

In many cases, it makes sense to leave the default font specification alone for most of the text on your site. That way, users can set their fonts as they choose, and you won't interfere with their personal preferences. If you do modify the fonts on the page, make sure that the fonts scale with the user's settings so that they can see the text at a size that is comfortable for them.

Take Advantage of All HTML Tags

It's easy to fall into the trap of using `<i>` or `<b>` instead of more specific tags when you need to add emphasis to something. For example, let's say you're citing a passage from a book. When you enter the book title, you could indicate to your users that it's a proper title by putting it inside the `<i>` tag, or you could use the `<cite>` tag. There are plenty of other underutilized tags as well, all of which provide some semantic meaning in addition to the text formatting they're associated with.

Even in cases in which you really just want to emphasize text, it's preferable to use `<em>` and `<strong>` over `<i>` and `<b>`. These tags provide a lot more meaning than the basic text formatting tags that are often used. Not all alternative browsers will take advantage of any or all of these tags, but conveying as much meaning as possible through your choice of tags won't hurt accessibility for sure, and will help some now and could help more in the future. There's no downside to taking this approach, either.

Frames and Linked Windows

Frames are, to put it bluntly, a barrier to accessibility. There are some workarounds available, but the bottom line is that if you're really concerned about accessibility, you should probably avoid frames. Using linked windows and pop-up windows can also be a huge hassle from an accessibility perspective.

If you opt to use frames, you should include titles for all of your frames, not just the document containing the frameset. Using regular browsers, the titles of these documents are suppressed. That's not necessarily the case with alternative browsers. Some will provide

17

links to the individual frames when you pull up the frameset, and having titles makes it easier for users to distinguish between them.

Forms

Forms present another thorny accessibility issue. Nearly all web applications are based on forms, and failure to make them accessible can cost you users. For example, large online stores have a serious financial interest in focusing on form accessibility. How many sales would Amazon or eBay lose if their sites weren't accessible? Some work on making sure the forms that enable you to purchase items are accessible can really pay off.

One key thing to remember is that disabled users often navigate using only the keyboard. As I mentioned when talking about links, assigning sensible `tabindex` values to your form fields can really increase both the usability and accessibility of your forms. The other advanced form tags, such as `fieldset`, `optgroup`, and `label`, can be beneficial in terms of usability as well.

Validating Your Sites for Accessibility

There's no reason to rely on luck when it comes to determining whether your site measures up when it comes to accessibility. Just as you can use the W3C validator to verify that your HTML files are standards compliant, you can use the WebXACT, the accessibility validator, to determine how well a page complies with accessibility guidelines. The validator can be found at http://webxact.watchfire.com. It can validate a site against the Section 508 guidelines mentioned earlier, or against the Web Content Accessibility Guidelines developed by the W3C.

Its operation is virtually identical to that of the HTML validator provided by the W3C. If you submit your page to the validator, it will generate a report that indicates which areas of your page need improvement, and will also provide general tips that can be applied to any page. It also prints out the full content of the page and adds in links to the report so that you can see exactly which places on the page the report refers to. Figure 17.5 is a screenshot of WebXACT's report on the digg.com page.

Another nice feature of WebXACT is that the report contains links to specific ways to address the issues it raises. For example, Figure 17.6 is the page that WebXACT links to when you have repetitive navigation links on a page.

WebXACT is provided free of charge by Watchfire, which is in the business of providing website management tools. The downside of the free version is that it validates only one page at a time. This isn't as bad as it sounds because most larger sites have a lot of common markup from page to page so if you fix an issue in one place, you can often fix it on all of your pages. However, Watchfire also offers commercial versions of WebXACT that can be installed on a server or used by a single user to validate entire sites.

FIGURE 17.5
An accessibility report generated by WebXACT.

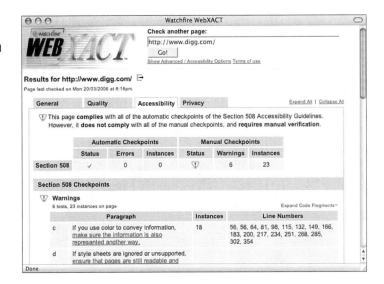

FIGURE 17.6
Advice from WebXACT on how to fix an accessibility issue.

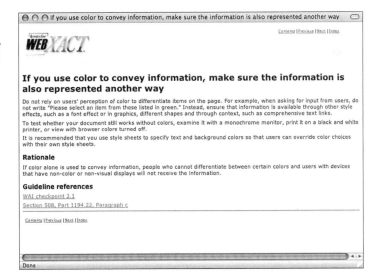

17

Further Reading

This lesson is really the tip of the iceberg when it comes to handling accessibility on websites. If you're going to make a commitment to creating an accessible site, you'll probably want to research the issue further. Your first stop should be online accessibility resources. The W3C provides a huge body of information on accessibility as part of their Web Accessibility Initiative. The home page is http://www.w3.org/WAI/.

If you maintain a personal site, you might also find Mark Pilgrim's online book, *Dive Into Accessibility* (http://diveintoaccessibility.org/), to be a useful resource. There are plenty of other sites that discuss accessibility as well. Just enter the word **accessibility** into your favorite search engine to get a list. The WAI also provides a list of resources at http://www.w3.org/WAI/References/.

There have also been several books written on web accessibility. Joe Clark's *Building Accessible Websites* is very well regarded. You can find out more about the book at the book's website: http://www.joeclark.org/book/. Other books include John Slatin and Sharon Rush's book, *Maximum Accessibility: Making Your Web Site More Usable for Everyone*, or *Constructing Accessible Web Sites*, which is a group effort from Glasshaus.

Summary

HTML 4.01 and XHTML 1.0 accommodate the needs of many visitors by providing three different approaches to website design. Hopefully, you now realize that the needs of your visitors also can affect the approach you use in your website design. The key is to anticipate those needs and try to address them as broadly as possible. Not every site has to be filled with multimedia that implements the latest and greatest web technologies. On the other hand, certain topics almost demand higher levels of page design. Listen to the needs of your visitors when you design your pages, and you'll keep them coming back.

Even though accessibility issues ostensibly affect only a small percentage of web users, they should not be ignored. Many accessibility-related improvements actually improve the web experience for most users. Leaving out disabled users by not accounting for them in your designs is inconsiderate, and can often be a poor business decision as well. Adding accessibility features to an existing site can be challenging, but when you build new sites from scratch, making them accessible can often be done with little additional effort. If I've convinced you of the importance of accessibility in this lesson, you'll probably want to dig into the resources listed previously for more information.

Workshop

As if you haven't had enough already, here's a refresher course. As always, there are questions, quizzes, and exercises that will help you remember some of the most important points in this lesson.

Q&A

Q Feedback from visitors to my site varies a lot. Some want my pages to use less multimedia, whereas others want more. Is there an easy way to satisfy both of them?

A You've already learned that you can provide links to external multimedia files. This is the best approach for visitors who want less multimedia because they won't see it unless they click the link.

You can also simply ask them which version of your site they want to see. I generally recommend building a site that works well for users regardless of their connection speed or browser capabilities, but in some cases it makes sense to create alternative versions of your site. You can start out with an entry page that allows your users to choose between the different versions of the site, or you can start out with the fancier page and provide a link to the text version that shows up regardless of their browser's capabilities.

Q I use a lot of external files on my website, and they can be downloaded from several different pages. Wouldn't it be more efficient to include a link to the correct readers or viewers on the pages where the external files appear?

A Although it's much easier for the visitor to download an external file and the appropriate reader or helper application from the same page, it might be more difficult for you to maintain your pages when the URLs for the helper applications change. A good compromise is to include a Download page on your website with links to all the helper applications that the visitor will need. After the visitor downloads the external file, she can then navigate to your Download page to get the helper application she needs to view that file.

Q If I don't make my site accessible, what percentage of my audience will I lose?

A Even if you weren't wondering about this yourself, there's a good chance your boss probably wants to know. Unfortunately, there's no hard and fast number. I've seen it reported that 10% of the population has disabilities, but not all of those disabilities affect one's ability to access the Web.

17

Q **Can I run into legal trouble if I don't bother with making my site accessible?**

A If you're in the United States, the answer to this question is no, unless you're working on a site for the federal government and are bound by Section 508.

Quiz

1. How do real-world user needs vary?

2. What are some important things to include on your site to help those who are new to computers or the Internet?

3. How does the HTML 4.01 or XHTML 1.0 Transitional specification help you accommodate the needs of more visitors?

4. True or false: It's better to have a lot of frames in a frameset because you can keep more information in the browser window at the same time.

5. What are the advantages and disadvantages of using HTML 4.01 or XHTML 1.0 Strict to fulfill the needs of your visitors?

6. True or false: To make a site truly accessible, no images can be used for navigation or links.

7. How should navigation be placed on a page in order to make it most accessible?

8. Name three attributes of tags aimed specifically at accessibility.

Quiz Answers

1. Different users will have different levels of experience. Browser preferences will vary. Some want to see a lot of multimedia, whereas others prefer none at all. Some prefer images and multimedia that are interactive, whereas others prefer simpler pictures that demonstrate a process or technique on how to do something. Other preferences are more specific to the interests of the visitors.

2. Include pages on your site that help the visitor find the information she's looking for. Also include pages that help them find their way around the site.

3. HTML 4.01 or XHTML 1.0 Transitional is designed to be backward compatible with older browsers. It enables you to use tags and attributes that are deprecated in the Strict specification.

4. False. Too many frames can be confusing for new users, and they may be too small to be useful when they're viewed at lower resolutions.

5. The disadvantage of using the Strict specifications is that if you adhere to them, some percentage of users won't see your site the way you designed it. The advantage is that you can use a lot of advanced techniques that make your site easier to create and work better with newer browsers.

6. False; however, you must use the images in an accessible manner.

7. Navigation should be placed after the main content on a page to make it accessible with users who must navigate the page in a linear fashion.

8. Some attributes designed to improve accessibility are the `title` attribute of the `<a>` tag, the `longdesc` and `alt` attributes of the `<img>` tag, and the `summary` attribute of the `<table>` tag.

Exercises

1. Design a simple navigation system for a website and describe it in a manner that makes sense to you. Then ask others to review it and verify that your explanations are clear to them.

2. Make a list of the topics that you want to discuss on your website. Go through the list a second time and see whether you can anticipate the types of people who will be interested in those topics. Finally, review the list a third time and list the special needs that you might need to consider for each user group.

3. Visit WebXACT, the accessibility validator and see how your site rates against the accessibility guidelines.

4. Make sure that all the `<img>` tags on your site have `alt` attributes. It's a good first step toward accessibility.

17

PART VI:
Going Live on the Web

LESSON 18:
Putting Your Site Online

The catchphrase "If you build it, they will come," from the movie *Field of Dreams* notwithstanding, just uploading your site to a web server somewhere doesn't mean that you'll attract many visitors. In fact, with millions of sites online already, some of them with thousands of documents, you'll need to promote your site if you want to build an audience.

In this Lesson

So, how do you entice people to come to your site? This lesson will show you some of the ways, including the following:

- What a web server does and why you need one
- Where you can find a web server to host your site
- How to deploy your website
- How to find out your URL
- How to test and troubleshoot your web pages
- Advertising your site
- Getting your site listed on the major web directories
- Submitting your site to search engines
- Using business cards, letterheads, and brochures
- Locating more directories and related web pages
- Using log files and counters to find out who's viewing your pages

What Does a Web Server Do?

To publish web pages, you'll need a web server. The server listens for requests for web browsers and returns the web pagees specified in those requests. Web servers and web browsers communicate by using the *Hypertext Transfer Protocol* (*HTTP*), a protocol created specifically for the request and transfer of hypertext documents over the Web. Because of this use, web servers often are called *HTTP servers*.

Other Things Web Servers Do

Although the web server's primary purpose is to answer requests from browsers, it's responsible for several other tasks. You'll learn about some of them in the following sections.

File and Media Type Determination

In Lesson 11, "Integrating Multimedia: Sound, Video, and More," you learned about content types and how browsers and servers use file extensions to determine file types. Servers are responsible for telling the browsers what kinds of content the files contain. Web servers are configured so that they know which media types to assign to files that are requested. In "Questions to Ask Your Webmaster" later in this lesson, you'll learn about some of the important questions you should ask your web presence provider or webmaster before you publish your pages.

File Management

The web server also is responsible for very rudimentary file management—mostly in determining where to find a file and keeping track of where it's gone. If a browser requests a file that doesn't exist, the web server returns the HTTP error code 404 and sends an error page to the browser. You can configure the web server to redirect from one URL to another, automatically pointing the browser to a new URL for files that have moved. Servers can also be set up to return a particular file if a URL refers to a directory on a server without specifying a filename.

Finally, servers keep log files for information on how many times each URL on the site has been accessed, including the address of the computer that accessed it, the date and, optionally, which browser they used, and the URL of the page that referred them to your page.

Server-Side Scripts and Forms Processing

In addition to serving up static documents like HTML files and images, most web servers also offer the option of running scripts or programs that generate documents on the fly. These scripts can be used to create catalogs and shopping carts, discussion boards, clients to read email, or content management systems to publish documents dynamically. In fact, any website that you find that does more than just publish plain old documents is running some kind of script or program on the server. There are a number of popular scripting platforms available for writing web applications. Which one is available for your use depends in part on which web server you're using. PHP is probably the most popular choice. It's easy to get started with and runs on most servers. Other popular choices include Active Server Pages (or ASP), which runs on Microsoft Windows, or Java Server Pages (JSP), which can run on most servers. The old standby is CGI, which stands for the Common Gateway Interface. It provides a way for the web server to talk to external programs written in just about any language. Traditionally the most popular choice for writing CGI scripts is Perl.

Server-Side File Processing

Some servers can process files before they send them along to the browsers. On a simple level, there are server-side includes, which can insert a date or a chunk of boilerplate text into each page, or run a program. Some of the access counters you see on web pages are run in this way. Also, you can use server-side processing in much more sophisticated ways to modify files on the fly for different browsers or to execute small bits of code embedded in your pages.

Authentication and Security

Password protection is provided out of the box by most web servers. Using authentication, you can create users and assign passwords to them, and you can restrict access to certain files and directories. You can also restrict access to files or to an entire site based on site names or IP addresses. For example, you can prevent anyone outside your company from viewing files that are intended for empoyees. It's common for people to build custom authentication systems using server-side scripts as well.

For security, some servers now provide a mechanism for encrypted connections and transactions using the *SSL (Secure Socket Layer)* protocol. SSL allows the browser to authenticate the server, proving that the server is who it says it is, and an encrypted connection between the browser and the server so that sensitive information between the two cannot be understood if it is intercepted.

Locating a Web Server

Before you can put your site on the Web, you'll need to find a web server. How easy this is depends on how you get your access to the Internet.

Using a Web Server Provided by Your School or Work

If you get your Internet connection through school or work, that organization may allow you to publish web pages on its own web server. Given that these organizations usually have fast connections to the Internet and people to administer the site for you, this situation is ideal.

You'll have to ask your system administrator, computer consultant, webmaster, or network provider whether a web server is available and, if so, what the procedures are for putting up your pages. You'll learn more about what to ask later in this lesson.

Using a Commercial Internet or Web Service

You may pay for your Internet access through an Internet service provider (ISP), or a commercial online service. Many of these services allow you to publish your web pages, although it may cost you extra. There might be restrictions on the kinds of pages you can publish or whether you can run server-side scripts. Ask your provider's help line or participate in online groups or conferences on Internet services to see how others have set up web publishing.

There are many organizations that have popped up that provide nothing but web hosting. These services, most commonly known as *web hosts*, usually provide a way for you to transfer your files to their server (usually FTP), as well as the disk space and the actual web server software that provides access to your files. They also have professional systems administrators onsite to make sure the servers are running well at all times.

Generally, you're charged a flat monthly rate, with added charges if you use too much disk space or network bandwidth. Many web hosts provide support for server-side scripts, and often install some commonly used scripts so that you don't even have to set them up for yourself. Most also enable you to set up your site with your own domain name, and some even provide a facility for registering domain names as well. These features can make using commercial web hosting providers an especially attractive option.

CAUTION | Make sure that when you register your domains, they are registered in your name rather than in the name of the hosting provider or domain registrar who registers them on your behalf. You want to make sure that you own the domain names you register.

To get your own domain name, you need to register it with an authorized registrar. The initial cost to register and acquire your domain name can be as low as $8 per year. Thereafter, an annual fee keeps your domain name active. Once you have your own domain name, you can set it up at your hosting provider so that you can use it in your URLs and receive email at that domain. Your site will have an address such as http://www.example.com/.

Many ISPs and web hosts can assist you in registering your domain name. You can register your domain directly with an authorized registrar such as Network Solutions (http://www.networksolutions.com/), Register.com, dotster.com, or godaddy.com. Most of these services also offer *domain parking*, a service that allows you to host your domain with them temporarily until you choose a hosting provider or set up your own server. The prices vary, so you should shop around before registering your domain.

NOTE

> The Ultimate Web Host List at http://webhostlist.internetlist.com/ is a good resource for finding and evaluating web hosting services. For more information, see Appendix A, "Sources for Further Information."

Setting Up Your Own Server

18

If you're really courageous and want the ultimate in web publishing, running your own website is the way to go. You can publish as much as you want and include any kind of content you want. You'll also be able to use forms, scripts, streaming multimedia, and other options that aren't available to people who don't have their own servers. Other web hosts might not let you use these kinds of features. However, running a server definitely isn't for everyone. The cost and maintenance time can be daunting, and you need a level of technical expertise that the average user might not possess. Furthermore, you need some way to connect it to the Internet. Many Internet service providers won't let you run servers over your connection, and putting your server in a hosting facility or getting a full-time Internet connection for your server can be costly.

Free Hosting

If you can't afford to pay a web hosting provider to host your website, there are some free alternatives. Yahoo Geocities (at http://geocities.yahoo.com/) provides free Web hosting, as does Google Pages (http://pages.google.com/). There are lots of other similar services as well, including services that host particular kinds of content like weblogs (http://www.blogger.com/), journals (http://www.livejournal.com/), or photos (http://www.flickr.com/). These are just some examples. The tradeoff is that the pages on these sites have advertisements included on them and that your bandwidth usage is generally sharply limited. There are often other rules regarding the amount of space you can use as well. Free hosting can be a good option for hobbyists, but if you're serious about your site, you'll probably want to host it with a commercial service.

Organizing Your HTML Files for Publishing

Once you have access to a web server, you can publish the website you've labored so hard to create. Before you actually move it into place on your server, however, it's important to organize your files. Also, you should have a good idea of what goes where to avoid lost files and broken links.

Questions to Ask Your Webmaster

The *webmaster* is the person who runs your web server. This person also might be your system administrator, help desk administrator, or network administrator. Before you can publish your site, you should get several facts from the webmaster about how the server is set up. The following list of questions will help you later in this book when you're ready to figure out what you can and cannot do with your server:

- **Where on the server will I put my files?** In most cases, someone will create a directory on the server where your files will reside. Know where that directory is and how to gain access to it.

- **What's the URL of my top-level directory?** This URL will usually be different from the actual path to your files.

- **What's the name of the system's default index file?** This file is loaded by default when a URL ends with a directory name. Usually it's `index.html` or `index.htm`, but it may be `default.htm`, or something else.

- **Can I run PHP, ASP, CGI, or other types of scripts?** Depending on your server, the answer to this question may be a flat-out "No," or you might be limited to certain programs and capabilities.

- **Do you support special plug-ins or file types?** If your site will include multi-media files (MP3, RealAudio, Shockwave, Flash, or others), your webmaster might need to configure the server to accommodate those file types. Make sure that the server properly handles special types of files before you create them.

- **Do you support FrontPage Server Extensions?** Microsoft FrontPage, a popular web authoring tool for Windows platforms, enables you to develop web pages and complete websites. To take full advantage of its features, however, the web server must have FrontPage Server Extensions installed on it. If you're interested in using FrontPage to design advanced pages, be sure to ask your ISP whether it supports the Server Extensions.

- **Are there limitations on what or how much I can put up?** Some servers restrict pages to specific content (for example, only work-related pages) or restrict the amount of storage you can use. Make sure you understand these restrictions before you publish your content.

- **Is there a limit to the amount of bandwidth that my site can consume?** This is somewhat related to the previous question. Most web hosts only allow you to transfer a certain amount of data over their network over a given period of time before they either cut you off or start charging you more money. You should ask what your bandwidth allotment is and make sure that you have enough to cover the traffic you anticipate. (The bandwidth allotment from most web hosts is more than enough for all but the most popular sites.)

- **Do you provide any canned scripts that I can use for my web pages?** If you aren't keen on writing your own scripts to add advanced features to your pages, ask your service provider whether it provides any scripts that might be of assistance. For example, many ISPs provide a script for putting a page counter on your home page. Others might provide access to form-processing scripts as well.

18

Keeping Your Files Organized with Directories

Probably the easiest way to organize your site is to include all the files in a single directory. If you have many extra files—images, for example—you can put them in a subdirectory under that main directory. Your goal is to contain all your files in a single place rather than scatter them around on your hard drive. You can then set all the links in those files to be relative to that directory. This makes it easier to move the directory around to different servers without breaking the links.

Having a Default Index File and Correct Filenames

Web servers usually have a default index file that's loaded when a URL ends with a directory name rather than a filename. One of the questions you should ask your webmaster is, "What's the name of this default file?" For most web servers, this file is called `index.html`. Your home page, or top-level index, for each site should have this name so that the server knows which page to send as the default page. Each subdirectory should also have a default file if it contains any HTML files. If you use this default filename, the URL to that page will be shorter because you don't have to include the actual filename. For example, your URL might be http://www.myserver.com/www/ rather than http://www.myserver.com/www/index.html.

CAUTION | If you don't put an index file in a directory, many web servers will enable people to browse the contents of the directory. If you don't want people to snoop around in your files, you should include an index file or use the web server's access controls to disable directory browsing.

Also, each file should have an appropriate extension indicating its type so the server can map it to the appropriate file type. If you've been reading this book in sequential order, all your files should have this special extension already and you shouldn't have any problems. Table 18.1 lists the common file extensions that you should be using for your files and multimedia.

TABLE 18.1   Common File Types and Extensions

Format	Extension
HTML	`.html, .htm`
ASCII Text	`.txt`
PostScript	`.ps`
GIF	`.gif`
JPEG	`.jpg, .jpeg`
PNG	`.png`
Shockwave Flash	`.swf`
AU Audio	`.au`
WAV Audio	`.wav`
MPEG Audio	`.mp2, .mp3`
MPEG Video	`.mpeg, .mpg`
QuickTime Video	`.mov`
AVI Video	`.avi`
Portable Document Format	`.pdf`
RealAudio	`.ra, .ram`

If you're using multimedia files on your site that aren't part of this list, you might need to configure your server to handle that file type. You'll learn more about this issue later in this lesson.

Publishing Your Files

Got everything organized? Then all that's left is to move everything to the server. Once your files have been uploaded to a directory that the server exposes on the Web, you're officially published on the Web. That's all there is to putting your pages online.

Where's the appropriate spot on the server, however? You should ask your webmaster for this information. Also, you should find out how to access that directory on the server, whether it's simply copying files, using FTP to put them on the server, or using some other method.

Moving Files Between Systems

If you're using a web server that has been set up by someone else, usually you'll have to upload your web files from your system to theirs using FTP, SCP (secure copy), or some other method. Although the HTML markup within your files is completely cross-platform, moving the actual files from one type of system to another sometimes has its drawbacks. In particular, be careful to do the following:

- **Watch out for filename restrictions**—If your server is a PC and you've been writing your files on some other system, you might have to rename your files and the links to them to follow the correct filenaming conventions. (Moving files you've created on a PC to some other system usually isn't a problem.)

  Also, watch out if you're moving files from a Macintosh to other systems. Make sure that your filenames don't have spaces or other funny characters in them. Keep your filenames as short as possible, use only letters and numbers, and you'll be fine.

- **Watch out for uppercase or lowercase sensitivity**—Filenames on computers running Microsoft Windows are not case sensitive. On UNIX and Mac OS X systems, they are. If you develop your pages on a computer running Windows and publish them on a server that has case-sensitive filenames, you must make sure that you have entered the URLs in your links properly. If you're linking to a file named `About.html`, on your computer running Windows, `about.html` would work, but on a UNIX server it would not.

- **Be aware of carriage returns and line feeds**—Different systems use different methods for ending a line. The Macintosh uses carriage returns, UNIX uses line feeds, and DOS uses both. When you move files from one system to another, most of the time the end-of-line characters will be converted appropriately, but sometimes they won't. The characters that aren't converted can cause your file to come out double-spaced or all on a single line when it's moved to another system.

18

Most of the time, this failure to convert doesn't matter because browsers ignore spurious returns or line feeds in your HTML files. The existence or absence of either one isn't terribly important. However, it might be an issue in sections of text that you've marked up with <pre>; you might find that your well-formatted text that worked so well on one platform doesn't come out that way after it's been moved.

If you do have end-of-line problems, you have two options. Many text editors enable you to save ASCII files in a format for another platform. If you know the platform to which you're moving, you can prepare your files for that platform before moving them. If you're moving to a UNIX system, small filters for converting line feeds called dos2unix and unix2dos may be available on the UNIX or DOS systems. And you can convert Macintosh files to UNIX-style files by using the following command line in UNIX:

```
tr '\015' '\012' < oldfile.html > newfile.html
```

In this example, oldfile.html is the original file with end-of-line problems, and newfile.html is the name of the new file.

Using FTP to Upload Files

In the preceding list of tips about moving files, I talked a little bit about FTP. If you already know how to transfer files using FTP, you can just skip this section.

Most web surfers have used FTP whether they know it or not. When you download a file from a remote site to save on your computer, sometimes it's transferred via FTP rather than HTTP. When you're publishing files to a website, the way you use FTP is a bit different.

When you download files from a public site, generally you log in anonymously—the browser takes care of that for you. When you publish files using FTP, you log in with a specific username and password.

NOTE

> You'll have to get the username and password you'll use to publish files using FTP from your Internet service provider or system administrator.

Another difference between file downloads using FTP and publishing files using FTP is that when you publish files, you'll probably use an interactive FTP session. In other words, rather than just connecting, uploading a file, and disconnecting in one step, you'll create an FTP session, upload or download files as needed, and then disconnect. You'll manually open and close the connection and perform the required tasks while that session is open.

One nice thing about FTP is that there are many clients available. First of all, all popular browsers can be used as FTP clients. That's why you can download files from FTP sites transparently using your browser. However, I recommend that you skip right past them and use something else to publish files. The FTP capabilities in web browsers were designed to make it easy to download one file, not upload an entire website.

One option that's often available is publishing files through your HTML editing tool. Many popular HTML and text editors have built-in support for FTP. You should definitely check your tool of choice to see whether it enables you to transfer files using FTP from directly within the application. Some popular tools that provide FTP support include Adobe Dreamweaver and HomeSite, Barebones BBEdit, and Microsoft FrontPage. Text editors like UltraEdit and jEdit support saving files to a server via FTP as well. There are many others.

If your HTML editor doesn't support FTP, or if you're transferring images, multimedia files, or even bunches of HTML files at once, you'll probably want a dedicated FTP client. FTP is common enough that there are many, many excellent FTP clients available. A list of some popular choices follows:

- CuteFTP (Windows)—http://www.globalscape.com/
- WS_FTP (Windows)—http://www.ipswitch.com/
- FTP Explorer (Windows)—http://www.ftpx.com/
- FileZilla (Windows)—http://filezilla.sourceforge.net/
- Cyberduck (Mac OS)—http://www.cyberduck.ch/
- Fugu (Mac OS)—http://rsug.itd.umich.edu/software/fugu/
- Transmit (Mac OS)—http://www.panic.com/transmit/
- Fetch (Mac OS)—http://fetchsoftworks.com/

18

How the FTP client is used varies depending on which client you choose, but there are some commonalities among all of them that you can count on (more or less). You'll start out by configuring a site consisting of the hostname of the server where you'll publish the files, your username and password, and perhaps some other settings that you can leave alone if you're just getting started.

CAUTION

> If you're sharing a computer with other people, you probably won't want to store the password for your account on the server in the FTP client. Make sure that the site is configured so that you have to enter your password every time you connect to the remote site.

Once you've set up your FTP client to connect to your server, you can connect to the site. Depending on your FTP client, you should be able to simply drag files onto the window that shows the list of files on your site to upload them, or drag them from the listing on the server to your local computer to download them.

Remote Management Tools

Most HTML editing tools enable you to manage and update the contents of your pages on a remote web server.

Microsoft's FrontPage is a web development tool aimed at small to medium websites. FrontPage provides a WYSIWYG page editor and a site manager for managing document trees and links, as well as a variety of server extensions that can be used with a variety of servers, ranging from Windows-based to UNIX servers.

These extensions enable Frontpage users to add a variety of features, including interactive discussion groups and other interactive features. These extensions also enable you to use FrontPage to upload files on the server as you make changes to your site. FrontPage enables you to publish your website to a remote server, regardless of whether it has the FrontPage Server Extensions installed.

Other site development and management tools, such as Adobe HomeSite, GoLive, and Dreamweaver (www.adobe.com), enable you to develop offline and then update the content on a remote server.

Troubleshooting

What happens if you upload all your files to the server and try to display your home page in your browser, and something goes wrong? Here's the first place to look.

I Can't Access the Server

If your browser can't even get to your server, this probably isn't a problem you can fix. Make sure that you have entered the right server name and that it's a complete hostname (usually ending in .com, .edu, .net, or some other common suffix). Make sure that you haven't mistyped your URL and that you're using the right protocol. If your webmaster told you that your URL included a port number, make sure that you're including that port number in the URL after the hostname.

Also make sure that your network connection is working. Can you get to other URLs? Can you get to the top-level home page for the site itself?

If none of these ideas solve the problem, perhaps your server is down or not responding. Call your webmaster to find out whether he or she can help.

I Can't Access Files

What if all your files are showing up as Not Found or Forbidden? First, check your URL. If you're using a URL with a directory name at the end, try using an actual filename at the end. Double-check the path to your files; remember that the path in the URL might be different from the path on the actual disk. Also, keep case sensitivity in mind. If your file is `MyFile.html`, make sure that you're not trying `myfile.html` or `Myfile.html`.

If the URL appears to be correct, check the file permissions. On UNIX systems, all your directories should be world-executable and all your files should be world-readable. You can ensure that all the permissions are correct by using the following commands:

```
chmod 755 filename
chmod 755 directoryname
```

TIP

Most FTP clients will allow you to modify file and directory permissions remotely.

18

I Can't Access Images

You can get to your HTML files just fine, but all your images are coming up as icons or broken icons? First, make sure that the references to your images are correct. If you've used relative pathnames, you shouldn't have this problem. If you've used full pathnames or file URLs, the references to your images may have been broken when you moved the files to the server. (I warned you....)

In some browsers, you get a pop-up menu when you select an image with the right mouse button (hold down the button on a Macintosh mouse). Choose the View This Image menu item to try to load the image directly. This will give you the URL of the image where the browser thinks it's supposed to be (which may not be where *you* think it's supposed to be). You can often track down strange relative pathname problems this way.

If you're using Internet Explorer for Windows, you can also select the Properties option from the menu that appears when you right-click on an image to see its address. You can check the address that appears in the Properties dialog box to see whether it points to the appropriate location.

If the references all look good and the images work just fine on your local system, the only other place a problem could have occurred is in transferring the files from one system to another.

My Links Don't Work

If your HTML and image files are working just fine but your links don't work, you most likely used pathnames for those links that applied only to your local system. For example, you might have used absolute pathnames or file URLs to refer to the files to which you're linking. As mentioned for images, if you used relative pathnames and avoided file URLs, you shouldn't have a problem.

My Files Are Being Displayed Incorrectly

Suppose you have an HTML file or a file in some multimedia format that's displayed correctly or links just fine on your local system. After you upload the file to the server and try to view it, the browser gives you gobbledygook. For example, it displays the HTML code itself instead of the HTML file, or it displays an image or multimedia file as text.

This problem can happen in two cases. The first is that you're not using the right file extensions for your files. Make sure that you're using one of the correct file extensions with the correct uppercase and lowercase.

The second case is that your server is not properly configured to handle your files. If all your HTML files have extensions of `.htm`, for example, your server might not understand that `.htm` is an HTML file. (Most modern servers do, but some older ones don't.) Or you might be using a newer form of media that your server doesn't understand. In either case, your server might be using some default content type for your files (usually `text/plain`), which your browser probably can't handle. This can happen with server-side scripts as well. If you put up `.php` files on a server that doesn't support PHP, the server will often send the scripts to the browser as plain text.

To fix this problem, you'll have to configure your server to handle the file extensions for the correct media. If you're working with someone else's server, you'll have to contact your webmaster and have him or her set up the server correctly. Your webmaster will need two types of information: the file extensions you're using and the content type you want him or her to return. If you don't know the content type you want, refer to Appendix E, "MIME Types and File Extensions."

Registering and Advertising Your Web Pages

To get people to visit your website, you need to promote it. The higher your site's visibility, the greater the number of hits.

A *hit* is a visit to your website. Be aware that although your site may get, say, 50 hits in a day, that doesn't necessarily mean that it was visited by 50 different people. It's simply a record of the number of times a copy of your web page has been downloaded.

There are many ways to promote your site. You can list it on major web directories and indexes, include the URL in your email signature, put the URL on your business cards, and so much more. The following sections describe each approach.

Getting Links from Other Sites

It doesn't take much surfing to figure out that the Web is huge. It seems like there's a site on every topic, and when it comes to popular topics, there may be hundreds or thousands of sites. Once you've done the hard work of creating an interesting site, the next step is to get other people to link to it.

The direct approach often works best. Find other sites like your own and send a personal email to the people who run them introducing yourself and telling them that you have a site similar to theirs that they may be interested in. If they are, there's a good chance that they'll provide a link to your site. Oftentimes, there's a quid pro quo involved where you might link to someone else's site and ask them if they're interested in linking to yours in return.

18

This doesn't mean that you should go out and pester people or email them repeatedly if they don't do as you request. The subtle approach often works best. If diplomacy isn't your strong suit, or even if it is, you might also want to look into some of the larger web directories as well. Many sites exist solely to direct users to other sites. Generally there's a process by which you can submit your site for inclusion in the directory. I'm going to discuss some of the larger directories individually but bear in mind that there are lots of other directories out there that are restricted to particular areas of interest. You should find the ones that are appropriate for your site and submit your URL to them as well.

Yahoo!

By far, the best-known directory of websites is Yahoo! at www.yahoo.com (see Figure 18.1), created by David Filo and Jerry Yang. This site started in April 1994 as a small, private list of David's and Jerry's favorite websites. Since then, it has become a highly regarded catalog and index of websites and is one of the most successful Internet companies out there.

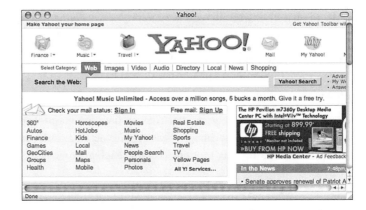

Yahoo! uses an elegant multilevel catalog to organize all the sites it references. To view the contents of any level of the catalog, first you select the hyperlink for the major category that most closely represents the information you're interested in. Then follow the chain of associated pages to a list of related websites, like the one shown in Figure 18.2. The following is the full URL of this page:

http://dir.yahoo.com/Computers_and_Internet/Data_Formats/HTML/

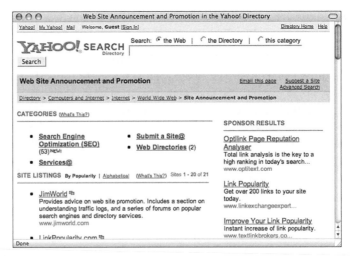

To add your site to Yahoo!, return to www.yahoo.com and select the category that's appropriate for your site. Work your way through any subcategories until you locate a list of sites that are most similar to your own.

Suppose that you've created a site that discusses camel racing. You navigate your way through the Recreation links, which then leads to Sports, which then has a category called Camel Racing. Yes, there really is a category like this:

http://dir.yahoo.com/Recreation/Sports/Camel_Racing/

When you scroll down to the bottom of this page, you see a Suggest a Site link. Click this link to display the Suggest a Site page. This page provides complete instructions for adding your site to Yahoo!. Currently, the process involves filling out four easy-to-understand forms.

NOTE

> Even though I'm discussing how to register for search engines individually, you may prefer to wait and register for them all at once. Later on in this lesson, I'll discuss some services you can use to do this.

18

CAUTION

> These days, it can take an awfully long time to get your site into the Yahoo! directory. If you run a noncommercial site, you can submit your site for free and take your chances. If you want to be listed as a commercial site, or you just don't feel like waiting, Yahoo! offers an express listing service that guarantees consideration within seven days for $299. To maintain your listing as a commercial site, you must continue to pay Yahoo! $299 a year.

After you submit your site, your request is processed by the folks at Yahoo!. Eventually, you'll find your site listed among the other camel racing pages!

dmoz: The Open Directory Project

The Open Directory Project at www.dmoz.org is a web directory, just like Yahoo!. It differs from Yahoo! in that it's maintained by volunteer editors who are responsible for maintaining individual categories in the catalog. The project was purchased by Netscape, which was in turn purchased by AOL, so it's technically an AOL property. Even so, it's still maintained by a volunteer staff.

Like Yahoo!, you can request that your site be added, and the editor of that category will check out your site and include it in the directory. The huge group of category editors ensure that sites are considered for inclusion on a timely basis. There's no charge for listing your site in the Open Directory.

One of the biggest advantages of having your site listed in the Open Directory Project is that everyone can publish its contents on their site. For example, Google (www.google.com) includes the contents of the Open Directory Project on its site. A screenshot of the dmoz home page appears in Figure 18.3.

FIGURE 18.3
The dmoz home page.

Yellow Pages Listings

Another popular method of promoting business sites is to register them with the growing number of Yellow Pages directories that have begun to spring up on the Web.

As a rule, Yellow Pages sites are designed specially for commercial and business web users who want to advertise their services and expertise. For this reason, most of the Yellow Pages sites offer both free and paid advertising space, with the paid listings including graphics, corporate logos, and advanced layout features. A free listing, on the other hand, tends to be little more than a hyperlink and a short comment. When you're starting out, free advertising is the best advertising. Of the Yellow Pages sites currently in operation, the Verizon SuperPages home page at www.superpages.com is one of the most popular (see Figure 18.4).

FIGURE 18.4
The Verizon
SuperPages home
page.

Private Directories

In addition to the broad mainstream web directories, many private directories on the Web cater to more specific needs. Some of these directories deal with single issues, whereas others are devoted to areas such as online commerce, education, business, and entertainment.

The best way to locate most of these directories is to use an Internet search tool such as Google (www.google.com) or MSN Search (search.msn.com). Alternatively, most of these directories are listed in such places as Yahoo! and dmoz, so a few minutes spent at these sites can be very beneficial.

18

Site Indexes and Search Engines

After you list your new site on the major directories and maybe a few smaller directories, you need to turn your attention to the indexing and search tools. The following are the most popular of these sites:

Google	www.google.com
Yahoo	www.yahoo.com
MSN Search	search.msn.com
Ask Jeeves	www.ask.com

Unlike web directories, which contain a hierarchical list of websites that have been submitted for inclusion, these indexes have search engines (sometimes called *spiders*) that prowl the Web and store information about every page and site they find. Users can then go to the sites and search for things using a full text search. In other words, whereas directories store the name and description of sites, search engines index the full contents of sites so that pages containing specific text can be found. After you publish your site on the Web and other people link to it, chances are that at some point a search engine will find it and index it. However, you don't have to wait. You can tell these indexes about your site and get it included on the list of sites to be indexed. Each of these search engines enables you to submit your site for indexing.

In the text that follows, I'm going to describe how to submit your sites to some of the popular search engines. There's a set of interlocking relationships among search engine providers that can make it difficult to keep track of who is providing search functionality for whom. The search engines listed previously maintain their own indexes. Once your site is included in their index, it will be available via all the search engines that use their index as well.

NOTE	The search engine descriptions are very brief, and due to the rapidly changing nature of the search engine industry, may be out of date by the time you read them. For more information on search engines, I strongly recommend Search Engine Watch at www.searchenginewatch.com.

Google

Google is currently the most popular search engine. Its search results are ranked based not only on how frequently the search terms appear on a listed page, but also on the number of other pages in the index that link to that page. So, a popular page with thousands of incoming links will be ranked higher than a page that has only a few incoming links.

This search algorithm does a remarkably good job of pushing the most relevant sites to the top of the search results. It also rewards people who publish useful, popular sites rather than those who've figured out how to manipulate the algorithms that other search engines use. Many sites that aren't dedicated to providing search functionality use Google's index, so getting into the Google index provides wide exposure. Statistics from November 2005 show that Google searches make up about half of the search engine market.

How Search Results Are Ranked

Every search engine has an algorithm that ranks sites based on their relevance. It might take into account how many times the keyword you enter appears on the page, whether it appears inside heading tags or in the page title, or whether it appears in text inside links. It might also take into account how high on the page your search terms appear. Such algorithms are trade secrets within the search engine industry, but some of them have been unraveled to greater or lesser degrees. Armed with this information, some site authors write their pages in such a way that search engines will give them a higher relevance ranking than they deserve. For example, some sites have really long titles with lots of information in hopes of appearing first in search results.

Yahoo!

Yahoo! has been around since 1994. They provide both a human-edited directory of the Web, which I discussed earlier, and web search. Yahoo! has leased their web index from other companies, including Google, in the past, but they currently maintain their own index. Yahoo!'s index includes not only HTML documents, but also PDF and Microsoft Office documents. Yahoo!'s search engine market share is about 25% as of November 2005.

MSN Search

MSN Search is Microsoft's web search offering. Like Yahoo! and Google, Microsoft maintains its own index of the Web. Like Google, MSN Search includes incoming links to your site to determine how to rank it. As of November 2005, searches at MSN Search make up about 10% of the market.

Ask.com

Ask.com is another search engine that maintains its own index. Ask.com indexes fewer pages than Google or Yahoo!. Ask.com was formerly known as Ask Jeeves and was notable for allowing users to submit their searches in the form of questions. Its basic approach is now similar to other search engines. Ask.com only controls about 2% of the search engine market as of November 2005, but is listed because like the other sites listed previously, it has its own index.

Search Engine Optimization

Not only do you want to make sure your site is included in the popular search engines, but you want to make sure that it shows up near the top of the results when people are

18

searching for topics that are related to your sites. If you create a site about model rail-roads, you want your site to appear as high as possible in the results for searches like "model railroad" and "model train."

Unfortunately, search engines don't publish instructions on how to make your site rank near the top of their index. Before Google, search engines ranked sites mostly on the basis of their content. The more prominently a term was placed on your website, the higher it would be ranked for that term. So if your model trains page had "model trains" in a page title, or in heading tags on the page, then that page would be more highly ranked for the terms "model train." That's why you sometimes see pages with lots and lots of words listed in the title—it's an attempt to improve search engine rankings for those words.

At one point, search engines enabled you to provide hints about your site by way of `meta` tags. There was a tag that enabled you to specify a description for the page, and another that enabled you to list keywords associated with each page. The content of the tags was invisible; it was only used to help search engines with indexing. Unfortunately, people who published websites immediately started abusing `meta` tags, putting in keywords that were not related to the page content, or putting in far too many keywords in order to try to gain a higher ranking. Now all of the popular search engines disregard `meta` tags entirely.

Search engines now consider not only what's on your site but also who links to it in determining the relevance of your pages, so the more sites that link to yours, the better your placement will be in search engine results. There are companies that sell search engine optimization services that attempt to exploit this method of improving search rankings by paying popular sites to link to your site, or even creating fake sites and fill-ing them with links to their clients. You should avoid these types of services, and be very wary of search engine optimization services in general.

Rather than worrying too much about how to make your site more friendly to search engines, you should worry about writing good HTML and making your site friendly for users. As your site gains in popularity, your search engine ranking will come along. One thing that can help is writing good, descriptive titles, and making sure to use heading tags for headings rather than just using large fonts.

Paying for Search Placement

All of the popular search engines have programs that allow you to pay for search place-ment. In other words, you can agree to pay to have a link to your site displayed when users enter search terms that you choose. Generally this service is priced on a per-click basis—you pay every time a user clicks on the link, up to a maximum that you set. Once you've used up your budget, your advertisement doesn't appear any more.

Most search engines display paid links separately from the regular search results, but this approach still provides a way to get your site in front of users who may be interested immediately. You just have to be willing to pay.

Business Cards, Letterhead, Brochures, and Advertisements

Although the Internet is a wonderful place to promote your new website, many people fail to consider some other great advertising methods.

Most businesses spend a considerable amount of money each year producing business cards, letterhead, and other promotional material. These days it's rare to see any of these materials without Web and email information on them. By printing your email address and home page URL on all your correspondence and promotional material, you can reach an entirely new group of potential visitors.

Even your email signature is a good place to promote your site. Just put in a link and the title or a short description, so that everyone you correspond with can see what you're publishing on the Web.

18

When you're promoting your website, the bottom line is lateral thinking. You need to use every tool at your disposal if you want to have a successful and active site.

How to Win Friends and Influence People

If you've created a site that's dedicated to a particular topic, one of the best ways to promote it is to jump in and join the community surrounding that topic. For example, if you create a web page dedicated to your favorite musical group, you might want to look into seeing whether there are online discussion boards or mailing lists devoted to that group. Not only might participating in those forums be enjoyable, but it also gives you an opportunity to promote your site.

Bear in mind, though, that most web users are quite jaded when it comes to naked self-promotion. Joining a popular Rolling Stones mailing list and immediately sending a message telling everyone to check out your site will only put people off. Instead, join up, follow the course of the discussion, and chime in when you have something interesting to add. If there's a page on your site that's relevant to the discussion, post a link to it.

Such participation is the very essence of becoming a full-fledged citizen of the web community. Nothing will increase the popularity of your site faster than becoming a respected member of communities related to your site. Even big companies have figured this out—rather than avoiding online forums where their products are discussed, many are now assigning employees to participate in those forums. The marketing jargon for this sort of thing is *evangelism*, and some companies have honed it to a science.

Finding Out Who's Viewing Your Web Pages

Now you've got your site up on the Web and ready to be viewed, you've advertised and publicized it to the world, and people are flocking to it in droves. Or are they? How can you tell? You can find out in a number of ways, including using log files and access counters.

Log Files

The best way to figure out how often your pages are being seen, and by whom, is to get access to your server's log files. How long these log files are kept depends on how your server is configured. The logs can take up a lot of disk space, so some hosting providers remove old logs pretty frequently. If you run your own server, you can keep them as long as you like, or at least until you run out of room. Many commercial web providers allow you to view your own web logs or get statistics about how many visitors are accessing your pages and from where. Ask your webmaster for help.

If you do get access to these raw log files, you'll most likely see a whole lot of lines that look something like the following. (I've broken this one up into two lines so that it fits on the page.)

```
vide-gate.coventry.ac.uk - - [17/Feb/2003:12:36:51 -0700]
   "GET /index.html HTTP/1.0" 200 8916
```

What does this information mean? The first part of the line is the site that accessed the file. (In this case, it was a site from the United Kingdom.) The two dashes are used for authentication. (If you have login names and passwords set up, the username of the person who logged in and the group that person belonged to will appear here.) The date and time the page was accessed appear inside the brackets. The next part is the actual filename that was accessed; here it's the index.html at the top level of the server. The GET part is the actual HTTP command the browser used; you usually see GET here. Finally, the last two numbers are the HTTP status code and the number of bytes transferred. The status code can be one of many things: 200 means the file was found and transferred correctly; 404 means the file was not found (yes, it's the same status code you get in error pages in your browser). Finally, the number of bytes transferred usually will be the same number of bytes in your actual file; if it's a smaller number, the visitor interrupted the load in the middle.

Access Counters

If you don't have access to your server's log files but you'd like to know how many people are looking at your web page, you can install an access counter. These counters look like odometers or little meters that say "Since July 15, 1900, this page has been accessed 5,456,234,432 times."

Many web counters are available, and some of them require you to install something on your server or use server-side includes. These days, there are a number of access counters that you can incorporate into your website without installing anything. They use JavaScript and images located on their own servers to keep track of the visitors to your site.

The web counter at www.digits.com is easy to set up and is very popular. If you have a site without a lot of hits (fewer than 1,000 a day), the counter service is free. Otherwise, you'll need to be part of the commercial plan, costing $30 and up.

After you sign up for the digits.com counter service, you'll get a URL that you must include on your pages as part of an <img> tag. When your page is hit, the browser retrieves that URL at digits.com's server, which generates a new odometer image for you.

You can find a list of other free counter services in Appendix A.

If you'd like to go a step further in collecting statistics using an access counter, check out Hitbox at www.hitbox.com. Its counter is invisible, and you can go to the Hitbox site to find out how many people have accessed your site, along with a lot of other information. It provides a lot of information for you and doesn't force you to deal with log analysis yourself.

18

Summary

In this lesson you published your site on the Web through the use of a web server, either one installed by you or that of a network provider. You learned what a web server does and how to get one, how to organize your files and install them on the server, and how to find your URL and use it to test your pages. You also learned the many ways that you can advertise and promote your site, and how to use log files to keep track of the number of visitors. At last, you're on the Web and people are coming to visit!

Workshop

As always, we wrap up the lesson with a few questions, quizzes, and exercises. Here are some pointers and refreshers on how to promote your website.

Q&A

Q I've published my pages at an ISP I really like. The URL is something like http://www.thebestisp.com/users/mypages/. Instead of this URL, I'd like to have my own hostname—something like http://www.mypages.com/. How can I do this?

A You have two choices. The easiest way is to ask your ISP whether you're allowed to have your own domain name. Many ISPs have a method for setting up your domain so that you can still use their services and work with them—it's only your URL that changes. Note that having your own hostname might cost more money, but it's the way to go if you really must have that URL. Many web hosting services have plans starting as low as $5 a month for this type of service, and it currently costs as little as $16 to register your domain for two years.

The other option is to set up your own server with your own domain name. This option could be significantly more expensive than working with an ISP, and it requires at least some background in basic network administration.

Q There are so many of those search engines! Do I have to add my URL to all of them?

A No, you don't have to, but think of the (vastly overused) analogy of the Internet as a superhighway. When you're driving down a real highway, there's usually a clutter of billboards that are clamoring for your attention. How many of them do you really notice, though? You remember the ones you see most frequently. Likewise, listing your page on multiple search engines makes it more visible.

Q In regard to web rings, what if I can't find a suitable place for the code that they want me to place on my home page? What alternatives do I have?

A It depends on the web ring and the person who runs it. Each web ring has a list of instructions that tell you how to add the code to your pages. Some of them are very particular about where you place it (for example, it must be on your home page), whereas others let you place it on any prominent page in your site. Others allow you to include graphics or just make a text-only mention of the web rings.

If your ringleader allows you to place the web ring code on a page other than your home page, be sure to provide a link to your web ring page on your home page. A simple text link such as "For a listing of the web rings to which this site belongs, please visit my Web Ring page" should do it.

Quiz

1. What's the basic function of a web server?
2. How can you obtain an Internet connection?
3. What are default index files, and what's the advantage of using them in all directories?
4. What are some things that you should check immediately after you upload your web pages?
5. Name some of the ways that you can promote your website.
6. What's a hit?
7. What are the advantages of using an all-in-one submission page to promote your site?

Quiz Answers

1. A web server is a program that sits on a machine on the Internet (or an intranet). It determines where to find files on a website and keeps track of where those files are going.
2. You can obtain an Internet connection through school, work, or commercial Internet or web services, or you can set up your own web server.
3. The default index file is loaded when a URL ends with a directory name rather than a filename. Typical examples of default index files are `index.html`, `index.htm`, and `default.htm`. If you use default filenames, you can use a URL such as http://www.mysite.com/ rather than http://www.mysite.com/index.html to get to the home page in the directory.
4. Make sure that your browser can reach your web pages on the server, that you can access the files on your website, and that your links and images work as expected. After you've determined that everything appears the way you think it should, have your friends and family test your pages in other browsers.
5. Some ways you can promote your site include major web directories and search engines, listings on business cards and other promotional materials, and web rings.
6. A hit is a request for any file from your website.
7. An all-in-one submission page enables you to submit your URL to several different site promotion areas and web robots at once. Some provide a small number of submissions for free and a larger number of submissions for an additional fee.

18

Exercises

1. Start shopping around and consider where you want to store your website. Call two or more places to determine what benefits you'll get if you locate your web pages on their servers.

2. Upload and test a practice page to learn the process, even if it's just a blank page that you'll add content to later. You might work out a few kinks this way before you actually upload all your hard work on the Web.

3. Visit some of the search engines listed in this lesson to obtain a list of the sites where you want to promote your web page. Review each of the choices to see whether there are special requirements for listing your page.

4. Design a new business card or brochure that advertises your company and your website.

LESSON 19:
Taking Advantage of the Server

Over the course of this book, you've learned a lot about designing web pages, and just about everything you've learned would work equally well whether you put your pages on a web server somewhere or you open them directly from your hard drive. Most web servers offer a lot more features than just serving up static web pages requested by users.

In this Lesson

I'll talk about some of the features provided by web servers that can make your life as a web developer easier. The following topics will be discussed:

- An overview of web applications
- A description of some popular web application platforms
- How to use server-side includes
- How to set up access control under Apache
- How to use Apache to redirect users

Web Applications

Static content makes up a huge part of the Web, but a lot of the action going on today is in the world of web applications. By taking advantage of server-side software, many companies and people are providing full-fledged applications over the Web. You can purchase goods from any number of online sites, read your email over the Web, or participate in discussion forums. Sites such as Yahoo! provide full personal information manager functionality over the Web, with email, calendaring, a to-do list, and an address book.

Let's talk about how web applications are created. As you know, when a browser wants a document that resides on a web server, it sends a request to that server using a URL. When a web application is in place, URLs point to programs instead of to static files. The program is passed any parameters (generally supplied by the user), and the output of the program is sent back to the browser.

When it comes to web applications, you can be as ambitious as you want to be. You can write a complex system that provides a web interface for an existing mainframe-based application, build a full-featured online store, or write a bit of code to include the same footer in all of your web pages. The scope of your effort is entirely up to you.

Even if you don't have any interest in writing your own web applications, there's a good chance that you might want to use applications someone else wrote with slight modifications, or that you'll be working with a programmer and modifying pages associated with a web application. My objective here is to explain the syntax used by these web application platforms well enough that you're not confused when you see files associated with them. Understanding JavaScript is a good start toward being able to build web applications, because JavaScript is a scripting language and the principles are not that different than the principles of most server-side scripts.

A huge number of languages are available for creating web applications. A few make up the lion's share of the market, but there are plenty of obscure platforms as well if you're interested in something esoteric. Let's look at some of the more popular ones that you may encounter.

CGI

If there's a platform for creating web applications that could be referred to as the old standby, it's CGI. CGI, which is short for *Common Gateway Interface*, is the original web application platform. When the NCSA web server was introduced, it included an interface to external programs. When a URL that points to a CGI script is requested, a script completely external to the web server is called and the output is sent back to the browser. The job of a CGI program is to process the data submitted to it (usually through an HTML form), and to generate a response (usually an HTML page).

Back in Lesson 10, "Designing Forms," I mentioned that forms have a couple of different submit methods, GET and POST, and explained how to choose which method to use. These methods are important when it comes to CGI programs (and other web applications), because they dictate how the data submitted by the user is provided to the program. When the GET method is used, the parameters are passed to the CGI program via an environment variable. When the POST method is used, they're passed to the program via standard input. If you don't know what either of those things is, don't worry about it. Just understand that they're handled in different ways, and that these days most web application platforms don't care—they give you access to the values passed in either way.

The nice thing about CGI is that it's simple and universal. Nearly all web servers support CGI, and it's easy to get started writing CGI programs because the interface is so simple. CGI has almost no infrastructure. You just put your program (which is written so that it gets input to the right place and prints out web content) in a directory set up to recognize requests for CGI programs, and the work is basically done. Other than generating web content, there's only one other hard and fast requirement for CGI programs—they have to generate the HTTP header that indicates what type of content the program generates.

Let's look at a simple example of a CGI program:

```
#!/usr/bin/perl

use CGI qw(:standard);

print header;

print "<html><head><title>Example</title></head><body>\n";
print "<p>Welcome, ", param('name'), ".</p>\n";
print "</body></html>\n";
```

This program, helpfully called example.pl, is written in Perl. This book isn't even about CGI programming, much less Perl, so I'll just provide a very cursory overview of how it works. When the CGI program is requested, the server loads the Perl interpreter, which in turn compiles and runs the script. The first line of the file indicates that this program is a script, and the location of the interpreter used to run the script. This is standard UNIX notation for script files.

The third line in the script imports the CGI library that is distributed with Perl. At one time it was an add-on for Perl, but because Perl became so popular for writing CGI programs and the CGI library took so much grunt work out of it, it became a standard part of the Perl distribution. Most people use it to extract the parameters submitted by the

19

user and make them easily accessible within the program. (It's thanks to the CGI library that the differences between GET and POST become invisible to the programmer. It checks for both GET and POST data and makes the data available to the programmer either way.) As you'll see on line 5, it's also used to generate the Content-type header that indicates what type of content is generated by the script. The default is text/html. To print the header, I just call the header subroutine, which is imported from the CGI library. If I weren't using the CGI library, I could generate the header by simply printing it out, like this:

```
print "Content-type: text/html\n\n";
```

The two line feeds (represented by \n\n) indicate that the script is done printing headers and that the remainder of the output is the body of the response.

Once the header has been generated, the rest of the script is devoted to printing out the body of the response: the web page that is displayed in the browser. This part of the script consists of three lines of code that print out a very simple HTML page. The only thing out of the ordinary here is the code that inserts the value of the name parameter. By calling param('name'), I retrieve the value of the name parameter that was submitted with the request. If the name parameter was not included, this value returns an empty string. (This script would be accessed by a form that includes an input field named name.)

Obviously this script is a lot simpler than most you'll see, but the idea is fundamentally the same regardless of what you ultimately use your CGI program to accomplish. As a web designer, one of the drawbacks of CGI is that you often wind up writing a program that has a bunch of HTML in it. That makes it difficult to prototype your pages or to create them using your favorite HTML editor. Web application platforms like Active Server Pages and PHP solve this problem by enabling you to embed script code within your HTML documents.

Active Server Pages

In the Microsoft world, Active Server Pages (or ASP) is the web application platform of choice. The approach with Active Server Pages is very different than the one taken with CGI programs. With ASP, you have pages that look a lot like HTML documents, except that there's some code mixed in as well. Unlike CGI, which is really an interface from a web server to external programs, support for Active Server Pages is built into Microsoft's Internet Information Server (IIS) web server.

IIS is able to distinguish ASP files from regular web documents by their extension. Generally, IIS is configured to treat any file with the extension .asp as an Active Server Page. ASP supports multiple programming languages—the two that are built in are JavaScript and VBScript, which is based on Visual Basic. VBScript is the default. When you write an ASP, you distinguish the code from the standard HTML by placing it inside special tags. For example, the following code would print out the string inside quotation marks (using VBScript):

```
<%
response.write("This is printed using code.")
%>
```

The scriptlet begins with `<%` and is closed with `%>`. Anything not enclosed in scriptlets is treated as standard HTML. In this code example, I use the `write` method of the `response` object to print out some text as part of the page. A shorter way to print out a string is to use the expression evaluator:

```
<%= "This is printed using code." %>
```

This scriptlet begins with `<%=`, which indicates that the only thing inside it will be an expression, and the results of the expression will be included as part of the content of the page. That example doesn't make it clear exactly how this works because it's just a static string. Take a look at this one:

```
<%= 2 + 2 %>
```

That expression would print out the number four. It could be used in a case like this:

```
<p>The sum of two and two is <%= 2 + 2 %>.</p>
```

This is a really, really simple example. ASP is used to create web applications of every level of complexity. At some point, it makes sense to stop throwing more and more code into your ASPs and start using external libraries instead. These libraries are generally created as COM objects—if you're familiar with Windows, they're `.dll` files. You can write code in Visual Basic or C++, bundle that code up into COM objects, and then use those COM objects from within your pages. For example, you can write a COM object to send email, or one that calculates sales tax on an order.

19

Using Includes

Regardless of the web application platform you use, you'll find yourself wanting to include files in other files all the time. If you've never used includes before, this may sound strange to use, but believe me, once you get used to it, you'll never want to go back. Let's say every page on your site has exactly the same footer, containing some navigational links, a copyright statement, and a link to send you email. Rather than keeping this content up to date on every single page on your site, by using includes, you can create one file, perhaps called `footer.html`, and include it on all the pages of your site. Then when one of the links changes, you have to update only one file. You've already seen how this approach can work with CSS files; there's no reason why it can't work for content as well.

Let's look at how includes are used in the world of ASP. This is actually a sneak preview of the section later in the lesson on server-side includes, because ASP reuses the SSI include syntax. The basic format of an include is

```
<!--#include file="footer.html" -->
```

As you can see, the `include` directive looks like an HTML comment. This is convenient in cases where your includes aren't recognized by the web server. Rather than printing out the code as part of the page, they're hidden by the browser because they're treated as comments.

The earlier `include` directive attempts to find a file called `footer.html`, read it, and include its contents in the page in place of the directive. If you use the `file` attribute in the directive, the file being included must be in the current directory or a directory below it. The path cannot include . or begin with /. For example, `../includes/footer.html` would not work, but `includes/footer.html` would.

If you need to use . or an absolute path, use the `virtual` attribute instead of `file`. Using `virtual`, you can access anything in the document root. When you use `virtual`, either of those two paths would be valid. You still can't include files that are outside the document root, but you shouldn't be doing that anyway.

When you use includes with ASP, if you include a file with the .asp extension, IIS will execute any scriptlets found in the file when it is included. This provides you with a capability above and beyond just including common content in your pages. If you have ASP code that you want to run on more than one page, you can put it in an included file. This enables you to create libraries of common code. This can be a huge timesaver.

JSP/J2EE

In the Java world, JSP is the Web equivalent to ASP. It's short for Java Server Pages. J2EE is short for Java 2 Enterprise Edition, and it includes web technologies such as Java Server Pages and servlets, along with other server-side technologies that are beyond the scope of this book. You might be familiar with Java applets. Applets are Java programs that are downloaded along with a web page and generally displayed inline on a page. There are Java applet games, Java applet news tickers, and Java applet banner ads. In fact, when Java was originally created, it was widely thought of purely in terms of applets.

Server-side web programming in Java began with Java servlets, which were in some ways the server-side analogue of Java applets. Servlets are also similar to CGI programs. The main difference between a servlet and a CGI program is that servlets have to run in the context of an application that's known as a servlet container. In this sense, they're more like ASP programs. Just as the IIS understands how to interpret and execute ASPs, the servlet container understands how to pass requests on to servlets and send the output back to the user. In some cases, the web server serves as the servlet container; in others, the servlet container is a separate application that is connected to the web server.

In any case, you can write servlets and deploy them on your servlet container. Once you've written a servlet and mapped it to a particular URL, it can respond to requests the same way a CGI program can. What does this have to do with Java Server Pages? Java Server Pages (or JSPs) are just a simpler way to create servlets. A JSP looks a lot like an ASP—it's an HTML page that optionally contains scriptlets and directives. In the JSP world, the scriptlets are written using Java. The trick here is that when a servlet container serves up a JSP, it converts it into a servlet, compiles that servlet into a Java class file, and then maps it to the path where the JSP is located. So, a JSP at /index.jsp is turned into a servlet that is called whenever that path is requested.

The syntax for JSPs is virtually identical to that of ASP files. Scriptlets are defined in exactly the same way. In Java, it looks like this:

```
<%
String aString = "This is a string.";
response.write(aString);
%>
```

The expression evaluation feature in JSP is also exactly the same as it is in ASP. To print out the value of aString without bothering with response.write(), use the following:

```
<%= aString %>
```

There are some other constructs associated with JSP as well. These directives follow this pattern:

```
<%@page language="Java" %>
```

The fact that it starts with <%@ indicates that it's a directive. page is the name of the directive and language is an attribute. This directive indicates that the language used in the scriptlets on the page is Java. In truth, this is the only valid option; JSPs must use Java as their programming language. Perhaps the most common attribute of the page directive that you'll see is the import attribute, which is used to indicate that a particular class is used on your page. If you're not a Java programmer, imports might be a bit confusing for you. Just remember that you'll see a lot of them of you work on complex JSPs.

There's also an alternative form of directives for JSPs that use an XML-based notation. To see how they differ from normal directives, let's look at how you include files in the JSP world. The first method uses a normal-looking include:

```
<%@include file="footer.jsp" %>
```

19

This directive includes a file called `footer.jsp` from the current directory in place of the directive. When you use the `include` directive, the included file is inserted at compile time. What this means is that the file is included before the JSP is converted to a servlet. For programmers, it means that code in the included file can interact with code in the files that include it. For example, you could set the copyright date in a variable in the including file, and reference that variable to print out the variable in the included file.

You can also include files using JSP's XML-style directives. To include `footer.jsp` using the XML directive, the following code is used:

```
<jsp:include template="footer.jsp" />
```

When you use this type of include, it's treated as a runtime include. This differs from the previous in that runtime includes are only included after the page has been converted into a servlet and run. The include is processed or read in separately at that point, which means that variables can't be shared between the included file and the including file.

The last common constructs you'll hear about in the JSP world are taglibs. To make things easier for people who aren't Java programmers, the developers of the J2EE specification created a way to provide custom tags (called taglibs, short for *tag libraries*) that you can use as part of your pages. Not only can programmers create their own custom tags, but there are a number of projects working to create standard custom tags that encapsulate common functionality needed by many web applications. The `taglib` directive is used to make a tag library available for a JSP:

```
<%@ taglib uri="/WEB-INF/app.tld" prefix="app" %>
```

The `uri` attribute provides the URL for the descriptor file for the tag library. The `prefix` attribute indicates how tags associated with the tag library are identified. For example, if there's a tag library tag called `blockquote`, it is differentiated from the standard `<blockquote>` tag by using the prefix, like this:

```
<app:blockquote>Some stuff.</app:blockquote>
```

Many programmers write their own tag libraries that provide functionality specific to their applications. However, Sun has also defined a standard set of tag libraries to provide functionality common to many applications. This group of libraries is called JSTL (Java Standard Tag Libraries). You can read more about JSTL at http://java.sun.com/products/jsp/jstl/.

You can find an actual implementation of JSTL at http://jakarta.apache.org/taglibs/doc/standard-doc/intro.html.

The JSTL tags provide functionality for things such as loops, conditional operations, and processing XML.

There's a lot more to building web applications using Java and J2EE than I've discussed here. I've just provided an overview for you in case you need to apply your HTML skills to a web application written in Java. Hopefully, when you run into one of these applications, you'll have seen enough here not to be confused by the JSP syntax.

PHP

PHP is yet another language that enables you to embed scripts in your web pages. ASP is really part of Microsoft's overall software development platform, and similarly, J2EE is part of the Java universe. PHP, on the other hand, is completely independent. Rather than building on a general-purpose language, PHP is a programming language unto itself. The language uses a C-like syntax that also has some things in common with Perl. Like ASP and JSP, it can be interspersed with your HTML. Usually, you'll find that PHP files have the extension .php, but the web server can be configured to treat any files as PHP files. You can even set things up so that files with the extension .html are treated as PHP files.

There are two ways to include script code in your pages:

```
<?php
echo("Hello.");
?>
```

There's also a more concise notation for adding scripts to your page:

```
<?
echo("Hello.");
?>
```

This was the traditional notation for adding PHP code to web pages, but it conflicts with XML, so <?php ?> was added to differentiate between the two. If you're starting out, you should stick with the <?php ?> notation because doing so could save you trouble later, and it's not that much more trouble.

19

One of the nicest things about PHP is that it's completely free, and can be easily installed to work with Apache, the most popular web server. For this reason, many, many web hosting providers include support for PHP with their hosting packages. It's fairly simple to install, and is neither large nor unwieldy, so you can run it yourself with little trouble. PHP is also easier to learn than some of the other systems because it's not just an extension of a larger programming environment. You can find out more about PHP at http://www.php.net/.

As I've done with the other technologies, let me explain how to include external files in your pages. In the PHP world, there are four functions that can be used to include external files in PHP documents. All of them are compile-time includes for the purposes of PHP. The functions are include(), require(), include_once(), and require_once().

Both `include()` and `require()` accept the path to a file as an argument. The difference is that if you use `include()` and the file cannot be read for some reason, a warning is printed but the page continues to be processed. If you use `require()`, a fatal error occurs if the included file cannot be read. `include_once()` and `require_once()` are exactly the same, except that if the file to be included has already been included earlier on the page, the include will be ignored. This may seem strange if you're thinking about including content, but it's helpful if you're including code. Let's say you have a file that sets up a bunch of variables used later on your page. It probably makes sense to use `require_once()` to make sure that those variables aren't set more than once.

Server-Side Includes

Now that I've described a number of popular web application platforms, let me describe something much simpler that you may find more useful, at least in the immediate future. Most web servers support an extension called server-side includes (SSI) that enable you to place directives in your pages that are processed by the server when the pages are downloaded. All directives follow the same format. The basic format is

```
<!--#directive attribute=value attribute=value .. -->
```

Note that SSI directives are cleverly disguised as HTML comments. The advantage is that if the server doesn't process the directives, the browser will ignore them. This is particularly useful when you're previewing pages that have SSI directives embedded in them locally.

Let's look at the directive in more detail. The directive name indicates how the directive should be used. In the ASP section earlier in this lesson, you saw that the `include` directive is used to include external files in an HTML document. The directive is followed by one or more `attribute` and `value` pairs. These pairs define how the directive is used. For example, the `include` directive has two possible attributes (which are mutually exclusive): `file` and `virtual`. The values associated with both of them are paths to files to include. As mentioned previously, the `file` attribute is used to load files from the current directory or below it. The `virtual` attribute indicates that the file can appear anywhere in the document root.

Here are a couple of examples of `include` directives:

```
<!--#include file="includes/footer.html" -->
<!--#include virtual="/includes/footer.html" -->
```

Any web server that claims to support server-side includes will support the `include` directive. Apache, the torchbearer for SSI, supports many other directives as well.

Table 19.1 contains a list of all the directives supported by Apache. You can read more about them at http://httpd.apache.org/docs/mod/mod_include.html.

TABLE 19.1   SSI Directives Supported by Apache

Directive	Usage
config	Enables you to configure the error message to be displayed if a directive fails, and the format for displaying date and time information and file size information.
echo	Prints out the value of an include variable.
exec	Executes a CGI program or command and includes the results in the page. (This directive is usually disabled for security reasons.)
fsize	Prints out the size of the specified file. The virtual and file attributes are used with this directive, just as they are with the include directive.
flastmod	Prints the date the specified file was last modified. Supports the file and virtual attributes.
include	Includes a file in the page.
printenv	Prints a list of all environment variables and their values.
set	Sets a variable to a value.

Using Server-Side Includes

Let's look at how you might use server-side includes on a real site. As I said before, includes are the most common SSI directives used on most sites. Using includes, you can save a ton of work by bundling up content that's common to more than one page into separate files that are included on each of those pages. Let's look at an example that demonstrates how to use SSI on a real site. On many sites, you'll find that navigational elements are shared among pages, and the header and footer are common to every page.

First of all, let's take a look at the files common to every page, the header and footer. Here's the source code to the header file:

```
<div id="header">
<img src="header.gif" alt="Baseball Online" /><br />
Welcome to the largest baseball site on the Web.
</div>
```

The header consists of a single <div> containing a banner image and the tagline for the site. I've assigned the ID header to the <div> so that I can use CSS to modify how it's presented. Now let's look at the footer. It contains some basic copyright information that's found on every page.

19

```
<div id="footer">
Copyright 2003, Baseball Online.<br />
Send questions to <a href="mailto:webmaster@example.com">webmaster</a>.
</div>
```

Now for the navigational elements for the site. If I were going the easy route, I'd just create one navigation file to be used on all the pages on the site, but that's not appropriate in many cases. One purpose of navigation is to enable users to move to various areas of the site. However, another purpose is to give users a sense of where they are on the site. So, instead of creating one navigation file to be used everywhere, I'm going to create three navigation files, one for each section of the site.

The content of the three files follows. First is the navigation for the games section:

```
<div id="navigation">
<a href="/">Home</a><br />
Games<br />
<a href="/teams/">Teams</a><br />
<a href="/leagues/">Leagues</a>
</div>
```

Here's the navigation for the teams section:

```
<div id="navigation">
<a href="/">Home</a><br />
<a href="/games/">Games</a><br />
Teams<br />
<a href="/leagues/">Leagues</a>
</div>
```

And, finally, here's the navigation for the leagues section:

```
<div id="navigation">
<a href="/">Home</a><br />
<a href="/games/">Games</a><br />
<a href="/teams/">Teams</a><br />
Leagues
</div>
```

Now that I've created all of my included files, I can stuff them in a directory called `includes` off of the root directory. In this example, they'll be called `header.html`, `footer.html`, `nav_games.html`, `nav_teams.html`, and `nav_leagues.html`. Now let's look at a real page that uses these includes:

```
<!DOCTYPE html PUBLIC '-//W3C//DTD XHTML 1.0 Strict//EN'
"http://www.w3.org/TR/xhtml1/DTD/xhtml1-strict.dtd">
<html xmlns="http://www.w3.org/1999/xhtml" xml:lang="en" lang="en">
<head>
<title>Games: A Games Page</title>
```

```
<link rel="stylesheet" type="text/css" href="/includes/styles.css" />
</head>
</head>
<body>
<!--#include virtual="/includes/header.html" -->
<!--#include virtual="/includes/nav_games.html" -->
<div id="content">This is the content for a games page.</div>
<!--#include virtual="/includes/footer.html" -->
</body>
</html>
```

As you can see, the page I created consists mainly of includes. There are a few other things to note as well. Both in the includes and in the main page, there are no tags that modify how the data is presented. Instead, I just put everything inside <div> tags with IDs. The linked style sheet in this document contains all the style rules for the page, and controls the layout of the entire page. Here's the source for the page once all the included files have been included by the web server:

```
<!DOCTYPE html PUBLIC '-//W3C//DTD XHTML 1.0 Strict//EN'
"http://www.w3.org/TR/xhtml1/DTD/xhtml1-strict.dtd">
<html xmlns="http://www.w3.org/1999/xhtml" xml:lang="en" lang="en">
<head>
<title>Games: A Games Page</title>
<link rel="stylesheet" type="text/css" href="/includes/styles.css" />
</head>
</head>
<body>
<div id="header">
<img src="header.gif" alt="Baseball Online" /><br />
Welcome to the largest baseball site on the Web.
</div>

<div id="navigation">
<a href="/">Home</a><br />

Games<br />
<a href="/teams/">Teams</a><br />
<a href="/leagues/">Leagues</a>
</div>

<div id="content">This is the content for a games page.</div>
<div id="footer">
Copyright 2003, Baseball Online.<br />
Send questions to <a href="mailto:webmaster@example.com">webmaster</a>.
</div>

</body>
</html>
```

19

Using Apache Access Control Files

Apache is the most popular web server, and is especially popular among ISPs that provide web hosting. For that reason, when I discuss features of web servers, I'm going to discuss Apache. You can apply the general techniques described here to any web server, but the specifics will apply only to Apache. Under Apache, assuming the server administrator has given you the right to do so, you can set up access control files that you can use to manage access to your directories, along with a lot of other things. These days, many kinds of server configuration directives can be used on a per-directory basis from the access file.

The access control file is generally named .htaccess. It can actually be named anything that the server administrator chooses, but .htaccess is the default, and there's really no good reason to change it. Because the filename begins with a period, it's a hidden file under UNIX. This keeps it from cluttering things up when you're looking for content files in a directory.

Apache configuration directives begin with the directive, and the rest of the line consists of the parameters associated with the directive. They're entered one per line. The format is usually something like this:

```
Directive valueForDirective
```

Sometimes the configuration directives are slightly more complex, but that's the general format. The first type of configuration I'll explain how to manipulate is actual access to the pages in the directory (and its subdirectories).

Managing Access to Pages

Controlling access to pages can be somewhat complex, mainly because Apache's access control system is very flexible. First, let's look at the access control directives themselves. The four you need to pay attention to are allow, deny, require, and order. The allow and deny directives enable you to control access to pages based on the IP address or domain name of the computer the visitor is using. Let's say you want to disallow all users from samspublishing.com (meaning that they're using a computer on the samspublishing.com network) from some pages on your site. You could just stick

```
deny from samspublishing.com
```

in your .htaccess file. These directives match parts of hostnames, so even if the user's hostname is firewall.samspublishing.com, he'll still be denied. By the same token, you can deny based on IP address:

```
deny from 192.168.1
```

In this case, anyone on the network 192.168.1.* would be denied. You can be as restrictive as you want. You could create a directive like this, if you wanted:

```
deny from com
```

Needless to say, this would prevent anyone on a .com network from viewing your pages. That's pretty harsh. If you're not careful, you can restrict everyone from seeing your pages. If that's what you intend to do, you can just use this directive:

```
deny from all
```

Why would you want to do that? Well, it makes more sense when combined with two other directives: order and allow. Using order, you can specify the order in which deny and allow rules are applied. allow is just like deny, except that it allows users that meet the rule you specify to see the pages. So, you can write rules like this:

```
order deny, allow
deny from all
allow from samspublishing.com
```

This restricts use of your pages to only people on the samspublishing.com network. Based on the order directive, the deny rule is applied first, shutting out everyone. Then if the user meets your allow rule, she's allowed in. The last directive in this family is require. This directive, rather than basic access on how the user's machine identifies itself, is used to require user authentication. Before you can use it, you need to set a few things up.

First, you'll need to create a file containing a list of usernames and passwords that can be used to access your site. Apache helpfully provides a tool to create these files, called htpasswd. It's invoked in the following manner:

```
htpasswd -c /usr/local/apache/passwords account
```

The arguments are as follows: the flag -c indicates that the password file should be created if it doesn't already exist. The next argument, /usr/local/apache/passwords, is the name of the password file. The last argument is the name of the account you want to create. The program will then ask you to type the password for the account and confirm it. Once you've done so, the account is created, along with the password file. At that point, you can add more accounts to your file by repeatedly running htpasswd (without the -c flag) and passing in new account names each time. The reason you can't just create a text file in a text editor is that the passwords are encrypted when they're saved in the file. htpasswd takes care of that.

You can also create groups of users by creating a group file. To create this file, just use your favorite text editor and use the following format:

```
groupname: account1 account2 account3 ...
```

19

Substitute *groupname* with a group name of your own choosing, such as `managers`, and then list all the accounts from your password file that are members of the group. Once you've set up your password file and (optionally) your group file, you're ready to start using the `require` directive. To set up what's referred to as an *authentication realm*, the following directives are used:

- `AuthType`—The authentication scheme to use. Except in rare circumstances, you'll use `Basic` here.
- `AuthName`—The name of the realm. This name will be displayed when the user is prompted to log in.
- `AuthUserFile`—The path of the password file you created.
- `AuthGroupFile`—The path to the group file, if there is one.

Now let's look at how these are used in the file:

```
AuthType Basic
AuthName "Administrator Files"
AuthUserFile /usr/local/apache/passwords
AuthGroupFile /usr/local/apache/groups
```

Once you've set up the authentication realm, you can start using `require` directives to specify who's allowed to see the pages and who isn't. The format for `require` directives is as follows:

```
require group administrators
require user fred bob jim betty
```

First, you specify whether the `require` directive refers to users or groups, and then you include a list of usernames or group names. If you included the previous directives in your `.htaccess` files, the users `fred`, `bob`, `jim`, and `betty` would be able to access the pages, along with any users in the `administrators` group.

Redirecting Users

Although `.htaccess` files were once associated strictly with access control, their capabilities were eventually expanded to encompass nearly all of the configuration directives for Apache. There's a full list of configuration directives for Apache 1.3 at http://httpd. apache.org/docs/mod/directives.html.

If you're using Apache 2.0, you can use http://httpd.apache.org/docs/2.0/mod/ directives.html.

I want to talk about two in particular: `Redirect` and `RedirectMatch`. First, let's talk a bit about redirection. Redirecting users from one URL to another is all too common. For example, let's say you have a directory called `aboutus` on your website, and you want to move everything to a directory called about. One common way of handling things so that your users don't get a dreaded 404 Not Found error when they go to the old URL is to put an index.html file in that directory that looks like this:

```
<html>
<head>
<title>Moved</title>
<meta http-equiv="refresh" content="1; url=http://www.example.com/about" />
</head>
<body>
<p>This page has moved to a
<a href="/about/">new location</a>.</p>
</body>
</html>
```

The <meta> tag basically tells the browser to wait one second and then proceed to the URL specified. The content on the page is there just to handle the rare case in which the user's browser doesn't do what the <meta> tag tells it to. This is how many people handle these sorts of cases.

There's one obvious problem, though. Let's say you had many pages in the aboutus directory. You'd have to create pages like this one to replace each of them. The other, slightly less obvious problem, is that these tags mess with the Back button. Unless users are careful, they'll go back to the redirect page, get redirected to the new page again, go back again, get redirected again, and on and on. To get back past a page that uses a <meta> tag to redirect users, you have to click the Back button twice in rapid succession.

Using the Redirect directive, you can solve this problem much more elegantly. Here's how it works:

```
Redirect /aboutus http://www.example.com/about
```

Any requests for URLs that begin with /aboutus will be redirected to the /about directory. Apache will also take everything after the path specified in the Redirect directive and append it to the target URL. So, a request for /aboutus/management.html will be redirected to http://www.example.com/about/management.html. This makes the redirection completely transparent to the user. You can even specify whether the redirect is permanent or temporary like this:

```
Redirect temp /aboutus http://www.example.com/about
Redirect permanent /aboutus http://www.example.com/about
Redirect seeother /aboutus http://www.example.com/about
```

You can indicate that /aboutus is gone without redirecting the user like this:

```
Redirect gone /aboutus
```

19

That's a more civilized thing to do than letting your users run into 404 errors.

If you need to match something other than the beginning of the URL, you can use `RedirectMatch`, which uses regular expressions as the matching part of the URL. There's no space here to discuss regular expressions, but I'll give you one example of how `RedirectMatch` works. Let's say you replace all of your `.html` files on your site with `.php` files so that you can use PHP includes for navigation. Here's the rule:

```
RedirectMatch (.*)\.html$ http://www.example.com$1.php
```

Let me break that down. It basically says that any URL ending in `.html` should be redirected to the same URL on the server `http://www.example.com` except that the `.html` ending should be replaced with `.php`. First, let's look at the URL to match, from end to beginning. It ends with `$`, which indicates that the string to be matched must be at the end of the URL. The `\.html` is the string to match. The `\` is in there to indicate that the `.` should actually appear in the URL, and not be treated as a regular expression metacharacter. The `(.*)` says "match everything up to the `.html`." The `.*` matches everything, and the parentheses indicate that the regular expression should remember what was matched. In the target URL, the part of the URL that was matched is retrieved and plugged in.

Summary

Throughout this book, I've talked about HTML, JavaScript, images, and other techniques that work regardless of whether your web pages live on a web server, on a CD-ROM, or in a work directory on your local hard drive. There's more to web servers, though, than just serving up static web pages when users request them, and this lesson was just the tip of the iceberg when it comes to exploring the additional capabilities of web server software. I discussed some popular web application development platforms. You probably don't need to know all of them, but if you do much web development, eventually you'll wind up using one of them or another. I also talked about how you can take advantage of server features such as server-side includes, access control, and redirection features built into the server to make your life as a web developer easier.

The key here is to take advantage of the features your web server offers to save yourself work and provide a better experience for your users. You should look into the web server that your pages will reside on for more ways to take advantage of it.

Workshop

This workshop contains some questions about HTML validation, as well as a quiz and exercises that will refresh your memory on what you've learned.

Q&A

Q How do I figure out which web server I use?

A If you don't know which web server your web pages reside on, you can ask the system administrator responsible for making sure it's up and running; he'll certainly know. Or you can use Netcraft's site to figure out the server software and operating system for your site. Just go to http://uptime.netcraft.com/up/graph/.

Enter the hostname of the computer where your pages are stored to get information about the software running on your server.

Q Does using the web application platforms require me to be a programmer?

A No more so than learning to use Dynamic HTML or JavaScript. There are some really simple things you can do to take advantage of these platforms, and at the same time you can write really complex applications as well, like the ones that power huge sites like Amazon.com and Yahoo!.

Quiz

1. What's the relationship between the web server and CGI programs?
2. What are the two standard languages associated with programming in Active Server Pages?
3. What are the two types of includes in the J2EE world?
4. In PHP, how do the `require()` and `include()` functions differ?
5. When using server-side includes, how do `virtual` and `file` includes differ?

Quiz Answers

1. CGI programs are standalone programs that are invoked by the web server. They produce data in a format that the web server understands how to send to the browser.
2. The two standard languages that can be used with ASP are VBScript and JavaScript.
3. In the J2EE world, there are compile-time includes and runtime includes. Code in compile-time includes can interact with code in the including file. Runtime includes must be independent.
4. If the file cannot be included when you use the `require()` function to include a file in PHP, the page fails to load. If `include()` is used, PHP proceeds with a warning.

19

5. When you use `virtual` includes with SSI, the file can exist anywhere under the document root. When you use `file`, the file must be in or below the current directory.

Exercises

1. Find out which web server you use and figure out how to apply includes to your website.

2. If you have a web application environment available for your server, find a site that offers free sample programs and take a look at some.

LESSON 20:

Understanding Server-Side Processing

At this point, you've learned how to publish websites using HTML. This lesson takes things a step further and explains how to build dynamic websites using scripts on the server. Rather than trying to explain several of the platforms described in Lesson 19, "Taking Advantage of the Server," I'm focusing on PHP in this lesson. PHP is the most common scripting platform provided by web hosts, can be easily installed on your own computer, and is completely free. It's also easy to get started with. Even if you wind up developing your applications using some other scripting language, you can apply the principles you'll learn in this lesson to those languages.

In this Lesson

- How PHP works
- How to set up a PHP development environment
- The basics of the PHP language
- How to process form input
- Using PHP includes

How PHP Works

Lesson 19 provided a brief introduction to PHP. You learned that PHP is a language that enables you to embed code processed by the server in your web pages. Normally, when a user submits a request to the server for a web page, the server reads the HTML file and sends its contents back in response. If the request is for a PHP file and the server has a PHP interpreter installed, then the server looks for PHP code in the document, executes it, and includes the output of that code in the page in place of the PHP code. Here's a simple example:

```
<html>
<head><title>A PHP Page</title></head>
<body>
<?php echo "Hello world!"; ?>
</body>
</html>
```

If this page is requested from a web server that supports PHP, the HTML sent to the browser will look like this:

```
<html>
<head><title>A PHP Page</title></head>
<body>
Hello world!
</body>
</html>
```

When the user requests the page, the web server determines that it is a PHP page rather than a regular HTML page. If a web server supports PHP, it usually treats any files with the extension .php as PHP pages. Assuming this page is called something like hello. php, when the web server receives the request, it scans the page looking for PHP code and then runs any code it finds. As you learned in Lesson 19, PHP code is set apart from the rest of a page by PHP tags, which look like this:

```
<?php your code here ?>
```

Whenever the server finds those tags, it treats whatever is within them as PHP code. That's not so different from the way things work with JavaScript, where anything inside <script> tags is treated as JavaScript code. The main difference is that all your <script> tags are supposed to be placed within the page header, whereas PHP tags can occur anywhere within a page.

In the example, the PHP code contains a call to the echo function. This function prints out the value of whatever is passed to it. In this case, I passed the text "Hello world!" to the function, so that text is included in the page. The concept of functions should also be familiar to you from the lesson on JavaScript. Just like JavaScript, PHP lets you define your own functions or use functions built into the language. echo is a built-in function.

Statements in PHP, as in JavaScript, are terminated with a semicolon. (You can see the semicolon at the end of the statement in the example.) There's no reason why you can't include multiple statements within one PHP tag, like this:

```
<?php
  echo "Hello ";
  echo "world!";
?>
```

PHP also provides a shortcut if all you want to do is print the value of something to a page. Rather than using the full PHP tag, you can use the expression tag, which just echoes a value to the page. Rather than using this:

```
<?php echo "Hello world!"; ?>
```

You can use this:

```
<?= "Hello world!" ?>
```

Replacing php with = enables you to leave out the call to the echo function and the semi-colon. This style of tag is referred to as a *short tag*.

Getting PHP to Run on Your Computer

Before you can start writing your own PHP scripts, you'll need to set up a PHP environment. The easiest approach is probably to sign up for a web hosting account that provides PHP support. Even if you do so, though, there are some advantages to getting PHP to work on your own computer. You can edit files with your favorite editor and then test them right on your own computer rather than uploading them in order to see how they work. You'll also be able to work on them even if you're not online. Finally, you can keep from putting files on a server that your users will be able to see without your having tested them first.

To process PHP pages, you need the PHP interpreter and a web server that works with the PHP interpreter. The good news is that PHP and the most popular web server, Apache, are both free, open-source software. The bad news is that getting PHP up and running can be painful, mainly because it's usually installed as an add-on to the Apache web server. So you have to get Apache to work, install PHP, and then get it to work with Apache.

20

Fortunately, if you're a Windows or Mac user, someone else has done this hard work for you. A tool called XAMPP, available for both Windows and Mac OS X, bundles up versions of Apache, PHP, and MySQL (a database useful for storing data associated with web applications) that are already set up to work together. You can download it at http://www.apachefriends.org/en/xampp.html.

If you're a Mac user, you also have the option of using MAMP, another free package that combines Apache, PHP, and MySQL. It can be downloaded from http://www.mamp.info.

Once you've installed XAMPP (or MAMP), you just have to start the application in order to get a web server up and running that you can use to develop your pages. To test your PHP pages, you can put them in the `htdocs` directory inside the XAMPP install directory. For example, if you wanted to test the `hello.php` page I talked about earlier, you could put it in the `htdocs` directory. To view it, just go to http://localhost/hello.php.

If that doesn't work, make sure that XAMPP has started the Apache server. If you're using MAMP, the steps are basically the same. Just put your pages in the `htdocs` folder, as with XAMPP.

The PHP Language

When you think about the English language, you think about it in terms of parts of speech. Nouns name things, verbs explain what things do, adjectives describe things, and so on. Programming languages are similar. A programming language is made up of various "parts of speech" as well. In this section, I'm going to explain the parts of speech that make up the PHP language—comments, variables, conditional statements, and functions.

Comments

Like HTML and JavaScript, PHP supports comments. PHP provides two comment styles—one for single-line comments and another for multiple comments. (If you're familiar with comments in the C or Java programming language, you'll notice that PHP's are the same.) First, single-line comments. To start a single-line comment, use `//` or `#`. Everything that follows either on a line is treated as a comment. Here are some examples:

```
// My function starts here.
$color = 'red'; // Set the color for text on the page
# $color = 'blue';
$color = $old_color; # Sets the color to the old color.
// $color = 'red';
```

The text that precedes `//` is processed by PHP, so the second line assigns the `$color` variable. On the third line, I've turned off the assignment by commenting it out. PHP also supports multiple-line comments, which begin with `/*` and end with `*/`. If you wanted to comment out several lines of code, you could do it like this:

```
/*
$color = 'red';
$count = 55; // Set the number of items on a page.
// $count = $count + 1;
*/
```

PHP will ignore all the lines inside the comments. Note that you can put the // style comment inside the multiline comment with no ill effects. You cannot, however, nest multiline comments. This is illegal:

```
/*
$color = 'red';
$count = 55; // Set the number of items on a page.
/* $count = $count + 1; */
*/
```

> **NOTE**
> The generally accepted style for PHP code is to use // for single-line comments rather than #.

Variables

Variables just provide a way for the programmers to assign a name to a piece of data. In PHP, these names are preceded by a dollar sign ($). Therefore, you might store a color in a variable called $color or a date in a variable named $last_published_at. Here's how you assign values to those variables:

```
$color = "red";
$last_published_at = time();
```

The first line assigns the value "red" to $color; the second returns the value returned by the built-in PHP function time() to $last_published_at. That function returns a time-stamp represented as the number of seconds since what's called the "Unix epoch."

One thing you should notice here is that you don't have to indicate what kind of item you'll be storing in a variable when you declare it. You can put a string in it, as I did when I assigned "red" to $color. You can put a number in it, as I did with $last_published_at. I know that the number is a timestamp, but as far as PHP is concerned, it's just a number. What if I want a date that's formatted to be displayed rather than stored in seconds so that it can be used in calculations? I can use the PHP date() function. Here's an example:

20

```
$last_published_at = date("F j, Y, g:i a");
```

This code formats the current date so that it looks something like "March 18, 2006, 8:47 pm." As you can see, I can change what kind of information is stored in a variable without doing anything special. It just works. The only catch is that you have to keep track of what sort of thing you've stored in a variable when you use it. For more information on how PHP deals with variable types, see http://www.php.net/manual/en/language.types.type-juggling.php.

Despite the fact that variables don't have to be declared as being associated with a particular type, PHP does support various data types, including string, integer, and float (for numbers with decimal points). Not all variable types work in all contexts. One data type that requires additional explanation is the array data type.

Arrays

The variables you've seen so far in this lesson have all been used to store single values. Arrays are data structures that can store multiple values. You can think of them as lists of values, and those values can be strings, numbers, or even other arrays. To declare an array, use the built-in array function:

```
$colors = array('red', 'green', 'blue');
```

This declaration creates an array with three elements in it. Each element in an array is numbered, and that number is referred to as the *index*. For historical reasons, array indexes start at 0, so for the preceding array, the index of red is 0, the index of green is 1, and the index of blue is 2. You can reference an element of an array using its index, like this:

```
$color = $colors[1];
```

By the same token, you can assign values to specific elements of an array as well, like this:

```
$colors[2] = 'purple';
```

You can also use this method to grow an array, like this:

```
$colors[3] = 'orange';
```

What happens if you skip a few elements when you assign an item to an array, as in the following line?

```
$colors[8] = 'white';
```

In this case, not only will element 8 be created, but elements 4 through 7 will be created as well. If you want to append an element onto an array, you just leave out the index when you make the assignment, like this:

```
$colors[] = 'yellow';
```

In addition to arrays with numeric indexes, PHP also supports associative arrays, which have indexes supplied by the programmer. These are sometimes referred to as *dictionaries* or as *hashes*. Here's an example that shows how they are declared:

```
$state_capitals = array(
  'Texas' => 'Austin',
```

```
    'Louisiana' => 'Baton Rouge',
    'North Carolina' => 'Raleigh',
    'South Dakota' => 'Pierre'
);
```

When you reference an associative array, you do so using the keys you supplied, as follows:

```
$capital_of_texas = $state_capitals['Texas'];
```

To add a new element to an associative array, you just supply the new key and value, like this:

```
$state_capitals['Pennsy\lvania'] = 'Harrisburg';
```

If you need to remove an element from an array, just use the built-in unset() function, like this:

```
unset($colors[1]);
```

The element with the index specified will be removed, and the array will decrease in size by one element as well. The indexes of the elements with larger indexes than the one that was removed will be reduced by one. You can also use unset() to remove elements from associative arrays, like this:

```
unset($state_capitals['Texas']);
```

Array indexes can be specified using variables. You just put the variable reference inside the square brackets, like this:

```
$i = 1;
$var = $my_array[$i];
```

This also works with associative arrays:

```
$str = 'dog';
$my_pet = $pets[$str];
```

As you'll see a bit further on, the ability to specify array indexes using variables is a staple of some kinds of loops in PHP.

20

As you've seen, there's nothing that distinguishes between a variable that's an array and a variable that holds a string or a number. PHP has a built-in function named is_array() that returns true if its argument is an array and false if the argument is anything else. Here's an example:

```
is_array(array(1, 2, 3));  // returns true
is_array('tree'); // returns false
```

As I mentioned before, it's perfectly acceptable to use arrays as the values in an array. Therefore, the following is a valid array declaration:

```
$stuff = ('colors' => array('red', 'green', 'blue'),
          'numbers' => array('one', 'two', 'three'));
```

In this case, I have an associative array that has two elements. The values for each of the elements are arrays themselves. I can access this data structure by stacking the references to the array indexes, like this:

```
$colors = $stuff['colors']; // Returns the list of colors.
$color = $stuff['colors'][1]; // Returns 'green'
$number = $stuff['numbers'][0]; // Returns 'one'
```

Strings

The most common data type you'll work with in PHP is the string type. A string is just a series of characters. An entire web page is a string, as is a single letter. To define a string, just place the characters in the string within quotation marks. Here are some examples of strings:

```
"one"
"1"
"I like publishing Web pages."
"This string
spans multiple lines."
```

Take a look at the last string in the list. The opening quotation mark is on the first line, and the closing quotation mark is on the second line. In PHP, this is completely valid. In some programming languages, strings that span multiple lines are illegal—not so in PHP, where strings can span as many lines as you like, as long as you don't accidentally close the quotation marks.

There's more to strings than just defining them. You can use the . operator to join strings, like this:

```
$html_paragraph = "<p>" . $paragraph . "</p>";
```

The $html_paragraph variable will contain the contents of $paragraph surrounded by the opening and closing paragraph tag. The . operator is generally referred to as the *string concatenation operator.*

Up to this point, you might have noticed that sometimes I've enclosed strings in double quotation marks, and that other times I've used single quotation marks. They both work for defining strings, but there's a difference between the two. When you use double quotation marks, PHP scans the contents of the string for variable substitutions and for special characters. When you use single quotation marks, PHP just uses whatever is in the string without checking to see whether it needs to process the contents.

Special characters are introduced with a backslash, and they are a substitute for characters that might otherwise be hard to include in a string. For example, \n is the substitute for a newline, and \r is the substitute for a carriage return. If you want to include a newline in a string and keep it all on one line, just write it like this:

```
$multiline_string = "Line one\nLine two";
```

Here's what I mean by variable substitutions. In a double-quoted string, I can include a reference to a variable inside the string, and PHP will replace it with the contents of the variable when the string is printed, assigned to another variable, or otherwise used. In other words, I could have written the preceding string-joining example as follows:

```
$html_paragraph = "<p>$paragraph</p>";
```

PHP will find the reference to $paragraph within the string and substitute its contents. On the other hand, the literal value "$paragraph" would be included in the string if I wrote that line like this:

```
$html_paragraph = '<p>$paragraph</p>';
```

You need to do a bit of extra work to include array values in a string. For example, this won't work:

```
$html_paragraph = "<p>$paragraph['intro']</p>";
```

You can include the array value using string concatenation:

```
$html_paragraph = "<p>" . $paragraph['intro'] . "</p>";
```

You can also use array references within strings if you enclose them within curly braces, like this:

```
$html_paragraph = "<p>{$paragraph['intro']}</p>";
```

One final note on defining strings is escaping. As you know, quotation marks are commonly used in HTML as well as in PHP, especially when it comes to defining attributes in tags. There are two ways to use quotation marks within strings in PHP. The first is to use the opposite quotation marks to define the string that you're using within another string. Here's an example:

```
$tag = '<p class="important">';
```

I can use the double quotes within the string because I defined it using single quotes. This particular definition won't work, though, if I want to specify the class using a variable. If that's the case, I have two other options:

```
$tag = "<p class=\"$class\">";
$tag = '<p class="' . $class . '">';
```

20

In the first option, I use the backslash character to "escape" the double quotes that occur within the string. The backslash indicates that the character that follows is part of the string and does not terminate it. The other option is to use single quotes and use the string concatenation operator to include the value of $class in the string.

Conditional Statements

Conditional statements and loops are the bones of any programming language. PHP is no different. The basic conditional statement in PHP is the if statement. Here's how it works:

```
if ($var == 0) {
  echo "Variable set to 0.";
}
```

The code inside the brackets will be executed if the expression in the if statement is true. In this case, if $var is set to anything other than 0, then the code inside the brackets will not be executed. PHP also supports else blocks, which are executed if the expression in the if statement is false. They look like this:

```
if ($var == 0) {
  echo "Variable set to 0.";
} else {
  echo "Variable set to something other than 0.";
}
```

When you add an else block to a conditional statement, it means that the statement will always do something. If the expression is true, it will run the code in the if portion of the statement. If the expression is not true, it will run the code in the else portion. Finally, there's elseif:

```
if ($var == 0) {
  echo "Variable set to 0.";
} elseif ($var == 1) {
  echo "Variable set to 1.";
} elseif ($var == 2) {
  echo "Variable set to 2.";
} else {
  echo "Variable set to something other than 0, 1, or 2.";
}
```

As you can see, elseif allows you to add more conditions to an if statement. In this case, I added two elseif conditions. There's no limit on elseif conditions—you can use as many as you need. Ultimately, elseif and else are both conveniences that enable you to write less code to handle conditional tasks.

PHP Conditional Operators

It's hard to write conditional statements if you don't know how to write a boolean expression. First of all, boolean means that an expression (which you can think of as a statement of fact) is either true or false. Here are some examples:

```
1 == 2 // false
'cat' == 'dog' // false
5.5 == 5.5 // true
5 > 0 // true
5 >= 5 // true
5 < 10 // true
```

PHP also supports logical operators, such as "not" (which is represented by an exclamation point), "and" (&&), and "or" (||). You can use them to create expressions that are made up of multiple individual expressions, like these:

```
1 == 1 && 2 == 4 // false
'blue' == 'green' || 'blue' == 'red' // false
!(1 == 2) // true, because the ! implies "not"
!(1 == 1 || 1 == 2) // false, because ! negates the expression inside the ()
```

Furthermore, individual values also evaluate to true or false on their own. Any variable set to anything other than 0 or an empty string ("" or '') will evaluate as true, including an array with no elements in it. So if $var is set to 1, the following condition will evaluate as true:

```
if ($var) {
   echo "True.";
}
```

If you want to test whether an array is empty, use the built-in function empty(). So if $var is an empty array, empty($var) will return true. Here's an example:

```
if (empty($var)) {
   echo "The array is empty.";
}
```

You can find a full list of PHP operators at http://www.php.net/manual/en/language.operators.php.

20

Loops

PHP supports several types of loops, some of which are generally more commonly used than others. As you know from the JavaScript lesson, loops execute code repeatedly until a condition of some kind is satisfied. PHP supports several types of loops: do...while, while, for, and foreach. I'll discuss them in reverse order.

foreach **Loops**

The foreach loop was created for one purpose—to enable you to process all of the elements in an array quickly and easily. The body of the loop is executed once for each item in an array, which is made available to the body of the loop as a variable specified in the loop statement. Here's how it works:

```
$colors = array('red', 'green', 'blue');
foreach ($colors as $color) {
  echo $color . "\n";
}
```

This loop prints each of the elements in the $colors array with a linefeed after each color. The important part of the example is the foreach statement. It specifies that the array to iterate over is $colors, and that each element should be copied to the variable $color so that it can be accessed in the body of the loop.

The foreach loop can also process both the keys and values in an associative array if you use slightly different syntax. Here's an example:

```
$synonyms = array('large' => 'big',
                  'loud' => 'noisy',
                  'fast' => 'rapid');

foreach ($synonyms as $key => $value) {
    echo "$key is a synonym for $value.\n";
}
```

As you can see, the foreach loop reuses the same syntax that's used to create associative arrays.

for **Loops**

Use for loops when you want to run a loop a specific number of times. The loop statement has three parts: a variable assignment for the loop's counter, an expression (containing the index variable) that specifies when the loop should stop running, and an expression that increments the loop counter. Here's a typical for loop:

```
for ($i = 1; $i <= 10; $i++)
{
  echo "Loop executed $i times.\n";
}
```

$i is the counter (or index variable) for the loop. The loop is executed until $i is larger than 10 (meaning that it will run 10 times). The last expression, $i++, adds one to $i every time the loop executes. The for loop can also be used to process an array instead of foreach if you prefer. You just have to reference the array in the loop statement, like this:

```
$colors = array('red', 'green', 'blue');
for ($i = 0; $i < count(array); $i++) {
  echo "Currently processing " . $colors[$i] . ".\n";
}
```

There are a couple of differences between this loop and the previous one. In this case, I start the index variable at 0, and use < rather than <= as the termination condition for the loop. That's because count() returns the size of the $colors array, which is 3, and loop indexes start with 0 rather than 1. If I start at 0 and terminate the loop when $i is equal to the size of the $colors array, it runs three times, with $i being assigned the values 0, 1, and 2, corresponding to the indexes of the array being processed.

while **and** do...while **Loops**

Both for and foreach are generally used when you want a loop to iterate a specific number of times. The while and do...while loops, on the other hand, are designed to be run an arbitrary number of times. Both loop statements use a single condition to determine whether the loop should continue running. Here's an example with while:

```
$number = 1;
while ($number != 5) {
  $number = rand(1, 10);
  echo "Your number is $number.\n";
}
```

This loop runs until $number is equal to 5. Every time the loop runs, $number is assigned a random value between 1 and 10. When the random number generator returns a 5, the while loop will stop running. A do...while loop is basically the same, except the condition appears at the bottom of the loop. Here's what it looks like:

```
$number = 1;
do {
  echo "Your number is $number.\n";
  $number = rand(1, 10);
} while ($number != 5);
```

Generally speaking, the only time it makes sense to use do ... while is when you want to be sure the body of the loop will execute at least once.

Controlling Loop Execution

Sometimes you want to alter the execution of a loop. Sometimes you need to stop running the loop immediately, and other times you might want to just skip ahead to the next iteration of the loop. Fortunately, PHP offers statements that do both. The break statement is used to immediately stop executing a loop and move on to the code that follows it. The continue statement stops the current iteration of the loop and goes straight to the loop condition.

Here's an example of how break is used:

```
$colors = ('red', 'green', 'blue');
$looking_for = 'red';
foreach ($colors as $color) {
  if ($color = $looking_for) {
    echo "Found $color.\n";
    break;
  }
}
```

In this example, I'm searching for a particular color. When the foreach loop gets to the array element that matches the color I'm looking for, I print the color out and use the break statement to stop the loop. Once I've found the element I'm looking for, there's no reason to continue.

I could accomplish the same thing a different way using continue, like this:

```
$colors = ('red', 'green', 'blue');
$looking_for = 'red';
foreach ($colors as $color) {
  if ($color != $looking_for) {
    continue;
  }

  echo "Found $color.\n";
}
```

In this case, if the color is not the one I'm looking for, the continue statement stops executing the body of the loop and goes back to the loop condition. If the color is the one I'm looking for, the continue statement is not executed and the echo function goes ahead and prints the color name I'm looking for.

The loops I'm using as examples don't have a whole lot of work to do. Adding in the break and continue statements doesn't make my programs much more efficient. Let's say, however, that each iteration of my loop searches a very large file or fetches some data from a remote server. If I can save some of that work using break and continue, it could make my script much faster.

Built-in Functions

PHP supports literally hundreds of built-in functions. You've already seen a few, such as echo() and count(). There are many, many more. PHP has functions for formatting strings, searching strings, connecting to many types of databases, reading and writing files, dealing with dates and times, and just about everything in between.

You learned that most of the functionality in the JavaScript language is built using the methods of a few standard objects such as window and document. PHP is different—rather than its built-in functions being organized via association with objects, they are all just part of the language's vocabulary.

If you ever get the feeling that there might be a built-in function to take care of some task, you should check the PHP manual to see whether such a function already exists. Chances are it does. Definitely check whether your function will manipulate strings or arrays. PHP has a huge library of array- and string-manipulation functions that take care of most common tasks.

User-Defined Functions

PHP enables you to create user-defined functions that, like JavaScript functions, enable you to package up code you want to reuse. Here's how a function is declared:

```
function myFunction($arg = 0) {
  // Do stuff
}
```

The function keyword indicates that you're creating a user-defined function. The name of the function follows. In this case, it's myFunction. The rules for function names and variable names are the same—numbers, letters, and underscores are valid. The list of arguments that the function accepts follows the function name, in parentheses.

The preceding function has one argument, $arg. In this example, I've set a default value for the argument. The variable $arg would be set to 0 if the function were called like this:

```
myFunction();
```

On the other hand, $arg would be set to 55 if the function were called like this:

```
myFunction(55);
```

Functions can just as easily accept multiple arguments:

```
function myOtherFunction($arg1, $arg2, $arg3)
{
  // Do stuff
}
```

20

As you can see, myOtherFunction accepts three arguments, one of which is an array. Valid calls to this function include the following:

```
myOtherFunction('one', 'two', array('three'));
myOtherFunction('one', 'two');
myOtherFunction(0, 0, @stuff);
myOtherFunction(1, 'blue');
```

One thing you can't do is leave out arguments in the middle of a list. So if you have a function that accepts three arguments, there's no way to set just the first and third arguments and leave out the second, or set the second and third and leave out the first. If you pass one argument in, it will be assigned to the function's first argument. If you pass in two arguments, they will be assigned to the first and second arguments to the function.

Returning Values

Optionally, your function can return a value, or more specifically, a *variable*. Here's a simple example of a function:

```
function add($a = 0, $b = 0) {
   return $a + $b;
}
```

The return keyword is used to indicate that the value of a variable should be returned to the caller of a function. You could call the previous function like this:

```
$sum = add(2, 3); // $sum set to 5
```

A function can just as easily return an array. Here's an example:

```
function makeArray($a, $b) {
   return array($a, $b);
}

$new_array = makeArray('one', 'two');
```

If you don't explicitly return a value from your function, PHP will return the result of the last expression inside the function anyway. For example, let's say I wrote the add function like this:

```
function add($a = 0, $b = 0) {
 $a + $b;
}
```

Because $a + $b is the last expression in the function, PHP will go ahead and return its result. That's the case for logical expressions as well. Here's an example:

```
function negate($a) {
   !$a;
}

negate(1); // returns false
negate(0); // returns true
```

Your function can also return the result of another function, whether it's built in or one you wrote yourself. Here are a couple of examples:

```
function add($a = 0, $b = 0) {
  return $a + $b;
}

function alsoAdd($a = 0, $b = 0) {
  return add($a, $b);
}
```

Processing Forms

You learned how to create forms back in Lesson 10, "Designing Forms," and although I explained how to design a form, I didn't give you a whole lot of information about what to do with form data once it's submitted. Now I'm going to explain how PHP makes data that has been submitted available to your PHP scripts.

When a user submits a form, PHP automatically decodes the variables and copies the values into some built-in variables. Built-in variables are like built-in functions—you can always count on their being defined when you run a script. The three associated with form data are $_GET, $_POST, and $_REQUEST. These variables are all associative arrays, and the names assigned to the form fields on your form are the keys to the arrays.

$_GET contains all the parameters submitted using the GET method (in other words, in the query string). The $_POST method contains all the parameters submitted via POST in the response body. $_REQUEST contains all the form parameters regardless of how they were submitted. Unless you have a specific reason to differentiate between GET and POST, you can use $_REQUEST. Let's look at a simple example of a form:

```
<form action="post.php" method="post">
  Enter your name: <input type="text" name="yourname" /><br />
  <input type="submit" />
</form>
```

When the user submits the form, the value of the yourname field will be available in $_POST and $_REQUEST. You could return it to the user like this:

```
<p>Hello <?= $_REQUEST['yourname'] ?>. Thanks for visiting.</p>
```

20

Preventing Cross-Site Scripting

You have to be careful when you display data entered by a user on a web page because malicious users can include HTML tags and JavaScript in their input in an attempt to trick other users who might view that information into doing something they might not want to do, such as entering their password to your site and submitting it to another site. This is known as a *cross-site scripting attack*.

In order to prevent malicious users from doing that sort of thing, PHP includes the `htmlspecialchars()` function, which automatically encodes any special characters in a string so that they are displayed on a page rather than letting the browser treat them as markup. Or, if you prefer, you can use `htmlentities()`, which encodes all of the characters that are encoded by `htmlspecialchars()` plus any other characters that can be represented as entities. In the preceding example, you'd really want to write the script that displays the user's name like this:

```
<p>Hello <?= htmlspecialchars($_POST['yourname']) ?>.
Thanks for visiting.</p>
```

That prevents the person who submitted the data from launching a successful cross-site scripting attack.

If you prefer, you can also use the `strip_tags()` function, which just removes all the HTML tags from a string.

Finally, if your form is submitted using the POST method, you should refer to the parameters using `$_POST` rather than `$_REQUEST`, which also helps to avoid certain types of attacks by ignoring information appended to the URL via the query string.

Once you have access to the data the user submitted, you can do whatever you like with it. You can validate it (even if you have JavaScript validation, you should still validate user input on the server as well), store it in a database for later use, or send it to someone via email.

Handling Parameters with Multiple Values

Most form fields are easy to deal with; they're simple name and value pairs. If you have a text field or radio button group, for example, you can access the value submitted using `$_REQUEST`, like this:

```
$radio_value = $_REQUEST['radiofield'];
$text_value = $_REQUEST['textfield'];
```

There are some types of fields, however, that submit multiple name and value pairs, specifically check boxes and multiple select lists. If you have a group of five check boxes on a form, that field can actually submit up to five separate parameters, all of which have the same name and different values. PHP handles this by converting the user input into an array rather than a regular variable. Unfortunately, you have to give PHP a hint to let it know that a field should be handled this way. (PHP has no idea what your form looks like; all it knows about is the data that has been submitted.)

If you include [] at the end of the name of a form field, PHP knows that it should expect multiple values for that field and converts the parameters into an array. This occurs even if only one value is submitted for that field. Here's an example:

```
<form action="postmultiplevalues.php" method="post">
  <input type="checkbox" name="colors[]" value="red" /> Red<br />
  <input type="checkbox" name="colors[]" value="green" /> Green<br />
  <input type="checkbox" name="colors[]" value="blue" /> Blue
</form>
```

When the form is submitted, you can access the values as you would for any other parameter, except that the value in the $_REQUEST array for this parameter will be an array
rather than a single value. You can access it like this:

```
$colors = $_REQUEST['colors'];
foreach ($colors as $color) {
  echo "$color<br />\n";
}
```

If the user selects only one check box, the value will be placed in an array that has only
one element.

Task: **Exercise 20.1: Validating a Form** ▼

One of the most common tasks when it comes to server-side processing is form validation. When users submit data via a form, it should be validated on the server, even if your
page includes JavaScript validation, because you can't guarantee that JavaScript validation was actually applied to the form data.

I'm going to use a simplified version of the user registration form from Lesson 10 in this
exercise. Figure 20.1 is a screenshot of the form I'll be using. Here's the HTML source:

Input ▼

```
<html>
<head>
<title>Registration Form</title>
</head>
<body>
<h1>Registration Form</h1>

<p>Please fill out the form below to register for our site. Fields
with bold labels are required.</p>

<form method="post">

<p><label for="name"><b>Name:</b><br />
<input name="name" /></p>

<p><label for="age"><b>Age:</b><br />
<input name="age" /></p>

<p><label for="toys[]"><b>Toys:</b></label><br />
<input type="checkbox" name="toys[]" value="digicam" /> Digital Camera<br />
```

20

```
<input type="checkbox" name="toys[]" value="mp3" /> MP3 Player<br />
<input type="checkbox" name="toys[]" value="wlan" /> Wireless LAN</p>

<p><input type="submit" value="register" /></p>
</form>
</body>
</html>
```

Output ▶

FIGURE 20.1
A simple user
registration form.

As you can see, the form has three fields—one for the user's name, one for the user's
age, and one that enables the user to select some toys he or she owns. All three of the
fields are required. The form submits to itself, using the POST method. I've specified the
action for the form using a built-in PHP variable that returns the URL for the page currently being displayed. That way I can make sure the form is submitted to itself without
including the URL for the page in my HTML. Here's the basic structure of the page:

```
<?php
// Form processing code
?>
<html>
    <head>
        <title>Page Structure</title>
        <style type="text/css">
            /* Page styles go here. */
        </style>

    </head>
    <body>
        <h1>Sample Page</h1>
        <!-- Print form errors here -->
        <form method="post" action="<?= $_SERVER['PHP_SELF'] ?>">
            <!-- Present form fields here -->
        </form>
    </body>
</html>
```

This structure is pretty common for pages that present a form and process that form as well. The PHP processor runs the scripts on the page from top to bottom, so all the form processing will take place before any of the page is presented. If this page were going to do more than just validate the form, it would probably redirect the user to a page thanking him or her for registering if the validation code found no errors. It would also probably save the values submitted through the form somewhere. In this case, though, I'm just explaining form validation.

As you can see, the form-processing code lives on the same page as the form itself, so the form will be submitted to this page. The validation code will live within the script section at the top of the page. My objective for this page is to make sure that the user enters all the required data and that the age the user enters is actually a number. To make things a bit easier on myself, I've written a function to do the actual validation for me.

Here's the function:

```
function validate() {
    $errors = array();

    if (empty($_POST['name'])) {
        $errors['name'] = 'You must enter your name.';
    }

    if (!is_numeric($_POST['age'])) {
        $errors['age'] = "You must enter a valid age.";
    }

    if (empty($_POST['toys'])) {
        $errors['toys'] = 'You must choose at least one toy.';
    }

    return $errors;
}
```

This function validates each of the fields on the form and then places all the errors in an associative array called $errors. When an error is detected, a new entry is added to the array with the name of the field as the key and the error message as the array value. Later on, I'll display the error messages and use the field names to mark the fields that have errors.

On the first line of the function, I declare $errors to store the errors found during validation. Next, I validate the name parameter. PHP has a built-in function called empty() that checks to see whether a variable is empty. In this case, I use it to check $_POST['name'], which was set automatically when the form was submitted. If that variable is empty, meaning that the user did not submit his or her name, I add an entry to $errors.

20

▼ Next, I validate the age field using PHP's is_numeric() function. I negate the condition with the not operator because it's only an error if the value in the field isn't numeric.

Finally, I check to make sure that the user has selected a toy. As you saw, this field is actually a check box group, meaning that the contents of the field are submitted as an array (assuming I've named the field properly). Again, I use empty() here. It works with regular variables and arrays, and it returns true if an array contains no elements. If there are no elements in the array, no toys were submitted, and the error is added to the array.

Once validation is complete, I return the value of the $errors variable to the caller. Here's the code I use to call the validate() function. It lives right at the top of the page:

```
$errors = array();

if ($_SERVER['REQUEST_METHOD'] == 'POST') {
    $errors = validate();
}
```

I'm going to check on $errors later in the page regardless of whether I validate the input, so I go ahead and declare it. To determine whether I should validate a form submission or display an empty form, I check the built-in variable $_SERVER['REQUEST_METHOD'] to see whether the request was submitted using the POST method. If it was, then I want to do the input validation. If not, then I just want to display the form.

If any parameters were submitted via POST, I run the validate() function I just described. There's one more line of code at the top of the page where most of my PHP code lives:

```
$toys = array('digicam' => 'Digital Camera',
    'mp3' => 'MP3 Player', 'wlan' => 'Wireless LAN');
```

It's an array that contains a list of all the check boxes to display for the toys field. It's easier to iterate over all the check boxes in a loop than it is to code them all by hand. If I need to add new toys to the list, I can just add them to the array definition and they'll automatically be included on the page. I'll show you how the code that displays the field works shortly.

Presenting the Form

Aside from validating form submissions, one of the other important functions of server-side processing is to prepopulate forms with data when they are presented. Many web applications are referred to as *CRUD applications*, where CRUD stands for create/update/delete. It describes the fact that the applications are used to mostly manage records in some kind of database. If a user submits a form with invalid data, when you

▼ present the form for the user to correct, you want to include all the data that the user

entered so that he or she doesn't have to type it all in again. By the same token, if you're ▼
writing an application that enables users to update their user profile for a website, you
will want to include the information in their current profile in the update form. This section explains how to accomplish these sorts of tasks.

However, before I present the form to the user, I'm going to provide a list of errors that
the user needs to correct before the form submission is considered valid. Here's the code
to accomplish that task:

```php
<?php if (!empty($errors)) { ?>
    <ul>
        <?php foreach (array_values($errors) as $error) { ?>
            <li><?= $error ?></li>
        <?php } ?>
    </ul>
<?php } ?>
```

I use the `empty()` function yet again to determine whether there are any errors. If there
aren't any, I can go ahead and present the form. If there are any errors, I present them in
a list. First, I create an unordered list; then I use a `foreach` loop to iterate over the errors.
The `$errors` variable is an associative array, and the error messages to present are the
values in the array. I use the built-in `array_values()`function to extract an array containing only the values in the `$errors` array, and iterate over that array using the `foreach`
loop. There's something interesting going on here. The body of the `foreach` loop is
HTML, not PHP code. Look closely and you'll see the opening and closing braces for
the `foreach` loop. Rather than sticking with PHP for the body of the loop, though, I go
back to HTML mode by closing the PHP script, and I use regular HTML to define the
list items. Inside the list item I use a short tag to present the current error message.

Separating Presentation and Logic

The point here is that it's common to mix PHP and HTML in this way. You create your
loop using PHP but you define the HTML in the page rather than in `echo()` calls
inside your PHP code. This is generally considered the best practice for PHP. You
should write as much HTML as possible outside your PHP scripts, using PHP only
where it's necessary to add bits of logic to the page. Then you can keep the bulk of
your PHP code at the top or bottom of your page or in included files in order to separate the presentation of your data and the business logic implemented in code. That
makes your code easier to work on in the future. As an example, rather than sprin-
kling the validation code throughout my page, I put it in one function so that a programmer can work on it without worrying about the page layout. By the same token,
I could have built the unordered list inside the validation function and just returned
that, but then my HTML would be mixed in with my PHP. Cleanly separating them is
generally the best approach.

20

▼ Once I've listed the errors, I can go ahead and present the form fields. Before I do that, let me show you one more thing I've added to the page. I included a style sheet that defines one rule—`label.error`. The labels for any fields with errors will be assigned to this class so that they can be highlighted when the form is presented. Here's the style sheet:

```
<style type="text/css">
label.error {
    color: red;
}
</style>
```

OK, now that everything is set up, let's look at how the `name` field is presented. Here's the code:

```
<p>
<?php if (array_key_exists('name', $errors)) { ?>
    <label for="name" class="error"><b>Name:</b></label>
<?php } else { ?>
    <label for="name"><b>Name:</b></label>
<?php } ?>
<br />
<input name="name" value="<?= strip_tags($_POST['name']) ?>" /></p>
```

This code is a lot different from the old code I used to present the `name` field in the original listing in this example. First, I include an `if` statement that checks to see whether there's an error associated with this field. To do so, I use the `array_key_exists()` function, which is yet another built-in PHP function. Remember that the keys in `$errors` are the names of the fields with errors. So if the `$errors` array contains an element with the key `name`, it means that this field was not valid.

If there is an error with the field, I include the attribute `class="error"` in the `<label>` tag for the field. When the form is presented, the label will be red, indicating to the user that he or she needs to fix that field, even if the user didn't bother to read the list of errors. If there isn't an error, the normal `<label>` tag is printed.

Once that's done, I just have to print out the `name` field, but in this case I need to include the value that was submitted for the field if it's available. I include the `value` attribute in my `<input>` tag, and I use a short tag to include the value of `$_POST['name']` as the value. Inside the expression evaluator, I've wrapped the variable containing the value for the field in the `strip_tags()` function. This PHP function automatically removes any HTML tags from a string, and it's used here to thwart any possible cross-site scripting attacks a malicious person might employ.

The age field is identical to the `name` field in every way except its name, so I'll skip that
▼ and turn instead to the `toys` field. Here's the code:

```
<p>
<?php if (array_key_exists('toys', $errors)) { ?>
    <label for="toys[]" class="error"><b>Toys:</b></label>
<?php } else { ?>
    <label for="toys[]"><b>Toys:</b></label>
<?php } ?>
<br />
<?php foreach ($toys as $key => $value) { ?>
    <input type="checkbox" name="toys[]"
    <?php if (in_array($key, $_POST['toys'])) { echo 'checked="checked" '; } ?>
    value="<?= $key ?>" /> <?= $value?><br />
<?php } ?>
</p>
```

As you can see, the code for marking the label for the field as an error is the same for this field as it was for name. The more interesting section of the code here is the loop that creates the check boxes. When I was describing the form-processing section of the page, I explained that I put all the toys inside the array $toys so that I could print out the check boxes using a loop. There's the loop.

The values in the <input> tags are the keys in the array, and the labels for the check boxes are the values. I use the associative array version of the foreach loop to copy each of the key/value pairs in the array into the variables $key and $value. Inside the loop, I print out the <input> tags, using toys[] as the parameter name to let PHP know that this field can have multiple values and should be treated as an array. To include the value for a field, I just use a short tag to insert the key into the value attribute of the tag. I use it again to print out the label for the check box, $value, after the tag. The last bit here is the if statement found within the <input> tag. Remember that if you want a check box to be prechecked when a form is presented, you have to include the checked attribute. I use the in_array() function to check if the key currently being processed is in $_POST['toys']. If it is, I then print out the checked attribute using echo(). This ensures that all the items the user checked before submitting the form are still checked if validation fails.

A browser displaying a form that contains some errors appears in Figure 20.2. Here's the full source listing for the page:

20

Input ▼

```
<?php
    $toys = array('digicam' => 'Digital Camera',
        'mp3' => 'MP3 Player', 'wlan' => 'Wireless LAN');

    $errors = array();

    if ($_SERVER['REQUEST_METHOD'] == 'POST') {
```

```
        $errors = validate();
    }

    function validate() {
        $errors = array();

        if (empty($_POST['name'])) {
            $errors['name'] = 'You must enter your name.';
        }

        if (!is_numeric($_POST['age'])) {
            $errors['age'] = "You must enter a valid age.";
        }

        if (empty($_POST['toys'])) {
            $errors['toys'] = 'You must choose at least one toy.';
        }

        return $errors;
    }
?>
<html xmlns="http://www.w3.org/1999/xhtml">
<head>
<title>Registration Form</title>
<style type="text/css">
label.error {
    color: red;
}
</style>
</head>
<body>
<h1>Registration Form</h1>

<p>Please fill out the form below to register for our site. Fields
with bold labels are required.</p>

<?php if (!empty($errors)) { ?>
    <ul>
        <?php foreach (array_values($errors) as $error) { ?>
            <li><?= $error ?></li>
        <?php } ?>
    </ul>
<?php } ?>

<form method="post" action="<?= $_SERVER['PHP_SELF'] ?>">

<p>
<?php if (array_key_exists('name', $errors)) { ?>
    <label for="name" class="error"><b>Name:</b></label>
<?php } else { ?>
    <label for="name"><b>Name:</b></label>
```

```php
<?php } ?>
<br />
<input name="name" value="<?= strip_tags($_POST['name']) ?>" /></p>

<p>
<?php if (array_key_exists('age', $errors)) { ?>
    <label for="age" class="error"><b>Age:</b></label>
<?php } else { ?>
    <label for="age"><b>Age:</b></label>
<?php } ?>
<br />
<input name="age" value="<?= strip_tags($_POST['age']) ?>"/></p>

<p>
<?php if (array_key_exists('toys', $errors)) { ?>
    <label for="toys[]" class="error"><b>Toys:</b></label>
<?php } else { ?>
    <label for="toys[]"><b>Toys:</b></label>
<?php } ?>
<br />
<?php foreach ($toys as $key => $value) { ?>
    <input type="checkbox" name="toys[]"
    <?php if (in_array($key, $_POST['toys'])) { echo 'checked="checked" '; } ?>
    value="<?= $key ?>" /> <?= $value?><br />
<?php } ?>
</p>

<p><input type="submit" value="register" /></p>
</form>
</body>
</html>
```

Output ▶

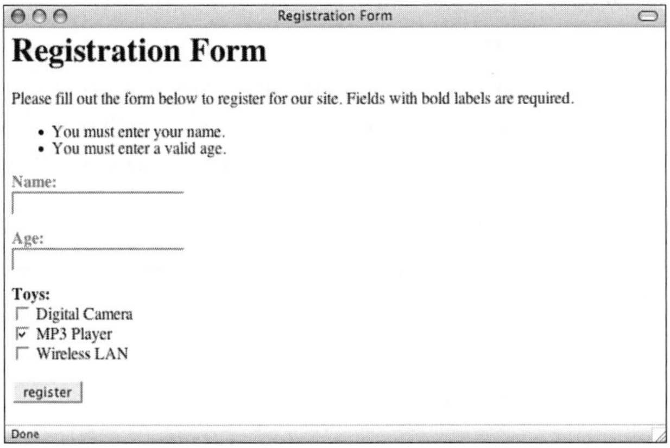

FIGURE 20.2
A form with some
errors that were
caught during
validation.

20

Using PHP Includes

In the previous lesson, you learned how to use server-side includes, which enable you to easily include snippets of web pages within other web pages. PHP and all other server-side scripting languages provide the same functionality, generally with the added benefit of giving you a lot more control over how includes are applied. With PHP, files are included using built-in functions. You can conditionally include files, specify which file to include dynamically, or even nest include function calls within included pages. Here's a simple example of an include call:

```
include("header.php");
```

On encountering that function call, PHP will try to read in and process a file named header.php in the same directory as the current page. If it can't find this file, it will try to find the file in each of the directories in its *include path* as well. The include path is a list of directories (generally specified by the server administrator) where PHP searches for files to include, and it's generally set for the entire server in a configuration file.

Four include-related functions are built into PHP: require, require_once, include, and include_once. All these functions include an external file in the page being processed. The difference between "include" and "require" is how PHP reacts when the file being included isn't available. If include or include_once is used, the PHP page prints a warning and continues on. If require or require_once is used, an unavailable include file is treated as a fatal error and page processing stops.

If you use require_once or include_once to include a file that was already included on the page, the function call will be ignored. If you use require or include, the file will be included no matter what.

PHP includes are like HTML links in that you can use relative or absolute paths in your includes. The difference is that absolute PHP paths start at the root of file system rather than the web server's document root. So if you wanted to include a file using an absolute path on a computer running Windows, you'd write the include like this:

```
require_once('c:\stuff\myfile.php');
```

That's almost never a good idea. You should always use relative paths where possible. In other words, if the included file is in the directory above the one where the including file is located, you should use a path like this:

```
require_once("../myinclude.php");
```

If the file being included is not stored with your other web documents, you should try to have that directory added to your server's include path rather than using absolute paths to access it.

CAUTION

> Never pass data entered by a user to any include function; it's a big security risk. For example, this would be inappropriate:
>
> ```
> require_once($_POST['file_to_include']);
> ```

Choosing Which Include Function to Use

Given these four very similar functions, how do you choose which makes the most sense to use? The most important factor in making that decision is the content of the file to be included. Generally there are two types of include files—snippets of markup that will be presented on your page, and PHP code libraries that provide code you are using on multiple pages throughout a site.

If the file you are including is a library, you just about always want to use `require_once`. If you're using code from the library on a page, chances are the page will not work if the library file is not available, meaning that you should use `require` rather than `include`. If the file contains library code, you're not going to want to include it more than once. Let's look at an example. You've written a library called `temperature_converter.php`. The contents of the file are shown here:

```php
<?php
function celsiusToFahrenheit($temp = 0) {
    return round(($temp * 9/5) + 32);
}
?>
```

This file contains one function, `celsiusToFahrenheit()`, which converts a Celsius temperature to Fahrenheit and then rounds the result so that the function returns an integer. Now let's look at a page that includes this file:

```php
<?php
require_once("temperature_converter.php");
?>
<html>
  <head>
    <title>Current Temperature</title>
  </head>
  <body>
    <p>Current temperature in Fahrenheit: <?= celsiusToFahrenheit(55) ?></p>
  </body>
</html>
```

20

As you can see, in this case the page won't have any meaning if the function in the library page is not available, so using `require` makes sense. On this page, it wouldn't matter whether I used `require` or `require_once` because there are no other includes.

Let's say that the page included another file, one that prints the current temperatures around the world. If that page also had a require() call for temperature_converter. php, the same code would be included twice. An error would cause the page to fail, because each function name can only be declared once. Using require_once ensures that your library code is available and that it is not accidentally included in your page multiple times.

On the other hand, if you're including content that will be displayed within your page, then include or require make more sense. You don't have to worry about conflicts, and if you're including something to be displayed on the page, chances are you want it to appear, even if you've already included the same thing.

Expanding Your Knowledge of PHP

PHP is a full-featured scripting language for creating web applications and even writing command-line scripts. What you've seen in this lesson is just a brief introduction to the language. There are more statements, lots more built-in functions, and plenty of other things about the application for which there isn't space to discuss in this lesson. Fortunately, an online version of the PHP manual is available that will fill in most of the blanks for you. You can find it at http://www.php.net/docs.php.

Also, shelves of books about PHP are available to you. Some that you might want to look into are *Sams Teach Yourself PHP in 24 Hours, 3rd Edition* (ISBN 0672326191), *Sams Teach Yourself PHP in 10 Minutes* (ISBN 0672327627). You might also look at *PHP and MySQL Web Development, 3rd Edition* (ISBN 0672326728).

There's more to PHP than just the core language, too. Lots of libraries have been written by users to take care of common programming tasks that you might run into. There's an online repository for these libraries called PEAR, which stands for PHP Extension and Application Repository. You can find it at http://pear.php.net/.

For example, the eBay website provides an API (application programming interface) that you can use to integrate your own website with eBay. You could write the code to use this API yourself, but a library in PEAR already exists. You can find it at http://pear. php.net/package/Services_Ebay.

This is just one of the many libraries you can obtain via PEAR. When you're writing your applications, make sure to check the PHP manual to ensure there's not already a built-in function to take care of whatever you're doing. If there isn't, you should check PEAR.

As I said before, I left out huge swaths of PHP functionality in this lesson for the sake of space. Here are some areas that you'll want to look into before developing your own PHP applications.

Database Connectivity

I mentioned CRUD applications already. A CRUD application is generally just a front end for a relational database, which in turn is an application optimized for storing data within tables. Databases can be used to store content for websites, billing information for an online store, payroll for a company, or anything else that can be expressed as a table. It seems like there's a relational database providing the storage for just about every popular website.

Because databases play such a huge role in developing web applications, PHP provides a lot of database-related functionality. Most relational databases are applications that can be accessed over a network, a lot like a web server. PHP is capable of connecting to every popular relational database. In order to communicate with relational databases, you have to use a language called SQL—the structured query language. That's another book unto itself.

Regular Expressions

Regular expressions comprise a small language designed to provide programmers with a flexible way to match patterns in strings. For example, the regular expression `^a.*z$` matches a string that starts with *a*, ends with *z*, and has some number of characters in between. You can use regular expressions to do much more fine-grained form validation than I did in Exercise 20.1. They're also used to extract information from files, search and replace within strings, parse email addresses, or anything else that requires you to solve a problem with pattern matching. Regular expressions are incredibly flexible, but the syntax can be a bit complex.

PHP actually supports two different varieties of regular expression syntax—Perl style and POSIX style. You can read about both of them in the PHP manual.

Sending Mail

PHP provides functions for sending email. For example, you could write a PHP script that automatically notifies an administrator by email when a user registers for a website, or sends users a password reminder if they request one when they forget their password. PHP also provides functions that enable your applications to retrieve mail as well as send it, making it possible to write web-based email clients and other such applications.

20

Object-Oriented PHP

PHP provides features for object-oriented development if you prefer that style of programming. The object-oriented features work differently between PHP 4, which is the version that's most commonly deployed, and PHP 5, the most recent version of the language. For more information on object-oriented PHP, refer to the manual.

Cookies and Sessions

Cookies are a browser feature that lets websites set values that are stored by your browser and returned to the server any time you request a page. For example, when users log into your site, you can set a cookie on their computers to keep track of who they are so that you don't have to force them to log in any time they want to see a password-protected page. You can also use cookies to keep track of when visitors return to your site after their initial visit. PHP provides full support for cookies. It also provides a facility called *sessions*. Sessions enable you to store data between requests to the server. For example, you could read a user's profile into his or her session when that user logs into the site, and then reference it on every page without going back and loading it all over again. Generally cookies are used with sessions so that the server can keep track of which session is associated with a particular user.

File Uploads

Back in Lesson 10, you learned about file upload fields for forms. PHP can deal with file uploads, enabling the programmer to access and manipulate them. With PHP, file uploads are stored to a temporary location on the server, and it's up to the programmer to decide whether to store them permanently and, if so, where to put them.

Summary

This lesson provided a whirlwind tour of the PHP language, and it explained how server-side scripts are written in general. Although the syntax of other languages will differ from PHP, the basic principles for dealing with user input, processing forms, and embedding scripts in your pages will be quite similar.

In the next lesson, you'll learn how to take advantage of applications that other people have written rather than writing them yourself. Just as PHP has lots of built-in functions to take care of common tasks, so too are there many popular applications that you can download and install rather than writing them from scratch yourself.

Workshop

The following workshop includes questions you might ask about server-side development, quizzes to test your knowledge, and two quick exercises.

Q&A

Q **At work, all of our applications are written using Active Server Pages. Why didn't you write about that?**

A There are a number of popular platforms for writing web applications. PHP has the advantage of running on a number of operating systems, including Windows, Mac OS X, and Linux. Furthermore, support for PHP is offered by many web hosting providers. Finally, as you'll learn in the next lesson, there are many applications already written in PHP that you can take advantage of. Knowledge of PHP can be helpful in working with them.

Q **Do I need a special application to edit PHP files?**

A Just as with HTML, PHP files are normal text documents. Some text editors have specialized features that make working with PHP easier, just as there are for HTML. If you're just starting out, using Notepad or any other regular text editor will work fine, but you'll probably want to find a more powerful tool for writing PHP if you find yourself programming in PHP a lot.

Q **How do I deploy PHP files to a server?**

A There are no special requirements for deploying PHP files. You can just transfer them to the server as you would regular HTML files. As long as the server is configured to handle PHP, you should be fine. The one thing you do need to be careful to do is to make sure your directory structure is the same on the server and on your local computer. If you are using includes and directory paths change, your includes will break.

Q **Are PHP scripts browser-dependent in any way?**

A All of the processing in PHP scripts takes place on the server. They can be used to produce HTML or JavaScript that won't work with your browser, but there's nothing in PHP that will prevent it from working with a browser.

Quiz

1. What is the difference between double and single quotes in PHP?
2. How do the `include_once` and `require_once` functions differ?
3. Which functions can be used to help avoid cross-site scripting attacks?
4. How do you declare an associative array in PHP?

20

Quiz Answers

1. In PHP, strings in double quotes are parsed for variable references and special characters before they are presented. Strings in single quotes are presented as is.

2. The `include_once` function does not return a fatal error if the file being included is not found. With `require_once`, if the file is not found, a fatal error occurs and the rest of the page is not processed.

3. You can use `htmlspecialchars()` to escape the characters used to generate HTML tags for a page. You can use `strip_tags()` to remove any HTML tags from a string. Either approach should prevent users from using malicious input to attempt a cross-site scripting attack.

4. Associative arrays are declared as follows:

```
$array = ('key' => 'value, 'key2' => 'value2');
```

Exercises

1. Get PHP up and running on your own computer.

2. Write a script that enables a user to show the current date and time on a web page.

3. Go to the PHP manual online and find a built-in function that wasn't introduced in this lesson. Use it in a script of your own.

LESSON 21:
Using Tools to Make Publishing Easier

Throughout the course of this book, you've learned how to build websites by hand, creating HTML pages one by one. In this lesson, you'll learn how to use applications to manage aspects of your website. These types of applications are generally called *content management systems*, and I'll explain how to install them and use them to keep track of your content so that it's easier to publish and maintain.

In this Lesson

- How content management systems came into being

- How to decide whether to use a content management system for your website

- What the common types of content management systems are

- How to work with packaged web applications in general

- How to install and use four popular content management applications—TypePad, WordPress, MediaWiki, and Coppermine

The Rise of Content Management

Content management systems were invented to deal with the complexity and tedium of managing large collections of HTML documents by hand. A content management system is an application that manages website content in a form that's convenient for editing and maintenance and publishes the content as HTML. Some content management systems generate HTML programmatically on the fly, whereas others generate static files and publish them. Most content management systems are web applications themselves. Users enter and manage content via HTML forms, and the content management system takes care of storing the content in a database of some kind. Generally content management systems provide some kind of facility for creating templates and then merge the content entered by users with the templates to produce a finished website. When templates are updated, all the pages that use those templates automatically have the changes applied to them.

Content management systems were initially deployed at the largest sites, such as online news sites, online catalogs, and technical sites that published lots of data. These systems were generally custom built and rather complicated. Content management eventually became an industry unto itself, with many companies producing large, expensive systems aimed at publishers, large corporate websites, and other customers who had lots of web content and a few hundred thousand dollars to spend to deploy a system to manage that content.

At the same time, content management systems aimed at individuals also became increasingly popular, except that they weren't called content management tools. Instead, they were called weblogging tools, wikis, photo gallery scripts, and so on.

These days, most websites are built using content management systems of some kind, and some of the largest and busiest websites utilize content management tools that were originally aimed at individuals running small sites. For example, one of the busiest sites on the Web, Wikipedia.org, is an encyclopedia written and edited by volunteers that was built using a content management system called a *wiki*. Wikis started out as a way to make it easy for individuals to quickly publish content on the Web without any knowledge of HTML. Now you can download and use MediaWiki, the tool behind Wikipedia, free of charge. You'll learn more about it later in this lesson.

Is a Content Management System Right for You?

It may seem odd to talk about using an application to manage your content now after you've worked through 20 lessons explaining how to build web pages from scratch. However, those skills will serve you well whether you use a content management system or not. Content management systems can take a lot of drudgery out of web publishing without limiting the amount of creativity you can apply in designing your web pages.

Some work is involved in learning, setting up, and customizing a content management system. When you're creating a website, it's probably easier to start with just a few static files and leave aside the content management system. As your site gets bigger, though, at some point the work involved with dealing with static files offsets the initial investment required to start working with a content management system. You have to figure out whether that initial time investment will pay off in the end.

Another common tradeoff with content management systems is that they vary in flexibility. Some, such as photo galleries, are built to handle very specific kinds of content. You wouldn't use photo gallery software to manage an online news site, for example. Others are more flexible. For example, the Mambo content management system is designed as a generic content management system for any type of content. Generally speaking, the more flexible a content management system is, the more work it is to set up. So if you know you're publishing a photo gallery, setting up a photo gallery package probably makes more sense than setting up a general-purpose content management system and customizing it to present photos.

In Lesson 18, "Putting Your Site Online," I talked about the various options for web hosting. A similar set of options is available when it comes to content management systems. You can write your own. This provides the most flexibility, but it can be a huge amount of work. You can install and manage an application that someone else wrote and customize it for your own needs. Generally to go this route you'll need your own server or at least an account with a web hosting provider. The final option is to subscribe to a hosted application. For many kinds of web applications, you can pay to subscribe to an application that's hosted by someone else. They make sure that the servers stay up and that the application is running properly, and you just focus on entering your content and making whatever customizations are available. Hosted applications are generally the least flexible, but they're also the easiest to get started with.

Types of Content Management Systems

Content management systems can be sorted into rough categories. As you've probably figured out, there's more to it than just deciding to use a content management system. You have to figure out what type of content you have and which content management system makes the most sense for you. In some cases, multiple content management systems may be the answer. You may prefer to publish your writing using a weblogging tool and to publish your photos using a photo gallery application. Here's a discussion of some common types of content management systems.

21

Weblogging Tools

It seems you can't escape the term *weblog* (or more commonly, *blog*) these days. A weblog is just a website where new items are published in reverse chronological order. The items can be articles, links, recipes, photos, or anything else. Generally the most recent items are displayed on the front page, the site maintains an archive of earlier material, and in many cases the site allows users to publish comments of their own. You can find weblogs on just about any topic of interest, and increasingly weblogs are integrated into other types of websites. For example, many magazines and newspapers publish weblogs as part of their sites. Companies are using weblogs to communicate directly with their customers. Political campaigns are using them to get their message out. In large part, the reason weblogs have taken off is that the format is easy to work with. You can publish short items as frequently as you like, and users know that when they visit the site they'll always see the latest and greatest information right up front. In this lesson, I'm going to discuss a weblogging package you can install yourself called WordPress as well as a hosted weblog tool called TypePad. Google also offers a hosted solution that's free to use called Blogger, which you can find at http://www.blogger.com. You may want to check that out as well.

Community Publishing Applications

Community publishing applications are similar to weblog tools in that they are usually built around publishing items by date right up front. They differ from weblogging tools in that they are more centered around providing features for all of the site's users, not just the site's author or authors. Generally these applications provide the ability for users to register as members of the site, submit stories, and engage in discussions among themselves. Sites that incorporate this kind of functionality include http://slashdot.org/ and http://digg.com/.

Some other popular community publishing applications include the following:

- **Slash (http://www.slashcode.com/)**—The software behind the popular website Slashdot.org, written in Perl.
- **Scoop (http://scoop.kuro5hin.org/)**—The software behind Kuro5hin. Scoop is similar to Slash and also written in Perl.
- **Drupal (http://drupal.org)**—A community publishing system written in PHP. The application is written in a modular fashion so that you can include only the features you want.
- **PostNuke (http://www.postnuke.com)**—Another community publishing system written in PHP.

Wikis

Wiki-style systems take the most radical and counterintuitive approach to content management. Most wikis not only allow anyone to view articles but also to edit them. Some wikis require users to register before they can view or edit articles, but the wiki philosophy is that every user is an editor. When most people hear about this concept, they imagine that the result will be anarchy, but as long as there is a critical mass of users who want the wiki to be useful, this type of system is resistant to attempted defacement. Wikis generally keep a history of changes made to every article, so it's easy to go back to an older version of a page if someone deletes things they shouldn't or otherwise submits unwanted changes.

The most famous wiki is Wikipedia (http://wikipedia.org), an online encyclopedia written and edited by volunteers. Not only can anyone view the articles in the encyclopedia, but they can also edit them. If you know something about Fargo, North Dakota that's not already in Wikipedia, you can look it up there and add your own information. Attempted vandalism is taken care of by volunteers who keep an eye out for it, and volunteers handle disputes over controversial content as well.

The name *wiki* comes from the name of the original wiki software, which was called WikiWikiWeb, taken from an airport bus route in Honolulu, Hawaii. To read more about the nature of wikis and their history, why not read about them in Wikipedia? The URL is http://en.wikipedia.org/wiki/Wiki.

Aside from the fact that everyone can edit the pages in a wiki, the other distinguishing feature of wikis is that they generally provide their own markup language instead of HTML. Generally wiki markup is less flexible than HTML, but also a bit easier to get the hang of. Unfortunately, wiki markup usually differs between wiki software packages, so learning MediaWiki's markup language won't help you out a whole lot if you start using TWiki, for example.

Wikis aren't right for every project. If you want to publish your poetry online, putting it up on a page where anyone can edit it probably isn't a good idea. On the other hand, if you need a site where a group can collaboratively write documentation for a project, a wiki can be a great choice. Here's a list of other popular wiki applications and hosts:

- **WikiWikiWeb (http://c2.com/cgi/wiki)**—The original wiki.
- **MediaWiki (http://www.mediawiki.org/)**—The software behind Wikipedia. I'll discuss it more later in this lesson.
- **TWiki (http://twiki.org/)**—A popular wiki package aimed at people who want to support collaboration on a project.

21

- **DokuWiki (http://wiki.splitbrain.org/wiki:dokuwiki)**—Another wiki designed for project collaboration. Unlike some other wikis, it does not require you to install a relational database such as MySQL to store its data.

You can find a comparison of various wiki software packages at http://en.wikipedia.org/wiki/Comparison_of_wiki_software.

There's also a list of hosted wikis that you can use at http://c2.com/cgi/wiki?WikiFarms.

Image Galleries

As digital cameras have grown more popular, so too has sharing photos online. There are many photo-sharing sites online that you can use to host your photos. Some popular choices include Flickr (http://flickr.com/), Kodak EashShare Gallery (http://kodakgallery.com/), Snapfish (http://snapfish.com/), and Fotki (http://fotki.com/).

If you just want to upload pictures and share them with your friends and family members, these sites provide an easy way to do that. In some cases, however, you may want to host your own image galleries. A number of popular image gallery applications are available that vary in terms of complexity and the extent to which they can be customized. The good ones take care of creating thumbnails of your images for you so that you can just upload your photos without dealing with image-editing programs yourself.

In this lesson, I'm going to discuss Coppermine, a popular image gallery application written in PHP.

General-Purpose Content Management Systems

There are far too many general-purpose content management systems to list here. Some content management systems are really just toolkits that enable you to build something on your own. Others are highly structured with tons of features that you control via configuration, rather than by writing code on your own. Here are some features that these general-purpose content management systems tend to have in common:

- **A templating system**—All content management systems provide some way for you to specify how your content will be laid out on the page, and how the pages containing the content will look. Most templates take the form of HTML files with special markers that indicate where each piece of content goes. In many cases, the templates are just regular PHP, JSP, or ASP pages. In other cases, the content management system will provide its own template language.

- **A data repository**—Content management systems produce web pages, but they usually store the data in some structured format, whether it's in a relational database or in XML files. When users enter data, it is stored so that the system can merge the data with the templates to generate HTML when the documents are published.

- **A workflow system**—Controlling who gets to edit which content as well as managing processes for moving content from draft to published status are big parts of many content management systems. Some provide very rigid systems that you have to work within; others let you modify the workflow to suit your own organization. Generally complex workflow features are part of larger content management systems. They're not very useful for individuals or small groups.

- **A system for writing and editing content**—All content management systems provide some way for you to get your content into the system. Some enable you to enter it using HTML forms; others provide integration with external tools such as Microsoft Word.

- **A system for publishing content**—Once content is in the repository and has been approved for publishing, a content management system has to merge that content with a template and publish it on a web page. Some content management systems produce actual HTML files; others generate the HTML on the fly for every request. Which approach is used usually depends on how much dynamic content appears on the page. Most content management systems that don't publish static files provide some mechanism for caching so that data that hasn't changed can be read from the cache rather than being generated dynamically.

Working with Packaged Software

So far, this book has been about building things from scratch. This lesson, on the other hand, is about applying tools to make building things a bit easier. However, as I've mentioned, using existing tools can be a job unto itself. Before you can start using MediaWiki to manage your content, you have to download it and get it installed on a server and configured properly. The same is true with any software package. Even if you go with a hosted solution, you still have to set things up so that the software enables you to accomplish your goals.

You may also be wondering at this point why you bothered to learn HTML, CSS, JavaScript, and everything else in between if you're going to let an application do your work for you. This is one of the most common misconceptions about this kind of software. Content management systems make some things more convenient, but you'll still apply all of the skills you learned over the course of the book to make your pages look the way you like.

21

Before discussing specific applications, I'm going to discuss some topics that pertain to nearly all applications of this kind—relational databases and deployment issues.

Relational Databases

In Lesson 20, "Understanding Server-Side Processing," and today, I've brought up the subject of relational databases more than once, but I haven't really explained what they are or how they work. Relational databases are by far the most popular data repository for web applications. There are a number of reasons for that:

- **They can scale from the smallest to the largest of applications.** You can start a website on a web hosting account on a server that's shared with 50 other people, and eventually wind up running 50 servers of your own and use a relational database to store your data the entire way.

- **They are very flexible when it comes to the types of data they can store.** All relational databases store their data in tabular format. Each record is a row in a table, and the columns describe the properties of each record. In other words, if you have a table to store information about people, every person will have the same properties. The actual structure of your tables can be customized to suit just about any task. You can create a table of links that has names, URLs, and descriptions for each link, or a table of invoices that lists the customer, amount, shipping address, and item ordered for each invoice. The columns in the table can be configured to hold numbers, dates, short strings, large bodies of text, or even binary files.

- **You can create relationships between tables.** That's where the "relational" in relational database comes from. You can relate articles to authors, invoices to customers, or even people to other people within the same table. The relational model is very, very powerful.

- **Relational databases use a standard query language called SQL (Structured Query Language).** Although some differences exist between database vendors, by and large if you know SQL you can work with just about any relational database.

- **Relational databases are popular.** The basic technology behind relational databases hasn't changed very much in the last 20 years, and they are the foundation of many business applications. What has changed is the fact that now several relational databases are freely available, providing powerful features once only associated with the most expensive software targeted at large corporations. Relational databases are so popular and common that using them for data storage for an application is often an easy decision.

Relational databases are usually deployed as a service that is accessible over the network, much like an HTTP server. The difference is that rather than using HTTP to communicate, the database will use its own proprietary protocol. Generally to communicate with a database, you will need some kind of client or library provided by the database vendor. PHP has clients for most popular relational databases built in, so you can just use the functions associated with your database and not install anything extra.

Most hosting providers that allow you to use PHP, CGI scripts, or some other scripting environment also provide access to relational databases. You may have to fill out a special form to have a database set up for you. Once it's set up, your hosting provider will give you the hostname of your database server and a username or password. You can use that information to access the database, or in the case of packaged software, you can use it to configure the software so that it can access the database.

Once a relational database is installed, all the administrative tasks—from creating specific databases to creating and managing users—are accomplished using SQL. So to configure a database for a particular application, you generally create a new user and database for it to use and then run an installation script that creates all the tables that the application needs and inserts the initial data into the database. Often your hosting provider will take care of creating the user and database, and you will run the installation script that builds the initial database.

The most common relational database offered by web hosting providers is MySQL. It's a free product produced by MySQL AB, a Swedish company. There are many other popular relational databases as well, including Oracle, Microsoft SQL Server, and PostgreSQL (another free database), but for web applications, MySQL is the leader. All the applications I'm going to discuss in particular work with MySQL. If you want to read more about it, the manual is available online at http://dev.mysql.com/doc/.

Deploying Applications

All the applications discussed in this lesson run on a web server. When it comes to hosted applications, you don't need to worry about the web server. That's the job of the application provider. In cases where you are installing your own applications, it's up to you to make sure your web server environment will work with your application. For example, all the applications I'm going to discuss in detail are written in PHP. If you are planning on deploying to a server running Microsoft Internet Information Services without PHP support, you won't be able to get these applications to run. Before you download and attempt to install an application, you should check its requirements to make sure the server on which you plan to deploy the application meets them.

21

If you lease server space from a web hosting provider, you may need to check with them before installing your software to make sure it's compatible with their environment. For example, in addition to big requirements such as PHP or MySQL, some software packages also require particular libraries or supplemental software packages in order to function properly. You may need to ask in order to find out whether your hosting provider has all the software you need running in their environment. In some cases, a hosting provider will actually install the software you need if you explain what you're trying to do.

There's another issue you might run into depending on what kind of access you have to your server. Generally two levels of access are available when it comes to web providers—FTP access and shell access. If you have FTP access, you're allowed to upload your files to the server, but you are not allowed to log into the server and run commands directly. Shell access provides a command-line interface to the server that enables you to edit files directly on the server, move things around, and generally use the server more like it's your own computer. If you don't have shell access to the server, you will have to edit the configuration files for your application locally on your own computer and then upload the files and test them on the server.

TypePad: A Hosted Weblogging Application

As I've said before, the shortest route to using a content management system is to sign up for a hosted application. You don't have to download the application, deal with a hosting provider, run installation scripts, or tweak configuration files. TypePad is a subscription service for publishing a weblog. It provides all the features you'd expect from a weblog—archives, user comments, and syndication feeds. You can use it without supplying your own domain name, as long as you're willing to accept a name that ends with "typepad.com," and you don't even have to modify the templates if one of the default themes is OK with you.

As soon as you've signed up for TypePad, you can start posting articles to your new weblog. Figure 21.1 contains a screenshot of the TypePad posting interface. It's fairly typical of the posting interfaces in most content management systems. For weblogs, the typical properties of an article are title, category, and the article text itself. You can enter all those values in this form. TypePad also includes some basic workflow features. You can publish the post immediately, save it as a draft, or schedule it to be published at a specific time.

To write a post and publish it, you just have to fill in the fields and click the Save button. At that point, your post will appear on the public web page for your weblog, as shown in Figure 21.2.

FIGURE 21.1
The TypePad pub-
lishing interface.

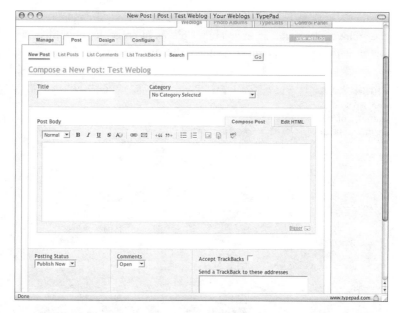

FIGURE 21.2
A public post on a
weblog.

Even for a relatively basic service such as TypePad, there are still a lot of configuration options. Figure 21.3 shows TypePad's author profile page. As you can see from the figure, TypePad's Control Panel has several tabs, all of which reveal various configuration options. This is one difference between hosted applications and applications you install and maintain yourself. Generally applications that you install yourself include configuration files that you must edit yourself, along with configuration forms like the ones found in TypePad.

One more thing to discuss regarding TypePad is how to modify the design for your pages. TypePad allows you to change both the theme and the layout for your pages. Themes alter the color scheme and visual appearance of your pages. Layouts dictate

21

where the various components of the page are placed, such as the weblog entries, links to the archive, photo galleries, and other pieces of content you publish. TypePad includes a set of themes you can choose from, as shown in Figure 21.4.

FIGURE 21.3
The TypePad author profile configuration page.

FIGURE 21.4
Selecting a theme in TypePad.

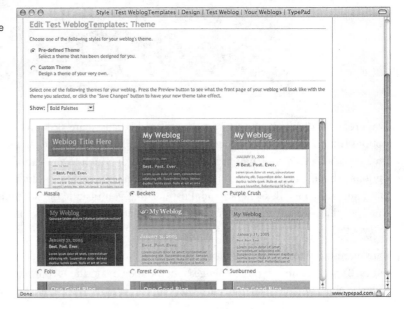

If you prefer to design something for yourself, TypePad provides that option as well. The degree of flexibility you have in modifying your design depends on which level of TypePad account you sign up for. Users with Pro accounts can edit the style sheet for their weblog directly.

There are several other subscription (and free) weblog services as well, including WordPress.com (http://www.wordpress.com), LiveJournal (http://www.livejournal.com), and Blogger (http://www.blogger.com). They all offer feature sets similar to TypePad.

WordPress

WordPress is a weblog publishing tool written in PHP. It's open-source software, so you are free to use it or modify it as you wish. You can download WordPress at http://wordpress.org/. The first step is to extract the file in the place where you want to install your weblog. The files in the archive are all inside a folder called wordpress, but you can move them into another directory if you like.

Once you've extracted the archive, you should copy the wordpress directory to a directory accessible as part of your website. If you want your weblog to reside at the root directory for your server, copy the files out of the wordpress folder and directly into your document root directory. Visiting the home page of your WordPress installation will quickly illustrate the difference between using a hosted service and running an application on your own. You're greeted with a request to create a configuration file, as shown in Figure 21.5.

FIGURE 21.5
WordPress needs a configuration file to get started.

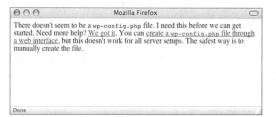

In your WordPress directory, you'll find a file named wp-config-sample.php. To set up WordPress, you need to copy this file to a file named wp-config.php and enter your database settings. If you are deploying WordPress to a server where you don't have a shell account and can't edit files directly, you must create and edit this file before you upload your files to the server.

21

I'm installing WordPress on my own computer, so I created the database and database user myself. If you are installing WordPress on a shared hosting account, chances are you've gotten the database login information from your hosting provider. In some cases, you may want to install several different applications, or perhaps even multiple installations of WordPress in the same database. In that case, you'll want to look at the following line in `wp-config.php`:

```
$table_prefix  = 'wp_';   // Only numbers, letters, and underscores please!
```

This is the string that WordPress puts on the front of the names of all the files it creates. If you already had one WordPress installation using a database, you'd want to change this prefix to something else so as to prevent the two installs from conflicting. I have created a database just for this purpose, so I'll leave the prefix as is.

Once you have `wp-config.php` in place, you can proceed with the installation. If you reload the index page in the WordPress directory, you'll be referred to `install.php`, unless there's a problem with your database configuration. If WordPress can't connect to the database using the settings you provided, it will print an error message. Make sure you have all the information on your database entered properly and test your database connection using this page until WordPress stops complaining.

In the first step of the actual installation, shown in Figure 21.6, you pick a name for your weblog and enter your email address. Once you've done that, WordPress creates all the database tables it needs and generates an account for you to log into the system. That's it for installation.

FIGURE 21.6
The WordPress installation page.

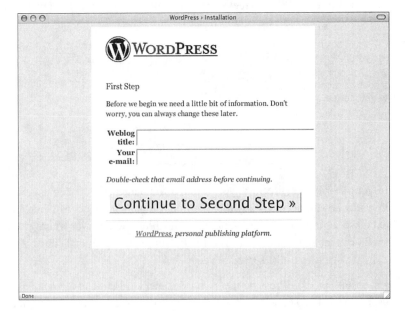

Once you've completed the installation, you're presented with the Dashboard for your weblog. It's not all that different from the Control Panel for TypePad. The posting page, shown in Figure 21.7, is even more similar to TypePad and most other weblog tools. You can enter the title and body of your post, along with some other optional information. The options on the right side enable you to mark your post as draft or published as well as categorize it. You can select from other options as well.

FIGURE 21.7
The posting page for WordPress.

The posting page isn't all that interesting. Where WordPress differs from TypePad is in how much control you have over the layout and design of your weblog. With WordPress, all the work you've done learning HTML, CSS, and PHP can really pay off. Clicking on the Presentation tab and then on Theme Editor enables you to edit all the files that make up the published side of your weblog from within your browser (see Figure 21.8).

You can see the actual source code for index.php, the main page of my WordPress site, in a <textarea> element. Any changes I make to the file will be saved to disk, and the next time I view the front page of my weblog, I'll see them.

Needless to say, if you know how to edit these files, you can customize WordPress to your heart's content. If you don't want to make changes to your WordPress theme by hand, you can download and install themes that other people have created at http://wordpress.org/extend/themes/. You can download the themes and place them within your WordPress installation so that they can be applied to your weblog. You can also use those themes as starting points to create your own custom theme.

21

FIGURE 21.8
Editing part of a
WordPress theme.

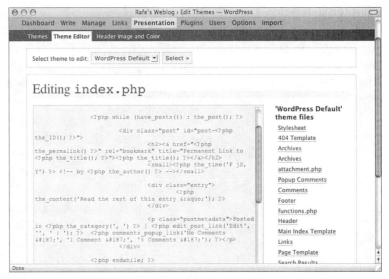

The functionality of WordPress can also be extended using plug-ins. This is yet another advantage of running your own installation of WordPress. Not only can you create your own themes and install themes created by other people, but you can also extend WordPress using plug-ins that you download or you can write the new functionality yourself. A directory of available plug-ins can be found at http://wp-plugins.net/. This directory contains hundreds of plug-ins for WordPress.

Installing plug-ins is straightforward. Let's say I want to install the Related Posts plug-in, which automatically lists posts related to the post currently being viewed in WordPress. First, I go to the download site and download the plug-in. Here is the site for Related Posts:

http://wasabi.pbwiki.com/Related%20Entries

Once I've downloaded the file, I just have to copy the plug-in itself into the `wp-content/plugins` directory in the WordPress installation directory. At that point, I can click on the Plugins tab inside WordPress and I should see that the Related Posts plug-in is installed, as shown in Figure 21.9.

Once the plug-in is installed and activated using the Activate button on the Plugin list, I can configure the options for the plug-in using the Related Posts Options tab that appears once the Related Posts plug-in is activated. Then all I have to do is go to my single-page archive post and find a spot for the `related_posts()` call to include the list of related posts.

FIGURE 21.9
The Related Posts
entry on the
WordPress Plugins
page.

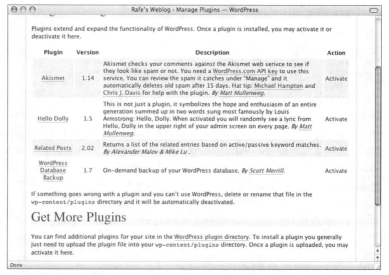

MediaWiki

Many applications are available for publishing wikis. I've chosen to discuss MediaWiki because it's written in PHP, so it can be installed at a wide range of web hosts, and because it is relatively simple to set up. MediaWiki is also widely adopted, and it's the plumbing for Wikipedia, the most popular wiki. Because of its popularity, the software is undergoing constant improvement, and a large collection of extensions is available for the software.

The main downside of publishing a site using MediaWiki is that it won't give you a great opportunity to use or improve your HTML skills. Content in MediaWiki is entered using MediaWiki's internal markup language. MediaWiki markup is translated into HTML tags, though, so even though you use different syntax, a knowledge of how web pages are constructed will still help you lay out your pages using MediaWiki's markup language. Here's an example of MediaWiki markup:

```
== Sample Heading ==

This is a paragraph.

This is a paragraph containing '''Bold text'''.

Here's an [http://www.example.com outbound link].
```

21

And here's the equivalent in HTML:

```
<h2> Sample Heading </h2>
<p>This is a paragraph.</p>
<p>This is a paragraph containing <b>Bold text</b>.</p>
<p>Here's an <a href="http://www.example.com">outbound link</a>.
```

The first thing you should notice is that unlike HTML, in MediaWiki markup, white space counts. When you skip lines between paragraphs, MediaWiki converts those breaks into paragraph tags. Headings are specified using equals signs. Two equals signs are converted to <h2>, four are converted to <h4>, and so on. MediaWiki markup can also be used to apply inline tags as well as block-level tags. As you can see, I used ''' to make some text bold, and I created an outbound link from the wiki. You can also use MediaWiki markup to create tables, include images in pages, and take on most of the other tasks that you can accomplish with HTML. There's a guide to MediaWiki's markup language at the following page:

http://meta.wikimedia.org/wiki/Help:Editing

This is a wiki page, and if you had some information to add to the discussion of wiki markup, you could add it.

Downloading and Installing MediaWiki

The download and installation process for MediaWiki is similar to the process for WordPress. To download the software, go to http://www.mediawiki.org/wiki/Download.

Find the most recent release and download that archive. Once you've expanded the archive, rename the folder, which probably has a name such as mediawiki-1.5.8. The name you give it will appear in the URL, so you probably want to pick mediawiki or just wiki. Upload or copy all the files into the document root of your server (or into the directory where you want the wiki to reside) and then go to the URL where you just uploaded the files. You'll see a page like the one in Figure 21.10, which indicates that you need to go through the MediaWiki installation process.

When you click on the setup link, the MediaWiki install script checks to make sure your server is configured properly and has the software that you need for MediaWiki to work. It also asks you to answer a few questions. Some are easy, such as the name of the site and the email address for the person running the site. Others are not so easy, such as the caching configuration. You can safely choose "no caching" for that one.

If MediaWiki is able to write to your configuration files (based on the permissions on those files and the privileges that the web server runs with), it allows you to enter all your database configuration settings right on the installation page. If you have root (administrator) access to your MySQL server, MediaWiki will even create a dedicated database and user for you. If you're using shared hosting, you'll probably have to enter the database name and login information for your database and then let MediaWiki create its tables. MediaWiki, like WordPress, lets you pick a prefix for your table names so that you can avoid naming conflicts if multiple applications use the same database. Once setup is complete, MediaWiki requests that you move the configuration file it created to the proper location, and then you can begin editing content.

FIGURE 21.10
MediaWiki needs to be installed.

If everything is set up properly, MediaWiki installation can be painless. Unfortunately, with these types of applications, there's always an opportunity for something to go wrong. If you run into trouble, check out the MediaWiki installation guide:

http://meta.wikimedia.org/wiki/Help:Installation

The settings for MediaWiki are found in the file LocalSettings.php, which MediaWiki may have generated for you. You can find a full list of configuration settings at the following location:

http://www.mediawiki.org/wiki/Help:Configuration_settings

MediaWiki will work fine with the default settings, but you'll probably at least want to add your own logo to replace the placeholder image. MediaWiki also supports themes, which are called *skins* in the MediaWiki world. A big list of skins that you can download and install can be found here:

http://meta.wikimedia.org/wiki/Gallery_of_user_styles

21

Users can change their personal settings to use any skin that's installed. To change the default skin for the site, edit the $wgDefaultSkin variable in your LocalSettings.php file.

Using MediaWiki

Once you've got MediaWiki set up however you like, you can start entering content of your own. In fact, if you go with the default installation, anyone who sees your site can start entering content of his or her own. Every page in a wiki has an edit link on it, allowing you to jump in and make changes. To add an internal link in MediaWiki, you enclose the name of the page in double square brackets, like this:

```
[[My New Page]]
```

When you click on the link, you'll be asked to fill in the body of the new page. That's all there is to it. You can also create a new page by entering its name directly into the URL. If you enter a URL, such as http://localhost:8888/mediawiki/index.php/Flying_Monkeys, and a page named "Flying Monkeys" does not exist, it will be created automatically. Wikis tend to grow organically; as people need new pages, they create them by linking to them. With a wiki, it's really easy to move content from one page to another, split one long page into several smaller pages, and generally manage your content however you see fit.

MediaWiki keeps track of every change made to every page. On each page you'll see a history tab that you can click on to see all the edits ever made to that page. The history page for the home page of my new wiki appears in Figure 21.11.

FIGURE 21.11
The edit history for a wiki page.

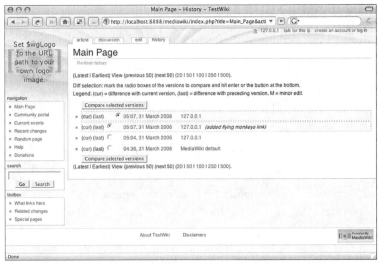

From the history page, you can compare revisions of a page or view the old revisions. To revert a page back to the old version, view that version, click on Edit, and then save the page. MediaWiki will warn you that you're replacing newer content, but if you're reverting changes, you can ignore the warnings.

Coppermine

Coppermine is a photo gallery package written in PHP. It is designed to make it easy to upload and present images within web pages. Like MediaWiki and WordPress, PHP, and MySQL, Coppermine also requires that you have one of two image-processing applications installed—GD or ImageMagick. (The most recent versions of PHP include GD.) Most web hosting providers will have at least one of these packages installed; many applications that have image-related features rely on these applications. If you run your own server, you'll have to install one of these applications yourself (assuming neither is already installed). You can download the Coppermine software at http://coppermine-gallery.net. You can read more about ImageMagick at http://www.imagemagick.org. If you want to install GD, its home page is http://www.boutell.com/gd/.

As with the other applications, Coppermine requires you to perform some tasks on the server. In this case, Coppermine needs permission to write to various directories in its installation. On servers running Linux or any other variety of UNIX, every application runs as a user. Usually Apache runs as the user apache or www, an account that is associated only with that server. Because the files in your account are most likely owned by you, not Apache, by default it won't have permission to write to those files. So if your application needs to save, modify, or delete files, you'll have to give Apache permission to do that. Generally, the easiest way to do this is to just give everyone write access to the file or directory. If you have a shell account, you can just do the following:

```
chmod 777 albums
```

This gives the owner, the owner's group, and everyone else access to read, write, and execute the files in the albums directory. Most FTP clients also enable you to change the permissions for files and directories. If yours doesn't, you should find a more full-featured FTP client. Coppermine needs permission to write to several directories, as shown in Figure 21.12.

Once I fix the file permissions, Coppermine asks for the same kinds of information that the other applications asked for. It needs to create an account for the administrator of the application, and it needs information about which database to use. Again, you can enter information supplied by your web hosting provider here or create your own database and user if you have the ability to do so. Coppermine also needs to know the path to the ImageMagick convert program. Here's where you might need help from your web hosting provider. If you don't have shell access yourself, they can probably tell you where that application is located, assuming it's installed.

21

FIGURE 21.12
Error messages
from Coppermine.

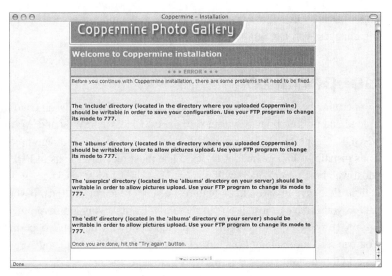

Once you've filled out the form correctly, Coppermine will automatically log you in with the account you just created.

Using Coppermine

Coppermine is very powerful, but with that power comes complexity. Not only can you share your own images with Coppermine, but you can also allow users to upload images and share them with one another. For that reason, it supports user registration as well as the ability to assign users to groups, giving them access to particular albums and categories of albums. For example, you could create a group for your family members to upload pictures to a family photo album and another group for your friends in the garden club to share pictures of their rose gardens.

The first step in testing Coppermine is to upload a picture. Before you can do that, you have to create an album to put it in. When you're logged in as an administrator, Coppermine provides an administrative toolbar that enables you to do things such as create albums, manage the list of users, and configure the application. Using the administrator's albums page, you can add a new album, as shown in Figure 21.13.

As you can see from the figure, I'm adding an album called "Family Photos." To add the album, all I have to do is click on the Apply Modifications button. Once that's done, I'm taken to my new, empty photo album. From there I can click on the Upload File link in the navigation area and upload a file using an HTML form. Coppermine enables you to upload multiple files at once in order to save time, but in this case I'm just uploading one file. Once the file is uploaded, I can assign it to an album and enter a title, description, and keywords for it, as shown in Figure 21.14.

FIGURE 21.13
Adding an album
to Coppermine.

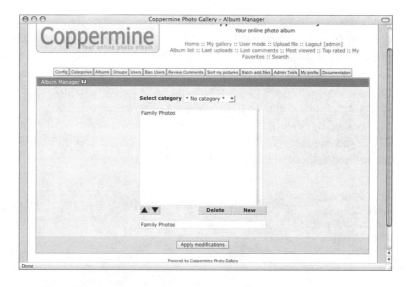

FIGURE 21.14
Describing an
image in
Coppermine.

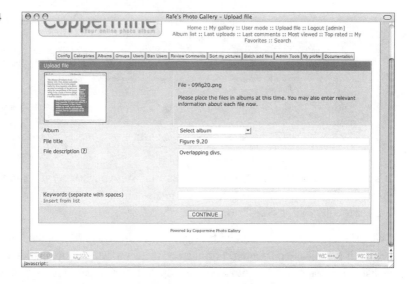

The image I uploaded was actually much larger than it appears in the figure. That's why you must have ImageMagick or GD installed in order to use Coppermine—it uses them to resize the images you upload. On this screen, I've assigned the image to the Family Photos album and have given it a name and description as well.

Once I'm done with that, the image appears in the album I assigned it to. Once an image has been included in an album, users can view, rate, and comment on it.

21

Aside from creating albums and uploading photos, you might also want to modify the configuration of Coppermine so that it works the way you want it to. There are a number of options that enable you to control the degree to which users are allowed to participate on your site. For example, if you don't want the general public commenting on your photos, you can disallow user registration and bar users from submitting anonymous comments. You can also change the appearance of your site, picking any of the themes that are installed by default, and changing the name and description of your gallery. In Figure 21.15, you can see what the configuration page of the site looks like once I've switched themes and updated my gallery's name and description.

FIGURE 21.15
The Coppermine configuration page after a theme change.

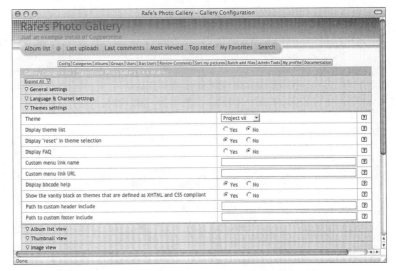

If none of the themes included with Coppermine suit your tastes, you can find more themes at the Coppermine website. You can also create themes of your own, just as you can for MediaWiki or WordPress.

There's a lot more you can do with Coppermine; this was just a quick introduction to getting it installed and running. Fortunately, there's a detailed manual at the Coppermine website that you can delve into if you wind up using Coppermine on your own website.

Other Applications

This lesson provided a very brief tour of a few popular web applications that you can use to go beyond building websites made up of static HTML pages. Not only are there lots of other applications out there, but there are lots of other categories of applications out there. You can find guest books, shared calendars, discussion boards, tools for sharing bookmarks, and everything in between. Also, even though I focused on applications written in PHP, there are equivalents of these applications written for many other platforms as well.

If you want to set up a wiki at work, and all your servers run Windows, you can use FlexWiki, which is written using ASP.NET. Its home page is http://www.flexwiki.com/default.aspx. If you want a weblogging tool written using Java and JSP, you can use Roller, which can be found at http://rollerweblogger.org/.

Companies are always trying to bridge the gap between hosted applications that are very structured and applications you can download and manage yourself, which are generally more flexible. For example, a company called Ning (http://www.ning.com) has built a hosted system for constructing your own applications. It is "hosted" in the sense that your applications reside on their servers and you don't have to worry about logging into the servers or managing them in any way. However, they provide their own programming language and database that you can use to build applications. Their tools are not as flexible as languages such as PHP or ASP.NET, but they can still be used to build a wide variety of applications. It remains to be seen whether Ning's concept takes off, but the overall trend in web application development continues to move toward giving people with limited programming skills more flexibility in the types of things they can deploy without writing applications on their own.

Spam

Applications such as weblogging tools and wikis enable you to build a relationship with your users by allowing them to contribute to your site, either by posting comments or contributing information of their own. Unfortunately, spammers looking to advertise their websites or raise their search engine rank also take advantage of these features by way of programs that seek out and automatically post to sites running common software, such as TypePad, WordPress, and MediaWiki (among others).

There are a number of approaches to combating spam. These days, most popular applications provide tools that attempt to prevent spammers from posting, but even so, some spam still makes it through. I mention this only to let you know that it's a risk of deploying these kinds of applications on the Web these days.

The most important thing to remember is that you shouldn't deploy one of these applications and then abandon it. A MediaWiki installation that goes unused will be overrun with spammers in no time. The same is true for the comments sections of weblogs as well. If you put up an application but then stop using it, you should remove the files or

21

configure your web server so that it is no longer publicly accessible. Not only will it keep spammers from filling up your databases with junk, but it will be an act of good citizenship on the Web.

Summary

The purpose of this lesson was to take you beyond the realm of HTML, CSS, and JavaScript and into the world of web publishing. These days, there's more to publishing on the Web than uploading HTML files to a server. Using free or inexpensive tools, you can build interactive websites that help you keep a handle on your content and make it easy to communicate with your users. You can apply your newfound skills to personalizing and improving these tools as well as to creating the content that you use them to publish.

Workshop

This final workshop contains some questions about content management systems, as well as a quiz and exercises.

Q&A

Q What about security? I've read about security holes in some web applications.

A A number of popular web applications have been found to have bugs that can cause security problems, and when you install an application, it's important to keep an eye on subsequent releases to make sure that you install updates that fix any security holes that arise. Deploying an application and not keeping it updated can leave you vulnerable not only to malicious users who want to break into your servers, but also spammers who look for problems with applications that can send mail to use them to deliver spam. The bottom line is that putting up an application on the Web places some responsibility on the person who deployed it to keep it up to date and prevent it from being used for nefarious purposes.

Q Is there a way to automatically keep my applications up to date?

A Some servers run operating systems with package managers. As long as you install your applications from packages supported by the package managers, you can let the operating system keep them up to date. Doing so generally requires that you run your own server. If you are using a web hosting provider, you're probably on your own when it comes to installing updates.

Q **Will my web hosting provider install and maintain any of these applications for me?**

A Some web hosting providers maintain installations of popular applications so that their customers don't have to install the applications themselves. For example, there's a list of web hosts that support WordPress at http://wordpress.org/hosting/. If you're sure which application you want to use, it may make sense to select your hosting provider on that basis.

Quiz

1. What are some of the tradeoffs between hosted applications and those you install yourself?
2. Why do some applications require you to change the file permissions on the server?
3. Why do most installable applications ask you to specify a prefix for table names in a database?

Quiz Answers

1. Hosted applications tend to be less work up front and easier to maintain, but offer less flexibility than applications you install yourself.
2. Applications that make changes to the file system, either because they store their data in files or because they allow users to upload files, generally require you to change the file permissions for specific directories when you install them.
3. Each application has its own table prefix in order to prevent naming conflicts when several applications use the same database. For example, several applications might have their own table called "users." Adding an application-specific prefix to it will prevent conflicts.

Exercises

1. Find out which operating system, application development environment, and database are available from your web host, if you have one. If you're working on internal projects, find out about your servers from the Information Technology department.
2. Install one of the applications mentioned in this lesson, or one you find yourself, and try it out.
3. Go forth and put your new web publishing skills to good use.

21

PART VII:
Appendixes

APPENDIX A:

Sources for Further Information

Haven't had enough yet? In this appendix, you'll find the URLs for all kinds of information about the World Wide Web, HTML, and developing websites. With this information, you should be able to find just about anything you need on the Web.

CAUTION	Some of the URLs in this appendix refer to FTP sites. They might be very busy during business hours, and you might not be able to access the files immediately. Try again during non-prime hours.
	Also, for mysterious reasons, some of these sites might be accessible through an FTP program but not through web browsers. If you're consistently refused by these sites using a browser, try an FTP program instead.

These sites are divided into the following categories and are listed in alphabetical order under each category:

- Access counters
- Browsers
- Collections of HTML and web development information
- Forms and imagemaps
- HTML editors and converters
- HTML validators, link checkers, and simple spiders
- Java, JavaScript, and embedded objects

- Log file parsers

- HTML style guides

- Servers and server administration

- Sound and video

- Specifications for HTML, HTTP, and URLs

- Server-side scripting

- Web publishing tools

- Other web-related topics

- Tools and information for images

- Web hosting providers

- Web indexes and search engines

Access Counters

Access counters without server programs
http://www.digits.com/

LiveCounter
http://www.chami.com/counter/classic/

Bravenet Counter
http://www.bravenet.com/webtools/counter/index.php

StatCounter
http://www.statcounter.com

Site Meter
http://www.sitemeter.com/

Extreme Tracking
http://extreme-dm.com/tracking/

Browsers

Internet Explorer
http://www.microsoft.com/windows/ie/

Lynx (text-based browser)
http://lynx.browser.org/

Links (alternative to Lynx with better table handling)
http://links.sourceforge.net/

Mozilla Firefox
http://www.mozilla.com

Seamonkey
http://www.mozilla.org/projects/seamonkey/

Netscape page
http://browser.netscape.com/ns8/

Opera
http://www.operasoftware.com

Safari
http://www.apple.com/safari/

wget
http://www.gnu.org/software/wget/wget.html

evolt Browser Archive (huge archive of old browsers)
http://browsers.evolt.org/

Collections of HTML and Web Development Information

CNET Builder.com
http://www.builder.com/

The home of the WWW Consortium
http://www.w3.org/

The Virtual Library
http://wdvl.com/

A

MSDN (Microsoft Developer's Network) Online
http://msdn.microsoft.com/

Mozilla Developer Center
http://developer.mozilla.org

AOL webmaster.info
http://webmaster.aol.com/

evolt.org
http://www.evolt.org/

A List Apart
http://www.alistapart.com/

W3Schools
http://www.w3schools.com/

Forms and Imagemaps

HotSpots (a Windows imagemap tool)
http://www.1automata.com/hotspots/index.html

Mapedit: A tool for Windows and X11 for creating imagemap map files
http://www.boutell.com/mapedit/

Poor Person's Image Mapper (web-based imagemap creation system)
http://www.pangloss.com/seidel/ClrHlpr/imagemap.html

HTML Editors and Converters

HTML-Kit
http://www.chami.com/html-kit/

TopStyle
http://www.bradsoft.com/topstyle/

HomeSite
http://www.macromedia.com/software/homesite/

HotDog (Windows)
http://www.sausage.com

1st Page
http://www.evrsoft.com/download/

Adobe Dreamweaver

http://www.macromedia.com/software/dreamweaver/

Adobe GoLive

http://www.adobe.com/products/golive/main.html

Microsoft FrontPage (Windows, Macintosh)

http://www.microsoft.com/frontpage/

BBEdit (Mac OS)

http://www.barebones.com/

HTML Validators, Link Checkers, and Simple Spiders

W3C Validator

http://validator.w3.org/

HTML Tidy

http://tidy.sourceforge.net/

WDG HTML Validator

http://www.htmlhelp.com/tools/validator/

CSE HTML Validator

http://www.htmlvalidator.com/

Java, JavaScript, and Embedded Objects

QuirksMode

http://www.quirksmode.org/

JavaScript Source

http://javascript.internet.com/

Sun's Java home page

http://www.javasoft.com/

JavaScript Reference

http://javascript-reference.info

Douglas Crockford's Wrrrld Wide Web

http://www.crockford.com/

script.aculo.us

http://script.aculo.us/

Dynamic Drive

http://www.dynamicdrive.com/

HotScripts.com

http://www.hotscripts.com/

Log File Parsers

Analog

http://www.analog.cx/

Webalizer

http://www.mrunix.net/webalizer/

Wusage

http://www.boutell.com/wusage/

AWStats

http://awstats.sourceforge.net/

HTML Style Guides

Tim Berners-Lee's style guide

http://www.w3.org/Provider/Style/Overview.html

The Yale HyperText style guide

http://www.webstyleguide.com/

NYPL Online Style Guide

http://www.nypl.org/styleguide/

Sun—Writing for the Web

http://www.sun.com/980713/webwriting/

Servers and Server Administration

Apache (UNIX, Windows)
http://httpd.apache.org/

Tomcat (UNIX, Windows)
http://jakarta.apache.org/tomcat/

Current list of official MIME types
http://www.iana.org/assignments/media-types/

Microsoft Internet Information Server (Windows NT)
http://www.microsoft.com/iis

Sound and Video

Audacity
http://audacity.sourceforge.net/

Apple iTunes
http://www.apple.com/itunes/

WinAmp (free sound player for Windows)
http://www.winamp.com/

QuickTime
http://www.apple.com/quicktime/

RealNetworks
http://www.realnetworks.com/

Windows Media
http://www.windowsmedia.com/

VLC
http://www.videolan.org/vlc/

mplayer plug-in
http://mplayerplug-in.sourceforge.net/

iSquint
http://www.isquint.org/

Specifications for HTML, HTTP, and URLs

HTML Specification and Info
http://www.w3.org/MarkUp/

XHTML 1.0
http://www.w3.org/TR/xhtml1/

HTML 4.01
http://www.w3.org/TR/html4/

The HTTP specification (as defined in 1992)
http://www.w3.org/hypertext/WWW/Protocols/HTTP/HTTP2.html

Cascading Style Sheets
http://www.w3.org/Style/CSS/

Information about HTTP
http://www.w3.org/Protocols/

Pointers to URL, URN, and URI information and specifications
http://www.w3.org/Addressing/

Server-Side Scripting

PHP
http://www.php.net/

The CGI specification
http://hoohoo.ncsa.uiuc.edu/cgi/interface.html

ASP.NET
http://www.asp.net/

The original NCSA CGI documentation
http://hoohoo.ncsa.uiuc.edu/cgi/

CGI.pm
http://search.cpan.org/dist/CGI.pm/

Web Publishing Tools

Blogger
http://www.blogger.com/

TypePad, Movable Type, and LiveJournal
http://www.sixapart.com/

WordPress
http://www.wordpress.com/

MediaWiki
http://www.mediawiki.org/wiki/MediaWiki

Drupal
http://drupal.org/

A

Other Web-Related Topics

Adobe Acrobat
http://www.adobe.com/prodindex/acrobat/main.html

Web security overview
http://www.w3.org/Security/Overview.html

Tools and Information for Images

Barry's Clip Art Server
http://www.barrysclipart.com/

Animation Factory
http://www.animationfactory.com

IrfanView
http://www.irfanview.com/

GraphicConverter
http://www.lemkesoft.de/en/index.htm

Web Hosting Providers

The List (worldwide list of Internet providers)
http://thelist.internet.com/

Web Indexes and Search Engines

Google
http://www.google.com/

Yahoo!
http://www.yahoo.com/

MSN Search
http://search.msn.com

Ask Jeeves
http://www.askjeeves.com

APPENDIX B:
HTML 4.01 Quick Reference

This appendix provides a quick reference to the elements and attributes of the HTML 4.01 language, as specified by the World Wide Web Consortium. It's based on the information provided in the *HTML 4.01 Specification*, W3C Recommendation 24 December 1999 (most current version at press time). The latest version of this document can be found at http://www.w3.org/TR/html4/.

To make the information readily accessible, this appendix organizes HTML elements by their function in the following order:

- **Common Attributes and Events**

  id, class, style, title, lang, dir, onclick, ondblclick, onmousedown, onmouseup, onmouseover, onmousemove, onmouseout, onkeypress, onkeyup, onkeydown

- **Structure**

  bdo, body, Comments, div, !DOCTYPE, h1...h6, head, hr, html, meta, span, title

- **Text Phrases and Paragraphs**

  acronym, address, blockquote, br, cite, code, del, dfn, em, ins, kbd, p, pre, q, samp, strong, sub, sup, var

- **Text Formatting Elements**

  b, basefont, big, font, i, s, small, strike, tt, u

- **Lists**

  dd, dir, dl, dt, li, menu, ol, ul

- **Links**

  a, base, link

- **Tables**

  caption, col, colgroup, table, tbody, td, tfoot, th, thead, tr

- **Frames**

  frame, frameset, iframe, noframes

- **Embedded Content**

  applet, area, img, map, object, param

- **Style**

  style

- **Forms**

  button, fieldset, form, input, isindex, label, legend, option, select, textarea

- **Scripts**

  script, noscript

NOTE

Table B.1, located at the end of the appendix, contains a list of character entities.

Within each section, the elements are listed alphabetically and the following information is presented where applicable:

- **Usage**—A general description of the element.
- **Start/End Tag**—Indicates whether these tags are required, optional, or illegal. Differences between HTML and XHTML are noted.
- **Attributes**—Lists the attributes of the element with a short description of its effect.
- **Deprecated**—Lists deprecated attributes; that is, attributes that are still supported in HTML 4.01 and in most browsers, but that are in the process of being phased out in favor of newer techniques, such as style sheets.
- **Empty**—Indicates whether the element can be empty.
- **Notes**—Relates any special considerations when using the element and indicates whether the element is new, deprecated, or obsolete.

Common Attributes and Events

The HTML 4.01 specification includes several attributes that apply to a significant number of elements. These are referred to as `%coreattrs`, `%i18n`, and `%events` throughout this appendix and are explained in the following section.

%coreattrs

Four attributes are abbreviated as `%coreattrs`:

- `id="..."` A global identifier
- `class="..."` A list of classes separated by spaces
- `style="..."` Style information
- `title="..."` Provides more information for a specific element, as opposed to the `title` element, which titles the entire web page

%i18n

Two attributes for internationalization (i18n) are abbreviated as `%i18n`:

- `lang="..."` The language identifier
- `dir="..."` The text direction (`ltr`, `rtl`)

%events

The following intrinsic events are abbreviated `%events`:

- `onclick="..."` A pointing device (such as a mouse) was single-clicked.
- `ondblclick="..."` A pointing device (such as a mouse) was double-clicked.

B

- onmousedown="..." A mouse button was clicked and held down.
- onmouseup="..." A mouse button that was clicked and held down was released.
- onmouseover="..." A mouse moved the cursor over an object.
- onmousemove="..." A mouse was moved.
- onmouseout="..." A mouse moved the cursor off an object.
- onkeypress="..." A key was pressed and released.
- onkeydown="..." A key was pressed and held down.
- onkeyup="..." A key that was pressed has been released.

Structure

HTML relies on several elements to provide structure to a document (as opposed to structuring the text within), as well as provide information that is used by the browser or search engines.

<bdo>...</bdo>

Usage	The bidirectional algorithm element is used to selectively turn off the default text direction. Default text direction is left to right, but can be changed (to render Hebrew text from right to left, for example).
Start/End Tag	Required/Required.
Attributes	lang="..."—The language of the document.
	dir="..."—The text direction (ltr, rtl).
Empty	No.
Notes	The dir attribute is mandatory.

<body>...</body>

Usage	Contains the content of the document.
Start/End Tag	Optional/Optional (HTML); Required/Required (XHTML 1.0).
Attributes	%coreattrs, %i18n, %events.
	onload="..."—Intrinsic event triggered when the document loads.
	onunload="..."—Intrinsic event triggered when document unloads.

Deprecated	The following presentational attributes are deprecated in favor of setting these values with style sheets:
	`background="..."`—URL for the background image.
	`bgcolor="..."`—Sets background color.
	`text="..."`—Text color.
	`link="..."`—Link color.
	`vlink="..."`—Visited link color.
	`alink="..."`—Active link color.
Empty	No.
Notes	There can be only one `body`, and it must follow the `head`.
	The `body` element can be replaced by a `frameset` element.

B

Comments `<!-- .. -->`

Usage	Inserts notes or scripts that are not displayed by the browser.
Start/End Tag	Required/Required.
Attributes	None.
Empty	Yes.
Notes	Comments are not restricted to one line and can be any length.
	The end tag is not required to be on the same line as the start tag.

`<div>...</div>`

Usage	Division element is used to add structure to a block of text.
Start/End Tag	Required/Required.
Attributes	`%coreattrs`, `%i18n`, `%events`.
Deprecated	The `align` attribute is deprecated in favor of controlling alignment through style sheets.
	`align="..."`—Controls alignment (`left`, `center`, `right`, `justify`).
Empty	No.
Notes	Cannot be used within a `P` element.

`<!DOCTYPE...>`

Usage	Version information appears on the first line of an HTML document and is a Standard Generalized Markup Language (SGML) declaration rather than an element.
Notes	Optional in HTML documents, but required in XHTML 1.0.

\<h1>...\</h1> **Through** \<h6>...\</h6>

Usage	The six headings (h1 is the uppermost or most important) are used in the body to structure information in a hierarchical fashion.
Start/End Tag	Required/Required.
Attributes	%coreattrs, %i18n, %events.
Deprecated	The align attribute is deprecated in favor of controlling alignment through style sheets.
	align="..."—Controls alignment (left, center, right, justify).
Empty	No.
Notes	Visual browsers display the size of the headings in relation to their importance, with h1 being the largest and h6 the smallest.

\<head>...\</head>

Usage	This is the document header and contains other elements that provide information to users and search engines.
Start/End Tag	Optional/Optional (HTML); Required/Required (XHTML 1.0).
Attributes	%i18n.
	profile="..."—URL specifying the location of meta data.
Empty	No.
Notes	There can be only one head per document. It must follow the opening html tag and precede the body.

\<hr>

Usage	Horizontal rules are used to separate sections of a web page.
Start/End Tag	Required/Illegal—See note for XHTML 1.0 requirements.
Attributes	%coreattrs, %events.
Deprecated	align="..."—Controls alignment (left, center, right, justify).
	noshade="..."—Displays the rule as a solid color.
	size="..."—The size of the rule.
	width="..."—The width of the rule.
Empty	Yes.
Notes	In XHTML 1.0, this tag should take the XML form of \<hr /> to ensure compatibility with older browsers.

`<html>...</html>`

Usage	The html element contains the entire document.
Start/End Tag	Optional/Optional (HTML); Required/Required (XHTML 1.0).
Attributes	%i18n.
Deprecated	version="..."—URL of the document type definition specifying the HTML version used to create the document.
Empty	No.
Notes	The version information is duplicated in the `<!DOCTYPE...>` declaration and therefore is not essential.

B

`<meta>`

Usage	Provides information about the document.
Start/End Tag	Required/Illegal—See note for XHTML 1.0 requirements.
Attributes	%i18n.
	http-equiv="..."—HTTP response header name.
	name="..."—Name of the meta information.
	content="..."—Content of the meta information.
	scheme="..."—Assigns a scheme to interpret the meta data.
Empty	Yes.
Notes	In XHTML 1.0, this tag should take the XML form of `<meta />` to ensure compatibility with older browsers.

`<span>...</span>`

Usage	Organizes the document by defining a span of text.
Start/End Tag	Required/Required.
Attributes	%coreattrs, %i18n, %events.
Empty	No.

`<title>...</title>`

Usage	This is the name you give your web page. The `title` element is located in the `head` element and is displayed in the browser window title bar.
Start/End Tag	Required/Required.
Attributes	`%i18n`.
Empty	No.
Notes	Only one title allowed per document.

Text Phrases and Paragraphs

You can structure text phrases (or blocks) to suit a specific purpose, such as creating a paragraph. This should not be confused with modifying the formatting of the text.

`<acronym>...</acronym>`

Usage	Defines acronyms.
Start/End Tag	Required/Required.
Attributes	`%coreattrs`, `%i18n`, `%events`.
Empty	No.

`<address>...</address>`

Usage	Provides a special format for author or contact information.
Start/End Tag	Required/Required.
Attributes	`%coreattrs`, `%i18n`, `%events`.
Empty	No.
Notes	The `br` element is commonly used inside the `address` element to break the lines of an address.

`<blockquote>...</blockquote>`

Usage	Displays long quotations.
Start/End Tag	Required/Required.
Attributes	`%coreattrs`, `%i18n`, `%events`.
	`cite="..."`—The URL of the quoted text.
Empty	No.

\<br\>

Usage	Forces a line break.
Start/End Tag	Required/Illegal—See note for XHTML 1.0 requirements.
Attributes	%coreattrs, %i18n, %events.
Deprecated	clear="..."—Sets the location where next line begins after a floating object (none, left, right, all).
Empty	Yes.
Notes	In XHTML 1.0, this tag should take the XML form of \<br /\> to ensure compatibility with older browsers.

B

\<cite\>...\</cite\>

Usage	Cites a reference.
Start/End Tag	Required/Required.
Attributes	%coreattrs, %i18n, %events.
Empty	No.

\<code\>...\</code\>

Usage	Identifies a code fragment for display.
Start/End Tag	Required/Required.
Attributes	%coreattrs, %i18n, %events.
Empty	No.

\<del\>...\</del\>

Usage	Shows text as having been deleted from the document since the last change.
Start/End Tag	Required/Required.
Attributes	%coreattrs, %i18n, %events.
	cite="..."—The URL of the source document.
	datetime="..."—Indicates the date and time of the change.
Empty	No.
Notes	New element in HTML 4.01.

<dfn>...</dfn>

Usage	Defines an enclosed term.
Start/End Tag	Required/Required.
Attributes	`%coreattrs`, `%i18n`, `%events`.
Empty	No.

...

Usage	Emphasizes text.
Start/End Tag	Required/Required.
Attributes	`%coreattrs`, `%i18n`, `%events`.
Empty	No.

<ins>...</ins>

Usage	Shows text as having been inserted in the document since the last change.
Start/End Tag	Required/Required.
Attributes	`%coreattrs`, `%i18n`, `%events`.
	`cite="..."`—The URL of the source document.
	`datetime="..."`—Indicates the date and time of the change.
Empty	No.
Notes	New element in HTML 4.01.

<kbd>...</kbd>

Usage	Indicates text a user would type.
Start/End Tag	Required/Required.
Attributes	`%coreattrs`, `%i18n`, `%events`.
Empty	No.

<p>...</p>

Usage	Defines a paragraph.
Start/End Tag	Required/Optional (HTML); Required/Required (XHTML 1.0).
Attributes	`%coreattrs`, `%i18n`, `%events`.
Deprecated	`align="..."`—Controls alignment (`left`, `center`, `right`, `justify`).
Empty	No.

`<pre>...</pre>`

Usage	Displays preformatted text.
Start/End Tag	Required/Required.
Attributes	`%coreattrs, %i18n, %events`.
Deprecated	`width="..."`—The width of the formatted text.
Empty	No.

`<q>...</q>`

Usage	Displays short quotations that do not require paragraph breaks.
Start/End Tag	Required/Required.
Attributes	`%coreattrs, %i18n, %events`.
	`cite="..."`—The URL of the quoted text.
Empty	No.
Notes	New element in HTML 4.01.

`<samp>...</samp>`

Usage	Identifies sample output.
Start/End Tag	Required/Required.
Attributes	`%coreattrs, %i18n, %events`.
Empty	No.

`<strong>...</strong>`

Usage	Stronger emphasis.
Start/End Tag	Required/Required.
Attributes	`%coreattrs, %i18n, %events`.
Empty	No.

`<sub>...</sub>`

Usage	Creates subscript.
Start/End Tag	Required/Required.
Attributes	`%coreattrs, %i18n, %events`.
Empty	No.

B

^{...}

Usage	Creates superscript.
Start/End Tag	Required/Required.
Attributes	%coreattrs, %i18n, %events.
Empty	No.

<var>...</var>

Usage	A variable.
Start/End Tag	Required/Required.
Attributes	%coreattrs, %i18n, %events.
Empty	No.

Text Formatting Elements

Text characteristics such as the size, weight, and style can be modified by using these elements, but the HTML 4.01 specification encourages you to use style sheets instead.

...

Usage	Bold text.
Start/End Tag	Required/Required.
Attributes	%coreattrs, %i18n, %events.
Empty	No.

<basefont>

Usage	Sets the base font size.
Start/End Tag	Required/Illegal—See note for XHTML 1.0 requirements.
Deprecated	size="..."—The font size (1 through 7 or relative; that is, +3). color="..."—The font color. face="..."—The font type.
Empty	Yes.
Notes	Deprecated in favor of style sheets. In XHTML 1.0, this tag should take the XML form of _<basefont /> to ensure compatibility with older browsers.

`<big>...</big>`

Usage	Large text.
Start/End Tag	Required/Required.
Attributes	`%coreattrs`, `%i18n`, `%events`.
Empty	No.

`<font>...</font>`

Usage	Changes the font face, size, and color.
Start/End Tag	Required/Required.
Deprecated	`size="..."`—The font size (1 through 7 or relative; that is, +3).
	`color="..."`—The font color.
	`face="..."`—The font type.
Empty	No.
Notes	Deprecated in favor of style sheets.

`<i>...</i>`

Usage	Italicizes text.
Start/End Tag	Required/Required.
Attributes	`%coreattrs`, `%i18n`, `%events`.
Empty	No.

`<s>...</s>`

Usage	Strikethrough text.
Start/End Tag	Required/Required.
Attributes	`%coreattrs`, `%i18n`, `%events`.
Empty	No.
Notes	Deprecated in favor of style sheets.

`<small>...</small>`

Usage	Small text.
Start/End Tag	Required/Required.
Attributes	`%coreattrs`, `%i18n`, `%events`.
Empty	No.

B

`<strike>...</strike>`

Usage	Strikethrough text.
Start/End Tag	Required/Required.
Attributes	%coreattrs, %i18n, %events.
Empty	No.
Notes	Deprecated in favor of style sheets.

`<tt>...</tt>`

Usage	Teletype (or monospaced) text.
Start/End Tag	Required/Required.
Attributes	%coreattrs, %i18n, %events.
Empty	No.

`<u>...</u>`

Usage	Underlines text.
Start/End Tag	Required/Required.
Attributes	%coreattrs, %i18n, %events.
Empty	No.
Notes	Deprecated in favor of style sheets.

Lists

You can organize text into a more structured outline by creating lists. Lists can be nested.

`<dd>...</dd>`

Usage	The definition description used in a dl (definition list) element.
Start/End Tag	Required/Optional (HTML); Required/Required (XHTML 1.0).
Attributes	%coreattrs, %i18n, %events.
Empty	No.
Notes	Can contain block-level content, such as the <p> element.

`<dir>...</dir>`

Usage	Creates a multicolumn directory list.
Start/End Tag	Required/Required.
Attributes	%coreattrs, %i18n, %events.
Deprecated	compact—Compacts the displayed list.
Empty	No.
Notes	Must contain at least one list item. This element is deprecated in favor of the ul (unordered list) element.

B

`<dl>...</dl>`

Usage	Creates a definition list.
Start/End Tag	Required/Required.
Attributes	%coreattrs, %i18n, %events.
Deprecated	compact—Compacts the displayed list.
Empty	No.
Notes	Must contain at least one <dt> or <dd> element in any order.

`<dt>...</dt>`

Usage	The definition term (or label) used within a dl (definition list) element.
Start/End Tag	Required/Optional (HTML); Required/Required (XHTML 1.0).
Attributes	%coreattrs, %i18n, %events.
Empty	No.
Notes	Must contain text (which can be modified by text markup elements).

`<li>...</li>`

Usage	Defines a list item within a list.
Start/End Tag	Required/Optional (HTML); Required/Required (XHTML 1.0).
Attributes	%coreattrs, %i18n, %events.
Deprecated	type="..."—Changes the numbering style (1, a, A, i, I) in ordered lists or bullet style (disc, square, circle) in unordered lists. value="..."—Sets the numbering to the given integer, beginning with the current list item.
Empty	No.

`<menu>...</menu>`

Usage	Creates a single-column menu list.
Start/End Tag	Required/Required.
Attributes	`%coreattrs`, `%i18n`, `%events`.
Deprecated	`compact`—Compacts the displayed list.
Empty	No.
Notes	Must contain at least one list item. This element is deprecated in favor of the `ul` (unordered list) element.

`<ol>...</ol>`

Usage	Creates an ordered list.
Start/End Tag	Required/Required.
Attributes	`%coreattrs`, `%i18n`, `%events`.
Deprecated	`compact`—Compacts the displayed list. `start="..."`—Sets the starting number to the chosen integer. `type="..."`—Sets the numbering style (`1`, `a`, `A`, `i`, `I`).
Empty	No.
Notes	Must contain at least one list item.

`<ul>...</ul>`

Usage	Creates an unordered list.
Start/End Tag	Required/Required.
Attributes	`%coreattrs`, `%i18n`, `%events`.
Deprecated	`compact`—Compacts the displayed list. `type="..."`—Sets the bullet style (`disc`, `square`, `circle`).
Empty	No.
Notes	Must contain at least one list item.

Links

Hyperlinking is fundamental to HTML. These elements enable you to link to other documents.

<a>...</a>

Usage	Used to define links and anchors.
Start/End Tag	Required/Required.
Attributes	%coreattrs, %i18n, %events.

charset="..."—Character encoding of the resource.

name="..."—Defines an anchor.

href="..."—The URL of the linked resource.

target="..."—Determines where the resource will be displayed (user-defined name, _blank [in a new unnamed window], _parent [in the immediate parent frameset], _self [in the same frame as the current document], or _top [in a full browser window that removes the frameset completely]).

rel="..."—Forward link types.

rev="..."—Reverse link types.

accesskey="..."—Assigns a hotkey to this element.

shape="..."—Enables you to define client-side imagemaps using defined shapes (default, rect, circle, poly).

coords="..."—Sets the size of the shape using pixel or percentage lengths.

tabindex="..."—Sets the tabbing order between elements with a defined tabindex.

Empty	No.

B

\<base\>

Usage	All other URLs in the document are resolved against this location.
Start/End Tag	Required/Illegal—See note for XHTML 1.0 requirements.
Attributes	href="..."—The URL of the linked resource.
	target="..."—Determines where the resource will be displayed (user-defined name, _blank, _parent, _self, _top).
Empty	Yes.
Notes	Located in the document head. In XHTML 1.0, this tag should take the XML form of \<base /\> to ensure compatibility with older browsers.

\<link\>

Usage	Defines the relationship between a link and a resource.
Start/End Tag	Required/Illegal—See note for XHTML 1.0 requirements.
Attributes	%coreattrs, %i18n, %events.
	href="..."—The URL of the resource.
	rel="..."—The forward link types.
	rev="..."—The reverse link types.
	type="..."—The Internet content type.
	media="..."—Defines the destination medium (screen, print, projection, braille, speech, all).
	target="..."—Determines where the resource will be displayed (user-defined name, _blank, _parent, _self, _top).
Empty	Yes.
Notes	Located in the document head. In XHTML 1.0, this tag should take the XML form of \<link /\> to ensure compatibility with older browsers. Most often used to load external style sheets.

Tables

Tables are meant to display data in a tabular format. Tables are widely used for page layout purposes, but you can generally create any layout based on tables more simply with Cascading Style Sheets.

`<caption>...</caption>`

Usage	Displays a table caption.
Start/End Tag	Required/Required.
Attributes	`%coreattrs, %i18n, %events`.
Deprecated	`align="..."`—Controls alignment (`left`, `center`, `right`, `justify`).
Empty	No.
Notes	Optional. Used inside the `table` element.

B

`<col>`

Usage	Groups columns within column groups in order to share attribute values.
Start/End Tag	Required/Illegal—See note for XHTML 1.0 requirements.
Attributes	`%coreattrs, %i18n, %events`.
	`span="..."`—The number of columns the group contains.
	`width="..."`—The column width as a percentage, pixel value, or minimum value.
	`align="..."`—Horizontally aligns the contents of cells (`left`, `center`, `right`, `justify`, `char`).
	`char="..."`—Sets a character on which the column aligns.
	`charoff="..."`—Offset to the first alignment character on a line.
	`valign="..."`—Vertically aligns the contents of a cell (`top`, `middle`, `bottom`, `baseline`).
Empty	Yes.
Notes	In XHTML 1.0, this tag should take the XML form of `<col />` to ensure compatibility with older browsers.

`<colgroup>...</colgroup>`

Usage	Defines two or more columns as a group.
Start/End Tag	Required/Optional (HTML); Required/Required (XHTML 1.0).
Attributes	%coreattrs, %i18n, %events.
	span="..."—The number of columns in a group.
	width="..."—The width of the columns.
	align="..."—Horizontally aligns the contents of cells (left, center, right, justify, char).
	char="..."—Sets a character on which the column aligns.
	charoff="..."—Offset to the first alignment character on a line.
	valign="..."—Vertically aligns the contents of a cell (top, middle, bottom, baseline).
Empty	No.

`<table>...</table>`

Usage	Creates a table.
Start/End Tag	Required/Required.
Attributes	%coreattrs, %i18n, %events.
	width="..."—Table width.
	cols="..."—The number of columns.
	border="..."—The width in pixels of a border around the table.
	frame="..."—Sets the visible sides of a table (void, above, below, hsides, lhs, rhs, vsides, box, border).
	rules="..."—Sets the visible rules within a table (none, groups, rows, cols, all).
	cellspacing="..."—Spacing between cells.
	cellpadding="..."—Spacing in cells.
Deprecated	align="..."—Controls alignment (left, center, right, justify).
	bgcolor="..."—Sets the background color.
Empty	No.

`<tbody>...</tbody>`

Usage	Defines the table body.
Start/End Tag	Optional/Optional (HTML); Required/Required (XHTML 1.0).
Attributes	`%coreattrs, %i18n, %events`.
	`align="..."`—Horizontally aligns the contents of cells (`left, center, right, justify, char`).
	`char="..."`—Sets a character on which the column aligns.
	`charoff="..."`—Offset to the first alignment character on a line.
	`valign="..."`—Vertically aligns the contents of cells (`top, middle, bottom, baseline`).
Empty	No.

B

`<td>...</td>`

Usage	Defines a cell's contents.
Start/End Tag	Required/Optional (HTML); Required/Required (XHTML 1.0).
Attributes	`%coreattrs, %i18n, %events`.
	`axis="..."`—Abbreviated name.
	`axes="..."`—axis names listing row and column headers pertaining to the cell.
	`rowspan="..."`—The number of rows spanned by a cell.
	`colspan="..."`—The number of columns spanned by a cell.
	`align="..."`—Horizontally aligns the contents of cells (`left, center, right, justify, char`).
	`char="..."`—Sets a character on which the column aligns.
	`charoff="..."`—Offset to the first alignment character on a line.
	`valign="..."`—Vertically aligns the contents of cells (`top, middle, bottom, baseline`).
Deprecated	`nowrap="..."`—Turns off text wrapping in a cell.
	`bgcolor="..."`—Sets the background color.
	`height="..."`—Sets the height of the cell.
	`width="..."`—Sets the width of the cell.
Empty	No.

`<tfoot>...</tfoot>`

Usage	Defines the table footer.
Start/End Tag	Required/Optional (HTML); Required/Required (XHTML 1.0).
Attributes	`%coreattrs`, `%i18n`, `%events`.
	`align="..."`—Horizontally aligns the contents of cells (`left`, `center`, `right`, `justify`, `char`).
	`char="..."`—Sets a character on which the column aligns.
	`charoff="..."`—Offset to the first alignment character on a line.
	`valign="..."`—Vertically aligns the contents of cells (`top`, `middle`, `bottom`, `baseline`).
Empty	No.

`<th>...</th>`

Usage	Defines the cell contents of the table header.
Start/End Tag	Required/Optional (HTML); Required/Required (XHTML 1.0).
Attributes	`%coreattrs`, `%i18n`, `%events`.
	`axis="..."`—Abbreviated name.
	`axes="..."`—axis names listing row and column headers pertaining to the cell.
	`rowspan="..."`—The number of rows spanned by a cell.
	`colspan="..."`—The number of columns spanned by a cell.
	`align="..."`—Horizontally aligns the contents of cells (`left`, `center`, `right`, `justify`, `char`).
	`char="..."`—Sets a character on which the column aligns.
	`charoff="..."`—Offset to the first alignment character on a line.
	`valign="..."`—Vertically aligns the contents of cells (`top`, `middle`, `bottom`, `baseline`).
Deprecated	`nowrap="..."`—Turns off text wrapping in a cell.
	`bgcolor="..."`—Sets the background color.
	`height="..."`—Sets the height of the cell.
	`width="..."`—Sets the width of the cell.
Empty	No.

`<thead>...</thead>`

Usage	Defines the table header.
Start/End Tag	Required/Optional (HTML); Required/Required (XHTML 1.0).
Attributes	`%coreattrs`, `%i18n`, `%events`.
	`align="..."`—Horizontally aligns the contents of cells (`left`, `center`, `right`, `justify`, `char`).
	`char="..."`—Sets a character on which the column aligns.
	`charoff="..."`—Offset to the first alignment character on a line.
	`valign="..."`—Vertically aligns the contents of cells (`top`, `middle`, `bottom`, `baseline`).
Empty	No.

B

`<tr>...</tr>`

Usage	Defines a row of table cells.
Start/End Tag	Required/Optional (HTML); Required/Required (XHTML 1.0).
Attributes	`%coreattrs`, `%i18n`, `%events`.
	`align="..."`—Horizontally aligns the contents of cells (`left`, `center`, `right`, `justify`, `char`).
	`char="..."`—Sets a character on which the column aligns.
	`charoff="..."`—Offset to the first alignment character on a line.
	`valign="..."`—Vertically aligns the contents of cells (`top`, `middle`, `bottom`, `baseline`).
Deprecated	`bgcolor="..."`—Sets the background color.
Empty	No.

Frames

Frames create new "panels" in the web browser window that are used to display content from different source documents.

`<frame>`

Usage	Defines a frame.
Start/End Tag	Required/Illegal—See note for XHTML 1.0 requirements.

Attributes	name="..."—The name of a frame.
	src="..."—The source to be displayed in a frame.
	frameborder="..."—Toggles the border between frames (0, 1).
	marginwidth="..."—Sets the space between the frame border and content.
	marginheight="..."—Sets the space between the frame border and content.
	noresize—Disables sizing.
	scrolling="..."—Determines scrollbar presence (auto, yes, no).
Empty	Yes.
Notes	In XHTML 1.0, this tag should take the XML form of <frame /> to ensure compatibility with older browsers. Margins should normally be set using Cascading Style Sheets.

<frameset>...</frameset>

Usage	Defines the layout of frames within a window.
Start/End Tag	Required/Required.
Attributes	rows="..."—The number of rows.
	cols="..."—The number of columns.
	onload="..."—The intrinsic event triggered when the document loads.
	onunload="..."—The intrinsic event triggered when the document unloads.
Empty	No.
Notes	Framesets can be nested.

<iframe>...</iframe>

Usage	Creates an inline frame.
Start/End Tag	Required/Required.
Attributes	name="..."—The name of the frame.
	src="..."—The source to be displayed in a frame.
	frameborder="..."—Toggles the border between frames (0, 1).
	marginwidth="..."—Sets the space between the frame border and content.

marginheight="..."—Sets the space between the frame border and content.

scrolling="..."—Determines scrollbar presence (auto, yes, no).

height="..."—Height.

width="..."—Width.

Deprecated   align="..."—Controls alignment (left, center, right, justify).

Empty   No.

\<noframes>...\</noframes>

Usage	Alternative content when frames are not supported.
Start/End Tag	Required/Required.
Attributes	None.
Empty	No.

Embedded Content

Also called *inclusions*, embedded content applies to Java applets, imagemaps, and other multimedia or programmatic content that's placed in a web page to provide additional functionality.

\<applet>...\</applet>

Usage	Includes a Java applet.
Start/End Tag	Required/Required.
Deprecated	align="..."—Controls alignment (left, center, right, justify).

alt="..."—Displays text while loading.

archive="..."—Identifies the resources to be preloaded.

code="..."—The applet class file.

codebase="..."—The URL base for the applet.

height="..."—The width of the displayed applet.

hspace="..."—The horizontal space separating the image from other content.

name="..."—The name of the applet.

object="..."—The serialized applet file.

vspace="..."—The vertical space separating the image from other content.

width="..."—The height of the displayed applet.

Empty	No.
Notes	Applet is deprecated in favor of the object element.

`<area>`

Usage	Defines links and anchors in a client-side image map.
Start/End Tag	Required/Illegal—See note for XHTML 1.0 requirements.
Attributes	shape="..."—Enables you to define client-side imagemaps using defined shapes (default, rect, circle, poly).
	coords="..."—Sets the size of the shape using pixel or percentage lengths.
	href="..."—The URL of the linked resource.
	target="..."—Determines where the resource will be displayed (user-defined name, _blank, _parent, _self, _top).
	nohref="..."—Indicates that the region has no action.
	alt="..."—Displays alternative text.
	tabindex="..."—Sets the tabbing order between elements with a defined tabindex.
Empty	Yes.
Notes	In XHTML 1.0, this tag should take the XML form of <area /> to ensure compatibility with older browsers.

`<img>`

Usage	Includes an image in the document.
Start/End Tag	Required/Illegal—See note for XHTML 1.0 requirements.
Attributes	%coreattrs, %i18n, %events.
	src="..."—The URL of the image.
	alt="..."—Alternative text to display.
	height="..."—The height of the image.
	width="..."—The width of the image.
	usemap="..."—The URL to a client-side imagemap.
	ismap—Identifies a server-side imagemap.

Deprecated	`align="..."`—Controls alignment (`left`, `center`, `right`, `justify`).
	`border="..."`—Border width.
	`hspace="..."`—The horizontal space separating the image from other content.
	`vspace="..."`—The vertical space separating the image from other content.
Empty	Yes.
Notes	In XHTML 1.0, this tag should take the XML form of `<img />` to ensure compatibility with older browsers.

B

`<map>...</map>`

Usage	When used with the `area` element, creates a client-side imagemap.
Start/End Tag	Required/Required.
Attributes	`%coreattrs`.
	`name="..."`—The name of the imagemap to be created.
Empty	No.

`<object>...</object>`

Usage	Includes an object.
Start/End Tag	Required/Required.
Attributes	`%coreattrs, %i18n, %events`.
	`declare`—A flag that makes the current object definition a declaration only.
	`classid="..."`—The URL of the object's location.
	`codebase="..."`—The URL for resolving URLs specified by other attributes.
	`data="..."`—The URL to the object's data.
	`type="..."`—The Internet content type for data.
	`codetype="..."`—The Internet content type for the code.
	`standby="..."`—Show message while loading.
	`height="..."`—The height of the object.
	`width="..."`—The width of the object.

usemap="..."—The URL to an imagemap.

shapes=—Enables you to define areas to search for hyperlinks if the object is an image.

name="..."—The URL to submit as part of a form.

tabindex="..."—Sets the tabbing order between elements with a defined tabindex.

Deprecated	align="..."—Controls alignment (left, center, right, justify).
	border="..."—Displays the border around an object.
	hspace="..."—The space between the sides of the object and other page content.
	vspace="..."—The space between the top and bottom of the object and other page content.
Empty	No.

<param>

Usage	Initializes an object.
Start/End Tag	Required/Illegal—See note for XHTML 1.0 requirements.
Attributes	name="..."—Defines the parameter name.
	value="..."—The value of the object parameter.
	valuetype="..."—Defines the value type (data, ref, object).
	type="..."—The Internet media type.
Empty	Yes.
Notes	In XHTML 1.0, this tag should take the XML form of <param /> to ensure compatibility with older browsers.

Style

Style sheets (both inline and external) are incorporated into an HTML document through the use of the style element.

<style>...</style>

Usage	Creates an internal style sheet.
Start/End Tag	Required/Required.
Attributes	%i18n.
	type="..."—The Internet content type.

`media="..."`—Defines the destination medium (`screen`, `print`, `projection`, `braille`, `speech`, `all`).

`title="..."`—The title of the style.

Empty	No.
Notes	Located in the `head` element.

Forms

Forms create an interface for the user to select options and submit data back to the web server.

`<button>...</button>`

Usage	Creates a button.
Start/End Tag	Required/Required.
Attributes	`%coreattrs`, `%i18n`, `%events`.
	`name="..."`—The button name.
	`value="..."`—The value of the button.
	`type="..."`—The button type (`button`, `submit`, `reset`).
	`disabled="..."`—Sets the button state to disabled.
	`tabindex="..."`—Sets the tabbing order between elements with a defined `tabindex`.
	`onfocus="..."`—The event that occurs when the element receives focus.
	`onblur="..."`—The event that occurs when the element loses focus.
Empty	No.

`<fieldset>...</fieldset>`

Usage	Groups related controls.
Start/End Tag	Required/Required.
Attributes	`%coreattrs`, `%i18n`, `%events`.
Empty	No.

`<form>...</form>`

Usage	Creates a form that holds controls for user input.
Start/End Tag	Required/Required.
Attributes	%coreattrs, %i18n, %events.
	`action="..."`—The URL for the server action.
	`enctype="..."`—Specifies the MIME (Internet media type).
	`onsubmit="..."`—The intrinsic event that occurs when the form is submitted.
	`onreset="..."`—The intrinsic event that occurs when the form is reset.
	`target="..."`—Determines where the resource will be displayed (user-defined name, `_blank`, `_parent`, `_self`, `_top`).
	`accept-charset="..."`—The list of character encodings.
	`method="..."`—The HTTP method (`post` or `get`).
Empty	No.

`<input>`

Usage	Defines controls used in forms.
Start/End Tag	Required/Illegal—See note for XHTML 1.0 requirements.
Attributes	%coreattrs, %i18n, %events.
	`type="..."`—The type of input control (`text`, `password`, `checkbox`, `radio`, `submit`, `reset`, `file`, `hidden`, `image`, `button`).
	`name="..."`—The name of the control (required except for `submit` and `reset`).
	`value="..."`—The initial value of the control (required for radio and checkboxes).
	`checked="..."`—Sets the radio buttons to a checked state.
	`disabled="..."`—Disables the control.
	`readonly="..."`—For text password types.
	`size="..."`—The width of the control in pixels except for text and password controls, which are specified in number of characters.
	`maxlength="..."`—The maximum number of characters that can be entered.

`src="..."`—The URL to an image control type.

`alt="..."`—An alternative text description.

`usemap="..."`—The URL to a client-side imagemap.

`tabindex="..."`—Sets the tabbing order between elements with a defined `tabindex`.

`onfocus="..."`—The event that occurs when the element receives focus.

`onblur="..."`—The event that occurs when the element loses focus.

`onselect="..."`—Intrinsic event that occurs when the control is selected.

`onchange="..."`—Intrinsic event that occurs when the control is changed.

`accept="..."`—File types allowed for upload.

Deprecated	`align="..."`—Controls alignment (`left`, `center`, `right`, `justify`).
Empty	Yes.
Notes	In XHTML 1.0, this tag should take the XML form of `<input />` to ensure compatibility with older browsers.

`<isindex>`

Usage	Prompts the user for input.
Start/End Tag	Required/Illegal—See note for XHTML 1.0 requirements.
Attributes	`%coreattrs, %i18n`.
Deprecated	`prompt="..."`—Provides a prompt string for the input field.
Empty	Yes.
Notes	This field is deprecated in favor of actual form controls.

`<label>...</label>`

Usage	Labels a control.
Start/End Tag	Required/Required.
Attributes	`%coreattrs, %i18n, %events`.
	`for="..."`—Associates a label with an identified control.
	`disabled="..."`—Disables a control.
	`accesskey="..."`—Assigns a hotkey to this element.

onfocus="..."—The event that occurs when the element receives focus.

onblur="..."—The event that occurs when the element loses focus.

Empty   No.

\<legend>...\</legend>

Usage   Assigns a caption to a fieldset.

Start/End Tag   Required/Required.

Attributes   %coreattrs, %i18n, %events.

accesskey="..."—Assigns a hotkey to this element.

Deprecated   align="..."—Controls alignment (left, center, right, justify).

Empty   No.

\<option>...\</option>

Usage   Specifies choices in a select element.

Start/End Tag   Required/Optional (HTML); Required/Required (XHTML 1.0).

Attributes   %coreattrs, %i18n, %events.

selected="..."—Specifies whether the option is selected.

disabled="..."—Disables control.

value="..."—The value submitted if a control is submitted.

Empty   No.

\<select>...\</select>

Usage   Creates choices for the user to select.

Start/End Tag   Required/Required.

Attributes   %coreattrs, %i18n, %events.

name="..."—The name of the element.

size="..."—The width in number of rows.

multiple—Allows multiple selections.

disabled="..."—Disables the control.

tabindex="..."—Sets the tabbing order between elements with a defined tabindex.

onfocus="..."—The event that occurs when the element receives focus.

onblur="..."—The event that occurs when the element loses focus.

onselect="..."—Intrinsic event that occurs when the control is selected.

onchange="..."—Intrinsic event that occurs when the control is changed.

Empty	No.

B

`<textarea>...</textarea>`

Usage	Creates an area for user input with multiple lines.
Start/End Tag	Required/Required.
Attributes	%coreattrs, %i18n, %events.
	name="..."—The name of the control.
	rows="..."—The width in number of rows.
	cols="..."—The height in number of columns.
	disabled="..."—Disables the control.
	readonly="..."—Sets the displayed text to read-only status.
	tabindex="..."—Sets the tabbing order between elements with a defined tabindex.
	onfocus="..."—The event that occurs when the element receives focus.
	onblur="..."—The event that occurs when the element loses focus.
	onselect="..."—Intrinsic event that occurs when the control is selected.
	onchange="..."—Intrinsic event that occurs when the control is changed.
Empty	No.
Notes	Text to be displayed is placed within the start and end tags.

Scripts

Scripting language is made available to process data and perform other dynamic events through the script element.

`<script>...</script>`

Usage	Contains client-side scripts that are executed by the browser.
Start/End Tag	Required/Required.
Attributes	`type="..."`—Script language Internet content type.
	`src="..."`—The URL for the external script.
Deprecated	`language="..."`—The scripting language, deprecated in favor of the `type` attribute.
Empty	No.
Notes	You can set the default scripting language in the `meta` element.

`<noscript>...</noscript>`

Usage	Provides alternative content for browsers unable to execute a script.
Start/End Tag	Required/Required.
Attributes	None.
Empty	No.

Character Entities

Table B.1 contains the possible numeric and character entities for the ISO-Latin-1 (ISO8859-1) character set. Where possible, the character is shown.

NOTE

Not all browsers can display all characters, and some browsers may even display different characters from those that appear in the table. Newer browsers seem to have a better track record for handling character entities, but be sure and test your HTML files extensively with multiple browsers if you intend to use these entities.

TABLE B.1   ISO-Latin-1 Character Set

Character	Numeric Entity	Character Entity (if any)	Description
	&#00;–&#08;		Unused
	&#09;		Horizontal tab
	&#10;		Line feed
	&#11;–&#31;		Unused
	&#32;		Space
!	&#33;		Exclamation mark
"	&#34;	&quot;	Quotation mark
#	&#35;		Number sign
$	&#36;		Dollar sign
%	&#37;		Percent sign
&	&#38;	&amp;	Ampersand
'	&#39;		Apostrophe
(	&#40;		Left parenthesis
)	&#41;		Right parenthesis
*	&#42;		Asterisk
+	&#43;		Plus sign
,	&#44;		Comma
-	&#45;		Hyphen
.	&#46;		Period (fullstop)
/	&#47;		Solidus (slash)
0–9	0–9		Digits 0–9
:	&#58;		Colon
;	&#59;		Semicolon
<	&#60;	&lt;	Less than
=	&#61;		Equal sign
>	&#62;	&gt;	Greater than
?	&#63;		Question mark
@	&#64;		Commercial at
A–Z	A–Z		Letters A–Z
[	&#91;		Left square bracket
\	&#92;		Reverse solidus (backslash)

B

TABLE B.1   continued

Character	Numeric Entity	Character Entity (if any)	Description
]	&#93;		Right square bracket
^	&#94;		Caret
—	&#95;		Horizontal bar
`	&#96;		Grave accent
a–z	a–z		Letters a–z
{	&#123;		Left curly brace
|	|		Vertical bar
}	&#125;		Right curly brace
~	&#126;		Tilde
	&#127;–Ÿ		Unused
			Non-breaking space
¡	&#161;	&iexcl;	Inverted exclamation
¢	&#162;	&cent;	Cent sign
£	&#163;	&pound;	Pound sterling
	&#164;	&curren;	General currency sign
¥	&#165;	&yen;	Yen sign
¦	&#166;	¦ or &brkbar;	Broken vertical bar
§	&#167;	&sect;	Section sign
¨	&#168;	¨ or ¨	Umlaut (dieresis)
©	&#169;	&copy;	Copyright
ª	&#170;	&ordf;	Feminine ordinal
‹	&#171;	&laqo;	Left angle quote, guillemet left
¬	&#172;	&not;	Not sign
	&#173;	&shy;	Soft hyphen
®	&#174;	&reg;	Registered trademark
¯	&#175;	¯ or &hibar;	Macron accent
°	&#176;	&deg;	Degree sign
±	&#177;	&plusmn;	Plus or minus
2	&#178;	&sup2;	Superscript two
3	&#179;	&sup3;	Superscript three

TABLE B.1 continued

Character	Numeric Entity	Character Entity (if any)	Description
´	&#180;	&acute;	Acute accent
µ	&#181;	&micro;	Micro sign
¶	&#182;	&para;	Paragraph sign
·	&#183;	&middot;	Middle dot
¸	&#184;	&cedil;	Cedilla
1	&#185;	&sup1;	Superscript one
°	&#186;	&ordm;	Masculine ordinal
›	&#187;	&raquo;	Right angle quote, guillemet right
1/4	&#188;	&fraq14;	Fraction one-fourth
1/2	&#189;	&fraq12;	Fraction one-half
3/4	&#190;	&fraq34;	Fraction three-fourths
¿	&#191;	&iquest;	Inverted question mark
À	&#192;	&Agrave;	Capital A, grave accent
Á	&#193;	&Aacute;	Capital A, acute accent
Â	&#194;	&Acirc;	Capital A, circumflex accent
Ã	&#195;	&Atilde;	Capital A, tilde
Ä	&#196;	&Auml;	Capital A, dieresis or umlaut mark
Å	&#197;	&Aring;	Capital A, ring
Æ	&#198;	&AElig;	Capital AE dipthong (ligature)
Ç	&#199;	&Ccedil;	Capital C, cedilla
È	&#200;	&Egrave;	Capital E, grave accent
É	&#201;	&Eacute;	Capital E, acute accent
Ê	&#202;	&Ecirc;	Capital E, circumflex accent
Ë	&#203;	&Euml;	Capital E, dieresis or umlaut mark
Ì	&#204;	&Igrave;	Capital I, grave accent
Í	&#205;	&Iacute;	Capital I, acute accent
Î	&#206;	&Icirc;	Capital I, circumflex accent
Ï	&#207;	&Iuml;	Capital I, dieresis or umlaut mark

B

TABLE B.1 continued

Character	Numeric Entity	Character Entity (if any)	Description
Đ	Ð	Ð or Đ	Capital Eth, Icelandic
Ñ	Ñ	Ñ	Capital N, tilde
Ò	Ò	Ò	Capital O, grave accent
Ó	Ó	Ó	Capital O, acute accent
Ô	Ô	Ô	Capital O, circumflex accent
Õ	Õ	Õ	Capital O, tilde
Ö	Ö	Ö	Capital O, dieresis or umlaut mark
×	×	×	Multiply sign
Ø	Ø	Ø	Capital O, slash
Ù	Ù	Ù	Capital U, grave accent
Ú	Ú	Ú	Capital U, acute accent
Û	Û	Û	Capital U, circumflex accent
Ü	Ü	Ü	Capital U, dieresis or umlaut mark
Y	Ý	Ý	Capital Y, acute accent
	Þ	Þ	Capital THORN, Icelandic
ß	ß	ß	Small sharp s, German (sz ligature)
à	à	à	Small a, grave accent
á	á	á	Small a, acute accent
â	â	â	Small a, circumflex accent
ã	ã	ã	Small a, tilde
ä	ä	ä	Small a, dieresis or umlaut mark
å	å	å	Small a, ring
æ	æ	æ	Small ae dipthong (ligature)
ç	ç	ç	Small c, cedilla
è	è	è	Small e, grave accent
é	é	é	Small e, acute accent

TABLE B.1   continued

Character	Numeric Entity	Character Entity (if any)	Description
ê	&#234;	&ecirc;	Small e, circumflex accent
ë	&#235;	&euml;	Small e, dieresis or umlaut mark
ì	&#236;	&igrave;	Small i, grave accent
í	&#237;	&iacute;	Small i, acute accent
î	&#238;	&icirc;	Small i, circumflex accent
ï	&#239;	&iuml;	Small i, dieresis or umlaut mark
	&#240;	&eth;	Small eth, Icelandic
ñ	&#241;	&ntilde;	Small n, tilde
ò	&#242;	&ograve;	Small o, grave accent
ó	&#243;	&oacute;	Small o, acute accent
ô	&#244;	&ocirc;	Small o, circumflex accent
õ	&#245;	&otilde;	Small o, tilde
ö	&#246;	&ouml;	Small o, dieresis or umlaut mark
÷	&#247;	&divide;	Division sign
ø	&#248;	&oslash;	Small o, slash
ù	&#249;	&ugrave;	Small u, grave accent
ú	&#250;	&uacute;	Small u, acute accent
û	&#251;	&ucirc;	Small u, circumflex accent
ü	&#252;	&uuml;	Small u, dieresis or umlaut mark
	&#253;	&yacute;	Small y, acute accent
	&#254;	&thorn;	Small thorn, Icelandic
ÿ	&#255;	&yuml;	Small y, dieresis or umlaut mark

B

APPENDIX C:
Cascading Style Sheet Quick Reference

Cascading Style Sheets (CSS) allow for advanced placement and rendering of text and graphics on your pages. Using style sheets, you can apply text, images, and multimedia to your web pages with great precision. This appendix provides a quick reference to CSS1, as well as those properties and values that are included in the CSS2 recommendation dated May 12, 1998. This is the most current version of this document at press time.

NOTE

This appendix is based on the information provided in the Cascading Style Sheets, Level 2 W3C recommendation dated May 12, 1998, which can be found at http://www.w3.org/TR/CSS21/.

To make the information readily accessible, this appendix organizes CSS properties in the following order:

- Block-level properties
- Background and color properties
- Box model properties
- Font properties
- List properties
- Text properties
- Visual effects properties
- Aural style sheet properties
- Generated content/automatic numbering properties
- Paged media properties
- User interface properties
- Cascading Style Sheet units

How to Use This Appendix

Each CSS property's description contains the following attributes:

- **Usage**—A description of the property
- **CSS1 values**—Legal CSS1 values and syntax
- **CSS2 values**—Legal CSS2 values and syntax
- **Initial**—The initial value
- **Applies to**—Elements to which the property applies
- **Inherited**—Whether the property is inherited
- **Notes**—Additional information

Deciphering CSS values is an exercise that requires patience and a strict adherence to the rules of logic. As you refer to the values for each property listed in this appendix, you should use the following scheme to understand them.

Values of different types are differentiated as follows:

- **Keyword values**—Keywords are identifiers, such as `red`, `auto`, `normal`, and `inherit`. They do not have quotation marks.

- **Basic data types**—These values, such as `<number>` and `<length>`, are contained within angled brackets to indicate the data type of the actual value used in a style statement. It's important to note that this refers to the data type and is *not* the actual value. The basic data types are described at the end of this appendix.

- **Shorthand reference**—Values that are enclosed in angled brackets and single quotation marks, such as `<'background-color'>` within the `background` property, indicate a shorthand method for setting the desired value. The values identified in `_background-color` are available for use in the `background` property. If you choose to set the background color for the document body, for example, you can choose to do so by using either body `{ background: red }` or body `{ background-color: red }`.

- **Predefined data types**—Values within angled brackets without quotation marks, such as `<border-width>` within the `'border-top-width'` property, are similar to the basic data types but contain predefined values. The available values for `<border-width>`, for example, are `thin`, `thick`, `medium`, and `<length>`.

C

When more than one value is available, they are arranged according to the following rules:

- **Adjacent words**—Several adjacent words indicate all values must be used but can be in any order.

- **Values separated by a bar "¦"**—A bar separates two or more alternatives, only one of which can occur.

- **Values separated by double bars "¦¦"**—The double bar separates two or more options, of which one or more must occur in any order.

- **Brackets "[ ]"**—Brackets group the values into statements that are evaluated much like a mathematical expression.

When evaluating the values listed in this appendix, the order of precedence is that adjacent values take priority over those separated by double bars and then single bars.

In addition to this, modifiers may follow each value or group of values. These are the following:

- *** (asterisk)**—The preceding type, word, or group occurs zero or more times.

- **+ (plus sign)**—The preceding type, word, or group occurs one or more times.

- **? (question mark)**—The preceding type, word, or group is optional.

- **{} (curly braces)**—Surrounding a pair of numbers, such as `{1,2}`, indicates the preceding type, word, or group occurs at least once and at most twice.

Block-Level Properties

Block-level elements are those that are formatted visually as blocks. A paragraph or a list, for example, is a block.

bottom, left, right, top

Usage	Specifies how far a box's bottom, left, right, or top content edge is offset from the respective bottom, left, right, or top of the box's containing block.
CSS2 Values	`<length>` | `<percentage>` | `auto` | `inherit`
Initial	`auto`
Applies to	All elements.
Inherited	No.
Notes	Percentage refers to height of containing block.

direction

Usage	Specifies the direction of inline box flow, embedded text direction, column layout, and content overflow.
CSS1 Values	`ltr` | `rtl`
CSS2 Values	`inherit`
Initial	`ltr`
Applies to	All elements.
Inherited	Yes.
Notes	See `unicode-bidi` for further properties that relate to embedded text direction.

display

Usage	Specifies how the contents of a block are to be generated.
CSS1 Values	`inline` | `block` | `list-item`
CSS2 Values	`run-in` | `compact` | `marker` | `table` | `inline-table` | `table-row-group` | `table-column-group` | `table-header-group` | `table-footer-group` | `table-row` | `table-cell` | `table-caption` | `none` | `inherit`
Initial	`inline`
Applies to	All elements.
Inherited	No.

float

Usage	Specifies whether a box should float to the left, right, or not at all. Floated elements are affixed to one side of the enclosing block so that other elements on the page can flow around them.
CSS1 Values	`none	left	right`
CSS2 Values	`inherit`
Initial	`none`
Applies to	Elements that are not positioned absolutely.
Inherited	No.

position

Usage	Determines which CSS2 positioning algorithms are used to calculate the coordinates of a box.
CSS2 Values	`static	<relative>	<absolute>	fixed	inherit`
Initial	`static`
Applies to	All elements except generated content.
Inherited	No.

C

unicode-bidi

Usage	Opens a new level of embedding with respect to the bidirectional algorithm when elements with reversed writing direction are embedded more than one level deep.
CSS2 Values	`normal	embed	bidi-override	inherit`
Initial	`normal`
Applies to	All elements.
Inherited	No.

z-index

Usage	Specifies the stack level of the box and whether the box establishes a local stacking context.
CSS2 Values	`auto	<integer>	inherit`
Initial	`auto`
Applies to	Elements that generate absolutely and relatively positioned boxes.
Inherited	No.

Background and Color Properties

HTML enables you to specify background and color properties for text, link, and back-grounds on a global basis in the document head; CSS provides similar properties that enable you to customize colors for individual elements (or for the entire page, if you prefer). The following properties affect foreground and background colors of elements.

background

Usage	Shorthand property for setting the individual background proper-ties at the same place in the style sheet.
CSS1 Values	[<'background-color'> || <'background-image'> || <'background-repeat'> || <'background-attachment'> || <'background-position'>]
CSS2 Values	inherit
Initial	Not defined.
Applies to	All elements.
Inherited	No.

background-attachment

Usage	If a background image is specified, this property specifies whether it is fixed in the viewport or scrolls along with the document.
CSS1 Values	scroll | fixed
CSS2 Values	inherit
Initial	scroll
Applies to	All elements.
Inherited	No.

background-color

Usage	Sets the background color of an element.
CSS1 Values	<color> | transparent
CSS2 Values	inherit
Initial	transparent
Applies to	All elements.
Inherited	No.

background-image

Usage	Sets the background image of an element.
CSS1 Values	`<uri>` I `none`
CSS2 Values	`inherit`
Initial	`none`
Applies to	All elements.
Inherited	No.
Notes	Authors also should specify a background color that will be used when the image is unavailable.

background-position

Usage	Specifies the initial position of the background image, if one is specified.
CSS1 Values	`[[<percentage> I <length>](1,2) I [top I center I _bottom] II [left I center I right]]`
CSS2 Values	`inherit`
Initial	0% 0%.
Applies to	Block-level and replaced elements.
Inherited	No.

C

background-repeat

Usage	Specifies whether an image is repeated (tiled) and how, if a background image is specified.
CSS1 Values	`repeat-x I repeat-y I repeat I no-repeat`
CSS2 Values	`inherit`
Initial	`repeat`
Applies to	All elements.
Inherited	No.

color

Usage	Describes the foreground color of an element's text content.
CSS1 Values	`<color>`
CSS2 Values	`inherit`

Initial	Depends on browser.
Applies to	All elements.
Inherited	Yes.

Box Model Properties

Each page element in the document tree is contained within a rectangular box and laid out according to a visual formatting model. The following elements affect an element's box.

border

Usage	A shorthand property for setting the same width, color, and style on all four borders of an element.
CSS1 Values	[`'border-width'` ‖ `'border-style'`	`<color>`]
CSS2 Values	`inherit`
Initial	Not defined for shorthand properties.
Applies to	All elements.
Inherited	No.
Notes	This property accepts only one value. To set different values for each side of the border, use the `border-width`, `border-style`, or `border-color` property.

border-bottom, border-left, border-right, border-top

Usage	Shorthand properties for setting the width, style, and color of an element's bottom, left, right, or top border (respectively).
CSS1 Values	[`'border-bottom-width'` ‖ `'border-style'` ‖ `<color>`]
	[`'border-left-width'` ‖ `'border-style'` ‖ `<color>`]
	[`'border-right-width'` ‖ `'border-style'` ‖ `<color>`]
	[`'border-top-width'` ‖ `'border-style'` ‖ `<color>`]
CSS2 Values	`inherit`
Initial	Not defined.
Applies to	All elements.
Inherited	No.

border-color

Usage	Sets the color of the four borders.
CSS1 Values	`<color> (1,4)	transparent`
CSS2 Values	`inherit`
Initial	The value of the `<color>` property.
Applies to	All elements.
Inherited	No.
Notes	This property accepts up to four values, as follows:
	One value: Sets all four border colors.
	Two values: First value for top and bottom; second value for right and left.
	Three values: First value for top; second value for right and left; third value for bottom.
	Four values: Top, right, bottom, and left, respectively.

C

border-bottom-color, border-left-color, border-right-color, border-top-color

Usage	Specifies the colors of a box's border.
CSS1 Values	`<color>`
CSS2 Values	`inherit`
Initial	The value of the `<color>` property.
Applies to	All elements.
Inherited	No.

border-style

Usage	Sets the style of the four borders.
CSS1 Values	`none	dotted	dashed	solid	double	groove	ridge	inset	outset`
CSS2 Values	`inherit`
Initial	`none`
Applies to	All elements.
Inherited	No.

Notes	This property can have from one to four values (see notes under border-color for explanation). If no value is specified, the color of the element itself will take its place.

border-bottom-style, border-left-style, border-right-style, border-top-style

Usage	Sets the style of a specific border (bottom, left, right, or top).
Values	Same as border-style.
Initial	none
Applies to	All elements.
Inherited	No.

border-width

Usage	A shorthand property for setting border-width-top, border-width-right, border-width-bottom, and _border-width-left at the same place in the style sheet.
CSS1 Values	[thin | medium | thick] | <length>
CSS2 Values	inherit
Initial	Not defined.
Applies to	All elements.
Inherited	No.
Notes	This property accepts up to four values (see notes under border-color for explanation).

border-bottom-width, border-left-width, border-right-width, border-top-width

Usage	Sets the width of an element's bottom, left, right, or top border (respectively).
CSS1 Values	[thin | medium | thick] | <length>
CSS2 Values	inherit
Initial	medium
Applies to	All elements.
Inherited	No.

clear

Usage	Indicates which sides of an element's box or boxes may not be adjacent to an earlier floating box.
CSS1 Values	none | left | right | both
CSS2 Values	inherit
Initial	none
Applies to	Block-level elements.
Inherited	No.

height, width

Usage	Specifies the content height or width of a box.
CSS1 Values	<length> | auto
CSS2 Values	<percentage> | inherit
Initial	auto
Applies to	All elements but non-replaced inline elements and table columns; also does not apply to column groups (for height) or row groups (for width).
Inherited	No.

margin

Usage	Shorthand property for setting margin-top, margin-right, margin-bottom, and margin-left at the same place in the style sheet.
CSS1 Values	<length> | <percentage> | auto
CSS2 Values	inherit
Initial	Not defined (shorthand property).
Applies to	All elements.
Inherited	No.

margin-bottom, margin-left, margin-right, margin-top

Usage	Sets the bottom, left, right, and top margins of a box, respectively.
CSS1 Values	<length> | <percentage> | auto

C

CSS2 Values	`inherit`
Initial	`0`
Applies to	All elements.
Inherited	No.

max-height, max-width

Usage	Constrains the height and width of a block to a maximum value.
CSS2 Values	`<length>` | `<percentage>` | `inherit`
Initial	100%
Applies to	All elements.
Inherited	No.
Notes	Percentages refer to the height of the containing block.

min-height, min-width

Usage	Constrains the height and width of a block to a minimum value.
CSS2 Values	`<length>` | `<percentage>` | `inherit`
Initial	`0`
Applies to	All elements.
Inherited	No.
Notes	Percentages refer to the height of the containing block.

padding

Usage	Shorthand property that sets `padding-top`, `padding-right`, `padding-bottom`, and `padding-left` at the same place in the style sheet.
CSS1 Values	`<length>` | `<percentage>`
CSS2 Values	`inherit`
Initial	Not defined.
Applies to	All elements.
Inherited	No.

padding-top, padding-right, padding-bottom, padding-left

Usage	Specifies the width of the white space within a box's top, right, bottom, and left sides.
CSS1 Values	`<length>` | `<percentage>`
CSS2 Values	`inherit`
Initial	`0`
Applies to	All elements.
Inherited	No.
Notes	Values cannot be negative. Percentage values refer to the width of the containing block.

C

Font Properties

Far more powerful than the font tags and attributes found in HTML 4.01, cascading style sheets enable you to affect many additional elements of a font. CSS1 font properties assume that the font is resident on the client's system and specify alternative fonts through other properties. The properties proposed in CSS2 go beyond that, actually enabling authors to describe the fonts they want to use, and increasing the capability for browsers to select fonts when the font the author specified is not available.

font

Usage	A shorthand property for setting `font-style`, `font-variant`, `font-weight`, `font-size`, `line-height`, and `font-family` at the same place in the style sheet.
CSS1 Values	`[['font-style' ‖ 'font-variant' ‖ 'font-weight']? 'font-size' [/'line-height']? font-family`
CSS2 Values	`caption` | `icon` | `menu` | `message-box` | `small-caption` | `status-bar` | `inherit`
Initial	See individual properties.
Applies to	All elements.
Inherited	Yes.
Notes	Percentages allowed on `font-size` and `line-height`. For backward compatibility, set `font-stretch` and `font-size-adjust` by using their respective individual properties.

font-family

Usage	Specifies a list of font family names and generic family names.
CSS1 Values	[[<family-name> | <generic-family> [,]* [<family-name> | <generic-family>]
CSS2 Values	inherit
Initial	Depends on browser.
Applies to	All elements.
Inherited	Yes.
Notes	<family-name> displays a font family of choice (Arial, Helvetica, or Bookman, for example). <generic-family> assigns one of five generic family names: serif, sans-serif, cursive, fantasy, or monospace.

font-size

Usage	Describes the size of the font when set solid.
CSS1 Values	<absolute-size> | <relative-size> | <length> | _<percentage>
CSS2 Values	inherit
Initial	medium
Applies to	All elements.
Inherited	The computed value is inherited.
Notes	Percentages can be used relative to the parent element's font size.

font-size-adjust

Usage	Enables authors to specify a z-value for an element that preserves the x-height of the first choice substitute font.
CSS2 Values	<number> | none | inherit
Initial	none
Applies to	All elements.
Inherited	Yes.
Notes	Percentages can be used relative to the parent element's font size.

font-stretch

Usage	Specifies between normal, condensed, and extended faces within a font family.
CSS2 Values	`normal` I `wider` I `narrower` I `ultra-condensed` I `extra-condensed` I `condensed` I `semi-condensed` I `semi-expanded` I `expanded` I `extra-expanded` I `ultra-expanded` I `inherit`
Initial	`normal`
Applies to	All elements.
Inherited	Yes.

font-style

Usage	Requests normal (roman or upright), italic, and oblique faces within a font family.
CSS1 Values	`normal` I `italic` I `oblique`
CSS2 Values	`inherit`
Initial	`normal`
Applies to	All elements.
Inherited	Yes.

C

font-variant

Usage	Specifies a font that is not labeled as a small-caps font (`normal`) or one that is labeled as a small-caps font (`small-caps`).
CSS1 Values	`normal` I `small-caps`
CSS2 Values	`inherit`
Initial	`normal`
Applies to	All elements.
Inherited	Yes.

font-weight

Usage	Specifies the weight of the font.
CSS1 Values	`normal` I `bold` I `bolder` I `lighter` I `100` I `200` I `300` I `400` I `500` I `600` I `700` I `800` I `900`

CSS2 Values	`inherit`
Initial	`normal`
Applies to	All elements.
Inherited	Yes.
Notes	Values `100` through `900` form an ordered sequence. Each number indicates a weight that is at least as dark as its predecessor. `normal` is equal to a weight of `400`, and `bold` is equal to a weight of `700`.

List Properties

When an element is assigned a `display` value of `list-item`, the element's content is contained in a box and an optional marker box can be specified. The marker defines the image, glyph, or number that's used to identify the list item. The following properties affect list items and markers.

list-style

Usage	Shorthand notation for setting `list-style-type`, `list-style-image`, and `list-style-position` at the same place in the style sheet.
CSS1 Values	`['list-style-type' || 'list-style-position' || 'list-style-image']`
CSS2 Values	`inherit`
Initial	Not defined.
Applies to	Elements with `display` property set to `list-item`.
Inherited	Yes.

list-style-image

Usage	Sets the image that will be used as the list item marker.
CSS1 Values	`<uri>	none`
CSS2 Values	`inherit`
Initial	`none`
Applies to	Elements with `display` property set to `list-item`.
Inherited	Yes.

list-style-position

Usage	Specifies the position of the marker box with respect to the line item content box.
CSS1 Values	inside	outside
CSS2 Values	inherit
Initial	outside
Applies to	Elements with display property set to list-item.
Inherited	Yes.

list-style-type

Usage	Specifies the appearance of the list item marker when list-style-image is set to none.
CSS1 Values	disc	circle	square	decimal	lower-roman	upper-roman	lower-alpha	upper-alpha	none
CSS2 Values	leading-zero	western-decimal	lower-greek	lower-latin	upper-latin	hebrew	armenian	georgian	cjk-ideographic	hiragana	katakana	_hiragana-iroha	katakana-iroha	inherit
Initial	disc
Applies to	Elements with display property set to list-item.
Inherited	Yes.

C

Text Properties

The following properties affect the visual presentation of characters, spaces, words, and paragraphs.

letter-spacing

Usage	Specifies the spacing behavior between text characters.
CSS1 Values	normal	<length>
CSS2 Values	inherit
Initial	normal
Applies to	All elements.
Inherited	Yes.

line-height

Usage	Specifies the minimal height of each inline box.
CSS1 Values	normal | number | <length> | <percentage>
CSS2 Values	inherit
Initial	normal
Applies to	All elements.
Inherited	Yes.

text-align

Usage	Describes how a block of text is aligned.
CSS1 Values	left | right | center | justify
CSS2 Values	<string> | inherit
Initial	Depends on browser and writing direction.
Applies to	Block-level elements.
Inherited	Yes.

text-decoration

Usage	Describes decorations that are added to the text of an element.
CSS1 Values	none | underline | overline | line-through | blink
CSS2 Values	inherit
Initial	none
Applies to	All elements.
Inherited	No.

text-indent

Usage	Specifies the indentation of the first line of text in a block.
CSS1 Values	<length> | <percentage>
CSS2 Values	inherit
Initial	0
Applies to	Block-level elements.
Inherited	Yes.

text-shadow

Usage	Accepts a comma-separated list of shadow effects to be applied to the text of an element.
CSS2 Values	none | <color> | <length> | inherit
Initial	none
Applies to	All elements.
Inherited	No.
Notes	You also can use text shadows with :first-letter and :first-line pseudo-elements.

text-transform

Usage	Controls the capitalization of an element's text.
CSS1 Values	capitalize | uppercase | lowercase | none
CSS2 Values	inherit
Initial	none
Applies to	All elements.
Inherited	Yes.

C

vertical-align

Usage	Affects the vertical positioning of the boxes generated by an inline-level element.
Values	baseline | sub | super | top | texttop | middle | bottom | text-bottom | sub | <percentage>
CSS2 Values	inherit
Initial	baseline
Applies to	Inline-level and table-cell elements.
Inherited	No.

white-space

Usage	Specifies how white space inside the element is handled.
CSS1 Values	normal | pre | nowrap
CSS2 Values	inherit
Initial	normal

Applies to	Block-level elements.
Inherited	Yes.

word-spacing

Usage	Specifies the spacing behavior between words.
Values	normal	<length>
CSS2 Values	inherit
Initial	normal
Applies to	All elements.
Inherited	Yes.

Visual Effects Properties

The following properties affect visual rendering of an element.

clip

Usage	Defines which portion of an element's rendered content is visible.
CSS2 Values	<shape>	auto	inherit
Initial	auto
Applies to	Block-level and replaced elements.
Inherited	No.

overflow

Usage	Specifies whether the contents of a block-level element are clipped when they overflow the element's box.
CSS2 Values	visible	hidden	scroll	auto	inherit
Initial	visible
Applies to	Block-level and replaced elements.
Inherited	No.

visibility

Usage	Specifies whether the boxes generated by an element are rendered.
CSS2 Values	visible	hidden	collapse	inherit

Initial	`inherit`
Applies to	All elements.
Inherited	No.

Aural Style Sheet Properties

Aural style sheets are provided for the blind and visually impaired communities. Page contents are read to the user. The aural style sheet "canvas" uses dimensional space to render sounds in specified sequences as page elements are displayed and selected.

azimuth

Usage	Enables you to position a sound. Designed for spatial audio, which requires binaural headphones or five-speaker home theater systems.
CSS2 Values	`<angle>` | `[[left-side` | `far-left` | `left` | `center-left` | `center` | `center-right` | `right` | `far-right` | `right-side]` || `behind ]` | `leftwards` | `rightwards` | `inherit`
Initial	`center`
Applies to	All elements.
Inherited	Yes.

cue

Usage	Shorthand property for `cue-before` and `cue-after`. Plays a sound before or after an element is rendered.
CSS2 Values	`cue-before` | `cue-after` | `inherit`
Initial	Not defined (shorthand property).
Applies to	All elements.
Inherited	No.

cue-after, cue-before

Usage	Plays a sound after (`cue-after`) or before (`cue-before`) an element is rendered.
CSS2 Values	`<uri>` | `none` | `inherit`
Initial	`none`
Applies to	All elements.
Inherited	No.

elevation

Usage	Enables you to position the angle of a sound. For use with spatial audio (binaural headphones or five-speaker home theater setups required).
CSS2 Values	`<angle>` l `below` l `level` l `above` l `higher` l `lower` l `inherit`
Initial	`level`
Applies to	All elements.
Inherited	Yes.

pause

Usage	A shorthand property for setting `pause-before` and `pause-after` in the same location in the style sheet.
CSS2 Values	`<time>` l `<percentage>` l `inherit`
Initial	Depends on browser.
Applies to	All elements.
Inherited	No.

pause-after, pause-before

Usage	Specifies a pause to be observed before or after speaking an element's content.
CSS2 Values	`<time>` l `<percentage>` l `inherit`
Initial	Depends on browser.
Applies to	All elements.
Inherited	No.

pitch

Usage	Specifies the average pitch (frequency) of the speaking voice.
CSS2 Values	`<frequency>` l `x-low` l `low` l `medium` l `high` l `x-high` l `inherit`
Initial	`medium`
Applies to	All elements.
Inherited	Yes.
Notes	Average pitch for the standard male voice is around 120Hz; for the female voice, it is around 210Hz.

pitch-range

Usage	Specifies variation in average pitch. Used to vary inflection and add animation to the voice.
CSS2 Values	`<number>` | `inherit`
Initial	`50`
Applies to	All elements.
Inherited	Yes.

play-during

Usage	Specifies a sound to be played as a background while an element's content is spoken.
CSS2 Values	`<uri>` | `mix?` | `repeat?` | `auto` | `none` | `inherit`
Initial	`auto`
Applies to	All elements.
Inherited	No.

C

richness

Usage	Specifies the richness, or brightness, of the speaking voice.
CSS2 Values	`<number>` | `inherit`
Initial	`50`
Applies to	All elements.
Inherited	Yes.

speak

Usage	Specifies whether text will be rendered aurally, and in what manner.
CSS2 Values	`normal` | `none` | `spell-out` | `inherit`
Initial	`normal`
Applies to	All elements.
Inherited	Yes.

speak-header

Usage	Specifies whether table headers are spoken before every cell, or only before a cell when it is associated with a different header than a previous cell.
CSS2 Values	once | always | inherit
Initial	once
Applies to	Elements that have header information.
Inherited	Yes.

speak-numeral

Usage	Speaks numbers as individual digits (100 is spoken as "one zero zero") or as a continuous full number (100 is spoken as "one hundred").
CSS2 Values	digits | continuous | inherit
Initial	continuous
Applies to	All elements.
Inherited	Yes.

speak-punctuation

Usage	Speaks punctuation literally (period, comma, and so on) or naturally as various pauses.
CSS2 Values	code | none | inherit
Initial	none
Applies to	All elements.
Inherited	Yes.

speech-rate

Usage	Specifies the speaking rate of the voice.
CSS2 Values	<number> | x-slow | slow | medium | fast | x-fast | faster | slower | inherit
Initial	medium
Applies to	All elements.
Inherited	Yes.

stress

Usage	Specifies the height of local peaks in the intonation of a voice. Controls the amount of inflection within stress markers.
CSS2 Values	`<number>` | `inherit`
Initial	`50`
Applies to	All elements.
Inherited	Yes.
Notes	A companion to the `pitch-range` property.

voice-family

Usage	Specifies a comma-separated list of voice family names.
CSS2 Values	`<specific-voice>` | `<generic-voice>` | `inherit`
Initial	Depends on browser.
Applies to	All elements.
Inherited	Yes.

C

volume

Usage	Specifies the median volume of a waveform. Ranges from `0` (minimum audible volume level) to `100` (maximum comfortable level).
CSS2 Values	`<number>` | `<percentage>` | `silent` | `x-soft` | `soft` | `medium` | `loud` | `x-loud` | `inherit`
Initial	`medium`
Applies to	All elements.
Inherited	Yes.
Notes	`silent` renders no sound at all. `x-soft = 0`, `soft = 25`, `medium = 50`, `loud = 75`, and `x-loud = 100`.

Generated Content/Automatic Numbering Properties

CSS2 introduces properties and values that enable authors to render content automatically (for example, numbered lists can be generated automatically). Authors specify style and location of generated content with `:before` and `:after` pseudo-elements that indicate the page elements before and after which content is generated automatically.

content

Usage	Used with `:before` and `:after` pseudo-elements to generate content in a document.
CSS2 Values	`<string>` | `<uri>` | `<counter>` | `attr(X)` | `open-quote` | `close-quote` | `no-open-quote` | `no-close-quote` | `inherit`
Initial	`empty string`
Applies to	`:before` and `:after` pseudo-elements.
Inherited	All.

counter-increment

Usage	Accepts one or more names of counters (identifiers), each one optionally followed by an integer. The integer indicates the amount of increment for every occurrence of the element.
CSS2 Values	`<identifier>` | `<integer>` | `none` | `inherit`
Initial	`none`
Applies to	All elements.
Inherited	No.

counter-reset

Usage	Contains a list of one or more names of counters. The integer gives the value that the counter is set to on each occurrence of the element.
CSS2 Values	`<identifier>` | `<integer>` | `none` | `inherit`
Initial	`none`
Applies to	All elements.
Inherited	No.

marker-offset

Usage	Specifies the distance between the nearest border edges of a marker box and its associated principal box.
CSS2 Values	`<length>` | `auto` | `inherit`
Initial	`auto`
Applies to	Elements with `display` property set to `marker`.
Inherited	No.

quotes

Usage	Specifies quotation marks for embedded quotations.
CSS2 Values	`<string>` | `<string>+` | `none` | `inherit`
Initial	Depends on browser.
Applies to	All elements.
Inherited	Yes.

Paged Media Properties

Normally, a web page appears as a continuous page. CSS2 introduces the concept of *paged media*, which is designed to split a document into one or more discrete pages for display on paper, transparencies, computer screens, and so on. Page size, margins, page breaks, widows, and orphans can all be set with the following properties and values. Unfortunately, these properties aren't supported by any current browsers.

C

marks

Usage	Specifies whether cross marks, crop marks, or both should be rendered just outside the page box. Used in high-quality printing.
CSS2 Values	`crop` | `cross` | `none` | `inherit`
Initial	`none`
Applies to	Page context.
Inherited	N/A.

orphans

Usage	Specifies the minimum number of lines of a paragraph that must be left at the bottom of a page.
CSS2 Values	`<integer>` | `inherit`
Initial	2
Applies to	Block-level elements.
Inherited	Yes.

page

Usage	Used to specify a particular type of page where an element should be displayed.
CSS2 Values	`<identifier>` `:left` | `:right` | `auto`

Initial	auto
Applies to	Block-level elements.
Inherited	Yes.
Notes	By adding `:left` or `:right`, the element can be forced to fall on a left or right page.

page-break-after, page-break-before

Usage	Specifies page breaks before the following element or after the preceding element.
CSS2 Values	auto I always I avoid I `left` I `right` I `inherit`
Initial	auto
Applies to	Block-level elements.
Inherited	No.

page-break-inside

Usage	Forces a page break inside the parent element.
CSS2 Values	avoid I auto I inherit
Initial	auto
Applies to	Block-level elements.
Inherited	Yes.

size

Usage	Specifies the size and orientation of a page box.
CSS2 Values	\<length\> I auto I portrait I landscape I inherit
Initial	auto
Applies to	Page context.
Inherited	N/A.

widows

Usage	Specifies the minimum number of lines of a paragraph that must be left at the top of a page.
CSS2 Values	\<integer\> I inherit
Initial	2
Applies to	Block-level elements.
Inherited	Yes.

Table Properties

The CSS table model is based on the HTML 4.01 table model, which consists of tables, captions, rows, row groups, columns, column groups, and cells. In CSS2, tables can be rendered visually and aurally. Authors can specify how headers and data will be spoken through attributes defined previously in "Aural Style Sheet Properties."

border-collapse

Usage	Selects a table's border model.
CSS2 Values	collapse I separate I inherit
Initial	collapse
Applies to	Table and inline table elements.
Inherited	Yes.

border-spacing

Usage	In separated borders model, specifies the distance that separates the adjacent cell borders.
CSS2 Values	<length> I <length> ? I inherit
Initial	0
Applies to	Table and inline table elements.
Inherited	Yes.

caption-side

Usage	Specifies the position of the caption box with respect to the table box.
CSS2 Values	top I bottom I left I right I inherit
Initial	top
Applies to	Table caption elements.
Inherited	Yes.

column-span, row-span

Usage	Specifies the number of columns or rows (respectively) spanned by a cell.
CSS2 Values	<integer> I inherit
Initial	1

C

Applies to	Table cell, table column, and table column group elements (`column-span`); table cell elements (`row-span`).
Inherited	No.

empty-cells

Usage	In the separated tables model, specifies how borders around cells that have no visible content are rendered.
CSS2 Values	`borders` I `no-borders` I `inherit`
Initial	`borders`
Applies to	Table cell elements.
Inherited	Yes.

table-layout

Usage	Controls the algorithm used to lay out the table cells.
CSS2 Values	`auto` I `fixed` I `inherit`
Initial	`auto`
Applies to	Table and inline table elements.
Inherited	No.
Notes	`fixed` table layout depends on the width of the table and its columns. `auto` table layout depends on the contents of the cells.

User Interface Properties

User interface properties enable customization of cursor appearance, color preferences, font preferences, and dynamic outlines.

cursor

Usage	Specifies the type of cursor that displays for a pointing device.
CSS2 Values	`<uri>` I `auto` I `crosshair` I `default` I `pointer` I `move` I `e-resize` I `ne-resize` I `nw-resize` I `n-resize` I `se-resize` I `sw-resize` I `s-resize` I `w-resize` I `text` I `wait` I `help` I `inherit`
Initial	`auto`
Applies to	All elements.
Inherited	Yes.

outline

Usage	Shorthand property for setting outline-color, _outline-style, and outline-width.
CSS2 Values	outline-color	outline-style	outline-width	inherit
Initial	See individual properties.
Applies to	All elements.
Inherited	No.
Notes	Similar to border property, creates an outline around visual objects such as buttons, active form fields, image maps, and so on. Using outline property rather than border property does not cause reflow when displaying or suppressing the outline. Outlines also can be nonrectangular.

C

outline-color

Usage	Specifies the color of the outline.
CSS2 Values	<color>	invert	inherit
Initial	invert
Applies to	All elements.
Inherited	No.

outline-style

Usage	Specifies the style of the outline.
CSS2 Values	Same as <border-style>	inherit
Initial	none
Applies to	All elements.
Inherited	No.

outline-width

Usage	Specifies the width of the outline.
CSS2 Values	Same as <border-width>	inherit
Initial	medium
Applies to	All elements.
Inherited	No.

Cascading Style Sheet Units

Several cascading style sheet attributes use standard units to define measurements, styles, colors, and other identifiers. Throughout this appendix, unit measurements have been enclosed within angle brackets (< >). The following section lists the values associated with each unit type.

<absolute-size>

Absolute sizes refer to font sizes computed and kept by the user's browser. The following values are from smallest to largest:

xx-small

x-small

small

medium

large

x-large

xx-large

<angle>

Angle values are used with aural style sheets. Their format is an optional sign character (+ or -) immediately followed by a number. The following are angle units:

deg	Degrees
grad	Gradients
rad	Radians

<border-style>

These properties specify the type of line that surrounds a box's border. The border-style value type can take one of the following:

none	Forces border width to zero
dotted	A series of dots
dashed	A series of short line segments
solid	A single line segment
double	Two solid lines, with the sum of the two lines and the space between them equaling the value of border-width

groove	Renders a border that looks as though it were carved into the canvas
ridge	Renders a border that looks as though it were coming out of the canvas
inset	Renders a border that looks like the entire box is embedded in the canvas
outset	Renders a border that looks like the entire box is coming out of the canvas

`<border-width>`

The border-width property sets the width of the border area. It can take one of the following values:

thin	A thin border
medium	A medium border
thick	A thick border
<length>	An explicit value (cannot be negative)

C

`<color>`

Colors can be defined by keyword (as defined in HTML 4.01) or by a numerical RGB specification. Following are the accepted formats:

Keyword:	aqua I black I blue I fuchsia I gray I green I lime I maroon I navy I olive I purple I red I silver I teal I white I yellow
#rgb	Example for blue: { color: #00f }
#rrggbb	Example for blue: { color: #0000ff }
rgb (integer range)	Example for blue: { color: rgb(0,0,255) }
rgb (float range)	Example for blue: { color: rgb(0%, 0%, 100%) }

`<family-name>`

Fonts can be specified by the name of a font family of choice. Examples of this are Arial, Times New Roman, Helvetica, Baskerville, and so on. Font family names that contain white space (tabs, line feeds, carriage returns, form feeds, and so on) should be enclosed by quotation marks.

`<frequency>`

Frequency identifiers are used with aural style sheets. The format is a number immediately followed by one of the following identifiers:

`Hz`	Hertz
`kHz`	Kilohertz

`<generic-family>`

Authors are encouraged to use generic font family names as a last alternative, in case a user does not have a specified font on his or her system. Generic font family names are keywords and must not be enclosed in quotation marks. The following are examples of each:

`serif`	Times New Roman, MS Georgia, Garamond
`sans-serif`	Arial, Helvetica, Futura, Gill Sans
`cursive`	Zapf-Chancery, Caflisch Script
`fantasy`	Critter, Cottonwood
`monospace`	Courier, MS Courier New, Prestige

`<generic-voice>`

Generic voices are the aural equivalent of generic font family names (refer to the preceding section) and are used in conjunction with `<voice-family>`. The following are possible generic voice values:

`male`

`female`

`child`

`<integer>`

An integer consists of one or more digits (0 through 9). It may be preceded by a - or a + to indicate the sign. See also `<number>`.

`<length>`

Lengths are specified by an optional sign character (+ or -) immediately followed by a number with or without a decimal point, immediately followed by one of the following unit identifiers:

Relative values

em	The font size of the relevant font
ex	The x-height of the relevant font
px	Pixels, relative to the viewing device

Absolute values

pt	Points (1/72nd of an inch)
in	Inches
cm	Centimeters
mm	Millimeters
pc	Picas (12 points, or 1/6 of an inch)

\<number\>

A number can consist of an integer, or it can be zero or more digits, followed by a dot (.), followed by one or more digits. A number may be preceded by a - or a + to indicate its sign. See also \<integer\>.

\<percentage\>

Percentage values are always relative to another value, such as a length. The format is an optional sign character (+ or -), immediately followed by a number, immediately followed by %.

\<relative-size\>

Relative sizes are interpreted relative to the font size of the parent element.
The following are possible values:

larger

smaller

\<shape\>

In CSS2, the only valid shape value is rect(\<top\> \<right\> \<bottom\> \<left\>, where the four descriptors specify offsets from the respective sides of the box.

\<specific-voice\>

Specific voice values are the aural style sheet equivalent of font-family. Values are specific names of a voice (for example: teacher, comedian, preacher, and so on).

C

`<time>`

Time units are used with aural style sheets. Their format is a number immediately followed by one of the following identifiers:

ms   milliseconds

s   seconds

`<uri>`

URI (Uniform Resource Indicator) values are used to designate addresses of page elements such as images. The format of a URI is url (followed by optional white space, followed by an optional single quote or double quotation mark, followed by the URI itself, followed by an optional single or double quote, followed by optional white space). To clarify, here is an example of the proper syntax:

```
body { background: url("http://www.foo.com/images/background.gif") }=
```

APPENDIX D:

Colors by Name and Hexadecimal Value

Table D.1 contains a list of all the color names recognized by Navigator 2.0 and Internet Explorer 3.0 (and later versions of both browsers, of course), and it also includes their corresponding Hexadecimal (Hex) Triplet values. To see all of these colors correctly, you must have a 256-color or better video card and the appropriate video drivers installed. Also, depending on the operating system and computer platform you're running, some colors may not appear exactly as you expect them to.

TABLE D.1   Color Values and Hex Triplet Equivalents

Color Name	Hex Triplet	Color Name	Hex Triplet
aliceblue	#f0f8ff	darksalmon	#e9967a
antiquewhite	#faebd7	darkseagreen	#8fbc8f
aqua	#00ffff	darkslateblue	#483D8b
aquamarine	#7fffd4	darkslategray	#2f4f4f
azure	#f0ffff	darkturquoise	#00ced1
beige	#f5f5dc	darkviolet	#9400d3
bisque	#ffe4c4	deeppink	#ff1493
black	#000000	deepskyblue	#00bfff
blanchedalmond	#ffebcd	dimgray	#696969
blue	#0000ff	dodgerblue	#1e90ff
blueviolet	#8a2be2	firebrick	#b22222
brown	#a52a2a	floralwhite	#fffaf0
burlywood	#deb887	forestgreen	#228b22
cadetblue	#5f9ea0	fuchsia	#ff00ff
chartreuse	#7fff00	gainsboro	#dcdcdc
chocolate	#d2691e	ghostwhite	#f8f8ff
coral	#ff7f50	gold	#ffd700
cornflowerblue	#6495ed	goldenrod	#daa520
cornsilk	#fff8dc	gray	#808080
crimson	#dc143c	green	#008000
cyan	#00ffff	greenyellow	#adff2f
darkblue	#00008b	honeydew	#f0fff0
darkcyan	#008b8b	hotpink	#ff69b4
darkgoldenrod	#b8860b	indianred	#cd5c5c
darkgray	#a9a9a9	indigo	#4b0082
darkgreen	#006400	ivory	#fffff0
darkkhaki	#bdb76b	khaki	#f0e68c
darkmagenta	#8b008b	lavender	#e6e6fa
darkolivegreen	#556b2f	lavenderblush	#fff0f5
darkorange	#ff8c00	lemonchiffon	#fffacd
darkorchid	#9932cc	lightblue	#add8e6
darkred	#8b0000	lightcoral	#f08080

TABLE D.1 continued

Color Name	Hex Triplet	Color Name	Hex Triplet
lightcyan	#e0ffff	olivedrab	#6b8e23
lightgoldenrodyellow	#fafad2	orange	#ffa500
lightgreen	#90ee90	orangered	#ff4500
lightgrey	#d3d3d3	orchid	#da70d6
lightpink	#ffb6c1	palegoldenrod	#eee8aA
lightsalmon	#ffa07a	palegreen	#98fb98
lightseagreen	#20b2aa	paleturquoise	#afeeee
lightskyblue	#87cefa	palevioletred	#db7093
lightslategray	#778899	papayawhip	#ffefd5
lightsteelblue	#b0c4de	peachpuff	#ffdab9
lightyellow	#ffffe0	peru	#cd853f
lime	#00ff00	pink	#ffc0cb
limegreen	#32cd32	plum	#dda0dd
linen	#faf0e6	powderblue	#b0e0e6
magenta	#ff00ff	purple	#800080
maroon	#800000	red	#ff0000
mediumaquamarine	#66cdaa	rosybrown	#bc8f8f
mediumblue	#0000cd	royalblue	#4169e1
mediumorchid	#ba55d3	saddlebrown	#8b4513
mediumpurple	#9370db	salmon	#fa8072
mediumseagreen	#3cb371	sandybrown	#f4a460
mediumslateblue	#7b68ee	seagreen	#2e8b57
mediumspringgreen	#00fa9a	seashell	#fff5ee
mediumturquoise	#48d1cc	sienna	#a0522d
mediumvioletred	#c71585	silver	#c0c0c0
midnightblue	#191970	skyblue	#87ceeb
mintcream	#f5fffa	slateblue	#6a5acd
mistyrose	#ffe4e1	slategray	#708090
navajowhite	#ffdead	snow	#fffafa
navy	#000080	springgreen	#00ff7f
oldlace	#fdf5e6	steelblue	#4682b4
olive	#808000	tan	#d2b48c

D

TABLE D.1   continued

Color Name	Hex Triplet	Color Name	Hex Triplet
teal	#008080	wheat	#f5deb3
thistle	#d8bfd8	white	#ffffff
tomato	#ff6347	whitesmoke	#f5f5f5
turquoise	#40e0d0	yellow	#ffff00
violet	#ee82ee	yellowgreen	#9acd32

APPENDIX E:
MIME Types and File Extensions

Table E.1 lists some the file extensions and MIME content types supported by many popular web servers. If your server doesn't list an extension for a particular content type, or if the type you want to use isn't listed at all, you'll have to add support for that type to your server configuration.

TABLE E.1 MIME Types and HTTP Support

MIME Type	File Type	Extensions
application/acad	AutoCAD Drawing files	dwg, DWG
application/arj		arj
application/clariscad	ClarisCAD files	CCAD
application/drafting	MATRA Prelude drafting	DRW
application/dxf	DXF (AutoCAD)	dxf, DXF
application/excel	Microsoft Excel	xl
application/i-deas	SDRC I-DEAS files	unv, UNV
application/iges	IGES graphics format	igs, iges, IGS, IGES
application/mac-binhex40	Macintosh BinHex format	hqx
application/msword	Microsoft Word	word, w6w, doc
application/mswrite	Microsoft Write	wri
application/octet-stream	Uninterpreted binary	bin
application/oda		oda
application/pdf	PDF (Adobe Acrobat)	pdf
application/postscript	PostScript	ai, PS, ps, eps
application/pro_eng	PTC Pro/ENGINEER	prt, PRT, part
application/rtf	Rich Text Format	rtf
application/set	SET (French CAD standard)	set, SET_application/sla
	Stereolithography	stl, STL
application/solids	MATRA Prelude Solids	SOL
application/STEP	ISO-10303 STEP data files	stp, STP, step, STEP
application/vda	VDA-FS Surface data	vda, VDA
application/x-csh	C-shell script	csh
application/x-director	Macromedia Director	dir, dcr, dxr
application/x-dvi	TeX DVI	dvi
application/x-gzip	GNU Zip	gz, gzip
application/x-mif	FrameMaker MIF Format	mif
application/x-hdf	NCSA HDF Data File	hdf
application/x-latex	LaTeX source	latex
application/x-netcdf	Unidata netCDF	nc, cdf
application/x-sh	Bourne shell script	sh

TABLE E.1 continued

MIME Type	File Type	Extensions
application/x-shockwave-flash	Flash movie	swf
application/x-stuffit	Stuffit Archive	sit
application/x-tcl	TCL script	tcl
application/x-tex	TeX source	tex
application/x-texinfo	Texinfo (Emacs)	texinfo, texi
application/x-troff	Troff	t, tr, roff
application/x-troff-man	Troff with MAN macros	man
application/x-troff-me	Troff with ME macros	me
application/x-troff-ms	Troff with MS macros	ms
application/x-wais-source	WAIS source	src
application/x-bcpio	Old binary CPIO	bcpio
application/x-cpio	POSIX CPIO	cpio
application/x-gtar	GNU tar	gtar
application/x-shar	Shell archive	shar
application/x-sv4cpio	SVR4 CPIO	sv4cpio
application/x-sv4crc	SVR4 CPIO with CRC	sv4crc
application/x-tar	4.3BSD tar format	tar
application/x-ustar	POSIX tar format	ustar
application/x-winhelp	Windows Help	hlp
application/zip	ZIP archive	zip
audio/basic	Basic audio (usually ∞-law)	au, snd
audio/x-aiff	AIFF audio	aif, aiff, aifc
audio/x-mpeg.mp3	MP3 audio	mp3
audio/x-mpegurl	URL resource of MP3 Audio	m3u, mp3url
audio/x-pn-realaudio	RealAudio	ra, ram
audio/x-pn-realaudio	RealAudio (plug-in)	rpm_plugin
audio/x-wav	Windows WAVE audio	wav
image/gif	GIF image	gif
image/ief	Image Exchange Format	ief
image/jpeg	JPEG image	jpg, JPG, JPE, jpe, JPEG, jpeg
image/pict	Macintosh PICT	pict

E

TABLE E.1 continued

MIME Type	File Type	Extensions
image/png	Portable Network Graphics	png
image/tiff	TIFF image	tiff, tif
image/x-cmu-raster	CMU raster	ras
image/x-portable-anymap	PBM Anymap format	pnm
image/x-portable-bitmap	PBM Bitmap format	pbm
image/x-portable-graymap	PBM Graymap format	pgm
image/x-portable-pixmap	PBM Pixmap format	ppm
image/x-rgb	RGB Image	rgb
image/x-xbitmap	X Bitmap	xbm
image/x-xpixmap	X Pixmap	xpm
image/x-xwindowdump	X Windows dump (xwd) format	xwd
multipart/x-zip	PKZIP Archive	zip
multipart/x-gzip	GNU ZIP Archive	gzip
text/html	HTML	html, htm
text/plain	Plain text	txt, g, h, C, cc, hh, m, f90
text/richtext	MIME Richtext	rtx
text/tab-separated-values	Text with tab-separated values	tsv
text/x-setext	Struct enhanced text	etx
video/mpeg	MPEG video	mpeg, mpg, MPG, MPE, mpe, MPEG, mpeg
video/quicktime	QuickTime Video	qt, mov
video/msvideo	Microsoft Windows Video	avi
video/x-sgi-movie	SGI Movieplayer format	movie
x-world/x-vrml	VRML Worlds	wrl

Index

Symbols

empty cells, creating, 224-225

empty-cells property (CSS), 758

enablejavascript attribute (QuickTime), 369

enctype attribute

<form> tag, 316, 718

f<form> tag, file, 323

endtime attribute (QuickTime), 369

equal sign (=), 395

equality operator, 398

equality operator (==), 398

escape codes

for HTML reserved characters, 146-147

URLs, 118

evangelism, 589-590

event handlers

<a> tags, 119

defined, 468

JavaScript, 394-395

onblur, 394

onchange, 394, 472

onclick, 394, 691

pull-down menus, 485

random link generator, 410-411

ondblclick, 691

onfocus, 394

onkeydown, 692

onkeypress, 692

onkeyup, 692

onload, 394

onmousedown, 692

onmousemove, 692

onmouseout, 423-424, 692

pull-down menus, 485

onmouseover, 394, 423-424, 692

onmouseup, 692

onselect, 394

onsubmit, 394, 416

onunload, 394

event-driven models of execution, 386

events. *See also* functions

event handlers. *See* event handlers

JavaScript, 392

list of, 691-692

evolt website, 681-682

ex unit (CSS), 275

exec directive, 605

exercises. *See also* samples

content, 45

HTML, 63-64

HTML tags, 91

links, 126

text formatting, 169

URLs, 23, 126

web browsers, 23

existence of objects, testing, 478

expressions, JavaScript, 396-397

eXtensible Markup Language (XML), 53

extensions

image files, case sensitivity, 172

web servers, 769-772

Extreme Tracking website, 680

F

face attribute

<basefont> tag, 700

<font> tags, 151, 701

family-name (<family-name> unit measurements, 761

fan sites, 29. *See also* content

FAQs, structuring, 37

Fetch, 577

fieldset tag, 717

file extensions, 574

web servers, 769-772

file formats

AVI (audio/video interleaved) files, 373

GIF (Graphics Interchange Format), 173, 214

JPEG (Joint Photographic Experts Group), 173-174, 214

MIDI (Musical Instrument Digital Interface), 372

MPEG (Moving Picture Experts Group), 372-373

PNG (Portable Network Graphics), 174

QuickTime files, 373

RealAudio, 373

RealVideo, 373

video, 374

WAV files, 372

Windows Media Video, 373

WMA (Windows Media Audio) files, 372

File Not Found errors, 579

File Transfer Protocol (FTP), 576-578

file upload controls, creating with i<input> tag, 322-323

file uploads, PHP, 646

filenames, 573-575

files

Apache access control files, 608-612

AVI (audio/video interleaved) files, 373

determining type of, 568

downloading form FTP sites, 20

file, URL anatomies, 122-123

file extensions, 574

File Not Found errors, 579

Filenames, 575

Filo, David, 581

Firefox (Mozilla), 18

Flash, interactivity of, 16

How can we make this index more useful? Email us at indexes@samspublishing.com

onmousedown event handler, 692

onmousemove event handler, 692

onmouseout event handler, 423-424, 692

pull-down menus, 485

onmouseover event handler, 394, 423-424, 692

pull-down menus, 485

onmouseup event handler, 692

onselect attribute

<input> tag, 719

<select> tag, 721

<textarea> tag, 721

onselect event handler, 394

onsubmit event handler, 394, 416

onunload attribute (<frameset> tag), 712

onunload event handler, 394

Open Directory Project (dmoz), 583-584

Opera, 19

Opera website, 681

DOM reference, 470

operators

JavaScript, 396-398

or operator, 417

string concatenation operators, 622

opinion gathering, 29

optimizing search engines, 587-588

<option> tag, 720

or operator (||), 417

order directive, 609

ordered lists, 75. See also numbered lists

creating, 704

organization. See also designs

websites, 506-507

organizing HTML documents, 572

default index files, 573-574

directories, 573

filenames, 573-574

web server setup, 572-573

orphans property (CSS), 755

outline property (CSS), 759

outline-color property (CSS), 759

outline-style property (CSS), 759

outline-width property (CSS), 759

overflow property (CSS), 748

o<option> tag, 325-327

P

<p> tag, 698

packaged software, 655-656

deploying applications, 657-658

relational databases, 656-657

padding (table cells), 231-232

padding property (CSS), 279-284, 740

padding-bottom property (CSS), 741

padding-left property (CSS), 741

padding-right property (CSS), 741

padding-top property (CSS), 741

page descriptions, creating, 156-157

page layout, 510-512

page layouts, HTML and, 49-50

page property (CSS), 755

page-break-after property (CSS), 756

page-break-inside property (CSS), 756

page-level styles (CSS), creating, 270

paged media, CSS properties, 755-756

pages. See web pages

Paint Shop Pro, 172

palette attribute (<embed> tag), 359

pan attribute (QuickTime), 369

paragraphs

formatting, 698

HTML tags for, 72-73

<param> tag, 360, 379, 716

parent target name, 454

parentheses () in method names, 391

parsing HTML documents, 49

password controls, creating with i<input> tag, 317-318

password protection, 569

passwords, creating for forms, 309-313

pathnames, linking local pages

absolute pathnames, 103-104

overview, 101

relative pathnames, 101-103

relative versus absolute pathnames, 104

pause property (CSS), 750

pause-after property (CSS), 750

pause-before property (CSS), 750

paying for search placement, 588

pc unit (CSS), 275

percent sign (%)

in email addresses, 121

modulus operator, 396

URL escape codes, 118

percentage (<percentage>) unit measurements, 763

percentage units (CSS), 275-276